THE
INTERNATIONAL
POLITICS
OF REGIONS

a comparative approach

LOUIS J. CANTORI and STEVEN L. SPIEGEL
University of California, Los Angeles

PRENTICE-HALL, INC., ENGLEWOOD CLIFFS, NEW JERSEY

C—13-473421-1
P—13-473413-0

Library of Congress Catalog Card Number 75-94428

Printed in the United States of America

Current printing (last digit):

10   9   8   7   6   5   4   3   2   1

PRENTICE-HALL INTERNATIONAL, INC., *London*
PRENTICE-HALL OF AUSTRALIA, PTY. LTD., *Sydney*
PRENTICE-HALL OF CANADA, LTD., *Toronto*
PRENTICE-HALL OF INDIA PRIVATE LTD., *New Delhi*
PRENTICE-HALL OF JAPAN, INC., *Tokyo*

For JOANIE *and* FREDI

CONTENTS

v

LIST OF TABLES

PREFACE

This volume began as a relatively simple attempt to collect a variety of readings on subordinate systems, a project developed over a series of wide-ranging luncheon discussions when both authors had first come to the Political Science Department at UCLA in the fall of 1966. It gradually mushroomed into an effort to set forth an analytical framework for the comparative study of regional international politics. The readings became a vehicle for demonstrating the relevance of this approach for previous work done in the field and for providing the reader with further information about the subjects discussed. We endeavored to show how the region or the subordinate international system is the intermediate unit of analysis between the nation-state on the one hand and the dominant system on the other. We set out to provide a rubric for viewing these international relations as the member states of the regions themselves perceive them, and not, as has too often been done by statesman and scholar alike, from the elevated and external vantage point of the bipolar confrontation.

The purpose of this framework is simply to begin the process of elaborating a "comparative regional international relations" approach. We seek to use what lessons can be learned from the past study of comparative politics, area studies, international relations, the various disciplines of the social sciences, and the more specific endeavors of international organization and international integration to evolve an approach which will elucidate and concentrate upon the dynamics of regional international politics. We believe that the domestic politics of a nation cannot be fully understood without reference to the neighboring environment in which that nation has developed, and that international politics cannot be fully comprehended if there is concentration only on the relations among the greatest of powers.

This book is part of an initial effort to define an approach. We are not yet at the stage of investigating hypotheses and forming propositions. We

ix

simply hope to show here the manner in which regions can be compared in the light of our framework. Even the ranking of regions on specific bases (e.g. social or economic factors) may be elementary, but it should serve to illustrate the direction of research which we have in mind. In the future lies the more fruitful task of attempting to correlate the variety of factors with which we are dealing.

The plan of this book is as follows: in the first chapter we set out the analytical framework upon which our work has been based. In the second, fourth, and sixth chapters we attempt to apply our framework empirically to the five subordinate systems which have been selected for study in this volume. The third, fifth, and seventh chapters include the readings discussed earlier. These have been selected to elucidate the approach of this volume, to demonstrate its fruitfulness, and also to provide the reader with the opportunity to gain a more complete understanding of the international politics within the five specific subordinate systems. In the last two chapters we demonstrate two ways in which the approach might be used. In Chapter 8 Professor Lynn Miller has sought to show its applicability to the study of regional international organizations, while in Chapter 9 we have attempted to provide a classification of the types of regional international systems which currently exist, based on the material presented earlier.

This approach, in essence, represents the marriage of the political science sub-fields of area-focused comparative politics and international relations. Not unexpectedly, this reflects Louis Cantori's primary scholarly concerns with comparative politics and Steven Spiegel's similar concern with international relations. Ideally, one approach has served to inspire the other.

It perhaps follows logically that the indebtedness of a co-authored work should be considerable. We both owe a substantial debt to our teachers and fellow students at the graduate schools of Chicago and Harvard Universities, from which we emerged in 1966, and to our colleagues at UCLA, who were at all times characteristically challenging and encouraging. The emphasis on regional studies by the UCLA Political Science Department provided an environment in which this project could be more easily pursued. Specifically, Professor Leonard Binder of the University of Chicago, author of a seminal article on the Middle East as a subordinate system [1] a decade ago, planted the seeds of which the present effort is a product.

A number of research assistants were especially helpful in the arduous mechanics of preparing a combination authored and edited volume of, literally, global scope. In particular, the Research Committee of the

---

[1] Leonard Binder, "The Middle East as a Subordinate International System," *World Politics*, X (April, 1958), 408-29.

UCLA Academic Senate must be thanked for its research support. The energy and enthusiasm of Mr. James Murray, until recently Political Science editor of Prentice-Hall, Inc., provided us with both encouragement and reassurance while preparing the volume. Finally, and in a much more personal vein, both authors owe far more than they might care to admit to their wives, and it is therefore appropriate that this book be dedicated to them. Proper recognition must also be made of the diversionary qualities of Gregory, Eric and Nadia Cantori, and Mira Sharone Spiegel.

Louis J. Cantori
Steven L. Spiegel

THE FIVE SUBORDINATE SYSTEMS
IN GLOBAL PERSPECTIVE

THE FIVE SUBORDINATE SYSTEMS
IN GLOBAL PERSPECTIVE

INTRODUCTION:
THE SUBORDINATE SYSTEM

It is the purpose of this book to analyze the role of the region in present-day international politics. We will consider regions to be areas of the world which contain geographically proximate states forming, in foreign affairs, mutually interrelated units. For each participant, the activities of other members of the region (be they antagonistic or cooperative) are significant determinants of its foreign policy; while particular members of certain regions may have extraregional concerns, their primary involvement in foreign affairs ordinarily lies in the region in which they find themselves. Under normal conditions they cannot accomplish successes elsewhere until they have achieved and are able to maintain a permanent position in their own area.

Modern theorists in the field of international relations have concentrated primarily upon the great powers or the dilemmas of foreign policymaking which all nations share. Because we lack empirical evidence and because outside hegemonies often exist, regional politics has been a missing link in the chain of explanation provided by political scientists. Regions have been considered exclusively as a part of area studies, without being compared with each other. They have been reduced (as, e.g., Latin America and East Europe) to extensions of the foreign policy of some powerful state. Sometimes "regionalism" has been studied exclusively in terms of regional organization. As a problem of area studies, the region has been analyzed as a geographic unit and its place in international politics considered on that basis. Relationships among the constituent states of a region, however, have never fully been studied, and as no systematic comparisons between region and region have been possible. By not considering the importance of regional international relations within regions, those scholars who were preoccupied with the state took too restricted a view, while those who concerned themselves with the international system as a whole had too broad a perspective.

The key positions which underlie our elaboration of a comparative approach to the study of regional international relations are that the region is an appropriate unit for analysis by students of international relations and that it possesses the appropriate parameters for generalization by students

1

of comparative politics. In short, ours is an attempt to study the region in terms of the shared features of all regions—hence comparisons become feasible—and to study the potentialities of these features for meaningful generalization in the study of international relations. Our concern with this type of comparative study sets our effort apart from other recent efforts to deal with regional international relations, which generally speaking, have been influenced by, and sometimes are directly derived from, studies of West European economic and political unification. The oftentimes explicit questions they are asking are: To what extent are the international relations of region X similar to those of West Europe? and, above all, What is the likelihood of integrating the region?[1] We, on the other hand, are concerned not so much with the question of integration as with the question of how best to devise an appropriate set of categories which will help us to analyse relations within a region, and to compare one region to another. Ultimately we seek information both about the internal nature of regional international relations and the manner in which they are related to the international system as a whole.[2]

One of the difficulties of dealing with the region has been the problem of definition, of delineation. Many regions are denoted by obvious geographic or cultural boundaries (e.g., the boundaries between maritime and mainland areas, political regimes, peoples), but most geographic and political boundaries are fluid and arbitrary, and may vary with technological and political conditions. While nation-states are defined by political developments and international relations are similarly defined but to a slightly lesser degree, regions are entities in international politics whose perimeters cannot wholly be determined by events. Subjective determinants consequently become necessary for gauging their boundaries.

All states are by their very existence participants in international politics, but global politics encompasses the ideological and political relationships (antagonistic or cooperative) which are worldwide in scope and which therefore primarily involve the most powerful of nations. In global political conflict there are no peripheral areas and both the region and the nation-state are loci of conflict. Regional political conflict, on the other hand, is conducted within the region, and the nation-state may be—and usually is— the sole theater of competition. The politics of a nation-state are confined to the sum total of political activities within its boundaries.

Such a delineation of three arenas of international politics—the globe, the region, and the nation-state—provides us with the basis of an analytical structure for the consideration of international politics. In international

---

[1] For representative works illustrating this concern with the West Europe experience, see Selected Bibliography at the end of this chapter, section labeled "Integration-Oriented."

[2] The present effort is consistent with the efforts of a number of scholars in recent years. See Selected Bibliography, "Subordinate System-Oriented" section.

politics, a system is the totality of relations which exist between the autonomous units in a particular arena; in this volume, the three arenas are represented as three systems: the dominant, the subordinate, and the internal.[3] *The dominant system, in the global arena, is the confrontation of the most powerful of nations; the subordinate system, in the region, is the total interaction of relations within that region; and the internal system, in the nation-state, is the totality of relations of the organizations which compose its domestic politics.* While for the present we are concerned with the region, a framework of three interconnected arenas in which international relations occur provides us with a more complete understanding of what is happening in the world today.

Each of these three systems of relationships is in turn composed of subsidiary systems which encompass the relations of a part of the area (globe, region, or state) under consideration, which constitute sector politics. It is possible to show that the dominant system has a core and a periphery and, as we shall see, it is demonstrable that subordinate systems also have cores and peripheries. The internal system of a state, on the other hand, also has a variety of component parts which may be dealt with by means of the concept of "political system" or by means of the distinction between the "modern" and "residual" sectors, especially (but not exclusively) of developing nations.[4]

[3] The authors, while aware of the suggestiveness of what we have to say for systems theory in political science, have deliberately sought to avoid using the technical vocabulary of systems theory as it appears, for example, in David Easton, *A Systems Analysis of Political Life* (New York: John Wiley & Sons, Inc., 1965); Morton Kaplan, *System and Process in International Politics* (New York: John Wiley & Sons, Inc., 1957); and O. R. Young, "A Survey of General Systems Theory," *General Systems*, IX (1964), 61–80.

As a consequence, we have attempted to define the concept of system in its simplest possible form: in terms of relationship or interaction. Charles A. McClelland has suggested that "Any system is a structure that is perceived by its observers to have elements in interaction or relationships and some identifiable boundaries that separate it from its environment." (*Theory and the International System* (New York: The Macmillan Co., 1966), p. 20). One of the tasks of this volume, then, becomes the effort of identifying the boundaries of each region in order to examine the relations of the states within each region and between regions. We have used the term "subordinate system" to apply to regions in order to stress the interactive nature of local areas. In this sense the term "subordinate system" should not be viewed as connoting an inferior order of activity, but rather as simply referring to a set of relations which constitutes a segment or part of the international system as a whole. (While we have chosen to equate subordinate systems with regions, it is possible in the study of international relations to use the term as well to apply to any grouping of more than one nation-state—e.g. NATO, The British Commonwealth, The Communist world.)

[4] For the use of the concept of "political system," see David Easton, *A Systems Analysis of Political Life* (New York: John Wiley & Sons, Inc., 1965), *passim;* for "modern" and "residual" sectors, see Aristide Zolberg, *Creating Political Order: The Party Systems of West Africa* (Chicago: Rand McNally & Co., 1966), p. 131.

The present authors are currently engaged on a larger, more comprehensive work in which the framework described here will be elaborated and in which the three levels of dominant, subordinate, and internal systems will be related to one another.

ADVANTAGES OF THE APPROACH

We can identify at least six advantages of including the subordinate (i.e., the regional) system in the study of international relations.

First, the concept of the subordinate system permits us to construct an intermediate unit. Instead of almost 150 independent states, we have 15 units to analyze.[5]

Second, a consideration of the subordinate system corrects the practice, on the part of some scholars and policy makers alike, of regarding all international relations from the viewpoint of the dominant system and, in so doing, of making erroneous judgments about the general or specific character of given events. Regional analysis implies to policy makers that many political crises and developments may not have been created by superpowers or, at least, may occur with only secondary reference to superpowers. The implication for theorists in international relations is that the systemic qualities of interdependence they attribute to the global arena may, in fact, be of limited relevance in regional international relations.

Third, the concept of the subordinate system permits area specialists, who often concern themselves with the study of a single country, to broaden their horizons and see the interrelated character of their specialized area. At the same time, the concept allows the generalist in international relations to achieve a more meaningful grasp of the unique characteristics of a given region without highly specialized preparation.

Fourth, from the comparison of sectors of the dominant, subordinate, and internal systems one may gain a broad understanding of the interaction among various parts of the international system. In particular, the analysis of the subdivisions of subordinate systems which we propose to make in this volume assists in the examination of the behavior of individual states at different levels of the international system.

Fifth, the concept permits scholars to investigate a relatively unexplored area: the comparative study of both contemporary and historical subordinate systems. In our own day, Europe has declined as the center of international politics; each region has regained its independence, providing opportunity for comparisons. Each region can be compared vertically, i.e., contemporary subordinate systems can be compared with earlier systems in the same regions, and horizontal comparisons can be made of subordinate systems which exist in various regions at the same time. The combination of the vertical and horizontal approaches may also be used for comparing a subordinate system in one region to another subordinate system in another

---

[5] See Table 1-1, Subordinate Systems of the World and Their Subdivisions, p. 8. For a virtually identical breakdown, independently arrived at, see G. Etzel Pearcy, "Geopolitics and Foreign Relations," *Department of State Bulletin*, L (March 2, 1964), 318–30. We wish to thank Professor John Sigler for calling this to our attention.

region and in a different historical period: e.g., a number of contemporary subordinate systems may be compared to past stages of European politics, or contemporary European politics may be used as a model for the future development of other subordinate systems.

Sixth, the notion of the subordinate system, by providing an intermediate conceptual focal point in the study of international politics, enables scholars to study the interactions of various levels of the international system. Many nations, for example, have recently become legally independent of their former European masters but have retained, both internally and externally, vestiges of their former dependence. Therefore, as the concept of the subordinate system emphasizes, attempts by more powerful states to control the weak retain significance in international politics. Historical patterns of hegemony, condominium, and competition for domination are still relevant models of types of activities which affect subordinate systems today.

THE IDENTIFICATION OF SUBORDINATE SYSTEMS

Nation-states are delineated by events, political practice, and (at least in part) membership in the United Nations. The dominant system, i.e., global politics, is more difficult to discern and its precise membership is a matter of constant conjecture, but there are at least a minimum of contenders for predominant status and therefore a minimum of potential configurations. There is also a degree of consensus among most observers: some form of bipolarity. Regional or subordinate systems, on the other hand, do not easily lend themselves to clear-cut identification: there are many alternatives, potential definitions, and groupings. Consequently, the determination of subordinate systems is difficult and complex.

Given the complications of identifying subordinate systems, the authors have attempted nonetheless to identify the subordinate systems which exist in the contemporary world. The results of their efforts are contained in Table 1-1, which is offered not as a final formulation, but rather as a suggestive and perhaps provocative postulation.

In approaching the study of subordinate systems, the authors have made decisions based on the following considerations:

Every nation-state (no matter how strong or how weak) is a member of only one subordinate system. There are two exceptions to this generalization: the most powerful states are also active in other subordinate systems besides their own; and there are a few states which exist on the borderline between two subordinate systems and may be considered to belong to both (e.g., Finland, Turkey, Afghanistan, and Burma).

All subordinate systems are geographically delineated—at least in part— by reference to geographical considerations, but social, economic, political, and organizational factors are also relevant. Consequently, members of subordinate systems are proximate, but they may not be precisely contiguous. *Size does not necessarily determine the existence of a subordinate system.* It may consist of one nation and be relatively large (the U.S.S.R.),[6] or it may consist of several nations and be relatively compact in area (the Middle East). Where only one nation is a member of a region we can say that the internal and subordinate systems are identical.

Within the boundaries of a subordinate system, there is a complex interaction between political, social, and geographic factors. It is this interaction which is most important in defining the limits of a subordinate system. For example, primarily political boundaries divide East and West Europe; social and political boundaries divide Latin America and North America; geographic boundaries help to identify the Middle East and divide North Africa from the rest of Africa.

Indigenous political relationships (antagonistic and cooperative), geographic factors, and social and historical backgrounds help to define a subordinate system. Thus, the authors believe that, despite the Organization of African Unity (OAU), the African continent is fragmented by a variety of local interactions, while in Latin America, despite great differences, the area is more interrelated.[7]

Outside powers play a role in defining a subordinate system. This is particularly true in East Europe, Southeast Asia, and Latin America.

Although geographic boundaries do not change and social factors rarely do, political and ideological factors are fluid. Consequently, the identity of a subordinate system is both tenuous and dynamic. For example, the nineteenth-century writer would probably have suggested the significance of the Central European subordinate system; but he certainly would not have found the nation-state of Israel in the Middle East.

We can thus conclude that a subordinate system consists of one state, or of two or more proximate and interacting states which have some common ethnic, linguistic, cultural, social, and historical bonds, and whose sense of identity is sometimes increased by the actions and attitudes of states external

---

[6] The Soviet Union has been considered a region in and of itself because with reference to social, political, and geographic factors it resembles many of the other subordinate systems.

[7] It is worth noting in this regard that Africa is almost twice as large as Latin America and that its population is also about twice as large.

Some readers may be surprised that the authors have not defined such areas as Scandinavia and Central America as separate subordinate systems. It is our position that were political integration to occur among such nations (Benelux and the British West Indies may be added), they would have a similar position in their subordinate systems (i.e., as part of the core or periphery) as they do now, even though their power within the system would be increased. For example, a United States of Central America would play a similar role to that played by Mexico or Venezuela as members of the Latin American core, and a United States of Scandinavia would relate to West Europe much as Great Britain does at present. Our subsequent analysis of cores and peripheries will further clarify the rationale for these judgments.

to the system. The seven foregoing basic generalizations, plus this definition, should be sufficient to enable us to at least tentatively identify a subordinate system. It will become clear, as we proceed to elaborate the components of our approach, that we are at the same time elaborating our definition.

Although it is relatively easy to identify any particular subordinate system, the specific membership of certain states poses some difficulty. In general this difficulty can be dealt with by asking whether or not a particular state could possibly be placed in another subordinate system. While there are occasionally difficult borderline cases (e.g., Burma, which might be placed in Southeast Asia or South Asia; and Afghanistan, which might be placed in the Middle East or South Asia), we shall try to show that in general each state can be included in one subordinate system. One of our major tasks, in this chapter, will be to explore methods of determining the precise membership of particular subordinate systems.

In Table 1-1, the authors have divided the globe into fifteen subordinate systems, each of which has been determined with reference to the considerations already discussed. (It is, of course, possible that other researchers— even using a similar framework—could come to slightly different conclusions.) In the present comparative exploration of the international politics of subordinate systems, we have chosen to concentrate on five of these areas: West Europe, the Middle East, West Africa, Southeast Asia, and Latin America. Before we proceed, however, we must indicate that the various countries in each subordinate system are actively interrelated. It is this dynamic inner relationship which helps us both to define each subordinate system and to compare various subsystems. We shall use the following analysis of the ways in which a state interacts on a regional level as a means of organizing our discussion of the five subordinate systems. The utility of the following research patterns in identifying subordinate systems should become clear as we proceed.

THREE SUBDIVISIONS OF THE SUBORDINATE SYSTEM

Granted that we have identified a subordinate system, it is possible to differentiate it further into three subdivisions: the core sector, the peripheral sector, and the intrusive system. In addition, we believe there are four pattern variables which are crucial to the demarcation of th. e subdivisions: (1) the nature and level of cohesion; (2) the nature of communications; (3) the level of power; and (4) the structure of relations. These variables are also crucial to the comparison of subordinate systems with diverse qualities.

The term "pattern variable" as used here means a general category which inter-connects several related factors. For example, the pattern variable of cohesion inter-connects social, economic, political, and organizational factors;

Table 1-1   SUBORDINATE SYSTEMS OF THE WORLD AND THEIR SUBDIVISIONS

REGION	CORE	PERIPHERY	INTRUSIVE SYSTEM
Middle East	United Arab Republic	Israel	U.S.
	Yemen	Turkey	U.S.S.R.
	Saudi Arabia	Iran	France
	Kuwait	†Afghanistan	Great Britain
	Iraq		West Germany
	Lebanon		People's Republic of
	Sudan		China
	Jordan		
	Syria		
	South Yemen		
	(Persian Gulf States)		
West Europe	France	*Northern:*	U.S.
	West Germany	*Great Britain	U.S.S.R.
	Italy	*Ireland	
	Belgium	*Switzerland	
	Netherlands	Iceland	
	Luxembourg	†Finland	
		*Denmark	
		*Sweden	
		*Norway	
		*Austria	
		Southern:	
		*Spain	
		*Portugal	
		†Turkey	
		Greece	
		Malta	
		Cyprus	
East Europe	Poland	*Albania	U.S.
	Czechoslovakia	*Yugoslavia	France
	Hungary	Finland	West Germany
	Rumania	East Germany	U.S.S.R.
	Bulgaria		People's Republic of
			China
U.S.S.R.	U.S.S.R.		
North America	U.S.	†Trinidad and Tobago	
	Canada	†Jamaica	
	.	†Barbados	
		†(West Indies Associated States)	
Latin America	Argentina	*Cuba	U.S.
	Bolivia	Trinidad and Tobago	U.S.S.R.
	Brazil	Jamaica	Great Britain
	Chile	Barbados	Netherlands
	Colombia	Guyana	France
	Costa Rica	Haiti	People's Republic of
	Dominican Republic	(Surinam)	China
	Ecuador	(West Indies Associated States)	
	El Salvador	(French Guiana)	
	Guatemala		
	Honduras		
	(British Honduras)		

Table 1-1 continued

REGION	CORE	PERIPHERY	INTRUSIVE SYSTEM
	Mexico		
	Nicaragua		
	Panama		
	Paraguay		
	Peru		
	Uruguay		
	Venezuela		
East Asia	People's Republic of China	*Taiwan	U.S.
		North Korea	Portugal
		South Korea	Great Britain
		*Mongolia	U.S.S.R.
		Japan	
		(Hong Kong)	
		(Macao)	
Southwest Pacific	Australia New Zealand	(Islands of South Pacific)	U.S. France
		Western Samoa	Great Britain
			U.S.S.R.
			Japan
Southeast Asia	*Maritime S.E. Asia:*	Singapore	People's Republic of China
	Indonesia	(Territory of New	
	Malaysia	Guinea)	Japan
	Philippines	(Territory of	Portugal
	Mainland S.E. Asia:	Portuguese Timor)	
	Laos	Burma	Australia
	North Vietnam		U.S.
	South Vietnam		France
	Cambodia		Great Britain
	Thailand		U.S.S.R.
South Asia	India	*Ceylon	U.S.
		*Nepal	U.S.S.R.
		*Bhutan	
		*Sikkim	
		Afghanistan	Great Britain
		Maldive Islands	People's Republic of China
		Pakistan	
		†Burma	
North Africa	Morocco	Mauritania	France
	Tunisia	Libya	U.S.S.R.
	Algeria		U.S.
		(Spanish Sahara)	People's Republic of China
			Spain
West Africa	Ivory Coast	Nigeria	U.S.
	Dahomey	Liberia	U.S.S.R.
	Guinea	Sierra Leone	France
	Senegal	Gambia	Great Britain
	Upper Volta	Ghana	Portugal
	Mali	(Portuguese Guinea)	
	Niger		
	Togo		
Southern Africa	South Africa	Malawi	U.S.
	Rhodesia	Malagasy Republic	Great Britain

Table 1-1   Continued

REGION	CORE	PERIPHERY	INTRUSIVE SYSTEM
	(Angola)	Lesotho	Portugal
	(Mozambique)	Botswana	
	(South West Africa)	Zambia	
		Swaziland	
		Mauritius	
Central Africa	The Congo (Kinshasa)	Central African	U.S.
	Rwanda	Republic	Belgium
	Burundi	Chad	People's Republic of
		Cameroon	China
		Gabon	U.S.S.R.
		Congo (Brazzaville)	France
		Equatorial Guinea	Spain
East Africa	Uganda	Ethiopia	U.S.
	Kenya	Somali Republic	U.S.S.R.
	Tanzania	(French Somaliland)	France
			People's Republic of
			China
			Great Britain

Note:
An asterisk (*) *indicates a state which is potentially part of the Core.* Parentheses *indicate a colony. Only the most important colonies (in terms of their effect upon the subordinate system) have been listed. A* dagger (†) *indicates a state which could possibly be a member of a second periphery.*

the pattern variable of power inter-connects material, military, and motivational factors. Each pattern variable should be viewed as referring to a segment of the elements and activities which constitute any individual subordinate system. Through the use of these four broad categories, or pattern variables, we will be able to sharpen the process of demarcating and comparing subordinate systems, by focusing on various aspects of the international relations of particular regions. By isolating specific, but related elements, we will elucidate both the differences and similarities between systems and sectors of systems.[8]

PATTERN VARIABLES

Nature and Level of Cohesion

By cohesion we mean the degree of similarity or complementarity in the properties of the political entities being considered and the degree of interaction between these units. The concept of cohesion plays a similar role in the consideration of regions to that which the concept of integration has played in the analysis of nation-states. In the study of comparative national politics

[8] For a more technical use of the term "pattern variable" see Talcott Parsons, *The Social System* (New York: The Free Press, 1951), pp. 46–51, 58–67, 101–12.

integration has been used to mean, "the problem of creating a sense of territorial nationality which overshadows—or eliminates—subordinate parochial loyalties."[9] When applied to the study of international relations the concept of integration can thus involve an assumption that the states being compared will lose their independence as they become more interlocked. Cohesion involves no such assumption. As states become more similar and more interactive, there is no guarantee that they will unite or federate; on the contrary, cohesiveness may as likely lead to disunity as to unity. When the term "integration" is applied to regions, it is usually assumed at a minimum that warfare does not exist among the members or that a more encompassing political institution results from the process: "Integration and security community...imply stable expectations of peace among the participating units or groups, whether or not there has been a merger of their political institutions" or "Political integration is the process whereby political actors in several distinct national settings are persuaded to shift their loyalties, expectations and political activities toward a new centre, whose institutions possess or demand jurisdiction over the pre-existing national states."[10] Not so with cohesion, for there is no direct correlation between cohesion and absence of warfare or between cohesion and a shift of political loyalty.

In this volume, we mean by *integration* the process of political unification or incorporation. Integration may include the unification of sectors of one nation-state or the federation of more than one nation-state to form a new whole. In either case, the process of integrating assumes, but proceeds beyond, the absence of military conflict. A condition in which nations cease to prepare for war against one another, but are not becoming unified, can be said to be one of *consolidation*. In cohesion, these units are homogeneous; they interact and there is complementarity—but there may also be conflict. In each case—integration, consolidation, and cohesion—there are stages and degrees.

In the Conclusion to this volume we will return again to these distinctions and discuss how they can be applied to all four pattern variables as a means of constructing a typology of subordinate systems. For the present, however, we will assume that neither consolidation nor integration can occur without a high degree of cohesion; and we will, therefore, compare subordinate systems on the basis of their relative degrees of cohesion. We will assume that cohesion makes integration and consolidation possible, but we will leave the results until a further assessment in Chapter 9.

9 Myron Weiner, "Political Integration and Political Development," in *Political Modernization*, ed. C. Welch, (Belmont, Calif.: Wadsworth Publishing Co., Inc., 1967), pp. 150–51. Reprinted from *The Annals*, CCCLVIII (March, 1965), 52–64.
10 The first quotation is from Karl Deutsch, "Security Communities," in *International Politics and Foreign Policy*, ed. J. Rosenau, (New York: The Free Press, 1961), p. 98; the second is from Ernst Haas, *The Uniting of Europe* (Stanford, Calif.: Stanford University Press, 1958), p. 16.

The concept of cohesion as discussed here can be further differentiated into its social, economic, political, and organizational elements. When we speak of "social" cohesion we are concerned with the similarity of component units, whereas when we speak of "economic" and "political" cohesion, complementarity becomes more important. Finally, interaction is most significant with reference to organizational cohesion and economic cohesion.

Under the rubric of *social cohesiveness,* attention is focused upon the contributive factors of ethnicity, race, language, religion, culture, history, and consciousness of a common heritage. The contrasts that these factors may present can be seen in the extremes of the Middle East subordinate system's high degree of social cohesion and Southeast Asia's extremely low degree of social cohesion. Under the rubric of *economic cohesiveness,* the focus is upon the distribution and complementarity of economic resources as well as on the character of trade patterns. The extremes of this factor can be seen in the West European system's high degree of economic cohesiveness and the West African and Middle Eastern systems' low degree. Under the rubric of *political cohesiveness* we are concerned with the manner in which the pattern and degree of complementarity of types of regime contribute or detract from the cohesion of a subordinate system. In this respect one could compare West Europe, with its multitude of reconciliatory or parliamentary-type regimes, and the Middle East, with its contrasting mobilizational and modernizing autocracies.[11]

Finally, under the rubric of *organizational cohesion* we should note the possible effects upon cohesion of membership in the United Nations and in regional organizations. The analysis of voting behavior in the United Nations

---

[11] For this classification of political systems, see David Apter, *The Politics of Modernization* (Chicago: University of Chicago Press, 1965), pp. 28–38, and Chaps. 9 and 11.

Apter's system of classification is based on two models, the sacred-collectivity model and the secular-libertarian model, and on three subtypes of these models. These five types of systems are then:
1. The reconciliation system (secular-libertarian model), in which given values and purposes generate legitimate authority and conflict between groups holding these values gives rise to public policy (e.g., Great Britain, United States).
2. The mobilization system (sacred-collectivity model) in which new values are created and whose leaders are attempting to work out a system of moral authority (e.g., Soviet Union, Guinea, Cuba).
From these two models there follow three variations or subtypes:
3. The modernizing autocracy with a traditionalistic ideology, associated with a monarch who represents the nation (e.g., Thailand, Morocco, Ethiopia).
4. The military oligarchy, similar to the preceding but with a military leader in place of the king (e.g., Indonesia, Ghana).
5. The neo-mercantilist society, also similar to the preceding two types but which has a "presidential monarch" (e.g., Tunisia, Ivory Coast).
Although in this volume we have dealt with political cohesion primarily in terms of complementarity of types of regimes, the authors intend to expand this category in their forthcoming volume to include the important considerations of political culture, class structure, bureaucracy, and political institutions. These subjects seemed beyond the scope of the present work.

has revealed the existence of groupings of states identifiable as Afro-Asian, Latin American, and so forth, all of which contribute in some degree to regional consciousness.[12] As for regional organization, we should note to what extent a regional organization is coterminous with the region's boundaries, contrasting, e.g., the European Common Market and the Arab League. If all members of a subordinate system or a sector of a subordinate system belong to a regional international organization, this tends to reinforce cohesion, particularly if the boundaries of the membership coincide with the system's or sector's boundaries.

Nature of Communications

The second pattern variable, the nature of communications, is divisible into four aspects: personal communications (mail, telephone, telegraph); mass media (newspapers, radio, television); exchanges among the elite (intra-regional education, tourism, diplomatic visits within the region); and transportation (road, water, rail, air). It is evident that literacy rates and differences in language will affect the first three and that geography and technological development will affect all four. Regions will differ from each other with the degree to which these four factors are present and applicable. Southeast Asia is weak in all four, for example as is West Africa, while West Europe has been able to outweigh linguistic differences by the sheer profusion of channels of communications and other pattern variables.

Level of Power

"Power," the third pattern variable, is defined here as the present and potential ability and the willingness of one nation to alter the internal decision-making processes of other countries in accordance with its own policies. We can isolate three broad aspects of a nation's power: material, military, and motivational. The *material* elements of power comprise the basis of a nation's capacity: these include its location and resources; the size, quality, and structure of its population; its economy and its industrial capacity (particularly to be measured by gross national product (GNP), per capita GNP, and production and consumption of energy); and the relative efficiency of its administration and government. The *military* elements of power comprise a nation's ability to wage war: its military techniques, weaponry, manpower, and efficiency. They also include the effect which scientific and technological developments have on the ability of stronger nations to increase their margin of superiority over weaker nations or of weaker countries to overtake the leaders. Finally, the *motivational* elements of power center on a nation's will to seek prestige and status in international affairs, and on its readiness to sacrifice consumer satisfaction

[12] For an analysis along these lines, see Bruce Russett, *International Regions and the International System* (Chicago: Rand McNally & Co., 1967), Chaps. 4, 5.

to build its material and military power. Motivation is influenced by such elements as ideology, national character and morale, nationalism, history, the personalities and abilities of particular statesmen, and diplomatic skill.

Because existing and potential[13] national strengths and weaknesses are frequently contradictory, it is difficult to produce a "power calculation" in order to compare states. Given the complexity of the process, the attempt to estimate the power of nations nevertheless produces valuable information about the distribution or balance of power among nations in a subordinate system. This analytical process also facilitates the comparison of the character of various subordinate systems.

It is possible to detect seven types of nation-states in the current period: primary powers, secondary powers, middle powers, minor powers, regional states, micro-states, and colonies. Which category a nation state belongs in depends on its degree of power and its range of influence.

PRIMARY POWERS. The primary powers (the U.S. and the U.S.S.R.), together with the secondary powers constitute the great powers, that is, nations which influence domestic politics and foreign policies of other countries in several areas of the world and which are individually superior to other nations materially, militarily, and in motivation. Primary powers are superior to secondary powers on the basis of these three factors, but both types compose the dominant system in international politics.

SECONDARY POWERS. Compared to primary powers, secondary powers (the United Kingdom, France, West Germany, Japan, and China) have a more limited capacity to participate in selected subordinate systems of the world.

MIDDLE POWERS. Middle powers (e.g., Italy, Canada, Australia, East Germany, Spain, Portugal, Brazil, India) are those states whose level of power permits them to play only decidedly limited and selected roles in subordinate systems other than their own.

Unlike the great powers, middle powers are not usually capable or desirous of attempting to alter the international relations of weaker nations. Their involvement is usually limited to specific kinds of economic, military, and political participation in isolated countries. For example, Canada has aided India in the peaceful development of atomic energy; Italian and Dutch oil companies have been active in North Africa and the Middle East; Poland, Czechoslovakia, and East Germany have often provided military and economic aid in conjunction with Soviet policies; and the Indians (although primarily involved with their own region) have cooperated sporadically with such other nonaligned nations as Egypt and Yugoslavia. One of the few major activities which middle powers pursue within weaker

---

[13] "Potential" applies to each factor of power (material, military, and motivational). An advanced state may be capable of growing further or may change in motivation as a result of altered international conditions or a new domestic regime. A developing state's potentiality may be long or short-term, depending upon its possible development and rate of growth.

areas is the possession of colonies (e.g., the Spanish and Portuguese holdings). MINOR POWERS. Minor powers are those states which play leading roles in the international relations of their own systems, either through regional activities or independent policies (e.g., Cuba, Algeria, South Korea, Taiwan, Pakistan, Egypt, Israel, Ghana, Indonesia, Rumania, Yugoslavia, Argentina, Mexico, Nigeria, Turkey, North Vietnam, New Zealand, and the Philippines). Most countries in this category attempt to alter, in their own favor, the direction of domestic and foreign policies in some countries within their region. Others, however, are thwarted within their own regions and express their potential influence in subordinate systems other than their own: Israel, and to a lesser extent Yugoslavia, Rumania, South Korea, Taiwan, and Cuba, are particular examples. Yet despite forays into other subordinate systems, these countries are still most active within their own regions, since they are not capable of the same intensity of involvement elsewhere as the middle and great powers. While the United States tends to have more entrenched influence with secondary and middle powers, the Soviet Union has closer relations with a greater percentage of the minor powers.

In comparison with the majority of middle powers, minor powers tend to be more unpredictable in their international associations, more ideological, and less industralized. They usually possess somewhat more material power than other countries in their own regional complex or are led by a highly motivated elite. They frequently seek independence from individual external powers in their attempt to influence or establish the elite of nearby countries which could become close allies. As a consequence, they are fickle followers of dominant powers; their relations with the great powers are not ordinarily designed to involve them in the manipulations of the dominant system, but rather to gain competitive advantages within their own subordinate system. The distinctive characteristic of these powers is that they are strong enough to attempt to use their relations with more powerful states as an instrument in the pursuit of independent regional goals.

Primary, secondary, middle, and minor powers are the active nations in current international politics. The passive nations are those countries which are so weak that in their international politics they are largely recipients of stronger power action. There are three types: regional states, micro-states, and colonies.

REGIONAL STATES. Regional states are defined as countries which are generally weaker than minor powers in material, military, and motivational power but which have a small degree of influence on the foreign scene because they are able on occasion to play a limited role in their own subordinate system. They also tend to have greater flexibility with reference to stronger powers than do micro-states and colonies. The regional states gain their influence either because they have a small degree of power which they are able to exert in their own region, because their territory is a meeting ground for larger powers, or because they are able to attain a degree of neutrality vis-à-vis the competition of greater powers. Regional states which exert some minimal influence in their own region include Greece, Hungary, Colombia, Venezuela, Iraq, Syria, Sudan, Tunisia, Morocco, North Korea, Ceylon, Kenya, Zambia, Ethiopia, Tanzania, and the Congo (Kinshasa). There have been revolutions, or at least some form of competition of greater powers, in every one of these countries, yet they are still not the weakest nations in their areas. They are distinctive, however, because a higher degree of internal convulsion exists in these states than in the minor powers.

Some regional states are able to gain neutrality through internal strength and the tacit agreement of stronger powers, e.g., Burma, Afganistan, and Finland. If she were stronger, Burma, for example, would attempt to use the greater powers to further her own policies, as the minor powers do.

MICRO-STATES. Micro-states are defined as nations which have little or no influence in international affairs because elements within the power calculation (e.g., economic status or geographic position) place them almost totally within the orbit of a stronger power. They are usually within an area of one great power's influence or are isolated former colonies which are still closely attached to their former protectorates.

Included in this group are many of the weaker countries of Latin America and other small countries such as Iceland, Luxembourg, Bulgaria, Jamaica, Mongolia, Liberia, Libya, Malta, Haiti, the Maldive Islands, Chad, Niger, Dahomey, Upper Volta, Togo, and Gambia. There are a few micro-states whose geographic position, material weakness, and internal political chaos cause them to be outright battlegrounds, rather than scenes of competition as are regional states. These include Cyprus and Yemen. Frequently, the government in power in a micro-state has even less substantive control over its population than the governments of regional states. As more smaller states gain independence and become able to bargain with the stronger nations, the number of micro-states is increasing.

COLONIES. Colonies are the few remaining political entities which have little or no independent motivational power. Examples include the Spanish Sahara, South West Africa, Portuguese Angola and Mozambique, British Honduras, Surinam, Hong Kong, and the French, British, and American colonies of the South Pacific. Since they have the least influence over their own territory, they have the lowest independent influence upon foreign affairs of any countries in the world, even though their potentialities may be greater than some of the regional and micro-states. As long as they remain dependencies, their role in international politics is one of complete passivity except for the occasional effects of dynamic liberation movements. Any immediate significance that colonies have is ordinarily a result of the foreign policy of the colonial power, although their territorial position and material power may lead us to predict for them a far more active part in international affairs once they have attained independence.

This categorization allows us to make an estimate of both the distribution and hierarchy of power within a subordinate system. West Europe is distinctive for the prevalence in it of secondary and middle powers. In Latin America there is only one middle power (Brazil), and a few minor powers (Argentina, Chile, Mexico), a few regional powers (Colombia, Peru, Venezuela) and many micro-states. In the Arab sector of the Middle East, congeries of regional and micro-states cluster around the one minor power; the United Arab Republic (U.A.R.), while the non-Arab states are all minor powers. The categories also facilitate the comparison of subordinate systems: the predominance of secondary and middle powers in West Europe indicates that its level of power is greater than that of either Latin America or the Middle East. Furthermore, as our twofold criteria of power and influence indicates, the role of a nation cannot be separated from its local base: Cuba, for example, might be much stronger politically were it located in Africa, and much weaker were it in West Europe. Location, because it is related to the opportunity for influence, affects ranking.

The ranking system, however, has not been determined in regional isolation. It can apply both universally and regionally because we have not assumed that the major state in each subordinate system must be accorded the status of a primary power. For example, the most powerful state in North America is a primary power, but the most powerful states in West Africa are only regional states. Thus this ranking system gives us some possibility—admittedly only approximate—of determining the relative strength of the individual members of any two subordinate systems, and also enables us to compare the countries within any one region.

Structure of Relations

The fourth pattern variable the structure of relations, is the character of the relationships among the nation-states that compose a subordinate system. It is important here to determine: (1) which states are cooperating and which are in conflict (*the spectrum of relations*); (2) the basis for their amity or antagonism (*the causes of relations*); and (3) the instruments which they use to effect their relations—e.g., types of weapons, ways of ameliorating conflict, methods of cooperation—(*the means of relations*).

THE SPECTRUM OF RELATIONS.[14] The structure of a system's interrelations can be described by reference to the conditions depicted in Table 1-2, which

---

[14] The concept of power, the seven types of nations, and the spectrum of relations are discussed in greater detail in a forthcoming book by Steven L. Spiegel to be published by Little, Brown and Company.

Table 1-2   SPECTRUM OF RELATIONS

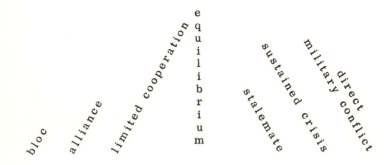

shows a spectrum extending from the close cooperation of a bloc to the exacerbated conflict of direct military confrontation.

Conditions of amity include: a *bloc,* in which two or more nations act in international politics as if they were one political entity; *an alliance,* in which they agree to aid each other in specified ways—usually including military means; and *tentative cooperation,* in which they coordinate their actions for specific purposes and over a very short period of time (days rather than weeks, weeks rather than months). From the opposite direction, *conditions of antagonism include: direct military conflict,* in which combat occurs between the troops of two opposing sides; *sustained crisis,* in which contending parties make persistent attempts, short of direct military conflict, to alter the balance of power between them; and *stalemate,* in which contention continues while neither side is prepared or able to alter the existing relationship. In direct military conflict, the means used to change the *status quo* are forceful and deliberate, but in sustained crisis the primary means of contention are more subtle: they include political maneuvering among neutral and independent states, arms races, limited local warfare between parties aligned on either side, vituperative exchanges, crises, and in general a chaotic atmosphere filled with tension. In stalemates, contention is at a lower level because both sides decide that, given existing conditions, they would prefer to live with the situation than face the consequences of attempting to upset the prevailing balance of forces.

Only when we arrive at *equilibrium* do we find a standoff in competitive power between two sides that is mutually acceptable. Whether or not an equality of power exists, the effect is the same; the statesmen of both sides not only accept the situation but prefer it to any foreseeable alternative. The *status quo* becomes a standard of the acceptable balance of power, and so long as neither side moves to alter it or perceives that it is being altered the equilibrium will continue. The difference between stalemate and equilibrium is that in a stalemate one or both sides would change conditions if they could and are seeking means of doing so; in equilibrium neither side believes that it would alter the balance of power even if it had the means to do so. Equilibrium is a prerequisite to most stages of amity—except the lowest forms of limited cooperation.[15]

THE CAUSES OF RELATIONS. States are, of course, not always consistent in their relations. In any relationship between two or more states there may be elements of conflict on one level and of cooperation on others. Many Latin American states (e.g., Peru, Chile, Bolivia) are in a stalemate with reference to border issues while they are allied in economic and diplomatic international organizations. Saudi Arabia and the U.A.R. have been in a sustained crisis in regard to Yemen but in an alliance in regard to Israel. It is therefore necessary to consider the relative significance of major issues which cause conflict or cooperation between particular states in a subordinate system. In Latin America, the effect of American influence has been to subordinate local issues to regional pursuits. Similarly, in the Middle East, intra-Arab disputes are muted by the confrontation with Israel.

When there is conflict, the nature of the disputed issues reveals the intensity of the contention. For example, border and economic disputes are usually less damaging to peaceful international relations in the region than racial, religious, ideological, and historical rivalries. Similarly, when there is cooperation, the reasons for collaboration indicate the strength of the cross-national ties. A common enemy is likely to be a stronger tie than mutual economic interest; under present conditions, economics is likely to be a stronger incentive to cooperation than religious ties.

THE MEANS OF RELATIONS. The spectrum of relations within a subordinate system is further elucidated by reference to the means which are used in such relations. The type of warfare (e.g., guerrilla vs. conventional) being carried on helps to explain the relations which exist. Moreover, the manner in which conflicts are ameliorated and terminated indicate the strength of particular conditions in the spectrum of relations. For example, conditions in Latin America, where an elaborate set of diplomatic devices exists for the settlement of many types of conflict, are very different from conditions in the Middle East, where cease-fires are arranged by intermediaries and there is little or no contact between the Arabs and Israelis. West Europe, where states are also likely in the current period to resort to established means of amelioration, is different from Southeast Asia, where guerrillas either emerge victorious or fade into the interior and where rare agreements are broken freely. Finally, the extent of established consultative devices and the range of ties between cooperating governments not only help to indicate

---

[15] The spectrum we have presented does not include nations which are "neutral" toward each other in the sense of noninvolvement in hostile relations. In current subordinate systems, equilibrium or stalemate in respect to two conflicting sides is frequently either the cause or the effect of neutral policies of individual states.

whether a bloc, alliance, or limited cooperation is in progress; they also hint at the durability of these relationships.

These three elements, then, provide a frame of reference for examining the prevailing nature of relationships within a subordinate system. They enable us to make comparisons with other subordinate systems, both with respect to the influence of what we shall call the "intrusive" system and the effect of levels of cohesion, power, and communications. As we shall see, these four pattern variables, when applied to a given subordinate system, unveil the existence of what we term "core" and "peripheral" sectors.

THE CORE SECTOR, THE PERIPHERAL SECTOR, AND RELATIONS BETWEEN SECTORS

The Core Sector

The core sector consists of a state or a group of states which form a central focus of the international politics within a given region. The core sector usually consists of more than one state and when it does they possess a shared social, political, and/or organizational background or activity. There may be more than one core sector within a given subordinate system.[16]

We can make our definition more specific and useful by examining a hypothetical core sector in terms of our four pattern variables: the level of cohesion, the nature of communications, the level of power, and the structure of its interrelations. The minimal conditions for the existence of a core sector can be determined by its *level of cohesion,* which requires a consideration of the degree of social, economic, and political similarity, complementarity, and interaction within the particular group of states. In addition, the factor of organizational cohesion would have to be considered. Thus, an analysis of the similarity or complementarity of social cohesiveness would take into account ethnic, linguistic, cultural, and historical similarities, while economic cohesiveness would depend upon the complementarity of natural resources as well as the patterns and the degree of trade within the core and with the periphery. Political cohesiveness would be determined by the similarities among regimes and the manner in which these might contribute to or detract from the cohesiveness of the core sector. For example, in West Europe the regimes of the core sector are relatively similar, while in the Middle East they are not. Organizational cohesion would be revealed

16 Generally, the identification of a core sector is assisted by the existence of an easily identifiable culturally heterogeneous peripheral sector. When the peripheral sector is not so heterogeneous, as, for example, in the West African Anglophonic peripheral sector, then such factors as degree of cohesion, size or geographical area, population, and economic wealth have to be considered in order to determine the political center of gravity of the subordinate system. In West Africa, it is the high level of cohesion relative to the periphery and the vastness of the Francophonic area which are the decisive factors.

by the extent to which an organization (e.g., the European Common Market and the West European core sector) coincides with a core sector. The degree of common memberships in international organizations, moreover, would be an indication of the extent of interaction within the core sector. It is evident that a knowledge of the degree of similarity or complementarity of these factors of cohesion will assist us to delineate a core sector. It is also evident that one type of cohesion may be more pronounced than others in a given core sector (e.g., the organizational in West Europe, and the social in the Middle East), while still other core sectors may be significantly united by all four elements of cohesion (e.g., North America, Southwest Pacific). Most often, however, one or more of the elements of cohesion, but not all of them, are significantly present in a core.

The second pattern variable, *the nature of communications,* should further inform us about the nature of a core sector in terms of personal communications, mass media, interchange among the elite, and transportation facilities. It is striking, for example, the extent to which the flow of communication within a subordinate system can be restricted to a core sector and fail to penetrate the peripheral sector (e.g., the Francophonic core sector of West Africa and the Anglophonic peripheral sector).

An analysis of the core sector in terms of *levels of power,* our third pattern variable, should inform us of the political capabilities contained within it. As in a region as a whole, the distribution of power within the core is revealing of the political processes at work. The primacy of France and West Germany in the Common Market, of Australia in the Southwest Pacific, of Algeria in North Africa, and of the Union of South Africa in Southern Africa may be contrasted with the rough equality among the participants in the cores of maritime Southeast Asia and East Africa. The degree of supremacy of the preeminent states of a core (e.g., United States in North America vs. the U.A.R. in the Middle East) can be contrasted with the position of weaker states (e.g., Canada in North America vs. Jordan, Yemen, and South Yemen in the Middle East), and the relative gap between strongest and weakest must also be assessed. Finally, in distinguishing the core from the peripheral sector it is important to note the relative power of each. The Middle East and West Africa are distinctive for the strength of their peripheral states vis-à-vis the core, while in Latin America and Southeast Asia the peripheries are particularly weak. In West Europe, the core and periphery come closer to approximating equality than in any of the cases just cited.

The fourth pattern variable, *the structure of relations,* completes the profile of a core sector. It is closely connected to the third variable, for it informs us of the dynamics of the exercise of power. Differing levels of power within a core sector will have profound consequences on its internal relations. The conflicts between the U.A.R. and Saudi Arabia, Brazil and Argentina, North

Vietnam and Thailand, Guinea and the Ivory Coast, among Indonesia, Malaysia, and the Philippines, and between Algeria and her two neighbors, Tunisia and Morocco, are related to power conditions within the core. The means of both conflict and cooperation are, moreover, directly connected to the level of power of the core—except where outside powers intervene and provide their own instruments of contention (e.g., jet fighters) or collaboration (e.g., international organization). The causes of relations, however, often involve wider issues than mere level of power. Cohesion and communications are especially significant in explaining the reasons for the particular structure of relations within the core. For example, the factor of political cohesion helps to explain the split within the Arab core; improved communications and political and organizational cohesion help to explain Franco-German reconciliation.

It can thus be seen that while the initial delineation of the subordinate system itself may be considered somewhat subjective, the application of the four pattern variables soon reveals the identity of the subordinate system and of the more well-defined core sector as well. In fact, our ability to delineate the core sector so sharply in turn assists us to define the subordinate system itself, as will be seen in the later discussion of the core sectors of the five regions we have selected for analysis.

Peripheral Sector

The peripheral sector includes all those states within a given subordinate system which are alienated from the core sector in some degree by social, political, economic, or organizational factors, but which nevertheless play a role in the politics of the subordinate system. While the core sector tends towards cultural, social, and political homogeneity, the peripheral sector is characteristically heterogeneous, and there is usually little interaction among periphery members. The minimal factor accounting for the inclusion of the member states of the peripheral sector in the subordinate system appears to be primarily geographical, although additional social, cultural, political, and historical factors exist. It follows, then, that peripheral sector, as compared with the core sector, is characterized by less cohesion, less communication, relatively unrelated levels of power, and much more fluid relations.

There are some exceptions, however, in areas where there tends to be some degree of homogeneity if not also cohesiveness (notably in the Anglophonic periphery of West Africa, groupings in the West European periphery, the Black states of the Southern African periphery and the Francophonic periphery of Central Africa). In West Africa, for example, a common British colonial experience and knowledge of the English language contribute to this comparative homogeneity. Where both the core and periphery are cohesive, it is necessary to assess the relative degree of cohesiveness and the locus of political centrality within the subordinate system before assigning the label "core."

One of the outstanding characteristics of the periphery is that its diplomatic orientation is typically outside of the region, i.e., peripheral states usually seek their diplomatic alignments outside of, rather than within, the subordinate system. This can be seen, for example, in the key role played by Nigeria, a member of the West African peripheral sector, in the founding of the OAU and in the membership of Iran and Turkey, members of the Middle Eastern peripheral sector, in CENTO (the Central Treaty Organization). Another characteristic of the peripheral sector is that it often serves as a geographic and diplomatic buffer between external powers. This largely geopolitical circumstance can be seen in Libya and Mauritania, which are buffers for the North African core sector, and in Burma, which is a buffer for the mainland Southeast Asian core sector.

ABERRATIONS IN THE PERIPHERY. The fluid nature of the periphery makes it occasionally necessary to qualify its delineation. A few of the states which we have described as peripheral are, by virtue of their activities, *divided between the peripheries of two subordinate systems.* In terms of our four pattern variables, this generally appears to occur when certain states (notably Turkey, Finland, Afghanistan, and Burma) can be identified with one subordinate system in terms of cohesion and communications while they interact with another in terms of power and the structure of relations. For this reason we have found it necessary to include specific states in two subordinate systems. Thus Finland shares common historical and organizational (Nordic Council) features with the Northern grouping of the West European periphery, but the Soviet Union draws it into the East European periphery, in terms of power and the structure of relations. Similarly, there are in Turkey strong historical and cultural elements which identify it with the Middle Eastern subordinate system, while in terms of power and the structure of relations (as expressed, e.g., in NATO membership and the dispute with Greece over Cyprus) it is more appropriately placed in the West European periphery. Afghanistan and Burma are somewhat similar cases. Afghanistan has ancient historical ties and continuing religious ties with the Middle East, but in terms of power and the structure of its relations it can be included in the South Asian periphery. Burma has historical, religious, and cultural ties with Southeast Asia, but it shares with India the common historical experience of British colonial rule and its population contains a sizable Indian minority. In addition, the Anglophonic area of the Caribbean appears to lie astride both the North American and Latin American subordinate systems, as elements of the four pattern variables and geography pull these micro-states in both directions in this period of transition from colony to independence.

Some degree of verification of the marginal character of borderline states is provided by the fact that our discussion of them reveals that they are always located in a periphery, and never a core. Thus, although borderline peripheral states are difficult to locate within a specific subordinate system, it is possible to examine their position by utilizing this comparative regional approach.

Further delineation is also required with respect to the West European periphery, because its large size and certain dichotomous features suggest that it can be divided into Northern and Southern groupings (see Table 1-1). The Northern peripheral states are more industrialized, more economically developed, and more democratically governed than the South; as a consequence, they are more likely to become a part of the core. They are also distinguished from the South because they are more Protestant and linguistically more Nordic, Anglo-Saxon, and Germanic. Yet, as we shall see in the course of our more specific discussion of the West European periphery in Chapter 4, this potential division within the West European periphery is offset by the organizational and economic cohesion of both parts of the sector with the core.

Relations Between the Sectors

As the definition of the peripheral sector indicated, the periphery is in part defined by its relationship to the core. In relations between the core and the periphery, alienation is a central factor, as was cohesion in our discussion of relations within a sector.

The core, as the center of political gravity in the subordinate system, relates individually to isolated states or to small groups of states in the periphery. Their alienation may arise for a variety of reasons. Geography is frequently a complement to other factors, but it is not ordinarily the only element leading to alienation from the core, and in fact may not be an element at all, as the case of Israel shows. In West Europe, geography has contributed to Great Britain's alienation from the core, but political developments have also been crucial. Were Britain to be admitted to the Common Market, she would thereby become a member of the core, since organizational cohesion is the most important element in determining the West European core. In the Middle East, on the other hand, social cohesion is extremely important in delineating the periphery; therefore, the three non-Arab states—Iran, Turkey and Israel—form the periphery.

The degree of alienation between the two sectors can perhaps be seen in the distinction between states with, and states without, the potentiality of becoming part of the core (e.g., Taiwan and Great Britain vs. Jamaica and Israel). A high degree of political and organizational cohesion in the core tends to breed peripheral states which are potential members of the core sector, while a high degree of social cohesion in the core tends to preclude peripheral states from having such potentialities (see Table 1-1).

There is frequently disaffection between the core and periphery. Among the fifteen subordinate systems of the world, some form of tension between the two sectors is especially severe in the Middle East, East Europe, Latin America, East Asia, and South Asia. Only in Southeast Asia and North Africa does tension within the core exceed the tension between the sectors. As for tension within the periphery, this hardly exists, because of the low level of interaction in the periphery. The major exceptions are Greece and Turkey (when Turkey is viewed as a member of the West European periphery); Albania and Yugoslavia in East Europe, the Koreas in East Asia, and Ethiopia and the Somali Republic in East Africa. States which are potentially part of the core and those which are not seem to be equally likely to find themselves in antagonistic relationships with their core. In some cases the differences which contribute to the difficulty of becoming part of the core create an antagonistic relationship with some or all of the core states (e.g., Israel, Pakistan, Mauritania), although frequently the potentiality of joining the core itself seems to create alienation and conflict (e.g., Taiwan, Albania, and Cuba).

INTRUSIVE SYSTEM

An intrusive system consists of the politically significant participation of external powers in the international relations of the subordinate system. While the core and peripheral sectors both involve the states located within the region, an analysis of almost every region reveals that these states are not the only ones which play a role in the activities of the subordinate system. As one would expect in an international system whose hierarchy consists of seven types of nations, external countries involve themselves in the international politics of subordinate systems other than their own. This pattern is absent only in the North American core and in the Soviet Union, where the level of power is extremely high. Additionally, in the core of North America, the level of cooperation between the two members, the United States and Canada, is extremely high.[17]

There are two types of externally based regional participation: politically significant involvement and politically insignificant involvement. *Politically insignificant involvement* comprises material aid, trade, economic investment, and cultural and educational efforts which do not usually produce participation in the balance of power of the region. Middle powers, and to some degree secondary powers, are most likely to undertake this type of involvement. Spanish involvement in the Middle East and Canadian aid to India are examples. Much of Japanese and West German aid (except West Germany's activities in East European politics and its Hallstein Doctrine)

---

[17] It might be suggested that French and British involvement in Canada is in form similar to intrusive action in other subordinate systems. The authors rejected this interpretation, however, both because of the indigenous power of Canada and its close relationship with the U.S.

has not been politically motivated or accompanied by a desire to participate in local international relations. These conditions may change, however.

Politically significant involvement, on the other hand, produces participation in the balance of power of the subordinate system and may affect the dominant system's balance as well. This participation is expressed by the possession of a colony; economic or military aid producing an alteration in the balance of power in the region; formal alliance, troop commitment, or any agreement which causes the external power to act in ways which resemble the types of actions that would ordinarily be taken by a country indigenous to the region. This type of involvement is also determined by reference to the objectives, power, motivation, location, and international position of the intruding nation. Since only politically significant members can be defined as being members of the intrusive system, we will primarily be concerned here with these types of external powers.

Even politically significant involvement by one state, once identified as such, has to be judged further in relation to other intrusive powers. Thus, for example, Australia and Portugal meet the minimum requirements for politically significant involvement in Southeast Asia, but their participation is nowhere near as significant as that of the United States, China, or the Soviet Union.

Methods of Participation and the Pattern Variables

We can isolate nine characteristic ways in which external powers participate in the politics of a given region. These are: multilateral arrangements; bilateral arrangements; trade and economic investment; possession of a colony; military intervention; subversion; the United Nations; cultural and educational activities; and propaganda. All of these are used in one situation or another by politically significant external powers, while a few—particularly the economic and cultural avenues—are used occasionally by those which are politically insignificant.

MULTILATERAL ARRANGEMENTS. Participation by means of a multilateral arrangement occurs when one or more external powers encourage or supervise the origination of a treaty or organization for the purpose of common defenses or economic enterprises in which both external and indigenous nations participate. NATO in West Europe, the Warsaw Pact in East Europe, SEATO in Southeast Asia, CENTO in the Middle East, and the OAS in Latin America are the most prominent recent defense oriented examples. Some recent multilateral economic arrangements are the Marshall Plan and its outgrowth, the Organization for Economic Cooperation and Development (OECD), the Soviet-sponsored Council for Mutual Economic Assistance (COMECON or CEMA) in East Europe, the Colombo Plan for Cooperative Economic Development in South and Southeast Asia, the

Aid India consortium, and the American-sponsored Alliance for Progress in Latin America.[18] It is the absence of concern on the part of the super-powers, the lack of direct threat of conquest, and the recent independence of the area which explain the near nonexistence of multilateral arrangements in most of Africa. The two major exceptions are the loose membership in the Commonwealth of most of the Anglophonic states and the much more significant Organisation Commune Africaine et Malgache (OCAM) membership of most Francophonic states.

BILATERAL ARRANGEMENTS. Bilateral arrangements are far more prevalent than multilateral ones; they may be subdivided into economic (including technical) assistance, military assistance, and mutual security treaties sometimes accompanied by the establishment of military bases. A primary example of the last is the American defense treaty with Spain. We may use the Middle East as an example of economic and military assistance: this region is of considerable strategic importance to greater powers because of geopolitical factors as well as its oil, and such arrangements have existed there in profusion. Both the United States and the Soviet Union have given sizable economic aid to the U.A.R. Soviet aid has been given liberally to Syria and, to a lesser extent, to Iraq. American and British aid has been extended to Saudi Arabia and Jordan. The pattern is in keeping with the general tendency of the superpowers to identify their own interests with either the radical or conservative bloc in the core sector of that region. Military arrangements in the Middle East have characteristically taken the form of barter deals and the outright sale or gift of arms and equipment. In the peripheral sector, military aid has been given by the Western powers to Iran and Turkey for defense against the Soviet Union,[19] and to Israel for defense against the Arabs. In the core sector, the pattern is a general tendency for Western states to give arms to Jordan and Saudi Arabia, and for Eastern states—recently joined by France—to provide arms for the United Arab Republic, Syria, Iraq, and Yemen.

TRADE AND ECONOMIC INVESTMENT. Trade is one of the most significant instruments for domination of subordinate systems by intrusive powers. Developing states are highly dependent upon a small range of exports; thus, an external power which purchases the bulk of a nation's exports gains considerable control over both its foreign and domestic policies. By skillfully manipulating its trade patterns, an external power may become essential

[18] It should be noted that in some cases the multilateral arrangements are not coterminous with the region to which they apply. They may include other nearby countries (e.g., Pakistan belongs to CENTO) or may exclude several nations within the particular region.

[19] Consistent with recent attempts by the U.S.S.R. to moderate its policies with respect to Iran and Turkey, the Russians have made military allotments to Iran and granted economic assistance to both.

to the economics of a region. Trade is a particularly important instrument when one external power is dominant in an area (e.g., the United States in Latin America and France in Francophonic Africa). It may also be a prime means of challenge to the ascendancy of an external power (e.g., West German trade efforts in East Europe and Soviet efforts in the Middle East).

Economic investment—by private groups from capitalist countries and, to a lesser extent, by governments of Communist nations—is a key means of intrusion. The involvement of a variety of American companies in West Europe has provided the grounds for Gaullists and others to claim undue American political and economic interference in their internal affairs; many of these same countries have, like the United States, been similarly accused for their activities in parts of the Middle East, Africa, Asia, and Latin America. Communist governments have on occasion performed functions similar to those carried out by Western companies. Examples include the Aswan Dam in Egypt, the Bhilai Russian-supported steel mill in India, Russian oil activity in Iraq, and the Chinese role in Yemen. While accusations of undue interference are not always justified, there is no question that economic investment may be an important means of influencing developments within, and ultimately between, the countries of a particular area.

POSSESSION OF A COLONY. Until 1945, colonies were the primary (although by no means the solitary) instrument for the involvement of great powers in the underdeveloped areas of the world. World Wars I and II were both caused in part by the attempt of challengers to acquire colonies for themselves, but in the present era of emerging nations, colonies have become a relic of a previous age. Only Portugal, and to a lesser extent Spain, have managed to hold onto a sizable number of their possessions, while Great Britain, France, Belgium, and the Nethelands have relinquished most of theirs. In those areas where colonies continue to exist, however, they still play a significant role in the dynamics of the intrusive system. This is particularly true in the Portuguese territories of Southern Africa and in British Hong Kong.

MILITARY INTERVENTION. Military intervention consists of the movement of the armed forces of an external power into a local area. There are three characteristic motives for military intervention: expanding one's area of control, the maintenance of the *status quo,* or the reinstatement of a prior condition. The Soviet military presence in Iran until 1948, throughout East Europe at the end of World War II, and the use of Soviet pilots in Korea are examples of expansionism. Examples of attempts to maintain the *status quo* include the American and British convoying of troops to Lebanon and Jordan, respectively, in 1958; American intervention in the Dominican Republic in 1965, and in Vietnam; and the stationing of troops from a variety of countries on both sides of the divided German territory. British and French action in the Suez crisis of 1956, and Russian intervention in the Hungarian crisis the same year, constitute examples of attempts—in one case unsuccessful, in the other successful—to reassert a former situation.[20]

SUBVERSION. Subversion consists of the covert use of force by agents of an external power—usually with the assistance of indigenous forces—to alter the political conditions within a country. Acts of subversion are by definition difficult to document, nonetheless a few comparatively recent examples have come to light. Examples of American subversion include Guatemala in 1954, the Cuban Bay of Pigs crisis in 1961, and the overthrowing of the Mossadegh regime in Iran in 1953. Examples of Soviet subversion include activities in Czechoslovakia in 1948, in Syria, and in the Congo (Kinshasa). Chinese attempts at subversion include actions in Burma, Thailand, Laos, Indonesia, and several countries of Africa.

UNITED NATIONS. The United Nations may on occasion be used as a means by which nations external to the region pursue their objectives within the intrusive system. The U.N. has been used by external powers, in numerous crises, to further their own interests and goals, even though the formal role of the U.N. in the crisis has not always been significant. Examples of such use of the U.N. during crises include sporadic efforts in the Middle East, and the crises in the Congo, Kashmir, Cyprus, and Southern Africa. Instruments available to intrusive powers through the United Nations include resolutions, peace observers, peace forces, and the use of the United Nations as a diplomatic sounding board or for purposes of mediation. Indeed, an external nation may use the debates in the United Nations as a means of expressing support for particular regimes with which it is attempting to gain or retain influence.

CULTURAL AND EDUCATIONAL ACTIVITIES. Cultural and educational activities are an important, but sometimes subtle means of involvement in the affairs of a subordinate system. External powers are able to affect regional attitudes through cultural exchange, through the teachers and technicians they send to indigenous countries and those who are sent to them from there for training, and by their assistance in local educational programs. The French, particularly, have characteristically been able to continue to foster the intellectual orientation of the middle and sometimes upper class toward French culture in many areas of the world, especially in those areas which were formerly French colonies, by making educational opportunities in France available to the local elite and by sponsoring the teaching of the

---

[20] There is a degree of ambiguity in both the Hungarian crisis and the Vietnam war, since it is possible to interpret the situations differently and reverse the classification we have given them. However, in the Hungarian case the Russians used force to reestablish a government; hence, we classify the action as a reassertion rather than continuation of the *status quo*. In Vietnam, the American effort may involve a rollback in certain areas, but in general the effort has been to uphold the present government in South Vietnam.

French language. In most areas formerly under French rule, the retention of an educational system along the French model continues to orient them towards French culture. Perhaps the major rival to French cultural efforts around the world has been the United States Information Agency (USIA) and its programs of cultural exchanges, libraries, and English-language instruction. The Peace Corps volunteers have served as an additional agency. The British, Russians, and Communist Chinese have been similarly active in attempts to make political gains through cultural and educational programs.

PROPAGANDA. Propaganda activities have become, in the age of competition for influence, a very significant means of achieving goals within local areas. Propaganda consists of communication which is designed to orient the views and actions of the recipient favorably in the direction of the originating agent. In this respect it may at times be similar to cultural and educational activities; however, there are specific acts which are intended almost solely as propaganda. These include broadcasts by the external power into the region, in indigenous languages: the Voice of America and Radio Free Europe are examples of American devices, but other countries have similar agencies. The Russians and Chinese have been particularly active throughout the developing world. Television, movies, magazines, books, newspapers, and art may be used to convey propaganda, even though they have a cultural and educational significance as well. Visits by leaders, either to or from an external country, are also usually subtle attempts to both create and convey propaganda.

The Intrusive System and the Pattern Variables

These characteristic ways of participation in the intrusive system have both positive and negative effects upon the four pattern variables of the subordinate system: cohesion, communications, power, and the internal structure of relations.

COHESION. The social, economic, political, and organizational aspects of the cohesion of a subordinate system is affected in a number of ways by the participation of an external power. *Social cohesion* can be enhanced by the educational efforts of an external power, if these efforts reinforce the pre-existing educational and linguistic patterns within the system. An example of this type of activity is the continued educational efforts of the French in their former colonies in North Africa and sub-Saharan Africa. Another way an intrusive power may affect social cohesion is to assist in the transfer of populations (e.g., the Russians, in moving the German and Polish populations westward after World War II). In general, however, external powers are less able to affect social cohesion as such.

Economic cohesion can be increased if economic assistance programs have as their aim the enhancement of economic complementarity through the encouragement of industrialization, improved methods of agriculture, or economic integration. Examples of external attempts to influence economic cohesion include American efforts in Latin America and West Europe, Russian efforts in East Europe, and British efforts in East Africa. In each case the purpose of external pressure and effort has been at least in part the encouragement of a division of labor within the region.

The effect of external participation upon *political cohesion* may be seen when the support of a given power serves to perpetuate a conservative, radical, or moderate regime in power, or to prevent a particular type of regime from coming to power, thereby reinforcing or reducing cleavages within the system. In addition, there are instances where the concern of an external power with regional security arrangements or economic arrangements have either contributed to or hindered the *organizational cohesion* of a subordinate system. Intrusive powers have been able to act whether or not they have actually been members of these international organizations (e.g., NATO, CENTO, COMECON).

COMMUNICATIONS. External powers influence communications within subordinate systems in a variety of ways. Economic assistance programs have aided mail delivery and telephone and telegraph facilities. In a variety of circumstances, they have also led to improvements in transportation systems and have expedited the introduction of radio and television. The activities of an external power in a region can also encourage interchange of elite groups. Diplomatic visits and education within the region have been promoted by intrusive powers. Moreover, students and diplomats have found themselves in contact with members of other elite groups of their own region, on the territory of an intrusive power, at its universities, and at conferences sponsored by it.

LEVEL OF POWER. It is upon the pattern variable of level of power that external powers have perhaps their greatest effect. External powers can promote the *material power* of members of subordinate systems by providing economic aid, food, technical assistance, favorable trade terms, birth control assistance, teachers, and administrative advice. Of more direct effect on the balance of power of a subordinate system is a change in *military power.* In ascending order of importance, the types of this kind of aid external powers can give members of the subordinate system are: economic aid which frees funds for arms purchases; grants or sales of arms and the training necessary for the use of these arms; transfer of the technology, know-how, and materiel necessary to permit indigenous manufacture of weaponry; and, finally, the commitment of troops.

Of the three factors of power, the *motivational factor* is here the most significant. Through their participation in the region, external powers may affect the political, social, and ideological direction which particular nations in the subordinate system follow. Exterior powers will decide whether to support existing governments or whether to support opposition or rebellious groups, and they may either moderate or encourage the desire of indigenous countries for increased influence of their own. External powers may then play an essential role in determining which elite comes to power in a large number of states of the region and which kinds of political institutions will prevail. In extreme cases, they may even affect the number of states which exist in the subordinate system.

Ideology must be considered as especially significant in shaping the direction which regional involvement by outside powers takes. It affects the degree of cooperation or conflict among the countries external to the region. It influences their choice of which nations they are willing to aid and it helps determine which nations are prepared to receive assistance from them. Involvement in the intrusive system may itself be related to the attempt, on the part of ideologically dynamic nations, to achieve fulfillment and self-justification and to prove the desirability of their ideology to other countries.

The intrusive system represents a series of risks for the indigenous countries of any subordinate system, in addition to the potential benefits we have already mentioned. As a consequence of its involvement with intrusive powers, a local state may lose whatever control it had over its own policies; in particular, the acceptance of material aid may lead to disequilibrium of the internal economy, to a dislodging of established social patterns, to the emergence of a trade dependence on an exterior power, or to a loss of political flexibility. The acceptance of military aid may upset the local balance of power and result in a net decrease of security for the recipient, either because the aid stimulates his adversaries to greater preparations or because it infuses him with a false sense of confidence (e.g., the Arabs in the Mideast War, 1967). Aid from external powers may also make the recipient a battleground for conflicts between members of the dominant system, particularly in terms of ideology. The greatest danger of external assistance is that it will infuse the local power with an ideological dynamism which will result in adventurous escapades with dire consequences. This assistance may become the catalytic agent in unifying potential local enemies which fear the recipient's possible adventurism.

STRUCTURE OF RELATIONS. As this analysis of the risks attendant upon the involvement of intrusive powers suggests, external powers affect and indeed, at times determine, the structure of relations within a subordinate system. The high degree of cooperation in both East Europe and Latin America is affected by the primacy of the Soviet Union and the United States, respectively, in these intrusive systems. It is interesting to note that when either the United States or the Soviet Union loses power in either of these regions, regional conflict tends to be aggravated. On the other hand, the competition of intrusive powers exacerbates conflict in the Middle East, Southeast Asia, East Asia, North Africa, and West Africa. In the Middle East and Southeast Asia particularly, sustained crisis and direct military conflict have become prevalent as the conflicts of both the dominant and subordinate system have fused.

The type of military aid and involvement of intrusive powers affects the *means of relations.* Consultation and amelioration is facilitated by one or more of the intrusive powers in West Europe, Latin America, East Europe, North Africa, and South Asia. In Southeast Asia and the Middle East, on the other hand, massive military aid has raised the level of conflict and made it far more dangerous. In addition, China has contributed to the turmoil in Southeast Asia through its conceptual and practical assistance in guerrilla warfare. The great influence of the intrusive powers upon the means of relations in Southeast Asia is attested to by the fact that regional wars are frequently accompanied by peace conferences attended by several great powers.

Intrusive powers usually have less of an influence on the *causes of relations* than on the other elements of the structure of relations. They may not be responsible for local religious and racial rivalries, but as we have already suggested they are capable of fanning the flames of contention by introducing ideological rivalries, by imposing their own political competitions on the area and by encouraging local adventurism. The division of Korea and of Vietnam may be cited as examples of external powers influencing local conflict. In like manner, although to a lesser extent, they can organize local blocs and alliances to support their policies (e.g., NATO, Warsaw Pact) and thereby enforce cooperation among local parties. In general, the experience of intrusive powers has been that it is easier to impose conflict than cooperation upon the members of a subordinate system.

Patterns of Involvement

The pattern of the participation of external powers in a subordinate system is the constant state of interaction between the balance of power among the external powers in the region and the balances among and between the peripheral and core nations. It is this dual and overlapping balance which forms the substance of international politics in the intrusive system. Like the periphery and the core, these two balances are constantly interacting and affecting each other. Under particular conditions and by means of the methods we have described, the "visiting" powers can affect the balance among the members of the subordinate system. Yet, under current conditions, the members of the subordinate system have a large measure of flexibility of their own. Diplomatic agility on their part can allow them to promote a stalemate between the outside contenders of the intrusive system, and they can use the balance between external powers to serve many of their own national interests.

An intrusive system—like any core, periphery, or any subordinate system as a whole—is a dynamic entity. Various external countries sporadically gain and lose influence or control within the intrusive system. In the course of this process, the identity of the intrusive powers changes as they gain or lose the ability and desire to seek involvement within the region. Moreover, as conditions in the dominant system and in the many subordinate systems change, the milieu of the particular intrusive system is affected accordingly.

The patterns of intrusive systems differ, in part, because of the variety of conditions under which they exist. The nature of the influence of an external power may vary according to the number of powers present, their degree of competition, and their degree of control. External powers may be completely absent in a region. This condition is more likely when the level of power of the member states is high, and it is enhanced when the structure of relations within the subordinate system is cooperative (e.g., North America) or when the region is an empire (e.g., the Soviet Union). The presence of a single external power in a region means that only one power has been able to establish a base of influence in the region (e.g., most of Latin America) or at least that it has prevented others from joining its intrusion. When there are several outside powers competing for influence in an intrusive system, conflict may be intense—particularly when the local powers are relatively weak (e.g., Southeast Asia, Middle East).

If external powers exercise a large measure of control, then there is likely to be a goodly number of colonies or micro-states in the region. When middle and minor powers and even regional states abound in a subordinate system, external powers usually find themselves forced to bargain and cajole for support. However, the degree of control and influence of the external powers is affected by their reciprocal relations. If they are cooperating with each other, their opportunities for control are enhanced even if the local countries are comparatively strong; if they are competing among themselves, then the flexibility of the indigenous countries is likely to be enhanced at their expense. Under most present circumstances, a heightened degree of conflict among the external powers is in turn likely to be reflected in tense conditions in the subordinate system, and vice versa. Thus, condominium and hegemony produce relative calm, while intrusive competition tends to produce regional strife.

The two superpowers in the current system are unwilling to establish a consortium in particular intrusive systems and unable to face direct conflict because of the danger of nuclear conflagration. As a result, three patterns of Soviet-American interaction in intrusive systems have developed: mutual noninvolvement, unilateral abstention, and restrained mutual involvement.

Mutual noninvolvement means that neither superpower participates in a politically significant manner in the area or state being considered. Although mutual noninvolvement in regions is theoretically possible, it does not occur in the current system. However, it does occur in particular countries, usually within peripheral sectors of subordinate systems, when these countries are either strong enough to exclude all intruders (e.g., Switzerland, Sweden, Ireland), are motivated to maintain an independent foreign policy (e.g., Singapore, Burma), or are under the influence of secondary or middle powers (e.g., Albania, Chad, Malagasy Republic, Jamaica, Gambia). Mutual noninvolvement is not necessarily limited to the peripheral sector (e.g., Communist China, Cambodia, Malaysia, Dahomey, and Togo); however, the peripheral states are particularly amenable to mutual non-involvement because, by the nature of their position in the subordinate system, they are forced into policies which are independent of most other states within the subordinate system. Unlike most core states, their security often seems best served by one of two extremes: avoidance of foreign entanglements, or the kind of increased outside relations which occurs in Britain, Israel, and Albania. When the peripheral state is fundamentally isolationist (by circumstance or by intent) mutual noninvolvement is most likely.

Unilateral abstention means that one of the superpowers has not involved itself in a subordinate system, or at least that it has avoided involvement in one of the sectors of that system. Unilateral abstention is more likely to occur in the core of a region than in its periphery, because the core is more cohesive and the foreign policies of its members are generally less individualistic. In Latin America, the United States is involved in the core sector while the Soviet Union involves itself in the major peripheral country. In West and East Europe, respectively, the Soviet Union and the United States have limited their influence, particularly in the cores. This process of unilateral abstention can also be seen in individual countries. An interesting example is East and Southeast Asia, where Chinese influence is checked, by design or by accident, by Soviet and American unilateral abstention in such countries as Mongolia, North Vietnam, North Korea, South Korea, Taiwan, and the Philippines.

Unilateral abstention tends to be less stable than mutual noninvolvement. Once one superpower has become involved in an area or a country, there are comparatively few major incentives to abstention by the other; thus, there is a tendency for unilateral abstention to be a fluid state which leads to mutual involvement. Possible motives to abstain which do exist include: the fear that involvement will bolster the position of a mutual antagonist (e.g., the Soviet-American attitude toward China in Asia); the calculation that the costs are too great (the Soviet Union in the Latin American core); the desire not to harm one's position in one's own area (e.g., the cores in East and West Europe); the fear of hurting one's ideological position (U.S.S.R. in the Southern Africa core); and the lack of a convenient inroad (e.g., the Soviet Union in the Southwest Pacific).

Restrained mutual involvement, is the third pattern of superpower involvement in the intrusive system which is short of both condominium and direct conflict. The essential factor which permits restrained mutual involvement in a country is mutual acceptance of the existing government. Attempted subversion of a regime supported by the other, while a very low-level type of overt conflict, nevertheless carries with it the possibility of affecting the balance in both the dominant and the subordinate systems. If both superpowers accept the regime in power, then their attempts to affect it politically, by aid and trade, provide a very different framework from that which occurs when one of then is alienated from the regime in power but nevertheless seeks influence among groups within its territory.

There are several levels of restrained mutual involvement. These extend from the temporary mutual acceptance of a local competition (e.g., Tanzania, Mali), to a more pronounced level of "division of labor" and toleration of the other power (e.g., Iran, Guinea, Ethiopia, Ceylon), to an implicit acceptance of the presence of the other side (e.g., India, Indonesia, Afghanistan, Pakistan), to an explicit and long-term acceptance of the presence of the other side (e.g., Austria, Finland, Yugoslavia). As the level of cooperation increases, the presence of the two primary powers becomes more stable. There is a kind of institutionalizing process at work which reinforces mutual involvement. Barring a change of regime within the recipient country or a major alteration of conditions within the subordinate system as a whole, the "logic" of mutual involvement is toward at least implicit if not also explicit acceptance, but as we shall see in Chapter 6, this process may be arrested at any time.

Whatever the precise nature of *mutual involvement* in any particular country, it is the most significant of the patterns of the intrusive system. As our illustrations have indicated, mutual involvement is more prevalent than either mutual noninvolvement or unilateral abstention. Numerous instances occur in both peripheral and core sectors. In addition, mutual involvement occurs more frequently in core states than mutual noninvolvement, and it occurs more frequently in peripheral states than unilateral abstention.

We have thus far discussed mutual involvement only in relation to individual countries. Obviously, it occurs in regions as well. And indeed, it is this pattern which is at the heart of the intrusive system. When both primary powers are involved in a subordinate system (and they are in most), the intrusive system is often explained to a great extent by the nature of their activities. The methods of participation, the patterns of involvement, and the manner in which each occurs in the core and peripheral sectors elucidate the nature of the overlapping balances of power of which the intrusive system consists.

Given the complexity and volatility of local balances, it must be emphasized, then, that limited competition in the intrusive system is prevented from constantly leading to direct conflict by the processes of mutual noninvolvement, unilateral abstention, and restrained mutual involvement. Of course, in particular circumstances, the primary powers engage in covert or overt support of opposite sides in an internal political conflict. As in Vietnam and Korea, they may even be indirectly opposed in a limited war. However, in the majority of situations, these three processes limit the total identity of the conflicts in the dominant and subordinate systems.

The primary powers are obviously not the only external powers which participate in intrusive systems. Secondary and middle powers have their own interests to pursue, and in the very process of their involvement in the intrusive system they too affect the balances in both the dominant and the subordinate systems. By challenging the primary powers, they may increase Soviet and American incentives for restraint with respect to each other (as has China in East, Southeast, and South Asia). If they are closely associated with one of the primary powers and willing to perform tasks for it, they may encourage unilateral abstention or mutual noninvolvement. They may support by their actions the policies of both primary powers (as has Japan in Indonesia and Great Britain in Malaysia). If they are independently oriented, they may encourage mutual noninvolvement by their insistence on maintaining an influence of their own in particular countries (as has France in West and Central Africa). Most important, secondary, middle, and even on occasion minor powers weaken the link between the dominant and subordinate systems in the intrusive system. Countries which are unable to compete with the two primary powers on an equal basis in the dominant system may be able to do so in the intrusive system. Their presence thus aids in reducing the congruence between the competitions in the global and regional arenas. At the very least, it necessitates calculations and considerations by the primary powers which are either unnecessary or impossible in the dominant system.

No matter what the restraints, the processes by which external and usually stronger powers intercede in the international politics of regions have far-reaching effects on the futures of subordinate systems. External powers can serve to intensify or reduce the level of conflict of subordinate systems. Their presence may encourage divisions or integrations among the nation-states of these areas. External powers may promote regional associations as a means of extending their control or of aiding the economic development of the indigenous states. On the other hand, their presence may limit regional cohesiveness and produce fissiparous tendencies. Whatever their effect, the external powers must be viewed as an integral part of the international politics of almost every region, without which the form of each subordinate system would be considerably dissimilar.

RELATIONS BETWEEN SUBORDINATE SYSTEMS

The final element of the international system to be considered here is the relationship between subordinate systems. We can distinguish two fundamental types of such relationships: that *oriented toward cohesion* and that *oriented toward power.* Relations which are oriented toward cohesion are based primarily (although not solely) on the effect of the first two pattern variables: cohesion and communications. They tend to occur among subordinate systems which are geographically proximate, have similar political and social backgrounds, and have a high degree of interaction. Examples of such relations between subordinate systems are the Middle East and North Africa, and Central Africa and West Africa. Power-oriented relations are influenced primarily by the pattern variables of level of power and the structure of internal relations, and are characterized by the presence of intrusive systems. The most powerful subordinate systems are the most highly interactive. In general, relations oriented toward cohesion exist between regions which are similar in power and power-oriented relations exist between subordinate systems unequal in power. Of course, subordinate systems do not always relate to each other as a whole; in particular cases, one sector or even country may be more important in determining the pattern of relations with another region. In particular cases then, we must investigate the countries or group of countries which relate to another system, as well as the role of the periphery and the core in these relations.

Let us select a single subordinate system by way of illustration. In the Middle East, relations with North America, the Soviet Union, West Europe, East Europe and, to a minor degree East Asia, are power-oriented. They are determined largely by the level of power and the spectrum of relations, with geographic proximity also playing an important role in some cases. On the other hand, the factors of cohesion and communications are particularly—although not solely—significant in the cohesive relations of most Middle Eastern states with North Africa and, to a much lesser degree, with West, East, and Central Africa. Factors of cohesion and geographic proximity are most important in the region's cohesive relations with South Asia and, to a lesser extent, in its cohesive relations with Southeast Asia, where the Islamic solidarity between most of the Middle East and Malaysia and Indonesia is the most significant influence. Israel, unlike the other states in the Middle East, conducts power-oriented relations with many countries in sub-Saharan Africa, Southeast Asia, and parts of Latin America.

Besides identifying the factors which contribute to relations between two or more systems, it is also necessary to form some estimate of the *intensity of relations* between subordinate systems. In this regard, one of the most significant indices is the degree of shared participation in international organizations, which may operate either toward cohesion or power. For example, OECD and NATO represent the cohesive interconnectiveness of West Europe and North America, but they also are significantly power-oriented. The Arab League is an indicator of the cohesive ties between the Middle East and North Africa, and the OAU links the various regions of Africa in a broader manner. To a lesser extent, power-oriented organizations encourage more cohesive relations between subordinate systems: the Colombo Plan has encouraged greater cohesive contacts between South and Southeast Asia; OCAM links Francophonic Africa; the British Commonwealth, in a much broader way, has served to increase incipient cohesive links between a variety of subordinate systems. In this way, international organizations like OECD, NATO, the OAU, OCAM, the Arab League, and the British Commonwealth can be viewed as supraregional in character; that is to say, they tend to function as aggregators of regions. By providing forums for greater interchange, they enable particular subordinate systems to intensify their interactions toward either cohesion or power.

Thus, relations between subordinate systems, while largely unstructured and uneven, can have a significant effect upon the international politics of particular areas of the world. The relationships between diverse subordinate systems, between individual countries in different regions, and between cores or peripheries of different regions, can affect local balances, local intrusive systems, and the dominant system. Consequently, in any complete analysis of the international system it is insufficient to consider each subordinate system in isolation. Its relationship to other systems must also be explored.

CONCLUSION

We have been engaged in an exploratory venture of attempting to characterize the nature of the international relations of regions. As our point of departure, rather than looking at these relations from a point on high in the international power structure, we have attempted to view them as systems of action unto themselves. We have not looked at them purely in terms of regional organizations, or, as has been customary in the study of international relations, as "regionalism."[21] And we have not looked at them, as some scholars have done recently, in terms of their potentialities for political integration.[22] Instead we have endeavored to treat the region as a unit of analysis unto itself, a unit which possesses its own internal dynamic processes. We have attempted to do this by means of an inductively arrived at classificatory system which can be used to specify how the subordinate system can be identified and what its component elements can be said to be: core sector, peripheral sector, and intrusive system. Our introduction of the four pattern variables—level of cohesion, nature of communications, level of power, and the structure of internal relations—was intended to

21 For example, see Norman J. Padelford and George A. Lincoln, *The Dynamics of International Politics* (2nd ed.; New York: The Macmillan Company, 1967), pp. 447 *ff*.

22 For an analysis based on several methods developed in the study of political integration, see Bruce M. Russett, *International Regions and the International System* (Chicago: Rand McNally & Co., 1967).

establish these matrical elements as of intrinsic importance to the delineation and understanding of the core and peripheral sectors and the intrusive system.

As part of the four pattern variables, we included a seven-step ranking system to estimate the level of power of each member state of the international system, as well as a spectrum of international relations which encompasses all conditions of cooperation and antagonism. We attempted to show, by means of these categories, that both antagonistic and cooperative relationships contribute to the delineation of a subordinate system and its sectors. Both antagonistic and cooperative relationships exist within the core and the peripheral sector and between the core and peripheral sectors, and these assist us in identifying a particular subordinate system.

We cannot fully understand the inner dynamics of a subordinate system, however, until the effects of politically significant participation by external powers in what we have called the "intrusive" system have been added. Only a consideration of the antagonism and cooperation inculcated within the subordinate system by external powers can provide a complete panorama of the full network of relations at work within any particular subordinate system. As we have seen, the support or withdrawal of support of an external power can radically alter the internal balance of a subordinate system.

As we have just stated, our attempt here has been to provide a schema for the comparison of the international relations of regions. We have sought to produce a basis for analyzing units of international relations of diverse social and political backgrounds. Any such effort runs the risk of ignoring crucial factors, on the one hand, or of magnifying minor elements, on the other. We have entertained such a risk in our conviction of the significance of beginning to categorize and illustrate the patterns and processes at work in the intermediate arena of the international system—the subordinate system. For in this era, of the collapse of European influence in international affairs and of the decolonization of formerly dependent peoples, the region has become one of the crucial units of international politics.

In the remainder of this volume we shall attempt to further elucidate the analysis presented in this chapter. The major focus of our effort will be to examine the core, the periphery, and the intrusive systems. In the first chapter of each section, we will present a further analysis of the five subordinate systems on which we will concentrate. In the second chapter, we will provide a series of readings designed to demonstrate in greater detail international relations in each of these five subordinate systems. The final two chapters of the volume return to the pattern we have established in this introduction. In Chapter 8, Professor Lynn Miller applies the comparative regional international relations approach to the study of international organizations, and in Chapter 9 we have attempted to provide a summary of our conclusions by suggesting a typology of subordinate systems.

SUGGESTIONS FOR FURTHER READING

Integration-Oriented

Deutsch, Karl *et al., Political Community and the North Atlantic Area* (Princeton, N.J.: Princeton University Press, 1957).

Etzioni, Amitai, *Political Unification: A Comparative Study of Leaders and Forces* (New York: Holt, Rinehart & Winston, Inc., 1965).

Haas, Ernst B., *The Uniting of Europe* (Stanford, Calif.: Stanford University Press, 1958).

Haas, Ernst B., "The Uniting of Europe and the Uniting of Latin America," *Journal of Common Market Studies*, V (June, 1967), 315–43.

Haas, Ernst B. and Philippe Schmitter, *The Politics of Economics in Latin American Regionalism: The Latin American Free Trade Association After Four Years of Operation* (Denver, Colo.: University of Denver Monograph, 1965).

International Political Communities: An Anthology (Garden City, N.Y.: Doubleday & Company, Inc., Anchor Books, 1966).

Kaiser, Karl, "The Interaction of Regional Subsystems: Some Preliminary Notes on Recurrent Patterns and the Role of Superpowers," *World Politics,* XXI (October, 1968), 84–104.

Nye, Joseph S., Jr., "Comparative Regional Integration: Concept and Measurement," *International Organization,* XXII (Autumn, 1968), 855–80.

Nye, Joseph S. Jr., ed., *International Regionalism: Readings* (Boston: Little, Brown and Company, 1968).

Nye, Joseph S. Jr., *Pan-African and East African Integration* (Cambridge, Mass.: Harvard University Press, 1965).

Russett, Bruce M., *International Regions and the International System: A Study in Political Ecology* (Chicago: Rand McNally & Co., 1967).

Subordinate System-Oriented

Aron, Raymond, *Peace and War: A Theory of International Relations,* trans. Richard Howard and Annette Baker Fox (New York: Doubleday & Company, Inc., 1966), pp. 389–95.

Binder, Leonard, "The Middle East Subordinate International System," *World Politics,* X (April, 1958), 408–29.

Bowman, Larry W., "The Subordinate State System of Southern Africa," *International Studies Quarterly,* XII (September, 1968), 231–62.

Brecher, Michael, "International Relations and Asian Studies: The Subordinate State System of Asia," *World Politics,* XV (January, 1963), 213–35.

Brecher, Michael, *The New States of Asia* (London: Oxford University Press, 1963), Chapters 3, 6.

Modelski, George, "International Relations and Area Studies," *International Relations* (London), II (April, 1961), 143–55.

Rosenau, James N., ed., *Linkage Politics: Essays on the Convergence of National and International Systems* (New York: The Free Press, 1969).

Young, Oran R., "Political Discontinuities in the International System," *World Politics,* XX (April, 1968), 369–92.

Zartman, William I., "Africa as a Subordinate State System in International Relations," *International Organization,* XXI (Summer, 1967), 545–64

part one

THE
CORE
SECTOR

2

COMPARISONS

We have defined the core sector as that portion of the subordinate system which consists of a state or a group of states which form a central focus of the international politics within a given region. Its most salient features (which tend to be opposite to those of the peripheral sector) are its relatively high degree of cohesiveness and the high intensity of diplomatic relations which are focused on the core sector. This point will be better understood when, in Chapter 4, we note the characteristic absence of relations within the peripheral sector.

In this discussion of the six core sectors of the five subordinate systems (Latin America, West Europe, West Africa, the Middle East, and Southeast Asia) for which we have selected illustrative readings, we hope to pursue these two characteristic themes and, in the process, provide some background on these areas in such a manner as to facilitate comparisons between them. Our discussions will again be phrased in terms of the four pattern variables: cohesion, communications, power, and the structure of internal relations.[1]

COHESION

We have defined cohesion as the degree of similarity or complementarity in the properties of the political entities being considered, and the degree

[1] Tables for Chapter 2 appear in the appendix to this volume.

of interaction of these units. As we have already observed it is the greater cohesiveness of the core sector which sets it apart from the characteristically uncohesive periphery. The elements of cohesion, the reader will remember, are social, economic, political, and organizational, and the degree of cohesiveness is determined by noting to what extent each of these elements reinforces another and to what extent the components of one of the elements has a similar reinforcing effect.

SOCIAL COHESION

Social cohesion can be said to consist of such elements as ethnicity, languages, religion, culture, history, and a consciousness of a common heritage. As we have just noted, we are concerned with the extent to which each of the foregoing build upon one another. If the cores of the five regions under examination are compared, this reinforcing process stands out. In what follows we will discuss the six core sectors of the five regions we have selected (Southeast Asia has two) in the order of decreasing social cohesiveness: the Middle East, West Europe, Latin America, maritime Southeast Asia, mainland Southeast Asia, and West Africa.[2]

The Middle Eastern Core[3]

The reinforcement of social cohesiveness can be seen clearly in the Middle Eastern core, where a population that is ethnically almost entirely (97.5%) Semitic is also nearly entirely Arabic-speaking. Adding to the fabric is the manner in which religious, cultural, and historical factors, and a general feeling of a common heritage, have compounded these basic ethnic and linguistic factors. The core is over 90% Muslim. The greatest concentration of non-Muslims is in Lebanon and the Sudan; the result being, in Lebanon, a kind of confessional politics and in the Sudan, a North (Muslim)—South (Christian) division. In consequence, both Lebanon and, until recently, the Sudan have been prevented from siding either with the radical Arab states (led by the United Arab Republic) or the conservative states (led by Saudi Arabia). The possession of a common language and religion, in particular, have resulted in a common Islamic cultural heritage. All the foregoing have in turn been impacted under the pressure of political history: from the sixteenth century until 1914 most of the area was united under Ottoman rule. The combined effect of the political decline of the Ottoman empire in the nineteenth century and the advent of European imperial interference have

---

2 Most of the following analysis is based on the data appearing in Table 2-1, Core Sector Cohesion, p.393. See the notes to that Table for a listing of the sources utilized.

3 The Middle Eastern core consists of: the United Arab Republic, Yemen, Saudi Arabia, Kuwait, Iraq, Lebanon, Sudan, Jordan, Syria, South Yemen, and the Persian Gulf sheikhdoms.

served to undermine the social cohesiveness of the area, but it is still one of the most socially cohesive core sectors in the world.

The West European Core[4]

The West European core, while fairly uniform racially, is characterized by national differences which are viewed in ethnic terms and by single languages (with the exception of the Flemish-Walloon division within Belgium) which are coterminous with national boundaries. Religion, however, tends to reinforce the social uniformity and counteract the linguistic diversity. France, Italy, Belgium, and Luxembourg are all more than 90 percent Roman Catholic, the Netherlands is about evenly divided, and West Germany is 44 percent Catholic. The political effects of a universal religion, however, began to weaken in Europe with the Reformation, about the time that they were reestablished in the Middle East. From this time on, political division began to undermine the sense of a common European cultural heritage, although this sense still remains strong.

The Latin American Core[5]

The Latin American core lacks a high degree of ethnic cohesion, and is extremely complex with respect to both religious and linguistic cohesion. Most of the Latin American states consist of Indian and mestizo (Indian and Spanish mixtures) majorities and white Spanish or Portuguese minorities; a few also have additional black and mulatto minorities. This ethnic diversity is overcome to a great extent by the widespread use of Spanish among the Spanish and mestizo populations (although Portuguese is spoken in Brazil); however, the Indian populations (which range from a high of 54 percent in Guatemala to near nonexistence in Uruguay) remain linguistically isolated. Roman Catholicism counteracts this absence of ethnic and linguistic homogeneity in that it is at least a majority religion, if not one of 90 percent or more of the population. However, the hold of Catholicism, like that of language, is strongest among those of Spanish descent and weakest among the Indian population. Whatever might have been the politically unifying effects of three centuries of Spanish rule was counteracted in the early nineteenth century by the winning of separate national independence by the present-day states. Thus it is cultural, and not so much political, history which contributes to the social cohesiveness of the area. We might note, by way of conclusion, that in contrast to West

---

[4] The West European core consists of the E.E.C. membership of: France, West Germany, Italy, Belgium, Netherlands, and Luxembourg.

[5] The Latin American core consists of: Argentina, Bolivia, Brazil, Chile, Colombia, Costa Rica, Dominican Republic, Ecuador, El Salvador, Guatemala, Honduras, Mexico, Nicaragua, Panama, Paraguay, Peru, Uruguay, and Venezuela.

Europe, social divisions occur in Latin America both *within* and *between* the members of the core.

The Maritime Southeast Asian Core[6]

The maritime Southeast Asian core evidences a greater degree of ethnic homogeneity than either Latin America or the mainland Southeast Asian core. What sets the maritime core apart from the mainland is the distinctively Malay character of all three core members.[7] Such ethnic uncohesiveness which exists is attributable to the Dutch and British practices of importing Indians and Chinese to work the rubber plantations and the tin mines of the area. Most of this importation of minority ethnic groups occurred relatively recently (in the nineteenth century) and under colonial auspices; hence, the post-independence feeling against these immigrant minorities is greater than against the combination of displaced indigenous peoples and the historically present Chinese populations of the mainland. Unlike the Buddhist mainland, the maritime core is characterized in religious terms by the presence of Islam in Indonesia (90%) and Malaysia (about 50%), and by Roman Catholicism in the Philippines (90%). With the important exception of the Malay empire (which gives Indonesia a historical precedent for its "greater Malaya" ambitions), the maritime core, in contrast to the mainland, is characterized both by the absence of wide spread local imperial traditions and the early date (sixteenth century) of the advent of European interference; thus the maritime core has been more profoundly affected by the European experience. One of the differences in the colonial histories of the mainland and maritime cores is that, with the exception of independent Thailand, the mainland shared the single experience of French culture while in the maritime core each country had a different experience (Philippines: Spanish and American; Indonesia: Dutch; and Malaysia: British). Nevertheless, the maritime core, with its greater ethnic, linguistic, and religious homogeneity, and its common pre-colonial history, appears to be more socially cohesive than the mainland core.

The Mainland Southeast Asian Core[8]

The mainland Southeast Asian core is ethnically not nearly as heterogeneous as the West African. Each of the members of the core possesses a single

[6] The maritime Southeast Asian core consists of: Indonesia, Malaysia, and the Philippines.

[7] A dramatic illustration of the potentialities of this common Malay ethnicity is the fact that it was the non-Muslim and Christian state of the Philippines that originated the idea of a Malphindo (Malaysia, the Philippines, and Indonesia) confederation; although admittedly to attempt to press its claims to Northern Borneo (Sabah) at the expense of Malaysia. See Bernard K. Gordon, *Dimensions of Conflict in Southeast Asia* (Englewood Cliffs, N.J.: Prentice-Hall, Inc., 1966), pp. 21–30.

[8] The Southeast Asian mainland core consists of: Laos, North Vietnam, South Vietnam, Cambodia and Thailand.

ethnic majority population, ranging from a low of 66% of lowland Laos in Laos, to highs of 85% Vietnamese and Khmers in North Vietnam and Cambodia, respectively. In general, language groupings coincide with ethnic groupings. While there remain significant numbers of unintegrated peoples (usually mountain-dwelling) in each of these countries, what is distinctive about the mainland core is that, like West Europe and unlike the Middle East, these major groupings are generally coterminous with national boundaries. Minorities in other countries within the core, however, tend to take on great political importance as objects of irredenta feelings (e.g., the Shans of Burma in Thailand, the Laos in Northeast Thailand, and the Khmers of Cambodia in South Vietnam), unlike much larger minority groups in West Africa. This probably attests to the deeper nationalism within the mainland Southeast Asian core. Religion provides a cohesive influence, since the major religion in Laos, Cambodia, and Thailand is Buddhism. Even in North and South Vietnam, Buddhism is extremely significant, although in South Vietnam there is a politically important Catholic minority and several minority sects. In both Vietnams there is an additional Chinese influence (Confucian and Taoist). History has done little to counteract the atomistic nature of the ethnicity of the mainland core, and in fact has abetted it. The major original surviving inhabitants of the area appear to be the Khmers of Cambodia who, under the pressure of succeeding invasions from the North and East by the Thai, Laotian, and Annamitic (Vietnamese) peoples, have been restricted to the lower Mekong river area. Each of these invading peoples long ago (as early as the thirteenth century) established its own political dynasty. The area's main cultural characteristics are of external origin: either from the North and China, or from the West and India. The period of largely French colonial rule began only in 1862 (in present-day South Vietnam) and, unlike West Africa and perhaps more like North Africa, the mainland core did not inherit an over-all central colonial administration at the time of independence, although all their elite spoke French.

The West African Core[9]

In contrast to the Middle Eastern, West European, and maritime Southeast Asian cores, and somewhat like the mainland Southeast Asian, the West African core is ethnically and linguistically extremely heterogenous. There are hundreds of ethnic groupings, and the separate identity of each is reinforced by its own separate language. The Mossi, in Upper Volta, and the Hausa, in Niger, are the largest ethnic groups within any single state in the core, and they comprise only 42% of the respective populations! Moreover, in Upper Volta, the three largest groupings comprise only

9 The West African core consists of: The Ivory Coast, Dahomey, Guinea, Senegal, the Upper Volta, Mali, Nigeria, and Togo.

about 50% of the population and, in Niger, only 62%. Islam functions, as Catholicism does in Latin America, to offset this heterogeneity to some extent, but the range of its adherents is from 90% in Mail to 8% in Togo, while animism is the religion of the majority in the Ivory Coast, Upper Volta and Dahomey. However, although Christianity is statistically almost infinitesimal in some states, the educational effects of the religion have resulted in a number of the members of the ruling elite in each state being members of that faith. While Islam and Christianity are thus potentially solidifying factors, in fact there exists a virtually universal political division throughout the core between the Northern Muslims and the Southern Christians.

Historically, the two most important factors are, first, that an indigenous system of empires was in relatively recent existence (e.g., the Mossi in Upper Volta, and the Fulani in Guinea and elsewhere) at the time of the late nineteenth-century advent of European rule, and, second, the uniting effect of the French colonial experience.

Thus, unlike Latin America, where three centuries of Spanish rule erased the memory of the Aztecs and Incas from the area's historical consciousness, the West Africans have been able to incorporate their indigenous political tradition into their nationalisms. In Latin America and, to some extent, maritime Southeast Asia, nationalism has been influenced more by European rather than local tradition; it would thus appear that their longer exposure to European science and ideas has resulted in a more solidified nationalism in these areas than in West Africa. The French colonial experience, which began in the seventeenth century but became most intense with the establishment of the administrative unit of Afrique Occidentale Française in 1895, ended only in 1958, but it was relatively short-lived and perhaps did not have as profound an effect upon the indigenous societies as might have been thought. One consequence, however, was to establish French as a single language of communication among the elite of the various countries, and another was that the highly centralized nature of French colonial administration sowed the ideal of regional unity. It is perhaps evident that, in terms of ethnic, linguistic, religious, and to a lesser extent historical factors, the West African core is the most socially uncohesive of the six cores.

Let us now reexamine our ranking of the six cores under discussion in order of decreasing social cohesiveness: the Middle East, West Europe, Latin America, maritime Southeast Asia, mainland Southeast Asia, and West Africa. The first three we have seen are generally cohesive in ethnicity, language, and religion: the Middle East in all three, West Europe in the first and third, and Latin America in the second and third. The maritime Southeast Asian core ranks below Latin America, because while it has a high degree of ethnic and linguistic cohesion, it does not possess a single language, but rather related ones. In addition, while the religion of Islam is numerically dominant, it is also true that half of Malaysia's population is Taoist or Buddhist and that nearly all of the Philippines are Christian. The mainland Southeast Asian core, on the other hand, is neither ethnically nor linguistically cohesive, and only religion (Buddhism) provides some degree of cohesion. West Africa is the least socially cohesive because of the multitude of ethnic and linguistic groupings which are reinforced by animism. Only Islam, and to a much lesser extent Christianity, have tended to promote religious cohesion, and in only a few of the states within the core.

ECONOMIC COHESION

In examining the factor of economic cohesion we focus upon two aspects: first, to what extent there exist complementary economic resources in the core; and second, what is the nature of trade patterns within the core sector. It is clear that the West European core in fact possesses such complementarity of economic resources. For example, there is iron and steel production in France and Germany, and agricultural production in Belgium and the Netherlands. The next core sector, among the five we are considering, to have at least the potential of complementarity is Latin America. For example, 33% of Argentina's exports are cereals; 92% of Venezuela's are crude petroleum; 85% of Chile's is copper and other metals; and 24% of Peru's are fish products. The general problem of reliance upon primary products among developing nations also exists in Latin America (e.g., oil, bananas, coffee). This dependence is even more widespread in West Africa, where Senegal, Mali, and Niger produce peanuts, and the Ivory Coast and Togo export coffee and cocoa. In the Middle East the primary products are cotton in the U.A.R. and oil in Iraq, Saudi Arabia, Kuwait, and elsewhere. The mainland Southeast Asian core produces mainly rice, although North Vietnam is potentially industrial because of its tin, zinc, and copper deposits. In the maritime core, only the Philippines is an important food exporter (coconuts and sugar); rubber and oil are the most important Indonesian exports, and rubber and tin are primary products in Malaysia.

This listing of the major economic products of the five core sectors enables us to see what the potentialities of economic complementarity are, potentialities which, an inspection of trade statistics reveals, are largely unrealized except in the West European core. There, the percentage of exports and imports within the core ranges from a low of 41 and 32.5, respectively, in Italy, and 36.5 and 37 in W. Germany to a high of 63 and 57 respectively, in Belgium. In the Latin American core, by way of contrast, the high is in Uruguay, 35% of whose imports come from within the core sector, and the low is in Venezuela and Mexico, where the figure is 3%. In the West African core, the high is 18%, in Upper Volta, and the low is 2.5% in the relatively affluent Ivory Coast. In the Middle East, three countries are comparable to Latin America: Syria sends 30.5% of her exports to other countries within the core area and buys 11.5% of her imports from them; Jordan exports 44% and imports 21%; Lebanon exports 57% and imports 13%. The remaining states have figures more like those of the U.A.R. (7.5% and 5.5%, respectively). Figures of less than 15% also occur in the Southeast Asian cores. There is little intra-core trade between the Philippines, Indonesia, and Malaysia in the maritime core, and only slightly more on the mainland (e.g., 11.1% and 1.3% in Thailand).

Thus in terms of economic cohesion, we can rank the cores in descending order as: West Europe, Latin America, the Middle East, West Africa, and the mainland and maritime cores of Southeast Asia.

POLITICAL COHESION

By political cohesion we mean the relative homogeneity of the types of regime in an area. Perhaps the most obvious significance of this element of cohesion is that it is a symptom of other underlying factors of cohesion. Thus, with the significant exception of the West European core sector, which is remarkably homogeneous (all the governments are reconciliation types), the cores we are considering are extremely heterogeneous. The Latin American core gives the appearance of being characterized by reconciliation systems; in fact, however, the military either controls the government or stands ready to take it over in most of the states comprising the Latin American core (e.g. Ecuador and Guatemala). The West African core, on the other hand, has mobilizational, neo-mercantilist and military oligarchies. The Middle Eastern core consists of mobilizational systems, military oligarchies and modernizing autocracies. The mainland Southeast Asian core consists primarily of modernizing autocracies (Laos, Thailand, and Cambodia); additionally, North Vietnam is a mobilizational system and South Vietnam is a military oligarchy overlain with reconciliation rhetoric. The maritime core of Southeast Asia consists of a limited modernizing autocracy (Malaysia), a reconciliation system (the Philippines) and a military oligarchy (Indonesia).[10]

ORGANIZATIONAL COHESION[11]

Organizational cohesion is of significance primarily in terms of membership in regional and extra-regional organizations. In addition, voting studies of the United Nations' General Assembly reveal the existence of bloc voting which presumably helps, in some degree, to promote regional consciousness. What seems to be of great significance in assessing the cohesive effects of

10 For a complete explanation of the type of regimes listed here see Chap. 1, footnote 11, p. 12.

11 For a more extensive treatment of the relation of formal regional organizations to subordinate systems, see Chap. 8, by Professor Lynn Miller.

such membership is the number of such organizations and the extent of common core participation in individual units. In the West European core sector for example, virtually all six core members belong to several important regional organizations, all of which coincide exactly with the boundaries of the core sector.

In the Latin American core, such wholesale membership does not exist, but eleven of the eighteen core sector members do belong to the Latin American Free Trade Association (LAFTA), and five others belong to the Central American Common Market (CACM). All eighteen belong to the Organization of American States (OAS), sizable groups belong to other such organizations as the International Coffee Agreement, and all belong to the Inter-American Development Bank. (It should be noted that none of these organizations coincide with the boundaries of the core sector.) A similarly high degree of membership in international organizations exists in the West African core. It is possible to speculate however, that such membership promotes even more cohesiveness because the organizations are exclusively Francophonic. Thus, it is generally only Guinea and sometimes Mali (of the eight core members) who are not associated with such groups as Organisation Commune Africaine et Malgache (OCAM), the European Economic Community (EEC), the franc zone, or the Conseil de l'Entente, although all are members of the Organization of African Unity. (Again, however, it should be noted that all of these organizations are not exclusive to the West African core and this perhaps weakens their specifically West African cohesive effects.) A similar kind of linguistic exclusiveness is found in the Arab League of the Middle Eastern core, as well as in the Council of Arab Economic Unity, and the Arab Common Market; a difference, however, is the greater practical effectiveness of the West African grouping. And, it should be added, the Arab League is a trans-core sector grouping, while the remaining ones are restricted to core membership. In Southeast Asia, the only grouping which approaches the total membership of the core, in both the maritime and mainland areas, is the Colombo Plan, and the Association of Southeast Asian Nations (ASEAN) includes the maritime core plus Singapore and Thailand. Otherwise common groupings are virtually non-existent.

CONCLUSIONS

This discussion of the relative cohesion of six core sectors reveals the manner in which the factors of social, economic, political, and organizational cohesion tend to reinforce one another and so promote cohesiveness. This successive reinforcement is epitomized in the West European core, and we can rank the remaining core sectors in terms of decreasing cohesiveness as follows: Latin America, Middle East, West Africa, the maritime Southeast Asia and mainland Southeast Asia. While in objective terms, the Middle

Eastern core sector is the most socially homogeneous (compared, e.g., to Latin America) its potential cohesiveness is obviated by the appeal for regional unity by the radical states (United Arab Republic, Syria, Iraq, and Yemen) and the strength of the resistance of the conservative states (Saudi Arabia, Jordan, Kuwait plus Lebanon, and the Sudan). The West African core tends to counteract the uncohesiveness of its social, economic, and political factors by participating in functional organizations which are Francophonic. The Southeast Asian cores, on the other hand, do not have memberships in regional organizations to offset a lack of cohesion in the other factors; the maritime core does possess considerably more ethnic and linguistic cohesion than does the mainland.

COMMUNICATIONS

The reader will recall that we are examining communications, the second of our four pattern variables, in terms of four factors: personal communications (mail, telephone, telegraph); mass media (newspapers, radio, television); exchanges among the elite (regional education, tourism, diplomatic visits, and so forth); and transportation (road, water, rail, air).[12]

PERSONAL COMMUNICATIONS

The incidence of the exchange of mail and of telephone and telegraph messages within the core sector is of obvious importance in attempting to assess the significance of communications. Unfortunately, a country-by-country breakdown of mail shipments is generally not available, and there is little information on communication within the core by telegraph and telephones—indeed, direct facilities do not always exist. In the West African core, for example, telephone communications between states were, until recently, routed through Paris.

MASS MEDIA

The extent of the exchange of newspapers and of radio and television communications within a core is difficult to estimate because, again, there is a lack of data. This is especially true of newspapers. Television transmission exists within many core sectors, but because of distances and other factors it is important only perhaps in West Europe and in the Middle East, and

12 For a partial listing of the sources upon which this section is based see Core and Peripheral sources, p. 407. (Appendix). In general, the kind of data in which we are interested, i.e., information about the reception of personal and mass media communications, differentiated by recipient country, is not available. This accounts for the general nature of much of what follows. Those who have been interested in analyzing the flow of such transactions have been able to utilize the undifferentiated data. See, for example, Bruce Russett, *International Regions and the International System: A Study in Political Ecology* (Chicago: Rand McNally & Co., 1967).

it is only in these core sectors that radio programs are deliberately beamed at other countries. Most European capitals broadcast such programs, and the Voice of the Arabs in Cairo broadcasts to the Middle Eastern core. Generally speaking, strikingly little transmission occurs within Latin America, West Africa, or Southeast Asia.

EXCHANGE AMONG THE ELITE

Only in the West European and Middle Eastern core sectors is there large-scale attendance at universities located within the core sector. In the West European core this exchange occurs among all the countries, but in the Middle East it takes place primarily in the Egyptian secular universities, at the religious university of al-Azhar and at the American University in Beirut (in Lebanon). Elsewhere, higher education abroad ordinarily means going outside the region, usually to the United States, Britain, France, or the Soviet Union. Such attendance undoubtedly heightens the student's sense of regional awareness, for especially in Paris, Moscow, and Cairo they tend to live, dine, and organize on a regional basis.

Tourism within the core sector also heightens regional consciousness. There is not enough data to allow us to compare the core sectors, but an assessment of each individual sector can be made. In West Europe, touring within the core sector is proportional to population figures. Tourists number in the millions. In the Middle East, such touring appears to be widely dispersed, although more concentrated in Syria, Lebanon, and Jordan. We do not know, however, whether our data are true tourist figures or whether in fact they represent seasonal shifts in employment or even nomadism. In Latin America, the data indicate a concentration of exchanges of tourists among the three major countries, Argentina, Brazil, and Chile. Data are not available for Southeast Asia and West Africa, but the annual migration of labor in West Africa is an equivalent phenomenon.

The existence of diplomatic representation in a core sector is a kind of minimal assurance of at least diplomatic contacts between constituent states. Five of the six core sectors generally maintain full diplomatic representation in each other's capitals. The significant exception is the West African core, where such representation is noticeably weak. In 1964, Senegal, Ivory Coast, Upper Volta, and Dahomey did not have diplomatic representation in five or more of the remaining seven West African states.[13]

TRANSPORTATION

An inspection of the available data and maps indicates a wide variance in the manner in which road, water, rail, and airline systems link the members of each core sector. Again, the West European core sector, by

---

[13] I. William Zartman, *International Relations in the New Africa* (Englewood Cliffs, N.J.: Prentice-Hall, Inc., 1966), p. 77.

comparison with the remaining five, has an intricate network of roads, of sea, river, and canal connections, of railroad lines, and of airlines. Making some allowance for geography (e.g., the islands of the maritime Southeast Asian core), an inspection of core and peripheral sector communications reveals that in terms of the number of all-weather roads and rail lines crossing frontiers, the core sectors can be ranked roughly as follows: West Europe, Latin America, the Middle East, maritime Southeast Asia, West Africa, and mainland Southeast Asia. In all of these areas, however, there are also numerous international and local airlines with frequent schedules. This appears to be especially the case in Latin America where, however, maritime linkages are most important.[14] Air services can provide only rather tenuous linkage, because a reliance upon them precludes the shipment of material and the movement of large groups of people.

POWER

In considering power, the third pattern variable, we are concerned with, first, an assessment of a given state's power in relation to the other states of the core sector and, second, with the attempt to rank these states according to our seven-step ranking system.[15] The level of power of a state can be determined by analyzing its material resources and its military and motivational qualities. Ranking the state involves an assessment of the degree to which this power is translated into influence within or outside the subordinate system. Because our assessment of power is a relational process largely restricted to the boundaries of the subordinate system, our major discussion will be concerned with specific core sectors rather than with comparing it with other regions.

In the examination of the material characteristics of power we have decided to focus upon three factors: the size of the population, the size of the gross national product (GNP), and the amount of energy, e.g. electricity and fuel consumed. As our criterion of military power, we have selected the single factor of total size of the armed forces. Finally, in considering motivation we will focus on the percentage of the gross national product (GNP) devoted to military expenditures. It must be appreciated that the selection of these five factors is in the nature of shorthand; when they are insufficient, we will introduce supplementary data.[16]

We shall discuss the West European, Latin American, maritime Southeast Asian, Middle Eastern, mainland Southeast Asian, and West African

14 Robert T. Brown, *Transport and Economic Integration of South America* (Washington, D.C.: The Brookings Institution, 1966), p. 216.

15 Most of the following discussion is based on an analysis of the data presented in Table 2-2, Core Sector Power, p. 399.

16 This discussion of power is largely based on the data appearing in Table 2-2, Core Sector Power, p. 399.

cores, in that order, and attempt to justify this ranking by way of conclusion. In each case, we will focus first upon the general problem, the existence or nonexistence of an equal distribution of power among the members of the core and, second, upon each core's special characteristics.

THE WEST EUROPEAN CORE

The West European core (with the exception of Luxembourg) possesses a generally high level of power and thus is devoid of the extremes of power which characterize the remaining core sectors. Even though a sizeable gap exists between France and Germany on the one hand and Belgium and the Netherlands on the other, all of these states are industrialized and economically advanced. Moreover, Italy occupies a midway position among the other four major states. Thus, the consumption of energy in West Germany, first in rank, is 246.59, and its military force is roughly 450,000 (second only to highly motivated France); the figures for Belgium, generally fifth in rank, are 44.32 and about 100,000, respectively. An unusual feature of the West European core is the uniformly relatively low percentages of GNP spent on defense: the figure for France is 4.4%; for Belgium, 2.9%.

These low percentages of GNP spent on defense—which have been declining steadily in recent years—are explained by reference to several factors: the generally placid nature of recent international relations in the core, the gradual abstention of West European states from major military activities in other parts of the international system, and the protection afforded by the United States through NATO commitments. Of particular importance is the relatively high GNP of West European states, which means that they actually can spend considerable amounts on defense compared to weaker countries, yet these sums appear as a low percentage of GNP. It is interesting to note that France maintains the largest military force and spends the highest percent of GNP on defense in the core. In the light of France's recent withdrawal from NATO's military apparatus, its continued military posture can be interpreted as part of President de Gaulle's foreign policy of *grandeur*.

The distinctive characteristic of power in the West European core is its general high level. France and Germany are secondary powers, Belgium, the Netherlands, and Italy are middle powers, and only tiny Luxembourg is a micro-state.

THE LATIN AMERICAN CORE

The Latin American core sector is characterized, in contrast to West Europe, by a profound disjuncture in power between seven states—Brazil, Mexico, Argentina, Chile, Venezuela, Colombia, and Peru—and the remaining eleven states. These seven states range from middle to regional, while the remaining states are considered micro-states.

Let us compare Peru, the lowest of the upper seven, with Uruguay, the highest of the lower eleven. The disjuncture is only hinted at by Peru's larger GNP ($4 billion vs. $1.5 billion) because Peru has a much larger population figure than Uruguay (11,650,000 in 1965 vs. 2,715,000 in 1965), respectively. It is clearer in the figures showing consumption of energy (6.84 vs. 2.49). The figures for total military forces (55,100 vs. 15,400) and the percentages of GNP devoted to defense (3.1 in 1967 vs. 1.5 in 1967) further illustrate the consistent nature of the disjuncture of power among the states of the Latin American core.

Among the upper seven, there is potentially an extreme disjuncture between the power of Brazil (which had a population of 81,301,000 in 1965) and that of the remaining six (e.g., second-place Mexico, which had a population of 40,913,000 in 1965). Moreover, Brazil's armed forces number 194,000 vs. second-ranked Argentina's 120,000. The disjuncture remains potential rather than actual, however, for reasons that may perhaps be hinted at in Brazil's third-place standing in energy consumption (after Mexico and Argentina), but the disjuncture is reinforced by its second-place standing in the percentage of GNP spent on defense.

On the basis of the foregoing and the data presented in Table 2-2, we can categorize Brazil as a middle power to indicate its exceptional character; Argentina, Chile, and Mexico as minor powers; and Colombia, Peru, and Venezuela as regional powers. (Venezuela is distinctively the most powerful of the regional states.) These seven states are then clearly distinguished from the remaining eleven micro-states of the Latin American core.

A peculiar feature of the Latin American core is the low percentage of GNP expended for defense by most states as compared with other regions. In this respect the area resembles West Europe. The comparatively weak Dominican Republic spent the highest percentage on defense in 1967—probably because of the political turmoil within that country during that period. Mexico and Colombia are distinctive among the top seven nations for their low expenditures on defense. These generally small military expenditures undoubtedly reflect the extraordinarily low level of conflict in the Latin American core. A high percentage of expenditures probably more accurately reflects the priority of the political demands of the country's military over the nation's genuine needs for security.

THE MARITIME SOUTHEAST ASIAN CORE

There is an appearance of the existence of a disjuncture of power in the maritime Southeast Asian core, between Indonesia on the one hand, and the Philippines and Malaysia on the other. This appears to be true of material, military, and motivational factors. However, the situation is unlike that on the mainland or in the Latin American core, in that the potential difference in power is not visible: Indonesia remains too weak for the present. We have therefore categorized all three as minor powers. Malaysia, the weakest, still has a military force of 32,600. The result of this relative balance of forces has been that in this core sector—characterized by a high degree of conflict over territory—no change in boundaries has occurred as a consequence of the confrontations between the three core members.

THE MIDDLE EASTERN CORE

The Middle Eastern core is characterized by the singular position of the United Arab Republic (U.A.R.) as the most powerful nation in this sector. The population, GNP, consumption of energy, and total armed forces of the U.A.R. range from nearly four times (population) to two times (size of military) those of its closest rival.[17] After the U.A.R., in terms of power, there comes a group of states consisting of Saudi Arabia, Iraq, and Syria. The rest rate somewhat lower.

The most astonishing aspect of our five-factor ranking system is the U.A.R.'s position as fourth in the motivational factor, percentage of GNP spent on defense. Ahead of it are ranked Jordan, Saudi Arabia, and Syria. It is possible that this could be explained in terms of the massiveness of Soviet military aid, but it is also possible that it really indicates that primacy is given to domestic development, an emphasis for which it is often criticized by its radical Arab critics. This motivational phenomenon will be discussed again, when we turn to the fourth pattern variable, the structure of relations.

The preceding suggests the appropriateness of labeling the U.A.R. a minor power and Saudi Arabia as a strong regional state, as well as placing Iraq, Syria, Kuwait, Sudan, Jordan,[18] and Lebanon in the same category. Only Yemen and South Yemen rank as micro-states. However, the presence of only one power above the rank of regional state indicates that the level of power is weaker in the Middle East than in Latin America.

THE MAINLAND SOUTHEAST ASIAN CORE

The power disjuncture in the mainland Southeast Asian core occurs between North Vietnam, South Vietnam, and Thailand on the one hand, and Laos and Cambodia on the other. The calculation of the power of these three states is made extremely difficult by the present war, however. In the absence of war, it appears that Thailand would be the most powerful state in terms of material assets (size of population, GNP and consumption of energy). Yet, in size of military forces and percentage of the GNP spent on defense, North and South Vietnam both seem to be much more powerful because of their present bellicose tendencies. It is obvious that this greater power

[17] Both comparisons are with Iraq.
[18] Were Jordan to lose the West Bank permanently, it would be reduced to a micro-state.

is largely the result of external support by the U.S.S.R., the People's Republic of China, and the United States.

On the basis of outside aid and internal capacity we rank North Vietnam and Thailand as minor powers, South Vietnam as a regional state, and Cambodia and Laos as micro-states. The tenuous nature of this ranking in the context of an ongoing war in the core must, however, be emphasized. We could say that were there no war, such a ranking might be quite different but, on the other hand, the stalemate which followed the Korean War and froze the power status of both Koreas is perhaps instructive and should lead us to the hypothesis that if a similar situation were to crystalize in North and South Vietnam, the results would be similar there. In other words, each state would achieve a stable degree of power relative to the other, and more viable classification would become feasible.

THE WEST AFRICAN CORE

The general level of power within the West African core sector is very low, as illustrated by the fact that Guinea has the largest military force and this consists of 4,800 men! Even in this depressed power situation, however, there exists a slight power disjuncture which separates the Ivory Coast, Senegal and Guinea from the remaining five core members in terms of material, and motivational elements of power. This is illustrated dramatically in the figures for the consumption of energy. While all the figures are fantastically low, compared to other areas, the Ivory Coast, Senegal, and Guinea have figures of .58, .51, and .34, respectively, while the figure for Mali, the next highest, is .09, and that for Niger, the lowest, is .04.

The core-wide phenomenon of a general low level of power accompanied by a disjuncture of power is well illustrated by categorizing as regional powers the Ivory Coast, Guinea, Senegal, and Mali on the one hand, and as micro-states Dahomey, Upper Volta, Niger, and Togo, on the other.

The extremely low figure of the military forces is symptomatic of the low level of conflict in the core sector. In this respect it is very similar to the Latin American core, the outstanding difference being that even when the military has become involved in politics it has not yet created pressure for increased military expenditures. Thus the diplomatic initiative shown by the Ivory Soast, Senegal, and Guinea has been based more on economic, ideological, and historical factors (they having been leaders of West African nationalism) than on a direct concerns for security.

CONCLUSIONS

In conclusion, we can make two general points about our pattern variable of power. The first is in reference to our tentative ranking of the six core sectors in terms of power, the second is in reference to the distinction that we have made between cores which are characterized by a manifest disjuncture in power and those which are not.

In regard to the first point, it must be emphasized that the ranking of the cores in the order of West Europe, Latin America, maritime Southeast Asia, the Middle East, mainland Southeast Asia, and West Africa is perhaps of more heuristic than explanatory value. That is to say, for the present exploratory venture into the nature of regional international relations we present such a ranking only in order to begin to elucidate differences between the various cores, without attempting to investigate fully the implications of such differences. It has proven difficult enough to rank individual states in terms of material, military and motivational elements of power without trying to assess what one may mean by "motivation" when speaking of an aggregate of states constituting a core.[19] Having made this qualification, however, we can note that the utilization of the seven-step ranking system is of some assistance in the ranking of the cores themselves. Thus, at the outset, there would be little controversy over ranking the West European core, with its membership of secondary and middle powers, as the most powerful, and the West African, with its four regional powers and three micro-states, as the least powerful. The Latin American core is perhaps only slightly more controversially placed second, considering its possession of the only other middle power (Brazil), three minor powers, and three regional states. Again, the fifth-place position of the mainland Southeast Asian core is explicable in terms of the precarious presence (due to outside assistance) of one minor power, two regional states, and two micro-states. On the other hand, whether the maritime Southeast Asian core should be ranked third, and the Middle East fourth, is more open to question. The presence of three minor powers (including Indonesia with its great potentialities) in maritime Southeast Asia, while there is only a single one in the Middle East, is the justification for this order. Nevertheless, it must be appreciated that the Middle Eastern core shares a high degree of motivation (a factor of power) which is similar to that of the West European core and it could be argued that this is sufficient reason to rank the Middle East higher.

Our second theme is the disjuncture of power within the six cores. Such disjuncture is manifest in the Latin American, mainland Southeast Asian, and Middle Eastern cores, and is less present in the West European, West African, and maritime Southeast Asian cores. What is striking is that it is in the cores with a profound disjunction of power that internal conflict is the greatest. This is evident in the mainland Southeast Asian and Middle Eastern cores. Latin America is an exception, perhaps because it possesses a comparatively high degree of cohesion and because American hegemony

---

[19] Although it is perhaps possible to speak of the existence of core-wide motivation in West Europe (NATO and the perceived Soviet threat) and the Middle East (the common Arab attitude towards Israel).

mutes a real conflict. The cores characterized by a less dramatic disjunction of power are distinguished by a high degree of cooperation or equilibrium (West Europe and West Africa). In maritime Southeast Asia, the level of conflict is high, but there the relative equality of power operates to create the diplomatic standoff characteristic of that core.

We shall now turn to the further discussion of the problem of cooperation and conflict among the six cores.

STRUCTURE OF RELATIONS

In considering the fourth pattern variable, the structure of relations, we are concerned to determine within each core sector: (1) the spectrum of relations (i.e., which states are in cooperation or conflict with one another); (2) the causes of relations (i.e., the basis for their amity or enmity); and (3) the means of relations (i.e., the instruments of war, types of amelioration of conflict and methods of cooperation). In a real sense this pattern variable encompasses the political effects of the preceding three. We shall deal with the six cores in terms of what is felt to be a decreasing order of the presence of cooperation: West Europe, Latin America, West Africa, maritime Southeast Asia, the Middle East, and mainland Southeast Asia.

WEST EUROPEAN CORE

Conflict in the West European core is at present extremely muted. We have already noted how this quiescent conflict may be related to the relative equal distribution of power amongst the states comprising this core. Only such issues as the admission of Britain to the European Common Market or its future political form have found the Benelux countries in mutual disagreement with France, while France itself continues to be concerned about Germany—a concern which is still shared by a variety of governments within the region. This relationship between France and Germany may be understood as a state of equilibrium obtaining between the two secondary powers. Otherwise, the extraordinary economic success of the Common Market, with its promise of increased political interaction, gives this core a very definite stamp of cooperation, and of such intensity that it is set apart from all other cores. Even the low level of conflict within the Latin American core sector, as we shall shortly note, is due to the limited nature of relations rather than to any cooperative spirit.

The causes of relations within the West European core tend to be four: The first, a cause of conflict, is France's refusal to permit Britain to enter the Common Market. The second, also of conflict, is France's further refusal to permit the granting of greater political authority to the political organs of the Market. The third, again of conflict, is France's reluctance to see

Germany reunited. The fourth, of cooperation, is the common desire to share the economic benefits to be derived from the Market, a factor which usually outweighs the other three.

The means of relations used in the conflict are France's exertion of its diplomatic strength with its underlying economic muscle: France is too strategic and economically strong to be tampered with within the Market arrangement. The means of ameliorating conflict and the method of cooperation tend to be the same, namely the utilization of the councils and organs of the European Common Market organization.

THE LATIN AMERICAN CORE

In the Latin American core sector, the spectrum of relations reveals a generally low level of conflict. Indeed, there has only been one extended war in the 20th Century, the Chaco War between Paraguay and Bolivia from 1928–1938. There are, however, a variety of disputes which include Peru vs. Ecuador, Chile vs. Peru and Bolivia, Argentina vs. Chile, and Argentina vs. Brazil, and these can be said to be in a state of low-keyed stalemate. Most of these concentrate on contested borders; the conflict between Bolivia and Peru with Chile is especially lingering, as it dates from the war of the Pacific (1879–1883). The conflict between Brazil and Argentina, the two most powerful states in Latin America, is a competition for prestige and influence.[20] Otherwise, Latin American relations are characterized by cooperation of the alliance variety, as is evidenced in LAFTA and the Central American Common Market. More generally as we observed when we considered economic cohesion and communications, there is an absence of both intense cooperation and conflict. As we noted in our discussion of power, this absence of intense conflict is achieved in spite of a marked disjuncture of power. It is in terms of boundary disputes, rivalry for prestige, and common economic concerns that one sees the causes of relations in the Latin American core.

The means of relations, in terms of conflict, tend to be arms races and military parades. Amelioration of conflict tends to be accomplished through commissions (e.g., the Inter-American Peace Committee established in 1940—though its first meeting was held in 1948). The Rio Treaty of 1948 gave Latin American countries a greater role in their own affairs than they had earlier, when the hegemony of the U.S. was more complete. These methods of cooperation clearly tend to be those more hemispheric (e.g., LAFTA, OAS, and so forth) than bilateral.

[20] See David Wood, *Armed Forces in Central and South America* ("Adelphi Paper," No. 4 [London: Institute for Strategic Studies, 1967]), pp. 6–7, for a useful listing of areas of tension in Latin America.

THE WEST AFRICAN CORE

In contrast to the West European and Latin American cores, the spectrum of relations within the West African core sector is characterized by a low level of stalemated conflict. Its major qualities are a deflated power situation and little sector-wide cooperation. As we shall also note is the case in the Middle Eastern core, the stalemated conflict has a radical—conservative dimension: Guinea, Mali and, on occasion, Senegal, as radical states and regional powers, have been pitted against the remaining micro-states under the conservative leadership of the Ivory Coast, also a regional state. On the side of cooperation there is the alliance-like phenomenon of the Common Organization of Africa and Malagasy, organized for common economic benefits.

The chief cause of relations among West African core states is the radical–conservative one. Its roots go back to 1948. At that point Houphouet-Boigny (the present president of the Ivory Coast) and Leopold Senghor (the present president of Senegal) took diametrically opposed positions on the future of French West Africa, which has now become the West Africa core. Senghor desired the separation of Francophonic West Africa from France, but thought that the area ought to be maintained as a single political unit. Houphouet-Boigny, on the other hand, called for the independence of individual states, but proposed that all maintain continued ties to France. This issue of "Balkanization" has continued to find expression in the repeated attempts of the radical states to unite (an example is the Ghana-Guinea union of 1958). To counter the ideological appeal of these efforts, the Ivory Coast first organized the Entente states (the Ivory Coast, Niger, Dahomey, Upper Volta, and recently Togo) into a grouping (Conseil de l'Entente) whose economic benefits from the Ivory Coast have ebbed and flowed. It was the Entente states which were to be the basis of OCAM. All the core members (except Guinea) have, in effect, accepted Houphouet-Boigny's position by maintaining, through OCAM and their continued presence in the franc zone, a special economic relationship with France. In short, the main impetus for cooperation has been the economic benefits to be derived from association with the former metropolitan country in the form of guaranteed markets and subsidies, rather than any special rewards to be gained from relationships with the other countries in the core.

The means of relations on the side of conflict have included at times assassination plots (e.g., against Houphouet-Boigny in 1963), but more often have been ideological demands and subsidies tantamount to economic blackmail (e.g., from Ghana to Guinea in 1958, and from the Ivory Coast to Niger and Upper Volta). The amelioration of conflict has often resulted from the collective diplomatic pressure exerted by the Entente states and other groups within the core.

MARITIME SOUTHEAST ASIAN CORE

The maritime Southeast Asian core has been characterized by a spectrum of relations which has fluctuated between a high degree of conflict and moderate cooperation. Both Indonesia and the Philippines (minor powers) have been, separately and at different times, close to direct military conflict with Malaysia (also a minor power). As for cooperation, there has been only the suggestion of a Malphindo grouping by the Philippines.

The cause of the conflict has been the territorial designs of Indonesia in its "Greater Indonesia" dream, and the claim of the Philippines on the specific territory of Sabah within Malaysia. The means of conflict have included the breaking off of diplomatic and trade relations, and the infiltration of guerrillas into Malaysia. Amelioration of conflict—when it has occurred— has been of a temporary and tenuous nature (e.g., the coming to power of Suharto in Indonesia, and the current abandonment of the "crush Malaysia" policy). The diplomatic standoff resulting from this constant high degree of tension is due to the relative equality of power individually possessed by all of the three minor powers who are seeking a place in the sun.

THE MIDDLE EASTERN CORE

The Middle Eastern core's spectrum of relations is characterized by a high degree of conflict, which is in turn offset by an even higher degree of cooperation, due largely to the shared felt threat of Israel. The major conflict continues to be between the conservative states—(Saudi Arabia, Jordan, Kuwait, and the Persian Gulf states (largely regional states, with the exception of the potential Persian Gulf micro-state[21])—and the radical states: the U.A.R., Iraq, Syria, Yemen, and South Yemen. (Of the radical states, the U.A.R. is a minor power; Iraq and Syria are regional states; and Yemen and South Yemen are micro-states). Lebanon and, until recently, Sudan have been in the middle. This conflict, until the recent withdrawal of Egyptian forces from Yemen, was a sustained crisis verging on direct military conflict. The results of the war in June 1967 reduced the sustained crisis among the Arab nations to the level of a stalemate. A further conflict is that between the radical states of the U.A.R. and Syria. Again, aftereffects of the June 1967 war reduced it to a low-order stalemate. As as result of that war there has been a greater emphasis upon cooperation, expressed in increased collaboration within the Arab League and the special military arrangements existing among all the Arab states. In addition, there is the direct monetary aid that the U.A.R. and Jordan have been getting from the oil-rich states of Saudi Arabia, Kuwait, and Libya as a subsidy for the

---

[21] This state may emerge from the present British-protected states of Bahrain, Muscat and Oman, Qatar and the Trucial States.

continued closure of the Suez Canal and the occupation of segments of their territory.

As to the causes of conflict within the Middle Eastern core, there is the ideological issue of republican socialism which is linked to the Arab nationalist cause, vs. the monarchical principle which is claimed as the defender of traditional Islam. Within the radical group, there is the further issue of whether Syria or the United Arab Republic is the most qualified ideological leader of Arab nationalism. On the side of cooperation, on the other hand, there is the very real, vivid, and mutual feeling of cultural and historical solidarity, already discussed in our section on cohesiveness, whose political tenuousness continues to be countered by the common Arab concern with Israel.

As far as the means of relations are concerned, conflict has taken the form of virtually direct, regular military conflict between radicals and conservatives (the U.A.R. vs. Saudi Arabia in Yemen), and of ideological haranguing via mass media in the case of the conflict among the radical states. The amelioration of conflict has most often occurred by means of the intervention of third-party Arab states (e.g., Algeria, Sudan, and Iraq in the case of Yemen). The method of cooperation continues to be the basic structural one set by the Arab League, but there are also *ad hoc* bilateral and multilateral arrangements when the occasion demands it.

THE MAINLAND SOUTHEAST ASIAN CORE

The mainland Southeast Asian core is characterized by conflict virtually unrelieved by cooperation. There is direct military conflict between North and South Vietnam and, on a much reduced level, between North Vietnam and Laos. In addition, there are the stalemated traditional conflicts between Cambodia and South Vietnam, and between Cambodia and Thailand and Thailand and Laos. Virtually the only cooperation occurs between Laos, Cambodia, and South Vietnam, in the Mekong River Development Project.

The causes of relations, largely conflict, are ideological as expressed in the civil war between North and South Vietnam; military and diplomatic, as between North Vietnam and Laos; and more traditional and historical (already alluded to in our discussion of cohesion) between Cambodia and Thailand, and particularly between South Vietnam and Cambodia. In all these conflicts, the minor-power status of North Vietnam and Thailand, and the regional-power status of South Vietnam result in their taking the initiative. The limited cause of cooperation is the practical one of improving the utilization of the water resources of the Mekong River.

In terms of means of conflict these are influenced largely by countries external to the region. Outside powers provide guerilla training and indoctrination, send supplies, materiel and weapons, and even dispatch advisors and troops. As a result, this core is distinctive for the use of both the most primitive and the most advanced instruments of conflict.

SUMMARY

In summarizing our discussion of the structure of relations within these six cores, we can note that the West European and Latin American cores are chiefly characterized by a high degree of cooperation of the alliance variety. The West African relations are perhaps best described as in equilibrium. The remaining three cores, the maritime Southeast Asian, the Middle Eastern, and the mainland Southeast Asian, can be characterized as being, respectively, in a stalemate, a sustained crisis, and a direct military conflict.

CONCLUSION

We now return to a consideration of the two themes—degree of cohesiveness and the extent of international relations within the core—with which we began this chapter. The pattern variables of communication and power will be dealt with as they have bearing on these two themes. As we have observed, it is the presence of a notable degree of both elements which assists us in, first, recognizing the existence of a subordinate system and, second, in making the distinction between the core sector and the peripheral sector. In order to better organize our conclusion, we will rank the cores according to the decreasing presence of these two elements—stating at the outset, however, that pronounced relationships among the countries, whether cooperative or conflictual, are almost given in the core while they can be totally absent in the periphery. This unvarying quality of relations within the core leads us to focus upon the other theme, and our ranking of the six core sectors depends primarily upon their cohesiveness. The order we have determined on is: West Europe, Latin America, the Middle East, West Africa, maritime Southeast Asia, and mainland Southeast Asia.

West Europe's prospects for cohesion appear dim at first sight because of its perceived ethnic and actual linguistic diversity. When the widespread racial uniformity and the majority character of Catholicism is noted however, as well as the historical and cultural memories of something called "European," one begins to see an aggregation of cohesive factors. This aggregation is further increased by economic, political, and organizational cohesion, and still further reinforced by a variety of communications, to the point where the West European core has become one of the most cohesive in the world.

As to internal regional relations, we have characterized them in the West European core as consisting largely of cooperation of the alliance (EEC) variety. Insofar as conflict occurs, it has taken the form of a stalemate revolving around the sublimated issues of the future role of Germany, Britain's entry into EEC, and whether or not the EEC itself is to make further encroachments upon individual national sovereignty.

The Latin American core has similarities and dissimilarities to the West European. It is likewise somewhat ethnically and to a degree linguistically noncohesive, but it is at the same time unlike West Europe. First of all,

Spanish is the language spoken by most Latin Americans. Secondly, cohesive economic and political factors tend to outweigh the lack of social cohesion in West Europe, but in Latin America these factors are absent and the balance is achieved by a greater sense of single cultural and religious identity than West Europe possesses. Communications are also rudimentary, so that the sole factor further reinforcing cohesion is organization, primarily the externally (U.S.) inspired OAS and the United Nations' Economic Committee for Latin America, the more indigenous CACM and LAFTA, and the supporting specialized groupings upholding these organizations.

Relations within the Latin American core are similar to West Europe's, in the general sense of there being an absence of conflict. In Latin America this lack of conflict is due less to an explicit quality of cooperation than to a state of equilibrium. The disjunction of power that we noted between the top seven most powerful states and the less powerful remaining eleven, is not translated into the direct suzerainty of the former over the latter. Such conflict as occurs is perhaps even more accurately described as sublimated than is the case in West Europe.

The high degree of social cohesion in the Middle Eastern core is, as we have noted, its most outstanding characteristic and stands in contrast to West Europe and Latin America. The "capital" of this quality is soon dissipated, however, because of the virtual absence of economic factors of cohesion and because, in terms of political cohesion, the radical mobilizational systems are aligned against the conservative modernizing autocratic ones. Somewhat counteracting these uncohesive qualities are the organizational ones of the Arab League and related groupings. Again, unlike those in West Europe and Latin America, they do not coincide with the boundaries of the core; more important, they function as passive forums for the underlying dynamics of the area rather than as organizations with a force of their own. The communications of the Middle Eastern core are second only to the West European in promoting the cohesion of the area, although, generally speaking, communications in West Europe, despite linguistic differences, are evenly balanced in importance over the gamut of personal communications, mass media, interchanges among the elite, and transportation, whereas, largely for technological and geopolitical reasons, mass media and especially the interchange among the elite for education tend to be of greatest significance in the Middle East.

Relations within the Middle Eastern core, in sharp contrast to those in West Europe and Latin America, but much like those in Southeast Asia, are characterized almost exclusively by stalemated conflict between two sets of antagonists, the radical and conservative groupings on the one hand and the ideological rivals of the U.A.R. and Syria on the other. This situation of conflict is characterized by the preeminent role of the U.A.R. and the profound disjuncture of power between it and the remaining Arab states. Such cooperation as exists in this context of stalemated conflict is largely accounted for by the direct military conflict between the core and the peripheral sector, i.e., the Arab-Israeli dispute.[22]

It is the West African core which begins to illustrate the great difference particularly in terms of cohesion between the West European, Latin American and Middle Eastern cores on the one hand, and the West African and Southeast Asian cores on the other. In contrast to the first three cores, West Africa possesses little social cohesion and little economic and political cohesion. Some degree of cohesion is contributed by the universal religions of Islam and Christianity (and as we noted, these tend to be in tension with one another). It is the elitist French culture, and especially organizational cohesion as expressed in OCAM, which persuades us to rank West Africa higher than the Southeast Asian cores in terms of cohesion. Communications, except perhaps for the phenomenon of interchange among the elite in French universities, does little to promote cohesion.

The West African structure of relations is perhaps influenced by the general low level and the relatively equal distribution of power. The spectrum of relations is characterized by equilibrium or tentative cooperation. Such conflict as occurs is of a low order of stalemate, and its causes tend to take the form of differences of opinion about core unity and the relationship of the core to France. The means of these relations tends to be diplomatic alignments.

The maritime Southeast Asian core, unlike West Africa's, possesses ample social cohesion but little economic, political, or organizational cohesion, and communications in no sense contribute anything to overcome these deficiencies. Nevertheless, the strength of the social cohesion is such that we are inclined to rank the maritime core as more cohesive than the mainland core.

The ranking of power appears to have little effect on the structure of relations in the maritime Southeast Asian core because it is relatively evenly distributed at the present (although Indonesia has by far the most potential for regional paramountcy). Perhaps as a result, while there are at times sustained crises which verge on direct military conflict, between Indonesia and Malaysia, and between Malaysia and the Philippines, relations have continued to be a standoff. The causes of relations have been territorial claims, the means, military and diplomatic. Cooperation has been practically nonexistent, except for the as yet unproved ASEAN; the sense of Malay identification which found expression in the Malphindo declarations of Indonesia and the Philippines may someday provide the basis for such cooperation.

The mainland Southeast Asian core is the least cohesive. Only the common religious factor of Buddhism, and slight common membership in such specific-purpose organizations as the Mekong River Development Project

22 See Chap. 4.

tend to offset this characteristic. As we noted with reference to Latin America, West Africa, and the maritime core, communications do not offset the uncohesiveness.

The power hierarchy of the mainland core has been profoundly but perhaps not unalterably affected by the Vietnamese conflict. North Vietnam, and especially South Vietnam, have been elevated by the infusion of war material to a position of power out of all correspondence to its natural base. It would be both a mistake and a misunderstanding of the present approach, however, to understand the Vietnamese conflict as the sole creature of the primary powers. On the contrary, as we have seen, the great powers have only enlarged one of several indigenous conflicts which makes the mainland core comparable only to the Middle East in terms of the amount of conflict present. The difference between the two cores is that, in the Middle East, conflict is expressed in alignments, whereas in the mainland Southeast Asian core it is expressed more atomistically, nation-by-nation. Thus conflict tends to remain stalemated, the causes of relations tend to be irredentist, and the means of relations tend to be diplomatic or even military.

3

READINGS

INTRODUCTION

We present here an array of articles dealing specifically with the core sectors of the five subordinate systems that were discussed comparatively in Chapter 2.

All of the articles are concerned with what we have called the pattern variable of the structure of relations. As we have noted before, this pattern variable in a sense is the dynamic expression of the preceding three variables—cohesion, communications, and power.

Stanley Hoffman's article on the West European core sector ("Obstinate or Obsolete? The Fate of the Nation-State and the Case of Western Europe") argues that contrary to the explicit arguments of several European statesmen and the implicit assumptions of some scholars, there is nothing inevitable about European political integration. In fact, he suggests that integration has not proceeded as far as some have maintained.[1] For our purposes this argument is of great interest primarily because, in developing it, Hoffmann lays bare the major causes of the structure of West European relations: 1) France's and other nations' concern about the reemergence of a powerful, nationalistic Germany, 2) France's opposition to the according of governmental qualities to the EEC machinery, and 3) France's concern to free herself and Europe from the hegemony of either primary power. The focus upon France is of course justified because of the central importance (on the Continent) of de Gaulle's past leadership.

In reading Professor Hoffmann's article the reader must thus consider the relatively peculiar conditions of the international politics of the West European core—whose members are somewhere between unification and separate national existence. He must consider the role of nationalism and

[1] Hoffmann's emphasis on the importance of the nation-state and the international system and his doubts about the significance of regional subsystems are not inconsistent with the approach of this volume, which refuses to equate regionalism with the integration process. There is nothing that is contradictory between his theme and the one put forward by the authors of this volume, because we are less concerned with regional integration than with devising comparative categories for the study of the subordinate system as the framework of the individual regional state's diplomatic activity.

the effect of "the diversity of domestic outlooks and external positions." He must consider why, according to Hoffmann, the nation-state has continued to exist in West Europe, despite so many apparent incentives to its demise; and he should consider, on the other hand, what has actually been accomplished on the road to unification.

Hoffmann skillfully analyzes the competing forces which affect the major problem of the West European core—the direction of its political future and the future of the nation-state. The reader must attempt to identify these forces, and he should analyze carefully Hoffmann's account of the differences in outlook between France and West Germany, and between what he calls the "resisters" and the "resigned ones." Finally, this article should lead the reader to consider the effects upon West European international politics of such diverse external factors as the perception of the Soviet threat, the balance of terror, the comparative temperature of the cold war, the present and former European colonial possessions, and most significantly, the "political collapse of Europe."

Robert Burr's article ("International Interests of Latin American Nations") is similarly broad in scope. It sketches in a general way the structure of relations of the Latin American core, emphasizing that these relations have to be understood as having conflict and cooperation as well as causes and means that exist independently of the United States hegemony in the area.

At the end of his article he shows that in this subordinate system the clear dominance of the United States plays a role in the relations of Latin American states to each other. We can add to his discussion that, since Burr's book was written, the leaders of the Latin American states met with President Johnson at Punta del Este, Uruguay, in April 1967 and declared their intention to create a region-wide Common Market by 1985. The problems and promises raised by this Common Market will likely be among the major issues of Latin American international relations in the years ahead.

In analyzing Professor Burr's article on Latin American international relations the reader should attempt to identify the major incentives to both cooperation and conflict in the Latin American area. He should note which factors have accounted for the inconsistency between the plethora of local disputes and the relative durability of the concept of inter-American collaboration.

The discussion by Abbas Kelidar ("The Struggle for Arab Unity") focuses on the failures in achieving Arab unity. In taking this focus Kelidar lays out the conflicts of the Middle Eastern core much as Hoffmann does for Europe. His theme, that the structure of relations in the area is best understood in terms of the contest for leadership of the movement toward unity, reveals the existence of the sustained, and at times direct (as in Yemen), military conflict of the intra-core rivalries between radical and conservative states and among the radical states themselves.

The reader of Mr. Kelidar's analysis of recent contentions within the Arab world should look for the reasons that account for the tensions in the Middle Eastern core between the cooperative goal of unity and the actual condition of hostility. He should compare the Arab approach to unity with the integration movements in the Latin American and West European cores. In each case the nation-state remains very much alive, but the dynamics of international politics are divergent. The reader may wish to compare the role of social cohesion in both the Latin American core and the Middle Eastern core; in particular, he may wish to compare the role of Catholicism and Islam in each and the effects of the Spanish (and Portuguese) and Arab languages respectively. He may wish to consider the effects of economics as an incentive to unity in each core. Finally, he should consider why it is that the Middle Eastern core—which is socially the most cohesive of the three—is the one which has the highest degree of contention.

From the volatile Middle Eastern core, we turn to a consideration of a core in which the question of unity has been a focal point of regional contention, only here on a much more reduced level. I. William Zartman's discussion of the West African core's structure of relations ("Alliances and Counter Alliances in West Africa") deals comprehensively with the diplomatic complexities which have resulted primarily from the differences in the radical and conservative regimes' views of the desirability of a united West Africa free of French control and a West Africa consisting of independent states still closely related to France. In the months after the book from which this is taken was written, major military coups took place in the peripheral sector nations of Ghana and Nigeria. These coups seem to have coincided with a cooling down of radical-conservative and Africa-wide conferences. Thus Zartman's account ends at a historic point in the relations of the area, yet at the same time it conveys the persistent underlying causes of West African relations.

In the ensuing material Professor Zartman does not limit his discussion to the West African states alone, and he thus demonstrates the effect which activities in neighboring African subordinate systems (e.g. the crises in Algeria and the Congo) have had upon the international relations of this area. Professor Zartman's discussion makes it possible to compare the radical-conservative split in West Africa with the one in the Middle East. One can gain considerable insight into the possibilities for comparing the international relations of diverse regions by considering the effects of each conflict upon the structure of each core's relations, by considering the relationship between the radical-conservative rivalry and political cohesion, and by comparing the distribution of power among the participants in each case. In particular, it is enlightening to contemplate why the level of hostility in West Africa has been so much more muted than in the Middle East and what relationship, if any, this lessened contention has to the lower degree of cohesion of the West African core.

Moreover, although Zartman's delineation of West Africa is slightly broader than our own, the reader should concentrate on the history of the radical-conservative division within the French West African core as delineated in Table 1-1 and on the attempt by Ghana to participate in the core and the effects of these efforts upon core-wide international relations.

Bernard K. Gordon's discussions of the indigenous conflicts which beset Southeast Asia ("A Political Region of Southeast Asia" and "Regionalism and Instability in Southeast Asia") illustrate very well our distinction between the mainland and maritime cores of that area. Thus in discussing the conflict of Cambodia with South Vietnam and the tenseness of Thai-Cambodian relations on the one hand, and Philippine and Indonesian actions against Malaysia on the other, he documents the mutual exclusiveness of these sets of conflicts. Instructive by its omission is the Vietnamese war because, as he points out, the involvement of the world's primary powers in both countries has largely removed them from localistic relations and made them a part of what we call the intrusive system.

On reading these selections by Bernard Gordon, the student of international politics can assay the critical importance of purely local conflicts and rivalries in the international politics of the Southeast Asian cores, and he can assess the causes of these conflicts, both the "modern" (post colonial) and "traditional" (pre-colonial) types. He can also compare the as yet dimly perceived quests for unity in both Southeast Asian cores with those in the other subordinate systems, and he can assess the reasons why calls to unity have a lesser potency in Southeast Asia than in the other four areas.

The student of international politics can also compare the role of conflict in the two Southeast Asian cores with its role in the other subordinate systems under discussion. In particular, he can be aware how the tensions of each Southeast Asian core compare to those of the Middle East: the level of conflict on the mainland is more similar to that of the Arab core, but the level of social cohesion in the maritime area is more similar to the Middle Eastern core. Similarly, West Africa's level of power resembles more closely the level of power of the Southeast Asian mainland than that of the maritime core, but West Africa's comparatively moderate structure of relations is more similar to the structure of relations of the maritime core.

Stanley Hoffmann

OBSTINATE OR OBSOLETE? THE FATE OF THE

NATION-STATE AND THE CASE OF WESTERN EUROPE

I

THE CRITICAL issue for every student of world order is the fate of the nation-state. In the nuclear age, the fragmentation of the world into countless units, each of which has a claim to independence, is obviously dangerous for peace and illogical for welfare. The dynamism which animates those units, when they are not merely city-states of limited expanse or dynastic states manipulated by the Prince's calculations, but nation-states that pour into their foreign policy the collective pride, ambitions, fears, prejudices, and images of large masses of people, is particularly formidable.[1] An abstract theorist could argue that any system of autonomous units follows the same basic rules, whatever the nature of those units. But in practice, that is, in history, their substance matters as much as their form; the story of world affairs since the French Revolution is not merely one more sequence

Reprinted from Stanley Hoffmann, "Obstinate or Obsolete? The Fate of the Nation-State and the Case of Western Europe," *Daedalus,* Journal of the American Academy of Arts & Sciences, 95 (Summer, 1966, "Tradition & Change,") 862–915, by permission of the publisher.

[1] See Pierre Renouvin et Jean-Baptiste Duroselle, *Introduction a l'histoire des relations internationales* (Paris, 1964).

in the ballet of sovereign states; it is the story of the fires and upheavals propagated by nationalism. A claim to sovereignty based on historical tradition and dynastic legitimacy alone has never had the fervor, the self-righteous assertiveness which a similar claim based on the idea and feelings of nationhood presents: in world politics, the dynastic function of nationalism is the constitution of nation-states by amalgamation or by splintering, and its emotional function is the supplying of a formidable good conscience to leaders who see their task as the achievement of nationhood, the defense of the nation, or the expansion of a national mission.[2]

This is where the drama lies. The nation-state is at the same time a form of social organization and—in practice if not in every brand of theory—a factor of international non-integration; but those who argue in favor of a more integrated world, either under more centralized power or through various networks of regional or functional agencies, tend to forget Auguste Comte's old maxim that *on ne détruit que ce qu'on remplace:* the new "formula" will have to provide not only world order, but also the kind of social

[2] In a way, the weaker are the foundations on which the nation rests, the shriller the assertions become.

organization in which leaders, élites, and citizens feel at home. There is currently no agreement on what such a formula will be,[3] as a result, nation-states—often inchoate, economically absurd, administratively ramshackle, and impotent yet dangerous in international politics—remain the basic units in spite of all the remonstrations and exhortations. They go on *faute de mieux* despite their alleged obsolescence; indeed, not only do they profit from man's incapacity to bring about a better order, but their very existence is a formidable obstacle to their replacement.

If there was one part of the world in which men of good will thought that the nation-state could be superseded, it was Western Europe. One of France's most subtle commentators on international politics has recently reminded us of E. H. Carr's bold prediction of 1945: "we shall not see again a Europe of twenty, and a world of more than sixty independent sovereign states."[4] Statesmen have invented original schemes for moving Western Europe "beyond the nation-state,"[5] and political scientists have studied their efforts with a care from which emotional involvement was not missing. The conditions seemed ideal. On the one hand, nationalism seemed at its lowest ebb; on the other, an adequate formula and method for building a substitute had apparently been devised. Twenty years

after the end of World War II—a period as long as the whole interwar era—observers have had to revise their judgments. The most optimistic put their hope in the chances the future may still harbor, rather than in the propelling power of the present; the less optimistic ones, like myself, try simply to understand what went wrong.

My own conclusion is sad and simple. The nation-state is still here, and the new Jerusalem has been postponed because the nations in Western Europe have not been able to stop time and to fragment space. Political unification could have succeeded if, on the one hand, these nations had not been caught in the whirlpool of different concerns, as a result both of profoundly different internal circumstances and of outside legacies, and if, on the other hand, they had been able or obliged to concentrate on "community-building" to the exclusion of all problems situated either outside their area or within each one of them. Domestic differences and different world views obviously mean diverging foreign policies; the involvement of the policy-makers in issues among which "community-building" is merely one has meant a deepening, not a decrease, of those divergencies. The reasons follow: the unification movement has been the victim, and the survival of nation-states the outcome, of three factors, one of which characterizes every international system, and the other two only the present system. Every international system owes its inner logic and its unfolding to the *diversity* of domestic determinants, geo-historical situations, and outside aims among its units; any international system based on fragmentation tends, through the dynamics of unevenness (so well understood, if applied only to economic unevenness, by Lenin) to reproduce diversity. However, there is no

[3] On this point, see Rupert Emerson, *From Empire to Nation* (Cambridge, Mass., 1962), Chap. 19 and Raymond Aron, *Paix et Guerre entre les Nations* (Paris, 1962), Chap. 11.

[4] E. H. Carr, *Nationalism and After* (London, 1965), p. 51. Quoted in Pierre Hassner, "Nationalisme et relations internationales," *Revue française de science politique*, XV, No. 3 (June, 1965), 499–528.

[5] See Ernst B. Haas' book by this title (Stanford, Calif., 1964).

inherent reason that the model of the fragmented international system should rule out by itself two developments in which the critics of the nation-state have put their bets or their hopes. Why must it be a diversity of nations? Could it not be a diversity of regions, of "federating" blocs, superseding the nation-state just as the dynastic state had replaced the feudal puzzle? Or else, why does the very logic of conflagrations fed by hostility not lead to the kind of catastrophic unification of exhausted yet interdependent nations, sketched out by Kant? Let us remember that the unity movement in Europe was precisely an attempt at creating a regional entity, and that its origins and its springs resembled, on the reduced scale of a half-continent, the process dreamed up by Kant in his *Idea of Universal History.*[6]

The answers are not entirely provided by the two factors that come to mind immediately. One is the legitimacy of national self-determination, the only principle which transcends all blocs and ideologies, since all pay lip service to it, and provides the foundation for the only "universal actor" of the international system: the United Nations. The other is the newness of many of the states, which have wrested their independence by a nationalist upsurge and are therefore unlikely to throw or give away what they have obtained only too recently. However, the legitimacy of the nation-state does not by itself guarantee the nation-state's survival in the international state of nature, and the appeal of nationalism as an emancipating passion does not assure that the nation-state must everywhere remain the basic form of social organization, in a world in which many

nations are old and settled and the shortcomings of the nation-state are obvious. The real answers are provided by two unique features of the present international system. One, it is the first truly *global* international system: the regional subsystems have only a reduced autonomy; the "relationships of major tension" blanket the whole planet, the domestic polities are dominated not so much by the region's problems as by purely local and purely global ones, which conspire to divert the region's members from the internal affairs of their area, and indeed would make an isolated treatment of those affairs impossible. As a result, each nation, new or old, finds itself placed in an orbit of its own, from which it is quite difficult to move away: for the attraction of the regional forces is offset by the pull of all the other forces. Or, to change the metaphor, those nations that coexist in the same apparently separate "home" of a geographical region find themselves both exposed to the smells and noises that come from outside through all their windows and doors, and looking at the outlying houses from which the interference issues. Coming from diverse pasts, moved by diverse tempers, living in different parts of the house, inescapably yet differently subjected and attracted to the outside world, those cohabitants react unevenly to their exposure and calculate conflictingly how they could either reduce the disturbance or affect in turn all those who live elsewhere. The adjustment of their own relations within the house becomes subordinated to their divergences about the outside world; the "regional subsystem" becomes a stake in the rivalry of its members about the system as a whole.

However, the coziness of the common home could still prevail if the inhabitants were forced to come to

6 See on this point my essay "Rousseau on War and Peace," in *The State of War* (New York, 1965).

terms, either by one of them, or by the fear of a threatening neighbor. This is precisely where the second unique feature of the present situation intervenes. What tends to perpetuate the nation-states decisively in a system whose universality seems to sharpen rather than shrink their diversity is the new set of conditions that govern and restrict the rule of force: Damocles' sword has become a boomerang, the ideological legitimacy of the nation-state is protected by the relative and forced tameness of the world jungle. Force in the nuclear age is still the "midwife of societies" insofar as revolutionary war either breeds new nations or shapes regimes in existing nations; but the use of force along traditional lines, for conquest and expansion—the very use that made the "permeable" feudal units not only obsolete but collapse and replaced them with modern states often built on "blood and iron"—has become too dangerous. The legitimacy of the feudal unit could be undermined in two ways: brutally, by the rule of force—the big fish swallowing small fish by national might; subtly or legitimately, so to speak, through self-undermining—the logic of dynastic weddings or acquisitions that consolidated larger units. A system based on national self-determination rules out the latter; a system in which nations, once established, find force a much blunted weapon rules out the former. Thus agglomeration by conquest or out of a fear of conquest fails to take place. The new conditions of violence tend even to pay to national borders the tribute of vice to virtue: violence which dons the cloak of revolution rather than of interstate wars, or persists in the form of such wars only when they accompany revolutions or conflicts in divided countries, perversely respects borders by infiltrating under them rather than by crossing them

overtly. Thus all that is left for unification is what one might call "national self-abdication" or self-abnegation, the eventual willingness of nations to try something else; but precisely global involvement hinders rather than helps, and the atrophy of war removes the most pressing incentive. What a nation-state cannot provide alone—in economics, or defense—it can still provide through means far less drastic than hara-kiri.

These two features give its solidity to the principle of national self-determination, as well as its resilience to the U.N. They also give its present, and quite unique, shape to the "relationship of major tension": the conflict between East and West. This conflict is both muted and universal—and both aspects contribute to the survival of the nation-state. As the superpowers find that what makes their power overwhelming also makes it less usable, or rather usable only to deter one another and to deny each other gains, the lesser states discover under the umbrella of the nuclear stalemate that they are not condemned to death, and that indeed their nuisance power is impressive—especially when the kind of violence that prevails in present circumstances favors the porcupine over the elephant. The superpowers experience in their own camps the backlash of a rebellion against domination that enjoys broad impunity, and cannot easily coax or coerce third parties into agglomeration under their tutelage. Yet they retain the means to prevent other powers from agglomerating away from their clutches. Thus, as the superpowers compete, with filed nails, all over the globe, the nation-state becomes the universal point of salience, to use the new language of strategy—the lowest common denominator in the competition.

Other international systems were

merely conservative of diversity; the present system is profoundly conservative of the diversity of nation-states, despite all its revolutionary features. The dream of Rousseau, concerned both about the prevalence of the general will—that is, the nation-state—and about peace, was the creation of communities insulated from one another. In history, where "the essence and drama of nationalism is not to be alone in the world,"[7] the clash of non-insulated states has tended to breed both nation-states and wars. Today, Rousseau's ideals come closer to reality, but in the most un-Rousseauan way: the nation-states prevail in peace, they remain unsuperseded because a fragile peace keeps the Kantian doctor away, they are unreplaced because their very involvement in the world, their very inability to insulate themselves from one another, preserves their separateness. The "new Europe" dreamed by the Europeans could not be established by force. Left to the wills and calculations of its members, the new formula has not jelled because they could not agree on its role in the world. The failure (so far) of an experiment tried in apparently ideal conditions tells us a great deal about contemporary world politics, about the chances of unification movements elsewhere, and about the functional approach to unification. For it shows that the movement can fail not only when there is a surge of nationalism in one important part, but also when there are differences in assessments of the national interest that rule out agreement on the shape and on the world role of the new, supranational whole.

The word nationalism is notoriously slippery. What I suggest is the following threefold distinction, which may be helpful in analyzing the interaction between the nation-state and the international system:

1. There is *national consciousness* (what the French call *sentiment national*)—a sense of "cohesion and distinctiveness,"[8] which sets one off from other groups. My point is that this sense, which tends to have important effects on international relations as long as it is shared by people who have not achieved statehood, is rather "neutral" once the nation and the state coincide: that is, the existence of national consciousness does not dictate foreign policy, does not indicate whether the people's "image" of foreigners will be friendly or unfriendly (they will be seen as different—nothing else is implied), nor does it indicate whether or not the leaders will be willing to accept sacrifices of sovereignty. One cannot even posit that a strong national consciousness will be an obstacle for movements of unification, for it is perfectly conceivable that a nation convinces itself that its "cohesion and distinctiveness" will be best preserved in a larger entity. Here, we must turn to the second category.

2. For lack of a better phrase, I shall call it the *national situation*. Any nation-state, whether pulsing with a strong "national consciousness" or not —indeed, any state, whether a true nation-state or a disparate collection of unintegrated groups—is, to borrow Sartre's language, thrown into the world; its situation is made up altogether of its internal features—what, in an individual, would be called heredity and character—and of its position in the world. The state of national consciousness in the nation is one, but only

---

[7] P. Hassner, *"Nationalisme,"* p. 523.

[8] Karl Deutsch, *Nationalism and Social Communication* (Cambridge, Mass., 1953), p. 147.

one, of the elements of the situation. It is a composite of objective data (inside: social structure and political system; outside: geography, formal commitments) and subjective factors (inside: values, prejudices, opinions, reflexes; outside: one's own traditions and assessments of others, and the other's attitudes and approaches toward oneself); some of its components are intractable, others flexible and changeable. Any statesman, whether he is a fervent patriot or not, must define the nation's foreign policy by taking that situation into account; even if he is convinced of the obsolescence of *the* nation-state (or of *his* nation-state), the steps he will be able and willing to take in order to overcome it will be shaped by the fact that he speaks—to borrow de Gaulle's language this time —for the nation as it is in the world as it is. He cannot act as if his nation-state did not exist, however sorry its shape may be, or as if the world were other than it is. The national situation may facilitate unification moves, even when national consciousness is strong. It may prove a formidable obstacle, even when national consciousness is weak. The point is that even when the policy-maker tries to move "beyond the nation-state" he can do it only by taking along the nation with its baggage of memories and problems—with its situation. I do not want to suggest that the situation is a "given" that dictates policy; but it sets complicated limits that affect freedom of choice.[9]

[9] A more systematic and exhaustive analysis would have to discriminate rigorously among the various components of the national situation; if the purpose of the analysis is to help one understand the relations between the nation-state and the international system, it would be particularly necessary to assess (1) the degree to which each of these components is an unchangeable

3. I will reserve the term "*nationalism*" for a specific meaning: it is one of the numerous ways in which political leaders and élites can interpret the dictates, or rather the suggestions, of the national situation, one of the ways of using the margin it leaves. Whereas national consciousness is a feeling, and the national situation a condition, nationalism is a doctrine or (if one uses a broad definition) an ideology—the doctrine or ideology that gives to the nation in world affairs absolute value and top priority. The consequences of such a preference may vary immensely: nationalism may imply expansion (that is, the attempt at establishing the supremacy of one's nation over others) or merely defense; it may entail the notion of a universal mission or, on the contrary, insulation. It may be peaceful or pugnacious.[10] It is less an imperative determinant of choice than a criterion of choice and an attitude which shapes the choices made. But whatever its manifestations, its varying content, it always follows one rule common to all the former, it always pours the latter into one mold: the preservation of the nation as the highest good. Nationalism thus affects, *at least* negatively, the way in which the freedom of choice left by the national situation will be used; indeed, it may collide with, and try to disregard or overcome, the limits which the situation sets.

The relation between nationalism

given (or a given unchangeable over a long period of time) or on the contrary an element that can be transformed by will and action; (2) the hierarchy of importance and the order of urgency that political élites and decision-makers establish among the components.

[10] See Raoul Girardet, "Antour de l'idéologie nationaliste," *Revue française de science politique,* XV, No. 3, 423–45; and P. Hassner, *ibid.,* pp. 516–19.

and the two other factors is compli- cated. Nationalism (in the sense of the will to establish a nation-state) is trig- gered by, and in turn activates, national consciousness in oppressed nationalities; but nationalism, in colonial areas as well as in mature nation-states, can also be a substitute for a still weak or for a fading national consciousness. In na- tion-states that are going concerns, national consciousness breeds national- ism only in certain kinds of national situations. The national situation may be assessed by a nationalist leader exactly in the same way as by a non- nationalist one; however, nationalism may lead the former to promote policies the latter would have rejected and to oppose moves the former would have undertaken. That bane of international relations theory, the national interest, could be defined as follows:

N.I. = National situation X outlook of the foreign policy-makers.

It is obvious that the same situation can result in different policies, depend- ing in particular on whether or not there is a nationalist policy-maker. It is obvious also that national interests of different nations will not be defined in easily compatible terms if those respec- tive outlooks are nationalist, even when the situations are not so different. But the same incompatibility may obtain, even if the outlooks are not nation- alistic, when the situations are indeed very different.[11]

II

Let us now look at the fate of the nation-states in the part of Europe oc-

[11] As will be stated more explicitly in part V, what matters is not the "objective" dif- ference detected by scholars or outsiders, but the "felt" difference experienced by political élites and decision-makers.

cupied by the so-called Six, that is, the continental part of Western Europe, first by examining the basic features of their national situations, then by com- menting upon the process of unifica- tion, later by discussing its results, and finally by drawing some lessons.

Western Europe in the postwar years has been characterized by three features which have affected all of its nations. But each of those features has never- theless affected each of the six nations in a different way because of the deep differences that have continued to divide the Six.

1. The first feature—the most hope- ful one from the viewpoint of the uni- fiers—was the temporary demise of nationalism. In the defeated countries —Germany and Italy—nationalism had become associated with the regimes that had led the nations into war, defeat, and destruction. The collapse of two national ideologies that had been bellicose, aggressive, and imperialistic brought about an almost total discredit for nationalism in every guise. Among the nations of Western Europe that were on the Allied side, the most re- markable thing was that the terrible years of occupation and resistance had not resulted in a resurgence of chauvin- ism. Amusingly enough, it was the Communist Party of France that gave the most nationalistic tone to its propa- ganda; on the whole, the platforms of the Resistance movements show an acute awareness of the dangers of na- tionalist celebrations and national frag- mentation in Western Europe. The Resistance itself had had a kind of supranational dimension; none of the national resistance movements could have survived without outside support; the nations whose honor they had saved had been liberated rather than victori-

ous. All this prevented the upsurge of the kind of cramped chauvinism that had followed the victory of World War I, just as the completeness of the disaster and the impossibility of putting the blame on any traitors crushed any potential revival in Germany of the smoldering nationalism of resentment that had undermined the Weimar Republic. There was, in other words, above and beyond the differences in national situations between indubitable losers and dubious winners, the general feeling of a common defeat, and also the hope of a common future: for the Resistance platforms often put their emphasis on the need for a union or federation of Western Europe.

However, the demise of nationalism affected differently the various nations of the half-continent. On the one hand, there were significant differences in national consciousness. If nationalism was low, patriotic sentiment was extremely high in liberated France. The circumstances in which the hated Nazis were expelled and the domestic collaborators purged amounted to what I have called elsewhere a rediscovery of the French political community by the French:[12] the nation seemed to have redeemed its "cohesion and distinctiveness." On the contrary, in Germany especially, the destruction of nationalism seemed to have been accompanied by a drop in national consciousness as well: what was distinctive was guilt and shame; what had been only too cohesive was being torn apart not by internal political cleavages, but by partition, zones of occupation, regional parochialisms blessed by the victors. The French national backbone had been straightened by the ordeal, although the pain had

12 See "Paradoxes of the French Political Community," in S. Hoffmann *et al., In Search of France* (Cambridge, Mass., 1963).

been too strong to tempt the French to flex nationalistic muscles; the German national backbone appeared to have been broken along with the strutting jaw and clenched fist of Nazi nationalism. Italy was in slightly better shape than Germany, in part because of its Resistance movements, but its story was closer to the German than to the French.

However, there were other elements in the national situation, besides patriotic consciousness, that also affected differently the various nations' inclination to nationalism. The defeated nations—Germany in particular—were in the position of patients on whom drastic surgery had been performed, and who were lying prostrate, dependent for their every movement on the surgeons and nurses. Even if one had wanted to restore the nation to the pinnacle of values and objectives, one could not have succeeded except with the help and consent of one's guardians —who were not likely to give support to such a drive; in other words, the situation itself set the strictest limits to the possibility of any kind of nationalism, expansive or insulating. The lost territories were beyond recuperation; a healing period of *"repli"* comparable to that which had marked the early foreign policy of the Third Republic was not conceivable either. One could not get anything alone, and anything others could provide, while limited, would be something to be grateful for.

On the other hand, France and, to a lesser extent (because of their much smaller size), Belgium and Holland were not so well inoculated. For, although the prevalence of the nation meant little in the immediate European context, it meant a great deal in the imperial one: if the circumstances of the Liberation kept national consciousness from veering into nationalism in one realm, the same circumstances tended to encourage such a turn with respect to the colonies. Cut down to size in Europe, these nations were bound to act as if they could call upon their overseas possessions to redress the balance; accustomed, through their association of nationalism with Nazi and Fascist imperialism, to equate chauvinism only with expansion, they would not be so easily discouraged from a nationalism of defense, aimed at preserving the "national mission" overseas. The Dutch lost most of their empire early enough to find themselves, in this respect, not so different from the German and Italian amputees; the Belgians remained serene long enough not to have nationalistic fevers about the huge member that seemed to give them no trouble until the day when it broke off—brutally, painfully, but irremediably. The French, however, suffered almost at once from dis-imperial dyspepsia, and the long, losing battle they fought gave rise continuously to nationalist tantrums of frustration and rage. Moreover, the French inclination to nationalism was higher because of an internal component of the national situation as well: there was in France one political force that was clearly nationalist, that had indeed presided over the Liberation, given whatever unity they had to the Resistance movements, and achieved in the most impressive way a highly original convergence of Jacobin universalist nationalism and of "traditionalist," right-wing, defensive nationalism—the force of General de Gaulle. His resignation had meant, as Alfred Grosser suggests,[13] the defeat of a doctrine that put not only a priority

[13] *La politique extérieure de la V République* (Paris, 1965), p. 12.

mark on foreign affairs but also a priority claim on *Notre Dame la France*. The incident that had led to his departure—a conflict over the military budget—had been symbolic enough of the demise of nationalism referred to above. But his durability, first as a political leader, later as a "capital that belongs to all and to none," reflected a lasting nostalgia for nationalism; and it was equally symbolic that the crisis which returned him to power was a crisis over Algeria.

2. The second feature common to all the West European national situations, yet affecting them differently, was the "political collapse of Europe." Europe did not merely lose power and wealth: such losses can be repaired, as the aftermath of World I had shown. Europe, previously the heart of the international system, the locus of the world organization, the fount of international law, fell under what de Gaulle has called "the two hegemonies." The phrase is, obviously, inaccurate and insulting: one of those hegemonies took a highly imperial form, and thus discouraged and prevented the creation in Eastern Europe of any regional entity capable of overcoming the prewar national rivalries. Nothing is to be gained, however, by denying that U.S. hegemony has been a basic fact of life. American domination has indeed had the kinds of "domination effects" any hegemony produces: the transfer of decision-making in vital matters from the dominated to the dominator breeds a kind of paternalism in the latter, and irresponsibility (either in the form of abdication or in the form of scapegoatism) in the former. But the consequences of hegemony vary according to its nature. The peculiar nature of this domination has also had unique consequences—better and worse than in the classical cases.

One may dominate because one wants to and can; but one may also dominate because one must and does: by one's weight and under the pressures of a compelling situation. This has been America's experience: its hegemony was "situational," not deliberate.

The effects have been better than usual, insofar as such hegemony restricted itself to areas in which European nations had become either impotent or incapable of recovery by self-reliance. It left the dominated with a considerable freedom of maneuver, and indeed prodded them into recovery, power recuperation, and regional unity; it favored both individual and collective emancipation. But the effects have been worse precisely because this laxity meant that each party could react to *this* common feature of the national situations (that is, American hegemony) according to the distinctive *other* features of his national situation, features left intact by the weight and acts of the U.S., by contrast with the U.S.S.R. American domination was only one part of the picture. Hence the following paradox: both America's prodding and the individual and collective impotence of Western European nations, now reduced to the condition of clients and stakes, ought logically to have pushed them into unity-for-emancipation—the kind of process Soviet policy discouraged in the other half of Europe. But the very margin of autonomy left to each West European nation by the U.S. gave it an array of choices: between accepting and rejecting dependence, between unity as a weapon for emancipation and unity as merely a way to make dependence more comfortable. It would have been a miracle if all the nations had made the same choice; the diversity of national situations has ultimately prevailed. To define one's position toward the U.S.

was the common imperative, but each one has defined it in his own way.

At first, this diversity of domestic outlooks and external positions did not appear to be an obstacle to the unification movement. As Ernst Haas has shown,[14] the movement grew on ambiguity, and those who accepted American hegemony as a lasting fact of European life as well as those who did not could submerge their disagreement in the construction of a regional entity that could be seen, by the former, as the most effective way for continuing to receive American protection and contributing to America's mission and, by the latter, as the most effective way to challenge American predominance. However, there are limits to the credit of ambiguity. The split could not be concealed once the new entity was asked to tackle matters of "high politics"—that is, go beyond the purely internal economic problems of little impact or dependence on the external relationship to the U. S.[15] It is therefore no surprise that this split should have disrupted unification at two moments—in 1953–54, when the problem of German rearmament was raised; and in 1962–65, when de Gaulle's challenge of the U. S. became global.[16]

[14] *The Uniting of Europe* (Stanford, Calif., 1958).

[15] See my discussion in "The European Process of Atlantic Cross-Purposes." *Journal of Common Market Studies* (February, 1965), pp. 85–101. The very success of internal economic integration raised these external issues far earlier than many expected. (Cf. Britain's application for membership, the problem of external commercial policy.)

[16] The latter case is self-evident; the first, less so, since the crisis over E.D.C. was primarily an "intra-European" split, between the French and the Germans over the return of the latter to arms and soldiery. However, there was more to it than this: EDC was accepted mostly by those who thought that Europe could and should not refuse to do

This is how the diversity of national situations operated. First, it produced (and produces) the basic split between those I would call the resigned ones, and those I would call the resisters. The resigned ones were, on the one hand, the smaller nations, aware of their weakness, realizing that the Soviet threat could not be met by Europeans alone, accustomed to dependence on external protectors, grateful to America for the unique features of its protection, and looking forward to an important role for Europe but not in the realm of high politics. Italy had, in the past, tried to act as a great power without protectors; yet not only were those days over, but also the acceptance of American hegemony provided the creaky Italian political system with a kind of double cushion—against the threat of Communism, but also against the need to spend too much energy and money on Italian rearmament. For the smaller states as well as for Italy, the acceptance of U. S. hegemony was like an insurance policy, which protected them against having to give priority to foreign affairs. On the other hand, Germany accepted dependence on the U.S. not merely as a comfort, but as a necessity as vital as breathing. West Germany's geographical position had turned it into the front line, its partition has contributed to imposing security as the supreme goal, the staunch anti-Communism of its leadership had ruled out any search for security along the lines of neutrality. There followed not only the acceptance of U. S. leadership but also the need to do everything

possible in order to tie the United States to Western Europe. Moreover, in West Germany's helpless position, the recovery of equality was another vital goal, and it could be reached only through cooperation with the most powerful of the occupying forces. Defeat, division, and danger conspired to making West Germany switch almost abruptly from its imperialistic nationalism of the Nazi era to a dependence which was apparently submissive, yet also productive (of security and status gains) under Adenauer.

As for the resisters, they, like the West Germans, gave priority to foreign affairs—only not in the same perspective. The French reading of geography and history was different.[17] To be sure, the present need for security against the Soviet Union was felt. But there were two reasons that the "tyranny of the cold war" operated differently in France. One, French feelings of hostility toward Russia were much lower than in Germany, and, although it may be too strong to speak of a nostalgia for wartime grand alliance, it is not false to say that the hope of an ultimate détente allowing for European reunification, for a return of the Soviets to moderation, and for an emancipation of the continent from its "two hegemonies" never died. The French time perspective has been consistently different from, say, the German: the urgency of the threat never over-shadowed the desire for, and belief in, the advent of a less tense international system. This may have been due not only to France's location, but also to other elements in France's national situation. Whereas Germany's continuity with its past was both wrecked and repudiated, France (like England) looked back to the days

---

what the U.S. had demanded—that is, rearm in order to share the defense of the half-continent with the U.S., and to incite the U.S. to remain its primary defender; EDC was rejected by those who feared that the Defense Community would freeze existing power relationships forever.

[17] There was, however, in France, a minority of "resigned ones," like Paul Reynaud.

when Europe held the center of the stage and forward to the time when Europe would again be an actor, not a stake: the anomaly was the present, not the past. Also, on colonial matters, France (more than England) often found little to distinguish America's reprobation from Soviet hostility. Two, France continued to worry not only about possible Soviet thrusts but also about Germany's potential threats: the suspicion of a reborn German national consciousness and nationalism has marked all French leaders. An additional reason for fearing the perpetuation of American hegemony and the freezing of the cold war, for hoping for a détente that would help Europe reunite, was thus provided by the fear that any other course would make Germany the main beneficiary of America's favors. Germany looked East with some terror, but there was only one foe there; when the French looked East, they saw two nations to fear; each could be used as an ally against the other—but for the time being the Soviet danger was the greater, and, should Germany be built up too much against the Soviets, the security gained by France in one respect would be compromised in another.[18]

There was a second way in which the diversity of national situations operated. As I have suggested, situations limit and affect but do not command choices. A general desire for overcoming the cold war and American hegemony did not mean a general agreement on how to do so. What I have called "the resistance" was split, and it is this split that has become

decisive for an analysis of the obstacles to European unification. Had all the resisters calculated that the best way to reach France's objectives was the construction of a powerful West European entity, which could rival America's might, turn the bipolar contest into a triangle, and wrest advantages from both extra-European giants, the "ambiguity" of a movement led by resigned as well as resisting forces might not have damaged the enterprise until much later. However, there was a sharp division over methods between those who reasoned along the lines just described—like Jean Monnet—and those who feared that the sacrifice of national sovereignty to supranational institutions might entail a loss of control over the direction of the undertaking. The latter consisted of two kinds of people: on the one hand, the nationalists who, as indicated above, were still very much around, exasperated by the colonial battles, anxious to preserve all the resources of French diplomacy and strategy in order, in the present, to concentrate on the fronts overseas and, later, to promote whatever policies would be required, rather than let a foreign body decide; on the other hand, men like Mendès-France, who were not nationalists in the sense of this paper, but who thought that the continental European construction was not France's best way of coping with her situation— they thought that priority ought to go to more urgent tasks such as the search for a détente, the liberalization of the Empire, the reform of the economy.[19]

The success of the European movement required, first, that the "resisters"

18 There is an impressive continuity in French efforts to preserve the difference between France's position and Germany's: from the préalables and protocols to EDC, to Mendès-France's Brussels proposals, to de Gaulle's opposition to any nuclear role for Germany.

19 France's "intergrationist resisters," like Jean Monnet himself, often chose not to stress the "resistance" aspect of their long-term vision, but nevertheless aimed ultimately at establishing in Western Europe not a junior partner of the U.S. but a "second force" in the West. Mendès-France's political

suspicious of European integration remain a minority—not only throughout the six but in the leadership of every one of the six, not only in Parliament but above all in the Executive, the prime decision-making force in every state: a requirement which was met in 1950–53 and in 1955–58, but not in the crucial months for EDC in 1953–54, and no longer after 1958. The movement proceeded after 1958 because of the dialectic of ambiguity; however, there was a second requirement for success: that the "minute of truth"—when the European élites would have to ask themselves questions about the ultimate political direction of their community—be postponed as long as possible; that is, that the cold war remain sufficiently intense to impose even on the "resisters" a priority for the kind of security that implied U. S. protection—a priority for the *urgent* over the *long-term important* as they saw it. This is precisely what was already, if temporarily, shaken by the brief period of nervous demobilization that followed Stalin's death, in 1953–54, and then gradually undermined by the third basic feature of Europe's post-war situation. But before we turn to it, one remark must be made: in French foreign policy, "resistance by European integration" prevailed over "resistance by self-reliance" only as long as France was bogged down in colonial wars; it was this important and purely French element in France's national situation whose ups and downs affected quite decisively the method of "resistance."[20]

vision never put the nation on top of the hierarchy of values; however, in 1954 (especially in his ill-fated demands for a revision of EDC at the Brussels meeting in August) as well as in 1957 (when he voted against the Common Market), his actual policies did put a priority on national reform over external entanglements.

[20] It is no coincidence if EDC was re-

3. The divisions and contradictions described above were sharpened by the third common feature, which emerged in the mid-1950's and whose effects have developed progressively since: the nuclear stalemate between the superpowers. The impact of the "balance of terror" on the Western alliance has been analyzed so often and well[21] that nothing needs to be added here; but what is needed is a brief explanation of how the two splits already discussed have been worsened by Europe's gradual discovery of the uncertainties of America's nuclear protection (now that the U. S. could be devastated too), and how some new splits appeared. For to the extent to which the stalemate has loosened up a previously very tight situation—tight because of the threat from the East and the ties to the U. S. —it has altogether sharpened previous differences in national situations *and*

jected six weeks after the end of the war in Indochina, if the Common Market was signed while war raged in Algeria, if de Gaulle's sharpest attack on the "Monnet method" followed the Evian agreements. The weight of the situation affected and inflected the course of even as nationalist a leader as de Gaulle, between 1958 and 1962. Even he went along with the "Monnet method," however grudgingly, right until the end of the Algerian War. It is not a coincidence either if the French leaders most suspicious of the imprisoning effects of the community of the Six from France were the ones who labored hardest at improving the national situation by removing the colonial burdens (Mendès-France, de Gaulle)— and if those French rulers who followed Monnet and tried to place the pride of a nation with a sharp but wounded patriotic sense in its leadership of a united Europe were the men who failed to improve the national situation overseas (the Mouvement Républicain Populaire, Mollet). The one French politician who sought both European integration and imperial "disengagement" was Antoine Pinay.

[21] Especially by Henry Kissinger in *The Troubled Partnership* (New York, 1965).

increased the number of alternatives made available to élites and statesmen. Greater indeterminacy has meant greater confusion.

First, the split between French "resistance" and German "resignation" has become deeper. The dominant political élites in Germany have interpreted the new national situation created by the balance of terror as merely adding urgency to their previous calculation of interest. The nuclear stalemate was, given Germany's position, deemed to increase the danger for the West: the U. S. was relatively less strong, the Soviet Union stronger, that is, more of a threat. Indeed, the Socialists switched from their increasingly more furtive glances at neutrality to an outright endorsement of the Christian Democratic interpretation. If America's monopoly was broken, if America's guarantee was weakened thereby, what was needed— in a world that was not willing to let Germany rearm with nuclear weapons, in a continent that could not really develop a nuclear force of its own capable of replacing America's and of matching Russia's—was a German policy so respectful of America's main concerns, and also so vigilant with respect to the Soviet Union, that the U. S. would both feel obligated to keep its mantle of protection over Germany and not be tempted into negotiating a détente at Germany's expense. German docility would be the condition for, and counterpart of, American entanglement. The German reaction to a development that could, if General Gallois' logic were followed, lead to the prevalence of "polycentrism" at bipolarity's expense was the search for ways of exorcising the former and preserving the latter. On the whole, the smaller nations and Italy, while not at all fearful about the consequences of polycen-

trism (on the contrary), were nevertheless not shaken out of their "resignation"; the mere appearance of parity of nuclear peril was not enough to make them anxious to give, or to make them domestically capable of giving, priority to an active foreign policy.

In France, on the contrary, the balance of terror reinforced the attitude of resistance: what had always been a goal—emancipation—but had in fact been no more than a hope, given the thickness of the iron curtain, the simple rigidity of the superpowers' policies in the days of Mr. Dulles, and Europe's inability to affect the course of events, now became a possibility; for the giants' stalemate meant increased security for the less great (however much they might complain about the decrease of American protection and use it as a pretext, their lament coexisted with a heightened feeling of protection against war in general). What the Germans saw as a liability was an opportunity to the French. Germany's situation, its low national consciousness, incited most German leaders to choose what might be called a "minimizing" interpretation of the new situation; France's situation, its high national consciousness and, after 1958, the doctrine of its leader, incited French political élites to choose a "maximizing" interpretation. The increasing costs of the use of force made this use by the superpowers less likely, American protection less certain but also less essential, Europe's recovery of not merely wealth but power more desirable and possible—possible since the quest for power could be pushed without excessive risk of sanctions by the two giants, desirable since power, while transformed, remains the moving force and *ultima ratio* of world politics. This recovery of power would help bring about the much desired prevalence of polycentrism over bipolarity.[22]

Secondly, as this feud shows, the balance of terror heightened the split over method among the "resisters." On the one hand, it provided new arguments for those who thought that emancipation could be achieved only through the uniting of Western Europe: individual national efforts would remain too ridiculously weak to amount to anything but a waste in resources; a collective effort, however, could exploit the new situation, make Western Europe a true partner of the U. S., and not merely an economic partner and a military aide-de-camp. On the other hand, those who feared that the "united way" could become a frustrating deviation reasoned that the theory of graduated deterrence justified the acquisition of nuclear weapons by a middle-size power with limited resources and that this acquisition would increase considerably the political influence as well as the prestige of the nation. The increased costs of force ruled out, in any case, what had in the past been the most disastrous effect of the mushrooming of sovereign states—a warlike, expansionist nationalism—but they simultaneously refloated the value of small or middle-sized nations, no longer condemned by the cold, bipolar war to look for bigger protectors or to agglomerate in order to assure their security. Moreover, the "united way" would be a dead-end,

since some, and not exactly the least significant, of the associates had no desire for collective European power at the possible expense of American protection. Not the least significant reason for the prevalence of the second line of thought over the first has been one important element of the national situation—the army: almost desroyed by its Algerian experience, it had to be "reconverted." In the circumstances of 1962, this meant inevitably a conversion to French atomic concerns. Its success builds up in turn a vested interest in the preservation of the new establishment—and increases the difference in national situations between France and a non-nuclear Germany.

Thirdly, the new situation affected European unification negatively not only by sharpening those splits but in two other ways as well. On the one hand, until then, opposition to a supranational entity had come only from a fraction of the "resisters"; in the early 1950's the U. S. had strongly—too strongly—urged the establishment of a European defense system which was not considered likely to challenge America's own predominance in the military area. In the 1960's, the U. S. no longer urged the West Europeans to build such a system. American leadership has developed a deep concern for maintaining centralized control over the forces of the alliance, that is, for preserving bipolarity, and a growing realization that Europe's appetite would not stop short of nuclear weapons. As a result, some of the "resigned ones," instead of endorsing European integration as unreservedly as when the situation of a dependent Europe in a cold-war-dominated world did not allow Europeans to entertain thoughts of genuine military "partnership" with the U.S., now for the first time showed

[22] One should not forget that the original decisions that led to the French *force de frappe* were taken before de Gaulle, or that the French opposition to a national deterrent came from men who did not at all object to his argument about the need for Europe as a whole to stop being a client of the U.S., and who thought that, indeed, America's nuclear monopoly in the alliance was obsolete.

themselves of two minds—they were willing to pursue integration in economic and social fields, but much less so in matters of defense, lest NATO be weakened. It is significant that the Dutch resisted de Gaulle's efforts, in 1960–62, to include defense in his confederal scheme and that the German leaders, in their quest for security, put their hopes in the MLF—a scheme that ties European nations one by one to the U. S.—rather than in a revised and rveived EDC. Inevitably, such mental reservations of those who had been among the champions of supranationality could only confirm the suspicions of those "resisters" who had distrusted the "Monnet method" since the beginning. Thus, the national situation of Germany in particular—a situation in which America's own policy of reliance on Germany as the anchor of U. S. influence on the continent plays a large role—damaged the European movement: the German leaders were largely successful in their drive to entangle the U. S., but found that the price they had to pay was a decreasing ability to push for European integration. European integration and dependence on the U. S. were no longer automatically compatible.[23]

On the other hand, even that minority of German leaders who began to read Germany's national interest differently did not really compensate for the weakening of the majority's integrating ardor. Increasingly, in 1963 to 1965, suspicions about the value of the policy of docility-for-entanglement were voiced by a group of Christian Democrats, led by Adenauer and Strauss. They still read the German situation in

terms of security first; but their faith in America's aptitude to provide it was shaken, and they saw that Germany had sufficiently gained from America's support not to have to behave as a minor any longer. Their nickname of German Gaullists is however totally unsuitable. To be sure, these men are "resisters" in the sense of turning away from America; they are close to the French "integrationist resisters," insofar as they propose a European defense effort and a joint European nuclear policy (rather than a purely German one). Nevertheless, their foreign policy goals are quite different from those of all the French resisters, integrationist or nationalist. The national situation of France made most French leaders agree on a common *vision,* described above, that can be summed up as the end of the cold war and a continent reunited with a Germany placed under certain wraps. That common vision coexists with the split on *policies* already discussed—the "European" policy (in which the wraps are organic, that is, the net and bonds of integration) *vs.* the "national" policy (in which the wraps are contractual). The national situation of Germany has made most German leaders, after the Social Democratic switch,[24] agree on a common *vision* deeply different from the French —a perpetuation of the cold war, histility to the Soviet Union, the hope for a reunification tantamount not merely to the thawing of the Eastern "camp" but to its disintegration, and with as few concessions as possible. Since 1963, this vision has coexisted with two different *policies:* the majority policy of reliance on the U. S., the minority policy of substituting a strong, tough

[23] Hence the rather vague or embarrassed formulas used by Jean Monnet's Action Committee for the United States of Europe with regard to defense in the past two years.

[24] The case of Erich Mende's Free Democrats is more complicated.

Europe for an increasingly less reliable, increasingly détente-happy U. S. At present, "resisters" are thus split not only on methods (French integrationists *vs.* French anti-integrationists) but also on objectives (French *vs.* German).

This long discussion of the different responses to common situations has been necessary in reaction to the dominant approach to European integration which has focused on process. The self-propelling power of the process is severely constrained by the associates' views and splits on ends and means. In order to go "beyond the nation-state," one will have to do more than set up procedures in adequate "background" and "process conditions." For a procedure is not a purpose, a process is not a policy. . . .

IV

We must come now to the balance sheet of the "European experiment." The most visible aspect is the survival of the nations. To be sure, they survive transformed: first, swept by the advent of the "age of mass consumption," caught in an apparently inexorable process of industrialization, urbanization, and democratization, they become more alike in social structure, in economic and social policies, even in physical appearance; there is a spectacular break between a past which so many monuments bring to constant memory, and a rationalized future that puts these nations closer to the problems of America's industrial society than to the issues of their own history. Second, these similarities are promoted by the Common Market itself: it is of no mean consequence that the prospect of a collapse of the Market should have brought anguish to various interest groups, some of which had fought its

establishment: the transnational linkages of businessmen and farmers are part of the transformation. Third, none of the Western European nations is a world power any longer in the traditional sense, that is, in the sense either of having physical establishments backed by military might in various parts of the globe, or of possessing in Europe armed forces superior to those of any non-European power.

And yet they survive as nations. . . . On foreign and defense policies, not only has no power been transferred to common European organs, but France has actually taken power away from NATO, and, as shown in part two, differences in the calculations of the national interest have, if anything, broadened ever since the advent of the balance of terror. As for intra-European communications, research shows that the indubitably solid economic network of EEC has not been complemented by a network of social and cultural communications,[25] the links between some of those societies and the U. S. are stronger than the links among them. Indeed, even in the realm of economic relations, the Common Market for goods has not been completed by a system of pan-West European enterprises: enterprises that find themselves unable to compete with rivals within EEC often associate themselves with American firms rather than merge with such rivals. Finally, views about external issues, far from becoming more compatible, appear to reflect as well as to support the divergent definitions of the national interest by the statesmen. French élite opinion puts Europe ahead of the North Atlantic partnership, deems bipolarity obsolete, is over-

[25] I am using here unpublished studies done under Karl Deutsch, especially by Donald J. Puchala.

whelmingly indifferent or even hostile to the U. S., and is still highly suspicious of Germany; only a minority comes out in favor of a genuine political federation of Western Europe and thinks that U. S. and French interests coincide. German élite opinion puts the North Atlantic entente ahead of Europe, believes that the world is still bipolar, is overwhelmingly favorable to the U. S., deems U. S. and German interests in agreement, is either favorably inclined toward France or at least not hostile, and shows a majority in favor of a European federation. There is no common European outlook. Nor is there a common "project," a common conception of either Europe's role in word affairs or Europe's possible contribution to the solution of the problems characteristic of all industrial societies.

It is important to understand where the obstacles lie. To some extent, they lie in the present condition of national consciousness. I mentioned earlier that there were at the start considerable differences from country to country. In two respects, similarities have emerged in recent years. There has been a rebirth of German national consciousness, largely because the bold attempt at fastening Germany's shattered consciousness directly to a new European one did not succeed: the existence of a German national situation has gradually reawakened a German national awareness, and thus reduced the gap between Germany and France in this area. Moreover, all the national consciences in Western Europe are alike in one sense: they are not like Rousseau's general will, a combination of mores and moves that define with a large degree of intellectual clarity and emotional involvement the purposes of the national community. Today's national consciousness in Europe is negative rather than positive. There is still, in each nation, a "vouloir-vivre collectif." But it is not a "daily plebiscite" *for* something. It is, in some parts, a daily routine, a community based on habit rather than on common tasks, an identity that is received rather than shaped. Thus Germany's sense of "cohesion and distinctiveness" is the inevitable result of the survival and recovery of a West German state in a world of nations, rather than a specific willed set of imperatives. In other parts, national consciousness is a daily refusal rather than a daily creation, a desire to preserve a certain heritage (however waning, and less because it is meaningful today than because it is one's own) rather than a determination to define a common destiny, an identity that is hollow rather than full and marked more by bad humor toward foreign influences than by any positive contribution.

To be sure, the negative or hollow character of national consciousness need not be a liability for the champions of integration: general wills *à la* Rousseau could be formidable obstacles to any fusion of sovereignty. However, the obstacle resides partly in the common nature of the present state of national consciousness, partly in the remaining differences. A patriotic consciousness that survives in a kind of nonpurposive complacency may not be a barrier to efforts at transcending it, but it is a drag: it does not carry forward or push statesmen in the way in which an intense and positive "general will" prods leaders who act on behalf of national goals, or in the way in which European federalists have sometimes hoped that enlightened national patriotisms would propel Europe's national leaders into building a new European community, into which those enlightened patriotisms would converge and merge. Moreover, two of the "national consciences" have raised obstacles: the French one because it remains too strong, the German one because it remains too weak. The French may not have a sense of national purpose, but, precisely because their patriotism has been tested so often and so long, because the pressures of the outside world have continued throughout the postwar era to batter their concerns and their conceits, and because modernization, now accepted and even desired, also undermines traditional values still cherished and traditional authority patterns still enforced, French national consciousness opposes considerable resistance to any suggestion of abdication, resignation, *repli*—so much so that the "Europeans" themselves have had to present integration as an opportunity for getting French views shared by others instead of stressing the "community" side of the enterprise.[26] Germany's national consciousness, on the other hand, remains marked by a genuine distaste for or timidity toward what might be called the power activities of a national community on the world stage; hence a tendency to shy away from the problems of "high politics" which a united Europe would have to face and whose avoidance only delays the advent of unity; a tendency to refuse to make policy choices and to pretend (to oneself and to others) that no such choices are required, that there is no incompatibility between a "European Europe" and an Atlantic partnership. In one case, a defensive excess of self-confidence makes unity on terms other than one's own difficult, and obliges integrationist leaders to use cunning and flattery and deceit (with often lamentable results—like the EDC

[26] On this point, see Raymond Aron and Daniel Lerner, eds., *France Defeats EDC* (New York, 1957).

crisis) ; in the other case, an equally defensive lack of self-confidence projects itself into the external undertakings of the nation and weakens the foundations of the common European enterprise.

And yet, if the "national consciousness" of the European nations could be isolated from all other elements of the national situation, one would, I think, conclude that the main reasons for the resistance of the nation-state lie elsewhere.

They lie, first of all, in the differences in national situations, exacerbated by the interaction between each of the Six and the present international system. . . . One part of each national situation is the purely *domestic* component. In a modern nation-state, the very importance of the political system, in the triple sense of functional scope, authority, and popular basis, is already a formidable obstacle to integration. It is comparatively easier to overcome the parochialism of a political system which, being of the night-watchman variety, has only a slender administrative structure, whose power consists of punishing, rather than rewarding, with the help of a tiny budget, and whose transmission belts to the mass of the people are few and narrow, than it is to dismantle the fortress of a political system which rests on "socially mobilized" and mobilizing parties and pressure groups, and handles an enormous variety of social and economic services with a huge bureaucracy. To be sure, it was the hope and tactic of Monnet to dismantle the fortress by redirecting the allegiance of parties and pressure groups toward the new central institutions, by endowing the latter with the ability to compete with the national governments in the setting up of social services. In other words, the authority of the new European political system would deepen as its scope broadened and its popular basis expanded. The success of this attempt at drying up the national ponds by diverting their waters into a new, supranational pool depended on three prerequisites which have not been met: with respect to popular basis, the prevalence of parties and pressure groups over Executives; with respect to scope, the self-sustaining and expanding capacity of the new central bureaucracy; with respect to both scope and popular basis, the development of transnational political issues of interest to all political forces and publics across boundary lines. The modern Executive establishment has one remarkable feature: it owes much of its legitimacy and its might to the support of popularly based parties and pressure groups, but it also enjoys a degree of autonomy that allows it to resist pressures, to manipulate opposition, to manufacture support. Even the weak Fourth Republic has evaded pressure toward "transnationalism" and diluted the dose of "bargaining politics" along supranational lines. The civil servants' careers are still made and unmade in the national capitals. Above all, each nation's political life continues to be dominated by "parochial" issues: each political system is like a thermos bottle that keeps warm, or lukewarm, the liquid inside. The European political process has never come close to resembling that of any Western European democracy because it has been starved of common and distinctive European issues. It is as if, for the mythical common man, the nation-state were still the most satisfying—indeed the most rewarding—form of social organization in existence.[27] As for what it can no longer provide him with by itself, the state can still provide it without committing

[27] See Rupert Emerson, *From Empire to Nation,* Chap. 19.

suicide, through cooperation, or the citizens can go and find it across borders, without any need to transfer their allegiance—or else there is, in any event, no guarantee that any form of social organization other than a still utopian world state could provide it. If we look at the issues that have dominated European politics, we find two distinct blocs. One is the bloc of problems peculiar to each nation—Italy's battle of Reds *vs.* Blacks, or its concern for the Mezzogiorno; Belgium's linguistic clashes; Germany's "social economy" and liquidation of the past; France's constitutional troubles and miraculously preserved party splintering. Here, whatever the transnational party and interest group alignments in Luxembourg, the dominant motifs have been purely national. The other bloc of issues are the international ones (including European unity). But here is where the *external* component of the national situation has thwarted the emergence of a common European political system comparable to that of each nation.

It is here that the weight of geography and of history—a history of nations—has kept the nation-states in their watertight compartments. It is no accident if France, the initiator of the process, has also been its chief troublemaker: for in those two respects France's position differed from everyone else's in the community, and was actually closer to England's. Historically first: for Germany, integration meant a leap from opprobrium and impotence, to respectability and equal rights; for the smaller powers, it meant exchanging a very modest dose of autonomy for participation in a potentially strong and rich grouping. France could not help being much more ambivalent, for integration meant on the one hand an avenue for leadership and the shaping of a powerful bloc, but it also meant on the other the acceptance of permanent restrictions to an autonomy that was indeed quite theoretical in the late 1940's, but whose loss could not be deemed definitive. For a once-great power, whose national history is long, and therefore used to rise and fall, inherits from its past a whole set of habits and reflexes which make it conduct its policy as if it were still or could again become a great power (unless those habits and reflexes have been smashed, at least for a while, as completely and compellingly as were Germany's); for this once-great power showed, as described above, a still vigilant national consciousness, often the more virulent for all its negativism; for the international system itself seemed to open vistas of increased freedom of action to middle-sized states. In other words, integration meant an almost certain improvement in the national situation of the other five, but for France it could be a deterioration or an adventure.[28] There is no better example than the nuclear problem: integration here meant, for France, giving up the possibility of having a force of her own, perhaps never even being

certain that a united Europe (with no agreement on strategy and diplomacy in sight) would create a common deterrent, at best contributing to a European force which would put Germany in the same position as France; but the French decision to pursue the logic of diversity, while giving her her own force, has also made a European nuclear solution more difficult and increased France's distance from Germany. Moreover, a geographical difference has corroborated the historical one: France had lasting colonial involvements. Not only did they, on the whole, intensify national consciousness; they also contributed to France's ambivalence toward European integration. On the one hand, as indicated above, the worse France's overseas plight became, the more integration was preached as a kind of compensatory mechanism. But, on the other hand, this meant that integration had to be given a "national" rather than a "supranational" color, to be presented as a new career rather than as a common leap; it meant that the French consistently tried to tie their partners to the prevalence of France's overseas concerns, much against these partners' better judgment; above all, it meant that there was a competition for public attention and for official energies, between the "load" of integration and the burden of the overseas mission. The great power reflex and the colonial legacy combine today in the policy of cooperation with the former imperial possessions, despite its costs: cooperation is presented as a transfiguration of the legacy, and a manifestation of the reflex.[29]

Thus, the national situations have multiplied the effects of differences between the shapes of the various national consciences. But the resistance of the

[28] England's refusal to join European integration, before 1961, could not fail to increase French reticence, for integration thus meant equality with Germany, and a clear-cut difference between France's position and England's, that is, a reversal of French aspiration and traditions. England has on the whole rejected the "resignation-resistance" dilemma—and as a result, both the aspects of its foreign policy that appeared like resignation to U.S. predominance and the aspects that implied resistance to decline have contributed to the crisis of European integration: for France's veto in January 1963 meant a French refusal to let into Europe a power that had just confirmed its military ties to the U.S., but Britain's previous desire to play a world role and aversion to "fading into Europe" encouraged France's own misgivings about integration.

[29] See Alfred Grosser, *op. cit.,* Chap. 4.

nation-state is not due only to the kind of loan of life that its inevitable entanglement in international affairs and the idle motion left by its past provide even to nations with a low national consciousness. It is due also to the impact of the revival of nationalism in France. Even without de Gaulle the differences analyzed above would have slowed down integration and kept some fire in the nation's stoves. But the personal contribution of de Gaulle to the crisis of integration has been enormous. Not only has he raised questions that were inescapable in the long run, earlier and more pungently than they would have been otherwise, but he has also provided and tried to impose his own answers. His impact is due to his style as well as to his policies. The meaning of de Gaulle has been a change in French policy from ambivalence toward supranational integration to outright hostility; from a reluctance to force one's partners to dispel the ambiguities of "united Europe" to an almost gleeful determination to bring differences out into the open; from a tendency to interpret the national situation as oppressively difficult to a herculean effort at improving all its components in order to push back limits and maximize opportunities. The meaning of de Gaulle has also been a change in the national situations of the others, leading to a sharpening of antagonisms and to a kind of cumulative retreat from integration. Each one of those meanings must be briefly examined.

Insofar as France is concerned, the key is provided by de Gaulle's concept of grandeur.[30] Greatness is a mixture of

pride and ambition—the nation shall not at any point leave the control of its destiny to others (which does not mean that he does not acknowledge the existence of irresistible waves with which the ship of state must roll, lest, precisely, it fall in the hands of others who would rush to a predatory rescue or to a plunder of the wreck). The nation must try at any point to play as full a role in the world as its means allow. The consequences are clear: First, the kind of supranational integration which would leave decisions on vital issues to majority votes or to executive organs independent of the states is out of the question; even if the interests and policies of France should happen to prevail for a while (as indeed they did as long as the Commission, in its drive for economic integration, remained very close to French ideas), there would be no assurance against a sudden and disastrous reversal. Second, extensive cooperation is not at all ruled out: on the contrary, such cooperation will benefit all participants as long as it corresponds to and enhances mutual interests. Third, however, it is part of the very ambition of grandeur that in such schemes of cooperation which aim not merely at exchanges of *services* but at the definition of common *policies,* France will try to exert her leadership and carry out her views: the degree of French cooperativeness will be measured by the degree of responsiveness of the others.

It is true that the General is an empiricist, and that his analysis of the European situation is to a large extent irrefutable. What could be more sensible than starting from what exists—the nation-states—refusing to act as if what does not yet exist—a united Europe—had already been established, and refusing to forget that each of the Euro-

30 For a more detailed analysis of this concept, see my article: "De Gaulle's Memoirs: The Hero as History," *World Politics,* XIII, No. 1 (October, 1960), 140–55.

pean nations is willy-nilly engaged in an international competition that entails a fight for rank and power? But pragmatism is always at the service of ends, explicit or not (the definition of a bad foreign policy could be: that which uses rigid means at the service of explicit ends, as well as that whose flexible means are not serving clearly-thought-out ends). De Gaulle's empiricism is a superb display of skill, but on behalf of a thoroughly non-empirical doctrine. It is obvious that his distrust of supranational integration, which, within Europe, could submit French interests to the dictates of others, and could expose Europe to the dictates of the "hegemonists," while it is perfectly comprehensible as a starting point, nevertheless results in a kind of freezing of integration and perpetuation of the nation-state. If his chief foreign policy objective were the creation of a European entity acting as a world power, his "empirical" *starting point* would be a most unrealistic *method*. But the fact is that such a creation is not his supreme objective, and Europe not his supreme value.

His supreme value remains the nation-state; his supreme political objective is the creation of a world in which the "two hegemonies" will have been replaced by a multipolar international system, whose "first floor" would be the numerous nations, endowed with and entitled to political integrity and independence, and whose "second floor" would be inhabited by the nuclear powers, in a role comparable to that of the late European concert. Again, the implications are clear: de Gaulle's doctrine is a "universalist nationalism," that is, he sees France's mission as world-wide, not local and defensive; but this means that Europe is just one corner of the tapestry; Eu-

rope is a means, not an end. "Things being what they are," it is better to have separate nation-states (whose margin of freedom is undoubtedly smaller than when the use of force was not so costly, whose capacity to shape history is also undoubtedly limited if their size, population, and resources are mediocre, but whose ability to behave as self-determined actors on the stage is enhanced precisely by the blunting of force and by the opportunities opened to other instruments of power and influence) than it is to have a larger entity, undoubtedly more able to act as a forceful competitor in the world's contests should it be coherent, but more likely to be incoherent, given the divisions of its members and the leverage interested outsiders possess over some of the insiders. The size of the unit is less important than its "cohesion and distinctiveness," for its effectiveness is not merely a function of its material resources: if the unit has no capacity to turn these to action, because of internal cleavages and strains, the only beneficiaries would be its rivals. In a contest with giants, a confident David is better than a disturbed Goliath. This is a choice that reflects a doctrine; the refusal to gamble on European unity goes along with a willingness to gamble on the continuing potency of the French nation-state; the determination to accept only the kind of Europe that would be France writ large[31] corresponds to a conviction that French policies could be made to prevail whether Europe contributes its support or not: "with Europe if they follow,

[31] Grosser, *op. cit.*, pp. 112–13, draws attention to Prime Minister Pompidou's statement: "France is condemned by geography and history to play the role of Europe."

without Europe if they do not," Europe is just a card in a global game. Schumpeter had defined imperialism as an objectless quest; de Gaulle's nationalism is a kind of permanent quest with varying content but never any other cause than itself.

As I suggested above, a nationalist leader is one whose reading of the national situation is likely to be quite different from the reading other leaders would give. De Gaulle's brand of nationalism being what it is—universalist, aimed at overcoming the "two hegemonies," exploiting both of the somewhat contradictory trends that dominate the present world (the conservation of the nation as its basic unit, the concentration of what one might call "final power" among the nuclear states)—it is not surprising that he has altogether liquidated a colonial burden that kept France away from every one of the routes he wanted to travel, and replaced it with an ambitious policy of cooperation with the "Third World." In a way, it is true, as some critics have charged, that this policy is a kind of self-consolation prize for the failure of his European policy; but in another sense it conforms deeply to his most vital designs and to his most constant habit of never relying on one line of policy only: In the first place, cooperation manifests France's universal destiny; in the second, it aims at consolidating a system of independent, if cooperating, nations; in the third, it tries to use the prestige thus gained as an elevator to the floor of the "big five," to which access has been denied so far by the "big two." It is clear that the first two missions rule out a concentration on Europe alone, that the second prevents in any case his putting any passion into overcoming the nation-state in Europe, that the third

is precisely a substitute for the "elevator" Europe has failed to provide. As a result, all that has made France's historical heritage and geographic position distinctive has been strengthened.

Every great leader has his built-in flaw, since this is a world in which roses have thorns. De Gaulle's is the self-fulfilling prophecy. Distrustful of any Europe but his own, his acts have made Europe anything but his. Here we must turn to the impact of his policy on France's partners. First of all, there is a matter of style: wanting cooperation not integration, de Gaulle has refused to treat the Community organs as Community organs; but, wanting to force his views about cooperation on partners still attached to integration, and attempting to impose his views about a "European Europe" on associates who might have settled for cooperation but only on behalf of another policy, de Gaulle has paradoxically had to try to achieve cooperation for a common policy in a way that smacked of conflict not cooperation, of unilateralism not compromise. Thus we have witnessed not just a retreat from the Monnet method to, say, the kind of intergovernmental cooperation that marks OECD but to a kind of grand strategy of nonmilitary conflict, a kind of political cold war of maneuver and "chicken." With compromises wrested by ultimatums, concessions obtained not through package deals but under the threat of boycotts, it is not surprising if even the Commission ended by playing the General's game instead of turning whatever other cheek was left; its spring 1965 agricultural plan was as outright a challenge to de Gaulle as de Gaulle's veto of January 1963 had been an affront to the Community spirit. Just as de Gaulle had tried to force Germany to sacrifice her farmers to the idea of a European entity, the Commission tried to call de Gaulle's bluff by forcing him to choose between French farmers' interests and the French national interest in a "European Europe" for agriculture, on the one hand, and his own hostility to supranationality and the French national interest (as seen by him) in the free use of French resources, on the other. Playing his game, the Commission also played into his hands, allowing him to apply the Schelling tactic of "if you do not do what I ask, I will blow up my brains on your new suit," and in the end buying his return at the price of a sacrifice of integration.[32] In other words, he has forced each member to treat the Community no longer as an end in itself; and he has driven even its constituted bodies, which still insist it is that, into bringing grist to his mill.

Second, his impact on his partners is a matter of policy as well. Here we must examine Franco-German relations. As long as he hoped that Germany would follow his guidance and provide the basis for the "European Europe" of his design, his attitude toward West Germany was one of total support of her intransigence toward the Communists. As soon as the increasing clarity of his own policy (half-veiled until the end of the Algerian ordeal and his triumph in the constitutional battle of October-November 1962) provoked German suspicion and reticence, as the U.S., in response to his challenge, consolidated its ties with a still loyal Germany and even promised her substantial rewards for her loyalty, he applied to Germany the shock tactics so effectively used on Britain and the U.S. during World War II: he made his own opening to the East and gradually

shifted away from the kind of celebration of a "new Germany" (heir to her greatness in her past but now willing to take her place as France's aide in the new "European Europe"), so characteristic of his German visit in the fall of 1962. He now resorts to carefully worded reminders to the Germans of their past misdeeds, of the risk which their loyalty to the U.S. entails for their reunification, and of the interest France and the Eastern states (including Russia) share in keeping Germany under permanent restrictions. Had Germany been willing to follow France, he would have given priority to the construction of a "half-Europe" that would thereafter have been a magnet (as well as a guarantee of German harmlessness) to the East. Germany's refusal leads him to put the gradual emergence of a "Europe from the Atlantic to the Urals"—indeed from the British Isles to the Urals[33] if not ahead of at least on the same plane as the development of the "European Europe" in the West; for the containment of Germany, no longer assured in a disunited Western Europe of the Six, may still be obtained in a much larger framework. The implications are important. First, there is a considerable change in Germany's national situation. On the one hand, its external component has been transformed. Whereas for more than fifteen years both the U.S. and France carried out tacitly Robert Schuman's recommendation—"never leave Germany to herself"—the Franco-American competition for German support, the Gaullist refusal to tie Germany to France in a federal Europe so to speak for the knot's sake (that is, unless Germany follows France), America's disastrous emulation of the sorcerer's apprentice

---

[32] See Thomas Schelling's *Strategy of Conflict* (Cambridge, Mass., 1960).

[33] See de Gaulle reference to England in his press conference of September 9, 1965.

in titillating Germany's interest in nuclear strategy or weapons-sharing, in the belief, or under the pretext, of anticipating her appetite, all of these factors have contributed to loosen the bonds between Germany and the West: to the European part of the West, because of the slump in integration, and even to the U.S., because of America's failure to follow up after raising in Germany hopes that should not have been raised, but which, once raised and frustrated, are unlikely to fade. On the other hand, and consequently, the domestic component of Germany's national situation has also been affected: Still concerned with security as well as with reunification, but less and less capable of believing that loyalty to their allies will deliver any goods, the German leaders and élites may well come to feel less dependent and less constrained. Of course, objectively, the external constraints remain compelling: a policy of self-assertion may not lead anywhere; an attempt at bypassing the nuclear restrictions of the Paris agreements is not likely to make the East Europeans and the Soviets any more willing to let East Germany go; and the price the Soviets may want to exact for reunification is not likely to increase German security. But the fact that Germany's ties to Western powers are weakening means at least potentially that the capacity to test those constraints by unilateral action may well be used. To be in a cell with a chain around one's ankles and the hope of being liberated by one's jailers is one kind of situation. To be in that cell without such a chain and with such hopes gone is another situation, although the cell has not changed.

In other words, although the impact of de Gaulle on Germany so far has not been a rebirth of German nationalism, it has been a transformation of the situation that gives to nationalism some chances—chances if not of external success, given the nature of the cell, then of being at least "tried." The temptation to use one's economic power and potential military might in order to reach one's goals and the example of one's allies competing for accommodation with one's foe are not resistible forever, especially if one's past is full of precedents. To be sure, a nationalist Germany may well find itself as unable to shake the walls or to escape through the bars as Gaullist France is unable to forge the "European Europe." But the paradox of a revisionist France, trying to change the international system to her advantage despite her complete lack of "traditional" grievances (lost territories, military discrimination, and so forth), next to a Germany full of such grievances, yet behaving in fact like a *status quo* power, may not last eternally. Of course, a less aggressively ambitious France might not have prevented Germany from trying to follow her own path one day: the possibility of someone else's imitative *ubris* is no reason for one's own *effacement;* but precisely because the "essence and drama" of nationalism are the meeting with others, the risk of contagion—a risk that is part of de Gaulle's gamble—cannot be discarded.

Thus the nation-state survives, preserved by the formidable autonomy of politics, as manifested in the resilience of political systems, the interaction between separate states and a single international system, the role of leaders who believe both in the primacy of "high politics" over the kind of managerial politics susceptible to functionalism, and in the primacy of the nation, struggling in the world of today, over any new form, whose painful establishment might require one's lasting withdrawal

from the pressing and exalting daily contest.

LATIN AMERICA

Robert N. Burr

INTERNATIONAL INTERESTS OF

LATIN AMERICAN NATIONS

Those who seek to resolve the problems in United States relations with Latin America generally overlook the fact that the countries of that area quite properly cling to certain overriding objectives common to all sovereign nations: the assurance of their physical safety, and the safe-guarding of the free development of their citizens' way of life. While it may at times be to their interests to contribute to the security of the United States, it is *their own* needs that are of primary interest to them. The erroneous assumption of the people of the United States that Latin American nations are primarily or exclusively cogs in the machinery of United States security is inimical to United States interests because it is both unrealistic and repugnant to the Latin American nations.

Reprinted from Robert N. Burr, *Our Troubled Hemisphere: Perspectives on United States-Latin American Relations* (Washington, D. C.: The Brookings Institution, 1967) pp. 75–88, by permission of the publisher.

COMMON WEAKNESSES

In pursuing their objectives the nations of Latin America have since their inception been forced to act from a position of weakness all the more acute in comparison with the mounting power of the United States. Today each of the Latin American countries is, by comparison with the world's greater powers, "undeveloped." Moreover, except in Brazil, Mexico, and Argentina, questions of limited area and/or population appear to place a stringent limit upon their power potential in the immediate future. In addition, the abject poverty of a great proportion of those countries' populations both subtracts from the effective manpower pool available for productive economic, political, and cultural activities and adds to the strength of those divisive internal and external forces that feed upon human misery and discontent.

Augmenting the generally weak position of the Latin American nations in their international relations is a specific weakness in the industrial sector, reflected both in per capita productive capacity and in total industrial capability. Combined with and closely related to that weakness is their dependence upon the export of a few primary commodities to the more highly industrialized nations of the world upon whom they must rely not only for sophisticated manufactures but for technical skills and investment capital as well.

Finally, most of the Latin American nations function with administrative, political, social, economic, and educational institutions that appear inadequate to cope with existing critical situations, much less to provide the impulse for any meaningfully expeditious modernization.

Thus, in terms of practical international politics, the Latin American nations must rely upon other than physical power to maintain their independence and sovereignty. At the same time they must press urgently to improve their power position, something they can achieve in today's world only through the modernization of their societies. In the effort to modernize, however, they must have foreign assistance of one kind or another; this in turn raises entirely new problems such as prevention of undue foreign political influence as an accompaniment of foreign skills and investment, safeguarding of national resources against excessive exploitation for the benefit of non-national interests, and avoidance of cultural imperialism.

The fact that the Latin American nations share these common problems and interests as well as their historical and cultural roots establishes in a limited way the basis for their coopera-

tive action in world affairs vis-à-vis the non-Latin American world. Among the Latin American nations themselves, however, there exist not only divisions that sharply differentiate the interests of each country from the others but unique national characteristics that strongly affect each state's international behavior.

NATIONALISM

Nationalism in Latin America is not the parvenu that it is in some of the world's other underdeveloped regions. It is the sum of long-felt distinctions among the countries of the region and of an historical process in which the people of each country have shared experiences in triumph and disaster and in severe conflict with other nations, both inside and outside Latin America. The sentiment of nationality in Latin America was at first the attribute of the small elite groups that assumed power upon independence and was often superficial and imitative of European nationalism. In some countries—for example, Nicaragua and Haiti—the nature of nationalism has changed little; in others nationalism is now deeply rooted and widely diffused.

After the middle of the nineteenth century in certain countries the process of technological modernization and the sense of nationalism tended strongly to encourage each other, one often providing an emotional stimulus for the other. Improved communications enhanced the sense of national geographic identity, helping to counteract the strong regional sentiments of some countries. As modernization progressed, societies became more complex; new groups emerged—professional, industrial, and labor—that turned to the national government for aid in fulfilling their aspirations, justifying their demands on the ground of the "national good." In many countries these developments imparted to nationalism a populistic character whereby the welfare of the less privileged elements of society became equated with the welfare of the nation. Latin American nationalism furthermore tended to become xenophobic, at times seeing foreign threats to national autonomy where none existed. Independence in foreign policy became a highly cherished desideratum. Things foreign became suspect per se. In particular foreign investment and enterprise—an integral part of the modernization process—became the target of hostile nationalistic sentiment, their denunciation becoming an especially useful political instrument.

The interacting phenomena of nationalism and modernization have contributed to the creation in Latin America of twenty very distinct peoples, each with an individualized sense of national destiny, a more or less sharply defined concept of its own national interest, and a desire to assert its distinctive international personality. Any Latin American political candidate or officeholder who wishes popular support cannot ignore the nationalistic ethos of his country.

INTRA-LATIN AMERICAN RIVALRIES

Above all, the Latin American nations are concerned with rivalries among themselves. Argentina and Brazil vie for influence especially in Paraguay and Uruguay, Chile is often involved in disputes with Peru and Bolivia, nations it deprived of valuable territories in the late nineteenth century War of the

Pacific. Peru and Ecuador have been almost constantly on the verge of conflict in recent years over a boundary dispute that supposedly was settled in 1942. Guatemala, which is viewed with suspicion by the other Central American nations because of its larger population and past attempts to dominate them, in turn views its larger neighbor Mexico with mistrust, referring to it as the "colossus of the north." Argentina and Chile have barely escaped recent military confrontation over an uncertain boundary and at the end of 1966 appeared to be involved in a rivalry for jet-fighter supremacy—a rivalry into which Peru was reported ready to enter in order to maintain its position vis-à-vis Chile.[1]

Such rivalries have always poisoned inter-American relations, and they still do. The Eleventh Inter-American Conference, scheduled to meet in Quito in 1959, has not yet convened, in part because the Ecuadoran government refuses to proceed with its arrangements until its dispute with Peru is settled in Quito's favor. In 1962 the endemic hostility between Haiti and the Dominican Republic threatened to break out once again and thus facilitate extension in the Caribbean of elements inimical to United States interests. In the same year Bolivia weakened the effectiveness of the Organization of American States (OAS) by suspending its membership because of a dispute with Chile. The indefinite postponement in 1966 of a summit meeting of American presidents suggested by Lyndon Johnson was attributed in part to conflicts and rivalries among the Latin American nations.[2] The United States government

[1] *The New York Times,* Oct, 24, 1966.
[2] *Ibid.*

often becomes involved in these conflicts as the respective rivals seek its moral and material support.

Intra-Latin American conflicts have a special significance for those who seek to understand the real interests involved in the foreign policies of the Latin American nations. That significance lies in the fact that the Latin American nations regard as "fighting matters" disputes that have little meaning for European and United States policymakers, who are both poorly informed of the historical and contemporary bases of such conflicts and inclined to deprecate the possible importance of any difficulties among the Latin American states. The world in which Latin Americans live possesses a dimension that is terra incognita in Europe and the United States.

The decisive element in intra-Latin American conflicts—the element that makes the game worth the playing—is the fact that the various disputants operate on a basis of rough parity in terms of international power. The conflicts assume tremendous psychological and political importance precisely because they allow the Latin American countries (as they are *not* allowed in disputes with the great non-Latin American powers) to act out the role of sovereign, independent states in accord with their nationalistic aspirations. These intra-Latin American contentions, other than those today involving Cuba, have no direct relationship with the cold war; nor are they linked to the general political objectives of the Latin American nations in dealing with the great powers. To most Latin Americans their own disputes are far more vital than a cold war between superstates with which they are altogether unable to identify emotionally. The United States must not fail to take this into account if it wishes to have a realistic understanding of the interests of the Latin American nations—an understanding upon which any viable United States policy must rest.

THE INTERNATIONAL LATIN AMERICAN HIERARCHY

Intimately related to past and present Latin American conflicts is another political concern based upon the hierarchy of powers that has developed in Latin America since its independence. Rank in this hierarchy is determined by such variables as population, size of territory, wealth, degree of modernization, quality of literary and artistic production, national unity, victories in war, and political stability. Brazil, Mexico, and Argentina are presently bunched together at or near the top of the pyramid. Brazil's position rests largely upon the size of its population and territory, its São Paulo industrial complex, its architectural contributions, and the optimism with which the country's articulate sectors regard its future. Mexico's high rank is derived in part from its large territory and population but perhaps even more from the apparent success of its social revolution and its successful expropriation of the oil properties of powerful United States interests. In addition Mexico has scored points for three decades of political stability, for its rapid strides toward industrialization, and for its tremendous cultural vitality. Although Argentina's position is somewhat less clear, its persistently high opinion of itself, its wealth, population, and territory, its past achievements, and the fact that it has traditionally challenged the hemispheric leadership of the United States entitle it still to a position near the top of the hierarchy of Latin American nations.

It is evident that the three nations that now occupy the top of the power pyramid have special quasi-vested interests in foreign affairs, and they cannot maintain their prestigious leadership positions in Latin America merely by echoing Washington's policies. This accentuates the demand of the Latin American countries for independent policies, formulated in accord with their national interests as they themselves see them and not as paternally interpreted by other powers. Those states seek, moreover, to assert what they regard as an earned right and proven ability to act autonomously in the sphere of foreign affairs. This conviction is strong not only among the "big three" but also in such countries as Chile, Uruguay, and Costa Rica which have achieved a high degree of political development, national consciousness, culture, and modernization, but which lack the wealth, population, and territory of Brazil, Argentina, and Mexico.

COMMON INTERNATIONAL INTERESTS

The relative impotence of the Latin American countries, their development needs, their nationalism, their rivalries with one another, and their desires to play meaningful and respectable international roles—all these factors not only influence foreign policy formulation in the Latin American nations but also give those states certain common interests in their relations with the United States. All wish, for example, to obtain from that country the maximum assistance possible, in order to become more developed and thereby to become stronger domestically and vis-à-vis the outside world. But at the same time, all those countries wish to obtain the assistance of the United States without succumbing to its preponderant power. The same considerations apply, in varying degrees, in their interests toward all non-Latin American powers that are stronger than they. A major common objective of the Latin American nations has therefore been the development of techniques appropriate to the achievement of those ends.

Three general avenues of approach have served the Latin American states in dealing with the stronger nations of the world: exploitation of great-power rivalries; the obtaining of self-denying commitments from outside powers; and cooperation among themselves in the effort to create a counterpoise to the strength of the great powers. The first of those approaches, which has been in use since the Latin American countries achieved independence, is exemplified by the way in which Colombia played upon the rivalries among Great Britain, France, and the United States in the nineteenth century to maintain control of the potentially valuable isthmus of Panama. More recently Mexico employed the threat of supplying oil to Nazi Germany to force the United States into a settlement of disputes produced by Mexico's expropriations of the properties of United States oil interests.

In seeking to obtain from the great powers self-denying commitments that would limit the use of their superior force, Latin Americans have supported such international organizations as the League of Nations, the United Nations, and the Organization of American States (OAS), all of which sought an international rule of law in which might would not necessarily be right. Above all, Latin Americans have been pressing for acceptance, in international law, of their doctrine of nonintervention.

THE NONINTERVENTION DOCTRINE

During the nineteenth century the Latin American nations, with the exception of Mexico, were generally successful in assuring their security as independent states, partly because of their will to rest great-power domination and partly because of great-power rivalries that combined with a lack of vital interests in the area to hold in check the extension of great-power political influence in Latin America. Consequently the failure of Latin American nations to gain great-power acceptance of the Calvo Doctrine prohibiting intervention was not, then, of decisive importance. However, when the United States achieved undisputed hegemony in the Western Hemisphere, it became impossible to maintain a great-power equilibrium and the countries to its south found themselves confronting an expanding, immense, and frightening power to which there was no effective counterpoise.

Following long and strenuous efforts, the Latin American states finally wrested from the United States acceptance of the doctrine of nonintervention. That acceptance was embodied in the Additional Protocol Relative to Non-Intervention, signed at the Inter-American Peace Conference in Buenos Aires in 1936 and ratified the following year by the United States. In that protocol the United States government joined with the governments of Latin America in stipulating as international law for the American nations that "...The High Contracting Parties declare inadmissible the intervention of any one of them, directly or indirectly, and for whatever reason, in the internal or external affairs of any other of the Parties."[3] Achievement of that doctrine's acceptance established a power structure theoretically favorable to Latin American interests, for at the same time that the United States was obligated not to interfere in Latin America's affairs, it was sure to protect that area against domination by any non-American power. In the foreign policies of the Latin American nations and in the minds and emotions of Latin American leaders the doctrine of nonintervention came to hold an almost sacred role, analogous to that of the Monroe Doctrine in the foreign policy of the United States and the minds of United States citizens. Just as the Monroe Doctrine sought to limit European activity, the doctrine of nonintervention attempted to limit United States activity. Just as the Monroe Doctrine was in time modified in response to the changing interests of the United States (as in the case of the Roosevelt corollary), so too has the doctrine of nonintervention been modified since its acceptance in 1937 by the United States.

The doctrine of nonintervention was originally considered by the United States government as merely a ban upon the unilateral use of armed force to impose the will of a stronger upon a weaker nation. However, the need shortly developed to broaden the scope

[3] Robert N. Burr and Roland D. Hussey, eds., *Documents on Inter-American Cooperation* (2 vols.; Philadelphia: University of Pennsylvania Press, 1955), Vol. II, 114.

of the doctrine. In the first place the Latin American nations made the crucial decision to preserve and develop the inter-American system instead of abandoning its power of original jurisdiction over Western Hemisphere affairs to the United Nations. Several motives were involved in that decision, including the desire for a preferential position in United States foreign aid programs; more significantly, Latin America's oligarchic, conservative governments feared that Russia might use its United Nations veto power to interfere with security measures for the Western Hemisphere.[4]

In retaining a regional system as the court of original jurisdiction in Western Hemisphere affairs the Latin American nations voluntarily limited the use of their historic technique of playing off one great power against another. It thus became urgent to restrict further the extent to which the preponderant power of the United States could be used by Washington in its dealings with the Latin American countries. Moreover, it was by now altogether clear that although Washington was committed to refrain from armed intervention except under multilateral auspices, it might easily use its economic and political power "indirectly" to intervene in the weaker Latin American states.

Motivation for and reaction to a Uruguayan proposal of 1945 pointed up the need for further revision in the doctrine of nonintervention. Montevideo, disturbed by the severe repression taking place in Peronist Argentina, proposed that the inter-American system adopt a principle that would make it possible to intervene collectively in behalf of the "elementary rights of man"; and Washington, itself involved in a serious political conflict with Buenos Aires, seconded that proposal. While Uruguay's suggestion was not approved, it did inspire fear that future attempts might be made to intervene collectively against a member government that happened to be following unpopular policies. Such an interventionist possibility might, it was feared by Latin Americans, lead to degeneration of the inter-American system into a weapon with which the United States could intervene in the affairs of the Latin American nations, wounding their sovereignty and independence.

To avoid both that possibility and the danger of intervention through nonmilitary means, the Latin American governments insisted that the OAS Charter include provisions outlawing both collective and unilateral intervention and both military and nonmilitary coercion. Thus, Article 15 stipulates that ". . . No State or group of States has the right to intervene, directly or indirectly, for any reason whatever, in the internal or external affairs of any other States. The foregoing principle prohibits not only armed force but also any other form of interference or attempted threat against the personality of the State or against its political, economic and cultural elements." The charter nevertheless made it clear that enforcement measures called for in the provisions of the Inter-American Treaty of Reciprocal Assistance for the preservation of the peace and security of the Western Hemisphere would not constitute intervention. However, it left undefined and subject to consultation the nature of the aggression, other than

[4] Arthur P. Whitaker, *The Western Hemisphere Idea* (Ithaca, N.Y.: Cornell University Press, 1954), p. 172.

armed attack, that might permit intervention under the terms of the treaty.

COLD WAR POSITION

Since the signing of the Charter of the OAS, the international power structure has been drastically modified. In 1948 the nuclear monopoly of the United States gave it uncontested military hegemony, both hemispheric and global. Now, with the Soviet Union's nuclear power providing a counterpoise to the influence of the United States and with the constantly increasing importance of Communist China, the Latin American nations are once more in a position to use the technique of exploiting great-power rivalries to their own advantage. In view of the tempting possibilities provided by the problems of the United States in its relations with China and the Soviet Union, it is remarkable that only Fidelista Cuba among the Latin American states has sought to counteract Washington's power by developing a strong counter-relationship with either Moscow or Peking. The explanation for that lies less in Latin American fear of Soviet aggression—for it is clear that the United States would not tolerate that—than in Latin America's preference for the United States' goal of a world order of "free and independent states" rather than the Sino-Soviet system of totalitarian communism. That predisposition has been reinforced by gradual disenchantment of many sympathizers with the Cuban experiment. And Castro himself has not only chafed under restraints imposed by Moscow but openly attacked Peking for its allegedly exploitative treatment of Cuba.

Yet if a world order of "free and independent states" is to come about, the international implications of the

Latin American nations' relative weakness must be taken into account. Those countries believe that they cannot be "free to choose their own futures and their own system so long as it does not threaten the freedom of others" while any possibility of great-power intervention in their destinies exists. While they have supported the United States when it seemed clearly menaced by outside aggression, they have been reluctant to approve United States proposals to give the OAS even limited powers to facilitate possible collective intervention in their affairs. Though the Inter-American Peace Committee of the OAS was authorized to investigate tensions in the Caribbean, including Cuban-supported subversion, it was required to obtain the assent of affected governments prior to entering their territory—a requirement that seriously impeded any effective field investigation at the same time that it protected national sovereignty. Brazil, Mexico, and other nations made clear their opposition to intervention in 1962 when they both supported United States action to remove Soviet missile installations from Cuba and stated that they would oppose the use of force to bring about the overthrow of Castro. Latin American fear that a proposed inter-American peace force might become an instrument of United States intervention has aroused sufficient opposition to convince the United States not to press for a decision on the matter.

The rigid adherence of the Latin American nations to the doctrine of nonintervention is due basically to their relative weakness. It is strengthened, however, by the conviction of progressive elements that any United States intervention would support conservative or reactionary sectors and thus delay urgent reforms.

Latin American opposition to virtually any kind of intervention, stronger than ever in the wake of the Dominican episode, makes it highly unlikely that the United States can in the near future build the OAS into an effective security instrument. Four alternative approaches to hemisphere security matters thus remain to Washington. It can adhere to the nonintervention doctrine and rely upon collective action under the Inter-American Treaty of Reciprocal Assistance, perhaps in this way risking the further encroachment of antagonistic elements in the Americas. It could develop a compromise position in which, under specified circumstances, unilateral intervention might be permissible if promptly followed by collective control. Or the United States might reevaluate its present policies with a view to finding new ways of achieving its ultimate objective—ways that would obviate the use of intervention. Or, finally, the United States might continue its currently announced policy of unilateral intervention when deemed necessary by Washington. The last course would almost certainly arouse constantly growing opposition among the Latin American nations, forcing them away from cooperation with the United States and into alternative policies consonant with their self-respect and their emphasis on sovereignty and independence. Among the alternative policies open to Latin American nations would probably be a strengthened movement for cooperative action exclusive of and inherently opposed to the United States.

INTER-LATIN AMERICAN COOPERATION

From the time of their independence the Latin American nations, and especially those of Spanish origin, have sought to build upon their common historical, cultural, and institutional heritage a structure of cooperation. In the nineteenth century several of those states attempted at various times but without success to counteract the power of the greater countries by combining their military and political forces. Much more recently, and with greater success, the Latin American nations have concertedly advanced their common economic interests. In 1948 they succeeded in securing creation of a Latin American-controlled United Nations Economic Commission for Latin America, which in turn became an important tool for further economic cooperation and paved the way for an important movement toward economic integration.

The movement for economic integration has had political as well as economic implications. Institutionalized with the General Treaty on Central American Economic Integration and in South America with the twelve-member Latin American Free Trade Association, economic integration has become a prime objective of many Latin American leaders, including those of the Christian Democratic parties which are assuming growing importance in several Latin American nations. The 1964 meeting in Caracas of the Sixth Latin American Congress of Christian Democracy revolved about the theme of economic integration in Latin America and approved a declaration that sharply emphasized the close connection between economic integration and politics. That Caracas declaration not only asserted that political integration was essential to economic and social integration but also proposed that steps be taken toward political union through the establishment of two supranational councils—one in the field of education, the other in economics—and of a Latin American parliament representing the legislative bodies of all the Latin American nations. At Caracas it was also advocated that the Latin American countries work within the framework of the OAS, in spite of its asserted inefficiency, to achieve several objectives, among them "...a unified attitude of vigorous defense by the Latin American States of their common interests in relations with the United States."[5]

Christian Democrat Eduardo Frei, President of Chile, took the occasion to insist that the United States intervention in the Dominican Republic had dramatized the need for economic integration as a way of achieving sufficient strength for the Latin American nations to act effectively in world affairs. In particular Frei urged that "...the twenty poor and disunited [Latin American] nations [form] a powerful and progressive union which can deal with the United States as an equal,"[6] and in addition play an important role in the OAS which, according to Frei,

presently serves only the interests of the United States. It is evident that the growing number of Latin American statesmen who are of Frei's persuasion see in economic integration the basis for combined political action whose primary target is no other than the United States.

Such a view was clearly reflected in 1966, at a meeting held in Panama to discuss reorganization of the OAS, when the Latin American representatives combined to seek approval of a document opposed by the United States that would place United States social and economic assistance to Latin America upon a contractual basis. Whatever the outcome of that effort may ultimately be, it is a clear indication of a growing readiness of the Latin American nations to act in concert against what they consider to be the unacceptable hemispheric posture of the United States. It is evident that further deterioration in United States–Latin American relations will serve to accentuate that tendency and perhaps ultimately to create a deep chasm whose effects upon the world position of the United States would be grave indeed. . . .

[5] *DECE,* (Santiago de Chile), I, No. 1 (June, 1964).
[6] *Política y Espíritu,* March–April, 1965.

MIDDLE EAST

Abbas Kelidar

THE STRUGGLE FOR ARAB UNITY

Most ideologues of Arab nationalism seem to speak in terms of having a mission for the Arab peoples. This is no more than the express intention of all nationalists to liberate, unite, and reconstruct the Arab world and revive its cultural traditions. It means that they will conduct a campaign to end Western influence and domination, to assemble a nation of all the Arabs, and to adopt revolutionary action against all evils, intellectual, economic, social, and political. They reject evolutionary processes of change because their society is not healthy enough to produce such change. Revolution in this context means an intellectual and moral change which requires a change in the social system of values. However, most observers of the Arab nationalist scene seem to take these ideas at their face value, never doubting their foundation in historical and social reality; or else they question the expression of Arab nationalist sentiment and unionist aims, whether made at the official or the popular level. It may be more profitable to the understanding of Arab politics to focus attention not so much

on the theme of the establishment of an independent and united Arab State —though recent developments in the Middle East have made this once more a burning issue—but on the failure to achieve such a political objective.

There is no doubt that Arabism as a belief constitutes a great source of social power; but when it is advocated by different leaders, expressing divergent interests, this power is dissipated. There is also no doubt that the Arabs have not been able to agree on the leadership of this movement and in recent history the orientations of the leadership have changed many times, reflecting the interests of local ruling groups in the separate nation-States. The adoption of the Arab nationalist cause by Egypt in 1956[1] and her subsequent union with Syria two years later gave President Nasir unquestionable command over the Arab revolutionary movement. But the emergence of a revolutionary regime under General Qasim in July 1958 revived Iraqi claims to the leadership of Arabism after they had been in abeyance under Nuri al-Sa'id since 1945. With Syria's secession from the union with Egypt in 1961, and the elimination of Qasim in

Reprinted from Abbas Kelidar, "The Struggle for Arab Unity," *The World Today,* monthly journal of the Royal Institute of International Affairs, London, Vol. XXIII (July, 1967) 292–300, by permission of the publisher.

[1] The Constitution of 1956 recognized for the first time that the Egyptian people were an integral part of the Arab nation.

1963, the issue of pan-Arab leadership became more of a contest between the so-called 'revolutionaries' and 'reactionaries', the 'revolutionaries' comprising such States as Egypt, Iraq, Syria, Algeria, and the Republic of Yemen, led by Nasir, while the 'reactionaries' consisted of Jordan, Saudi Arabia, Tunisia, and Morocco, with no accepted leader.

REVOLUTIONARY SOCIALISM

In recent years, however, the concept of Arab unity has been accompanied by the idea of revolutionary socialism, which has tended to over-shadow nationalist hostility to the West. Anti-colonialism has remained the rallying-cry, but ever since 1958 there has been a shift of emphasis in the radical political currents in the Arab world, and this was given a strong impetus by the rise of the United Arab Republic and the Republic of Iraq. The appearance of these two republics on the Arab political scene led to the identification of the opponents of Arab unity as the 'reactionaries', i.e. the hereditary monarchs, oligarchic politicians, and wealthy land-owners and businessmen who had found it easier to protect their political and economic interests by keeping the Arab world divided. Their alleged reliance and co-operation with the Western Powers was held to be simply a facet of their reactionary outlook. At first sight, the division in the Arab world looks like a contest between the monarchies, with their accepted and traditional basis of legitimacy, and the newly established republics, seeking a fresh formula to legitimize their rule by responding to the political aspirations of the masses in their own territory and further afield. But on closer examination it is clear that the division is really

a struggle for the leadership of the Arab world by the contending parties. Furthermore, this division is not as clear-cut as many people seem to think, nor has it any real ideological basis. The differences between the 'revolutionaries' and the 'reactionaries', no matter how real they may have been, have had to give way from time to time to political exigencies. The support and active cooperation offered to Egypt, Syria, and Jordan by the other Arab States, regardless of their previous political identification, was highlighted in the Arab-Israeli war [of June 1967].

Following the foundation of the Syrian-Egyptian union in 1958, radical notions of nationalism and revolutionary socialism acquired a particular significance from the character of the union's principal architects: President Nasir of Egypt and the Ba'th party of Syria. Their ideological outlooks appeared very similar: both believed in the need to remove the last vestiges of foreign domination in the Arab world, both professed their conviction of the desirability of a policy of positive neutrality between the Great Powers, both advocated comprehensive Arab unity and called for the social, political, and economic reconstruction of the area under the central direction of the State. Both partners in the union believed that these objectives could be achieved only by revolutionary action. The fact that they had different backgrounds and entertained different notions of how these objectives were likely to be accomplished did not trouble them at the time of the union's inauguration. It is interesting, however, to point out that, though the Ba'th leaders took Nasir to task for seeking reconciliation with the so-called reactionary elements in later years, it was, ironically enough, the Ba'th leaders with their doctrinaire teachings of revolutionary socialism, and not the pragmatic Nasir, who spent the last years before 1958 in collaboration with 'reactionaries' like Shukri al-Quwatly and Sabri al-Asali.[2]

The establishment of the U.A.R. was seen as the finest achievement of the movement for radical nationalism and revolutionary socialism. A tumultuous wave of enthusiasm greeted the union in the two countries concerned and in the rest of the Arab world. It was regarded as the turning-point in the history of the movement; the initiative had passed to the revolutionary nationalists who expected the peoples of the other Arab States to rise against their oppressors and join the union. Iraq and Jordan were quick to protect themselves with a federation of their own, but the Iraqi revolution in July 1958 soon brought this to an end. It also blurred the distinction that had been developing between 'reactionaries' and 'revolutionaries.'

QASIM VERSUS NASIR

The emergence of General Qasim in Iraq posed a challenge to the revolutionary leadership of the U.A.R. The problem was that Qasim, unlike Nuri al-Sa'id, was no reactionary but an Arab revolutionary whose behaviour did not conform to the conventional expectations of the leadership in the U.A.R. He failed to join the march towards Arab unity and refused to acknowledge Nasir as the leader of the revolutionary movement. Qasim went further by actively combating Nasir's influence in Iraq and imprisoning his

[2] For useful studies of recent inter-Arab politics see Patrick Seale, *The Struggle for Syria* (London: O.U.P. for R.I.I.A., 1965), and Malcolm Kerr, *The Arab Cold War 1958–64* "Chatham House Essay," No. 10.

admirers and supporters, including the late President 'Arif. Moreover, he showed that he enjoyed considerable popular support among the Iraqis and particularly among the slum-dwellers of Baghdad. Revolutionary Iraq under Qasim, therefore, became an enemy which had to be countered. But this was not easy. Had Qasim been another 'reactionary,' he would not have been a serious threat and the counter-attack would have been clear and familiar. Qasim had also become a threat to the integrity of the Egypt–Syria union; for the U.A.R. leadership was faced with the problem that if Iraq, under such a revolutionary regime, would not join the union, there was little hope that other countries would do so.

To oppose Qasim, Nasir had to adjust his position *vis-à-vis* the other Arab countries, such as Jordan and Saudi Arabia—an adjustment which compromised his leadership in the eyes of his revolutionary followers. In April 1959 the U.A.R. sought to condemn Iraq at a meeting of the Arab League Council, but Jordan and Saudi Arabia would not agree unless they were given assurances by the U.A.R. leaders that the independence and integrity of their regimes would be respected. This seems to have been agreed, for soon afterwards diplomatic relations were restored between Jordan and the U.A.R. and King Sa'ud paid a State visit to Cairo. In order to face the challenge of Qasim and growing Communist influence in Iraq, Nasir also mended his relations with the United States, which he had previously condemned for supporting 'reactionary' President Sham'un in the Lebanon. The shift in alignments caused great dismay and disappointment among the more militant enthusiasts of revolutionary nationalism inside and outside Syria, and especially among the Ba'thists, who felt that Nasir had betrayed the Arab revolution.

The leadership of the U.A.R. was to be undermined further in 1961 by Qasim's claims to the newly independent State of Kuwait, and the Amir's prompt invocation of his defence treaty with Britain. In principle, the U.A.R. leadership could not very well object to the Iraqi claim, since it was committed to the cause of unity and to the termination of the privileged position of the oil-rich sheikhs. Furthermore, Iraq was as revolutionary and egalitarian as the U.A.R. But this was no time for logic. Qasim had to be stopped. Nasir was able to defend Kuwait's independence on the ground of the principle of self-determination, which he often declared to be the basis of Arab unity; but his prestige was not enhanced when he had to cooperate with Jordan and Saudi Arabia in creating a force under the auspices of the Arab League to replace the British troops in the Gulf. He had yet again compromised his leadership by enjoying the support of the 'reactionary' kings and the approval of an imperialist Power.

EGYPTIAN WITHDRAWAL

In September 1961 the union between Egypt and Syria collapsed. Egypt's explanation for Syria's secession was simple. The union had failed because it was stabbed in the back by the Syrian wealthy class, the 'reactionaries', who had been affected by the programme of socialist legislation which Nasir had decreed in July 1961. These reactionaries, with the help of the Western Powers and the Arab monarchs, had bribed and subverted a clique of officers in the Syrian army to carry out a *coup* to restore the old regime and to repeal the socialist reforms. However, the

Syrian secession brought to an end all the anomalies under which the U.A.R. leadership had suffered. Egypt contracted out of active Arab politics, and instead declared an ideological war on all the conservative 'reactionary' regimes in the area. She withdrew behind the barricades of socialist reconstruction at home. Egyptian troops were withdrawn from Kuwait, since it was no longer possible to co-operate with 'reactionary' Jordan and Saudi Arabia, or with 'secessionist' Syria. The revolutionary regime of Qasim in Iraq was also explained away in ideological terms: he was a 'deviationist'. A further ideological shift took place with the distinction made between Egypt as a 'revolution' and Egypt as a 'State'. The editor of *al-Ahram* put it as follows: 'As a State, Egypt deals with all Arab governments, whatever their forms or systems. She takes her place beside them in the Arab League and at the United Nations and concludes defence, trade, and other pacts with them. . . . As a revolution, Egypt should deal only with the people.' He went on to say that this did not mean that Egypt would interfere in the domestic affairs of other countries, adding, however, that since she believed in the oneness of the Arab nation, 'We have no right to separate ourselves from the struggle of other citizens of our nation.'[3]

Egypt's self-imposed isolation did not last long. In 1963 the Ba'th party seized power not only in Syria but also in Iraq. Egypt welcomed the *coup* which overthrew the Qasim regime in February; a month later the Ba'th was in power in Damascus. With the re-emergence of the Ba'th, the alliance of the revolutionary elements in Arab politics was to be renewed. Negotiations started in Cairo for a tripartite union between

3 *al-Ahram*, 29 December 1962.

Egypt, Iraq, and Syria in September 1963, but they were inconclusive. Nasir was not so willing to work with the Ba'thists this time. Meanwhile, the Ba'th in Iraq was overthrown by President 'Arif, a supporter of Nasir. In the new alignment between Iraq and Egypt, Ba'thist Syria found herself in the same position as the old Qasim regime in Iraq: Syria under the Ba'th was as revolutionary as Egypt under Nasir and Iraq under 'Arif, yet she remained out of step by claiming to be more radical than the others. Ideological orientations were no longer sufficient to unite them, and Egypt would tolerate no rivals for her bid to be the only revolutionary leader of the pan-Arab movement.

By the end of 1963, the Arab world was witnessing the collapse of any semblance of solidarity in either the reactionary or the revolutionary camp. Syria was quarrelling with Egypt and Iraq; Egypt and Saudi Arabia were feuding over the Yemen; Algeria was fighting with Morocco; and Morocco was irritated by Tunisia's recognition of Mauritania. Egypt and Syria found it ideologically convenient to be hostile to 'reactionary' Jordan, Morocco, and Saudi Arabia. None the less the general lines of division had become clear. The revolutionary States were pitted against the conservative and moderate regimes: Egypt, Algeria, Iraq, Syria, and the Republic of the Yemen against the others. But of all the feuding parties, the rivalry between Egypt and Syria for the leadership of the revolutionary movement was the most intense.

ISLAM VERSUS PAN-ARABISM

In December 1963 a radical change took place in the Egyptian position. Ideological confrontation with the Arab 'reactionary' rulers was aban-doned to make way for the first Arab summit conference. The catalyst of this occasion was Israel: Arab monarchs and presidents were called to Cairo to deliberate on projects to prevent Israel's diversion of the Jordan waters. The other purpose of the conference was to check Syrian jingoism against Israel, and to find a face-saving formula for the withdrawal of Egyptian troops from the Yemen by means of a direct approach to King Sa'ud. After two years, however, this method of consultation between the Arab Heads of State had failed to achieve unity, and the summit conferences collapsed without solving any of the outstanding Arab problems. Nasir made one more bid to extricate his forces from the Yemen with his visit to King Faysal[4] in August 1965. The failure of the Jedda agreement, followed by the abandonment of the summit conferences, renewed the struggle for Arab leadership, with the emergence of Faysal as a contender. Faysal called for the establishment of an Islamic alliance in which all the Muslim States would participate. In Egypt, this was seen as a threat to Arab nationalism, and an attempt to reconstitute a regional defence pact like the old Baghdad Pact. Syria condemned Faysal and on 27 January 1966 called for an emergency conference in Damascus of the five revolutionary Arab States to counter the projected alliance.

Throughout 1966, and until the war broke out between the Arabs and the Israelis in June of [1967], the main dividing line between the 'revolutionaries' and the 'reactionaries' has been that between the supporters of King Faysal's Islamic alliance and of President Nasir's pan-Arabism. In December 1966 Nasir launched his bitterest attack on the 'reactionary elements' in

---

4 King Sa'ud was deposed by his brother Faysal in November 1964.

the Arab world.[5] He accused King Faysal, and President Habib Bourguiba of 'being ready to sell the Arab nation in the same manner as ex-King 'Abdullah sold it in 1948, and the way Nuri al-Sa'id and Prince 'Abdel Illah of Iraq sold Palestine in 1948'. Referring to the political situation, he said that Nuri al-Sa'id and 'Abdel Illah had been replaced by others even less reputable. In a review of the discussions on united Arab action over the previous three years, he claimed that Egypt had been ready to let bygones be bygones but that King Faysal had made a deal with the Americans and deposed his brother, and that King Hussain had seized the opportunity to obtain funds from the summit conferences and from King Faysal. Faysal, in Nasir's words, had launched the Anglo-American-inspired Islamic alliance while Hussain wagged his tail. He concluded by saying that the Arabs could have no confidence in Faysal, Hussain, or Bourguiba. Egypt, on the other hand, was not immune from criticism. By maintaining her troops in the Yemen, she laid herself open to the charge of conducting a fratricidal war —a charge which Hussain and Faysal lost no time in making. 'Revolutionary' Syria taunted the Egyptian leadership for turning a blind eye to the Arabs' main enemy, Israel. Egypt was condemned by 'reactionaries' and 'revolutionaries' alike for her continued acceptance of the U.N. emergency force on her border with Israel.

Nasir, under great pressure from his rivals and critics, had to act. In 1963 he had called for an Arab summit meeting to contain the Syrians, who were clamouring for war with Israel

over the Jordan waters, by committing them to a general unified Arab policy. At the time, this was seen as a clear indication that he was not prepared to be dragged into war with Israel provoked by the Syrians. By 1967, however, conditions in the Arab world had changed. Though Nasir was still at war with the supporters of King Faysal's Islamic alliance and committed to protect the Republican regime in the Yemen, Syria had produced a new regime in February 1966, more radical than the one that had been in power since March 1963. This regime manifested a more militant attitude towards Israel and gave active support and encouragement to Palestinian commandos operating inside Israel and on her borders with Jordan. It also advocated radical notions of nationalism and socialism, and made some friendly overtures to the Egyptian leadership by focusing attention on the danger from King Hussain, who was thought to have supported an attempted *coup* by some Syrian officers in September 1966. Nasir, with Iraq and Algeria engrossed in their own internal problems, was left with only Syria and Sallal of the Yemen—both of them insecure—in his revolutionary camp. Thus in November 1966, relations between Syria and Egypt were brought closer than they had been since the Syrian secession in September 1961. A defence pact was signed and diplomatic relations resumed.

In some circles, it was thought that Nasir had obtained a promise, in return for Egyptian help in the event of an attack on Syria by Israel, that Syria would not provoke serious incidents on the border. But the incidents continued to grow in importance, culminating in the air battle on 7 April 1967 when four Syrian *MiGs* were shot down by

---

[5] In a speech at Port Said on 23 December 1966, reported in *al-Ahram* the following day.

the Israeli air force. On 20 April the Egyptian Prime Minister paid a visit to Damascus to discuss defence arrangements. At the beginning of May, there was talk of an imminent Israeli invasion of Syria. On 15 May Syrians and Egyptians had further talks to implement the joint defence treaty, and on 17 May the Egyptian Government moved troops into Sinai and asked the U.N. emergency force to leave. On 30 May King Hussain flew into Cairo to conclude a similar defence pact with Egypt and on 4 June Iraq joined as a third party; on the morning of 5 June war broke out.

The question that now has to be asked is: did Nasir want war with Israel in May 1967, when he shunned it in November 1966, or was he trying to make a grand gesture of strength in order to restore his command over the Arab leadership? In spite of his decision to close the Strait of Tiran to Israeli shipping, all the evidence would indicate that he was aiming at the latter policy rather than the former. Indeed, a case could be made that in fact what he wanted was nothing more than the maintenance of the *status quo*. By stating that Egypt would attack Israel only if Syria was attacked, he would have discouraged Israel and protected Syria, and at the same time restored his leadership of the Arab revolutionary movement and his reputation as the champion of the Arab cause in Palestine. But this was not to be.

FUTURE OF THE ARAB LEADERSHIP

The other question that has to be asked is: what is to become of this leadership following the disastrous defeat of the Arab armies? President Nasir has secured his position by acceding to the popular demands in Egypt and other Arab countries protesting against his attempted resignation on 9 June [1967]. However, in the final analysis the security of his position must depend on the attitude of the remnants of his army. King Hussain, who tried to insure the safety of his throne by signing a defence pact with Egypt, has enhanced his reputation as a courageous man but has lost the west bank of the Jordan. The Syrians are too insecure to last long. President, 'Arif of Iraq does not have the aptitude to be a popular leader. King Faysal, who has come out of the war unscathed, suffers from several handicaps if he is to assume the mantle of pan-Arab leadership, the least of these being his position as a traditional ruler of a relatively backward country.

This leaves President Houari Boumedienne of Algeria, but it is very doubtful if the Arab world could be led from North Africa. Nevertheless, President Nasir in his abortive resignation speech declared that there was a need for 'a unified voice on the part of the entire Arab nation, that is a safeguard for which there is no substitute in these conditions'. The Arabs, in their anger and grief at what has befallen them, are seeking to hold a summit conference, the purpose of which, as *al-Ahram* put it, is 'to work out a plan to erase the effects of the present setback and to adopt a unified stand on forthcoming conspiracies'.[6]

There is no doubt about the genuineness of the Arab desire for unity in the face of the defeat they have suffered, but whether Arab emotion can be translated into concerted political action remains to be seen. Judging by past experience this seems doubtful.

6 *al-Ahram,* June 12, 1967.

The obvious differences in their political orientations have kept them divided, and the diversity of political institutions and forms of government, and the differences in levels of economic and social development among the various States, further complicate the issue. The one element which remains identifiable to all Arabs, in spite of the differences between their rulers, is Islam. An Arab anywhere in Moroc-co, the Yemen, or Iraq accepts Arabism more readily if it is equated or linked with Islam, and this applies with equal validity to the Egyptian, who has always been conscious of being both an Egyptian and a Muslim. This may favour King Faysal's assumption of the pan-Arab leadership, but the other differences among the Arab States are bound to throw up rivals.

WEST AFRICA

by I. William Zartman

ALLIANCES AND REGIONAL UNITY IN WEST AFRICA

[*The underlying issue in the international relations of the Francophonic states of the West African core has been that of "Balkanization." As early as 1948 there began to be a divergence between those political leaders like Houphouet-Boigny (now president of the Ivory Coast) and Leopold Senghor (now president of Senegal) who took contrary positions on the future of*

Reprinted from I. William Zartman, *International Relations in the New Africa* (Englewood Cliffs, N. J.: Prentice-Hall, Inc., © 1966) pp. 17–26, 34–45, by permission of the publisher. In the larger work from which this selection is taken, Professor Zartman has chosen the label Western Africa to encompass what has been the very real interaction between the alliance systems of West and North Africa. Thus the reader will encounter in this reading a distinction between Western Africa on the one hand and West Africa on the other.

French West Africa which has now become the West African core. Senghor desired the separation of Francophonic West Africa from France but thought that the area ought to be maintained as a single political unit. Houphouet-Boigny, on the other hand, called for the independence of individual states but proposed that all maintain continued ties to France. By 1958 and the referendum of that year to decide on whether to adopt the latter position, Senghor had changed his position slightly but the issue remained. Guinea was the only state to decide not to have continued ties with France but she enjoyed considerable sympathy from the then Soudan (presently Mali) and opposition elements in most other West African core states. So strong was the growing sentiment in agreement with the radical position that the remaining moderate states were obliged to seek independence, although a reading of the article, "France's New Role in Africa," reprinted later in this volume will indicate to the reader the attenuated character of this "independence." (Editors)]

There were two major reasons behind the drive for alliances and regional unity in West Africa between 1950 and 1961.[1] One was the ideology of unity, expressed as federation in AOF [French West Africa] and as African unity by Ghana and other radical states. The other was the desire to avoid isolation, made particularly sharp in West Africa because of the interdependence and powerlessness of the states. Of all the classical ways to increase national power rapidly, the only two open to the new states were the manipulation of symbols and the creation of alliances. Ratification of the French constitution gave Senegal and Soudan the possibility of working for federation, as their territorial assemblies instructed their governments to do when they voted to accede to autonomy. A conference of federalists was called in Bamako for the end of December 1958. Ivory Coast and its like-minded RDA

[1] Where not specifically attributed, historical events are taken from the following newspapers and periodicals: *New York Times, West Africa* (London), *Le Monde* (Paris), *Africa Report* (Washington), *Al-Istiqlal* (Rabat), *La Nation Africaine* (Rabat), *Petit Marocain* (Rabat), *L'Avant-Garde* (Casablanca), *Révolution Africaine* (Algiers), *El-Moudjahid* (Algiers), *Jeune Afrique* (Tunis,), *Mauritanie Nouvelle* (Nouakchott), *L'Unité Africaine* (Dakar), *Agence France Presse-Guinée* [AFP-G] (Conakry), *Horoyo* (Conakry), *Essor* (Bamako), *Agence France Presse-Côte d'Ivoire* [AFP-CI] (Abidjan, *Abidjan Matin, Fraternité* (Abidjan), *Ghana Times* (Accra), *Daily Ghanaian* (Accra).

[African Democratic Rally] ally, Niger, were absent, but four other autonomous states of AOF were represented. The Senegal-Soudanese initiative meant a shift of allies for Soudan, which abandoned its RDA alliance with Ivory Coast. Dahomey's presence was a consequence of its PRA [African Regroupment Party][2] alliance, but Apithy also sought in federation an answer to his country's real economic problems—an uncertain venture because Dahomey's hinterland, Niger, had already excluded itself from the group. Dahomey would not be contiguous to the other federal territories if Upper Volta, with its key geographic position, was not also a member. Upper Volta's representatives to the Bamako Conference were only observers, and Premier Yameogo was not among them. Like Dahomey, Upper Volta lacked a charismatic national leader, and its many competing political figures considered the prospects of federation in terms of its economic effects as well as in terms of their political interests. The Bamako Conference prepared the way for a federal constituent assembly meeting in mid-January 1959 in Dakar, at which a federal constitution was unanimously accepted. It provided for a Federation of Mali, made up of the four West African republics and with autonomous status within the Franco-African Community. Before the end of the month, the constitution was adopted by constituent assemblies in Senegal, Soudan, and Upper Volta.[3]

[2] [The RDA and PRA are political parties with a French West African wide organization.]

[3] Federalist delegations had been sent in early January to Ivory Coast, Mauritania, Niger, and Togo to persuade their governments to join, without success; Hubert Maga (see below) was one of the delegates to Ivory Coast. *La Semaine en Afrique Occidentals,* January 3, 1959.

Only one of the two reasons for regional alliances was shared by the Ivory Coast leadership: the desire to avoid isolation. Houphouet-Boigny's antifederalist stand had left him in danger of opposing all formal governmental alliances and relying simply on RDA organization ties. But these ties had shown themselves to be outmoded and fragile in the face of the Mali Federation; Soudan and Upper Volta were following their own path, as Guinea had already done. At the risk of inconsistency, therefore, Houphouet-Boigny had announced as early as October 1958 that he was considering the formation of a loose, nonpolitical, economic-cooperation formula for the autonomous states of West Africa, including a customs union and a solidarity fund.[4] After a period of hesitation in early 1959, during which he observed the progress of the Federation, he set about to turn his RDA alliance of political organizations into a structure for economic cooperation among states. The third PDCI [Ivory Coast Democratic Party] congress, in mid-March, had the appearance of an interterritorial RDA meeting at which federalists and antifederalists presented their various points of view, Houphouet-Boigny again referred to his idea of a "Council of Union."

The first open defection from the Mali alliance was Upper Volta, whose constituent assembly, exactly a month after it had unanimously accepted the Mali constitution, by a bare majority adopted a constitution disassociating the Voltaic Republic from the Federation. Citing economic arguments, Premier Yameogo declared that his country had revised its stand on the Federation because "it did not want to choose

4 The original interview was given to *Carrefour* (Paris), October 15, 1958.

between Dakar and Abidjan." After a referendum approving the constitution and new general elections giving most of the assembly seats to the antifederalist wing of the local RDA section, Yameogo's strengthened government signed bilateral agreements on April 4, 1959, setting up a Council of the Entente with Ivory Coast. Upper Volta had chosen Abidjan. Three days later, its contiguity with Ivory Coast established, Niger followed suit. The new "anti-Federation" thus established was a flexible organization which provided for economic harmonization, political consultation, and a Solidarity Fund through which Ivory Coast could aid the poorer members.

In Dahomey Premier Apithy too had found himself opposed to the political exclusiveness and economic rigidity of the Mali Federation, which, he felt, was contrary to his federalist views and to the economic welfare and sovereignty of his country. His stand was supported, not by his own party or by the majority of the Dahomeyan assembly, but by the UDD [Dahomeyan Democratic Union], the local section of the RDA. At the end of January Apithy resigned from the Dahomeyan section of the PRA and reconstituted his old Dahomeyan Republican Party (PRD) in opposition to the Mali Federation. When new elections were held in early April to choose the assembly and government that would decide on membership in the Mali Federation, the results were almost identical with those of 1957, for the country was gerrymandered into political fiefs. However, the UDD (RDA), which had received more votes than the winning PRD but less than a third the number of its assembly seats, claimed that the new government was illegal, demanded new elections, and occupied parts of the country to enforce its protests. Houphouet-Boigny sent in RDA Premier Diori from Niger to mediate the dispute; when that failed, he negotiated personally with Apithy's representative in Abidjan. As a result, new elections were held in late April on the basis of a predetermined PRD-UDD apportionment. The outcome, however, was a three-party deadlock, with the UDD (RDA) now refusing the good offices of Houphouet-Boigny's envoys. The party also rejected Apithy and turned instead to the leader of the third Dahomeyan party, the Dahomeyan Democratic Rally (RDD), Hubert Maga, who was finally chosen premier in mid-May. Maga had not been party to the May negotiations among Ivory Coast, Niger, and Upper Volta and had to be convinced of Dahomey's economic interest in the Entente. On May 29, 1959, Dahomey signed a multilateral agreement with the other three members of the Entente, and in October of the following year, the RDD asked to join the interterritorial RDA party alliance.

When the legislative assembly of the Mali Federation met in Dakar on April 4, 1959, only Senegal and Soudan were represented. Modibo Keita of Soudan was chosen to head the federal government, while Senghor was elected president of the assembly and of the new federal party. To avoid a deadlock between the separate political organizations of the two states, a conference had been held in Dakar at the end of March to create a combined African Federalist Party (PFA). In addition to its Soudanese and Senegalese sections, the PFA also included associated organizations outside the Federation: Sawaba in Niger, the PRA remnant in Dahomey, the leftwing RDA federalists and later a new National Voltaic Party (PNV) in Upper Volta, and a new National

Union Party (UNM) of the southern (Senegalese-affiliated) population in Mauritania.[5] The *renversement des alliances* was thus complete; Senegal and Soudan, united in the Mali Federation, had a cautious ally in Mauritania and weak movements to support in three other states. Once the institutions of the new regional-unity organization were in place on both the territorial and the political levels, the leaders of the Federation could once more turn their attention to the demand for independence.

The Malian request for independence was not accepted by President de Gaulle until December. The news caused Houphouet-Boigny again to consider an important policy reversal. The same month, in an Entente meeting in Niamey, he promised that the four states would not be left behind by the Malian move, if only they would stick together. Franco-Malian negotiations, which began in January, ended in April with an agreement for independence on June 20, 1960. In February, Houphouet-Boigny and Senghor met in Paris to begin the process of *rapprochement;* the following month, missions from the two Mali states visited Abidjan. At the end of May, Houphouet-Boigny himself went to Dakar to declare his hope for "a broad union between Mali and the Council of the Entente"; soon after, he announced that he would request im-

[5] All the associated, minority parties except the UNM were soon to be charged with subversion. The UNM merged with the ruling PRM (which had an observer delegation at the Dakar PFA conference) after the Federation broke up. In addition, the small Guinea-based National Committee for a Free Ivory Coast also claimed association with the PFA; *La Situation politique en Côte d'Ivoire et l'indépendance nationale* (Conakry: Comité Nationale, 1959).

mediate independence, with agreements with France to be negotiated only after admission into the United Nations. Thus, on alternate days in the period August 1–7, 1960, Dahomey, Niger, Volta, and Ivory Coast also attained their independence. The Council of the Entente, meeting in Abidjan during the Ivory Coast independence celebrations, decided to harmonize the political and economic structures of the four member states and to establish identical constitutions for each.

Although the Entente was strengthened in August through the achievement of independence and some reinforcement of unity among its members, the tensions inherent in the Mali Federation soon brought about its collapse.[6] These tensions were partly organic: the hastily devised federal constitution uniting only two states while providing no mediatory institution between them, and the imbalance between richer, smaller Senegal and poorer, larger Soudan. But the tensions were also

6 This analysis, and the later section in Chap. III, subscribe to the causes of the breakup as described in Crowder, *Senegal: A Study in French Assimilation Policy* (New York: Oxford University Press, 1962), pp. 61–62, somewhat more than to the description by Thomas Hodgkin and Ruth Schachter Morgenthau in "Mali," in Coleman and Rosberg (eds.), *op. cit.*, pp. 241–46, particularly in the matters of direct French interference and of differences of opinion over the Algerian war. Hence, this analysis is closer—although not uncritically—to the Senegalese view, given in *Livre blanc sur le coup d'état manqué du 19 au 20 août 1960 et la proclamation de l'indépendance du Senegal* (Dakar: Ministry of Information, 1960), than to the Malian version, given in *Le Mali continue...* (Bamako: USRDA, 1960 [Extraordinary Party Congress Record]) and Modibo Keita, *Le Mali en marche* (Bamako: Secretariat of State for Information, 1962). For an insightful analysis on a different level, see Foltz, *op. cit.*

ideological: Soudan, with a well-organized party section, had announced as early as April 1959 that it favored a strong unitary federal government. The Soudanese were radicals in economic and foreign policy, while Senegal was liberalist and favorable to France. There was also a rivalry between both the personalities and the beliefs of the leaders: the Soudanese were opposed to Senghor as PFA candidate for federal president in the coming August elections. It was little wonder, then, that when Federal Premier Keita of Soudan dismissed Defense Minister Mamadou Dia of Senegal and declared a state of emergency on August 19, 1960, the Senegalese interpreted this as a Soudanese attempt to take over their country. On August 20, 1960, Senegal declared its independence from the Mali Federation, arrested Keita and the Soudanese ministers, and sent them back to Bamako. On September 22nd, Soudan declared the Federation ended and proclaimed its own independence, adopting the name of Mali. Thus two new states in West Africa achieved their independence, but at the cost of unity, and both were now isolated from any allies.

Houphouet-Boigny's reaction was skillful. Although neither of the formerly federated states could admit the correctness of his predictions and join the Entente, both needed allies. Senegal's need was partially political, and Ivory Coast continued a gradual development of better relations that overlooked the PRA-RDA and Dakar-Abidjan rivalries of the past. Mali's need was economic, and Houphouet-Boigny made an unpublicized visit to Bamako immediately after the rupture to assure Mali of his support, despite the bad blood that the RDA rupture had caused earlier. An Ivory Coast mission and then an exchange of visits by the premiers of the two states in early September completed the negotiation of arrangements whereby Abidjan would replace Dakar as Mali's supply port. The agreement benefited both sides, but it was made with a minimum of offense to Senegal.

The members of the Ghanaian alliance system did not have to contend with problems of independence, but they encountered other basic obstacles to successful unity. Like the defunct Mali Federation, the Guinea-Ghana Union contained only two members. The states were not contiguous (they were separated by Ivory Coast), but the gulf between them was more than geographical: they spoke different languages; their two strong leaders were potential rivals; their levels of modernization and their systems of government were different; and they profoundly misunderstood and sometimes even mistrusted each other. Only their common radical ideology and their similar party structures provided grounds for agreement. The fragility of this agreement was revealed in the Conakry declaration of May 1959, negotiated during Nkrumah's trip to Guinea. The statement of "Basic Principles of the Union of Independent African States" was couched mainly terms of policy coordination and made no provision for common political institutions.

Talk of union disturbed President Tubman in Monrovia. After the initial Guinea-Ghana announcement of 1958, a Guinean mission had to be dispatched to Liberia to assure Monrovia of Conakry's intentions and to negotiate a counterbalancing treaty of friendship, commerce, and navigation. In response to the 1959 Conakry declaration, Tubman called a conference of the heads of the three independent West African states to clarify the problem of unity.

(Another stimulus to a West African meeting was the impending French atomic test in the Sahara, announced in early July 1959.) The resulting Sanniquellie meeting of mid-July dashed Nkrumah's hopes for concrete measures of union; a ten-point declaration proposed a Community of Independent African States similar to the union of the Conakry declaration, with no political institutions, and with national identity, constitutional structure, and future policies and relations specifically excluded from unification.[7] The community idea, according to which all African states would simply seek friendly and harmonious relations among themselves, was Tubman's view of African unity. It had been reflected in his emphasis on mutually beneficial economic ties with Guinea, and it was in sharp opposition to Ghana's drive for leadership of African political unity. Nkrumah felt that he had been betrayed by his ally, Touré, but he did agree to place the declaration before a proposed Special Conference of Independent African States.

Despite the weaknesses of their union, Ghana and Guinea continued to cooperate in spreading independence during the following months. Like Ghana, Guinea also carried on its West African policy at two levels. Groups such as the National Committee for the Liberation of Ivory Coast, the Study Group for the Questions of Benin and the Committee of Dahomeyans in Guinea carried out political warfare and open pressure against the Entente

[7] A good review of events leading to Sanniquelli is found in Lawrence A. Marinelli, *The New Liberia* (New York: Praeger, 1964), pp. 122–29, 187–98. Information has also been gathered from interviews with Fodé Cissé. For a full report of speeches, see *La Première conférence au sommet* (Monrovia: Liberian Information Service, 1959).

states from Guinean sanctuary. To an increasing extent, however, Guinea also developed conventional diplomatic influence in neighboring states through visits and agreements. In May 1960, Tubman came to Conakry to strengthen frontier and economic agreements, and in July Touré went to Accra and Lomé to confer on unity and economic cooperation. As independence spread throughout West Africa in 1960, Guinea's diplomatic contacts increased and the causes for bad relations with other states in the region fell away. In Abidjan on the way home from Accra, Touré even suggested that he would be willing to meet Houphouet-Boigny. A rapid return visit by an Ivory Coast minister prepared the way for a border meeting between the two former RDA leaders in September. Guinea, however, was not ready to go further by shifting alliances and renouncing its radical ideology.

The same duality of methods continued to characterize Ghanaian policy. Surrounded by states that were not independent until mid-1960, and thereafter by governments that were suspicious if not hostile, Ghana's radical regime saw itself the focus of a colonialist and then neocolonialist encirclement that aggravated its sense of isolation. Between the Ivory Coast elections of April 1959 and Houphouet-Boigny's public warning to Nkrumah in January 1960 to cease intervention in neighbors' affairs, Ghana armed and aided the dissident Sanwi movement in southeast Ivory Coast. Beginning in October 1959 and continuing after Togolese independence on April 27th, Ghana accelerated its campaign to annex Togo, turning formerly sympathetic Olympio sharply against Nkrumah. A Ghanaian attempt at *rapprochement* with Ivory Coast was coincident with and as limited in scope

as Guinea's. After Nkrumah indicated in July that he was ready to meet Houphouet-Boigny, an important Ivory Coast delegation was sent to Accra in August, the two heads of state met briefly on the border in mid-September, and diplomatic relations were opened in October, although the proposed state visit of Houphouet-Boigny to Accra never took place.

The breakup of the Mali Federation in August 1960 had important repercussions on the Guinea-Ghana Union and on the trend of moderation in the two states. Economic assurances from Ivory Coast did not solve the problem of political isolation for the radical regime of the new Mali Republic. In November 1960 in Bamako and again in early December in Siguiri, Touré and Keita met to discuss unity between the two states and with Ghana[8]; on Christmas Eve the heads of the three radical states met in Conakry, where Ghana offered a $11.2 million loan to Mali. A committee was instructed to prepare the accession of Mali to a revised and strengthened Guinea-Ghana Union, and the second meeting of the three heads of state, in Accra at the end of April 1961, ended in the creation of a new radical alliance: the Union of African States. Institutions were to include a political preparatory committee and an economic committee, with the supreme executive organ being quarterly conferences of the heads of state. The significant characteristic of Union—borrowing a page from the RDA and the PRA-PFA experiences—was the provision for a coordination com-

[8] Gabriel D'Arboussier had been sent by Senegal to Ghana in mid-September 1960 to secure Ghanaian neutrality in the aftermath of the Federation's breakup, but without success, since Keita had got there a week earlier.

mittee for mass organizations (parties, women's groups, trade unions, and youth movements) to develop "a common ideological orientation which is absolutely necessary for the development of the Union." The counter-Entente was expanding, breaking the isolation of Ghana and supporting its ideological bent.

In order to eliminate completely Ghana's isolation and at the same time cut off Ivory Coast from its allies, it was necessary to reverse the ties of alliance held by Upper Volta and join it to the UAS, thus achieving contiguity among the three UAS members. Nkrumah lost no time in putting this strategy into effect, aided by the current dissatisfaction of Volta with the economic arrangements of the Entente.[9] At the end of June, at the frontier town of Paga, Nkrumah and Yameogo knocked down a wall (specially constructed for the purpose) to symbolize the establishment of a customs unions between them. However, neither Guinea nor Volta's neighbor, Mali, took part in this arrangement (there was no customs union between them or with Ghana), and there is much reason to believe that Yameogo was merely using his Ghana agreements to strengthen his hand with Ivory Coast; by August, he had achieved a favorable revision of financial arrangements with Ivory Coast and reaffirmed his solidar-

ity with the Entente. This rebuff to Ghana's efforts to consolidate the UAS was followed by a letdown in the activities of the Union itself. The three heads of state met in late June 1961 in Bamako, but never again within the framework of their alliance. "Mass organizations" were never unified, and the preparatory and economic committees made no progress toward unification. The only effective bond among the three states was their radical ideology, manifest internally in their African Socialist economies and mobilization parties, and externally in their suspicion of continuing European influence. Nevertheless, after four years of foreign-policy maneuvering and reversals, the West African alliance structure had crystalized into two interlocking systems, with Ghana, surrounded by the four Entente states, allied to Guinea and Mali in the UAS. Coastal powers large and small—such as Senegal, Liberia, Togo, and Nigeria—conducted their foreign policy without allies, only with enemies, looking for ties with other West African states but unable to accept or qualify for membership in either of the two alliance systems.

[*In the period 1960–63 the already crystallized West African conservative and radical groupings became the nuclei of groupings of states drawn from all over the African continent. As Zartman notes, it is often said that the two groupings of first the Brazzaville states and later the Monrovia states on the one hand and the Casablanca states on the other came into existence as a result of the issues of the early 1960's of the Congo and Algeria. In fact as we have already noted these groupings existed in incipient form within the West African subordinate system. Thus it was the Entente states under the leadership of Houphouet-Boigny of the*

---

[9] The *rapprochement* was aided by a flurry of diplomatic activity between Upper Volta and the UAS states. Yameogo visited Mali and Ghana and Touré visited Upper Volta in May; Malian and Guinean delegations visited Upper Volta in May and June. Mali claimed that Volta's rejection of military agreements with France made it "acceptable" to the UAS. But no multilateral ties were negotiated to buttress the Accra agreements of May 22nd and the Paga agreement of June 27th.

Ivory Coast which called a meeting at Brazzaville, Congo in December, 1960 which all the African Francophonic states attended except, significantly, Guinea and Togo while Mali sent only an observer. This meeting of moderate states prompted a response in the meeting of radical states (Guinea, Ghana and Mali plus Morocco, the provisional Algerian government, the U.A.R., Ceylon plus a lesser representative of Libya) at Casablanca in January, 1961. On the two major African issues of the Congo and Algeria the two groups took opposite respective positions: the moderates supported Kasavubu against Lumumba and mediation between France and Algeria rather than outright independence. From the Brazzaville meeting there followed in September, 1961, the establishment of the African and Malagasy Union (UAM) for purposes of economic cooperation among African moderate Francophonic states.

Meanwhile in March, 1961, the West African peripheral state of Nigeria took the diplomatic initiative of attempting to reconcile the two larger moderate and radical groupings. At first this effort only resulted in the expansion of the moderate grouping into the Monrovia grouping in May, 1961, to include all except the Casablanca group. After further meetings and diplomatic activity of the Monrovia group in 1962 the moderate and radical elements were brought together in the May, 1963, meeting at Addis Ababa which was to see the founding of the Organization of African Unity—the moderates had carried the day. (Editors)]

THE AFRICAN CONTEXT OF WEST AFRICAN RELATIONS

The Addis Ababa summit meeting of May 22–26, 1963, marked a turning point in the foreign policies of Western Africa, as of the entire continent. Previous ideological differences by no means disappeared, but they were submerged in the combined atmosphere of euphoria and seriousness that reigned at the meeting. When they appeared later, they were contained within the institution set up at the conference, the Organization of African Unity (OAU), and were subject to a number of ground rules for keeping intra-African disputes on a manageable level.[10] These rules all reflected the dominant position of the moderates, solidly organized in the UAM [African and Malagasy Union] alliance and its Monrovian outgrowth. They included notably a declaration against subversion, political assassination, and interference in internal affairs, taken from the Lagos charter, and provision for an arbitration commission for the peaceful settlement of disputes, along the lines of a detailed Tunisian proposal. In exchange for the predominance of moderate theses on intra-African relations, the radicals obtained greater attention to the problems of colonial Africa, particularly the Portuguese territories and South Africa. A Liberation Coordination Committee of nine—Guinea, Algeria, Senegal, Nigeria, Tanganyika, Uganda, Congo, Ethiopia, and the UAR—was established to administer aid to anti-colonial liberation movements. In this exchange, the Ghanaian federalist thesis of African unity was left by the wayside. The OAU was established on the basis of an Ethiopian draft, along lines drawn from both the Casablanca and Monrovia charters, and it included an annual summit meeting, a council of foreign

[10] See Boutros Boutros-Ghali, *The Addis Ababa Charter* (New York: Carnegie Endowment for International Peace, 1964 [International Conciliation Series No. 546]); Marinelli, *op. cit.*, pp. 138–40.

ministers, a secretariat, and a number of special commissions. Liberia, Nigeria, and Ethiopia were most active in drawing up the charter, and the definition of *unity*—solidarity and cooperation among sovereign and equal states— vindicated the ideas consistently expressed by Western Africa's oldest independent state since Tubman's first meetings with Touré in 1958.

Four elements made for the success and impact of the Addis Ababa meeting. One was the careful preparation, resulting from the efforts of the Casablanca and Monrovia Groups almost from their beginnings and from Tunisia's work toward North African harmony and a third Conference of Independent African States. A foreign-ministers' meeting at Addis Ababa immediately preceding the summit meeting set up an agenda and completed the year of preparations. Another element was the nearly universal attendance, which indicated that the local issues of the past had been relegated to a second level—although by no means resolved—and that the traditional divisions between Black and Arab Africa, between English and French-speaking states, between radicals and moderates, and among rival personalities were not important enough to prevent a common meeting. Furthermore, the impressive attendance imposed on the delegates the need to come to some agreement. In the middle of the conference, when spirits had begun to flag because of an apparent lack of harmony, a speech by Emperor Haile Selassie reminded the heads of state that the foreign press, only too conscious of the failures of past attempts at unity, was scornfully predicting failure again at Addis Ababa. The speech roused the delegates and impressed them with the need for more than formal attendance.

Third, the results of Addis Ababa combined the aims of previous groups, alliances, and organizations, eliminating rivals by absorbing their purposes. Goals of political consultation, economic cooperation, and assistance to independence movements were taken over from the Conference of Independent African States, the Casablanca and Monrovia Groups, and the AAPO [All African Peoples Organizaiton]. In June, Touré, who called for the abolition of all subgroups, announced the dissolution of the UAS [Union of African States]; the collapse of the May meeting of the Casablanca Group brought the end of this alliance. The Entente and the UAM both faded and then changed in nature, and the Monrovia Group dissolved into the OAU.

Finally, the Addis Ababa meeting meant an effective resting place in the search for African unity. Agreement on a specific formula did not destroy the arguments of those states—like Ivory Coast—which wanted no interference by a supranational institution, nor of those—like Ghana—which believed in the creation of a Pan-African federation. But it did establish an initial consensus, and working institutions based on that consensus. Only when these had been tried and tested for several years could it be determined whether or not they were adequate to the needs and wishes of their members and to the changing African situation.

Western African relations immediately put the OAU institutions to the test. Most serious was the outbreak of hostilities between Morocco and Algeria over their undelineated border. Initial military action along a frontier that had been troubled by incidents for several months broke out in early October 1963, and continued despite bilateral negotiations and attempts at mediation by Tunisia, Ethiopia, and the Arab League. Later in the month, on the suggestion of Algeria, the matter was carried before a special quadripartite summit meeting of the OAU at Bamako, where Hassan II, ben Bella, Keita, and Haile Selassie worked out a cease-fire agreement. The Bamako declaration also called for an urgent meeting of the OAU foreign ministers at Addis Ababa in mid-November to create a special arbitration commission. The commission—composed of Mali, Senegal, Ivory Coast, Nigeria, Sudan, Tanganyika, and Ethiopia—met at Abidjan in early December, in Bamako in late January and late April, and in Casablanca and Algiers in May. The "Africanization" of the problem brought several results: it symbolized North Africa's membership in the African world, and showed the greater vitality of the OAU over the Arab League. By giving the new organization of Addis Ababa something to do, the border war both put it to the test and prolonged its life. The OAU succeeded in stopping the war because the rest of Africa was more deeply committed to unity than to either belligerent, and because an armistice fit in with both Morocco's goal (to bring the unsettled border to Algeria's attention) and Algeria's aims (to end the war that it was losing). The OAU did not succeed in establishing the frontier because it was impossible to make a technical decision either on the border or on the "war guilt," and because it still did not have the authority to make a political decision on either matter.

The work of the Liberation Coordination Committee was less effective in Western Africa. Meeting in Dar es-Salaam in late June, the Committee of Nine drew up a report recognizing the government-in-exile of Holden Roberto as the authentic Angolan nationalist movement and requesting a budget of $4.2 million for support of nationalist movements. But no agreement was to be had on recognition of a single movement in Portuguese Guinea, although a subcommittee (Algeria, Guinea, Senegal, Nigeria, and Congo) interviewed representatives of rival Portuguese Guinean groups in Conakry in late July, and recommended the formation of a United Action Front based on the militant African Independence Party (PAIGC). Senegal disagreed and vetoed endorsement of the Conakry-supported PAIGC when the matter came up before the foreign-ministers' conference of the OAU in Dakar in early August. The Committee of Nine had also made the decision to turn over coordination of support to the exiled movements' host countries (in most cases, Congo or Tanganyika), thus giving up most of its functions. This position caused increased dissatisfaction among radical states, culminating in an open attack on the committee in the Ghanaian press—an attack immediately endorsed by Algeria. When the new state of Gambia became the seventeenth independent state in Western Africa in mid-February 1965, it was not as a result of any action by the OAU.

The existence of a continental organization challenged the *raison d'être* of the remaining alliances of Western Africa. The UAM held its first meeting after Addis Ababa in Cotonou in late July, under attack from Touré, who felt that all alliances should give way to the OAU and who preferred to deal individually with the former members of AOF. The results were ambiguous. Togo was admitted as the fourteenth member and Ivory Coast was proposed as a member of the United Nations

Security Council, but the UAM office in the United Nations was dissolved in favor of an OAU caucus and the "evolution" of the Group in relation to the OAU was proposed. Most of the smaller members remained dependent on the alliance for security and thus were interested in its continuing existence; a period of reflection was therefore granted before scheduling a new meeting in 1964 in Dakar. The heads of state met in the Senegalese capital in early March, without Houphouet-Boigny and the presidents of Equatorial Africa. Particularly after the initiative provided by the host, Senghor, and the current president of the UAM, Yameogo, the "evolution" was begun: the political organization—UAM—was dissolved as unnecessary, and the institutions for harmonization of economic and communications matters were reconstituted as the African and Malagasy Union for Economic Cooperation (UAMCE). Foreign ministers of the states in the new organization met for the first time in Nouakchott in late April, but the absence of the ministers of the three Entente states and the Centrafrican Republic prevented the final signing of the new charter. Another time of reflection was scheduled before a second meeting in Nouakchott in 1965.

Within the Western African membership of the UAM, old rivalries were also pressing toward new constellations. Most important was the long-standing political and economic competition between Dakar and Abidjan. The Entente fell into somnolence after Addis Ababa. During 1963, plots against the president were discovered in Ivory Coast, the RDA government of Maga was overthrown in Dahomey, and a quarrel broke out between Dahomey and Niger. Entente meetings were held among only Houphouet-Boigny, Diori, and Yame-

ogo in Abidjan in late 1963 and throughout 1964. Ignoring Dahomey and the Entente, Houphouet-Boigny turned to his old RDA allies, and in April 1964 invited Diori, Yameogo, Touré, and Keita to Bouake to discuss means of controlling internal subversion; in September, he brought Diori and Yameogo with him to meet Senghor in Bobo-Dioulasso. In mid-August, on Tubman's suggestion he also met in Monrovia with Touré and Albert Margai (who had succeeded his late brother as premier of Sierra Leone), to study the possibility of a West African free-exchange zone; important ministerial delegations of the four countries met again in the Liberian capital to continue negotiations in mid-February 1965. Senegal too was preoccupied with internal economic and political problems incident to the consolidation of Senghor's new regime, after a confrontation between Senghor's and Dia's followers in December 1962 led to the imprisonment of the premier. But Dakar also moved to restore its commercial and political leadership in West Africa, beginning first with a *rapprochement* with Mali and then by promoting economic cooperation among the four Senegal River states: Senegal, Mali, Guinea, and Mauritania. Senegal's interest in an economic UAM was part of its campaign to make the organization acceptable to Guinea and Mali, and bring them back into cooperation with their former AOF partners. The rivalry between Dakar and Abidjan concerned primarily these two states, which lay between Ivory Coast and Senegal and could serve as markets for both; unfortunately, they could serve as close allies for neither, for their basically radical attitudes clashed with the more moderate outlook of both Senghor and

Houphouet-Boigny. Economic rivals but political allies, Senegal and Ivory Coast failed to realign the basic elements of West African affinities and conflicts in 1963 and 1964.

Probably the most important shift in policy on regional cooperation after Addis Ababa concerned the outlook of newly independent Algeria. After coming to power in the fall of 1962, ben Bella followed the patterns of sympathy formed during his stay in Cairo (before his capture by the French), and turned to developing a close relationship with the Arab Middle East and especially with Nasser's Egypt. Missions to Cairo by Khider, Defense Minister Haouri Boumedienne, and Foreign Minister Mohammed Khemisti in late 1962, however, brought back disappointing impressions. Nasser's visit to Algiers in May 1963 was a festive occasion and Egypt aided Algeria in time of need, notably during the Algero-Moroccan war, but ben Bella looked elsewhere for a primary field of action. His experience at Addis Ababa, selected African support for the FLN during the Algerian war, and the apparent opportunities for action and Algerian leadership in Africa—all combined to turn his attention to his own continent. Disappointment was not long in appearing. The Liberation Coordination Committee temporized, the OAU in general was dominated by the moderates, and the African states proved little susceptible to Algerian leadership. If Addis Ababa marked a turning toward Africa by Algeria, the Dakar meeting of the OAU foreign ministers in August, at which ben Bella (then Algeria's foreign minister) could observe for himself the bickering and indecision, was the beginning of a turning away. More promising were possibilities of North African cooperation, despite the border war with Morocco. Algeria perceived that

unity was more meaningful and more likely through a functionalist (or economic) approach than through a federalist (or political) one. The economic agreements concluded with Tunisia in September and November 1963 were the first result of bettered relations with one neighbor. They were followed by the meeting of ben Bella, Bourguiba, and Nasser at the celebrations over the French evacuation of Bizerte in mid-December. Hassan II stayed away in protest over the border affair, and although this conflict slowly lost fire, relations were kept strained by the infiltration of armed bands from Algeria into Morocco. Nevertheless, Algeria used new opportunities, such as the problem of relations with the European Common Market, to move toward greater economic cooperation with its two neighbors. In late November, Morocco, Algeria, Tunisia, and Libya met in Rabat and Tangier to try a new approach to Maghreb unity. Using the OAMCE [African-Malagasy Organization for Economic Cooperation] as a model, the four states planned their unity on economic lines, creating a permanent consultative committee of economic ministers and a center for industrial studies.

Many of Western Africa's problems found a fitting denouement in the second OAU summit held in mid-July 1964 in Cairo. As had become customary at such meetings, the occasion was used for the reconciliation of bickering states. Bourguiba brought together Hassan II and ben Bella. (It was not until ten months later, however, that the two heads of state finally met on their own soil, in the Moroccan town of Saidia, and that ben Bella at last agreed to study the frontier issue.) Hassan's presence at the conference, in alphabetical order next to Mauritania, marked a noticeable relaxation of Moroccan irredentist pressures, and permitted the two delegations to agree on the cessation of radio propaganda.

On the other hand, the 1963 Togo incident had its parallel in 1964, when Congo's new premier, Moise Tshombé, was banned from attending. Unfinished business at Cairo consisted mainly of strengthening and completing the original structure of the Addis Ababa organization problems which the foreign ministers had not tackled at Lagos and Addis Ababa and had not solved at Dakar and Cairo. A resolution specifying the legitimacy of colonial frontiers was introduced by Touré and passed, and a renewed plea for immediate political unity by Nkrumah was turned into a weaker resolution recommending study of the Pan-Africanist approach. Agreement was finally reached on three matters: the site of a permanent seat (Addis Ababa in preference to Dakar or Lagos), the choice of a permanent secretary-general (Guinean Telli Diallo in preference to the UAM candidate, Emile Zinsou) with four assistants (from Nigeria, Algeria, Dahomey, and Kenya), and the location of the third heads-of-state meeting (Accra, in September 1965). A potential item of unfinished business that received little attention was the matter of the undissolved regional units. Partly because their value was recognized, partly because there was increased interest in new regional groupings, and partly as an antidote to Nkrumah's insistence on continental political unification, organizations of regional cooperation were spared from attack.

Despite the reconciliations and the progress achieved at Cairo, one dispute —Congo—continued to worsen. The national government of Tshombé, facing widespread dissidence from the Congolese Liberation Movement (MLC), turned to mercenaries for sup-port when an appeal for troops addressed to other African governments (including Nigeria and Liberia) was rejected; the MLC rebels, in turn, benefited from military and diplomatic aid from Algeria, Ghana, Guinea, Mali, and others. The issue at stake involved more than a simple personality or government; it was a clash between two basic ideological concepts. One claimed the right to interfere in the internal affairs of another state in the name of a higher value, "Africanity," and saw in Congo an overt colonial threat against the entire continent; the other rejected subversion and interference in the affairs of a sovereign state and viewed the African system as a concert of states designed to defend the new independence from any threat. Broadly, the argument between unity (orthodoxy) and independence (sovereignty), or between the revolutionary and conventional policies, had broken out again over Congo.

The effects were evident in a number of policy changes. For Ghana, there was a return to the tools of subversion (after it had apparently suspended their use upon appeals in the OAU). For Algeria, there arose a new opportunity for leadership in Africa, which was added to continued policies of cooperation in the Maghreb; this basic orientation was not changed by the military coup of June, 1965, that replaced ben Bella with his former vice-president, Col. Haouri Boumedienne. For the Entente, the need to tighten cooperation became evident, and active efforts were made to solve the Dahomey-Niger dispute by recalling Dahomey to the fold instead of merely giving support to Niger; in a meeting of the Entente states in mid-January, Ahomadegbe met with the delegates of the other three states and the alliance was complete for the first time in over a year. Houphouet-Boigny proposed common citizenship and increased cooperation (although they were not implemented before the target date of July 1965) and overtures on membership were favorably greeted by Togo, which was also undergoing a period of tense relations with Ghana.

The most significant changes concerned the UAMCE. When the heads of member states met in Nouakchott in mid-February to sign the new organization's treaty, they were confronted with a strong group of Entente allies who had returned to play their original role of a core group in the larger organization and who were now convinced by the weakness of the OAU and the upsurge of radical, subversive activity in Africa that a political bloc of moderates was necessary. The UAMCE was scrapped before it was inaugurated, and in its place was established an Afro-Malagasy Common Organization (OCAM) "to strengthen cooperation and solidarity...in order to speed up political, economic, social, technical, and cultural development." The same final communiqué condemned Ghanaian subversion by name and supported the legal government of Tshombé in Congo. Immediately after Nouakchott, the moderate group went to Nairobi for the OAU foreign ministers' meeting. There their number was large enough to block any radical proposal for official support to the rebels, although not quite enough (largely because of absences) to push through full approval of Tshombé. Instead, they used OCAM for the purpose, admitting Congo to membership at a meeting held in Abidjan in May (total membership remained the same, however, because Mauritania withdrew in disagreement with both the fact and the manner of Congo's joining).

In 1965, the new states of Western Africa were beginning a second distinct stage in their developing relations. By its universality and its modest charter, the OAU created at Addis Ababa embodied a temporarily satisfying definition and institutionalization of the elusive unity slogan, while at least outwardly legitimizing and consolidating the independence of the participants. Western Africa had become part of a continental system of international relations, of which it was the initiator. The frantic search for alliances to overcome isolation was temporarily arrested as the states digested their newly found unity. By 1965—as at the 1960–61 midpoint of the previous stage—the unity idea was again torn by ideological differences triggered by an outside event. Instead of looking for unity as the highest goal, radicals and moderates— split on the new Congo question— looked for unity on their own terms and were unanimous only in deploring the ineffectiveness of the OAU. Unlike 1960–61, however, the second year of the OAU did not see the formation of rival groups. Toward the end of the year, the three major conferences to which Western Africa was host—the Arab League meeting in Casablanca in September; the Afro-Asian or "second Bandung" conference in Algiers, postponed from June to November and then *sine die;* the third OAU summit in Accra, postponed from September to October—all had notable defections and meager results. The development of intra-African relations by 1965 showed also the durability of the inchoate, artificial, colonial-inherited state. This durability was not inherent, for much of the leaders' foreign effort (and a good part of their domestic activities) was required to shore up their new creation. But at least the states lasted, creating their own legitimizing mythology, while regional or continental unification faltered, despite a mythology already established.

[*The events of the post-1963 period are consequently to be understood in the perspective of this article. Thus the formation of the Common Organization of Malagasy and African States in 1965 represented the success of the Ivory Coast-led Conseil d'Entente in expanding its appeal. With the downfall of Kwame Nkrumah of Ghana in 1966 and Modibo Keita of Mali in November, 1968, and with Guinea seeking increased ties with the United States and France, the radical impetus for regional unity and severance of ties with France has diminished. At least for the moment, the moderate faction in West Africa appears to have carried the day. However, the basic division still remains as is illustrated by the fact that the Ivory Coast i.e., Homphouet-Boigny has given diplomatic recognition to the breakaway regime of Biafra while Singhor has argued against doing so precisely in terms of his aversion to the "Balkanization" of Africa.*[11] *(Editors)*]

[11] [Léopold Sédor Senghor, "Si on bent la paix au Nigeria," *Jeune Afrique,* 416 (December 29, 1968), 24.]

SOUTHEAST ASIA

Bernard K. Gordon

A POLITICAL REGION OF SOUTHEAST ASIA

This [article] deals with the international politics of Southeast Asia. More precisely, it deals with the conflicts, and the scope of potential cooperation, among the nations of this region. But is that suggesting too much?—*Is* there a political "region" of Southeast Asia? In this context, one specialist on Asian affairs recently wrote that, unlike Europe or the Middle East, Southeast Asia cannot be regarded as a regional unit, but "must be considered as an aggregate of territories."[1] Another expert, a decade earlier, also denied that there is a "region" of Southeast Asia; it is instead, he argued, "merely a place on the globe where certain groups of people, holding little in common, live contiguous to one another."[2]

These views, while perhaps accurate in the past, do not now describe reality.

Reprinted from Bernard K. Gordon, *The Dimensions of Conflict in Southeast Asia* (Englewood cliffs, N. J.: Prentice-Hall, Inc. © 1966) pp. 1–8, by permission of the publisher.

[1] P. M. A. Linebarger, "The Psychological Instruments of Policy in Southeast Asia," in William Henderson ed., *Southeast Asia: Problems of United States Policy* (Cambridge, Mass.: The M.I.T. Press, 1963), pp. 227–28.

[2] Nathaniel Pfeffer, "Regional Security in Southeast Asia," *International Organization* (August, 1954), pp. 311–15.

Today, at least three factors force us to consider Southeast Asia as a region. The first is the awareness by Southeast Asia's leaders of the many similar problems they share in common, largely in the area of economic development. Their awareness comes from—for example—regular participation in meetings of the United Nations Economic Commission for Asia and the Far East (ECAFE), and from involvement in many special groups, like the United Nations Conference on Trade and Development in 1964. In addition to sharpening leaders' awareness of their common problems, these meetings add greatly to intra-regional communications, which in turn contribute to consciousness of the "region." No longer do leaders in Bangkok and Manila depend, as they once did, on London and Washington for their knowledge of each other.

The second factor which makes Southeast Asia a "region" is the widespread incidence of conflict, along with some attempts at cooperation, in the area. Both conflict and cooperation are forms of communication; both have led to an unprecedented involvement, by Southeast Asia's leaders, in the affairs of neighbors. Some of this involvement is disruptive, such as Indonesia's campaign against Malaysia; other aspects, such as the plan to establish an Asian Development Bank, are potentially constructive. But in any event Southeast Asia's leaders—and it is the leadership with which we must be concerned if we are to judge whether the area qualifies as a "region"—have been thrown together as never before. Thus, when one critic, seeking to deny that the area is a region, charges that "knowledge of the region as a unit is not yet diffused to the populations which inhabit it,"[3]

we must ask: how important is that charge within the context of Southeast Asia? Narrow elites, both relatively and absolutely smaller than in the West, dominate the political and economic affairs of all developing nations. Southeast Asia, essentially a village society in which 80 to 90 per cent of its population is rural-agricultural, is no exception. Even in Europe, where consciousness of "region" is high and institutions like the European Economic Community exist to bring about economic and perhaps even political integration, there is a gap between elite attitudes and popular understanding on this subject. In Southeast Asis, with its high illiteracy and underdeveloped communications, the gap between popular understanding and elite attitudes is necessarily much wider. The region's leaders, however, have been thrust into intimate contact with their neighbors, often through conflict; the communications developed as a result are one factor which perhaps more than anything else compels us to accept the fact that a sense of "region" does now exist in Southeast Asia.

The third incentive to accepting the concept of "region" is that a major political force—Communism—has been precisely such an incentive for forty years. The careers of Ho Chi Minh and Tan Malaka, the Indonesian revolutionary, are symbolic. Ho, as Comintern and Soviet agent specially responsible for Indochina and nearby areas in the 1920s and '30s, moved constantly throughout the region.[4] Tan Malaka, "Comintern agent for Southeast Asia and Australia," was similarly well traveled.[5] Marxism stressed that there

---

[3] Linebarger, *Psychological Instruments of Policy.*

[4] Ellen Hammer, *The Struggle for Indochina* (Stanford, Calif.: Stanford University Press, 1954), p. 82.

[5] Arnold Brackman, *Indonesian Communism* (New York: Frederick A. Praeger, Inc., 1963), p. 23.

were common elements in the plight of the Asian peoples and that their independence depended on a Communist victory in all countries. In 1928 the Chinese Communist Party stated that "the triumph of Communism in China . . . could not fail to influence neighboring Asia, particularly India, Indochina, Java, and Korea."[6] Today, little has changed, as North Vietnam's Premier recently stressed:

We must see the situation in the Indochinese peninsula against the background of the general situation in Southeast Asia and . . . with the situation in the southern part of our country. Here we must lay bare the British imperialist scheme in the setting up of Malaysia, aimed at consolidating the British colonialist domination in the countries within that bloc, strengthening the British military base of Singapore, and directly threatening the Republic of Indonesia.[7]

In sum, the incentives for examining the "region" of Southeast Asia derive from the perspective of communications—based on both conflict and cooperation—as well as from Communism. Evidence from each perspective suggests that the nations in Southeast Asia are much more than an unrelated aggregate of states. It indicates that we can learn things of importance by examining the *region*—not only for what we learn about each of the nations separately, but also about the politics among these nations generally and the concept of "regionalism" in particular. In the process we can also come to understand the region's instability, for instability is the one feature of Southeast Asia that gives the region much of its contemporary importance.

Political Conflict in Southeast Asia.

6 *Ibid.*
7 From the Premier's report at the first session of the National Assembly of North Vietnam, June 27, 1964 (Hanoi: VNA International Service in English).

Many of the conflicts that divide the nations of Southeast Asia are not really new. The aggravations of existing sores sometimes may give the appearance of "new" tensions, but many of today's problems derive in large part from actions taken long ago. Thus, except for the war in Vietnam, the global conflict between the Communist and non-Communist world has not played a major part in the tension among Southeast Asian nations. Indeed, that war has effectively removed the two Vietnams from much of the region's international politics,[8] and our study therefore deals with the foreign policies of the other states: Thailand, Burma, Cambodia, Indonesia, the Philippines, and Malaysia (along with Singapore).[9]

What kinds of issues contribute to tensions among these nations? Do they differ from those that have led other states in other times to distrust one another? The answer to both questions is very closely tied to the nature of politics in Southeast Asia. These are states that are both old and new. Some writers have called them *the developing countries;* others have used the phrase *nations in transition;* and Professor Fred Riggs has made a strong case for using the term *prismatic societies.* He suggests that, instead of applying the label *traditional society* to an undeveloped nation, we think in terms of a *fused society.* In a traditional, or "fused" society, as he points out, a

8 An exception is in the efforts of Cambodia to improve relations with the Hanoi regime: Prince Sihanouk of Cambodia has repeatedly said that he does not expect South Vietnam to retain its independence for long, and he wants to be on good terms with the eventual winner in the Vietnamese struggle.
9 The foreign policies of these nations in comparison with Vietnam's have not been so extensively analyzed. On the "two Vietnams," see Bernard B. Fall, *The Two Vietnams* (New York: Frederick A. Praeger, Inc., 1963).

single structure—whether it be tribe, clergy, or monarchy—performs the basic political functions for the society. Modern, advanced states, on the other hand, have established separate and almost innumerable structures for performing necessarily more complicated functions. Riggs calls these *refracted societies*—"in which for every function, a corresponding structure exists."[10] Prismatic society, he stresses, lies between the extremes of fused and refracted societies and is so called "because of the prism through which fused light passes to become refracted."[11]

The states in Southeast Asia each appear to fit the description of a prismatic society: they exhibit many practices of traditional society, while aspiring to the norms and methods of refracted societies or modern states. Both levels may exist side by side in a single nation, and this can lead to a multitude of internal tensions.[12] This duality has a clear impact on foreign affairs, both

in the sorts of disputes that become important and in the methods used to deal with them. Border disputes, for example, are among the most familiar causes of international conflict, and we will be dealing with one of these: the Philippines' claim to North Borneo. The nations involved seem closer to being refracted societies than any others in Southeast Asia. In fact, the Philippines and Malaysia have tended to deal with their problem in ways that might be expected among refracted states. They have sought, for example, to avoid resorting to the threat or use of force—a virtue popular among the politically advanced nations although not universally practiced by them. A markedly different style of foreign-policy choices, and quite distinct methods of implementing policy, will emerge when the foreign policies of Cambodia and Indonesia are discussed. There, the notion of the prismatic state probably will become more apparent, for the practices of these two nations are relatively less familiar to us than are the methods used by the Philippines and Malaysia.

Territoriality: Western Legalisms and Ancient Empires. Border disputes, ostensibly a "familiar" aspect of international politics, have different roots in Southeast Asia, and traditional Western concepts do not quite seem to fit. For example, the Khmer kingdom associated with Angkor did not wield the kind of political authority, or sovereignty, in all parts of its territory that Westerners associate today with the word *empire* or *kingdom*. Generally speaking, states and empires in Southeast Asian history seldom embodied the territorial implications of sovereignty that developed in the West. The sultans who ruled over different parts of what are now Malaya and Indonesia were not sovereign in the usual Western

---

[10] Fred W. Riggs, "International Relations as a Prismatic System," *World Politics,* XIV, No. 1 (October, 1961), 149.

[11] *Ibid.*

[12] For example, in reviewing a study of political development in Iran by Leonard Binder, Riggs noted that some leading Iranians, according to Binder, condemn "traditional practices such as nepotism. . . ." But, as Riggs points out: "Nepotism. . . cannot be identified as a traditional system. Hereditary office and ascriptive recruitment are prescribed by the traditional system. It is only the superimposition of norms which substitute achievement-oriented rules, making the appointment of relatives illegal, that creates nepotism. It is this illegality, the contradiction between formal prescription and effective practice, a glaring discontinuity between the ideal and the actual, which is the hallmark of the prismatic condition. Thus what appear as contradictions in Binder's frame of reference are not contradictory in terms of the prismatic model. They are what we expect to find." (Fred Riggs, "The Theory of Developing Politics," *World Politics,* XVI [October, 1963], 163.)

sense, for they themselves were—to varying degrees and from time to time —subject to the imperial rule of China. When they were at odds with one another or, later, when some of them were engaged in wars against the European powers, they frequently sought the aid of China. The Chinese often regarded these territories as part of China, though not as integral parts. Some, like present-day Vietnam (Annam), were more closely integrated with Chinese fortunes, and the imprint of Chinese cultural, political, and administrative tradition is very clear there.

Thus the concept of "dual sovereignty," one not too meaningful in Western thinking since the time of Jean Bodin, was not uncommon in Asian history. Its imprecision was paralleled by vagueness on the extent of territory too. Consider, for example, the ancient empire of Majapahit. Modern Indonesians sometimes think of their state as the ultimate successor to Majapahit. Many writings drawn from the thirteenth-century inscriptions known as the *Nagarakertagama,* however, suggest that the "boundaries" of Majapahit included what is now Indonesia, and more. Nevertheless, modern historians increasingly question whether familiar notions of a far-flung domain apply to Majapahit,[13] for that empire does not appear to have exercised the kind of centrally-directed and organized control that Rome wielded in

Gaul or the British Isles; and certainly it did not approach the authority of the eighteenth- and nineteenth-century British Empire. Instead, the "empire" of Majapahit may more accurately be interpreted as a series of rulers who considered themselves the supreme authority of a wide realm of islands and mainland territories in Southeast Asia. Majapahit was a sea-based empire with outposts in a variety of places. In those outposts it probably was sovereign; but only a few miles inland imperial rule ended.

Today's leaders, however, are not often familiar with findings of modern historiography; even if they were, there seems little likelihood that they would disregard the old myths. Contemporary Asian leaders tend to accept the ancient legends insofar as they relate to the extent of some ancient empires, and we can probably only applaud their interest in preserving rich histories and traditions. The political significance of their interest, however, is that modern Southeast Asian leaders are products of much *Western* thinking about the nation and state. To their mind, just as to ours, the state necessarily implies territory. It is the essential ingredient of the state and of the nation.

Not surprisingly, therefore, these leaders may get just as incensed about seemingly worthless pieces of territory as have their counterparts in European and American history. The precise charting of a boundary, probably never very important to some of the ancient kingdoms and empires,[14] can now—

---

[13] D. G. E. Hall concludes: "So far as the ascertainable facts go, the state of Majapahit was limited to East Java, Madura, and Bali." *A History of Southeast Asia* (2nd ed.; London: Macmillan & Co., Ltd., 1964), p. 83. In Professor Cady's new book a similar conclusion is reached: While Gaja Mada, the actual ruler of Majapahit (1330–64) boasted of his conquests, Cady points out, they were still extensive. "He claimed control over Bali, Macassar, parts of

Borneo, . . . all of lower Sumatra, and the Sunda area in Western Java, *but much of this control probably amounted to little more than receipt of vassal tribute.*" John F. Cady, *Southeast Asia: Its Histotrical Development* (New York: McGraw-Hill Book Company, 1964), p. 141. Emphasis added.

[14] International conflict in Southeast Asia

because of this superimposition on Asian traditions of Western legalisms about sovereignty and the state—lead to some quite intense disputes among the independent states of Southeast Asia.

One source of the problem is that many of today's independent nations are successor states to what were merely *parts* of the same kingdom or "empire" in the dimly recorded past. The European colonial powers, for their own reasons, often divided territories that had previously been part of a larger unit. Thus some of the lines the French drew around Laos, Annam, Cochin-China, and Cambodia were meaningful and some were not. Yet those demarcations have become today's "fixed" boundaries. In other cases old territorial divisions that were the result of pre-European intra-Asian conflicts were sometimes hardened by the Europeans, in moves related largely to intra-European diplomacy, as they administered and "protected" the separate territories as part of their empires or spheres of influence.

Even the Japanese, the last outsiders, contributed to these patterns. During World War II Japan "returned" to Thailand certain parts of French Indochina. Later, under pressure from the victorious Allies, the Thais relinquished those territories, but many Cambodians today fear that Thailand still covets their land. Similarly, as World War II drew to a close, the Japanese military decided that the former Dutch East Indies were readier for independence than was British Malaya. Thus when Indonesia—under Japanese sponsorship —proclaimed its independence, it included only the former Dutch territories. If Japan had decided differently, what is now Malaysia and Singapore might have been part of Indonesia. Many Malaysian leaders fear that Indonesia will try to "correct" that accident of history.

Of course not all the scores of invasions and conquests which have shaped Southeast Asian history find parallels in present territorial conflicts among the now-independent states. Yet even the briefest glance at the ethnographic map of Southeast Asia reveals the effects of the region's checkered history. Indeed, the very concept of Southeast Asia as an historical and geographic entity is likely to bring to mind an image of loosely extended and overlapping empires. That history has left us with an area especially fertile in disputes over who owns what, and dozens of population islands surrounded by ethnically different peoples. Often these communities do not live in harmony with one another, and some look across national borders for support.

Thus the Shan peoples of Burma, many of whom desire more autonomy or even independence, look to the adjacent and ethnically similar Thai for support. Until recently they were not always disappointed. Similarly with regard to the Muslim, or Moro, population of the southern Philippines. These people have hardly been integrated into Philippines society and culture; instead they have much closer commercial, cultural, and religious ties with Indonesians in nearby islands.

These illustrations, at least, concern dissidence within a framework of relatively well-defined borders. But in a

---

in the pre-European period was more commonly concerned with the control of a given commodity trade, trading routes, and the cities and entrepôts which were centers of trade—and thus of income. For the rich history that sentence so brutally passes over, see Cady, *Southeast Asia*, Chaps. 2 to 4, 7 to 8; and Hall, *History of Southeast Asia*, pp. 12–204.

number of cases—as between Cambodia and South Vietnam—the borders are not so generally agreed on. And in other instances, where borders are clearly defined, there are some openly competing claims to the same tract of land. One illustration is the dispute between South Vietnam and Cambodia over the ownership of some tiny islands; another is the Philippines' claim to North Borneo. Yet at least one dispute over territorial "ownership" appears to have been resolved when the World Court awarded the Prah Viharn Temple to Cambodia in 1962. (The temple dispute threatened to enflame even further the relations between Thailand and Cambodia[15]) Finally, there are also some "latent" disputes which can be anticipated but which have not yet erupted into open conflicts among states. These will be touched on, but it is probably best to focus attention on those territorial disputes which have already aggravated international politics in Southeast Asia. . . .

THE MAJOR DIVISIVE FORCES IN SOUTHEAST ASIA

Aside from the war in Vietnam, which now involves forces whose interests go beyond those of the Southeast Asian nations, conflicts in Southeast Asia seem to fall roughly into two categories: those that have roots deep in

[15] For details on that affair, see L. P. Singh, "The Thai-Cambodian Dispute," *Asian Survey,* XI, No. 8 (October, 1962), 23–26.

Reprinted from Bernard K. Gordon, "Regionalism and Instability in Southeast Asia," *Orbis,* X (Summer, 1966), 438–57, by permission of the publisher. *Orbis* is a quarterly journal of world affairs published by the Foreign Policy Research Institute of the University of Pennsylvania.

Asia's history, before the period of European colonialism, and those that stem primarily from much more recent events. The disputes between Cambodia and her neighbors, Thailand and both Vietnams, illustrate the first type: old fears and animosities reinforced by modern events. The argument between the Philippines and Malaysia over the sovereignty of North Borneo is more clearly an illustration of the second type. It reflects no long-standing interest of Filipinos or Malaysians in the affairs of the other, nor is it accompanied by that centuries-old mutual dislike and distrust which exists between Cambodians and Vietnamese (or Thais). In contrast, the controversy between Indonesia and Malaysia is a combination of both types. It is modern, in terms of the sources of Indonesia's ideological attitude toward Malaysia, and very old too, because of some historical relationships among the territories that make up Indonesia and Malaysia today.

Indonesia and Malaysia: Temporary Quarrel? One of the most promising recent developments in Southeast Asia is the decision of Indonesia's new leaders, which became apparent soon after the eclipse of President Sukarno, to call off the "confrontation" with Malaysia. By the early summer of 1966 the new government in Djakarta was seeking actively to terminate this conflict, which had led to small-scale guerrilla actions in Borneo and Malaya. Finally, after several months of searching for a mutually face-saving accommodation, the two parties brought confrontation to a close in August 1966.

Yet Indonesia's "crush [ganjang] Malaysia" policy, had, since late 1962, caused a serious disturbance in an unstable area. It is important to understand what led to the hostility toward

Malaysia in the first place. Indonesia is, after all, the fifth most populous state in the world, the largest state in the region; any lasting effort at stability or regional cohesion in Southeast Asia must take Indonesia into account.

The view that the policy was essentially Sukarno's has been widely accepted. Thus it has been argued that Indonesia's hostility to Malaysia derived from Sukarno's need to provide circuses rather than bread, and from his "balancing" position between the army and the Indonesian communists. Confrontation, in this view, was a perfect issue on which nationalists, soldiers and communists could readily agree, and just another of Sukarno's "nation-building" methods.

While there are elements of truth in this view, it misses a vital point: Indonesia's attitude toward Malaysia goes much deeper than Sukarno's immediate requirements of the 1962–1965 period. Thus, while Sukarno's successors seek an end to the policy of confrontation, because it is tactically expedient to end it, the attitudes that generated the policy will continue. This is because Indonesian leaders share a number of ideas and attitudes about their nation's role in the region, most of which envisage some sort of Indonesian influence and dominance in Southeast Asia.

Among the most important ingredients of Indonesia's Southeast Asia policy is a body of thought which advocates a "Greater Indonesia." Evidence of this thesis is found as early as 1945 in the statements of Indonesia's nationalist leaders, including Sukarno. Over the objections of Mohammand Hatta[1] and others, two-thirds of the

leaders who proclaimed an independent Indonesia in 1945 believed that their country's territory should include Malaya, all of Borneo, and parts of southern Thailand. Sukarno himself went further when he said:

I have on one occasion in my life dreamt of a pan-Indonesia, which will include not only Malaya and Papua (New Guinea) but also the Philippines.... I myself am convinced that the people of Malaya feel themselves [to be] Indonesians, belonging to Indonesia and as one of us.... Indonesia will not become strong and secure unless the whole Straits of Malacca is in our hands.[2]

Clearly, this sort of thinking can support a crude territorial expansionism—which in Indonesia has been reinforced by other pre-Malaysia attitudes concerning Malaya.

First, Singapore, included in the Malaysia concept, represented to many leading Indonesians a host of negative symbols. To them, this Chinese-run entrepôt, with its banking and processing facilities, bore a large share of the responsibility for the historic and, in their mind, continuing economic "bleeding" of Indonesia. Add to this resentment the bitterness that many Indonesian leaders have felt toward the Malayan government of Tunku Abdul Rahman since 1958–1959, when, according to them, both Malaya and Singapore shielded and assisted Indonesian rebels during the insurrection against the central government. Indeed, events during that period strained Djakarta's diplomatic relations with Kuala Lumpur and reinforced Sukarno's conviction that control of

---

[1] Hatta shared with Sukarno the leadership of Indonesia's independence movement, and served as Indonesia's Vice President until 1956.

[2] "The Territory of the Indonesian State," in *Background to Indonesia's Policy Towards Malaysia* (Kuala Lumpur, 1964), pp. 20–21. This consists of a translation of part of the records of the 1945 meetings which laid the foundations for Japan's grant of independence to Indonesia.

the "whole Straits of Malacca" is a requirement of Indonesian security.

Then, too, there is the curious mixture of contempt and apprehesion with which many Indonesians regard Malaya, and which has contributed to hostility. "Contempt" is perhaps too strong a term, but there is definitely an attitude in Djakarta that Malaysia is an "upstart" as a spokesman for Malay peoples; that Indonesia is culturally superior to Malaya; and that Indonesia is the natural leader of all ethnic Malays. The other side of the coin, a certain Indonesian apprehension about Malaya, derives from the latter's economic prosperity and its relative political stability. This has occasionally led Djakarta to fear that some Indonesians (particularly those on Sumatra) might attempt to emulate their neighbors' example, and apply in Indonesia the free-enterprise model so successful in Malaya's economic development. There has even been concern in Indonesia regarding Sumatran secessionist feelings, which tend toward either independence or association with Malaya.

The final element that contributed to hostility toward Malaya derived from Indonesia's heavily ideologized politics. This was of course most apparent in the last years of Sukarno's "guided democracy." During that period the official Indonesian world view increasingly regarded all nations as divided into two camps: the old established forces and the new emerging forces. Indonesian leaders considered Malaysia to be one of the old established forces, or at least a product of those forces,[3] and frequently asserted that a fundamental tenet of Indonesia's ideology was to work for the dissolution of those

forces. Even General Jani, among the officers slain by communist activists during the night of the attempted coup on September 30, 1965, maintained that Indonesians have an obligation to aid national liberation movements— particularly those along their own borders.[4] As a result of this conviction, Indonesians of many political persuasions were perfectly willing to give both overt and covert support to measures designed to disrupt the government of Malaysia and replace it with one more inclined to the views of Indonesia's leaders. General Nasution, who barely escaped assassination that same night, and disagrees with Sukarno on many other matters, also spoke frequently of the need to destroy Malaysia. Before the confrontation was announced he issued orders that led (as he later disclosed) to the training of "more than 6,000 anti-British, anti-Malaysia rebels in the Northern Borneo territories."[5]

All these factors combined to form an anti-Malaya political base in Indonesia that could support the foreign policy goals of the "Greater Indonesia" thesis. Since "Greater Indonesia" implied Indonesian dominance over the territories slated for Malaysia, and since many Indonesians were already unfriendly to the Kuala Lumpur government that was spearheading the Federation idea, it was not difficult for Indonesian leaders to fashion a "ganjang Malaysia" policy. The opportunity came in December 1962, as a direct result of an abortive revolt in Brunei, which Indonesia may or may not have initiated but certainly supported. The Brunei revolt set back, at least tem-

---

[3] On this point see Donald E. Weatherbee, "Indonsia and Malaysia: Confrontation in Southeast Asia," *Orbis*, Summer, 1962, p. 339.

[4] See Jani's statement reported in the *Washington Post*, February 2, 1963, that his troops were "awaiting the order" to move in support of people in Borneo "struggling for independence."

[5] *New York Times*, September 3, 1963.

porarily, the plans for the Malaysian Federation, and Djakarta responded by dropping any restraint previously shown with regard to its ultimate goals concerning the Malaysia territories. At that point Sukarno launched the confrontation and declared his intention to "ganjang Malaysia."

The thesis that Indonesia's decision was mainly the product of internal forces operating on Sukarno—that "components of the Indonesian ruling group were eager to embrace some new foreign crisis"[6]—must be rejected. Had a "foreign crisis" indeed been required —which some leading authorities doubt[7] —Indonesia had other targets from which to choose. Portuguese Timor, surrounded by Indonesia, would have been an ideal candidate for "liberation," particularly considering the negative image of Portugal in the United Nations and elsewhere. Certainly no important group inside Indonesia and no major foreign power would have strongly opposed a campaign to "liberate" Timor. Indeed, on every conceivable ground a confrontation over Timor, rather than against Malaysia, would have better served Indonesia's "need for a foreign crisis" —if that had been Indonesia's need. But that was not the case, for Timor can be seized at any time, while the

6 Donald Hindley, "Indonesia's Confrontation with Malaysia: A Search for Motives," *Asian Survey,* June, 1964, p. 909.
7 Herbert Feith, weeks before confrontation was launched, wrote that Indonesia's territorial ambitions had been satisfied by the New Guinea settlement, and the army leaders "would almost certainly oppose an agitational campaign" for Timor or Borneo. Finally, he wrote, Indonesia's need for "functional equivalents" to the New Guinea campaign could be met by tackling internal problems. ("Indonesia's Military Hardware," mimeo., 1962, p. 4. A slightly shortened version of this article was published in *Nation* [Sydney], November 3, 1962.)

instability surrounding the Malaysia proposal in 1962 presented an opportunity not to be missed. Indonesia's confrontation decision resulted, not from any alleged internal "need," but from a set of external goals reinforced by the conditions of its internal environment.

Indonesia's leaders expected their opposition to Malaysia would lead with relative ease to important changes in the nature of the proposed new state. Djakarta had two goals. The immediate one no doubt was at least to delay the formation of Malaysia. The second was probably to assure that Malaysia, if it had to come, would be more loosely constructed than the federation then planned. This was not an unreal goal, because the fear of Kuala Lumpur's domination, especially in Sarawak, Singapore and Brunei, was well known (Brunei never did join, while Singapore later left Malaysia). If such a looser Malaysia had been established, its separate parts might then have been attracted into some sort of *confederation* with Indonesia and the Philippines, and that in turn would have provided Indonesia with an opportunity eventually to incorporate all or parts of Malaysia. Singapore would have been the only difficult pill to swallow, but it could have been effectively "sugar-coated" by the other, more clearly "Malay," communities.

But Malaysia, as proposed by London and Kuala Lumpur, proved to be more difficult to undermine than President Sukarno anticipated. Confrontation did not achieve success in delaying significantly, altering the nature of, or "crushing" Malaysia. Indeed, Indonesia herself ran into difficulties during the second half of 1963 in her pursuit of these goals. Sukarno's several efforts to negotiate with Malaysia after mid-1963, as we will see below, strongly suggests that he realized the price of confrontation—the decidedly negative economic and political effects within Indonesia—might be too high. Therefore, he resolved, probably by June 1963, to attempt to end the confrontation.

By that time, however, the policy had developed a dynamism of its own within Indonesia, particularly among Indonesia's communists and their associates. To the Indonesian Communist Party (PKI), confrontation combined many advantages. First it meant that economic stabilization could not be undertaken in Indonesia. Second, it provided a legitimate method for opposing Malaysia, and for fostering national liberation movements in Borneo. Finally, of course, confrontation had once again placed the PKI at the forefront of an Indonesian movement championed by Sukarno.

For these reasons, Sukarno's wish to modify the confrontation was obstructed by its very dynamism, and the efforts he and Subandrio exerted were faltering and in the end unsuccessful. Nevertheless, during 1963 and 1964, they tried on at least three occasions, in Manila, Bangkok and Tokyo, to extricate themselves, and each time Sukarno's dilemma became more clear: how to give in without appearing to. The records of the effort, the Tokyo meetings with the Tunku and the Philippines President, show that Sukarno even seized upon a vague proposal for an Afro-Asian commission to end the conflict.[8] But on each occasion Indonesia insisted upon conditions —for example, prolonging Indonesian guerrilla activities while negotiations were in progress—that were intolerable to Malaysia.

When Sukarno lost power, the effort that he began, to reach a compromise settlement, was resumed, but under far better conditions. With the PKI demolished, and with men in office who are committed to more rational economic measures, the difficulties that Sukarno believed he faced no longer impede the process of ending confrontation. Indeed, the first moves to restore a measure of stability came on the heels of Singapore's separation from Malaysia in 1965, an event caused by reasons internal to Malaysia. Almost immediately, Indonesia offered to resume trade and other ties with Singapore. Soon afterward, Indonesia's new Foreign Minister, Adam Malik, made it clear that he would do more than simply normalize trade with Singapore. He wanted to find some way to hold talks with Malaysian leaders, end the embarrassing confrontation, and direct Indonesia's energies to economic development, which confrontation had helped to sabotage for three years.[9]

But it should be stressed that the end to confrontation at this time is not a "good guys, bad guys" proposition. Indonesia's anti-Malaysia policy was not an invention of Sukarno and Subandrio, which automatically disappears as they leave the scene. Sukarno himself attempted to find an end to confrontation because it brought more liabilities than assets *at the time,* but he would have continued to pursue certain foreign policy goals even had he

[8] For a full discussion on this point and extracts from the Tokyo and other "summit" meetings, see Bernard K. Gordon, *Dimensions of Conflict in Southeast Asia* (Englewood Cliffs, N. J.: Prentice-Hall, Inc., 1966), pp. 98–116, especially the section called "Hypothesis For Sukarno's Tactics."

[9] By May 1966, press stories from Kuala Lumpur confirmed what had been unofficially rumored for some time: that with the aid of Japanese and Thai officials, senior officials of the Indonesian and Malaysian governments had already been in direct contact in order to bring an end to confrontation. *Washington Post,* May 12, 1966.

been able to terminate confrontation. Sukarno's successors are seeking to end confrontation, and will probably succeed because it is expedient, not because they like, more than Sukarno does, today's Malaysian regime. A distaste for and distrust of the whole Malaysia concept will continue, for the genesis of the "crush-Malaysia" campaign lay in Indonesia's objective goals and subjective attitudes. Those goals do not necessarily call for the extension of formal Indonesian sovereignty over adjoining territories. They do imply, however, a dominant Indonesian influence in Malaya, and, in the view of some leading Indonesians, Djakarta's dominance in all of insular Southeast Asia.

With the end of confrontation, those objectives and attitudes will not cease to exist. Should another opportunity arise under circumstances again susceptible to a catalyst (like the Brunei revolt), Indonesia may be expected to resume a foreign policy which seeks to establish regional dominance. . . .

Filipino Adventurism: The Claim to North Borneo. The Philippines have also been involved in a dispute with Malaysia since 1962–1963. This controversy, too, seems now to be coming to an end. But the Philippines-Malaysia dispute differs from Indonesia's confrontation in two important respects. First, it is unlikely to be revived, and secondly, it does appear to have revolved heavily around a single person: former Philippines President Diosdado Macapagal.

The controversy arose because of a Philippine claim to North Borneo, now the Malaysian state of Sabah. While the claim derives from conflicting interpretations of a grant of land made by the Sultan of Sulu in 1878, it had to all intents and purposes lain dormant until the election of President Macapagal in 1961. At about the same time, a group of the Sultan's heirs gave notice that a formal claim to the territory would be presented to Great Britain, which still exercised sovereignty in North Borneo. A well-known Manila attorney, "Nick" Osmeña, represented them, and he reportedly let it be known that his clients would accept compensation in cash for their rights to Sabah. Estimates of the asking price run between $20 and $40 million.

Soon afterward, in early 1962, a series of colorful Manila press stories appeared demanding the "return" of North Borneo to the Philippines. Precisely at this time, when the proposals to establish Malaysia—which would incorporate North Borneo—were being discussed throughout Asia, President Macapagal made a famous declaration. He announced that the Philippines government had succeeded to the Sultan's claim, and was going to press for ownership of North Borneo, or Sabah, as a matter of sovereignty and national security. Ever since, relations between Kuala Lumpur and Manila have been troubled.

The claim itself has met with no success, but there have been several important consequences for international politics in Southeast Asia. First, in order to weaken the proposal for formation of Malaysia, and Malaysia itself once it became a reality, the Philippines entered into a year-long embrace with Indonesia. This step aggravated many leading Filipinos, some of them leaders of Macapagal's own party. When Malaysia was established, Manila refused to recognize the new government and recalled the Philippines Ambassador; this led to a break in diplomatic relations with Kuala Lumpur. These strained relations in turn forced the cessation of all activities in the Association for Southeast Asia (ASA), the group which the Philippines, Malaya and Thailand had set up in 1961 as Southeast Asia's first indigenous effort at practical regional cooperation.

Since that time, there have been a number of efforts to improve Philippines-Malaysia relations,[10] including some while Macapagal was still President, for he must have realized that his anti-Malaysia posture had not received wide support at home. The new President of the Philippines, Ferdinand Marcos, even while he was a leader of Macapagal's party and President of the Senate, became increasingly bitter in his denunciations of Philippines policy during this period. Marcos, former Vice-President Pelaez, and many others felt that Manila's suddenly warm relationship with Indonesia was a particularly foolish move. As a result, it is very likely that with Marcos as President, the Philippines will attempt to restore the previously good relationship with Kuala Lumpur, and it is likely too that ASA activities will be resumed during 1966.[11]

Nevertheless, leading Malaysian officials feel that the Philippines government, during former President Macapagal's term of office, sacrificed those formerly good relations in favor of two charlatans: Sukarno and Osmeña. The Tunku and his associates regarded Manila's efforts to cooperate with Indonesia during 1963–1964 as a cynical attempt to bring pressure on the Borneo claim. This policy of transparent expedience sorely distressed the Tunku, and some Philippines officials were in turn irritated by Malaysia's attitude that the Borneo claim was simply not negotiable. Thus, while ties between the two countries will be resumed soon, it is clear that the dispute over North Borneo eroded a large portion of the mutual trust that had developed between the two governments. It may not be quickly rebuilt.

Thailand and Cambodia: Diplomacy by Recrimination. Unlike the Philippines and Malaysia, Thailand and Cambodia have had relations with each other for centuries, and between them nothing like mutual trust has ever been present. While there are few material issues dividing them today, a legacy of historical enmity embitters their every contact. Cambodia fears, for example, that Thailand still covets at least two Khmer provinces, lands which were in fact "returned" to Thailand by her Japanese allies in World War II.[12] On top of this, Prince Sihanouk of Cambodia has long suspected Thai involvement in attempts to overthrow him. Almost daily he charges that Thailand harbors his enemies and permits an anti-Sihanouk radio station to broadcast from Thailand. This has led him to launch venomous attacks on all Thai leaders;

---

[10] Consular ties were resumed after a year.

[11] ASA completed its first meeting in three years in Kuala Lumpur on April 30, 1966 with recommendations for 29 economic and cultural projects to be undertaken by the revived three-nation association. On August 3, 1966, ASA convened its third meeting of Foreign Ministers, a strong indication that the group is no longer moribund.

[12] On April 1, 1966 a new twist was added when Cambodia's official broadcasting station charged that "As everyone knows, the Bangkok leaders are not content with only coveting Khmer provinces and trying to nibble portions of our territory, they also look hungrily at Laos, Burma and Malaysia. These expansionists, Thais of Southeast Asia, have always tried to expand their country at the expense of...all their neighboring countries."

when Thailand's former Premier, Marshal Sarit, died late in 1963, Sihanouk decreed that Cambodia should begin a period of "national rejoicing." These days the Prince's favorite target is Thailand's Foreign Minister, Thanat Khoman, who generally returns the barbs with the implication that the Prince is no longer sane.

In addition to this personal bitterness, Thai leaders, already anxious about communist gains in Laos and Vietnam, believe that Sihanouk will turn Cambodia over to the communists without a struggle. This is unlikely, for Sihanouk has made his distrust of Asia's communists very clear, yet the relations between the two countries are not improved by their mutual public recriminations and threats. For example, General Praphat, nominally second in command in Thailand, but in the view of many the real power in the country, has declared that "we must...put an end to the most vile acts of Sihanouk...."[13]

Against this background it is difficult to envisage any significant improvement in Cambodian-Thai relations—especially under their present leaderships. It is true that Cambodia has participated, under UN auspices, in the Mekong River project, but it is also true that Cambodia has steadfastly declined to participate in other, perhaps more immediately important efforts at cooperation in the region. She did not, for example, join ASA, and her bitter relationship with Thailand may inhibit Sihanouk from participating in other practical cooperative undertakings. Part of his reason may indeed be his desire to avoid too close a connection with Western-associated states like the Philippines and Malaysia, for fear of alienating Peking, but some

[13] From a press conference statement of Praphat, reported by the Cambodian government on March 20, 1964.

part of his thinking will continue to derive from the historic Cambodian fears of Thailand.[14]. . .

CAMBODIA AND VIETNAM: BOUNDARY DISPUTES

Cambodia's fear of Thailand today centers on Thai irredentism and the "lost" provinces, but its fear of Vietnam has a firmer basis: the possibility of outright absorption by Vietnamese imperialism. Thus, although Cambodian leaders distrust Thailand, their animosity toward the Vietnamese appears to be far deeper and more widespread.[15] For one thing, Cambodians

[14] For a full discussion see Bernard K. Gordon, "Cambodia: Where Foreign Policy Counts," *Asian Survey,* September, 1965.

[15] Attitudes toward the Thai seem ambivalent, and it was consistent with the practice of earlier Cambodian kings that Prince Sihanouk took up brief residence in Bangkok in 1953, as part of his preindependence campaign to embarrass France. There was also upset in Bangkok, "where the arrival of a monarch whose ancestors had been vassals of the Siamese Crown caused Marshal Phibul's government some embarrassment." Donald Lancaster, *The Emancipation of French Indochina* (London: Oxford University Press, 1961), p. 274. This visit, it should be pointed out, has never been forgotten by Sihanouk nor forgiven, for he feels that he was not given proper treatment in Bangkok. One account states that the Thai government, surprised by his unannounced arrival with a company of thirty-four others, "admitted him as a political refugee and lodged him in Bangkok's most luxurious hotel. But it refused to let him head a government-in-exile or to use Thailand as his intermediary for presenting Cambodia's case to the United Nations." Virginia Thompson and Richard Adloff, *Minority Problems in Southeast Asia* (Stanford, Calif.: Stanford University Press, 1955), p. 189.

Reprinted from Bernard K. Gordon, *The Dimensions of Conflict in Southeast Asia* (Englewood Cliffs, N. J.: Prentice-Hall, Inc., ©1966) pp. 46–48, 67.

have an intimate knowledge of the energies and skills of the Vietnamese. In Phnom Penh alone, Vietnamese now account for 28 per cent of the city's population, and there are at least 350,000 in the country as a whole.[16] These Vietnamese, along with the Chinese inhabitants of Cambodia, dominate the nation's economy, but there is a difference: it was the Vietnamese whom the French employed to administer their Cambodian protectorate. French colonialism in Indochina (Cambodia and Laos in particular) involved relatively few Frenchmen—in 1937 there were only about 4000 French officials and 11,000 French military personnel in all of Indochina.[17] The size of the territories and the almost total absence of trained Cambodians meant that the administration had to be entrusted to someone else. In Laos and Cambodia, it was entrusted to the Vietnamese. They ran the government offices, while the Chinese infiltrated the economic sphere:

Thus, whereas Vietnamese were employed as clerks in the French-staffed civil service

[16] Charles A. Fisher, *Southeast Asia: A Social, Economic and Political Geography* (London: Methuen & Co., Ltd., 1964), p. 570. Thompson and Adloff, *op. cit.,* p. 174, state that in 1944 there were about 250,000 Vietnamese in Cambodia. This would seem to indicate that, even after World War II, and allowing for statistical inaccuracies, the movement of Vietnamese into Cambodia under French auspices probably continued. The Khmers, in their own capital city, are a distinct minority; for, in addition to the Vietnamese population of 28 per cent, the Chinese account for another 30 per cent of the city's total.

[17] Lancaster, *Emancipation,* p. 63, fn. 11. Professor Bernard Fall, in conversations with this author, has reported that in 1925 there were (excluding French schoolteachers) only about 1000 French civil servants in all of French Indochina. These figures are consistent with the information provided by Thompson and Adleff, *op. cit.,* p. 172, who report that there were just 506 French officials before World War II.

and in French business houses, ... the local Chinese community...profited from the Cambodian distaste for commerce and lack of business acumen to engage in economic activities on an extensive scale....[18]

Whenever a Khmer came into contact with government power, it was usually a Vietnamese face he saw; the thousands of Vietnamese minor officials were visible evidence of Cambodia's subjection to foreign rule. This fact, coupled with the Cambodians' knowledge of Vietnam's expansionist tendencies in the past (which resulted in its acquisition of Cochin-China), has contributed to their widespread animosity toward Vietnam and the Vietnamese. Thus most observers conclude that Cambodians, although they do not trust the culturally similar Thais, generally harbor a much deeper hatred and fear of the Vietnamese.

Beyond these historic enmities, there have arisen many more problems which have intensified Cambodian-Vietnamese tensions since independence. Of these, the territorial disputes are only the most obvious....

The essential characteristic of Cambodia's foreign policy, therefore, is its negative quality, and its fundamental source is Cambodia's uncertainty about its continued existence. Thus the problems in which Cambodia is involved and which Sihanouk chooses to emphasize, whether they concern ethnic irredentism or border disputes, are absolutely different in nature from the seemingly similar problems facing other states in Southeast Asia.

The Philippines' claim to Sabah, for instance, has almost no relation to its national existence. In the foreign policies it adopts—whether disruptive or conciliatory—it can reasonably afford even to make mistakes, for few (if any)

[18] *Ibid.,* p. 70.

of these foreign policies are central or basic to its continued existence.[19]

Cambodia, however, can afford few real mistakes in foreign policy. Although there is no significant internal dissension, the fact that the continued existence of the state itself cannot yet

be taken for granted sheds new light on the seemingly erratic and disconnected moves that Cambodian leaders make in foreign affairs. For some years to come, Cambodia cannot be expected to participate in actions that would seem to "stabilize" the environment in Southeast Asia, such as attempts at regional cooperation. As long as the basic condition of Asia's international politics is instability, Cambodia must retain her capacity to benefit from that instability.

[19] This is well understood by Philippine leaders. As Vice-President Pelaez (himself engaged at the time in a preconvention contest for the presidential nomination) remarked to the author in October 1964: "No election in this country was ever won or lost on any foreign-policy issue."

SUGGESTIONS FOR FURTHER READING

West Europe

Aron, Raymond, "Is the European Idea Dying?" *Atlantic Community Quarterly,* V (Spring, 1967), 37–47.

Calleo, David P., *Europe's Future: The Grand Alternatives* (New York: Horizon Press, 1965).

Clark, W. Hartley, *The Politics of the Common Market* (Englewood Cliffs, N.J.: Prentice Hall, Inc., 1967).

Deutsch, Karl W., Lewis J. Edinger, Roy C. Macridis, and Richard L. Merritt, *France, Germany, and the Western Alliance: A Study of Elite Attitudes on European Integration and World Politics* (New York: Charles Scribner's Sons, 1967).

Haas, Ernst B., *The Uniting of Europe* (Stanford, Calif.: Stanford University Press, 1958).

Heathcote, Nina, "The Crisis of European Supranationality," *Journal of Common Market Studies,* V (December, 1966), 140–71.

Lindberg, Leon N., "Integration as a Source of Stress on the European Community System," *International Organization,* XX (Spring, 1966).

————, *The Political Dynamics of European Economic Integration* (Stanford, Calif.: Stanford University Press, 1963).

Liska, George, *Europe Ascendent* (Baltimore, Md.: Johns Hopkins University Press, 1964).

Pickles, Dorothy, *The Uneasy Entente* (New York: Oxford University Press, Inc., 1966).

Serfaty, Simon, *France, de Gaulle and Europe* (Baltimore: Johns Hopkins University Press, 1968).

Willis, F. Roy, *France, Germany, and the New Europe: 1945–67* (Stanford, Calif.: Stanford University Press, 1968).

Latin America

Alexander, R. J., *Today's Latin America* (Garden City, N.Y.: Anchor Books, Doubleday & Company, Inc., 1962).

Bailey, Norman A., *Latin America in World Politics* (New York: Walter and Co., 1967).

Goldrich, Daniel, "Inter-American Politics: Limited Thoughts on the Unthinkable," *World Poltics,* XVII (October, 1964), 143–57.

Haas, Ernst B., and Phillipe C. Schmitter, "Economics and Differential Patterns of Political Integration: Projections about Unity in Latin America," *International Organization,* XVIII (Autumn, 1964), 705–37.

Huelin, David, "Economic Integration in Latin America," *International Affairs,* XI (July, 1964), 430–40.

Lieuwen, Edwin, *Generals vs. Presidents: Neo-Militarism in Latin America* (New York: Frederick A. Praeger, Inc., 1965).

Maier, Joseph, and Richard W. Weatherhead, eds., *Politics of Change in Latin America* (New York: Frederick A. Praeger, Inc., 1964).

Nehemkis, Peter, *Latin America: Myth and Reality* (New York: Alfred A. Knopf, Inc., 1964).

Snow, Peter B., *Government and Politics in Latin America: A Reader* (New York: Holt, Rinehart & Winston, Inc., 1967).

Szulc, Tad, *The Winds of Revolution: Latin America Today and Tomorrow* (New York: Frederick A. Praeger, Inc., 1963).

Tannenbaum, Frank, *Ten Keys to Latin America* (New York: Alfred A. Knopf, Inc., 1962).

Tomasek, Robert D., ed., *Latin American Politics* (Garden City, N.Y.: Doubleday & Company, Inc., 1966).

The Middle East

Berger, Morroe, *The Arab World Today* (Garden City, N.Y.: Doubleday & Company, Inc., 1962).

Binder, Leonard, "The Middle East as a Subordinate International System," *World Politics,* X (April, 1958), 408–29.

———, *The Middle East Crisis: Background and Issues* (Chicago: The University of Chicago Center for Policy Study, 1967).

Hurewitz, J. C., "Regional and International Politics in the Middle East," in *The United States in the Middle East,* ed. G. Stevens (Englewood Cliffs, N.J.: Prentice-Hall, Inc., 1964).

Kanovsky, E., "Arab Economic Unity," *The Middle East Journal,* XXI (Spring, 1967).

Kerr, Malcolm, *The Arab Cold War: 1958–1967: A Study of Ideology in Politics* 2d. ed., rev. New York: Oxford University Press, Inc., 1967).

———, " Coming to Terms with Nasser': Attempts and Failures," *International Affairs,* XLIII (January, 1967), 65–85.

Lenczowski, George, "Radical Regimes in Egypt, Syria, and Iraq: Some Comparative Observations on Ideologies and Practices," *The Journal of Politics,* XXVIII (February, 1966), 29–57.

Rivlin, Benjamin, and Joseph S. Szyliowicy, eds., *The Contemporary Middle East: Tradition and Innovation* (New York: Random House, Inc., 1965).

West Africa

Grundy, Kenneth W., "Political Power and Economic Theory in 'Radical' West Africa," *Orbis,* VIII (Summer, 1964), 405–24.

Hargreaves, John P., *West Africa: The Former French States* (Englewood Cliffs, N.J.: Prentice-Hall, Inc., 1967).

Hodgkin, Thomas, "The New West Africa State System," *University of Toronto Quarterly,* XXXI (October, 1961), 74–82.

Rodney, William, "The Entente States of West Africa," *International Journal,* XXI (Winter, 1965–66), 1–13.

Senghor, Leopold S., "West Africa in Evolution," *Foreign Affairs,* XXXIX (January,1961).

Welch, Claude E., Jr., *Dream of Unity: Pan-Africanism and Political Unification in West Africa* (Ithaca, N.Y.: Cornell University Press, 1966).

Zartman, I. William, *International Relations in the New Africa* (Englewood Cliffs, N.J.: Prentice-Hall, Inc., 1966).

Zolberg, Aristide, "French-Speaking West Africa," *Current History*, XXXXV (December, 1963).

Southeast Asia

Bone, Robert C., *Contemporary Southeast Asia* (New York: Random House, Inc., 1962).

Brackman, Arnold, *Southeast Asia's Second Front* (New York: Frederick A. Praeger, Inc., 1966).

Brecher, Michael, *The New States of Asia: A Political Analysis* (New York: Oxford University Press, Inc., 1963).

Buchanan, Keith, *The Southeast Asian World* (London: G. Bell & Sons, Ltd., 1967).

Butwell, R., "Malaysia and the Impact on the Internatinoal Relations of S.E. Asia," *Asian Survey*, IV (July, 1964), 940–46.

Crozier, Brian, *South-East Asia in Turmoil* (Baltimore: Penguin Books, Inc., 1965).

Gordon, Bernard K., *The Dimensions of Conflict in Southeast Asia* (Englewood Cliffs, N.J.: Pretnice-Hall, Inc., 1966).

Hunter, Guy, *South-East Asia: Race, Culture, and Nation* (New York: Oxford University Press, Inc., 1966).

Pauker, Guy, "Political Doctrines and Practical Politics in Southeast Asia," *Pacific Affairs*, XXXV (Spring, 1962), 3–10.

Vanderbosch, Amry and Richard Butwell, *The Changing Face of Southeast Asia* (Lexington: University of Kentucky Press, 1966).

part two

THE
PERIPHERAL
SECTOR

4

COMPARISONS

We have defined the peripheral sector as including all those states within a subordinate system which are alienated from the core in some degree by social, political, economic, and/or organizational factors but which nevertheless play a role in the politics of the subordinate system. In our discussion of the peripheral sectors of West Europe, Latin America, West Africa, the Middle East, and Southeast Asia we shall pursue three major themes: (1) the degree of alienation from the core sector; (2) the degree of non-cohesiveness within the peripheral sector; and (3) the typical orientation of peripheral states in international relations outside their own region. These three themes will be pursued by the systematic discussion of our four pattern variables: cohesion, communication, power, and the structure of relations. It is with reference to the first of these themes, i.e., the degree of alienation from the core, that we shall also be noting a further phenomenon: namely, the possession by a peripheral state of the potentiality of belonging to the core of its region. A state usually possesses this potentiality when only a single factor is the cause of its alienation—the probability being that, if this factor changed, relationships would also be altered. Thus, we shall have to be concerned not only with alienation between the core and periphery, but with linkages between the two, as well.[1]

COHESION

It is obvious that cohesion is the most strategic pattern variable in our present context, both in terms of alienation from the core and in terms of the lack of cohesiveness of the peripheral sectors. We shall pursue these two themes under the four rubrics of social, economic, political, and organizational cohesion.

SOCIAL COHESION

As was our *modus operandi* in Chapter 2, we have ordered our analysis of social cohesion in terms of the decreasing cohesion of the five peripheries under discussion: West Europe, Latin America, West Africa, the Middle East, and Southeast Asia.

The West European Periphery[2]

The West European periphery is distinctive both for its inner cohesiveness and its overlapping linkages to the core. Within the periphery itself, as we suggested in Chapter 1, there is a broad division between the North and the South. The North is more industrialized and more democratic. Socially, the North is generally Germanic, Nordic, or Anglo-Saxon, and predominantly Protestant (with the exception of Catholic Ireland and Austria, and of Switzerland, which contains a slight Protestant majority). The Southern periphery is socially less cohesive, less developed economically, and contains far fewer democratic regimes. Spain and Portugal are, of course, Catholic and Latin in orientation; Malta is also largely Roman Catholic. The Greeks and the Greek Cypriots are Orthodox, while the Turks and the Turkish Cypriots are Muslim.

This loose division between North and South within the periphery is somewhat offset by the core itself. Both the North and South have close links to the various parts of the core. The Northern states relate, in terms of social cohesion especially, to West Germany and the Low Countries, while the Southern Catholic countries have close ties with France and

---

1 Most of the analysis in this chapter is drawn from Tables 4-1, 4-2, and from the sources indicated thereon. Tables for Chapter 4 appear in the Appendix to this volume.

2 The West European periphery consists of two groupings. In Northern Europe are Great Britain, Ireland, Switzerland, Austria, Iceland, Denmark, Sweden, and Norway. In Southern Europe are Greece, Cyprus, Malta, Spain, and Portugal. Finland, in the North, and Turkey, in the South, are borderline peripheral states and as such are not included on the tables.

Italy. Many countries in the periphery have socially cohesive bonds with most of the core (particularly Austria and Switzerland). The core, then, serves as a kind of unifying link between the various parts of West Europe. Even within the periphery, however, there are a variety of interconnections. Between the two major international organizations in the periphery, the Nordic Council and EFTA[3], there is only one nation—EFTA's Portugal—which is located in the Southern periphery. Nevertheless, traditional British interest in the Mediterranean states (as well as in Portugal) provides historic ties between the two sections of the periphery. Our analysis of economic cohesion will further illustrate this point. Accordingly, as might be expected in a subordinate system whose core is identified by reference to organizational cohesion, relationships in West Europe are varied and diverse, and often bypass patterns established by social cohesion.

The Latin American Periphery[4]

The alienation of the Latin American periphery from the core sector is well expressed in ethnic, linguistic, religious, and historical factors. It is striking that Cuba, a member of the Latin American peripheral sector because of the ideology of its regime, is the only state among all of the peripheral sectors we are considering which is linked in all these ways to the core sector. But even Cuba shares few of these factors with the remaining members of the Latin American peripheral sector. We consider Cuba as being potentially part of the core.

In general, the pre-colonial indigenous populations of the Latin American peripheral states were replaced by slaves from Africa, and they differ markedly from the Indian and Spanish ethnicity of the core. Also, these states tend to be predominantly Protestant rather than Catholic. In addition, all these states, except Cuba and Haiti, had a colonial experience which was largely under Britain rather than Spain or France (in the case of Haiti).[5]

In most regions it is typical to find only one, or at most two, pattern variables which either link the peripheral sector to the core or promote the cohesiveness of the periphery. Indeed, in a manner perhaps similar to the thus far unsuccessful Common Market in East Africa, the cohesiveness

[3] The Nordic Council consists of Denmark, Finland, Iceland, Norway, and Sweden. EFTA consists of Norway, Denmark, Sweden, Britain, Austria, Switzerland, and Portugal; Finland is an Associate Member.

[4] The Latin American periphery consists of Barbados, Guyana, Jamaica, Trinidad and Tobago, Haiti, and Cuba.

[5] For an excellent discussion of the abortive West Indies Federation that includes a general discussion of these problems, see Amitai Etzioni, "A Union That Failed: The Federation of the West Indies (1958–1962)" in the volume by the same author, *Political Unification: A Comparative Study of Leaders and Forces* (New York: Holt, Rinehart and Winston, 1965), pp. 138–83.

of the Anglophonic periphery in Latin America has been due to pressure from colonial powers rather than to internal pressure. In both cases the British provide the major impetus, except of course that the East African movement is rooted in the core and forms one of the central foci of the subordinate system, while in the West Indies the British influence lies in the periphery and is far less important to the region as a whole.[6]

The West African Periphery[7]

The West African periphery has a multitude of irredentist ethnic ties which link it to the core (a result of artificial colonial boundaries having divided tribal groupings), but only a few have had any real or potential political implications (e.g., the Hausa of Nigeria in Niger, the Assinis of Ghana in the Ivory Coast). In addition, there are only distant historical memories of the imperial organizations which linked the two sectors. For example, the centralized French colonial administration of the core, and the fact that French was spoken there while English was the language of the periphery, served to separate the two sectors. These circumstances especially promoted the noncohesiveness of the periphery, because the British administration of the West African colonies was never centralized. In the peripheral sector, only the English speech of the elite and, to a lesser extent, Protestant Christianity serve to promote its cohesiveness and offset a multitude of ethnic and linguistic groupings. Nevertheless, such is the degree of non-cohesiveness of the peripheries that the common use of English is enough to cause us to rank this periphery only below West Europe and Anglophonic Latin America in cohesiveness.

The Middle Eastern Periphery[8]

In the Middle East, the peripheral sector is linked to the core mainly through the prevalence of the religion of Islam in Turkey and Iran—even though in Iran, an almost completely Shiite (unorthodox) country, there

6 See Joseph S. Nye, Jr., *Pan-Africanism and East African Integration* (Cambridge, Mass.: Harvard University Press, 1965).

7 The West African periphery consists of Nigeria, Liberia, Sierra Leone, Gambia, and Ghana.

8 The Middle East periphery consists of Iran, Israel, and Turkey. As we have already noted, Turkey has immensely strong cohesive ties to the core. Even so, because of its level of power and its structure of relations, some scholars argue that Turkey can be viewed as being in West Europe. Turkey shares this ambivalence of subordinate system identification with Finland, Afghanistan, and, to some extent, Burma, as well as the Anglophonic periphery of Latin America. In this Chapter and in Chapter 6, we will generally treat Turkey as a part of the Middle East periphery, although she will be discussed with reference to West Europe when it is considered appropriate.

are doctrinal differences with the Sunni (orthodox) core. All three of the peripheral countries have common historical ties to the core. None of these factors, however, operates to promote even minimal cohesiveness. Thus it is impossible to speak of ethnic, linguistic, or, as we have just observed, even religious factors of cohesion, and there is a corresponding lack of a common history within the sector. Both Iran and Turkey are heirs to a recent independent and even contentious (Ottoman vs. Persia) relationship, and Israel is a recent phenomenon, though its claims hark back to the ancient past.

The Southeast Asian Peripheries

Burma, the single peripheral state of the *mainland Southeast Asian periphery*, is related to the core of the region by the irredentist minorities of the Shan people (who link it to Laos and Thailand) and the Kachin people (who link it to Thailand), as well as by the common religion of Buddhism. Singapore, the single peripheral state of the *maritime periphery*, is related to the core by reason of its common British colonial experience and its short-lived presence in Malaysia. It is ethnically divided from the Malay core by its majority Chinese population and its Chinese character, despite the existence of minority Chinese populations in Malaysia and Indonesia, and to a lesser extent in the Philippines. Indeed, ethnic factors were paramount in its secession from Malaysia in 1965.

Conclusions

We can note that while a single element of social cohesion, or at most two, serve to link the peripheries to the core (and thus to justify our identification of the five subordinate systems in terms of the common properties of the core and peripheral sectors), in fact these linkages are tenuous—except in the West European periphery—and then they are stronger in the North. There is slightly more social cohesiveness in the peripheral sectors of West Europe, Latin America, and West Africa, and less in the Middle East and Southeast Asia. As we shall soon see, however, this slight degree of social cohesiveness should not be unduly emphasized, because economic and organizational cohesion tend more to bind the periphery to the core than to cement the countries within the periphery.

ECONOMIC COHESION

In our discussion of economic cohesion, we are concerned primarily with trade relations and how they affect the relations between the core and the periphery as well as the cohesiveness of the periphery.[9] We shall frame our discussion in terms of two kinds of data: first, the identification of the major trading partners in either the core or the periphery; and second, the percentage of total trade these relations represent. In general, as we shall see, there is little economic cohesion.

The West European Periphery

Once again, it is the West European peripheral sector which is the most cohesive. An investigation of trade patterns within the peripheral sector gives evidence of a high degree of complementarity, expressed in the central importance of the United Kingdom as a trading partner. When we analyze trade among members of the periphery, only Austria does not have the United Kingdom as her major trading partner. Even when the trade figures are compared with figures for trade with the core countries, the United Kingdom still is the major trading partner of all the peripheral states except Austria, Sweden, and Switzerland. The United Kingdom's chief trading partner in the region, however, is West Germany. The organizational parameters which partially determine these patterns are, of course, EFTA in the periphery and the European Economic Community (EEC) in the core.

The phrase "partially determine" is used advisedly, because Austria, Sweden, and Switzerland are EFTA members, and yet they trade principally with West Germany, while Spain, which is not an EFTA member, has the United Kingdom as a major trading partner. In further illustration of this point (and also in illustration of the alienation between the core and the periphery), the figures for total trade (see Table 4-1) reveal that, of fifteen members of the peripheral sector, only five (Switzerland, Austria, Spain, Greece, and Turkey) trade more with the core than the periphery. Significantly, three of these five are members of the Southern peripheral subgroup which we have already identified in our discussion of social cohesion.

The fact that one-third of the West European periphery has such strong economic ties to the core bears out what we have been observing all along— namely, the uniqueness of the West European subordinate system. The unique characteristic here is the "balance" of economic cohesion within the periphery and between the sectors. The United Kingdom is, moreover, enough of an economic focal point to offset in some degree the North-South division of the periphery which we have just shown to have its economic corollary. That is to say, enough members of the North and South groupings have Britain as a primary trade partner so as to perhaps partially overcome

---

[9] We will discuss the economic cohesiveness of the peripheries in no special order because, as we will discover, with the exception of West Europe they possess no distinctive cohesive quality which sets them apart from one another.

their division. A further unusual feature of the West European periphery is the extent to which a major proportion of its members' total trade is with other members of the subordinate system.

The West African Periphery

Brisk trade within the region is manifestly not the case in the remaining peripheries under discussion. These areas are primary-crop producers.

Thus, in the West African periphery (in January through July, 1966) Nigeria had the largest volume of trade (about $463 millions of exports and $403 millions of imports), and her trade with the core was only about $2.0 millions of exports and $.4 millions of imports. Over 75% of Nigeria's remaining trade was with the developed areas. Her most important West African trade partner, in terms of exports, was another peripheral state, Ghana. Niger, a member of core, was second.[10] Ghana also tends to have over 75% of its trade with the developed areas. Her imports from Africa were $4 millions and her exports close to $7 millions; and her total imports and exports were about $206 and $169 millions, respectively. Consistent with Ghana's position as a peripheral state, Ghana traded more actively with Nigeria than with the core states of Mali and the Upper Volta, although the figures and margin of difference were small.[11] Thus, these three key peripheral states—Nigeria, Ghana, and Sierra Leone—all have more than 75% of their trade with developed countries. Moreover, only Ghana's major African trading partners are in West Africa, and these are in the core sector. Nigeria's primary African trade is outside the West African region; within it, Ghana is her major trading partner. Sierra Leone is very similar to Nigeria in this regard, her major trade being with Nigeria.

The data in Table 2-1 (based on trade figures for all of 1966) reveals that neither the trade within the periphery nor that between the periphery and the core is large enough to promote any cohesiveness. Only Ghana's imports from the core reach 2.5% of her total imports; the remaining countries import less than 1%.

The Middle Eastern Periphery

Like the countries in the West African periphery, Iran, Turkey, and Israel have over 75% of their trade with developed countries. Iran's total exports were around $1196 millions, and her imports were $841.5 millions; of this she exported about $0.5 million each to Israel and Turkey, and imported $6.7 million from Israel, but nothing from Turkey. Iran traded much more with the Middle Eastern core but primarily with the Persian Gulf states.

[10] *Direction of Trade* (I.M.F.), March, 1967, pp. 52–53. It should be noted, however, that Rhodesia was Nigeria's most important African trading partner during this period.

[11] *Ibid.*, November, 1967, p. 29. Figures for Ghana are for portions of 1967.

She exported almost $39 millions to Aden (but imported virtually nothing); almost $10 millions to Kuwait (and imported almost $5 millions), and she sent about $7 millions to Muscat-Oman (and imported less than $3 millions).[12] Iran, in 1966, sent 6% of her exports to the core and received from there only 2%; her total trade with the periphery was less than 0.5% of her totals. Turkey's trade with the other peripheral countries was also small. Out of total exports of $275.5 millions, she sent almost $4 millions to Israel and almost nothing to Iran; she imported over $446 millions, but less than $6 millions from Israel and only $0.2 million from Iran. She traded much more with core sector members, particularly Lebanon and Iraq, to whom she exported over $12 and $2 millions, respectively, and from whom she imported $0.1 and $11.1 millions, respectively. Again, for the whole of 1966, 5% of both imports and exports of Turkey were with the core and only 2% and 1% of her exports and imports, respectively, represented trade with the periphery. Israel's total exports were close to $305 millions, and her imports were $374 millions. Only $5.5 millions were exported to Iran, and only $0.5 million was imported; less than $4 millions went to Turkey and a little more than $1 million of her imports came from that country. She had no trade at all with the core members.[13] It should be noted, however, that Israel has been linked to Iran in an "invisible" manner by the use of third parties to ship Iranian oil to Israel.[14]

Thus it can be seen that only minimal trade relations exist between members of the Middle East periphery and that the most important trade relations of Iran and Turkey are with core members. The effect, of course, is to promote the cohesiveness of the subordinate system as a whole (except for Israel), but trade has little effect upon the cohesiveness of the periphery.

The Latin American Periphery

Cuba, much like Israel, is politically isolated in her subordinate system, and this also affects her economic isolation. She has no trade with other members of the periphery, and her only trading partner in the core is Mexico (insignificant because it involves almost none of her $686 millions of exports and only $3.5 millions of her $865 millions of imports).[15] Of the remaining five states of the periphery, Guyana has practically no trade with the core, though she does 11.5% of her trade with the periphery. Trinidad and Tobago has particularly extensive trade relations with the core (2% of her exports and 38% of her imports), and she also conducts some trade

[12] *Ibid.*, April, 1967, p. 39. Figures for Middle East Periphery are for portions of 1966 and 1967.

[13] *Ibid.*, December, 1967, pp. 67, 35. Figures cover portions of 1967.

[14] This importation is so large that it promises to place Israel in serious competition with the Egyptians for the shipment of oil via proposed pipelines from the Red Sea to Mediterranean ports. *The New York Times*, June 16, 1968.

[15] *Direction of Trade* (I.M.F.), April, 1967, p. 23. Figures are for 1965.

with other periphery members (4% of her exports and 1.5% of her imports). Jamaica trades slightly more in the periphery and Barbados trades equally with both the core and periphery. Haiti's trade with either is practically nonexistent.

Except for Cuba and Haiti, then, the Latin American peripheral countries trade equally among themselves and with the core. Because trade is relatively little altogether, the percentages here are higher than in all the sectors under discussion except West Europe and the special case of maritime Southeast Asia.

The Southeast Asian Periphery

Burma's peripheral status is evidenced in the fact that its largest trading partner is India, followed by Ceylon, and then by the People's Republic of China. Of total exports of $156 millions, she sends almost $37 millions to India, over $16 millions to Ceylon, and almost $14 millions to China; of total imports of $120 millions, she receives from them $5, $1, and $8 millions, respectively. In the Southeast Asian subordinate system, her only important trading partners are Indonesia (exports over $8 millions and imports $1 million) and Singapore (exports $5 millions, imports almost $3 millions), and they are in the maritime and not the mainland area.[16] In 1966, therefore, Burma sent 12.5% of her exports to the maritime area and received 4.5% of her imports from there, and her trade with the mainland core accounted for less than 1% of her exports and of her imports.

Singapore does a far greater percentage of her trade with her own core than with the mainland (32% and 2.1% of her exports, respectively and 23% and 0.6% of her imports). These high trade figures for Singapore can be explained in part by this city-state's former membership in Malaysia, which means that the relationship between the two is developed and complex and includes a comparatively high degree of trade. Moreover, Sukarno had cut off Indonesian trade with Singapore when it joined Malaysia, but the formerly close trade relations between Indonesia and Singapore are now gradually being resumed, further increasing Singapore's trade ties to the core.

Conclusions

Economic factors, then, provide an almost equal linking and cohesive effect within the West European periphery. The same situation obtains, but on a vastly diminished scale, in Latin America. Only linkages between the core and periphery are present in the Middle East and, by necessity, Southeast Asia. Both types of linkages are largely absent in West Africa. Excepting West Europe and maritime Southeast Asia, the percentages which we have

[16] *Ibid.*, August, 1967, p. 13. Figures are for portions of 1966.

been dealing with are diminutive. The overwhelming percentage of the trade of the countries in these regions is characteristically with developed, rather than underdeveloped, areas.

POLITICAL COHESION

The reader will recall that, when we speak of political cohesion, we are concerned with the degree of similarity or difference among the types of regimes. The reconciliation type is prevalent in the *West European periphery* (with the important exceptions of the authoritarian regimes of Portugal, Greece, and Spain). In the other peripheral sectors under discussion, the types of regimes do not either distinguish them from the core nor contribute to the cohesiveness of the periphery. Instead, the very variety of types of regime is symptomatic of the noncohesiveness of the periphery.

The Middle Eastern periphery consists of two reconciliation systems (Israel and Turkey) and one modernizing autocracy (Iran). *In West Africa* there are three military oligarchies (Nigeria, Ghana, and Sierra Leone) and two reconciliation systems (Gambia and Liberia); in *the Latin American periphery* there is the Cuban mobilizational system, the neo-mercantilist dictatorship of Haiti, and the reconciliation systems of Guyana, Jamaica, Trinidad and Tobago, and Barbados. In *the Southeast Asian periphery,* Burma is a military oligarchy and Singapore is a reconciliation system.

It is generally true that a similarity of government becomes politically significant only when other social and economic factors are present. These are not present in the peripheral sectors under discussion, except the West European.

ORGANIZATIONAL COHESION

Here we are concerned with determining to what extent membership in regional or international organizations affects the cohesion of the peripheral sector and its alienation from the core. To begin with, and in keeping with its high degree of cohesiveness, only the West European periphery has an organization which includes most of its members (EFTA). In all other cases, common membership in such organizations is shared with the core. For example, half of the Latin American periphery belongs to the OAS. Cuba has been suspended and Guyana is not a member. States in the West European periphery belong to NATO; members of the West African periphery belong to the Organization of African Unity (OAU), and Greece and Turkey are associate members of the European Common Market. Common organizational membership may not exist at all. For example, in the Middle Eastern periphery, only Iran and Turkey belong to the Central Treaty Organization (CENTO), and in the Southeast Asian periphery, only Singapore belongs to the tenuous Association of Southeast Asian Nations

(ASEAN) grouping founded in August 1967, to which Indonesia, Malaysia, the Philippines, and Thailand also belong.

The partially coterminous nature of the EFTA organization with the West European periphery undoubtedly is a cohesive factor, but its logically alienating effect from the core is perhaps offset by the strength of the economic and social cohesive factors we have already noted. Common membership of states from the core and the periphery in OAU, OAS, NATO, and ASEAN, on the other hand, undoubtedly diminishes the degree of alienation between the sectors. Still, few or no such organizational factors are at work in the Middle East or in mainland Southeast Asia. Thus, organizational cohesion rarely operates within the periphery, although it often helps to mitigate its alienation from the core.

CONCLUSIONS ABOUT COHESION

We can now turn to an over-all view of the linkage between the core and periphery and the noncohesiveness of the periphery.

It is evident that the West European and Latin American peripheries are more strongly linked to the core and have greater cohesion than the others. This is especially true in West Europe, where the ethnic and religious ties within the periphery are progressively reinforced by economic, political, and organizational elements. The Anglophonic states in the Latin American periphery, on the other hand, are socially only weakly linked to the core but are more strongly linked to each other. The Middle Eastern periphery has rather tenuous religious and historical ties linking it to the core, and slightly stronger economic bonds; in contrast, the periphery itself is almost totally noncohesive. The Southeast Asian peripheries which consist of the single states of Burma and Singapore have social and (in Singapore particularly) economic linkages to their respective mainland and maritime cores. The West African periphery is largely devoid of linkages to the core, and possesses little cohesiveness.

COMMUNICATIONS

The general uncohesiveness of the peripheral sector is further revealed in terms of the second pattern variable, communications. Two factors appear to be operative here: first, linguistic differences; and second, the level of technological development. As is perhaps evident by now, *the West European periphery* is something of an exception because, in virtually all categories of communications (personal, mass media, exchange among the elite, and transportation), linguistic differences appear to be overcome by the political and economic pull of the core sector. In another region, *Singapore* still has comparatively close communication links with Malaysia as a result of their now defunct union. In the remaining peripheries there tends to be little communication between core and periphery and among the peripheral states themselves. Cuba is perhaps the only exception in terms of core-periphery relations (e.g., the beaming of propaganda to the core) while, also in the *Latin American periphery,* the ill-fated West Indies Federation indicates the existence of telephone and telegraph linkages. Such linkages are still rudimentary in *the West African periphery,* and practically nonexistent in *Burma.* In the Middle East political factors are paramount in inhibiting communications between Israel and the Arab core.

Technological factors operate particularly in reference to transportation. Again, the situation is much as it is in the core sectors. The most concrete data we have is about roads and rails. The existence of a multitude of such linkages, both between the sectors in West Europe (assisted by widespread ferry services), and within the periphery, sets it dramatically apart from the others under discussion. The only possible exception might be the West European Southern peripheral grouping, where the technological level of such countries as Greece and Spain is more comparable to non-European areas. In the Latin American periphery, water and distance are the chief barriers to increased communications within the sector. In West Africa, the Middle East, and Southeast Asia, it is distance and lack of financial resources that limits communication; in these areas, it is unusual to find more than one, or even one, hard-surfaced road or railroad between two countries.

POWER

Here we shall again examine the manner in which three factors—material resources, military strength, and motivation—determine a hierarchical ordering of states in the peripheral sector. We shall employ our seven-step ranking system—primary, secondary, middle, minor, and regional powers, micro-states, and colonies, and look for the existence or nonexistence of disparate groupings of states in terms of level of power.

THE WEST EUROPEAN PERIPHERY

The hierarchical ordering of the West European states reveals that, as in the core, there is a graduated rather than abrupt distribution of power. There is a single secondary power (the U.K.), four middle powers (Sweden, Spain, Switzerland, and Portugal),[17] three minor powers (Norway, Denmark, and Austria), two regional powers (Greece and Ireland), and three micro-states (Cyprus, Malta, and Iceland). There is, of course, a great difference between the standing and reserve armed forces of Britain (518,300), Sweden (760,000), and Switzerland (520,000), on the one hand, and Denmark's

---

[17] Spain, and especially Portugal, are middle powers because both states continue to possess colonies in Africa and Southeast Asia.

45,000 men, on the other.[18] Still, even Denmark has enough troops and sufficient supporting material power to exercise some diplomatic leverage. In fact, perhaps only Ireland (with a total armed force of only 13,000) and the three micro-states (Cyprus, Malta, and Iceland) possess too small a population and too little strength to be able to exercise diplomatic influence.

THE MIDDLE EASTERN PERIPHERY

The distribution of power in the Middle Eastern periphery is more equal. True, Turkey, with a population of 31.4 millions, and Iran with one of 25.8 millions, seem to dwarf Israel's population of 2.6 millions. In fact, however, as the successive Arab-Israeli conflicts have shown, qualitative and motivational factors—the size of its highly competent mobilized reserve forces, and the percentage of the GNP spent on defense—give Israel power perhaps second only to Turkey's, and greater than Iran's. Such an ordering of states according to power is inherently subjective, but whatever the specific hierarchy, the three states can all be described as minor powers, i.e., states which play a major role in their own subordinate system. This can be said certainly of Israel in its conflict with the Arab core, and of Iran in its continued diplomatic involvement with the core. On the one hand, Iran has provided recent diplomatic support for the Arab states; on the other, she has had periodic situations of tension—particularly with Saudi Arabia, over the power vacuum in the Persian Gulf following British withdrawal, and with Iraq, over alleged Iranian assistance to Iraq's Kurdish insurgents.

THE WEST AFRICAN PERIPHERY

The ranking of the states of the West African periphery reveals the existence of two minor powers (Nigeria and Ghana) and three micro-states (Liberia, Sierra Leone, and Gambia). Although the general level of power in the periphery is low, the disjunctive of power is greater than in the core. Ghana and Nigeria represent the two most powerful states in this region, whereas the other three states are among the weakest in this subordinate system. Nigeria actually has the potential for becoming the paramount power in the area, as is suggested by the difference (in approximate terms) between her 57 million people and Ghana's 8 million, her GNP of $5 billions and Ghana's of nearly $2 billions, and her consumption of 18 million metric tons of energy vis-à-vis Ghana's less than a million. However, the civil war in Nigeria and Ghana's high level of motivation—moderated in the post-Nkrumah period—have served to offset the effect of material differences.

[18] This graduated power is stated in terms of conventional armed forces and the material support for these forces. The U.K.'s nuclear capability of course makes for a very great distance in power between it and the remaining states. See Table 4-2 for a breakdown of West Europe's armed forces without the addition of reserve units.

As far as the other three countries of the region are concerned, Sierra Leone and Liberia represent typical West African micro-states, while the Gambia is the weakest of all West African states. Although the material and military differences between Ghana on the one hand and Sierra Leone and Liberia on the other are minimal in universal terms, in the West African context they are considerable. In general, then, the West African periphery is characterized by a similar low level of power as in the core. The two most powerful states (Ghana and Nigeria) possess, in a sense, potential rather than realized power.

THE SOUTHEAST ASIAN PERIPHERIES

Burma and Singapore—the one withdrawn, the other cosmopolitan—are both regional states. Each, though isolated within the Southeast Asian subordinate system, manages to have a limited degree of influence within the area. In part, this role can be explained by their strategic locations, the interest of intrusive powers in them, the distinctiveness of their respective positions and, in Burma's case, her capacity for influence on the mainland.

THE LATIN AMERICAN PERIPHERY

The disparity in power between Cuba, a minor power, and the other members of the Latin American periphery, (Jamaica, Trinidad and Tobago, Guyana, Barbados, and Haiti), which are micro-states, is immense. In terms of population, Cuba's is 7.6 millions and that of Haiti (which ranks second) is 4.7 millions. Cuba's military forces number about 120,000; Haiti is second with about 5,500, and the others have only miniscule armies.

CONCLUSIONS ON POWER

The distribution of power in the five peripheries under discussion is generally graduated in West Europe and relatively equal in West Africa and the Middle East. Only in the Latin American periphery is there a sharp disjuncture in power (between Cuba and the remaining states). Southeast Asia's peripheries are difficult to characterize because they consist of single states.

When we compare the peripheries with the cores, we note the general equality of power of the two sectors in West Europe, West Africa and the Middle East, and the inequality of power of the two sectors in Latin America and Southeast Asia. The nature of the core is such that, almost by definition, one would not find an instance of a core being dominated by a periphery.

THE STRUCTURE OF RELATIONS

It will be recalled that at the beginning of this chapter we noted three outstanding features of the peripheral sector: (1) it is alienated from the core sector; (2) it is noncohesive; and (3) it is typically oriented outside the region in its international relations. In the present discussion of the fourth pattern variable, the structure of relations, we shall pursue three parallel themes—the nature of the relations between the core and periphery, the relations within the sector, and the sector's relations outside of the region. In doing so, we shall discover that one important result of the periphery's noncohesiveness is the relative lack of importance of relations within the sector and the greater importance of other relations. In our examination of these relationships, we shall have three considerations: the spectrum of relations (how the states are related to one another in terms of cooperation and conflict); the causes of relations (the issues characteristic of the periphery); and the means of relations (how these relations are carried out).

THE WEST EUROPEAN PERIPHERY

The exceptional nature of the West European subordinate system continues to be illustrated in our discussion of its peripheral sector. It is clear that, while there is a low order of conflict (of the stalemated variety) between France and Britain, in general the relations between the core and the periphery ranges from equilibrium to alliance membership (e.g., NATO). The causes of the Anglo-French conflict are Britain's desire to enter the Common Market and France's opposition because of the threat that a powerful Britain would present to France's present hegemonic ambitions in the core. Promoting cooperation, on the other hand, has been the increasingly reduced common awareness of a Soviet military threat to West Europe. The means of dealing with conflict between the sectors have been French diplomacy and "technical" arguments about the poor state of the British economy intended to preclude Britain from Common Market membership. The means of cooperation have included a common military organization (NATO), although France has withdrawn from its military commitments and now participates only politically.

The West European periphery is a major exception in terms of the extent of relations among its member states. This is especially noteworthy because these relations are generally cooperative. To the extent that conflict occurs, it is extremely localized (e.g., the sustained crisis between the U.K. and Spain over Gibraltar, and the more serious sustained crisis over Cyprus, which verges continuously on direct military conflict between Greece and Turkey). The causes of cooperation are largely common economic benefits. The cause of conflict, in the case of Gibraltar, appears to be prestige. The Cyprus case has its immediate roots in the tension between a Greek majority and a Turkish minority population, but Turkish–Greek rivalries are centuries old, dating back to the original Ottoman conquest of the Greek peoples in the fourteenth century, and they were reexpressed in the Turkish–Greek war of 1922. The means of cooperation tend to be organizational, (EFTA and the Nordic Council).[19] The means of conflict in Gibraltar tend to be the cutting off of access between it and the mainland, and general harassment. The means of conflict in Cyprus have been a combination of supplying arms to the respective populations and diplomatic posturing, including the shifting of troops and ships.

The relations of this peripheral sector to other subordinate systems are largely cooperative (in terms of the spectrum of relations) with the U.S., in the face of a perceived Soviet threat to West Europe (the cause of relations). The means of relations are military alliances, expressed organizationally in NATO and in military-base rights in Spain. The special relationship between the United States and Britain (for historical and cultural reasons) should also be noted. In addition, because of its historic role as a colonizer, and particularly because of the continued secondary-power status of Britain, the West European periphery plays a key role in virtually all the subordinate systems of the world.[20]

In conclusion, what is unusual about all the international relationships of the West European periphery, in comparison to the other peripheries that we shall discuss, is the generally low level of conflict and the extensive and cooperative relations within the sector.

THE LATIN AMERICAN PERIPHERY

An examination of the same three sets of relationships in the Latin American periphery reveals a more usual pattern. There is conflict with the core and a low level of relations within the sector, but there are fewer than usual relations with countries in other regions. Cuba is constantly in a sustained crisis, verging toward direct military conflict, with most of the core, the cause of these relations being her messianic brand of socialistic ideology. The means range from propaganda to the landing of armed guerillas. The remainder of the peripheral states exist in either a state of equilibrium with the core or engage in limited cooperation through the OAS, but the major exceptions are the Venezuela-Guyana border dispute, and the underlying hostility between Haiti and the Dominican Republic.

A generally low level of relations of an equilibrium type exists within the sector, especially between Cuba and the remaining states. Among the former British colonies, limited cooperation appears to exist in the aftermath of the externally inspired West Indian Federation which broke up in 1962.

The orientation of relations to states outside the region is clearest in Cuba, whose diplomatic isolation in the Western Hemisphere and ideological

---

[19] For an excellent discussion of the Nordic Council, see Amitai Etzioni, "A Stable Union: The Nordic Associational Web (1953–1964)," in the same author's *Political Unification,* pp. 184–228.

[20] The nature of West European participation in the other four subordinate systems under discussion here is discussed in Chap. 6, The Intrusive System: Comparisons.

commitments has forced it into uneasy alliances with the Soviet Union and the People's Republic of China. The means of this alliance have largely been barter agreements in which Cuban sugar has been exchanged for military and economic aid. The external relations of the remaining states is limited by their small size, their weakness, and their continued dependence upon Britain and the U.S. for aid and security.

THE WEST AFRICAN PERIPHERY

The nature of the West African periphery's relations has been profoundly affected by the 1966 military coups in Ghana and Nigeria, and by the continuing civil war in Nigeria. As to relations with the core, Ghana, before 1966 (under Nkrumah) had pursued such a militant, ideologically inspired foreign policy that it temporarily overcame noncohesive factors and became a member of the core through political union with Guinea (in 1958) and Mali (in 1960). The means of this policy were largely diplomatic, accompanied by some economic assistance from Ghana to Guinea. Since the coups, however, relations between the core and periphery are best described as in equilibrium. The only exceptions to this have been the high degree of economic cooperation along the Senegal River, between tiny Gambia and Senegal, and the recent tension between Ghana and Guinea over Nkrumah's presence in Guinea.

Relations within the sector have changed since the coups. There had been, at times, almost a sustained crisis, characterized by mutual charges of subversion between Nigeria and Ghana; now there is equilibrium. The two countries had had active relations outside the region (e.g., Nigeria played a key role in founding the OAU); these relations have declined. We should also note that American involvement in Nigeria (economic) and Soviet involvement (the supplying of arms to the Fededral government of Nigeria) have coincided with less dependence upon Britain.

In short, the structure of relations in West Africa's periphery is now characterized by a low degree of activity. All three sets of relations (between the sectors, within the sector, and outside the region) can be best described as in equilibrium. It should be noted, however, that with the diplomatic activity which surrounded the civil war in Nigeria (e.g., the recognition by Tanzania, Gabon, Zambia, and Ivory Coast of the Nigerian secessionist regime of Biafra, and attempts in Uganda and by the OAU to negotiate a settlement of the civil way), Nigeria has become unusually involved in external relations.

THE MIDDLE EASTERN PERIPHERY

The Middle Eastern periphery perhaps best typifies peripheral sector relations. There is strong conflict with the core, little by way of relations within the periphery, and pronounced relations outside the subordinate system.

Relations between the core and periphery (which are relatively equally balanced in power) are of course dominated by the continuing sustained crisis and direct military conflict between the Arabs and Israelis. At one point, Iran had been courted by Saudi Arabia and Jordan, as a potential member of a conservative Islamic Congress against the U.A.R.-led Arab radical states. This suggestion of cooperation has been offset by the planned withdrawal of the British presence from the Persian Gulf by 1971, which has increased tension between Saudi Arabia and Iran, and even more between Iraq and Iran, over who is to fill the power vacuum. Turkey's relation to the core is best described as in an equilibrium brought about by its orientation outside the subordinate system. The causes of relations between the sectors are the challenged legitimacy and existence of Israel and the potential power rivalry over control of the Persian Gulf and its oil reserves. The means of relations, in the case of Israel and the Arab states, have been conventional war, retaliatory raids, and incipient guerrilla warfare. Iran and Saudi Arabia have resorted to diplomatic and public statements over the Persian Gulf, but there are indications that a common appreciation of Egyptian interests in the area may force them into cooperation. Iraqi relations with Iran are further confused, however, by border disputes and by differences over the position of the minority Kurds in Iraq.

There has been a low level of relations within the sector taken as a whole, and these can perhaps best be described as in equilibrium, although there has been limited *de facto* economic cooperation between Israel and Iran. In addition, Iran and Turkey have achieved a degree of military cooperation as members of CENTO.

The common membership in CENTO of Iran and Turkey, and Turkey's membership in NATO, are symptomatic of the most outstanding characteristic of Middle Eastern peripheral relationships, namely its orientation outside the subordinate system. Iran and Turkey have been in a cooperative alliance with the U.S. and West Europe, and Israel has been in a more tacit alliance with the U.S.; the Israelis have also been involved in technical assistance programs, especially in sub-Saharan Africa. The cause of these relations has been security: for Iran and Turkey, security against the historic Russian threat; for Israel, against the Arab states and, implicitly, the Soviet Union. The means of relations have been military cooperation and diplomacy, extensive American economic and military assistance to Iran and Turkey (until recently); and extensive American public and private economic aid, as well as some military assistance, to Israel. Until 1967, Israel's relations with France were also very close.

THE SOUTHEAST ASIAN PERIPHERIES

The pursuit of the theme of these relationships is limited in an obvious way, in both the mainland and maritime Southeast Asian peripheries, by the presence of a single state in each. Burma, the single mainland peripheral state, has a stalemated relationship with Thailand, a member of the core. The cause of the conflict is Thai support of the separatist tendencies of the Shan peoples, and the means are largely diplomatic. Relations within the sector do not exist, except perhaps in terms of domestic politics. Relations outside the subordinate system have, until 1967, been typically in equilibrium —in keeping with Burma's neutral foreign policy. Since that date, Burma has been in a sustained crisis with the People's Republic of China caused by Chinese interference in domestic politics. The means of conflict have been diplomacy and the encouragement of insurgency.

Singapore, the member of the maritime periphery, has been independent only since 1965. Little can be said about its relations except to note that its smallness and its diplomatic isolation dictate relationships characterized by cooperation or at least equilibrium. Thus, for example, Singapore still remains linked to Malaysia, which is responsible for its defense and can station troops there.[21] In her relations outside the subordinate system, Singapore has pursued a policy of nonalignment but has been heavily dependent, economically and for security, on a British base which will be removed by the end of 1971.

IMPLICATIONS

We can now evaluate the three themes—relations between the sectors, within the periphery, and with other regions—with which we began this section. In terms of relations with the core, only the West European periphery and the maritime Southeast Asian periphery can be said to be in a cooperative relationship. The West African periphery and part of the Latin American periphery are in a state of equilibrium with their respective cores, Middle Eastern, Latin American, and mainland Southeast Asian peripheries are in varying degrees of conflict with their cores. The causes of these relations vary. In West Europe they are common considerations of security (against the Soviet Union). In maritime Southeast Asia, Singapore's former federation with Malaysia accounts for a still cooperative relationship. Relations with the core in West Africa and part of Latin America are nearly nonexistent. In other parts of Latin America, and in the Middle East, there is conflict over expansionism. Finally, there are irredentist goals in the mainland Southeast Asian core, but we should note that there is a very high degree of stalemate in present Thai-Burmese relations and that Burmese relations with the core as a whole verge on equilibrium.

Relations within the periphery are generally characterized by equilibrium, the only exception being the relatively high degree of cooperation found in West Europe. What is perhaps most remarkable, considering the great lack

[21] Michael Leifer, "Singapore Leaves Malaysia," *World Today,* XXI (September, 1965), 363.

of cohesion in these peripheries, is the universal absence of conflict among them, caused in some degree by the disparate and therefore unconflicting interests of these states. As is often characteristic of an equilibrium, the causes (issues) and the means of relations tend to be muted. In cooperative West Europe the issues tend to be mutual economic advancement (EFTA and the Nordic Council), and the means organizational and diplomatic.

Relations outside the subordinate system are more prevalent. To the extent that they are initiated by the peripheral sector member, they are intended to be cooperative in nature, although, as with the Chinese in Burma, this relationship can change to conflict. The causes tend to be economic or military assistance, sought because of the diplomatic isolation of the state in the noncohesive periphery (e.g., Cuba and Israel). In the West African periphery, relations outside the region are oriented primarily toward the African continent (e.g., Nigeria and the OAU), but occasionally they include appeals to outside powers for assistance. Burma seeks isolation and so does Singapore, but to a lesser extent. The causes of the relations between the West European peripheral sector and external countries have also been economic assistance and security, and the means have been diplomatic, whether multilateral arrangements (e.g., NATO or OECD) or bilateral (as between Spain and the U.S.).

CONCLUSION

In concluding this chapter, we can again return to the manner in which the three themes—alienation from the core, noncohesiveness, and relations outside the subordinate system—are related to and follow from one another.

In terms of alienation from the core, our two extremes were West Europe, with its multiple linking factors of ethnicity, religion, organization, economy, and communication, and West Africa, where we found only slight irredentist ethnic and historical ties. In between the extremes, one could rank the maritime and mainland Southeast Asian peripheries, the Latin American, and the Middle Eastern, in order of increasing alienation from the core. Because of the noncohesiveness of the peripheries, it is extremely difficult to rank them. In Latin America, for example, Cuba is potentially part of the core, but she is alienated by the current structure of relations. The Anglophonic states are not in conflict with the core, but neither are they cohesive with it. In the Middle East, Turkish and Iranian relations with the core are very different from those of Israel. In Southeast Asia, the single-state quality of the periphery makes it easier for contacts to develop with the core, even though the subordinate system as a whole is characterized by lack of cohesiveness. The ties of the West African periphery with the core are weak, but they produce little conflict. The ties of the Middle Eastern periphery to its core are strong, and they produce intense conflicts.

Granting the tenuousness of the linkage of these peripheries to the core, then, it frequently appears to be the case that the linkages are significant enough to account for a greater intensity of relations between the two sectors than within the periphery. This is especially the case in the Middle Eastern periphery, where religious, economic, and historic ties with the core are stronger than with fellow members of the periphery, even for Israel. It is also true, though perforce, in Southeast Asia. In the Latin American periphery, on the other hand, the situation is mixed. Cuba has more in common with the core than with Haiti or with the remaining Anglophonic states. These, unlike most peripheral states, tend to be oriented more toward each other than toward the core, for linguistic, ethnic, religious, and historic reasons. The West African periphery's internal bonds, its cultural and linguistic exposure to Britain, are stronger than its vague ties to the Francophonic core, and both sets of relations can best be described as in equilibrium. The case of West Europe is more difficult to judge in relative terms because (as our analysis of the North and South indicated) these states often have ties to each other, and because the United States and Great Britain also tend to play a unifying role. Nevertheless, the enthusiasm of many of these states for some form of association with the core indicates that in general the relationship between the sectors is more important here.

As the last three examples (the Latin American Anglophonic states, West Europe, and to a lesser extent West Africa) suggest, when peripheral states interact to a higher degree than in other peripheries, they are likely to be united, at least in part, by a common intrusive power. Moreover, in their external relations, the periphery members (especially those which are isolated) often attempt to manipulate the security objectives of the intruding powers toward their own ends. These ends may in fact coincide, as for example in the case of the encouragement of American involvement with Britain against the common Soviet antagonist, or in Iran's and Turkey's membership in CENTO in order to contain their historic Russian enemy. If they do not coincide, they may mix—as, for example, past American support of Israel, with the objective of containing communism, mixed with Israel's own primary concern with the Arab states. The objectives may even be quite different—as in the case of American military assistance to Portugal as a NATO ally, the objective of which is the containment of communism, while Portugal's own major military concern is the pacification of her African colonies of Portuguese Guinea, Angola and Mozambique.

We can conclude, in light of the foregoing, that the peripheral sector's chief characteristic, noncohesiveness and lack of internal relations, is compensated for, in some degree, by stronger bonds with the core and relations with countries in other parts of the world.

5

READINGS

INTRODUCTION

Each of the following articles illustrating the peripheral sector deals, in its own context, with the problems of states isolated and alienated from the focal center of international politics in its own subordinate system. There has been no attempt here to deal with every peripheral country in the five regions. It is indicative of the isolation of peripheral states—even from one another—that there is little scholarly writing dealing with the peripheral sectors as units (unlike the core sectors, which have been widely studied). Therefore the articles presented here focus on the primary problems that highlight the periphery and often distinguish it from the core.

Both alienation from and linkage to the core are in a sense the central subjects of "What Kind of Europe?," a chapter by Miriam Camps in a recent book, *European Unification in the Sixties*. Here Mrs. Camps analyzes Franco-British relations in the light of Gaullist efforts to prevent British entry into the Common Market. She examines the implications of possible British inclusion in the common market—for the future of EEC, for the future of European political union, and for the future of West Europe as a whole. She is more optimistic than Professor Hoffmann concerning the resilience of the integration movement and the flexibility of the nation-state. Mrs. Camps deals primarily with core potential, and she believes that the British will most likely soon be members of the core. She may be correct, and, as we have suggested, members of the West European periphery (e.g., Britain, Denmark, Norway, and Ireland) have the highest core potential of any countries we have discussed. But the reader must judge whether Mrs. Camps's optimism is justified and whether the British have become as "European" as she claims. He must also attempt to assess from her arguments, and from those of Professor Hoffmann earlier, how far European unification would proceed even if the British were admitted to the European Economic Community.

This article also tests the efficacy of our emphasis on economic and organizational cohesion as the criteria for dividing West Europe into its core and peripheral sectors. As Mrs. Camps suggests, the British and other peripheral states have a variety of social and political ties to Europe. In defense matters states such as Norway, Denmark, and Great Britain are closely tied to the core. The Camps piece analyzes these ties, but in the final analysis the reader must judge for himself both concerning the direction which European relations are taking and concerning the relative appropriateness of using the EEC and EFTA as a basis for the current division of Europe into core and peripheral areas.

Kevin Devlin, in his article "The Permanent Revolutionism of Fidel Castro," shows that the Cubans have attempted to become a funnel through which communist thought flows to the Latin American world. His article contributes to our greater comprehension of the complex interplay between the communist movement and Cuba on the one hand and between Cuba and the Latin American core on the other. Devlin demonstrates the role of Cuba in the spectrum of left wing groups in Latin America (communist and noncommunist alike), and he analyzes the present and potential effect of Cuba upon domestic politics within core nations generally.

In contradistinction to the two articles on West Europe, Devlin's article deals with the opposite of core potential. He analyzes the efforts of the Cubans to expand the periphery in Latin America and ultimately, perhaps, to lead the core ideologically. The major West European peripheral states seek to join their core; Cuba seeks to undermine the Latin American core and eventually to alter its nature. Devlin assesses the likelihood of future Cubas, using the Venezuelan and Bolivian experiences as the basis for his discussion. From it the reader can estimate how great a threat to the core Cuba is and how the tensions between the Latin American core and periphery can be described.

As we have seen, one characteristic of peripheral states is their increased relations with states external to their own subordinate system. Devlin deals with the complex position which Cuba has as the Latin American member of the Communist world. The reader should consider Cuba's peculiar role in the Latin American area that results from her Communist and leftist-oriented—but yet independent—policies. This article permits comparison of Cuba's and Britain's relations to their cores and evaluation of the contrasting and fascinating linkages of Cuba to the core that make her a prime example of an estranged peripheral state that nevertheless possesses core potential.

The selections by Camps and Devlin are concerned largely with relations between the core and periphery, while the last three articles in this section deal with the problems of three peripheral countries: Israel in the Middle East, Ghana in West Africa, and Burma in Southeast Asia. Each of these articles deals with the unique problems that these states face—Israel's confrontation with the Arab world, Ghana seeking post-Nkrumah stability, and Burma, at the crossroads of Southeast Asia, pursuing a policy of complete isolation.

Leonard J. Fein investigates the effects upon Israel of its alienation from the Arab core in "Israel and the Arab Nations," from his book, *Israel: Politics and People.* He attempts to show how conflict with the core has become one of the ever present verities of Israeli national life, affecting foreign relations, social and political integration, and the fabric of polity and society alike.

Fein's article displays the factors in Israeli life and in Israel's position in the Middle East that make Israel an almost archetypal peripheral state. As Fein puts it, Israel is in a "peculiar position in a land to which it feels such deep attachment in a region where it feels so very alien." Not only the more obvious elements of the structure of relations but also the more subtle factors of social and political cohesion separating Israel from the Arab core are presented in Fein's essay. How the Israelis have reacted to their unenviable position in the subordinate system of the Middle East and the effects of external hostility on Israeli life are treated. Israel's externally imposed situation contrasts with Britain's only partial alienation from the West European core and with Cuba's self-inflicted estrangement. This article allows the reader to consider again the social, economic, and political factors that have caused the divisions between core and periphery in each of the subordinate systems thus far discussed.

Ghana is a peripheral state in a position different from that of the other peripheral states we have analyzed. As we have seen, the West African core and periphery are loose entities which were molded into their present form by the colonial powers. In Ghana the early leadership of Kwame Nkrumah, which brought primary concentration of Ghana's relations with other states, has, since the 1966 coup, been replaced by a period of domestic orientation. Whereas in Israel the external threat has molded the content of politics within the domestic arena, in Ghana domestic developments have shaped the country's reactions to its neighbors—both those in the periphery and those in the core. While the threat to the Israelis occurs externally and is a unifying factor, in Ghana the "enemy"—personified by Kwame Nkrumah —is an internal, divisive factor. It is interesting to suggest that in the other major West African peripheral state, Nigeria, internal concerns and conflicts are similarly primary; but in Nigeria's case they are presently far more unstable. One of the ironies of the 1960's in the West African periphery is that early contention and pro-Eastern sympathies within Ghana gave way to a more pro-Western and stable stance, while early stability and democracy in Nigeria gave way to civil war and a modicum of Russian and East European influence.

In the light of these conditions in West Africa, the article by Claude E. Welch, Jr., "Ghana: The Politics of Military Withdrawal," stresses internal conditions within its subordinate system. The present moderation of Ghana in West Africa contrasts with Ghana's earlier and more volatile relationship to the rest of the subordinate system as given in Professor Zartman's analysis. More important, perhaps, the article by Professor Welch presents an appropriate opportunity to analyze the dilemmas and frustrations that face a typical developing nation currently and to evaluate the effects of these dilemmas upon regional international politics, especially those within the periphery and between the core and periphery. Thus, Welch's discussion of the new regime's internal dilemmas in both politics and economics should serve as an indication of the types of factors which affect international relations in subordinate systems throughout the developing world.

Of the several peripheral states we have discussed here, Burma occupies a peculiar position on the periphery of South and Southeast Asia and as the neighbor of an intrusive power—China. Ghana has entered a period of increasingly domestically-oriented policy, but as John H. Badgley points out in "Burma's China Crisis: The Choices Ahead," Burma may well be emerging from a period not only of domestic orientation but of neutralism and nonalignment accompanied by extreme isolation as well. Burma's position as a peripheral state is unique. Unlike Britain she has little internal strength of her own on which to depend. Unlike Cuba she does not seek to promote an ideology or to support revolution within the core. Like Israel she faces hostile neighbors, but Burma's problems are caused to a greater degree by domestic turmoil and by geopolitics; no matter what the nature of a Burmese regime or of her neighbor's regimes, the Burmese would likely have to walk a tightrope to maintain some degree of autonomy. Nor does Burma possess either the internal resources or the diplomatic flexibility that circumstances and geography allow Ghana.

Badgley shows us that as a result of these conditions Burmese attention is focused primarily on China rather than on either India or the mainland Southeast Asian states. The Burmese have sought to enhance their security not so much in estrangement as in isolation from that core. Consequently, Badgley's article stresses the fluctuations of Sino-Burmese relations and the dilemmas of the foreign policy alternatives faced by Burma rather than emphasizing the relations of core and periphery.

This article reveals the reasons for Burmese isolation from the core. What gains Burma could achieve from closer association with the other Southeast Asian mainland states, and what threats, if any, they represent to her security are important questions. Professor Badgley explores the variety of alternatives which the Burmese face in international affairs—particularly in light of the crisis in relations with China since 1967.

The framework provided in the previous sections can be applied, as a means of understanding the concrete forms of peripheral relations, to the details of peripheral states in five subordinate systems given by these articles.

The materials of these articles can be considered in terms of the relations of the core with the periphery, of the relations within the periphery, of the relations of members of a periphery with states outside their subordinate system, and of the consequences for domestic politics of a state's being a part of a periphery. In all the immediately following articles the major theme is the causes and effects of the alienation of the particular peripheral state under discussion. The reader should seek to differentiate the types of alienation and the reasons for their existence. In this manner the puzzling aspects of foreign policy and the prospects of peripheral states should be clarified.

WEST EUROPE

Miriam Camps

WHAT KIND OF EUROPE?

What are the prospects for British membership? How will the [European Economic] Community now develop? What kind of "Europe" seems likely in, say, the next decade? These are not questions that can be answered today with any confidence. And a glance back at the number of unforeseen developments affecting the Community that have happened since the beginning of 1963 underlines the folly of making predictions. Nevertheless, the events of the last few years, the interests of the countries involved, and the way attitudes are evolving, both on the Continent and in the United Kingdom, seem to point to a few rather tentative conclusions. . . .

Provided General de Gaulle relinquishes power in the next few years it seems reasonably safe to predict that the Community will survive the backwash of the NATO crisis, that the British interest in Europe will continue to grow, and that the United Kingdom will become a member of the Community—accepting the Treaty of Rome and its long-term political implications—soon after a change of government

Reprinted from Miriam Camps, *European Unification in the Sixties* (New York: McGraw-Hill Book Company, 1966, copyright © 1966 by Council on Foreign Relations, Inc.) pp. 196–235, by permission of the publisher.

in France. If, however, General de Gaulle were to remain in power for the full seven years of his present term of office (or even longer) there might be great temptations to form new patterns. It is possible that the British would become "European" enough in a few years time so that some British initiative and a realignment around the United Kingdom might be a natural development. It is also possible that the veto would endure, that the Community would remain a customs union of the Six, and that the British would become progressively linked to the European market by industrial ties but would not join the EEC. (The analogy of the Canadian relationship with the United States suggests itself, although it can not be pressed very far.) It seems rather more likely, however, that the French veto would, in time, be lifted in the sense that negotiations with the British would be given a green light. However, assuming continuing disagreements on defense, a government headed by General de Gaulle would probably seek to use the expansion of the Community to transform it into a loose economic arrangement shorn of its integrative pressures and its political overtones. . . .

The timing of General de Gaulle's departure from the political scene thus seems likely to be of considerable importance to the way things now develop between the British and the Six. It will also be important to the way things develop internally in the Community. The next section looks at the way the Community of the Six seems likely to develop while General de Gaulle remains in power. It is followed by some speculation about the way things might develop if he were to yield power, even to another Gaullist, some time between, say, 1967 and 1970, and the British were to join the Community soon thereafter.[1]

THE SHORT-TERM OUTLOOK FOR THE COMMUNITY

As long as General de Gaulle remains at the head of the French government it is difficult to see the Six making any significant progress toward common policies in fields not covered by the existing treaties or any very rapid progress toward the kind of economic union—with common, community policies supplanting separate national policies—that seemed in prospect a few years ago.

Although for a time in the early sixties the French seem to have hoped that the Five would accept French views as the basis of a collective European foreign policy, it was never very

[1] It seems reasonably clear that although many aspects of French policy will not change with a change in government in France, any successor government will be rather more "European" in its policies. All the important opposition leaders have made their position plain on this point. Another Gaullist would doubtless pursue the general line laid down by de Gaulle, but no successor is likely to have quite the same exalted view of France as an independent power as General de Gaulle has had or to have quite his imperviousness to domestic pressures and the wishes of his Common Market partners.

probable that the Germans would have felt the *force de frappe* offered them enough protection so that they could take the risk of loosening their ties with the United States. Whatever the dangers in the past, and they were probably quite small, General de Gaulle had gone so far in alienating the Germans —by his flirtation with Moscow and, more deeply, by his reversal of the earlier French policy of treating the Germans as equals—that this possibility had become very remote before General de Gaulle opened his attack on the NATO arrangements early in 1966. General de Gaulle's press conference on February 21, 1966, and the subsequent French moves to withdraw from the NATO structure would seem to have eliminated any possibility of finding common ground among the Six on defense questions while General de Gaulle remains in power. The alternative road to a common view in foreign policy and defense—that General de Gaulle would modify his own views to bring them into line with those of his partners—has also never seemed very likely; it is almost inconceivable today. . . .

If the Community were allowed to develop into an economic union along the lines envisaged by the Treaty of Rome and spelled out in more detail by the Commission in the Action Program and in its subsequent proposals (both those that have been published and those known to be in prospect[2]) national freedom of action on matters affecting foreign policy would become increasingly restricted. Perhaps if France's partners had been willing to

[2] In particular, the Commission's proposals of March 30, 1965, which were the pretext for the crisis, and the plans for a monetary union that the Commission has been working on for some time.

accept General de Gaulle's view of the policies the Europe of the Six should follow on foreign policy and defense the French would not have objected to the development of an economic union along these lines, for then the restraints on national freedom of action would have been far less important. Since the rest of the Six are clearly not prepared to accept French foreign policies as Community policies it seems probable that the French will continue to oppose —as they had started to do even before the crisis—any new commitments which restrict national freedom of action in any important way. All common policies come, of course, in this category. The French may also seek to loosen some of the more restricting commitments they have already undertaken.

The French can also be expected to continue to oppose the transfer of any real power from national authorities to central institutions, since any such transfer restricts the scope of the national authorities and is inconsistent with General de Gaulle's concepts of how relations among states should be organized. The objection to central institutions and the objection to common policies are closely related, but they are logically distinct. It would be possible, although not very easy, to have common policies elaborated by intergovernmental discussion and implemented entirely by national authorities. . . .

In short, as long as General de Gaulle is in power in France, it seems reasonable to expect that French efforts will be directed toward securing the economic benefits of the Common Market at a minimum cost in terms of interference with, or limitation on, national freedom of action. There is, of course, a contradiction here, for it is becoming increasingly clear to everyone —and, not least, to French industry— that many of the economic advantages of the Common Market can be expected to come precisely from the consequences of looking at and treating six (or more) economies as a single economic unit rather than, as General de Gaulle tends to do, as six separate units which have agreed to free trade and to make certain limited agreements of other kinds with one another. However, the whole trend of Gaullist thinking and particularly the crisis in the Community in 1965 make it difficult to believe that General de Gaulle will be prepared to accept any new arrangements which significantly impair the French government's control over the French economy even though such arrangements might, in fact, be very advantageous for France. . . .

"Organized cooperation" on the Gaullist model can, of course, lead to a more integrated European economy, as did the "organized cooperation" encouraged by the OEEC (Organization for European Economic Cooperation). And the existence of cooperation over a wide field obviously makes a later move to common policies easier than it would be if there were no prior experience of working together. The familiarity with each others' problems gained from cooperation in the OEEC, and the warm personal relationships formed during the early days of the OEEC, made the tasks of the Six far easier than they would otherwise have been. There is, however, a difference in kind between a number of governments deciding, on the one hand, to delegate powers to common institutions and to act in common and only in common for certain purposes, and their deciding, on the other hand, that it is to their mutual advantage to free trade and to remove various impediments to movements of manpower and capital, and to encourage research or scientific developments by national fiscal or financial measures. The first type of action is envisaged by the Treaty of Rome and is what makes the Common Market an exciting new experiment; the second type of action is eminently useful, but it is not different in kind from the organized cooperation that the EFTA, the OEEC—OECD, and other traditional intergovernmental organizations have shown themselves well suited to perform.

It is important to be clear about this point, because there is frequently a tendency in "European" circles to assume that any kind of action by the Six countries—particularly if it is formally launched by the Community institutions—is necessarily progress toward the goal of European union. If the goal is eventually reached, organized cooperation on an intergovernmental basis will doubtless have helped. But organized cooperation on a Six-country basis even when promoted by Community institutions does not lead necessarily and inescapably to the goal of European union.

On the assumption that the "Europeans" cannot hope for much more than a holding operation until there is a change of policy in Paris (or a realignment of the European countries pursuing the goal of union) then cooperation, where possible, is useful, both in itself and to lay the groundwork for later, more radical, action. But it should be recognized for what it is, and not seen as evidence of a change of heart on the part of the French government and of a new "post-Luxembourg" willingness to accept the "logic" of the Common Market. It is nothing of the sort. On the contrary, all signs point to continuing French

resistance to the "logic" of the Common Market, that is the built-in propulsion toward an economic-political union. Not unlike the attitude of the British government during the OEEC period and, again, during the free trade negotiations, the French attitude today seems to reflect a willingness to undertake a considerable measure of practical cooperation with her Common Market partners but to draw the line at any action which would effectively transfer the power of decision in matters of any significance to non-French hands or which would create a system with a dynamic of its own that would, over time, inescapably limit French freedom of action.

Despite the similarities between the French position today and the British position in the past, there is, of course, the significant difference that the Gaullists endorse the objective of a distinctively European construction—a power group with a policy of its own. The British position of the 1950s was more logical, for unlike the Gaullist position it was internally consistent in refusing both the limitations on national freedom of action and in questioning the objective of a "European Europe." General de Gaulle's position, in contrast, rests on a fundamental contradiction. But because the Gaullist objective of a "European Europe" has some features in common with the "European" objective, the kind of Six-country cooperation that may still be possible while General de Gaulle remains in power is not necessarily incompatible with European objectives and may, in the long term, assist the process.

Unless he is prepared to take France out of the Common Market, General de Gaulle cannot, of course, completely arrest the integrating process and the gradual encroachment on French independence of action that has already been set in train by the progress of the Common Market to date. The settlement of the crisis seems to show that he has concluded that the disadvantages of that course of action (not least the electoral risks[3]) are likely to be greater than the advantages. However, a government that is determined to throw sand into the gears can do a lot to slow down the *engrenage* in which the "Europeans" put their trust. . . .

The Common Market is now probably irreversible in the sense that it is almost impossible to see the Six re-erecting tariffs and the other barriers to trade that have been torn down since 1958 and returning to their earlier systems of agricultural protection. But it is by no means "irreversible" in the sense in which this word is frequently used by some "Europeans." There is no iron law of "spill over" nor an irresistible internal dynamic that is bound to carry the Six to full economic union and beyond that to some form of political union. Again, recent history is instructive.

Despite the claims made in earlier days, those closest to the scene and those most accustomed to talk of irreversibility were probably rather more doubtful whether the Community would survive the 1965 crisis than were those farther from the scene and less emotionally committed to the thesis that the unification of Europe had be-

[3] *The Observer*, February 20, 1966, reported that the French government had received the results of a secret poll of a sample of 2,500 people investigating why people who had previously voted for de Gaulle had voted against him in the 1965 election. The largest group (more than 40 per cent) was dissatisfied with social programs. But more than a third feared that General de Gaulle was out to destroy the Common Market.

come an inevitable development. But to some extent the two groups were talking about different things. The fear of the "Europeans" was not that the Six would go back to the pre-Community days but, rather, that the Community would be transformed into something looser with less promise of developing eventually into "Europe." This transformation might have occurred either by the Five yielding completely to the French and turning the Community into an intergovernmental organization of a more traditional kind, or by a break between the Five and the French followed by an arrangement on a broader, looser basis between the Five and the EFTA countries. Characteristically, some of the strongest "Europeans" were more alarmed at the prospect of the second than at the prospect of the first. The Community has been "saved" in the sense that neither of these things happened in January 1966, but either of them might still occur.

Even with no new decisions, the interdependence among the Six grows every day simply as the result of the steps already taken. But so, too, does the interdependence of the industrialized countries of the West. It will take something more than the simple departure of General de Gaulle from the scene to ensure that the Common Market becomes, in the end, more than a roundabout route to a Western European customs union or to an Atlantic low-tariff club.

THE LONGER-TERM OUTLOOK

Despite the skeptics and today's unpromising signs, it seems probable that the "something more" that is needed to carry the process of European unification further does exist, and that once

General de Gaulle has left the scene the process will again acquire momentum, provided the change in France is not too delayed. As indicated above, the proviso may well be of crucial importance.

Doubts about the probability, and also the validity, of the development of something that could legitimately be called a European union have been intensified by General de Gaulle's attacks on the Community and the NATO, but they would have arisen in any case, for many of the factors that formerly pushed in this direction no longer exist, or have a greatly diminished force. There is no imminent external threat, no sense of imperative need, no dynamic leader. Many of the strongest "Europeans" are old men. Europe is prosperous. The "German problem" does not exist in the acute form it took in the fifties. The nation-state which in Western Europe, at least, was supposed to be in decline has reasserted itself. "Gaullism" will not disappear with General de Gaulle. The present French government has given a new emphasis to nationalism, but it has probably only accentuated a tendency that was bound to appear in any case as a consequence of prosperity, stability and *détente*. "Gaullism" is, in part, a sport, a phenomenon that depends on the exceptional personality of one man whose return to power in 1958 was an accident of history. But "Gaullism" is also, in part, a reaction to the process of losing sovereignty—both the "planned" loss of sovereignty that has been occurring in the Communities and the "unplanned" loss of sovereignty that has come from the shift in power from the former great powers in Western Europe to the two super-powers.

There are today few signs of the popular enthusiasm, the leadership, the sense of need, that would seem to be required if the European countries were to achieve anything like a federation within, say, the next decade. Nevertheless, the evidence of the resilience and the durability of the European idea is impressive. The differences with the French have led, at times, to near stagnation in the Community, but the Six have shown an ability and a determination to absorb differences of view that on any rational calculation should have destroyed the Community. And three years after the veto the British are far more "European" than they were when membership in the Community seemed imminent.

In the world of the sixties European union is not a necessity but a matter of choice for the governments and the peoples involved. It is probably the best road to the kind of society and the role in the world the key Western European countries seem to want. But it is difficult to make a convincing case that either their economic prosperity or their political freedom depends upon it. It is not surprising, therefore, that the enthusiasm and the emotionalism that characterized the European movement in the early postwar years when many people on the Continent quite genuinely felt that union offered the only hope of restoring an acceptable economic and political system in Europe has disappeared.

Those who talked of "making Europe" and dreamed of a federation in a decade are growing old and somewhat disillusioned. But so, too, are those who dismissed all talk of European union as unreal and Utopian. Both groups are being replaced by a new generation that accepts European unity as a long-term goal and, what is more important, sees nothing very revolutionary or controversial in the fact that it should do so. This matter-of-fact assumption that Western Europe is in the process of uniting, and that the process is both desirable and more or less inevitable, is widespread on the Continent and growing in the United Kingdom. It is not an attitude that leads to rapid or dramatic changes, but it is one that seems likely to sustain a slow but continuing process of unification.

Today the safe prediction for the future is that the Western European countries—i.e., the Six joined in a few years' time by the United Kingdom and some of the other EFTA countries—will become a customs union with an agricultural policy based broadly on the system of the Six. But, for a number of reasons, the process seems unlikely to stop there.

Although it is true that some of the arguments for a European union that appeared most persuasive in the past have lost their force, some of them are still valid and some have assumed new forms. An economic union may not today seem necessary for prosperity, but on both sides of the Channel there is a strong and growing belief that the only road to a technologically advanced economy that is indigenous in character, rather than increasingly controlled by American industry, lies in organizing industries on a European rather than a national basis. Much of the new British interest in Europe stems from this consideration. And much of the new French interest in British membership, which is detectable in some quarters, comes from their recognition that the British have a sophisticated industrial base and spend appreciably more on research and development in industries such as aircraft, electronics, and atomic energy than does any other Western European country.[4] The technological and scientific pressures for "European" action seem likely to grow as the lead the United States already has in these fields continues to lengthen. And European action will mean more than the removal of tariffs.

There are also persuasive reasons arising from the situation in Germany for continuing down the road toward union, although the "German problem" presents itself in rather different terms today than it did in the past. In the fifties the need to put the relationship between Germany and France on a new basis seemed to many people the most compelling reason for trying to build a community within which the old nationalisms could be replaced by a new loyalty. Franco-German relations are not today as warm and harmonious as many people in both countries would like them to be, but a new relationship exists between the two countries and also between Germany and her other neighbors in Western Europe. There is inevitably, if unfortunately, some lingering mistrust of the Germans in Western Europe which shows itself in various ways, perhaps most clearly in the continuing British reluctance really to accept the Germans as equals in the defense field. But the earlier argument that European union was necessary to ensure peaceful relations between Germany and her Western neighbors now has little meaning. And the earlier argument that, for Germany, the road to equality and the end of occupation and discriminatory controls lay through participation in a European union has

[4] In 1962 research and development expenditures, per capita in U.S. dollars, were as follows: Federal Republic, 20.1; France, 23.6; United Kingdom, 35.5; United States, 93.7 (source: *The OECD Observer*, February 1966).

been so overtaken by events that, today, the willingness to treat the Germans as equals has become in the eyes of many continentals the test of whether or not the British have become "good Europeans."

Although these aspects of the question are radically changed, there is still a need to give the Germans an emotional and practical alternative to German reunification, for no acceptable basis for German reunification yet exists. Pressures in the Federal Republic for some progress toward German reunification have always been most apparent when progress toward European unity has been halting and uncertain. It is not surprising that these pressures are conspicuous today. They seem likely to become increasingly important as Germany grows stronger and as a new generation comes to power that has no personal sense of guilt for the Hitler period.[5] For the present, the German government needs the prospect of continuing progress toward a European union if these pressures are to be contained. But, somewhat paradoxically, the Germans also need to feel that the two policies—German reunification and European unification—are complementary and not true alternatives if they are to go much further down the road toward union. Unless an acceptable connection between the two policies is clearly seen and agreed upon, both in the Federal Republic and in the other countries of the Community, the Germans will inevitably be reluctant to give up their own freedom of action.

As discussed further below, the development of the Community (expanded

to include the United Kingdom) may, in the long term, offer a way to an acceptable solution to the problem of German reunification. The path ahead is not very clearly seen today, and any substantial pressure for European unification as the road to German reunification lies in the future. Nevertheless, the desire to play a more important part in the eventual settlement in Central Europe is one of the factors turning thoughts, in the United Kingdom as well as in the Six, to the advantages of collective action. With the appearance of signs of a *détente* between the United States and the Soviet Union following the settlement of the Cuban missiles crisis, the Germans became increasingly alarmed that their future might be settled by some deal between the two superpowers. General de Gaulle's attempt to exploit this fear and to induce the Germans to see in his Europe the road to reunification seems to have failed, but he has brought home the need for agreement among the Western European countries on the question of German reunification, as well as the dangers that lie in the lack of any agreed Western Policy on this central issue.

The desire for a bigger voice in the settlement of this key issue is, of course, only one aspect of the general proposition that only through unity can Europe regain its proper place in the world and exercise the influence that is both its right and its duty. The desire to increase European influence, or power, has always been one of the motives for unity. Today it is by far the most compelling pressure pushing in that direction. It is the connecting thread that links together the economic, political, and military arguments that now seem most persuasive. And it has provided the common ground between

---

[5] For a persuasive British statement of the importance of giving the Germans a "European alternative" to a purely national policy, see Kenneth Younger in *The Listener*, November 25, 1965.

the "Gaullists" and the "Europeans" that has enabled the Community to continue despite the profound differences between the member countries about the methods by which Europe is to unite and about its relationship with the United States.

If, as now seems probable, the British again seek to join the Community they will do so because—whatever Mr. Wilson may say today—they have decided that they can best maximize their power, both economic and political, by acting as a part of a European complex rather than by acting independently, or as a junior partner to the United States, or as an elder sister to the Commonwealth. If the French let the British join the Community it will be because the French have reached similar conclusions about their own role in the world, or, more accurately, because the French have rejected the Gaullist illusion that France can gain the power they want through independence and have returned to the analysis of French interests which led them to take the leadership in promoting the Communities of the Six. Put another way, if the French and British do come together within the Community framework[6] both governments will have decided that their interests lie in creating a workable, cohesive European grouping. The reasons that have led them to this decision will compel them to make the new group an effective one.

Both Britain and France are coming to the end of a long and difficult period of decolonization. Both countries have found it hard to adjust to their diminished roles in the world. Both believe

[6] The qualification "within the Community framework" is important. Obviously what follows would not be true if the French and British governments made it their common cause to transform the EEC into a broad free-trade area.

that they have contributions to make to the world—cultural, intellectual, political, technological, and scientific—that entitle them to an influence that is quite disproportionate to the real influence either, alone, can now exert. Unlike the other countries in Western Europe, they both, rightly or wrongly, think in big power terms. They feel instinctively that what happens elsewhere in the world is their concern and something for which they have a certain responsibility, although in the last few years the French view of their world role has been an eccentric and unhelpful one. And both countries in their hearts believe that the other one is the only European country with which it can fairly be classed.

The attractions of an Anglo-French partnership are so obvious that the temptation will be to give that relationship too high a priority and to repeat on an Anglo-French basis the mistakes General de Gaulle has made by treating the rest of the Five, and particularly the Germans, as a useful chorus which is expected to come in on the refrains, but is not allowed to sing any of the principal parts. The consequences of any such policy, like the consequence of General de Gaulle's policy, would be to strengthen German ties with the United States and to defeat the larger purpose of establishing a European group with an identity of its own. However, if this temptation can be avoided, the underlying strong similarity of interests between the British and the French in having the Community become a group which can exercise effective influence in the world should be a powerful pressure toward union. For only a group that can find its way to common policies and common institutions can use its power effectively.

Although the pressures pushing the Six and the United Kingdom to form some kind of effective union seem likely to prove stronger in the long term than the pulls in other directions —and the inertia—that today threaten the process, the "building of Europe" seems likely to be a slower and much more pragmatic process than it has been in the past. At times the pace can probably be deliberately forced by careful contriving by the institutions at the center. But one of the lessons of the last fifteen years would seem to be that it is usually counterproductive to try to take a very big leap forward. The EDC failed, the ambitious original conception of Euratom was watered down in the negotiations (and further watered down by the French after it was established), the Commission's attempt [in 1965] to manipulate the governments into taking a giant step forward would probably have failed even had the French played by the rules of the treaty and the conventions of the Community.

A strong and imaginative Commission can use conflicting pressures to push governments to opt for a Community solution and to speed up a process that has been started, as it did in twice accelerating the pace of tariff adjustments and in pushing through the common agricultural policy. But the kind of integration by stealth that M. Monnet was able to accomplish in the halcyon days of the Schuman Plan is unlikely again to become practical politics. To an even greater extent than was true in the past, the future development of the Community seems likely to be a slow, organic one, with integration occurring partly as a consequence of past actions, partly as the product of new policy decisions which have been undertaken quite deliberately in full awareness of their consequences.

There is clearly a spill-over effect at work in the Community. But, as the Six have demonstrated, the spill-over process is much more effective when there is acceptance of the principle of moving toward further integration than it is when there is not. If spill-over were irresistible, the Six would now have a common commercial policy and a common monetary policy. Governments now know about the virtues, and the dangers, of *engrenage*. And progress in the future is not likely to result from decisions taken half blindly without adequate thought about the consequences. The strongest reason for thinking that something like a federation may one day be formed in Western Europe is not because the pressures of a customs union will force the governments irresistibly to federate, although a customs union undoubtedly sets up pressures pushing in that direction, but because it seems probable that the key governments will decide that a federation is an acceptable long-term goal. They are unlikely to give progress toward that goal a high priority, because there is unlikely to be any great need to do so. But once it is accepted that a federation, however loose or far off, is at the end of the road down which they are traveling it will become easier for governments to settle many of the problems that arise by going farther down the road toward union than by taking separate national action. The more clearly the eventual goal is accepted the more the process of integration tends to feed on itself.

The Community is today a mixed system, a construction that is *sui generis*, which cannot be equated with either a federal state or an international organization in the conventional sense, although it has some of the attributes of each. It promises to remain a mixed system for a long time, with the members acting collectively for some purposes, individually for others with the amount of coordination of policy and of common action depending on the extent to which the interests of the member countries coincide and with the advantages to be gained from common action.

Although the "Community method," the dialogue between the Council of Ministers (representing the governments and the separate national interests) and the independent Commission (representing the common interest) survived the Gaullist attack in 1965, the effect of the crisis—both the crisis itself and the settlement early in 1966—was to tip the balance of power in the Community away from the institutions at the center and toward the governments. This may well be a temporary shift. But no very radical advance toward an institutional system that is more "supranational" than the Community system was when it was working best (i.e., 1959–62) seems probable for quite a number of years. Until there is a change of attitude in Paris the problem will continue to be to preserve a system that makes it possible to give any effective expression to the common interest.

If sometime between, say, 1968 and 1972 the British join the Community, they will be followed by a number of other countries—Denmark, certainly, and probably Norway and Ireland. The Community institutions are already cumbersome and slow moving, and simply adding new members, however "European-minded" they may then be, will add to the difficulties. Perhaps the occasion can be used for some streamlining and, hopefully, for more delegation of power to the Commission. The Council of Ministers has always been far too involved in details, and, following the crisis and the Luxembourg

settlement, the foreign ministers seem likely to become even more burdened with the minutiae of Community decisions. But, on the assumption that it is the present British government that finally takes the United Kingdom "into Europe," it is stretching credibility too far to believe that Mr. Wilson's known distaste for a strong Commission will change overnight into acceptance of the need for greater delegation of authority to the Commission if only to prevent the machine from seizing up.

Following British entry and a change of attitude in Paris, some improvements in the system will doubtless be made. But broadly the Community method as it has evolved during the last fifteen years seems likely to persist for some time, perhaps for another decade. With all its imperfections it is an institutional innovation that has "worked," albeit slowly. And it has now acquired a kind of sanctity simply because it has been under attack, in the early days from the British, more recently and with greater vigor from the Gaullists. Tampering with the system, even in the name of efficiency, has become suspect; it is likely to remain so until the new members have been absorbed and confidence in France has been restored....

One of the unfortunate by-products of the fact that the "Europeans" have been on the defensive for so long, and also of the stagnation that the Community has suffered during the last year or two, is that there has been a sterility in "European" thought and a tendency to continue to think in the patterns of the fifties. At a time when the "Europeans" have been trying above all to save and to protect what they have built, they have, naturally enough, resisted change and experimentation for fear that any tampering with their construction would open the path to its complete destruction. Had the "Europeans" felt confident of success they would have dared to experiment, and had the Community been developing rapidly the simple fact of having to deal with new problems would have stimulated new thoughts. Inevitably there has been a tendency to look nostalgically at the plans that are gathering dust in the files and to think of returning to the previous pattern when the Gaullist road block is removed. There are, unhappily, few signs anywhere today of creative new thought and of a willingness to experiment—either with institutional or substantive questions—that were characteristic of the "Europeans" a decade ago. Similarly, in the United Kingdom the effect of having been blocked in 1963 has made some of the British "Europeans" more committed than ever to a "European doctrine" that is becoming slightly musty. They have learned their "European lessons" too well.

THE PROBLEM OF "POLITICAL UNION"

. . . In any meaningful sense, an agreement of a "political union," like any other major step toward a more integrated Europe, is very unlikely so long as General de Gaulle remains in power.

What are prospects after that? On the perhaps optimistic assumption made in this chapter that the key governments—France, the Federal Republic, and the United Kingdom—will eventually decide that their interests lie in forming a cohesive European group able to act as a unit externally for many purposes, the question of going beyond the Treaties of Rome and Paris will certainly arise. It would be unfortunate if before that time comes

some new thought had not been given to the problem, for the argument has been a singularly sterile one and both the assumptions and prescriptions of the past are rather archaic.

Perhaps the first thing to be done is to get rid of the term "political union." Dr. Hallstein is, of course, right in maintaining that the Economic Community is a political phenomenon. The task in the future will be to decide on the areas beyond those already defined by the existing treaties in which the Community countries want to act in common and then to agree on the institutional arrangements that will make it possible for them to do so most effectively. The kind of Europe that is likely to emerge in, say, the next decade will be determined partly by the dynamics of the commitments undertaken within the framework of the existing treaties, partly by the reasons for unity that now and in the future are likely to seem important to the key governments, and partly by the developing pattern of international life into which the Community must fit.

In the past the "motor" of unification has been the pressures set up by trade liberalization. These will continue to be important. So, too, will the pressures of the common agricultural policy. But the desire for technological equality with the Soviet Union and the United States will also be a powerful factor in the future, with consequences for the way the Community approaches questions such as the organization of capital markets and economic planning. In the longer term the desire for the increase in power and influence that comes from common policies and collective action seems likely to become the most important propellant toward unity.

In the field of foreign policy, the central issue on which the European countries will want to maximize their power will presumably be the settlement in Central Europe. At present views on this issue divide rather than unite the key countries. Is it possible to conceive of a common policy emerging, in time, in this critical field? If it is not, the prospects for a union with a common foreign policy eventually developing in Western Europe are bleak. But provided the *détente* between the United States and the USSR continues, perhaps an approach on which all the countries in an enlarged Community could agree can be envisaged.

The possibility of seeking an acceptable solution to the problem of the division of Germany through the further development of the Community and a far-reaching form of association between East Germany and the Community would seem to be well worth exploring. By this means a *de facto* unification of the German people might eventually be achieved, although no single German state would be re-created.[7] The process of establishing such a relationship would obviously be a gradual one, extending, no doubt, over many years. The sequence of events might be something as follows.

First, the Community's relations with Poland, Czechoslovakia, and other Eastern European countries would be normalized. This process has, of course, already been started. Then, a gradual modification might be made in the

relations between the Community and Eastern Germany. A protocol to the Treaty of Rome provides that interzonal trade is to be considered as internal German trade. By building on this protocol, the question of recognition of Eastern Germany could be sidestepped, initially at least, and very likely for the duration of the Ulbricht regime. As a first step toward the new relationship, the existing interzonal trade arrangements might become arrangements relating to the Community as a whole. Later, and by gradual steps, the arrangement between Eastern Germany and the Community might be extended to the free movement of capital and labor as well as goods. Eventually, the economic and social relationships between Eastern Germany and the Community might be not too dissimilar from those existing between the members of the Community. Clearly, the Community itself would have to develop much further toward a real union before an association that would be comprehensive enough to satisfy the Germans could become a practical possibility.

Would such an arrangement be acceptable to the other interested countries—Germany's neighbors in Europe, the Soviet Union, and the United States?

The real interests of the United Kingdom, France, Italy, and the Benelux countries would seem, in the long run, to be very much the same, whatever the differences among them appear to be today. Although these countries have no strong national interest in a reunited Germany, they have a very strong interest in a stable and peaceful situation in Central Europe. And they have strong political and economic interests in having participation in the process of European

---

[7] In this connection it should be noted that M. Monnet's Action Committee for the United States of Europe in its declaration adopted in Bonn on June 1, 1964, referred to the eventual "reuniting of the Germans in the European Community" as "an essential condition for peace." The declaration adopted by the Committee at its meeting on May 8–9, 1965, in Berlin, contained a similar reference.

unification remain the policy of the Federal Republic. An alliance-free reunited Germany would be a destabilizing factor, whether or not it was technically neutralized. A reunited Germany which was appreciably the strongest partner in a loose alliance of Western states would raise psychological and other problems. But a *de facto* unification of the German people achieved by means of a far-reaching form of association between Eastern Germany and a strong Community might well seem to be an attractive arrangement to this group of countries.

The United States' interest is essentially one of seeing that the existing balance of power does not shift against it. Such an arrangement would improve the present balance. Why, then, should it be acceptable to the Soviet Union? Presumably it would not be today. But provided the *détente* between the Soviet Union and the United States continues, provided the cohesion of the Atlantic Alliance can be maintained (with or without France), and provided the Federal Republic continues to refuse all political deals with the East, the Soviet Union may well come to regard the development of a unified Western Europe more benignly than it has in the past. Presumably the Soviet Union would rather see the Federal Republic effectively integrated into a strong community than it would see either a weak community dominated by a strong Federal Republic, or a Federal Republic following in "Gaullist" footsteps and pursuing an independent national policy. The Soviet Union and the Eastern European countries may, therefore, come to regard British membership in the Community and a far-reaching form of integration in Western Europe as being to their advantage. This seems even

more probable if as a result of the formation of an effective European union there were a change in the nature of the military links between the Federal Republic and the United States. A reorganization of NATO defense arrangements on a "two-pillar" basis, even though a strong transatlantic link remained, would doubtless be regarded by the Soviet Union as an improvement on present arrangements. If the price of a real integration of the Federal Republic in Western Europe and, consequently, of a change in some of the bilateral German—United States' defense arrangements, were, as it may well prove to be, a freer relationship between Eastern Germany and the Community, would the price always seem to the Soviet Union to be too high?

Whether or not something along these lines suggests a possible approach to the problem of German reunification, it is clear that until the relationship between German reunification and European unification is much more seriously and widely discussed and until some common agreement is reached among the members of the European Community on the nature of and the steps to an acceptable eventual settlement of the German problem, there is little prospect of a union with a common foreign policy emerging in Western Europe, no matter how often foreign secretaries may meet or what the powers of initiative vested in an independent Commission.

Defense has always tempted the "Europeans" as a short cut to political union, but there is little reason to believe that it is a short cut that will be any easier to take in the future than it has been in the past. On the contrary if, as seems probable, the result of the NATO crisis is to increase the "interdependence" between Germany and the United Kingdom, on the one hand, and the United States, on the other, the lack of symmetry between the economic organization of Europe and the defense organization of Europe seems likely to become rather more pronounced for the next few years.

It is just possible that the British might still take the opportunity provided by the NATO crisis to propose a European defense community as a first step toward the reshaping of the alliance on to a "two-pillar" basis. But it seems much more probable that the effect of General de Gaulle's attack on the NATO system will be to retard the development of a "European pillar" and hence any real reshaping of the Alliance. An integrated Atlantic defense system can be maintained without France, but an integrated European defense system without France could only be a political maneuver, although possibly quite a useful one.

On the assumption made in this chapter that the process of integration will continue, common action in the defense field will clearly develop eventually. It is not improbable that a future French government would propose turning the *force de frappe* into a "European" *force de frappe* if the British would agree to do the same with their nuclear weapons. The nuclear issue is not dead, but sleeping. But, for a number of reasons, it would seem to be a mistake to reawaken it too soon.

If the nuclear issue were forced in the near future—by the Germans, by the French, or by the United States —the effect might well be to halt, possibly even to reverse, the "Europeanization" of the Wilson government. There is obviously a problem of nuclear equality for the Germans that must, in the long term, be solved. Presumably it will

eventually be solved either by putting the British and French nuclear weapons under a collective "European" control or by letting obsolescence reduce the importance of the British and French systems. The former has seemed a rather more probable development, given the European uneasiness at complete nuclear dependence on the United States. But the political organization of Europe that would make it possible to elaborate a workable control system will not exist for many years to come. Moreover, as discussed above, the kind of union that could support a nuclear weapons system only seems likely to develop if the key countries—the United Kingdom, France, and Germany—can agree on a common approach to the problem of German reunification. This, in turn, will obviously have a bearing on the nuclear role the Europe of the future will want to have. These are long-range questions that will have to be discussed and agreed; but they are not questions that will be settled quickly.

The relationship between European unification and German reunification also has a bearing on the arrangements made for the neutral countries of the EFTA, on the assumption that within the next few years the United Kingdom, Denmark, and Norway join the Community, and Portugal negotiates a "Greek-type" association with it. In the past, the "Europeans" and their supporters in the United States have tended to feel that Sweden and Switzerland, unlike Austria, were indulging in the luxury of neutrality at the expense of others, and that there was, therefore, little reason to encumber the Community with additional association arrangements on their behalf. Today these attitudes are changing, and they seem bound to continue to change. If, as seems probable, the Community completes an association arrangement with Austria it will be difficult, in fact, to maintain that what can be done for Austria cannot be done for the other two neutrals, despite the differences in the origins of their policies of neutrality.[8] Moreover, it now seems almost certain that the EFTA will have become a full free trade area before the question of British membership has been settled.[9] It is almost unthinkable that, given the history of the last few years and the affair of the surcharge, the British would agree to raise their tariffs against their EFTA partners.

Much of the "European" opposition to association arrangements under Article 238 of the treaty[10] has, in the past, stemmed from the feeling that such arrangements would be a drag on the development of the Community. To some extent this view arose because association arrangements under Article 238 were regarded as lineal descendants of the original free trade area proposal. At the time of the free trade area negotiation, the British would have been in the "outer" group and the Community was barely formed; there were, therefore, good grounds for fearing that the wider group would supplant the narrower group. Opposition

to association arrangements has also stemmed from the fact that there are very real difficulties in working out satisfactory association arrangements between a highly industrialized country, such as Austria, and the Community. And the difficulties tend to be greater the closer the form of association that is sought.[11] The essential problem is, of course, how to give the associated country an adequate voice in the formulation of those policies that affect it directly (e.g., modifications in the Community's external tariffs) without creating a situation in which the tail wags the dog.

The reasons that have aroused apprehension in the past seem likely to apply with diminished force in the future. At a time when the benefits of the Community were mainly those derived from participating in a larger area of free trade it was difficult to conceive of forms of association that did not, in effect, give the advantages of membership without the disciplines and restraints of membership.[12] In the future, as the benefits from participation in the Community tend to come increasingly from common policies, the trade benefits will lose some of their special significance. The more cohesive the Community itself becomes the easier it should be to find meaningful forms of association with it. And once

[8] A parallel agreement between the Community and the Swiss would of course strengthen the Austrian position that there is nothing inconsistent between an association with the Community and political neutrality.

[9] Under the present schedule the reduction of tariffs among the EFTA countries (except for Portugal which has a longer timetable) will be completed at the end of 1966.

[10] Article 238 provides for the association of other European countries with the Community. The African countries are associated under a special convention, and a special section (Part IV) of the treaty.

[11] "European" thinking on the problem of association has, in the past, tended to assume the opposite, that is that an association arrangement with other European countries should be as nearly as possible a replica of the Treaty of Rome. This line of reasoning is probably faulty and another legacy of the free trade area negotiations.

[12] Much of the "European" coolness to the provision for an elimination of tariffs in Title I of the Trade Expansion Act derived, of course, from the fact that tariff discrimination was the cement that held the Common Market together.

the British are in the "core group" there will be little force of attraction in the "outer group."

Apart from these reasons for thinking that some form of association with the neutrals is probable, it seems likely that the political advantages of having a category of relationship which has many of the economic advantages but none of the political-defense overtones of the Community will become increasingly attractive to a number of the Community countries as a way of extending the Community's contacts with the Eastern European countries, with Finland and Yugoslavia in the near future, later, perhaps, with Poland and Czechoslovakia, and probably in a somewhat different form with Eastern Germany. This seems particularly likely to be true if it is a Labour government which finally takes the United Kingdom into the Community, for one of the most pervasive arguments against membership that is found particularly, but not only, in Labour circles is that the unification of Western Europe will harden the dividing line between East and West in Europe.

In the early sixties the Community of the Six might have developed quite rapidly into a federal union had General de Gaulle chosen to make common cause with the "Europeans" and had

he seen his destiny, and that of France, as the creator of a new federal Europe. He chose another course, and the "Europe" of Schuman, de Gasperi, and Adenauer is no longer the possibility it once seemed. The "Europe" of tomorrow will almost certainly include the British, the Norwegians, the Danes, and the Irish. It is likely to be rather blurred at the edges with various kinds of special arrangements, south to the Mediterranean countries and Africa, east to the neutrals and perhaps some of the smaller countries of Eastern Europe. It is unlikely for many years to become a system that can fairly be described as a federal union. Perhaps what is happening in Western Europe is the pioneering of a new form of relationship among states, perhaps it is the building of an infrastructure of a European federation. It is much too soon to tell. However, if the enlarged Community is to be an effective force in the world, it must have a high degree of cohesion and the will and institutions to enable collective action to be taken. These seem likely to develop, in time; for the essential reason that is impelling the key countries in Western Europe to come together is, at bottom, the desire to play a larger and more effective role in the world.

Kevin Devlin

THE PERMANENT REVOLUTIONISM
OF FIDEL CASTRO

This revolution will never be anyone's satellite or be subjected to anyone's conditions...it will never ask anyone's permission to maintain its posture, whether it be in ideology or in domestic or foreign affairs."—*Fidel Castro, March 13, 1967.*

H. L. Mencken once remarked that no married woman could ever have absolute trust in her husband: the utmost she could achieve, said the sage of Baltimore, was "the wary confidence of the American pickpocket that the policeman on the beat will stay bought." The Soviet leaders have learned from hard experience that in the case of Fidel Castro such wary confidence would be misplaced—the charismatic leader of the Cuban revolution simply will not stay bought, even at the rate of an estimated one million dollars a day.

The root of the trouble lies in the fact that Castro is not content to be the leader of the Cuban revolution. Driven both by an evident sense of personal destiny and by a shrewd perception of self-interest, he openly aspires to leadership of the Latin American revolution, looking to a day when

Reprinted from Kevin Devlin, "The Permanent Revolutionism of Fidel Castro," *Problems of Communism* (January–February, 1968), 1–11, by permission of the publisher, United States Information Agency.

the Cordillera of the Andes will be the Sierra Maestra of a continent aflame with anti-Yanqui passion.

By the mid-1960's this claim to regional leadership—together with a rare combination of political independence and economic dependence—had given the Cuban regime a unique place in the new, increasingly diversified international Communist movement. If the regional role is unique, so are the ideological and organizational issues which it raises. In no other part of the world have non-Communist forces become so deeply involved in the transformation of communism; nowhere else does one find such complex patterns of factionalism, such shifting networks of left-wing relationships. Cuba is the key piece in that kaleidoscopic and bewilderingly intricate mosaic.

COMMUNISM SUI GENERIS

Castro's victory over a corrupt dictatorship was in itself a refutation of Leninist teaching on the avant-garde role of the Communist party, enabled by its command of "scientific" doctrine to interpret and shape historical developments. The "old" Cuban Communist party, the People's Socialist Party (PSP), scrambled onto the Castroist band-wagon at the eleventh hour, having previously criticized the guerrilla struggle against Batista as "adventurist" —a lesson which other Latin American Communist parties have not forgotten. For a time after Castro proclaimed his faith in Marxism-Leninism, it seemed that the Communists were in the process of taking over the regime by dominating the Integrated Revolutionary Organization (ORI), formed in 1961 by the merger of the PSP and Castro's July 26 Movement. But in March 1962 Castro suddenly ousted and exiled Anibal Escalante, the Communist who controlled the ORI machine; and from then on old-guard Communists like Blas Roca and Carlos Rafael Rodriguez retained their posts in the top leadership by hewing to Castro's line.[1]

A basic feature of that line, clearly expressed in Castro's Second Declaration of Havana (1961) and in Che Guevara's work *La guerra de guerrillas* (1960),[2] was a regional emphasis on revolutionary voluntarism. This call to arms, strengthened by the intoxicating example of the "First Territory of Free America," made a considerable appeal

[1] After the expulsion of Escalante, Castro carried out an extensive purge of the country's political and economic apparatus. Thus, all six of ORI's provincial secretary-generals were old-guard Communists; two acceptable to Castro were allowed to keep their posts and the rest were removed. The ORI itself was replaced by the Castroist-dominated United Party of the Socialist Revolution (PURSC), which had still not held its founding congress when it became the Cuban Communist Party in October 1965.

[2] English edition, *Guerrilla Warfare* (New York, 1961). Guevara's main theses were that the "subjective conditions" for a successful revolution could be created by determined action, even when they did not exist beforehand, and that in Latin America the best hope of success lay in mobilizing the peasantry and not the urban proletariat. Both arguments clearly challenged the theory and practice of almost all the Latin American Communist parties.

to rank-and-file Communists throughout South America. It also appealed to a few of the Communist leaderships, particularly in the period between the Bay of Pigs debacle of April 1961 and the Cuban missile crisis of November 1962. Prominent among those who rallied to the call was the leadership of the Venezuelan Communist Party (PCV), which in 1961 had joined the Movement of the Revolutionary Left (MIR) and other radical-leftist elements in Venezuela to form the National Liberation Front (FLN). This was the political arm of the Armed Forces of National Liberation (FALN), which embarked on a campaign of rural guerrilla fighting and urban terrorism with the declared aim of overthrowing the reformist government of the ex-Communist President Romulo Betancourt. The Venezuelan guerrillas were hailed by both the Russians and the Chinese—with the result that in 1963–64 the PCV adopted a distinctly neutralist position in the Sino-Soviet conflict. But the most enthusiastic support came from the beleaguered revolutionary citadel across the Caribbean and it was not merely moral support: in late 1963 a huge cache of arms shipped from Cuba was discovered on the Venezuelan coast.

As it turned out, however, the PCV leadership was far from wholeheartedly united in its commitment to violence[3] —particularly after the striking failure of the FLN's attempt to intimidate voters in the elections of December 1963, in which a turn-out of more than 90 percent of the Venezuelan electorate

[3] In an interview broadcast by Havana Radio on November 19, 1966, the Venezuelan guerrilla leader Elías Manuit said that the PCV leadership's decision in 1962 to launch an armed struggle was taken by a majority of one vote.

chose another reformist Democratic Action president, Raul Leoni, to succeed Betancourt. Two years of internal party dissension followed, resulting in an eventual split in the leadership and a flagrant attempt at intervention by the Cubans (more of which shortly). These developments have emphasized anew the question of Cuba's role in Latin America—and in the international Communist movement.

HAVANA AND MOSCOW

The Caribbean missile crisis of October 1962 was not only a watershed in the history of the Cold War but a turning point in Cuban-Soviet relations. The settlement of the crisis by the Soviet and United States leaders over Castro's head was of course a humiliating blow to his prestige and his regional revolutionary stature; but there was another side to it. Under the settlement, restoring the mutually acceptable limits of super-power confrontation in the Caribbean as in Berlin, the Soviet Union agreed not to try to make Cuba a potentially offensive base of Soviet power, while the United States agreed not to invade the island. The outcome of the crisis therefore removed the main obstacle to Soviet acceptance of Castro's claim, first made in April 1961, that his was a socialist regime, and hence part of the socialist camp.

The negotiated acceptance of Castro's membership application took place during his first visit to Russia in April-May 1963. But Castro did not come to Moscow cap in hand. The joint communiqué which registered the outcome of the talks was a compound of compromises, concessions and covert bilateral opportunism.[4] In this it set the pattern

for the shifting balance of convergent and divergent interests which has characterized Soviet-Cuban relations, and which has been remarkably little affected by Cuba's economic dependence on the USSR. Thus, a few months after the Moscow agreement, Cuba—alone among the "pro-Soviet" regimes—refused to ratify the nuclear test-ban treaty (which Castro clearly regarded as an ominous exercise in Soviet-American detente); and while the Sino-Soviet conflict sharpened during the second half of 1963, Cuba reaffirmed its neutralism.[5] On the other hand, the Cuban emphasis on revolutionary voluntarism was modified during the year or so following Castro's visit to Moscow.

In 1964, however, Latin American developments—notably the Brazilian coup in April and President Frei's electoral victory in Chile in September,

---

[4] *Pravda*, May 25, 1963. In this communiqué the Russians belatedly recognized the Cuban regime as a "socialist" one, but with a special status: it did not belong to Comecon or to the Warsaw Pact, so that Cuban-Soviet relations would be a matter for repeated bilateral settlement. The compromises in the communiqué were fairly obvious. Thus it gave full Cuban approval to the Soviet treatment of the missile crisis: against that, it described Castro's First and Second Declarations of Havana as being "of historic significance for the national liberation struggles of the people of Latin America," but qualified this in turn by noting that it was for each national revolutionary vanguard to decide its own form of struggle (*i.e.,* peaceful or violent). It expressed the Soviet line on such ideological issues as peaceful coexistence; on the other hand, it made no mention of the Albanian rebels whom the Cubans had refused to condemn.

[5] Significantly, it was the "old Communist" organ, *Hoy* (October 2, 1963) and not the "Castroist" *Revolución*, organ of the July 26 Movement, which was chosen to make the declaration that "Cuba wishes to maintain fraternal links with the entire socialist world, and will not allow itself to be separated from this or that country which is part of it." In November 1963 the Cubans gave practical expression to this stand by sending a diplomatic mission to Tirana.

which dashed Brazilian and Chilean Communist hopes of advancing on the "peaceful road"—led Castro gradually to resume his regional role, never really abandoned, as champion of the guerrilla struggle. At the same time the fall of Khrushchev (accepted by the Cubans with noncommittal equanimity) offered the opportunity for another reappraisal of Cuban relations with the USSR and with the "old guard" party leaderships of Latin America. Following a meeting of Latin American Communist parties held in Havana toward the end of 1964, a joint communiqué was issued indicating that the pro-Soviet parties had pledged themselves to step up the campaign of "solidarity with the people and government of Cuba...giving it an even more decisive and organized character."[6] They also promised more "active support" to the armed struggle in certain selected countries: "the Venezuelan, Colombian, Guatemalan, Honduran, Paraguayan and Haitian fighters" were specifically mentioned. In return, the Cubans recognized the right of each party to determine its own path in accordance with local circumstances. Without abandoning their neutralist stance, the Cubans also accepted generally pro-Soviet formulas (such as the call for an end to public polemics), including one on the international conference issue which implied that they would, after all, attend the "preparatory" meeting to be held in Moscow in March 1965. Perhaps the most significant phrase in the communiqué, however, was one condemning "all factionalist activity, whatever its character or source." This was obviously directed against the Chinese (secessionist pro-Chinese Communist parties already existed in Brazil and Peru, and were soon to appear in Colombia and Bolivia, while Maoist factions were active in most other Latin American countries). But, as the phrase "whatever its character or source" suggested, it also applied to the Cubans—and two years later the Venezuelan CP was to accuse Castro of violating this agreement. In short, an attempt was made to institutionalize Cuban relations with the other parties and to place limitations on Castro's claim to regional leadership. Given geopolitical realities and the character of the Cuban revolution, the attempt was bound to fail, and sooner rather than later.

TROUBLE IN VENEZUELA

Even as the communiqué was being drawn up, the Venezuelan guerrilla struggle, on which Castro placed such high hopes, was already faltering and becoming a source of intraparty dissension. The reason was that Castroist voluntarism was not standing the test of reformist reality: it had become increasingly clear during 1964 that the guerrilla-terrorist campaign was not going to succeed, and was merely antagonizing the Venezuelan masses. In April 1965 the seventh plenum of the PCV Central Committee reflected the leadership's dilemma—while reaffirming the party's commitment to the guerrilla alliance, it also adopted a five-point "minimum program" acceptable to "the majority of the people," aimed at achieving a "democratic peace," in which the PCV and the MIR would function as legal opposition parties.[7]

This attempt to combine incompatible postures began to collapse in January 1966. At the same time that the Venezuelan (FLN) delegation to the Tricontinental Conference in Havana

---

[6] *Pravda,* Jan. 19, 1965.

[7] See Saverio Tutino, *"Incontro con i comunisti nel territorio libero universitario,"* *L'Unità* (Rome), Sept. 26, 1965.

was joining in a Castroist chorus of commitment to revolutionary violence, three imprisoned leaders of the PCV Machado—were drafting a document the brothers Gustavo and Eduardo Machado—were drafting a document urging the abandonment of the guerrilla struggle. Thereafter events moved rapidly toward an open split and Cuban intervention.

In March 1966 Faría was released from prison under a conditional amnesty and went into exile in Moscow. In the same month Douglas Bravo, guerrilla commander and leader of the hardline faction, issued a "Manifesto of Iracara," calling for an intensification of the armed struggle; the PCV Politburo promptly moved to suppress it.[8] Early in April 1966 the eighth plenum of the Central Committee decided to "abandon the armed struggle in order to incorporate the party in the movement for the integration of the national Left," as a Politburo spokesman put it.[9] A few weeks later Bravo and four other guerrilla commanders notified the Politburo that they had decided to reorganize the FLN and the FALN "provisionally" under a separate politico-military leadership. In reply the Politburo issued a bulletin (May 18, 1966) condemning Bravo for having "arbitrarily proceeded to establish a parallel and objectively divisive center,"[10] and suspended him from the Central Committee (expulsion from the party was to follow).

At this point the Cubans intervened, extending recognition and open support to the dissident guerrillas, and publicizing hard-line statements issued by a permanent mission which the dissidents had established in Havana. In late August 1966 the PCV Politburo sent the Cuban Central Committee a letter protesting bitterly against "the open support given by leaders of the Cuban CP to factionalist elements;... [against the] displacement of the legitimate representatives of our party in the posts to be created within the secretariat of the Tricontinental Organization, in the Latin American Solidarity Organization and in other bodies, [posts] which without any doubt belong to us;...and [against] the acceptance [by Cuba] of a seditious 'delegation of the FALN.' "[11]

The Cuban response to this protest was to step up support for the Venezuelan dissidents, who were described by Cuban spokesmen and media as "true Communists" in rightful rebellion against the capitulationist policies of the "pseudo-revolutionaries." The interparty quarrel reached a climax with a speech by Castro on March 13, 1967, in which he denounced the PCV leaders as "accomplices of imperialism." This phillippic amounted to a declaration of ideological and organizational war against a fraternal party; more important, Castro raised issues which went far beyond the Cuban-Venezuelan feud, posing a challenge in continental —not to say global—terms:

Our position regarding Communist parties is based strictly on revolutionary principles. Those parties which unhesitatingly follow a revolutionary line we will support in spite of everything. Those parties which call themselves Communist or Marxist and believe themselves to have a monopoly on

[8] For an analysis of the manifesto from a right-wing viewpoint see the supplement to *Este y Oeste* (Caracas), June 15–30, 1966. (*Translations on International Communist Developments* [TICD], Washington, DC, No. 871, pp. 162–80.)
[9] See "Il P. C. venezolano cesserà la guerriglia," *Avantil* (Rome), April 8, 1966.
[10] The bulletin was published in *Confidencial* (Caracas), No. 32 (TICD, No. 895, pp. 13–16).

[11] See *La Republica* (Caracas), Sept. 3, 1966 (TICD, No. 889, pp. 125–29).

revolutionary feeling, but who are really monopolizers of reformism, we will not treat as revolutionary parties. If in any nation those who call themselves Communists do not know how to fulfill their duty, we will support those who—even though they do not call themselves Communists—behave like real Communists in the struggle. . . . What defines a Communist is his action against oligarchies, action against imperialism and, *on this continent, action in the armed revolutionary movement*.[12]

In their official reply to this "ignoble and over-bearing" speech, the Venezuelan Communist leaders lashed out against Castro's presumptuousness in claiming the right to decide who was and who was not a "true Communist." Accusing him of setting himself up as "an untouchable revolutionary oracle," the statement proclaimed the "absolute independence" of the PCV: if an "anarchic adventurous group" was willing to submit to Cuban directives, the Venezuelan Communist Party was not.[13]

This was like erecting a barbed-wire fence to keep out the tide. Some weeks later a young Cuban was killed and two others captured as they landed on the Venezuelan coast with a group of native guerrillas. Castro's reply to subsequent charges of aggression was to convene his Central Committee (for the first time) and issue a belligerent statement boasting that "we have aided and will continue to aid all those revolutionary movements which are struggling against imperialism, in whatever part of the world."[14] In other words, Cuban intervention in the internal

struggle of the Venezuelan Left would go on.

The Cuban stance, and the justification advanced for it, challenged the interests not only of the Venezuelan party but of all the Communist leaderships of Latin America. Even the most militant of them could not accept the subversive doctrine that revolutionary violence was the only criterion of a party's vanguard role. Thus, the Guatemalan Labor Party (PGT), one of the few Communist parties conducting a guerrilla struggle,[15] hastened to dissociate itself from a statement in which two of its representatives in Havana hailed the March 13 speech as "epoch-making in its exposure of pseudo-Marxists and pseudo-revolutionaries."[16] The Guatemalans were clearly disturbed by the Cuban leader's insistence that the title of "avant-garde" did not belong to a national Communist party by prescriptive, doctrinally-based right,

[12] Supplement to *Granma* (weekly English edition), March 19, 1967; emphasis added.

[13] The statement, signed by seven PCV Politburo members, was published in *Ultimas Noticias* (Caracas), March 17, 1967.

[14] *Le Monde* (Paris), May 20, 1967.

[15] In Colombia Communists conduct one of the two lingering guerrilla campaigns (the other being led by the Castroist Movement of Workers, Students and Peasants—MOEC), but the party still holds that "guerrilla action is not at present the principal form of struggle" (interview with Secretary-General Vieira in *L'Humanité*, [Paris] June 3, 1966). Even in Guatemala Communist commitment to the guerrilla struggle has been wavering in the face of army action and counter-terrorism by right-wing organizations. Thus, in a *World Marxist Review* article of February, 1967, a party spokesman, José Manual Fortuny emphasized that the election of the reformist President Mendez Montenegro in 1966 had opened up new opportunities for "open, legal organization of the masses" in conjunction with a continued armed struggle, and added pointedly, quoting a Central Committee resolution, that if the Army stopped anti-guerrilla operations, the guerrilla force (FAR) would confine itself to "retaliatory action in the event of repressions."

[16] Letter signed by Gabriel Salazar and José Maria Ortiz Vides, *Granma* (English edition), March 26, 1967.

but had to be won by revolutionary action—and that a non-Communist movement could pass the test while Communists failed.

THE TRICONTINENTAL CONFERENCE

Castro's March 13 speech confirmed what was already obvious: that the quarrel between the Cuban and Venezuelan Communist parties, sensational though it was, was merely part of a wider pattern of regional developments. The dominant motif of this pattern has been the growth of "Castroism" as an independent force—one which has had a radically disruptive impact on the traditional Communist order in Latin America since the early 1960's, and particularly since the Havana Tricontinental conference of January 1966.

At the time it was held, the Havana conference seemed to many observers to be dominated by the familiar Sino-Soviet confrontation—an impression strengthened by conflicting propaganda claims, and also by the struggle over such basic issues as voting procedures (the Chinese unsuccessfully pressing for the "unanimity-veto" formula) and the formation of a new tricontinental organization (with which the Russians vainly hoped to replace the Afro-Asian Peoples' Solidarity Organization). In fact, however, the one who gained most from the conference was the *tertius gaudens*—Fidel Castro. This was not merely due to the emphasis placed on revolutionary voluntarism—*à la cubaine* and not *à la chinoise*—in the conference resolutions. More important was the fact that the conference gave Castro the institutional means for promoting his policies both regionally and, to a lesser extent, internationally.

Opportunistic Chinese support—given despite the public rift announced

by Castro's denunciation of the Peking regime on the eve of the conference[17]—helped to make Havana the headquarters of the new Tricontinental Secretariat instead of Cairo (the Soviet delegation had initially supported the Egyptian claim). Havana was also made the headquarters of two other new organizations: a Latin American Solidarity Organization (OLAS) to provide support for national liberation movements throughout the continent and a committee for aid to such movements throughout the world. A Cuban leader, Osmany Cienfuegos, later became secretary-general of the Tricontinental Secretariat—on which neither the Soviet Union nor China was represented—and another Cuban, Haydée Santamaria, was named secretary-general of the OLAS.

Cuban activities before, during and immediately after the conference foreshadowed the bold use that the regime was to make of these institutional levers. The decisions of the International Preparatory Committee on the accreditation of delegations showed Cuban influence more clearly than that of either the Russians or the Chinese.[18]

[17] Castro attacked the Chinese on Jan. 2, 1966, for having cut rice-for-sugar exchanges; a month later (in *Granma*, Feb. 6, 1966) he stepped up the attack, accusing them not only of "criminal acts of economic aggression" but of attempting to subvert Cuban officers and officials by disseminating propaganda through Peking's Havana embassy. The sugar-rice trade was later quietly resumed. Significantly, Castro's attack was not couched in ideological terms, nor was it part of a sustained campaign; he maintained his neutralist posture.

[18] The Cubans would have joined the Chinese in excluding Yugoslav observers, and the Soviets in excluding all Latin American pro-Chinese factions except the Dominican MPD. Again, they supported the Mexican Castroist MLN's opposition to the accreditation of Lombardo Toledano's PPS, which led to the withdrawal of the pro-Soviet Mexican CP.

During the meeting itself Castro organized a sort of conference within a conference, holding prolonged discussions behind closed doors with the Latin American delegations, during which he reportedly urged on the Jacobin Left the regional lessons of the Cuban revolution. In the months following the conference the Cubans asserted their independent revolutionary line by attacking Yugoslavia (no longer a Communist regime, declared *Granma* flatly), the pro-Chinese factions ("paper revolutionaries"), Latin American governments both rightist and reformist, and the "peaceful-way" illusions of unnamed fraternal parties. They were more guarded in their criticism of the Soviet Union; but Castro cut close to the bone in a May Day speech in which he questioned whether "any nation can undertake the building of communism in a single country, without productive forces and technology being first developed in the rest of the underdeveloped countries."[19]

The Cuban line continued to harden. In August Castro acquired another important organizational lever, when the Latin American Student Congress convened in Havana to hear Armando Hart preach the gospel of regional violence, and proceeded to set up a permanent Havana-based organization (OCLAE) with the aim of "promoting the fighting solidarity of Latin American students in their struggle against imperialism."[20] At the same time the Cubans were pressing for the formation of national committees of the Latin American Solidarity Organization (OLAS)—often with the enthusiastic participation of the Jacobin Left, while local Communists dragged their feet. Declarations by the Havana secretariats of the OCLAE, the OLAS, and the

[19] *Granma* (English edition), May 8, 1966.
[20] *Ibid.*, Aug. 14, 1966.

tricontinental organization regularly followed the militant Cuban line—as when the last announced in November 1966 that, in accordance with a hitherto secret resolution of the Tricontinental Conference, Cuba and North Korea were setting up "schools for the training of political cadres for the revolutionary movements" of their respective continents.[21]

THE "SOLIDARITY" CONFERENCE

The most significant development, however, was the Cuban regime's careful preparation, beginning in the fall of 1966, for the "First Latin American People's Solidarity Conference," eventually held in Havana from July 31 to August 10, 1967.[22] Organizationally and ideologically, the OLAS conference was "rigged"; the Castroist outcome was preordained. A number of important Latin American Communist parties either were not invited or did not come—those of Venezuela, Brazil, Argentina and Ecuador, for example. Only three delegations, those of Uruguay, Costa Rica and El Salvador, were controlled or dominated by moderate, old-guard Communists. Some eight to

[21] Radio Havana, Nov. 18, 1966.
[22] An important feature of this tactical planning was the preparatory committee's circulation of detailed questionnaires about social, economic, political and cultural conditions in individual countries. By March 1967 these requests for data had gone out to 197 "progressive" groups throughout the continent—of which number the official Communist parties could account for no more than one-fifth at most—and an OLAS official was explaining frankly that the purpose was to "establish a common revolutionary strategy for Latin America" (*New York Times*, March 27, 1967). By the time the OLAS conference opened, the interim results had been compiled in 14 volumes, and a large staff was at work in Havana upon what had become a permanent research project, in the service not of sociology but of regional revolution.

ten others were divided between moderates and hard-liners, and were consequently hamstrung on critical issues by the rule that each delegation had only one vote and must reach agreement in order to cast it. A majority of the delegations was Castroist-dominated, Jacobin leftists surrendering happily to the overwhelming ambiance of revolutionary voluntarism expressed in the conference's slogan, "The duty of a revolutionary is to make revolution."

But if Castroist sentiment was dominant, it did not go unopposed. The closing session of the conference was, in fact, delayed by two days because of old-guard opposition to two resolutions —one condemning the "rightist" leadership of the Venezuelan Communist Party; and another, even more controversial, criticizing the policy of "certain socialist countries" which gave trade credits and technical assistance to Latin American governments. Rodney Arismendi, the Uruguayan Communist leader, tried to play the mediating role which he had often before assumed, but the only result was that the resolution criticizing Soviet relations with Latin American regimes passed by 15 votes to 3 (Uruguay, Costa Rica and El Salvador), with 9 absentions (the divided delegations)—was not made public. This made little difference. Castro, who had already criticized Soviet-Latin American relations in his March 13 speech, let the anti-Soviet cat out of the bag in his stormy closing address:

Anything that implies financial and technical aid to any of these countries means repression of the revolutionary movement . . .the least that we can expect from any state in the socialist camp is that it deny [such] aid to any of these governments.[23]

[23] Radio Havana, Aug. 10, 1967.

In its intransigent militance, Castro's address with its bitter denunciation of the "reactionary mafia elements in the revolutionary movement" (*i.e.*, the softline, old-guard Communist leadership) was a fitting conclusion to the proceedings of the conference. The 20-point General Declaration simply ignored and thereby disposed of the doctrinal subtleties advanced by old-guard theorists. Pertinent sections insisted, without qualification, that armed struggle was "the primary path of the revolution in Latin America," to which all other forms of struggle must be subordinated, and that the peoples of "those countries where this is not considered an immediate task" had better "consider it an inevitable prospect."[24] This challenge to the vanguard role of each national Communist party, and to its right to decide its own strategy and tactics, was strengthened by the powers which the OLAS statutes adopted by the conference assigned to the Havana-based (and Cuban-dominated) Permanent Committee:

The Permanent Committee can propose the enlargement or reduction of the national committees. These propositions shall be discussed with the national committee, *whose composition may be changed to find a unanimous solution. If no agreement is reached, the Permanent Committee shall make the decision.*[25]

OLD-GUARD REACTIONS

The OLAS conference, then, appeared to marke a further strengthening and institutionalization of Castroism as a regional force. Yet the appearance was somewhat deceptive. In the first place, this new "regional revolutionary

[24] *Ibid.*
[25] *OLAS Statutes,* Chap. 2. Emphasis added.

international," as some observers saw it, was not an international in the old, hierarchically disciplined, Comintern sense. The Cubans might dominate—not control—the Permanent Committee and the Havana missions; they did not dominate, let alone control, the constituent parent organizations in other countries. The alliance between member organizations in individual countries was a precarious and fitful one, and it was questionable how well it would withstand the strains of a prolonged waiting for the Godot of successful revolution. Moreover, Cuban propaganda could not conceal the fact that most of the Jacobin Leftist organizations attending the conference were insignificant fringe groups: the Yugoslav comment that "many delegations consist of quite unknown personalities, representing groups and organizations which have no influence in their countries," was unkind but not unfair.[26]

Moreover, the Cuban challenge to the old guard Communist leaderships is so far more of ideological than of practical significance. In their resistance to Castroist *Gleichschaltung* these parties have considerable advantages: their organizational strength and habitual discipline: their opportunistic response to local realities: the still persisting disarray of the Jacobin leftists: and, finally, Soviet support. Husbanding these primarily defensive strengths, they try to minimize the disruptive impact of Castroism while keeping their vanguard-role powder dry: their reaction is still predominantly discreet and indirect.

This cautiously defensive stance also characterized their attitudes to the OLAS conference. Before the confer-

ence a wave of articles in national and international Communist organs took ideological issue with Castroism which was never named as such but described as "petty-bourgeois revolutionism" or some similarly transparent periphrasis. After the conference, the Venezuelans vehemently condemned the "divisionist meeting" at which they had been denounced. A PCV Politburo statement described OLAS as "a base anti-Communist and revisionist pseudo-revolutionary group" and expressed confidence that "no Communist party will follow the Cuban leader in his adulteration of principles."[27] The Ecuadrorean and Argentine parties explained in marginally polemical terms why they were not attending the meeting, while the Chilean and Costa Rican parties, which had sent delegations, dissociated themselves quietly but firmly from conference documents which, according to Castro's closing speech, had been adopted unanimously.

THE SINO-SOVIET FACTOR

Soviet reactions to the new thrust of the Castroist offensive were also expressed cautiously and indirectly. Thus, on August 9, while the conference was going on, a "Radio Peace and Progress" broadcast in Spanish to Latin America quoted approvingly from a report published in the French Communist Party daily, criticizing the "violent anti-Communist and anti-Soviet diatribes of 'ultra-revolutionary' groups" which used "the language customary for some years in Peking."[28]

[26] Tanjug, Aug. 1, 1967. The failure of the Chilean Socialist leader Salvador Allende to attend the conference was significant.

[27] *Ultimas Noticias* (Caracas), Aug. 20, 1967.

[28] *L'Humanite,* Aug. 4, 1967, quoted by Radio Paz y Progresso (Moscow), Aug. 9. In his closing speech to the conference Castro referred scornfully to this attack by "neo Social Democrats in Europe."

Even before the OLAS conference, however, the divergence between Cuban and Soviet interests in Latin America was frequently obvious. In general, the Soviet leaders, recognizing the determined strength behind the US presence in the region, are not sanguine about revolutionary struggles. Moreover, the advent of another Communist regime in Latin America would raise serious economic and political problems for the Kremlin: the commitment to defend and subsidize one Cuba is onerous enough. Moscow's preference for political and diplomatic action, aimed at furthering its own and weakening US state interests, is manifest in its attempts to promote relations with Latin American governments condemned by Cuba.[29]

If the Castroist offensive has threatened the interests of the Soviet Union and of the old guard party leaderships, it has also involved Cuban condemnation of the pro-Chinese secessionists (and of the Trotskyists), who represent an ideological challenge to Castro's regional influence. The results of Chinese intervention in the area have often been exaggerated partly because Castroist movements are sometimes loosely described as "pro-Chinese." Only in Peru do the secessionists offer any real threat to the official Communist parties: only in Colombia are they taking a subordinate part (with the MOEC) in a guerrilla struggle. Chinese intervention, such as it is, has been aimed not at promoting anti-imperialist struggles but at gaining peripheral

ground in the Sino-Soviet conflict—and Castro is bent upon proving the irrelevance of that struggle for the Latin American revolution.

THE NEW IDEOLOGY

At the same time, Castro has still to prove the relevance of Castroism for Latin America. On one level as we have seen, this means an effort at institutionalization, exerted mainly through the OLAS, the OCLAE and other Havana-based regional organizations. On another level it means developing some ideological superstructure on the foundation of revolutionary voluntarism. Part of this work of ideological elaboration has been done by a new school of young Castroist "ideologues" at the University of Havana, whose vigorous critiques of sanctioned dogmas, and particularly of Soviet textbooks, have enlivened a publication with the characteristically iconoclastic title of *El Caimàn Barbudo* (*The Bearded Alligator*). However, Castroism has found its most impressive intellectual exponent not in a Cuban but in the young French scholar, Régis Debray—whose capture, trial and imprisonment for guerrilla activity in Bolivia have made world headlines in recent months, especially in connection with the death of Che Guevara.

Debray had abandoned a brilliant academic career to spend 1966 in Cuba —having already, at 26, visited the island several times, toured extensively in Latin America, and written with insight and enthusiasm about the continental revolution. Prolonged discussions with Castro and other Cuban leaders, and access to many unpublished documents, gave him an unrivalled background for his short book, *Revolución en la Revolución?* [*Revolu-*

[29] Two examples have particularly angered the Cubans. In 1966 Moscow signed a $100 million credit agreement which made the right-wing Brazilian regime the leading recipient of Soviet aid in Latin America after Cuba; and early in 1967 it signed an agreement for $57 million worth of credit and technical aid to the reformist Chilean regime.

tion within the Revolution?].[30] Published in Havana early in 1967, it was at once publicized by the Cuban press and radio: here were the lessons of the Cuban revolution for Latin America, analyzed with sophistication and enthusiasm—and expounded, most usefully, by a European outsider.

Debray summed up his primary thesis in a *Granma* interview (English edition, Feb. 5, 1967): "The Latin Americans have a gold mine in their neighborhood, and they were looking for paper currency elsewhere." By "paper currency" he meant the entire range of the revolutionary theory and practice of the Russians, the Chinese and the Vietnamese. In his book he dismissed the bulk of Communist strategic doctrine as being obviously inapplicable to Latin America. Like his Cuban sponsors, he argued that the primary task on the Latin American continent is "the development of guerrilla warfare and not...the strengthening of existing parties or the creation of new parties."[31] More precisely, the guerrilla force must develop its own, independent politico-military authority:

Fidel Castro says simply that there is no revolution without a vanguard; that this vanguard is not necessarily the Marxist-Leninist party; and that those who want to make the revolution have the right and the duty to constitute themselves a vanguard, independently of these parties.[32]

[30] An English translation by Bobbye Ortiz from the author's French and Spanish, under the title *Revolution in the Revolution?* has been issued as a special number of *Monthly Review* (New York), July–August 1967. References are to this version.
[31] *Revolution in the Revolution?* p. 116.
[32] *Ibid.,* p. 98. Debray's book contains a critique of previous revolutionary practice, including the concepts of "armed self defense" (upheld by the Colombian Communists), of "spontaneism" (the Trotskyist hopes of arousing the masses), of hetero-

Here we have an essentially pragmatic, functional approach to the specific problems of the Latin American revolution. Revolutionary action—through rural guerrilla struggles, as a general rule—is the test. It is a test open to all leftist groups that choose to undertake it, with no privileged position for the established Communist parties. Indeed, in this perspective these parties would be, at best, eventually absorbed, for out of the single politico-military leadership demanded by guerrilla warfare is to grow the future ruling party of the socialist revolution *if* the Cuban success can be repeated.

FAILURES AND SETBACKS

But there, precisely, is the rub. The last and most important level on which Castroism has yet to prove itself is that of practice. So far, it has produced more rhetoric than results. Apart from the small-scale, sporadic outbursts that have from time to time erupted in various countries in Central America and elsewhere—and have been quickly suppressed—serious guerrilla campaigns have developed in Guatemala, Venezuela, Peru, Colombia and Bolivia. Peru has been a great disappointment to Castro: the guerrilla struggle launched in 1965 by the Revolutionary Leftist Movement (MIR) was virtually crushed within six months. In three of the other four countries, campaigns which the Cubans hailed with a fanfare of extravagant predictions have made no headway or have been reduced to marginal proportions—as in Guatemala, for example, where of late the main result of the diminished cam-

geneous "national fronts" (as advocated by the old guard Communist leaderships) and of "armed propaganda" (as practiced by the Chinese and Vietnamese).

paigns of the Communist-controlled Rebel Armed Forces and the rival November 13 Movement has been to provoke a deplorable wave of right-wing counter-terrorism.

The greatest setback, however, has occurred in Bolivia; and it has involved not only Debray, the French evangelist of Castroism, but also the movement's most prominent figure after Fidel himself—Ché Guevara.

Following Guevara's mysterious disappearance from the Cuban scene in 1965, Castro indicated that his former lieutenant had gone to serve the revolutionary cause in other lands. Yet speculation based on known or assumed differences between the two persisted, and his whereabouts—not to mention his standing with Castro—were a subject of much debate. The first solid indication of Guevara's current preoccupations came when the Cubans, with much fanfare, published a manifesto in his name in April 1967, called "Message to the Peoples of the World through the Tricontinental."[33]

In its militant emphasis on the need to wage armed struggle against the imperialists in as many countries as possible, Guevara's manifesto was reminiscent of Chinese teachings on "people's war." But whereas the Chinese stressed the necessity of ideologically-motivated struggle, rejecting any prospect of collaboration with the "revisionists," Guevara condemned such dogmatism. Taking up a theme which Castro had sounded more discreetly on occasion, he denounced both the USSR and China (clearly, though not by name) for having kept up their "war of abuse and maneuvering," instead of moving together to "make Vietnam an inviolable part of the socialist world, running, of course, the risk of war on a global scale—but also forcing a decision upon imperialism." In view of this shared "guilt," and the fact that a Sino-Soviet reconciliation appeared "extremely difficult, if not impossible," the guerrilla fighters of the Third World—"we, the dispossessed"—could not take either side; their task, rather, was to confront imperialism with "two, three or many Vietnams."

While the Cubans were publicizing his manifesto, Guevara—as became clear subsequently—was engaged in precisely the task of trying to create "another Vietnam" in the inhospitable terrain of southeast Bolivia. The force of perhaps 100 men which Guevara assembled for this purpose, and which was pushed into premature action by a chance encounter with Bolivian troops in late March 1967, represented something new. First, it was strikingly international in composition.[34] Secondly, although Communist (both pro-Soviet and pro-Chinese), Castroist and Trotskyist parties in Bolivia hailed the guerrilla struggle, none was able to claim leadership or even partial control of it.[35] Again the area of struggle had been chosen by a shrewd strategist—inaccessible and thinly populated so that, given moderate luck, there would be time for careful preparation; but conveniently near the borders of Paraguay and Argentina, and not too far from the tin-mining centers with their own tradition of proletarian rebellion. For several months the guerrillas, well-armed and disciplined, inflicted a series of humiliating defeats on Army detach-

34 A Bolivian Army communiqué of June 11, 1967, claimed that the force was known to include at least 17 Cubans, 14 Brazilians, 4 Argentinians and 3 Peruvians.

35 See Carlos María Gutierrez, "Bolivia: Otra forma de guerrilla," *Política* (Mexico City), May 15–31, 1967.

33 *Granma Weekly Review,* April 23, 1967.

ments. But the tide turned—in part because the guerrillas failed to win the support of the Indian peasants. By September, troops were closing in on harried and divided remnants of the force. On October 8 the leader identified by fingerprints as Guevara was captured, and died next day, having apparently been shot after capture.[36]

In a speech on October 15, and again at a memorial rally on October 18, Castro acknowledged that Guevara had been leading the Bolivian struggle, and that he had been killed. Calling this "a tremendous blow for revolutionary movements" in Latin America, the Cuban leader suggested that the defeat might have been the result of Guevara's having "acted in an excessively aggressive manner."[37] By subtly attributing the Bolivian setback to his old comrade's impetuous militance, he thus reasserted his own charismatic leadership, while at the same time laying Castroist claim to the exemplary legend of Guevara, the dedicated revolutionary.

But the failure of the Bolivian venture has other roots and is of wider significance: it points to the unlikelihood of either "another Cuba" or "other Vietnams" in the foreseeable future. Castro's capacity to exploit anti-Yanqui nationalism and the forces re-

leased by the travail of social and economic modernization is considerable, but it is limited. For one thing, while the fact that Cuba is an island has helped Castro to maintain his regime, it is also the main obstacle to the fulfilment of his grandiose continental dreams. The flood of angry young men pouring into Cuba for "training" in the early 1960's has diminished to an unimpressive trickle. As a further consequence of this isolation, the aid that Cuba can give to foreign revolutionary movements must mainly take the form of inspiration, advice and propaganda: the direct intervention which has occurred in Venezuela and Bolivia is the exception. Meanwhile, the Castroist offensive serves to heighten Latin American governments' distrust of Cuba and their vigilance against subversion.

One observer has remarked that "the effect of Cuba on the hemisphere has been like the salt in a stew: little has really been added, but all the tastes have been accented."[38] The metaphor is apt and perceptive. However, something new *has* been added to the Latin American Left—a revolutionary movement of a new type which directly challenges the old, and which contributes, out of proportion to its power base, to the ideological erosion and polycentric transformation of international communism.

---

[36] The report of Guevara's death may still be questioned, because of the Bolivian authorities' action in cremating the body; but the weight of evidence, including the Cuban reaction, leaves little room for doubt.

[37] Radio Havana, Oct. 18, 1967; *New York Times,* Oct. 20.

[38] Kalman H. Silvert, "A Hemispheric Perspective," in John Plank, ed., *Cuba and the United States: Long-Range Perspectives,* (Washington, DC, 1967), p. 136.

Leonard J. Fein

ISRAEL AND THE ARAB NATIONS

Before 1967, Israel had fought two wars with the Arab states, one for survival, in 1948, and one for security, in 1956. Many Israelis, perhaps even most, expected that some day a third round would come, though few expected it so soon. And few were sanguine about Israel's prospects in the event of a third round. That public concern was widespread was confirmed by the Cantril survey,[1] which showed that almost 50 per cent of the Israelis mentioned war with the Arabs as one of their "fears for the nation," that 30 per cent mentioned war in general, and that 9 per cent feared an end to national independence. War was by far the most pervasive fear, and this was true for every subgroup within the population, whether defined by class, ethnicity, time of immigration, political affiliation, sex, educational attainment, region, religion, age, or occupation. Similarly, peace with the Arabs was the chief hope for the nation, for the population as a whole, and for all but two

Reprinted from Leonard J. Fein, *Israel: Politics and People* (Boston, Mass.: copyright © 1967, 1968, by Little, Brown and Company, Inc.) pp. 263–77, by permission of the publisher.

[1] Hadley Cantril, *The Patterns of Human Concerns* (New Brunswick, N.J.: Rutgers University Press, 1966).—Editor

subgroups within it.[2] Even when asked to express personal fears and hopes, many Israelis mentioned war and peace.

Everything that happened in Israel happened against the background of the threat of war, against the realization that Israel's destiny, in the most fundamental sense, was not in its own control. More than 57,000,000 people live in the seven nations which declared war on Israel in 1948, and which have yet to make peace with her. They outnumber the Israelis by better than twenty to one. Together, these seven nations contain an area about the size of India, well over 1,000,000 square miles; pre-1967 Israel was about the size of New Jersey, less than 8,000 square miles; Israel had altogether 613 miles of land borders, and across each and every one of those miles was a hostile neighbor.

Although the Six Day War created a new balance in the Middle East, the military considerations, for the most part, were unchanged. In the absence

[2] The two exceptions were white-collar workers, for whom peace was a close second to technological advancement, and members of Herut, Israel's most militantly aggressive political party, for whom war was again behind—though not by much—technological advance.

of lasting peace, the long-range prospects were much as they had been. The relative advantage the Arabs enjoy in manpower and territory may mean less and less in an era of pushbutton war, when technology rather than manpower determines victory. Yet, quite apart from the greater economic resources which the Arabs can bring to bear on the military balance, their massiveness has a marked psychological effect. The Israelis know that the Arab stake in any war is minimal. After the bullets—or missiles—have stopped flying, the worst the Arabs can fear, in hard military fact, is a relatively minor loss of territory and a high number of casualties. Israel's stake, however, is total; it can be permanently crippled, even destroyed. It lacks entirely a fallback position, both because its territory is so small and so vulnerable, and because the Arabs have repeatedly asserted that their goal is its annihilation.[3] In their own view, Israelis had few negotiable assets until 1967, for the outstanding issues between Arabs and Israelis which might have been bargained over, such as the repatriation of Arab refugees or a return to the boundaries set by the United Nations, were matters of vital national concern.

Israelis are fond of saying that two secret weapons have enabled them to survive—their own realization that there is no alternative, and Arab disunity. The knowledge that the only alternative to staving off the Arab threat is total destruction provides them, no doubt, with an important resource. It impels the nation to make greater sacrifices, and its army to be more tenacious, than they might were the issues less compelling than life and death. But again, human will seems destined to become decreasingly relevant as a national military resource as war itself becomes increasingly impersonal. And Arab disunity, except in the most tangential ways, is not a matter which Israel can affect. Hence Israel's active response to the Arab threat has not rested merely on such "secret weapons," but instead has been directed to developing both military and political deterrent strength.

Military Deterrence. The military deterrent is enormously expensive. It involves a commitment to maintaining the Israel Defense Forces at a level which will cause any potential aggressor serious pause, no mean feat when the potential aggressor involved has both income and manpower far in excess of the prospective defender. Estimates of Israel's actual defense expenditures vary widely, ranging from about 200 to almost 400 million dollars a year; even a relatively low estimate suggests that at least 7 per cent of Israel's gross national product [GNP] goes directly for defense needs.[4] And the 7 per cent figure excludes (1) classified expenditures and (2) the vast supportive contributions made to the defense effort by other sectors of the economy. Thus the location of new agricultural settlements is generally more a response to military exigencies than to economic planning. A proper

[3] The major military consequence of the Six Day War was to reduce the vulnerability of Israel, for the time being, by shifting its lines of defense to Arab areas.

[4] Estimates are available from various sources, including the official Israeli figures as they appear in the UN *Statistical Yearbook* as well as reports published regularly by the Institute for Strategic Services in London. A figure of $385 million was cited by *The New York Times* of December 24, 1963. Several sources give 9 or 10 per cent of GNP as a best estimate.

accounting system would charge the losses to the economy generated by introducing such noneconomic considerations into economic planning against the account of the defense establishment, thereby considerably increasing the size of that account. And, after these several calculations were made, the cost of taking large numbers of people out of the economy, perhaps the most significant, however indirect, would still have to be added.

The standing army in Israel is usually thought to be relatively small, numbering as it does only 70,000 men. That is a small number, however, only in relation to the total strength available after mobilization, which stands at over 250,000 men. It is not small as a percentage of the total population; indeed, it is the highest proportion of men in uniform in the Near East, it is higher than in the U.S., the U.K., Cuba, and most other countries. The strength of the defense forces is based on universal military training, lasting 30 months for men and 20 months for women.[5] (The figure of 70,000 for the standing army includes conscripts. The professional military numbers only about 12,000.) Moreover, men are liable for reserve duty through the age of 49, and women until they are 34; such duty involves up to one day per month plus one month per year of active service.

The combination of relatively many people in uniform and the small size of the country have made the military presence highly conspicuous. Even were it more hidden, however, Israelis would hardly have been able to escape the awareness of danger. Hardly a week of Israel's history before the Six Day War went by without some new border inci-

[5] In January, 1968, the term of duty was extended to 36 months.

dent, and the press reports fully on relevant developments in the Arab countries. Tel Aviv, the center of Israel's largest concentration of population, was 12 miles from the Jordanian border until that border was pushed eastward in the most recent war; no place in Israel was more than 70 miles from a hostile nation. There was—and remains, only marginally diminished—in short, an immediacy and a constancy to the threat of war which few nations experience so totally.

One learns to live with it. Jerusalem, for nineteen years divided close to its downtown center by a wall which marked the national boundary, joined to the rest of the country by a narrow land corridor, scene of occasional exchanges of gunfire, did not seem, to the casual visitor, an abnormal city. One needed to have the source of tension pointed out; it was by no means palpable. So, too, for its residents. Their brows were no more furrowed, their walk no more furtive, than those of people in more normal climes. They worked, and played, and bought, and learned, much as they might have elsewhere. This equanimity bespeaks no superhuman stamina, no extraordinary character. Around the world, there are many people who have come to terms with hazard, whether natural or of man conceived. Perhaps an as yet unexecuted psychoanalytic study might reveal the human costs of such adjustment; they are not manifest. It is no small matter to be threatened with extinction from nearby year-in year-out. But people have a wondrous capacity for learning to walk with danger, for adapting and repressing and surviving. It is possible, of course, that in making peace with the threat of war one must attach to the threat an inevitability which in turn sustains it; this we do not really know. It is clear, at the same time, that one major source of Israel's strength has been the presence of a defender marked by competence and invested with confidence.

Thus the defense forces, quite apart from their sometime deterrent impact on the Arab states, are a source of high morale to the Israelis. The army is not only taken for granted, it is honored. However much the earlier tradition of the Jew eschewed the military, Israelis have come to know the armed forces as their lifeline. No subtle reasoning is required for this knowledge, no complex extrapolation about what might happen if there were no Israeli army. It was clear before 1967, and it became still plainer in six long days in June of that year. The alternative is clear and present, as is the danger.

The army does more than reassure Israelis. It undertakes explicit responsibilities in education and integration, and it implicitly provides the most manifest symbol of Israel's nationhood, undiluted by political debate, unencumbered by ideological baggage, unblemished by scandal. There is no question that the army is seen as the most "pure" and certainly most efficient of Israel's institutions.

Yet with all the respect that is accorded it, with all the homage it receives, with all the purity of purpose and command that is imputed to it, the principle of civilian control is unquestioned. Its sharpest tests came in the protracted period of haggling after Sinai, when the army was visibly disconcerted by being forced to sacrifice its military gains under United Nations pressure. The Government, however reluctantly, acceded to that pressure, and, despite massive misgivings among many leading military figures, there

was neither hesitation nor public expression of disapproval. This, no doubt, bewilders many who have imputed a special character to "the military mind." However bewildering, Israel has managed to maintain its military forces as a citizens' army. Although some Israelis believe that in the early years of statehood, there was a minor possibility of military putsch, it is hardly likely that anyone in Israel today is seriously concerned with such a possibility. It is so far from likely, so almost literally inconceivable, that it is totally discounted.

One puzzles over this, and wonders why it should be so. The reasons are at best unclear; most likely, they depend upon an interplay of factors ideological, institutional, and cultural. The antimilitary tradition, though generally overcome, provides a residue of concern, and hence of security. The nature of reserve service, and the small size of the professional army, militates against a sharp cleavage between citizen and soldier. The policy of early retirement of staff officers, prevents, in part, a full-blown professionalism. Finally, the army has a present job to do, and it is fully supported in that job by the organs of the State. It is not frustrated by inactivity, nor at odds with Government policy. There is, after all, little room for option in that policy. Israel's concern has been—and is—security, not conquest. The recent expansion of Israel's borders was neither planned nor anticipated. It resulted from a war Israel hoped to avert, and it was justified in the Israeli view exclusively (save for Jerusalem) on the basis of security considerations. At least until the Six Day War, very few Israelis would have preferred a battle to a lasting peace arrangement. The policy of containment—a containment, be it noted, defended for nineteen years within Israel's own territory—has room for innovation only at the margins. Hence there is little ground for the emergence of a radical cleavage between civil and military wings.

Diplomatic Perspectives. Though Israelis take great pride in the competence of the military, and Israel takes great pains to preserve and expand that competence, it is quite clear to all that military proficiency is not a sufficient deterrent, at least over the long run. Strategic estimates vary widely, but it is commonly believed in Israel that there is a natural limit to Israel's capacity to compete with the Arab nations in armed might. Some gloomily predict that the limit will be reached several years hence; others expansively maintain, their arguments more weighty following the recent war, that at least a decade will pass before the Arabs can hope to overpower Israel. In either case, much sustenance must be derived from faith—faith in continued Arab disunity, faith in a major international détente which will encompass the Near East, faith even in a turn of heart among the Arabs, and chiefly in Egypt. Again, these are matters beyond Israel's control, and the faith may be wishful thinking bred by desperation. It is a strange juxtaposition, this—a new State, still somewhat surprised to find itself taken seriously, proud, intensely proud of its successes, and yet, on the crucial question of survival, at the mercy of others, save for the passing might of its own armies.

There is, however, more to it than this. For aside from its investment in military power, Israel has sought to increase its international political capital. The development of a political deterrent has been less costly, but hardly less taxing, than maintaining a military edge. Israel was never enthusiastic about relying on major power guarantees. After the Sinai Campaign of 1956, when England and France were unwilling to follow through the initial victory, Israel's policy planners became still more reluctant to take any guarantee seriously. Then, too, reliance on others grew less meaningful as Egyptian capacity to deal a severe first strike before any guarantee could become operative increased. Finally, the crushing blow to those who sought alliances was delivered by the total ineffectuality of other powers in intervening with Nasser in 1967. The hasty removal of United Nations Emergency Forces from the Gaza border, and the closing of the Straits of Tiran, were hard evidence that Israel could enjoy support from the major powers only if and as their needs were to coincide with her own (and not always then), and that her own tactic ought therefore to be a persistent effort at persuading those powers of the coincidence of interests.

This task was greatly complicated by what Israel perceived as American overcommitment to Nasser. In the Israeli view, America was deluded in its apparent persuasion that Nasser was the chief bulwark against Communist penetration of the Near East. Israelis argued, to the contrary, that Nasser was the key destabilizing element in the region, and that withdrawal of American support from Nasser might well have led to a significant reduction of tensions in the area. They rejected, at least for the record, the view that only the continued American relationship with Nasser provided the Near East with what stability it did enjoy. (It was difficult for the Israelis to refrain from reminding the U.S., in 1967, that "we told you so.")

Whatever the "facts" of the matter, the difference in view limited Israel's readiness to place great trust on repeated American pronouncements of support, or on such guarantees of territorial integrity as were—or are—sometimes proposed. All such efforts and proclamations alter the tactical conditions of a prospective confrontation. They force the recognition that no protracted land war will be fought between Israel and the Arabs, for intervention would surely come in a matter of days at most. But the strategic question is left untouched, for what Israel fears is what it must assume to be a growing Arab capacity to deliver a swift, crippling, and irretrievable blow. And even the strength of Israel's armies is little protection against such a possibility.

In addition to concerning itself with both defensive measures against sudden and massive devastation and—perhaps—with the development of second strike capacity, Israel has sought to overcome that early isolation which, it was felt, might lead the Arabs to believe that no one would much regret Israel's demise. The policy of developing international ties, of making allies and influencing nations, has obviously been more than a response to the Arab-Israel dispute alone. It has been, in at least as great a measure, a way of overcoming the anxieties of isolation, the insecurity that issues from finding that no one takes you seriously. The isolation is geographic: Israel's land borders are virtually sealed; it is diplomatic: Israel is systematically excluded from the regional councils of Afro-Asian states, and is effectively barred from participating in numerous international conferences whose sponsors are forced to choose between Israel and the Arabs; it is, to some degree, economic:

the Arab states maintain a boycott, which enjoys only limited success, and bar all direct trade with Israel, an economic fact of some importance. The psychological impact of these several forms of isolation is heightened also by Israel's own sense of difference, based on such things as its Jewishness, with all the uniqueness that implies, its language, unspoken elsewhere, and its peculiar position in a land to which it feels such deep attachment in a region where it feels so very alien.

A partial remedy to the ensuing loneliness has been the systematic development of ties to other countries, and especially to the new nations of Africa and Asia. The policy of pursuing such ties was first seen as a way of "leapfrogging" the Arab encirclement, and every success was greeted with high enthusiasm and not a little surprise. The new relationships are now viewed more realistically and more naturally, and have resulted in more than a rebuff to the hostile Arab states. Israel sends large numbers of its citizens to other nations on foreign aid projects of one kind or another, and plays host each year to thousands of visitors from developing nations, come primarily to study in her institutions. Out of this has come quite meaningful political benefit—Egypt is no longer able to find widespread endorsement for its hostile statements from the new nations —and also, perhaps more significant, another kind of reward, less tangible but more durable—a sense of relevance, the security of acceptance and friendship.

These paragraphs suggest a kind of permanence about Arab-Israel hostilities which may mislead. Some observers, perhaps too rational in their view, assert the increasingly difficult burden of the Near Eastern arms race, and conclude that the time is not far off when lack of resources will put an end to what has been a steady escalation, leading the parties to welcome plans for regional arms control. Others profess to find good omens elsewhere, in political developments inside the Arab world. In Israel, however, no sense of imminent relief is present, no sighting of an end, or even of a beginning to an end, of hostility—not even in the aftermath of the Six Day War. The continuing tension, the occasional aggravation, and the ever present possibility of another major conflict, now postponed, but not precluded, are accepted as part of the environment, to be protested against, to be prepared for, to try to circumvent, but neither to forget nor to wish away.

Inevitably, such massive preoccupation affects the society, both directly and indirectly. The military threat diverts, as we have seen, much of the nation's resources. It places Israel in a rather uncomfortable position in its international relations, for it can never be viewed solely in its own right, but must always be juxtaposed against the Arab world. It provides, in limited measure, an issue for political debate within the country, although the basic format of Israel's policy—more properly, Israel's response—is generally taken for granted. Less directly, and more beneficently, it provides to Israel an undoubted source of unity, an issue so preeminent and so undisputed as to make all other cleavages seem trivial. The "ifs" of history are frustrating questions, because unanswerable. But one may speculate that if there had been no massive threat to Israel's existence, the several social conflicts which have thus far been contained might well have proved uncontainable. Against the urge to give domestic ideo-

logical conflict its head, there had always been the looming foreboding that beyond a certain point lay disaster, doom doers ready and waiting to exploit the first immobilizing crisis. No one can know, but it may well be that Israel's is an example of a nonworking multiparty system which works, which works because of factors extraneous to the system itself. And no one can know, but it may well be that the degree of social integration which has been achieved, the capacity Israel has demonstrated to handle the vast immigration, has owed much to the unifying symbol of the army, and to the integrative experience of the army itself, to the always evident fact that, in this most important institution, in this one institution which may make the difference between national—and personal—life and death, there is neither East nor West. On the contrary. Westerners may feel more easy and more comfortable with others of similar background, with tourists and visitors of "their own kind"—but they know, as do the Easterners, that it is the massive immigration since 1948 which has provided the man-power Israel requires for her survival, and that all the good wishes and sympathies of other more congenial guests are as nothing against the gift of blood of young Israelis, whatever their complexion and whatever their cultural sophistication. In Israel, as far as we can see into the future, that gift remains an operative distinction, and quite probably a useful one.

At the same time, the apparently endless conflict exacerbates Israel's quest for identity, for it raises once again, and now in the most direct way, the issue of what Israel is to be. Is this country a European enclave at the Afro-Asian crossroad, or shall it be, in some still uncertain way, a part of the Near East? Neither view is easy, nor is any other, but so long as the essential abnormality of Israel's position among its neighbors remains, no honest selection is possible. Instead, and Israelis are most sensitive to this, the land which embraced the eternal stranger has itself now become stranger to its region; the walls of hostility which bar passage from Israel to Lebanon and Syria and Jordan and Egypt are no less barriers to national normalcy than the ghetto walls of Europe in their day.

WEST AFRICA

Claude E. Welch, Jr.

GHANA: THE POLITICS OF MILITARY WITHDRAWAL

Two years have passed since army and police officers toppled the regime of President Kwame Nkrumah. When and how civilian government will be restored remains unclear, despite the efforts of Ghana's top leaders to assure a smooth transition. Less than a week after the coup, the National Liberation Council, composed of coup leaders, announced that its members had no political ambitions and were "anxious to hand over power to a duly constituted representative civil government as soon as possible." Noble sentiments, these, but difficult to carry out. The 24 months of army control have illustrated how difficult it would be to re-

Reprinted from Claude E. Welch, Jr., "Ghana: The Politics of Military Withdrawal," *Current History*, (February, 1968), 95–100, 113–14, by permission of the publisher.

turn to civilian rule while major economic and political problems remain unresolved.

Since February 24, 1966, Ghanaian politics has operated within a context of financial retrenchment, revelations of mismanagement under Nkrumah, and gropings toward civilian participation. The timetable for reforms pledged by the National Liberation Council (N.L.C.) has lengthened. What seems to be emerging is a coalition of top army and police officers, some politicians who previously opposed Nkrumah and selected civil servants. The N.L.C. retains unchallenged control. This new group of leaders—moderate in policy; respectful of Ghana's heritage; more concerned with resolving domestic problems than strutting on the pan-African stage—has installed collective leadership under General Joseph

Ankrah, leadership utterly distinct from the personal political machine Nkrumah built.[1]

How stable is the new coalition? Might the economic vicissitudes of fiscal retrenchment undercut the support the National Liberation Council currently enjoys? Can elections be further delayed while the country resolves its financial problems? Such are the imponderables of Ghana today.

In 1966 the N.L.C. confronted three major obstacles. Pledged to restore Ghana "to an even keel politically, socially and economically," in the words of General Ankrah, the N.L.C. viewed its role first of all as curative, purging the state of Nkrumahist elements. Second, the ruling junta confronted a grave economic situation: foreign currency reserves had been reduced 80 per cent in less than a decade; crushing external debts, many of them short-term, neared $1 billion; inefficient import regulations brought crippling shortages of vital materials; world prices for cocoa, Ghana's main export, had fallen to a 20-year low. Third, and most important, the National Liberation Council confronted substantial political problems in shepherding the people through a difficult transitional period. The population— and its would-be political leaders—had to be reeducated to handle the changed conditions. Support had to be built for policies, such as fiscal austerity and currency devaluation, that would adversely affect large sections of society. These obstacles would challenge even the most skilled politician, and the members of the N.L.C., all professional officers, had little experience in the

[1] Henry L. Bretton, *The Rise and Fall of Kwame Nkrumah: A Study of Personal Rule in Africa* (New York: Frederick A. Praeger, Inc., 1966), pp. 41–100.

rough-and-tumble arena of Ghanaian politics.

RESTORATION OF DEMOCRACY?

Shortly after Nkrumah's overthrow, Ankrah announced that the N.L.C. would "run the affairs of this country until true democracy based on the popular will of the people and not on the will of one man alone has been fully restored." "True democracy" implies many attributes but in February, 1966, few democratic prerequisites existed. Voting registers were out-of-date and likely falsified in many constituencies; political parties were ill-organized (parties opposing Nkrumah's Convention People's party had been declared constitutionally illegal early in 1964, and the C.P.P. itself was banned by the N.L.C. after the coup); and repressive policies had diminished press freedom.

The N.L.C. might have pursued two alternative strategies to restore democracy. On the one hand, the military rulers could have established coalition of civilians not tainted by association with Nkrumah, then retired to the barracks within a very short period. Alternatively, the N.L.C. might have attempted to create "true democracy" under its direct aegis, attempting to create and channel political awareness without civilian intermediaries.

Neither strategy was selected. Faced with a situation of bewildering complexity, the Council reacted pragmatically. Its members agreed on the urgency of reform, and found it increasingly difficult to disengage themselves from control. The result has been a shifting level of civilian influence in what remains (despite the protestations of the N.L.C.) a government clearly directed by the men who overthrew

Nkrumah. A brief review of events since the coup makes this point clear.

THREE N.L.C. STEPS

After an initial period of hesitation, members of the N.L.C. took over cabinet positions. But increasing insistence from former politicians who had opposed Nkrumah, coupled with recurrent promises by General Ankrah about civilian rule, indicated that an expanded role for civilians was essential. In July, 1966, a 23-member "Political Committee" was named; its membership list read like a "Who's Who" of erstwhile Ghanaian politicians—two founders of the United Gold Coast Convention (a party established in 1946 to bring self-government "in the shortest possible time"), and several prominent opponents of Nkrumah. The Committee was instructed to examine the enactments, decisions and policies made since the coup d'etat. However, its advisory powers were severely limited. Apart from giving a number of talented and highly educated men a symbolic role in the government, the Political Committee accomplished little. But it should also be pointed out that the institutional context for decision-making remained amorphous. Until the N.L.C. decided to admit unequivocal civilian participation, uncertainties and frustrations were bound to occur.

Following the creation of the Political Committee, the N.L.C. established a constitutional committee. The committee, named in September, 1966, was not to prepare and ratify a constitution, but was to collect varying opinions from the citizenry. From such evidence, the committee would prepare a draft constitution for subsequent debate and ratification by a constituent assembly. The committee's activities were limited.

The grass-roots consultation was not fully carried out. Although conclusive evidence is not available, it seems likely that the N.L.C. did not wish to awaken unrealistic hopes of a rapid return to civilian rule. Civic reeducation lagged behind the pace the military leaders had foreseen. As Colonel A. A. Afrifa noted in March, 1967,

It may be necessary to let the people get used to their newly won freedom and to familiarize themselves with the qualities that they require from potential leaders before they are called upon to go to the polls.

He added that the return to civilian rule would also require destruction of the image of the Convention People's party and removal of factors, particularly economic factors, that led to the coup. Once again, the N.L.C. did not carry through with a policy it had apparently supported. Continued economic uncertainties appeared far more pressing than a rapid transition to an elected government.

The third major step taken by the N.L.C. came on June 30, 1967, with the establishment of a 21-member Executive Committee; two-thirds of the members were civilians. The most significant positions—interior, external affairs, defense, and finance—remained in N.L.C. hands. The Executive Committee was charged with "general direction and control" of the government, but these prerogatives were subject to the powers of the N.L.C. The majority of the men brought into the cabinet were not former politicians, but rather highly trained former civil servants, educators and technocrats. Their major task was to help establish the "even keel" which the N.L.C. had sought for 16 months. Formation of a National Advisory Committee, replacing the Political Committee established a year earlier, followed on July 11, 1967; the 31-member board was chaired by K. A. Busia. Economic reforms appeared paramount, and it was not fortuitous that currency devaluation occurred less than two weeks after the naming of the Executive Committee and a matter of days after creation of the advisory committee.

UNRESOLVED ISSUES

Several steps remain before complete civilian rule returns to Ghana. N.L.C. members realize that sweeping reforms cannot simply be promulgated in an official gazette, nor guaranteed by a well-intentioned elected government. Reorientation requires time, energy, support, awakened civic consciousness and responsibilities, and a firm economic foundation. To achieve "true democracy" may require a written constitution. This, in turn, requires examination by a constitutent assembly of the draft prepared by the constitutional committee; choice of the constitutent assembly requires delimitation of constituencies, preparation of new voting registers, and a fundamental decision by the N.L.C. as to whether campaigns for the constituent assembly should be fought on a partisan or a non-party basis. Basic issues thus remain unresolved. Should all former C.P.P. members be barred from public life? Can "true democracy" flourish without political parties? Has the economic situation sufficiently improved to encourage the army to make good its promises of returning to the barracks? Until clear answers are forthcoming, the N.L.C. may expect rising criticism which, thus far, has been successfully contained.

The army itself presents one potential danger to the National Liberation Council. The apparent ease with which Nkrumah and many other African politicians were ousted by army leaders does not pass unnoticed. Once officers have demonstrated that a simple show of force may topple a government, other members of the military may be tempted to mutiny. A series of counter-coups, of dissent and rebellion in the army, seem a possible outcome of military intervention.

The N.L.C. faced its first significant internal challenge on April 17, 1967. Officers of a reconnaissance regiment stationed near Ho (90 miles northeast of Accra, the capital) conspired to overthrow the ruling group by assassinating its leading members and seizing radio facilities in Accra. A dawn attack on the residence of General E. K. Kotoka (the main agent in the overthrow of Nkrumah) resulted in the death of four members of the regular army, including Kotoka. The leader of the revolt, 25-year-old Lieutenant Samuel Arthur, claimed during his trial that promotions of junior officers were not being granted rapidly enough. In other words, complaints about internal army matters had been transformed from barracks' gripes into incentives to rebel. Lieutenant Arthur and coconspirator Lieutenant Moses Yeboah were executed before a large crowd on May 9, long-term imprisonment was given other soldiers implicated in the plot, and 489 persons were placed in protective custody. The lesson was clear. The N.L.C. would be threatened by other counter-coups unless it maintained a high degree of cohesion and surveillance in the armed forces. Restoration of civilian rule, therefore, depended in part on military unity of purpose.

ECONOMIC RETRENCHMENT

Nkrumah left an economic shambles behind. By tropical African standards,

Ghana was, and remains, one of the continent's wealthiest states, with an annual per capita income greater than $250. Blessed with extensive foreign exchange reserves at independence, the state suffered from numerous extravagant and misguided economic ventures. General Ankrah did not mince his words: Nkrumah "brought Ghana to the brink of economic disaster by mismanagement, waste and unwise spending." To document the former government's profligate financial policies and endemic corruption, the N.L.C. doubtless gained support as the extent of financial manipulation became public. However, fundamental reforms proved necessary, and the medicine chosen—financial retrenchment through austerity and deflation—was bound to be unpalatable.

Four basic economic difficulties confronted the N.L.C. on the morrow of the coup. A severe, adverse balance of overseas payments had practically exhausted Ghana's external reserves. Budget deficits had been the rule, not the exception; inflation and food shortages had directly affected the articulate urban sectors of the population. In the face of a slowdown of economic activity, it became increasingly difficult to find employment, particularly for school leavers. (Between 1965 and 1970, an estimated 752,000 middle school leavers* will enter the labor force; but in the decade 1954–1964, the number of jobs in the modern sector of the economy grew from 225,000 to 350,000.)[2] Any major attempts at

* Editor's note: Middle school leavers are those who have completed the American equivalent of less than eight grades, i.e., those who do not go on to secondary education.

[2] Figures from Walter Birmingham, *et al.*, eds., *A Study of Contemporary Ghana*, Vol. II, (Evanston, Ill. Northwestern University Press, 1967), pp. 232–33.

deflation would have direct impact on the rate of unemployment—the political and security risks of a large jobless urban group must not be underestimated.

One factor in Ghana's economic plight was the drain on state resources from state firms. Thirty-seven such companies were established under the Nkrumah regime, few of which proved profitable. A few weeks after the coup, Ankrah decided to restrict the extent of the governmental economic participation that had proved so costly. Active state participation, he noted, "will be limited to certain basic and key projects." The private sector of the economy would remain the most significant, in terms of both output and employment. Joint private-government enterprises, and cooperative ventures, would also be encouraged.

Compared with pre-1966 policy, the National Liberation Council's economic priorities placed far greater stress on private initiative. State firms were reorganized. Three were sold to Ghanaian businessmen, and private participation was encouraged. Several United States firms, including Firestone Rubber, Abbot Laboratories, and Intercontinental Hotels (a Pan American subsidiary), agreed to assume responsibility for former state firms. To reduce the continuing financial drain, one-third of the farms operated by the Farms Corporation were closed; Ghana Airways reduced its operating deficit by cancelling orders for surplus aircraft, returning several Ilyushin aircraft to the Soviet Union, and arranging traffic pools with Nigeria Airways.

The most significant economic step of 1967 occurred in July, with the devaluation of the *cedi* from $1.40 to $.98. Currency devaluation is a well-known device to improve a state's export position and reduce imports. The

30 per cent devaluation was offset by increased prices for cocoa (a move that helped reduce discontent among the politically influential farmers of Ashanti), elimination of import duties on food, milk, and other essential goods, and a 5 per cent salary increase for civil servants. Devaluation indirectly boosted the sagging timber and gold mining industries, whose rising costs had made profitable operation unfeasible.

The overall, long-range effects of the government's actions cannot be assessed at this juncture. Brigadier A. A. Afrifa claimed that the devaluation would "reactivate the economy, increase production and employment, and set the stage for more accelerated development in the future"—but these assertions must be taken with due caution. It should be noted that the International Monetary Fund had urged devaluation, and acceptance of this advice bears witness to the willingness of the N.L.C. to turn to expert advice, even at the cost of politically unpopular side effects at home.

The 1967–1968 budget, like its immediate predecessor, stressed consolidation. (The N.L.C. scrapped the budget Nkrumah had prepared immediately before his ouster, and instead introduced a special budget in August, 1966.) Official projections allowed for a slight surplus: estimated recurrent expenses of $297 million, development expenses of $88 million, and estimated receipts of slightly over $385 million. Ghana also called on Harvard University to furnish a team of economists to work out a new development plan. The "Seven-Year Development Plan" prepared by the Nkrumah government earlier had been rejected by the N.L.C. as overambitious and unrealistic.

Reckless financing by the Nkrumah regime also confronted the N.L.C. with a serious foreign debt problem. Shortly after the coup, it was estimated that repayment of external commitments would consume a quarter of all foreign exchange earnings—funds urgently needed for development. Many of the debts resulted from pre-financing arrangements made by contractors. Rates of interest were high, and the economic utility of several projects remains debatable. In this situation, the Council confronted a basic dilemma. It wished to demonstrate its fiscal responsibility by meeting debts accumulated under Nkrumah. However, the government could not meet the heavy commitments of funds necessary for debt servicing. The only solution lay in considerably expanded international assistance and debt rescheduling, to allow the Ghanaian economy a breathing spell.

During 1966 and 1967, the bulk of Ghana's financial commitments (more than $560 million) were rescheduled. Economic assistance, drawn mainly from the International Monetary Fund and from Western states, reached $70 million in 1967. The balance of payments deficit, however, could not be eliminated. The Ghanaian economy remains hobbled by a lack of spare parts and raw materials. Ironically, the import licensing regulations established by the Nkrumah government to save foreign exchange may have gravely weakened the country's position. For example, insufficient amounts of insecticide were imported in 1965–1966, thereby reducing the cocoa crop.

Serious economic dislocations remain, in spite of the N.L.C.'s sincere and extensive retrenchment efforts. More than half the local industrial capacity is unutilized, owing to the lack of raw materials. The heavy public investments of the past decade did not increase the economy's rate of growth, and the burgeoning population (the average Ghanaian mother bears more than seven children) has absorbed any rise in per capita gross national product. The economy as a whole remains primarily dependent on cocoa, and though the N.L.C. has fortunately profited from rising world prices, the vagaries of the international market may jeopardize overall economic recovery.

Economic stagnation brings other problems in its train. Great internal migration in Ghana, particularly from the villages to urban centers, has compounded unemployment. Rural underemployment has become urban unemployment, since most educated youth scorn jobs that appear menial or "traditional." Only an extraordinarily rapid expansion of the modern sector of the economy can absorb these internal migrants. Given the basically cautious and pragmatic economic policies espoused by the Council, creation of jobs for jobs' sake appears unlikely. Unemployment can be reduced only by a basic change in attitudes, whereby the school leaver does not automatically escape to the city to avoid what he sees as a sterile, uninteresting, and unprofitable life in "the bush."

FOREIGN POLICY COMMITMENTS

Preoccupation with domestic reconstruction has reduced Ghana's role in international affairs under the N.L.C., as contrasted with the flamboyant, pan-African aspirations of Nkrumah. The coup d'etat brought three basic shifts in emphasis in Ghanaian foreign policy. First, relations with the neighboring French-speaking states (Ivory Coast, Togo and Upper Volta) improved

markedly. Good fences do not necessarily make good neighbors—but the decision of Ghana and Upper Volta to demarcate their border bore witness to more cordial relations.

The second shift occurred in intra-African politics. Nkrumah's vision of African unity was grounded on an unshakable belief in the necessity for political union. Almost alone among African leaders, he argued for a continental government—an assertion contrary to the basic trends in African politics.[3] The N.L.C. members, stressing internal solidarity and development, were far more in tune with their fellow rulers than was Nkrumah. Ghana thus came to work more closely with other African states on such issues as Rhodesia, and South West Africa, and to aid, through the Organization of African Unity, independence movements in Portuguese territories.

Far more cordial relations with Western states represented the third change. The earnest efforts of the Council to regain economic equilibrium and restore political choice won strong approval in Washington, London and Bonn. General Ankrah's visit to Great Britain, Canada and the United States in October, 1967, further helped to cement the ties his government had carefully nurtured.

The growing schisms and eventual civil war in Nigeria directly involved Ghana. On several occasions, Ankrah offered to mediate between the federal government and the secessionist Biafran regime of Colonel Odunegwu Ojukwu. In January, 1967, he arranged a meeting of Nigerian leaders at Aburi, a

[3] Claude E. Welch, Jr., *Dream of Unity: Pan-Africanism and Political Unification in West Africa* (Ithaca, N.Y.: Cornell University Press, 1966), p. 357.

palatial country estate built (but never occupied) by Nkrumah. The agreement reached quickly broke down, in a welter of claims and counter-claims.[4] When fighting erupted in July, Ankrah redoubled his efforts at mediation; in November, as an official delegate of the Organization of African Unity, he visited Lagos in an unsuccessful effort to halt the conflict. Ghana's major foreign policy efforts during 1967 thus came to naught, the victim of an unfortunate clash between primordial sentiments of tribalism and political desires for national unity.

LESSONS TO BE LEARNED

During 1967 the N.L.C. continued to follow the paths of economic responsibility, pragmatic political adjustment and limited collaboration with civilians. The regime was courageous. Staking their claim to historical renown on financial reconstruction, the members of the National Liberation Council attempted to postpone full transition to civilian rule until the economic situation had been righted.

During its early months, the N.L.C. gained support as the saviour of the country from despotism. Revolution against the Nkrumah government—its corruption and inefficiency, its denial of basic political rights, its unresponsiveness to public opinion—provided a valuable cushion of support for the army and police officers. However, support based on distaste for a previous regime cannot be expected to endure. Support must be built on a new basis. The Council is staking its claim on economic recovery. Ghana required extensive financial surgery—including

4 For a discussion of Nigeria, see John D. Chick, "Nigeria at War," *Current History,* LIV (February, 1968), 65–71, 113.

amputation of state firms that only drained away resources. Yet many factors that affect the Ghanaian economy lie beyond the N.L.C.'s control. Foremost among these is the world market price for cocoa.

In the absence of effective international price arrangements, a bumper crop might drive down the funds Ghana would receive per ton, and thereby jeopardize the mainstay of the Ghanaian economy. Ghana's growing local industries require markets, particularly in Africa, but other states, anxious to develop their own industrial capacity, may be unwilling to enter into extensive trading relationships. Although the debt rescheduling provides an opportunity for reconstruction until early 1969, the creditor countries expect Ghana to repay thereafter according to the old schedules. In other words, she must expend nearly $140 million in fiscal 1969–1970 for debt servicing, contrasted with $14 million in the current fiscal year.

At the current time, Ghanaian politicians seem strangely muted. The symbolic participation in decision-making provided by the Political Advisory Committee has definite limitations. If the professions of a return to civilian rule are accurate, one should expect increasing tensions as the time of transition nears. Former supporters of Kwame Nkrumah will demand a share in governing. Ethnic tensions may intensify. The unhappy urban unemployed offer fertile ground for radical political appeals, for developing a style of leadership far removed from the conservative pragmatism of the N.L.C. Disaffected young elements of the armed forces may attempt, as did Lieutenant Arthur, to overthrow the regime and substitute a government of far different policies. The possibility of an implicit alliance of ex-Nkrumahist politicians, urban unemployed and junior officers, linked by their opposition to the well-educated former opposition politicians and senior officers comprising the Political Advisory Committee and the National Liberation Council, must not be overlooked.

It is easy to overthrow a despised regime: a few skirmishes, the seizure of main communications facilities, and the incarceration of the former leader's assistants usually suffice. Thus far, restoring civilian rule has proved infinitely more complex.

SOUTHEAST ASIA

John H. Badgley

BURMA'S CHINA CRISIS:
THE CHOICES AHEAD

The middle ground in Asia has eroded, and the efficacy of neutralism is in doubt. The Asian international scene has changed in the past four years as though it had passed through a cataclysmic war. The Bandung spirit of Afro-Asian amity died with the Sino-Indian border conflict in October 1962. The transition to a new power arrangement was symbolized in June 1967 as Burma and Cambodia, the last of Asia's important neutrals, joined India and Indonesia, as well as those states aligned with the United States, in being denounced by China. Burma's twenty-year friendship policy toward China appeared to be bankrupt.

For Asia's former neutrals, the process of forming a new China policy is not

yet completed, but there can be no doubt about the direction in which Burma's Bogyoke Ne Win and his Revolutionary Council are being pressed. China's Maoists have their last levers of domestic influence in Burma—an insurgent communist party and the Chi- would be a major policy shift; yet Ne since the insurrection began in May 1948 has any Burmese government been so challenged at home and abroad. A major ally to counter the Chinese pressure may become essential, yet the choice is traumatic, for never in Burma's 900-year history has a free government aligned itself with a foreign power outside the Irrawaddy-Salween region. For Burma to enter into such an alliance against China would be a major policy shift; yet Ne Win is already modifying the isolationist policy which so weakened Burma economically that Peking could hope to overthrow the government with a rejuvenated insurrection.

Reprinted from John H. Badgley, "Burma's China Crisis: The Choices Ahead," *Asian Survey,* VII (November 1967), 753–61, by permission of the publisher. The article has been revised by the author for this volume.

THE NATURE OF THE CRISIS

The new challenge to the Rangoon government began in April 1967, when the Communist Party of Burma (CPB or White Flag), led by Thakin Than Tun, (later assassinated by a Chin student), became divided over the policy of continued insurrection. Since the coup of March 2, 1962, Bogyoke Ne Win had led the coalition of colonels and civilians, which governed with considerable revolutionary socialist devotion. Consequently, the alternative ideological program of the communists, who had been underground since 1948, was severely undermined. Their *raison d'être* seemed to be only a compulsion for power and a vision of a Burma aligned with China against the Soviet bloc as well as the West.

A former disciple of Thakin Than Tun who defected to the Ne Win government in early June 1967 was reported in the press to have revealed details of the split that ended in the "dismissal" of Goshal (Thakin Ba Tin) and Yebaw Htay, two of the five CPB politbureau members. Two weeks after the exposé, Radio Peking, in a complete reversal policy, commenced unprecedented propaganda attacks on the Ne Win government. Overnight the *paukpaw* (kinfolk) relationship, so carefully cultivated during the Bandung era, had changed to enmity. The Bogyoke's government was labeled "puppet of the revisionists and capitalists," and the Burmese people were asked to overthrow a "bastard gang that held power by opposing the true revolutionary forces." On July 3, 1967, Peking made official its decade-old covert support of the White Flags as a "true liberation movement," and allowed two leading Burmese Communist insurgents to address a mass rally with Chou En-lai.

In the two weeks between the defector's exposé and the policy reversal announced in Peking, a series of anti-Chinese eruptions within Burma changed the personal respect that characterized the attitude of most Burmese toward China. In two Rangoon schools Chinese students of Burmese nationality came to class on June 22 wearing Mao badges in place of the appropriate identity pins. Teachers asked that the Maoist pins be removed; the students refused until the principal intervened. Later in the afternoon an embassy car appeared with "older men" who distributed new pins as well as Maoist literature. Photographers were on the scene, and the offending students attacked them as well as several techers. The outbreak was subdued, but the following day a mob of Burmese students attacked the Chinese students. The next day some six hundred students from the predominantly Chinese schools were removed to a nearby army base. When parents came to claim them, student "leaders" barricaded the doors and refused to leave for two days. Students who escaped claimed several of these "leaders" had flown in from China after Red Guard training. Demonstrations broke out in other Chinese schools as well as around the Communist Chinese embassy, where eventually a mob broke in, killed one technician, and injured others.

During the next week rioting spread throughout Rangoon, so disturbing the city that neighborhood protective associations, *kin,* were formed, as they had been in 1942 during the Japanese invasion. (Normally Burmese get along well with Chinese, but more than a hundred thousand Burmese of Indian extraction live in Rangoon, and their presence may explain why more than fifty residents of the Chinese quarter were killed. Injuries ran much higher.) Anti-Maoist demonstrations followed in most Burmese towns, and by the first week in July genuine support for Bogyoke Ne Win was probably at its highest point since the 1961 coup. The continuing Peking radio attacks against their government solidified the Burmese against a foreign power as has no event in a decade.

Since July, anti-Maoist demonstrations have been nurtured by the government and carefully reported in the press. Every major town and many villages have held marches against the Maoist regime. More recently a new activity, work demonstrations in which "mental and physical workers" donate their holidays to increased productivity, has been encouraged against China, which has continued to malign the Ne Win regime over Radio Peking.

THE TURN IN BURMESE POLICY

What possible goal could the Peking government have had when it made such a major miscalculation? Or was it a miscalculation? If not, is this then a prelude to more forcible action? Has the Burmese government taken steps in the past year that would warrant such a severe threat?

One can answer these questions best in reverse order. A series of actions by the Burmese government does indeed suggest a decision to gradually reenter regional and international activities, even at the risk of good relations with China. The decision was presaged by Ne Win's frank criticism, in October 1965, of his government's failure to develop Burma's economy by pursuing an excessively radical nationalization policy. Two months later a warm reception was given Senator Mike Mansfield, who also visited Cambodia. Mansfield, the first high-ranking American political figure encouraged to enter Burma since the 1962 coup, had extended discussions with Ne Win and his closest advisers. The Senator, whose sympathy for Burma's and Cambodia's neutral foreign policy has been well defined, reportedly suggested that the Bogyoke visit the United States the following year, an offer that Ne Win subsequently accepted. In September 1966, he met with President Johnson in Washington, and they discussed "matters of mutual concern." A $35-million allocation made in 1958 was exhausted in 1967, but no subsequent agreement has been revealed.

Earlier in the year several American political commentators were given two-week visas to travel in Burma and interview high officials. Correspondents from major Western newspapers entered for the first time in four years, and the reporting on Burma's economic problems was astonishingly forthright.

The groundwork was laid for renewed international aid to pull the country out of the depression its excessive nationalization had created. Rice exports, which in pre-World War II days had averaged two million tons per year, had declined to 600,000 tons in 1967 and 320,000 tons in 1968. The need for revised internal policies as well as external assistance was also demonstrated by shortage and poor distribution of basic commodities, such as rice, fish paste, and cooking oil. Currently, the World Bank and the International Monetary Fund are considering Burma's needs, and trade missions have visited Malaysia, Singapore and Thailand, seeking new commercial ties. However the government did fail to develop these tentative gestures in 1967 or 1968.

Solutions to economic problems were not the only goals sought by the regime's reentry into the world. In 1966 Ne Win visited Pakistan and India. In January, 1967, India and Burma commenced negotiations on their long-disputed boundary. Within three weeks an agreement was reached, and the treaty was signed on March 10. Although five and a half miles of territory remained undefined, the agreement went beyond the territory China claimed as its own, where the three boundaries meet. Two months later the Burma-Pakistan border was agreed upon, if not demarcated, settling another outstanding issue that the Maoists apparently had hoped to exploit by supporting such frustrated minority leaders as Nagas and Bengalis in this ethnically tangled region stretching from Assam to the Naaf River and over to the Ganges delta.

Meanwhile, the Burmese government began to give internal publicity to its decision to host the annual Colombo Plan Conference in November, 1967. The invitations, extended at the 1966 meetings in Karachi, were so discreet that the Foreign Office allegedly was not informed until the Bogyoke's representative returned from the conference. The Revolutionary Council had previously played down its relationship to the Colombo group and emphasized the need for Burma to develop alone without foreign aid. India is one of the major recipients of Colombo Plan aid (much of which is American-financed); Burma's decision to identify with the program so closely marked a clear departure from its earlier "neutral" policy

(a euphemism for a policy acceptable to Peking).

Most recently Burma has moved in other technical fields toward a position that Peking must find irritating. In June, a team from the Information Ministry toured India, analyzing radio and telecommunications facilities. Several Burma Broadcasting operators are assigned to work in Washington with the Voice of America "to gain experience." In public health and medical research, various delegations of Burmese specialists have visited laboratories around the United States since 1966. Between two and three hundred students have gone to Eastern Europe and the Soviet Union for technical training while Chinese offers of assistance have gone unanswered. In September 1967, the few resident Burmese students and the Ambassador were withdrawn from China. The government has given considerable press coverage to the activities of the various Asian regional organizations such as the Asian Development Bank, the Association for Southeast Asia, the Southeast Asia Education Ministers Council, the Economic Commission for Asia and the Far East, and ASPAC (the Asian and Pacific Conference). In sports, the Burmese have recently entered many trans-Asian competitions (all boycotted by China) in tennis, golf, boxing, soccer, track, and swimming. Considerable publicity was given the 1968 Olympics, and quasi-Olympic symbols are now used freely for internal athletic activities.

There can be no doubt that Burma is moving back into an international life that was temporarily rejected in 1962. At that time some viewed Burma's policy as subservient to the People's Republic of China, despite the Burmese government's increasingly careful scrutiny of internal activities by the resident Chinese minority and infiltrating Chinese communist provocateurs. That policy resulted in the closure of the whole internal Chinese language press as well as the nationalization of the Chinese banks. On July 13, 1967, the legitimate channel of communication for the Chinese, the Burmese language newspaper *Ludu,* which had been pro-Peking since its founding, was closed. In all probability, the contacts with the Soviet Union, Japan, and other European powers will be advanced in the near future.

This could not be viewed as a policy success for a Peking bent on restructuring international relations.

THE LARGER ARENA

The course of events just described is in some respects unique to Burma, but it quite parallels the experiences of Burma's nonallied neighbors. India and Indonesia have, of course, long since earned Peking's hostility. Specifically, both diplomatic delegations suffered grave indignities in Peking. And in Djakarta, New Delhi, and Rangoon, Chinese diplomats were injured by mobs, a tragedy the Maoists exploited by flying the injured and the ashes of the dead back to Peking on special planes which were met by huge crowds demanding redress for the attacks. Cambodia's more recent difficulties follow the same pattern, with students wearing Mao badges, with Radio Peking belaboring Sihanouk's regime for its repression of the Red Guard movement, and with Sihanouk's removal of two pro-Peking cabinet ministers.

Peking's vitriolic verbal blasts have been shared by such a disparate crowd as the governments of East Germany,

Bulgaria, France, the Soviet Union, Kenya, and, of course, all the American allies in Asia. The evidence is strong that Burma's experience is not unique, but rather that the apparent "miscalculation" which cost so much Burmese good will is part of a global tactic. What motivations and goals the Maoists may have has been the subject of enormous debate, but what is evident from the Burmese experience is that local conditions are not an important consideration for Peking theorists behind the current strategy. In my view, Burma went as far as possible to accommodate the Peking radicals as well as its own socialists who had totalitarian proclivities. For four years, with the goal of reducing the political pressure that had broken the U Nu administration, it pursued both a domestic and foreign policy that set back economic development a full decade At last, with the trends all downward, Bogyoke Ne Win reached out tentatively and cautiously for a renewal of links with the outside world, links that could help Burma regain its economic footing.

It may well be that analysts in Peking did not perceive the delicate shift in Burmese policy over the past two years, or that the shift was reported and ignored, or that it was perceived, reported, and responded to. In any event, the result was the same, for China deliberately incited its covert political groups in Burma, the White Flag Communists and the Chinese students, to attack the government. The reaction against China and Burmese of Chinese extraction was immediate and so predictable that some have suggested the whole affair was an Indian or CIA plot. But the evidence makes such a cleverly demonic move both improbable and unnecessary. More likely,

Peking simply ignored its diplomatic and overseas communities in Burma and sacrificed everything in the pursuit of the inner logic surrounding the Cultural Revolution and the Red Guard movement.

The Maoists also may have sensed a losing cause and switched to a new policy, gambling desperately that the Burmese government of Bogyoke Ne Win would be weak enough to fall in the ensuing violence. Now the tactic has failed and the Rangoon government faces a new set of choices in foreign policy. Since Than Tun's death, and the accompanying fratricide of top level White Flags, Burma's insurgent communist movement has lost central direction.

FOREIGN POLICY ALTERNATIVES FOR BURMA

In one sense Burma is playing a new ball game, for the rules are different from any that have applied in the past. The principle around which other foreign policy considerations always clustered was the relationship with China. In the two decades since independence, every Rangoon government has worried over its long frontier with China, which is indefensible without major military aid. Post-colonial leaders reached the same conclusion as did all but the most bellicose of the pre-colonial monarchs. That conclusion was that Chinese hegemony should be acknowledged so that China would leave Burma alone. By the seventeenth century, tribute missions were traveling frequently enough to Peking, usually every ten years, to institute the relationship as a tradition, and with only a few dramatic exceptions the system worked until the British came on the scene.

The relationship since 1948 has func-

tioned in rather the same fashion for the same reasons. The analogy with Finland is often made, for there Russian dominance is axiomatic. Like Finland, Burma had no concrete evidence that any neighboring power could oppose her dominant neighbor in a real confrontation. After the Korean war, the only potential non-Asian power with that capability, the United States, seemed to have little taste for land fighting in Asia. Finally, and more important, the Burmese government had so much domestic strife that any significant great power involvement threatened to lead to another Korea, and later, another Vietnam.

For a time Burma was faced with an implacable China with expanding nuclear capability. The Maoists were delivering their worst propaganda attacks and may also have aided the insurgents. (The insurgents control perhaps a tenth of the population and nearly two-fifths of Burma. The CPB is only one of five insurgent groups, three of which are communal—the Shan, Karen, and Kachin.) Should China's belligerency have increased, the Ne Win government would have had no choice but to seek outside aid or risk a coup led by more militant anti-Chinese, by anti-communists within or outside the military or by both. The factor that may change Ne Win's perspective of the ball game is the ample evidence that both the United States and the Soviet Union can deliver the most sophisticated arms to Southeast Asia. The United States is clearly willing to spend considerable fortune and blood in defense of Asian allies, but it is uncertain, given the unpopularity of the Vietnam war, about taking on new commitments.

If Rangoon chooses, it can eventually seek association with SEATO or that cluster of states that already has nuclear defense arrangements with the United States: Korea, Japan, Taiwan, the Philippines, South Vietnam, Thailand, and Pakistan. Another choice would be to strike for the same sort of loose nuclear umbrella arrangement that India has with both the Soviet Union and the United States. A third alternative would be to seek major Soviet aid, as Indonesia did, suggesting a bilateral alliance of potential use against both China and the American cluster. A fourth possibility would be a mutual defense pact with the ex-neutrals, Indonesia, and Japan. These four choices are alternatives that Burma never felt free to make before. In the face of a Chinese threat which could become quite concrete, Burma could select one of these four alternatives and establish a historic precedent.

From the Burmese perspective, all these policy choices have disadvantages. To align with the U.S. and its allies would directly contradict previous policy. It would encourage the same American cultural subversion that Suharto has labeled Indonesia's second most dangerous threat. It would mean inviting China's most powerful enemy to a position directly on her border, a border that is as much a threat for China as for Burma. It would risk severe domestic disturbance, for an entire generation of Burmese has been reared on an ideology that labels the U.S. a colonial power. For many, an American presence would be as distasteful as a Chinese occupation.

The "loose nuclear umbrella arrangement" would suffer the same disadvantages perceived by India: ardent nationalists regard joint Soviet-American aid as unreliable and too distant in the event of attack from China. Furthermore, the nationalists see both powers as bent on interfering in India's domestic affairs—the U.S. through its economic aid and CIA activities, the USSR through its Communist Party ties and military aid. The technical problems posed by parallel commitments from the Soviets and American would be considerable, requiring the Burmese military to learn the use of both types of weapons. Lastly, it would mean asking the two superpowers to cooperate more closely than may be politically possible for either one, given the tension arising from the Vietnam and Middle East wars.

The third choice, inviting a unilateral Soviet presence, would be as great a strategic threat to China as would an American presence, given the Maoist perspective of the world. Furthermore, it would mean intimate cooperation with a communist state that has covertly aided the insurgents within the past decade. The Burmese army would have to be retooled and retrained in the use of Soviet weapons (they now have mostly American and British arms). Finally, as both the Vietnamese and the Middle East crises demonstrate, the Soviet Union might not be willing to commit its troops in the event of a major war.

The fourth alternative, while politically the most inviting of any new policy to the Burmese public, offers only limited military capability. Neither India nor Indonesia will be able to afford the export of substantial numbers of troops for many years to come. It is questionable how capable their brigades would be when fighting on foreign soil. To ask only for weapons and communications aid from either power would be politically acceptable to many Burmese but scarcely adequate to meet any serious Chinese invasion or insurgent buildup.

A modification of the fourth alternative, aid from Japan or Pakistan, might serve some short-term advantage in alerting the world to Burma's defense needs; but again, with a serious Chinese confrontation such aid would be puny. Other possible allies, Great Britain or the European powers, are less promising than the United States in terms of their defense interests. Militarily, Europe has forgotten about Asia, leaving security problems there to be solved by the superpowers and the Asians themselves.

Related to this last alternative could be an intensification of relations with Burma's Buddhist neighbors, Laos, Cambodia, and Thailand. Both U Nu and Ne Win have engaged more closely with Thai leaders because of the range of interrelated problems affecting both states. Their long common frontier is mutually indefensible and intermittently penetrated by smugglers, insurgents, and even tourists. Both worry that the other might be made a hostile launching area by a major power; the Thai fear that China might use Shan or Burman insurgents against Thailand, while the Burmese government has ample evidence that Karen, Shan, and KMT insurgents do receive aid from sources in Thailand. In an effort to attenuate these mutual fears over the past decade, the respective governments have repeatedly renewed pledges of respect for one another's territorial integrity, planned annual consultation, and even conducted joint border patrols. Neither side appears to be satisfied with the other's efforts, and the relationship remains prickly. As for Laos and Cambodia, despite shared problems of domestic insurgency, need to accommodate the major powers, peasant distrust of central government, and propinquity as well as cultural affinity, the Burmese pay little heed to their neighbors' internal affairs. Even the similar foreign policies of Sihanouk

and Ne Win since 1962 have not drawn these two powers into a closer affiliation. Perhaps the compelling reason is that none of the parties is capable of doing anything serious to, or for, the other without outside assistance. All three are buffer states.

IMPLICATIONS FOR THE UNITED STATES

The military confrontation between Burma and the Maoist regime is still unlikely, despite the heated exchange of mid-1967. But the sudden buildup of tension confirms the views of apologists for U.S. Vietnam policy and suggests that "leaving Asian problems for Asians to solve" may not be in the best interests of many Asians or of the status-quo industrial powers either. As one goes over Burma's alternatives in this current crisis, it is apparent that the Soviet and American presences in Asia offer important new possibilities. Without either power Burma would be forced to kowtow to China in the current crisis just as other weak powers throughout the world have done in the face of overwhelming pressure. Or Burma could fight as Finland did in 1939, or Poland in 1940, and suffer the same grievous losses.

Some have argued that China would not challenge the legitimacy of a neutral government that refused alliance with the United States or the Soviet Union. Such a view may have been correct once, but the crisis that Burma is now facing in its relations with China sustains the opposite position. Burma has pursued a foreign and domestic policy that was as correct as possible without being subservient to China; tragically, its reward is a foundering economy and a weakened bureaucracy that makes the country unusually vulnerable. In the face of the same unreasonable Chinese hostility that encouraged Peking to support the Indonesian communist insurrection, Ne Win must now seek an alternative course.

Should Burma turn to the United States for some form of renewed assistance, it would be doubly tragic if its request was ignored. Undoubtedly, the most acceptable form of support on both sides would come through international or regional agencies. In this sense the Burmese case is not unlike that of Indonesia, Malaysia, India, and the other nonsocialist states on China's border. Consequently, it would behoove the U.S. Congress to reconsider its current determination to cut back foreign aid at any cost. In a real sense, the reward for Vietnam casualties is already forthcoming in the Burma crisis. The extremists in Peking have overplayed their hand, and, as never before, the most neutral of Asia's states is free to modify its opposition to the West and pursue a more liberal and outward-looking policy. Such a policy, which would invite outside assistance as well as a return to a mixed domestic economy, could return Burma to the condition of rapid development characteristic of the mid-1950's. To ignore the Burmese plight would save money in the short run, but would incur far greater long-run costs if the Maoists prevail in China.

SUGGESTIONS FOR FURTHER READING

West Europe

Brown, Neville, "British Arms and the Switch towards Europe," *International Affairs,* London, XLIII (July, 1967), 468–82.

Camps, Miriam, "Britain and the European Crisis," *International Affairs* (London) (January, 1966), pp. 45–54.

———, *European Unification in the Sixties: From the Veto to the Crisis* New York: McGraw-Hill Book Company, 1966.

Comyns, Cair R., "Spain and the Common Market," *World Today* (June, 1964), pp. 249–55.

Jensen, W. G., *The Common Market.* London: G. T. Foulis & Co. Ltd., 1967.

Kitzinger, Uwe, "Britain's Crisis of Identity," *Journal of Common Market Studies,* VI (June, 1968), 334–57.

Rodó, Laureano López, "Spain and the E.E.C.," *Foreign Affairs,* XLIV (October, 1965), 127–33.

Rosecrance, R. N., *Defense of the Realm: British Strategy in the Nuclear Epoch.* New York: Columbia University Press, 1968.

Schopflin, George A., "EFTA: The Other Europe," *International Affairs* (London), XL (October, 1964), 674–84.

Von Bonsdorff, Goran, "Regional Cooperation of the Nordic Countries," *Cooperation and Conflict,* I (1965), 32–38.

Latin America

Abel, Elie, *The Missile Crisis.* Philadelphia: J. B. Lippincott Co., 1966.

Bonsal, Philip W., "Cuba, Castro, and the United States," *Foreign Affairs,* XLV (January, 1967), 260–76.

Corkran, Herbert, Jr., *From Formal to Informal International Cooperation in the Caribbean.* ("Arnold Monograph Series.") Dallas: Southern Methodist University, 1966.

Draper, Theodore, *Castro's Revolution.* New York: Frederick A. Praeger, Inc., 1962.

Goldenberg, Boris, *The Cuban Revolution and Latin America.* New York: Frederick A. Praeger, Inc., 1965.

Horowitz, Irving, "Cuban Communism," *Transaction* (October, 1967), pp. 7–15.

Pachter, H. M., *Collision Course: The Cuban Missile Crisis and Coexistence.* New York: Frederick A. Praeger, Inc., 1963.

Springer, Hugh W., *Reflections on the Failure of the First West Indian Federation.* ("Harvard University Center for International Affairs Occasional Paper.") Cambridge, Mass.: 1962.

Middle East

Draper, Theodore, *Israel and World Politics: Roots of the Third Arab-Israeli War.* New York: The Viking Press, Inc., 1968.

Gilead, B., "Turkish-Egyptian Relations: 1952–57," *Mid-East Affairs,* X (November, 1959), 356–65.

Howard, Michael, and Robert Hunter, *Israel and the Arab World: The Crisis of 1967*. London: Institute for Strategic Studies, 1967.

Laqueur, Walter, *The Road to Jerusalem: The Origins of the Arab-Israeli Conflict*. New York: The Macmillan Company, 1968.

Mango, Andrew J. A., "Turkey and the Middle East," *The Political Quarterly,* XXIII (April–June, 1957).

Marlowe, J., "Arab-Persian Rivalry in the Persian Gulf," *Journal of Royal Central Asian Society,* LI (January, 1964), 23–31.

Prittie, Terence, *Israel: Miracle in the Desert*. New York: Frederick A. Praeger, Inc., 1967.

Safran, Nadav, *The United States and Israel*. Cambridge, Mass.: Harvard University Press, 1963.

Stevens, Wiley, "L'Iran et Le Monde Arabe," *Chronique de Politique Etrangere,* XX (March, 1967), 119–32.

West Africa

Feith, Edward, "Military Coups and Political Development: Some Lessons from Ghana and Nigeria," *World Politics* (January, 1968), pp. 179–93.

Flint, John E., *Nigeria and Ghana*. Englewood Cliffs, N.J.: Prentice-Hall, Inc., 1966.

Penter-Brick, S. K., "The Right to Self Determination: Its Application to Nigeria," *International Affairs,* London, XLIV (April, 1968), 189–202.

Post, K. W. J., "Is There a Case for Biafra?" *International Affairs,* London, XLIV (January, 1968), 26–39.

———, "Six Views of the Nigerian War," *Africa Report,* XIII (February, 1968), 8–24.

Thompson, W. S., "New Directions in Ghana," *Africa Report,* XI (November, 1966), 18–22.

Williams, David, "How Deep the Split in West Africa?" *Foreign Affairs,* XL (October, 1961), 118–27.

Southeast Asia

Bradley, C. P., "Rupture in Malaysia," *Current History,* L (February, 1966), 98–105.

Emery, F., "Singapore Is Afraid that Time Is Running Out," *New York Times Magazine* (April 28, 1968) pp. 28–29.

Holmes, Robert A., "Burmese Domestic Policy: The Politics of Burmanization," *Asian Survey,* VII (March, 1967), 188–97.

Johnstone, William C., *Burma's Foreign Policy: A Study in Neutralism*. Cambridge, Mass.: Harvard University Press, 1963.

Leifer, M., "Singapore Leaves Malaysia," *World Today,* XXI (September, 1965), 361–64.

Trager, Frank N., "Burma: 1967—A Better Ending Than Beginning," *Asian Survey,* VIII (February, 1968), 110–19.

———, *Burma: From Kingdom to Republic*. New York: Frederick A. Praeger, Inc., 1966.

Warner, D., "Singapore and Malaysia: A Divorce of Inconvenience," *Reporter,* XXXIV (April 7, 1966), 44–46.

part three

THE

INTRUSIVE

SYSTEM

6

COMPARISONS

Having discussed the core, the periphery and the relations between them, we move now to the processes and problems of the intrusive system—the subordinate system when it is considered as including those external powers with politically significant involvement.[1] We will discuss this segment of regional international politics with reference to the framework that was established in the opening chapter. We will first apply the nine methods of participation discussed there to the five regions with which we are concerning ourselves in this volume. We will then proceed to a brief analysis of the effect of participation by intrusive powers upon the four pattern variables. As part of both sections of the discussion, the patterns of involvement (unilateral abstention, mutual noninvolvement, and mutual involvement) will be illustrated.[2]

THE METHODS OF PARTICIPATION

The reader may recall that we identified nine methods of participation in the intrusive system. These were: multilateral arrangements; bilateral

[1] See Chap. 1.
[2] Tables for Chap. 6 appear in the Appendix to this volume.

arrangements; trade and economic investment; possession of a colony; military intervention; subversion; the United Nations; cultural and educational activities; and propaganda. We now move to a detailed analysis of these nine methods. The ordering of the material as listed here allows us to consider first the three foremost political, economic, and military means of intrusion: multilateral arrangements, bilateral arrangements, and trade and economic investment. The three intervening methods—colonies, military intervention, and subversion—have uneven significance. The possession of a colony can be of the most crucial importance in molding a subordinate system and, in the past, often was. Military intervention and subversion are frequent, although not consistent, means of intrusive influence upon subordinate systems. The final three methods—the United Nations, cultural and educational activities, and propaganda—are all primarily political, rather than military or economic. They are intended as more subtle, indirect, and cheaper instruments of policy of intrusive powers.

MULTILATERAL ARRANGEMENTS

The ability to organize multilateral arrangements in an area is an indication of particular strength on the part of an intrusive power. Only a state with extensive contact, influence, and power in a particular subordinate system is in a position to participate in this way. In a roughly descending ranking, the present major Western powers with the ability to organize states multilaterally are the United States, France, and Great Britain; the major Communist powers are the Soviet Union and China.

The United States

It is not surprising that the United States, the most powerful nation in the world, has been especially active in the organization of multilateral arrangements—particularly in Latin America and West Europe but, to a lesser extent, in Southeast Asia and the Middle East also. We will discuss American multilateral arrangements in this order, because it represents a declining pattern of ascendancy.

In Latin America, the United States maintains the most paramount influence of any intrusive power in any of the five subordinate systems under discussion. It is involved or consulted in almost every one of the multilateral arrangements of the area, particularly in the core. In the diplomatic arena, the United States has participated in the Organization of American States (OAS), often attempting to use it for its own purposes during major crises. In economic affairs there have been a variety of institutions which the United States has either supported, organized, or joined. These have included the Inter-American Development Bank, the Alliance for Progress, The Central American Common Market (CACM),[3] The Latin American Free Trade

---

[3] For an excellent account of the American role in CACM, see Joseph Nye,

Association (LAFTA), and the as yet incipient Latin American Common Market. It is only in the mid-1960's that the United States has moved into a position of any thoroughgoing enthusiastic support for economic multilateral institutions in Latin America, although the record indicates that American support is a necessary (though insufficient) condition for success.[4] The Americans have in general preferred bilateral economic relations and have often acted unilaterally in the diplomatic and military spheres. In fact, American political policy in Latin America has frequently fluctuated between adherence to a renovated form of the Monroe Doctrine and championship of the principles of cooperation and nonintervention contained in the Charter of the OAS, concluded at Bogota in 1948.

Contradictory attitudes toward multilateralism have not characterized American involvement in the politics of *West Europe,* however. There the United States has vigorously supported indigenous European cooperation, largely through economic means, the ultimate goal being a United States of Europe. Even when the United States has participated in economically oriented institutions, the major goal has been a United Europe. Thus, the Organization of European Economic Cooperation (OEEC), which the Marshall Plan instituted (and which is now called the Organization for Economic Cooperation and Development (OECD)), had as one of its major initial purposes the encouragement of a greater degree of European cooperation. The crowning results of this policy were the European Coal and Steel Community (ECSC), the European Economic Community (EEC), and the European Atomic Energy Community (EURATOM). In the mid-1960's, under the Johnson Administration American enthusiasm for a United Europe began to wane in the wake of Gaullist economic, political, and military strategy and Common Market necessities, but the United States continued to be a primary supporter of British entry into the Common Market.[5] Hence, as American enthusiasm for Latin American integration increased in the light of the disappointing Alliance for Progress and the Dominican crisis,[6] it began to decline slightly in Europe in the light of the Gaullist assault and the lessening Soviet threat.

With regard to military multilateral organizations in West Europe, America's approach has been slightly different from its approach to economic organizations. Whereas the United States has, in general, encouraged European economic institutions but did not join them, it has participated

---

"Central American Regionalism," in his *International Regionalism* (Boston: Little, Brown and Company, 1968), pp. 414–19.

[4] For an account of the American change in attitude toward economic integration in Latin America, see Christopher Mitchell, "Common Market, The Future of a Commitment: Punta del Este and after," *Inter-American Economic Affairs,* XXI (Winter, 1967), 73–88.

[5] However, American support for Great Britain cannot be construed as being definitely pro-integration. British entry could increase American influence and loosen the Common Market.

[6] Mitchell, *op. cit.*

actively in the North Atlantic Treaty Organization (NATO). This institution has played the same role in West Europe—as the central focus of American military and diplomatic policy—as the OAS has played in Latin America.

In Southeast Asia, the United States has similarly concentrated on both economic and military multilateral institutions. The Americans have joined the Southeast Asian Treaty Organization (SEATO) as they joined the OAS and NATO, and have actually fought a war in part to uphold this multilateral organization. The diffuse nature of Southeast Asian politics and the relatively weaker position of the United States there has meant that SEATO has had far less support within the subordinate system than the OAS and NATO have had in Latin America and West Europe. Only the Philippines and Thailand actually joined; Laos, Cambodia, and South Vietnam were covered by a special protocol.

In Southeast Asia, as in the other two areas, the United States has supported organizations whose membership was limited to indigenous countries. For example, the U.S. has supported the Asian and Pacific Conference (ASPAC), the MeKong Development Committee, and the Association for Southeast Asian Nations (ASEAN), as well as institutions in which it participates (e.g. the Colombo Plan, the MeKong Basin Program, and the Asian Development Bank). The Americans have supported regional organization in Southeast Asia almost as enthusiastically as they have supported integration in West Europe. However, the lower levels of cohesion, of economic and political development, and of tranquility have meant more limited success in this area.

In the Middle East, the Americans have been unable to organize a multilateral economic institution. In military security affairs, a weak organization called the Central Treaty Organization (CENTO), and the multilateral guarantees contained in the Eisenhower Doctrine, have been the only steps—however unsuccessful—which the Americans have accomplished. The United States remains largely uninvolved *in West Africa* and has not sponsored any multilateral arrangements in that subordinate system.

France

No other intrusive power has attempted to sponsor multilateral institutions on the level of the United States. The French have maintained their paramount position in *West Africa*—particularly, of course, in the core—in the postcolonial period. Their major organization in that area, *Organisation Commune Africaine et Malgache* (OCAM), resembles the pattern the Americans have used elsewhere. The French, unlike the Americans, have tended to view integration as a hindrance to their hegemony rather than as an asset to their strength. Their activity in West Africa can thus most easily be compared to past American efforts in Latin America. The French do not participate, to any politically significant extent, in multilateral organizations in the other areas we are studying. Typical is their nearly moribund participation in SEATO.

Great Britain

The British Commonwealth serves as a declining, but still persistent, force in international affairs. In the regions we are studying, British influence is most important in the peripheries of *West Africa* and *Latin America,* and in Malaysia and Singapore in *Southeast Asia.* The British have from time to time sponsored efforts at integration and economic cooperation, but these have been neither dramatic nor successful. The major effect of the Commonwealth, in terms of regional international politics, has been to provide a focus for partial cooperation and at least mutual identification in the periphery of West Africa and in the Caribbean. Whether or not the Commonwealth will become a focus for future multilateral organizations or will be even further diluted, only time can tell. Certainly some form of British-encouraged multilateral organization appears more likely in the Carribean than in West Africa, where the British appear to be losing influence to the French, Americans, and Russians especially in the light of the complexities created by the Nigerian civil war.

The Soviet Union

With the exception of East Europe, the communist states have been much less successful than the West in organizing multilateral arrangements as a means of intrusion into particular regions. Indigenous communist parties out of power have long been an instrument more of subversion than of multilateralism. As in West Europe, when they lose their subversive character they also tend to become more independent of the communist bloc. The international communist movement has become as polycentric as the British Commonwealth, and even in East Europe it has become less effective in regional politics. The Russians have been so removed from multilateral arrangements that they have even failed to support Cuban Fidel Castro's organization, known as the Organization of Latin American Solidarity (OLAS), whose purpose is to unite the left-wing forces attempting to overthrow intrenched pro-American regimes. The orthodox pro-Moscow Communists in Latin America have themselves been largely unenthusiastic to this instrument of the followers of Fidel.[7]

Communist China

The Chinese have been even less successful with multilateral arrangements. Their attempts to organize anti-Soviet support within the communist

[7] Herbert S. Dinerstein, "Soviet Policy in Latin America," *American Political Science Review,* LXI (March, 1967), 86.

movement—particularly in Asia—have largely failed. At the summit of their effort in 1964, they maintained support of a broad number of communist parties, particularly Asian, but by 1968 their position in the communist world was declining and they had broken with such major advocates and sympathizers as the Japanese party and majority Indian party. Even the North Vietnamese and North Koreans appeared to have moved into a neutral position between them and the Soviet Union, and presumably leaned slightly toward the latter.

The Chinese attempted a kind of supraregional multilateral arrangement, centered in Indonesia, under the leadership of the then Indonesian President Sukarno. The New Emerging Forces (NEF), as it was called, became moribund with the failure of the communist coup in Indonesia in October, 1965. This development followed the failure of the Chinese to exclude the Russians from the Afro-Asian conference in Algeria, which was then canceled because of lack of agreement among the countries involved. The Chinese had apparently hoped to use the conference to advance their own foreign policy, which could have had significant repercussions in the Middle Eastern core and throughout Southeast Asia.

BILATERAL ARRANGEMENTS

For most intrusive powers, bilateral arrangements are more significant than multilateral. We are referring here to governmental disbursements (loans or grants), or other economic arrangements made between an intrusive and a local power. We are also concerned with the grant or sale of military equipment, and with bilateral defense treaties, which are often connected with base agreements. These treaties tend to tie the intrusive power closer to the local state, and usually are indicators of stong programs of military and economic aid.

When we view all forms of bilateral relations combined, three patterns emerge in our five regions: (1) in West Europe and Latin America, there is a high degree of unilateral dominance; (2) in the Middle East and Southeast Asia, there are a variety of intrusive states which are active and politically significant; and (3) in West Africa there is a mixed pattern in which there is a dominant power (France), but other states are also active. We will use these three patterns as a basis for our discussion of bilateral arrangements, because thereby we will be able first to examine the most simple arrangement (dominance of a single intrusive state); second, the most complex (the competitive situation); and finally, the most unusual (the situation where there is both dominance and competition).

West Europe

West Europe represents the most celebrated and successful case of foreign aid yet recorded. Here *the United States*—through a combination of multilateral and bilateral programs only suggested by the Marshall Plan and NATO—assisted the wartorn West European countries to accomplish a stunning recovery in the aftermath of the devastation of World War II. From 1946 to 1952, American aid to Europe (both economic and military) represented 69% of the American aid budget.[8] Even though this percentage had declined to 11 by 1965, the United States had still provided more aid to West Europe in the postwar period than any other intrusive power had granted to another subordinate system. Indeed, American aid to Europe—military and economic—represented nearly half of American foreign aid through 1957.[9] The total military assistance to West Europe between 1946 and 1965 can be estimated at $18,000 millions and the total economic assistance at $23,600 millions. During this time only recently independent Malta and highly stable Switzerland did not receive some form of aid. As Table 6-1 indicates, the greatest recipients of military aid were France, Turkey, Italy, Greece, the Benelux countries, the U.K., and West Germany, in that order. The greatest recipients of economic aid were, in order, the U.K., France, Italy, West Germany, Turkey, and Greece. Although aid programs of all types have tapered off as the European states themselves became strong enough to be aid-givers, American programs in West Europe were in general massive, broad and, with the possible exception of parts of the Southern periphery (Spain, Portugal, Greece, Cyprus, Malta, Turkey) highly successful.

With West Europe, the *Soviet Union*—the other intrusive power—has had a minimal degree of bilateral interaction. In the core and the Northern periphery, its most spectacular arrangement has been the agreement with former President De Gaulle to cooperate in mutual research endeavors.[10] The only other country to receive even minor Soviet aid is Turkey—which, as we have already indicated, is a borderline peripheral member of West Europe.[11] Generally, however, as Marshall Shulman points out, the Russians have attempted to increase their economic, political, and technological contacts with West Europe.[12] In addition, the Cyprus dispute and the increased Russian interest in the Mediterranean have led to recent low-level deals with Cyprus and reported Russian flirtation with Malta.

[8] David A. Baldwin, *Foreign Aid and American Foreign Policy* (New York: Frederick A. Praeger, Inc., 1966), p. 33.

[9] *Ibid.* These percentages include several totals for East Europe as well as West, but the West received the overwhelming majority of the sums involved.

[10] The following are examples of the kinds of projects the two governments are pursuing: On October 9, 1967, French meteorological equipment was launched from the USSR's Heyss Island rocket base in the Arctic. French and Russian scientific officials announced on June 9, 1968, an agreement for placing French scientific equipment aboard a Soviet lunar probe toward the end of 1968. The USSR had previously agreed to launch France's projected Rousseau satellite in 1972.

[11] Turkey will be discussed as part of the Middle East.

[12] Marshall D. Shulman, " 'Europe' versus 'Détente,' " *Foreign Affairs*, XLV (April, 1967), 395.

Besides American and Soviet aid to West Europe, there have been two other types of aid within this area that resembles intrusive action. First, in the Southern periphery, several countries have also been granted foreign aid by their neighbors to the north. There is, of course, considerable precedent for this activity. It should be remembered that Cyprus and Malta were British colonies until 1960 and 1964, respectively. The British also had prime Western responsibility for Greece and Turkey until 1947, when they found it impossible to continue for economic reasons and the American government made the far-reaching decision to replace that aid. Additional economic aid granted to the Southern periphery includes *moderate sums* granted by West Germany and Great Britain to Cyprus, Malta, Greece, Spain, and Turkey.

Second, although the United States has been overwhelmingly dominant in grants and sales of arms to West European countries, it is interesting to note that there has been a gradual rise in indigenously produced arms within Europe—especially in West Germany, Sweden, France, and Great Britain. Thus, a minor amount of the sales of arms formerly handled by the United States are now managed either by indigenous European production or by transactions within Europe. The French nuclear force has been the most spectacular indication of Europe's comparatively small, but growing, independence in armaments.

Latin America

In Latin America, the political superiority of the *United States* is greater than in West Europe, but in the realm of foreign aid the U.S. has received slightly more competition, both from a reawakened European interest in the area and from mild Soviet attempts to make inroads. American aid to this subordinate system has increased steadily, especially in the post-Castro period. From 1946 to 1948, it was only 2% of the total spent by the U.S. on foreign aid. It rose to 11% in 1959, dropped to 8% in 1960, and rose as high as 22% in 1965.[13] Indeed, as American aid to Europe has declined, the slack has been absorbed by greater interest in all three Asian regions as well as Latin America (and, in part, by a decline in the percentage of GNP spent on foreign aid). Joan Nelson reports that, in the Marshall Plan era, economic assistance alone represented about 2% of the American GNP and about 11% of the federal budget, and that in 1966 it absorbed only about 0.29% of the GNP and 1.9% of the budget. She reports that even when expenditures for military aid, contributions to international organizations, Food for Peace, and Peace Corps are added, costs have dropped from a peak of 28% of federal expenditures, in 1947, to 4.4% in 1966.[14] American aid to Latin America, then, has increased—in relative terms and

---

[13] Baldwin, *Foreign Aid*, p. 22.
[14] *Aid, Influence and Foreign Policy*, (New York: The Macmillan Company, 1968) pp. 6–7.

in the light of the general decline in this form of American foreign involvement.

American aid to Latin America has been broad and far-reaching, even though not massive. Foreign aid has been granted to all countries in the subordinate system at one time or another. Bilateral economic grants and loans have roughly followed the size of Latin American states. Thus, Brazil, the region's largest state, has received the most economic aid: from 1946 through 1965, it amounted to $1,590 million. Although much more went to some European countries, it is worth noting that in terms of average annual assistance (from 1960 to 1965), Brazil was the fifth highest recipient of U.S. aid (see Table 6-3). Argentina's share of the aid total is not as large as might be expected, however; the reasons include her relatively high development and nationalistic traditions. Aid to Venezuela is also surprisingly low, because of her comparatively high standard of living. Among the weaker countries of Latin America, Bolivia and Guatemala have received especially large amounts of American aid. The U.S. had supported the nationalist revolution in Bolivia since 1952. The United States has been concerned about communist intrusion in Guatemala since 1954, and has been willing to give extra amounts of aid to assure security.

Because of the importance of the military in Latin American countries, military aid is very significant. The U.S. has furnished military assistance at various times to all Latin American countries except the minor Caribbean states and Guyana, but the assistance has served various competing and contradictory programs. To grant arms solidifies American influence with indigenous armed forces, but it exacerbates local arms races, identifies the U.S. with the military establishment, and leads to the growth of local forces in order to maintain the equipment. To receive arms—even on favorable terms—often means, in addition, the sacrifice of important funds for economic development. On the other hand, many governments are so intimately tied to the military that not to sell arms to them risks the lessening of American influence. These states may turn to a European government in any case, make a less favorable deal, and end up paying even greater development costs.[15] In the final analysis, some of the criteria by which the United States determines the level of military assistance to particular countries are: The internal importance of the military and its role in keeping the country pro-American; the nature of particular arms races (e.g., Peru vs. Chile, Chile vs. Argentina); and, a criterion of gradually increasing significance, the extent of internal subversion (e.g., Bolivia, Colombia, Venezuela, Guatemala).

Other noncommunist intrusive states have given sporadic economic aid to Latin American states. In 1965, Brazil and Chile were among the five recipients of the largest French aid to non-franc countries. The same two

[15] Harold A. Hovey, *United States Military Assistance: A Study of Policies and Practices,* (New York: Frederick A. Praeger, Inc., 1965), pp. 244–49.

countries were the only major recipients, outside Asia, of Japanese aid in 1965.[16] They were among the recipients of grants given by Germany for technical assistance.[17] Brazil and Peru were among the six recipients of the largest amounts of German aid when figures for German financial assistance in 1965 are added.[18] The French have concentrated on the dramatic (e.g., De Gaulle's trip to Latin America in the spring of 1964 and controversial arms deals), but the British have made a broader range of grants to several Latin American states in recent years, and in 1965 they too were especially generous to Brazil and Chile.[19] They have concentrated, in particular, on their colonies and the members of the Commonwealth in the region. Although Argentina did not receive large amounts of aid in 1965, she did in earlier years—especially from West Germany, Great Britain and France.[20]

Military assistance is a crucial indicator of at least potential influence. The French are becoming active, against American desire, in offering military programs. For example, their sale of twelve Mirage jet fighters to Peru in 1968 touched off a heated controversy between the U.S. and Peru. That other Western powers have also been active can be seen from the fact that, from June 1966 to June 1967 alone, Chile, Venezuela, and Brazil made significant deals with Great Britain, West Germany, and Canada, respectively.[21]

Leaving Cuba aside for the moment *the U.S.S.R.'s* foreign aid to Latin America has been limited to loans to Argentina, Brazil, and Chile.[22] Trade has been far more important in Soviet dealings with Latin America than aid, but in general Soviet actions have reflected the tacit admission that the U.S. is the supreme power in this area of the world. Even in the 1950's, the Russians were willing to deal with Peron of Argentina and Batista of Cuba.[23] Their prevailing and rather consistent attitude seems to be that any loosening of American influence—even if accomplished through established governments—is a plus for Russian interests.

16 Organization for Economic Cooperation and Development, *The Flow of Financial Resources to Less-Developed Countries: 1965* (Paris, 1967) p. 85.

17 *Ibid*, p. 80.

18 *Ibid*. In 1964, Germany's aid surpassed that of Great Britain and became the third largest source of economic assistance after the U.S. and France. Wolfe W. Schmokel, "Germany in the Underdeveloped World," *Current History*, L (May, 1966), 281–88.

19 Great Britain, Ministry of Overseas Development, *British Aid: Statistics of Official Economic Aid to Developing Countries* (London: Her Majesty's Stationery Office, 1966) pp. 21–23.

20 Organization for Economic Cooperation and Development, *Development Assistance Efforts and Policies of the Members of the Development Assistance Committee,* A Report by Willard L. Thorp (September, 1967) pp. 131–32.

21 *The Military Balance 1967–1968.* (London: The Institute for Strategic Studies. September, 1967). See also Geoffrey Kemp, "Rearmament in Latin America," *The World Today*, XXIII (1967), 375–84.

22 See Table 6-1, p. 409

23 Marshall I. Goldman, *Soviet Foreign Aid* (New York: Frederick A. Praeger, Inc., 1967), Chap. 9.

In Cuba, the Russians received an unexpected and, as it turned out, an extraordinarily expensive windfall. Castro has not always been willing to cooperate in every way with his Soviet sponsors, and as of 1966 he had cost them approximately $592 millions in grants, loans, and technical assistance,[24] and probably a considerable additional sum in military assistance. Given the variety of Soviet foreign and defense commitments elsewhere, it is possible to suppose that the Russians would not necessarily favor another Cuba in the Western Hemisphere.

Since *the Chinese* have been much less willing to cooperate with established governments, their assistance in Latin America has been limited to Cuba. Indeed, the Chinese maintain diplomatic relations with no other country in Latin America. However, although China extended a loan of 60 millions to Cuba in 1960, and by the middle of the decade their trade had reached considerable proportions, the Chinese program there must be regarded as an almost total failure.[25] In January 1966, the Cubans chose to work with the Russians rather than the Chinese for economic reasons and because of specific grievances. The result was a lessening of the friendly relations between China and Cuba, although limited economic and diplomatic relations were maintained.[26] In terms of foreign aid, then, Chinese influence in Latin America is at present negligible.

The Middle East

Thus far we have dealt with two areas in which American influence is supreme. In the Middle East and Southeast Asia, conditions are considerably different. In the Middle East, the U.S. and the Soviet Union now share primacy—and other powers, particularly Britain, France, China, and West Germany occasionally spar for a smattering of influence.[27] Here the United States is on the defensive, her influence decreasing and her position—particularly in the core—diminishing.

In the periphery, *the United States* remains dominant. Turkey has continued to be the largest beneficiary of both American military and economic aid in the area. Between 1946 and 1965, she received more than twice as much economic assistance as Brazil (the Latin American leader), and less than only the U.K., France, and Italy in West Europe. The United States has also conducted strong programs in Iran and in Israel. And though economic aid has declined as Israel has grown stronger, military sales have

---

[24] *Ibid.*

[25] Alexander Eckstein, *Communist China's Economic Growth and Foreign Trade* (New York: McGraw-Hill Book Company, 1966), p. 305.

[26] Kevin Devlin, "The Permanent Revolutionism of Fidel Castro," *Problems of Communism,* XVII (January–February, 1968) 5.

[27] We have chosen to concentrate on the major intrusive powers, and hence the programs of the East European states and the small West European states have not been included in our discussion. It is worth noting, in particular, that East European programs often accompany Soviet efforts, especially in the Middle East.

gradually increased as the U.S. and Israel have become more closely identified.

The United Arab Republic (U.A.R.) in the core, has received twice as much economic aid as any other Arab state. Indeed, from 1960 to 1965 the U.A.R. ranked seventh in the average annual economic assistance granted by the U.S. (see Table 6-3). Nevertheless the U.S. has never granted military aid to the U.A.R., and its influence and aid has steadily declined. In the period following the Six Day War, relations were cut off by Egypt and no aid was granted by the United States. Food for Peace, first suspended in 1965, was cut off again in 1966.[28] The Middle-East Arab nation which has received the highest per capita assistance in recent times is the kingdom of Jordan. American aid and influence has come to settle here, in Lebanon, and in Saudi Arabia. Indeed, Saudi Arabia has become the strongest ally of the U.S. in the core and has received more military aid from the United States than any Middle-Eastern Arab country except Iraq., whose formerly close relations with the U.S. ended with the coup there in 1958.

Although *the French* were the major suppliers of the Israeli military before the Six Day War, Gaullist relations with the Arabs had improved gradually but steadily after the Algerian War.[29] As part of their gradual program of improving relations with the Arabs, the French have concentrated on Iraq, with mixed success. They have also maintained relatively close relations with the Lebanese. With the decline in importance of the Suez Canal and the British decision of July 1967 to withdraw its military presence east of Suez, the Middle East has become less and less significant for the formerly paramount United Kingdom. Outside of their colonies and protectorates, moderate amounts of British aid have gone to Turkey and Jordan, and there have been occasional sales of arms to several Middle East countries.[30]

The West Germans have been active in the periphery, especially in Israel and Turkey. Their relations with the Arab core were muddied by a crisis in 1965, when a combination of West German concern over Arab flirtation with East Germany and Arab concern over West German ties with Israel rose to a crescendo. The result was the establishment of West German diplomatic relations with Israel and the termination of diplomatic relations by several Arab states with West Germany. As Table 6-3[31] indicates, between

28 Joan Nelson, *Aid, Influence, and Foreign Policy,* pp. 118–19.
29 Eric Rouleau, "French Policy in the Middle East," *The World Today* XXIV, (May, 1968).
30 See Table 6-2, pp.412, Organization for Economic Cooperation and Development, *Geographical Distribution of Financial Flows to Less Developed Countries: 1960–64* (Paris: 1966), and OECD, *Geographical Distribution of Financial Flows to Less Developed Countries: 1965* (Paris, 1967).
31 p.416.

1960 and 1965 Israel received the second largest amount of German economic assistance (although the largest part of the sum came from reparations), Turkey the fourth, and the U.A.R. the tenth.

While changing fortunes, regimes, and events have peppered the Middle Eastern political salad, over the broad period since their efforts first began *Soviet programs* have generally moved forward. As to the periphery, the Soviet Union—despite extending early diplomatic recognition and assistance —has not advanced aid to Israel since 1949. Turkey and Iran have traditionally been, respectively, antagonistic and neutral toward the Russians; in the 1960's, however, decreased American involvement, an atmosphere of detente, and the Cyprus issue provided the Russians with new opportunities to wean both these countries from staunchly pro-American stances. The Russians have provided broad but light economic aid to Iran and, even more surprisingly, some measure of military aid. Although neither country has turned even vaguely anti-Western, the success of the policy was symbolized in June 1967, when the Turks allowed Russian ships to exit freely through the Dardanelles.

The Russians' program in the core has been even more spectacular and successful. They have granted some type of foreign aid to every Middle-Eastern Arab country except Saudi Arabia, Kuwait, Lebanon and Jordan. The U.A.R. is (along with India) one of the two non-communist countries in which Soviet aid has been most ambitious and successful.[32] The Aswan Dam is symbolic of a variety of activities, which have included steel mills, oil refineries, and agricultural machines.[33] The second largest recipient of Soviet economic aid in the core is Iraq, but Syria has also become an extremely important client of the Soviet Union and, interestingly enough, the Russians have been involved in strategically located Yemen since 1956— even when its government was a royalist regime. In addition, increasingly large amounts of aid have gone to the Sudan and to South Yemen since its independence in 1967. As to military aid, the Russians have become the prime supplier of arms to the Arab core. After they failed to intervene on behalf of the Arabs in the Six Day War, they resupplied most of the Arab forces, at a cost that may have run as high as $2 billions. Although barter arrangements (e.g., Egyptian cotton) had previously been used to repay Soviet arms grants, it appears that the arms in this case were supplied relatively free of economic charge. The U.A.R. has been the primary recipient of Soviet military aid, but all recipients of regular aid have also been supplied and, in June 1967, the Sudan joined the list of Soviet arms recipients.

The Chinese have maintained a program in the Middle East, paying

[32] Goldman, *Soviet Foreign Aid*, p. 61.
[33] *Ibid.*, Chap. 8.

particular attention to the U.A.R., Syria, and Yemen—but it is only in Yemen that they can be said to have been a competitive force.[34] They have, however, suffered from a lack of financial resources, and consequently their impact cannot be compared with that of the U.S. or the U.S.S.R. In the Middle East, foreign aid has become expensive, but, as in other subordinate systems, the Chinese have found it possible to be competitive in other ways.

Southeast Asia

In Southeast Asia, as in the Middle East, intrusive powers have rivaled each other. *American aid* has soared, due in large measure to the Vietnam War in the mainland core, the Indonesian coup, and the impending British withdrawal from the maritime core. Even before the Vietnam War was escalated, in 1965, the country had already received more American economic aid than any other nation in Southeast Asia, even more than such favored recipients of American aid as Brazil, Turkey, and Taiwan. From 1960 to 1965, it ranked fourth on the average (see Table 6-3). Since 1965, economic aid has increased significantly in South Vietnam, Thailand, and Laos, and although the amounts of military aid to these countries are classified information, we know that they have been very high. In the Southeast Asian area, the only country not to receive at least economic aid has been North Vietnam, although the Americans have experienced a kind of on-again off-again arrangement with Burma, Cambodia, and Indonesia. The Burmese and Cambodians have been antagonistic to a variety of donors, and their efforts at neutrality have achieved only moderate success. The Indonesians, on the other hand, swung from a pro-Soviet and pro-Chinese position, before the 1965 coup, to a more pro-American and pro-Japanese position afterwards— and the size and significance of American aid programs also changed. Unlike the Indonesians, the Filipinos—formerly under American colonial rule—have remained consistently pro-American and have been rewarded accordingly.

Until 1967, Malaysia and Singapore maintained very strong relations with *Great Britain*. In July 1967, however, when the British announced that after 1971 they would no longer be able to maintain their position east of Suez, the stage was set for a slight realignment in these two countries which will most likely entail the increased involvement of Australia and, especially, of the U.S. The British have contributed minor amounts of aid to almost every Southeast Asian state, but it is possible that even this assistance may eventually be decreased.

The French have not been a major factor in mainland Southeast Asian politics since they withdrew after their defeat in Indo-China in 1954. They

---

34 U.S. Congress, Joint Economic Committee, *An Economic Profile of Mainland China*, 90th Congress, 1st sess., 1967, (Washington, D.C.: Government Printing Office), Vol. II, 612.

were never a factor in the maritime core, although they have given small amounts of aid to Indonesia.[35] It is interesting, however, that Cambodia, Laos, and South Vietnam have continued to be among the principle recipients of French foreign aid outside the franc area. The French have also attempted to nurture their relations with North Vietnam, and so General de Gaulle must have viewed the choice of Paris for initial peace negotiations in 1968 with a good deal of satisfaction.

The Japanese have become a powerful, but reluctant, major influence throughout Southeast Asia with respect to economic aid. They have already largely superseded the French and British and show every sign of becoming more important in the future. They have thus far largely concentrated on Asian countries (over 90% of their aid, in 1965). From 1960 to 1965, the major recipients of Japanese aid in Southeast Asia were, in that order, Indonesia, Burma, the Philippines, South Vietnam, Thailand, and Cambodia (see Table 6-3). Outlays to Indonesia have increased considerably since the coup there. The Germans have also had an extensive program throughout Southeast Asia, which has now surpassed both the British and French efforts, but is smaller than that of the Japanese.[36]

Soviet policy in Southeast Asia has been characterized by a diverse series of successes and failures. In the maritime core, the only opportunity the U.S.S.R. has had is in Indonesia. Here the peculiar combination of corruption, inflation, and Sukarno's ambition contributed to very poor results even though the economic program was the Russians' fourth largest in the noncommunist world (the others being in India, the U.A.R., and Afghanistan).[37] Their military assistance program was similar to the one in the U.A.R., equipping and training the armed forces. Yet, under Sukarno the Russians progressively became less influential than the Chinese. Under the new regime they appear to be less influential than the Western powers, particularly the United States.

In the mainland core, however, Russian influence has gradually increased. One of the major early decisions by the successors to Khrushchev seems to have been to reverse his apparent policy of withdrawal from Southeast Asia, a decision which seems as much related to the Sino-Soviet conflict as to any particular developments within Southeast Asia.[38] Thus, when the bombing of North Vietnam began on February 7, 1965, Premier Kosygin was in Hanoi, heading a high-level Soviet delegation. Since that time, Soviet assistance to North Vietnam has increased dramatically, far surpassing anything the Chinese were capable of providing. In addition, the Russians

[35] John L. Sutton and Goeffrey Kemp, *Arms to Developing Countries, 1945–1965* ("Adelphi Paper," No. 28 [London: Institute for Strategic Studies, 1966]).
[36] Organization for Economic Cooperation and Development, 1960–64 and 1965.
[37] Goldman, *Soviet Foreign Aid*, p. 206.
[38] T. W. Wolfe, *The Soviet Military Scene: Institutional & Defense Policy Considerations* (Santa Monica: The RAND Corporation, 1966), pp. 109–10.

have maintained their loose foothold in Laos[39] and, especially, Cambodia, through limited economic and military aid. They have also suffered from Burma's frequent discrimination against foreigners, even those providing aid.

Southeast Asia is an area of extremely strong *Chinese interest,* but the Chinese have been unable to establish durable ties with any government in the area. Between 1953 and 1965, Communist China committed and provided more aid to North Vietnam than to any other country in the world.[40] This assistance seems in the long run to be less productive than the Chinese might have hoped since Russian influence increased gradually in Vietnam as a result of the exigencies of the war. The Chinese have promised more aid to Indonesia than to any other nonaligned country, but have actually granted more to Cambodia than to any other noncommunist nation. In Indonesia a very strong and apparently successful program was completely destroyed, while in Cambodia the results have been more satisfactory, even though the Chinese have suffered sporadically from Prince Sihanouk's accusations that they were subverting his regime. With Burma, formerly China's third highest recipient of foreign aid, relations have deteriorated sharply, since 1967, into mutual hostility.

Thus, in assessing the results of Southeast Asian bilateral arrangements, we conclude that the Americans seem to have been the most successful (despite or perhaps because of the Vietnam conflict) in gaining the political and diplomatic support of those they sought to aid, while, of the remaining powers, the Chinese appear to have made the worst record and the Russians to have obtained very mixed results. It is necessary to add, however, that in the turmoil-ridden politics of Southeast Asia, any momentary gains or superiorities are likely to be both ephemeral and Pyrrhic.

West Africa

In West Africa—an area in which only Liberia was independent before 1957—we find the mixed pattern of dominance and competition. *France* is the major intrusive power, but several other competitors are also moderately active. Since the area is exceptionally weak, it takes fewer funds to attain influence. West Africa has therefore attracted a variety of intrusive countries seeking to gain substantial rewards at a relatively low cost.

In the West African core the French have no rivals (except in Guinea) although minor programs are being carried out by the United States (especially in Upper Volta and Senegal) and Germany. Table 6-3 indicates that, as recipients of French economic aid from 1960 to 1965, Senegal and the Ivory Coast rank fifth and eighth respectively. Liberia, the sixth highest recipient of *German* foreign aid, was the only other West African recipient among the top ten to be aided by a major Western donor. In the periphery,

---

39 The Russians appear at various times to have aided both sides in Laos.
40 Eckstein, *Communist China's Economic Growth,* pp. 306–7, 161–68.

which has British ties, the United States is surprisingly active in the two most powerful countries, Nigeria and Ghana.[41] Despite its varied program in West Africa, the *United States* has decided to gradually discontinue its bilateral programs in the smaller countries of sub-Saharan Africa in favor of a more regional approach.[42] Although the British are less involved in this area than one might at first expect, the appropriate American agencies appear to assume that the Europeans will continue to carry the heavy part of the burden in this area and that American aid is more effectively channeled through multilateral agencies.

In military aid, the French are again predominant. They have bilateral defense agreements with Dahomey, the Ivory Coast, the Niger, Senegal, and Togo. Upper Volta has refused to sign a defense agreement, but has received French military assistance. Gambia, Sierra Leone, Nigeria, and Ghana have all received some form of British military assistance, and the United States has small programs in most of these countries. Both Israel and West Germany have been surprisingly active in providing military training.[43]

The most volatile and interesting cases in West Africa (outside of Nigeria, where there has been civil war) have been Ghana, Guinea, and Mali. The *Russians and Chinese* have been, at one time or another, most active in these countries. Ghana was ruled, until February 1966, by the "Sukarno of West Africa," Kwame Nkrumah, and under his dictatorship the Russians gradually established themselves by means of significant, though rather unsuccessful, economic programs, military training, apparently $1 million worth of military equipment by 1961 alone and, most important of all, growing influence.[44] The Chinese also committed themselves to generous loans, yet, while Nkrumah was on a friendship visit to Peking, he was toppled from power by an army coup. The Soviet Union, particularly, lost a major bastion in West Africa. As in Indonesia, large-scale military assistance was insufficient to assure durable primacy for the Russians.

In Guinea, enigmatic Sekou Touré has led his country in a dizzying round of political somersaults while several intrusive powers have vied for political supremacy. At the time of independence in 1958, the Guineans rejected French ties and turned to the Russians, but in 1961 the Soviet Ambassador was expelled and American influence increased even though Soviet assistance continued on a more moderate scale. By November, 1966, American economic aid had been suspended over a diplomatic incident, and the Guineans began again to flirt with France,[45] but by late 1968 relations with the

[41] Organization for Economic Cooperation and Development, 1960–64, and 1965.
[42] Joan Nelson, *Aid Influence and Foreign Policy*, pp. 105–8.
[43] This paragraph is based on material contained in David Wood, *The Armed Forces of African States* ("Adelphi Paper," No. 27 [London: Institute for Strategic Studies, 1966]).
[44] Goldman, *Soviet Foreign Aid*, p. 174.
[45] Joan Nelson, *Aid, Influence and Foreign Planning*, p. 109.

United States had warmed again. Meanwhile, relations with China have remained generally cordial. By 1963, for example, Guinea had used more Chinese economic aid than any other African country.[46] The Soviet Union and China have in the past both supplied military equipment.[47]

In the other French "rebel" in West Africa, Mali, the French staged a comeback of sorts in the mid-1960's, but the Chinese have remained on good terms at a relatively low cost. The Russians, who have spent more in military and economic aid than the Americans and Chinese combined,[48] have suffered the burden of the leader in that their mistakes have been most obvious. Nevertheless, Mali's relations with China appear to be fairly satisfactory.

Conclusions

We have examined as fully as possible, given the space available, the bilateral relations of the major intrusive powers within these five subordinate systems. We have identified the major patterns of participation which will recur, with minor variations, throughout the remainder of this chapter. In Latin America and West Europe, the United States is supreme but occasionally challenged. In the Middle East and Southeast Asia, there is an extreme degree of intrusive conflict. In West Africa, France is dominant in the core but there is a measure of competition throughout.

TRADE AND ECONOMIC INVESTMENT

The methods covered by the term *bilateral arrangements* involve official relations, disbursements of economic and military assistance, defense treaties, and military bases. *Trade* involves the exchange by two countries of goods and products; *economic investment* refers to the involvement of private enterprise in the economy of the recipient country. As we shall presently indicate, the communist nations occasionally use instruments similar to those employed by the private agencies of intrusive capitalist economies.

In a variety of contexts, trade and economic investment are at least as important in the intrusive process as aid or the more formal device of bilateral treaties. Trade creates a dependence of the weaker country upon particular products and goods received, especially of developing nations which need a reliable market. Once they become dependent upon an intrusive power for the sale of their major products, the door is opened to increased political influence.

Communist countries work at a distinct disadvantage when it comes to economic investment. Western intrusive powers (e.g., the U.S., West Germany) often have far larger programs within particular countries than

46 Eckstein, p. 307.
47 Goldman, p. 206.
48 *Ibid.*, pp. 177–78.

their aid figures suggest. Private companies are frequently involved in diverse projects, and thereby promote intrusive influence. While indigenous resentment against outside private projects may entail political debits, their efficiency is frequently appreciated relative to local operations and often even to official intrusive efforts. The Soviet Union and other communist countries have attempted to compensate for their inability to pursue private investment by arranging barter deals in return for military and economic aid programs. Leo Tansky reports that "From the Soviet viewpoint, the development of industry is an important aspect of its aid program. Through this device it seeks to pre-empt or replace private capital in industry by performing the same function."[49]

The Russians have thus been able to argue that their intrusive program has advantages over Western approaches (e.g., dependability as a trading partner, and the special credits they can advance).[50]

In the following analysis we will attempt to deal broadly with the five regions. Since we have already compared the patterns of bilateral arrangements, we will use our discussions here to point out where trade and investment reinforce aid patterns and where there are particular divergencies.

West Europe

In West Europe, trade does not reveal the real extent of American involvement (see Table 6-4). Here the major intrusive power, *the United States,* accounts for only 10% to 15% of the exports and imports. These low figures can be explained in part by the Common Market and EFTA, which orient trade within the subordinate system. Some of the countries which do not belong to EFTA or the EEC (Spain, Turkey, and Iceland) trade more with the U.S. than do other West European states.[51] However, an indication of American strength in this region emerges when we consider that many of the major West European countries have trade deficits with the U.S. (e.g. United Kingdom, France, Italy, and the Netherlands).

The real extent of the American intrusion into West Europe is actually revealed by private investments. The fear of higher Common Market and EFTA tariff walls forced American companies to invest directly within the core and accelerated a development which had already been in operation—what Servan-Schreiber, in his European best-seller, called *Le Défi Américain*

---

[49] Leo Tansky, "Soviet Foreign Aid to the Less Developed Countries," U.S. Congress, Joint Economic Committee, Subcommittee on Foreign Economic Policy, *New Directions in the Soviet Economy,* 89th Congress, 2nd Session (Washington, D.C., Government Printing Office) Part IV, 1966, p. 955.

[50] William D. Smith, "Soviet Entry into Mideast's Oil Affairs Has some Pedestrian Trappings," *New York Times,* Part III, May 5, 1968.

[51] American trade with Turkey may well decrease as her association with the Common Market (begun on December 1, 1964) becomes more pronounced.

(*The American Challenge*). American superiority has now been transferred from the public realm (e.g. OECD, NATO) to the private sector, and here the full extent of American managerial and technological prowess has been demonstrated. In the field of electronics alone, American corporations control 15% of the production of consumer goods (e.g., TV, radio, recording devices); 50% of the production of semi-conductors (which now replace electronic tubes); and 80% of the market for integrated circuits (miniature units crucial to guided missiles and the new generation of computers).[52] The Americans have also managed to concentrate on other essential industries; among them agricultural equipment, synthetic rubber, chemicals, and automobiles. In 1964, for example, American firms controlled 24% of EEC's automobile production: 40% in West Germany, and 20% in France.[53] The growing interest of the private sector of the American economy in Europe can be seen when we consider that, from 1955 to 1964, direct American investments in Europe increased sevenfold, while they increased fourfold elsewhere and while European investments in the U.S. increased two and a half times. In 1966, American investments in Europe increased by $2.2 billions, or 16%, over 1965. By the end of 1966, the cumulative value of American investments in West Europe had reached $16.2 billions. Nearly half this sum ($7.6 billions) represented investments in the core countries, including $3.1 billions in West Germany alone. The remainder was invested in peripheral countries, nearly two-thirds of it in the United Kingdom.[54]

Although American investments in West Europe increased by 20% from 1960 to 1964, they still represent only a minor percentage of European national income.[55] Nevertheless, there is growing European concern over American control of certain essential industries, and a gradual realization that Europe is unable to compete with the United States technologically, that it is deficient in higher education,[56] in research and development, and in methods of scientific and industrial management.[57] Servan-Schreiber states that "The American challenge is not basically industrial or financial. It is, above all else, a challenge to *our intellectual creativity and our ability*

---

52 I. J. J. Servan-Schreiber, *The American Challenge,* trans. Ronald Steel (New York: Atheneum Publishers; 1968), p. 13.

53 Auber de la Rue, "Perspectives Economiques entre Les Etats-Unis et l'Europe," *Politique Etrangere,* No. 4–5 (1967). p. 461.

54 *The Americana Annual; 1968* (New York: Rand McNally & Co.), p. 273.

55 As a percentage of national income, direct American investments in 1963 were: for Great Britain, 0.5; Germany, 0.4; France, 0.35; Italy 0.3; and the Netherlands 0.8. From Gérard-F. Bauer, *"Les investissement américains en Europe,"* *Revue Economique Et Sociale* (May, 1966), p. 137.

56 Servan-Schreiber reports that, according to a recent study by Professor Dimitri Chorafas, 43% of the American population between the ages of 20 and 24 are students. The comparable figures are 24% in the U.S.S.R., 16% in France, 7.5% in Germany, and 7% in Great Britain (*The American Challenge,* p. 73).

57 John Diebold, "Is the Gap Technological?" *Foreign Affairs,* XLVI (Jan. 1968), 276–91.

to turn ideas into practice."[58] Whatever the causes, in the period when West Europe has supposedly recovered from the devastation of World War II, the effects of American dominance are felt almost as strongly as at the height of the Cold War. The manifestations of that dominance, however, have now been radically transformed.

As we have already indicated, the intrusion of *the U.S.S.R.* into West Europe is not a major factor. This can be seen from the generally low trade figures with West European countries, especially the most important ones. Indeed, several of the stronger West European countries have arranged for their own private investment in the Soviet Union. The most spectacular of these arrangements occurred in August 1966, when Italy's Fiat company arranged a deal of $800 millions with the Russians, to help improve their automobile production, which had until then been comparatively minor. France's Renault and Peugeot companies have also been cooperating with the Russians, and the British have arranged to construct a variety of chemical plants in the Soviet Union.

Latin America

In Latin America, trade and investment figures clearly suggest the dominance of *the United States.* In most cases, Latin American states conduct at least one-third (and usually more) of their trade with the United States.[59] In addition, American companies undertake large investments in Latin America. Although Cuba has been eliminated as an opportunity for private investment, and American investments in oil-rich Venezuela declined in the early 1960's,[60] nevertheless private investment is the single most significant means of intrusion by the United States in Latin America. Indeed, in 1966 these investments represented 21% of American private investment abroad.[61] The United States accounts for about 40% of the total invested by foreign states in Brazil; 75% in Chile (in 1964) ; 50% in Colombia (in 1965) ; 51% in Peru (in 1961).[62] Even though the total value of American assets in the core and periphery combined was lower than in West Europe at the end of

[58] Servan-Schreiber, *The American Challenge.* p. 101. Italics in original.

[59] See Table 6-4. It should be noted that, despite the higher percentages of Latin American trade with the United States, the volume of the trade is lower than America's trade with Europe. In 1966, the total volume of American trade with West Europe was $16.7 billions, and only $9.5 billions with Latin America. These figures are explained by the higher GNP of the European states. International Monetary Fund and the International Bank for Reconstruction and Development, *Direction of Trade: A Supplement to International Financial Statistics, Annual 1962–1966,* pp. 348–49.

[60] Norman A. Bailey, *Latin America in World Politics* (New York: Walker and Co., 1967), pp. 109–10.

[61] The corresponding figure for Europe is 30%. *Britannica Book of the Year: 1968* (Chicago: Encyclopedia Britannica, Inc., 1968), p. 444.

[62] Compiled from Moshe Y. Sachs, ed. and publ., *Worldmark Encyclopedia of the Nations: 1967,* (New York: Worldmark Press, 1967) Vol. III.

1966 ($16.3 billions in Europe vs. $11.5 billion in Latin America, of which $9.9 billions were in the core),[63] these figures are still staggering when the generally lower level of the Latin American GNP (in comparison with the West European GNP) is considered. In West Europe, direct American investments accounted for less than 1% of national income, but in Latin America, governments collect 15% of all their revenues from American companies.[64] Only a consideration of private investments can reveal the breadth of American influence within Latin America. These investments have often served as a major political issue in particular countries, as in the early days of the Castro regime in Cuba, and in the 1968–69 controversy between the U.S. and Peru over the military junta's expropriation of the holdings of the International Petroleum Co., Ltd. (a subsidiary of Standard Oil of New Jersey).

Other Western countries are active in Latin America but, as in foreign aid, their influence often complements rather than detracts from American investment. Surprisingly, German trade, as Table 6-4 shows, is often measurably higher than British trade, although the British are still active in their former colonies. Private investors from a variety of European countries are involved (thus reducing the singular influence of any), the British, and then the Germans, being the most active. The French conduct a particularly low level of trade in this subordinate system, perhaps a sign of their underlying weakness were they to decide to seriously challenge the U.S. on a grand scale. *Soviet* and, even more, *Chinese trade* are not significant.[65] However, the Soviet Union, and even China, have conducted occasional trade with a small number of Latin American countries—particularly since Castro's accession to power. The most important of these appear to have been Argentina, Brazil, Uruguay, Mexico, and Chile. Except in Cuba, none of these arrangements have developed politically crucial ramifications. Since the Soviet Union took over the major purchases of Cuban sugar (shortly after Castro came to power) arguments between the two countries over this sugar trade have been a major element in Cuban-Soviet relations, exacerbating a series of negotiations that have not always been mutually gratifying.[66] Nevertheless, in 1965, trade with the U.S.S.R. represented almost 50% of Cuban trade, and it is reasonable to assume that after the split with China in January 1966, Cuban trade with the Soviet Union and East Europe rose even higher.

---

63 *Britannica Book of the Year, 1968* (Chicago: Encyclopedia Britannica, Inc., 1968), p. 44.

64 J. Lloyd Mecham, *A Survey of United States-Latin American Relations,* (Boston: Houghton Mifflin Company, 1965), pp. 191–92.

65 The available figures are particularly high, however, because of the Argentine wheat sent to the Soviet Union and China in the 1963–1964 period.

66 Goldman, *Soviet Foreign Aid,* Chap. 9.

Middle East

In the Middle East, as in Cuba, trade has been an important instrument for increasing dependence upon *the Soviet Union*. The Russians' penchant for trading by barter, instead of (less profitably) paying cash for the goods they purchase, has been well demonstrated here. Soviet trade figures for 1966 do not appear to be very high until they are compared to the early 1950's, when Soviet trade to the area was far smaller.[67] Moreover, when trade figures from other communist countries are added to Table 6-4, the extent of their effort in the Middle East becomes clearer. For example, exports from the U.A.R. to the Soviet Union were valued at $142.6 millions in 1966, but when Egyptian exports to Cuba, North Korea, and the East European states are added, they total $156.8 additional millions. Similarly, the U.A.R.'s imports from the Soviet Union totaled $93.7 millions, but other communist states (except China) accounted for $153 additional millions. The other progressive Arab states for which figures are available—Syria, Sudan, and Iraq—all have comparable accounts.[68]

Returning to the figures in Table 6-4, we can see that the percentage of exports transmitted to the Soviet Union are highest from Syria and the U.A.R., the two countries in the subordinate system most dependent upon the Russians for economic and military aid.[69] Exports to the U.S.S.R. have been encouraged, especially in the U.A.R., in return for Soviet economic and, even more, military aid. The close relationship between Soviet trade and aid is described by Hertha Heiss:

Although the USSR maintains trading relationships with more than forty developing countries, roughly two thirds of its total exports have been directed to a relatively small group of countries in the area; namely, India, the United Arab Republic, Indonesia, Iraq, and Afghanistan, which also have been the largest recipients of Soviet aid.[70]

The results of the increased trade are increased political and economic revenues to the Russians, and the increased dependence of developing countries upon them. Despite the fact that Russia is an oil exporter, there

[67] According to the *United Nations Statistical Abstract 1965,* Soviet and East European exports to the Middle East were valued at $290 millions for 1960, compared to $85 millions in 1953; imports in 1960 were $130 millions, and in 1953, $26 millions.

[68] International Monetary Fund, *Direction of Trade, 1962–1966;* trade figure are presented for each Middle Eastern country named above.

[69] The actual and potential influence of Communist China can be seen in the fact that, in 1966, its trade with Syria and the Sudan rivaled that of the Soviet Union.

[70] "The Soviet Union in the World Market," U.S. Congress, Joint Economic Committee, *New Directions in the Soviet Economy,* 89th Congress, 2nd Sess. (Washington, D.C.: Government Printing Office), Part IV, 1966, p. 925.

are reports that she has been using aid arrangements more and more frequently to acquire oil. Like the U.S., which also has vast reserves, the Soviet Union may be beginning to find it advantageous to import oil. Unlike Western oil companies, the Russians can offer a variety of tangible assistance for oil concessions and thus offset in part their lack of private investment.[71]

The Russians are by no means alone in the Middle East. The all-important oil industry is largely owned by *Western interests:* 53.4%, by Americans; 27.9%, by the British; 8.7%, by the Dutch; 6.0%, by the French.[72] In Iraq, which has been one of the Middle East countries closest to the Soviet Union, there are still branches of 73 British companies, of 24 American companies, 23 French, and 19 West German. The British have 22 bank branches in the Middle East; the West Germans, 8 (all in Lebanon); the Americans, 7; and the French, 5 (4 in Lebanon). The British maintain 78 insurance company branches throughout the region; the French, 14; the Americans, 5; and the Russians, 1.[73]

This impression of lingering Middle East activity by the Western powers is reiterated by the trade figures. The U.S. is active economically, not only in the periphery and in the conservative Arab states where it is relatively strong politically but in the "progressive" and left-leaning Arab regimes as well. While the U.A.R. exports heavily to the U.S.S.R., it imports heavily from the U.S. Similar comments can be made about the other Western intrusive powers. Despite considerable gains by communist countries since 1955, a very significant amount of Middle East trade is still conducted with the West.

Southeast Asia

In Southeast Asia, trade figures suggest the importance of Japan as both a market for goods and as a source of needed items. It is interesting to contrast the high level of Japanese trade with this subordinate system with the relatively low level of Communist Chinese and Soviet trade (excepting with North Vietnam). Otherwise, trade figures reflect former colonial patterns and the increased influence of the United States (as indicated by its large imports from Southeast Asia). (See Table 6-4). The figures for foreign investments are similar. The French are active in Cambodia and South Vietnam; the British in Malaysia; the Americans, in the Philippines, Laos, and South Vietnam. The two most chaotic situations for foreign investors have been in Burma and Indonesia. In Burma, nationalization of industry in 1963 brought the elimination of private foreign investment. In Indonesia,

[71] Smith, *N.Y. Times,* Part III, p. 3.
[72] "High Stakes in the Middle East," *Fortune,* LXXVI (September, 1967), 80–83.
[73] Compiled from *Europa Yearbook: 1967* (London: Europa Publications, 1967).

the Dutch had been the principle foreign investors until the dispute over West Irian resulted in the nationalization of Dutch enterprises and assets, with adverse consequences for the Indonesian economy.[74] Many were returned in the post-Sukarno period. The Americans, West Germans, and Japanese have been especially active in Indonesia since October 1965.

West Africa

The pattern of West African trade and foreign investment is similar to that of Southeast Asia. The colonial experience has shaped the situation, although the Americans (and here the Germans, instead of the Japanese) are making inroads into the colonial tradition. The Russians and, to a lesser extent, the Chinese have occasional success.

In trade the French and British have clearly retained their former leading positions, although less so with respect to the "wayward" former colonies— Guinea, Mali, Ghana. The United States and Germany are the primary intrusive traders with Liberia, and the U.S. has clearly taken up the French and British slack in Guinea and Ghana. In the latter two countries and Mali, the Russians retain a influential level of trade, but it is likely to decline in Ghana. As might be expected, Guinea and Mali conduct significant elements of their trade with China (see Table 6-4).

In West African foreign investments there are few surprises. These follow the colonial pattern, except in Ghana, where the Americans and Germans have joined the British in its involvement, in the post-Nkrumah period; in Mali, where "planned socialism" brought private foreign investment to a standstill in 1961; and in Guinea, where there has been some limited American investment and from which the French have largely withdrawn.

Conclusions

We can conclude, then, that in general trade and foreign investment reinforce the trends established in our examination of bilateral arrangements. In particular, colonial patterns suggest broad tendencies—especially in Southeast Asia and West Africa. In the Middle East, the Russians have made significant inroads; and in Latin America, the Americans retain their dominance. In West Europe the Americans have established a new primacy, largely through private investment.

POSSESSION OF A COLONY

In the five regions under consideration, colonies either serve as a focus of tension and dispute or simply allow the colonial power an opportunity to play a surrogate role as a member of the subordinate system.[75] In none of

[74] Compiled from *Worldmark Encyclopedia: 1967*.

[75] For the sake of simplicity, we are here lumping together colonies, dependent territories, protectorates, condominiums, and trust territories.

these areas is a colony a key to major control or influence within the region. *In West Europe,* neither of the intrusive powers possesses a colony. Although British control of Gibraltar has become a major source of contention with Spain, this is by definition a problem between two peripheral states rather than an intrusive one.

In West Africa, where every independent member of the system except Liberia has received its sovereignty since 1957, only tiny Portuguese Guinea remains as a colony. Although an element of the anticolonial conflict which highlights Southern African international politics spills over onto the West Africa scene, the major effect upon West African international politics is to allow Portugal to play a minor role in the West African subordinate system. Any influence which the Portuguese might have upon neighboring countries is limited by an enforced isolation.

In Southeast Asia, similarly, the effect of past colonies is more significant than those of the present. There are three minor exceptions. The first lies in the complex of islands which compose the nation of Indonesia. The Indonesians were able, in 1962, to oust the Dutch from the western section of New Guinea (West Irian), but the eastern section of that island—still controlled by Australia—remains a potential bone of contention despite its current relative tranquility. Nearby Portuguese Timor constitutes a colonial enclave within the Indonesian organism, but until now the two have been able to coexist. Finally, Brunei is a British-protected sultanate on the northern tip of Borneo which decided not to join the Federation of Malaysia.

In Latin America there are a variety of colonial entities. Although the major states of this subordinate system have been independent since the end of the first quarter of the nineteenth century, this region still contains the widest variety of colonies of any under discussion. The United States, the paramount intrusive power, leases the Panama Canal Zone in the core and owns Puerto Rico and the Virgin Islands, as well as some minor islands in the periphery. British Honduras, in Central America, and Surinam (Netherlands Guiana) and French Guiana, on the northeastern coast of South America, symbolize the lingering European presence within this subordinate system. To the west of South America, the British possession of the Falkland Islands is a festering sore of contention with Argentina. The most concentrated set of colonies in the subordinate system is owned by the British in the periphery: Bermuda, the Bahama Islands, and the West Indian Associated states, among others. These, in conjunction with former colonies already granted independence—Jamaica, Barbados, Guyana, and Trinidad and Tobago—serve as a basis for a concrete British influence in the Latin American periphery. Despite the declining involvement of the British worldwide, they have maintained their primacy in this area. Although there is American and Canadian activity, it does not interfere with the

British position. The assorted picture of Caribbean colonies is completed when we added the French-owned islands of Guadeloupe and Martinique and the Netherlands Antilles. The profile of Latin American colonial possessions thus established is a peppering of relatively minor entities which are primarily located in proximate areas of the Caribbean, Central America, and the northeastern tip of South America. Their chief function in the subordinate system is to provide threads of influence for minor intrusive powers.

The most politically sensitive colonies of the regions we study are in *the Middle East*. International politics in the Persian Gulf area have been anesthetized for the last 100 years by British possession of a coastal ring of oil-rich colonies and protectorates. Now that British withdrawal from east of Suez is scheduled by late 1971, the Persian Gulf is in the process of reemerging as a major focus of Middle Eastern subordinate and intrusive politics, one which promises to be second in importance only to the Arab-Israeli question. The former South Arabian Federation (which contains the one-time British base of Aden) became the independent South Yemen People's Republic in November 1967, after considerable local turmoil. The future of Bahrain, Muscat and Oman, Qatar, and the Trucial States will be decided by competition among Iran, Saudi Arabia, Iraq, and the U.A.R., and between the United States and the Soviet Union. No matter what the precise results, the decline of British influence here is destined to have more profound consequences on the international politics of this subordinate system than any other anticipated colonial development within any of our five regions.

We can conclude that, in terms of the intrusive system, colonies have no influence in West Europe and little in West Africa and Southeast Asia. In Latin America their primary significance is their large number, particularly in terms of their potential for some day swelling the ranks of the periphery and possibly making it slightly more important in the subordinate system as a consequence. It is only in the Middle East that colonies currently have political significance—and here because of their proximity to each other, their oil and, most important of all, their impending independence.

MILITARY INTERVENTION

In dealing with military intervention by intrusive powers, we should note that a low-level type of participation usually begins as soon as military equipment of almost any kind is sold or granted to a country. Technicians and officers acquainted with the use and maintenance of the equipment are often dispatched with the weapons. However, we covered this type of involvement under the military aspects of bilateral arrangements. The method of participation which we are here calling "military intervention" refers to a greater commitment of personnel than is ordinarily involved in a grant or sale of arms. It covers the spectrum of intrusive activities which necessitate the transfer of troops, whether as advisors (in larger numbers than required by ordinary technical assistance) or for actual military action.

In the opening chapter of this volume, we discussed three types of intervention, the key variable being the purpose of the action: expansion of control, maintenance of the *status quo,* or reversion to a former status. Most of the acts of intervention which have occurred recently in the five regions under consideration have been to maintain *the status quo.* As we shall presently indicate, subversion is frequently a more appropriate means of accomplishing both expansion and reversion.

There are a few examples of action designed to expand control or accomplish reversion to a former status, primarily *in the Middle East.* An unsuccessful attempt at reversion occurred when the British and French failed in their objective in the 1956 Suez crisis. Expansionism can be illustrated largely by the actions of the Soviet Union, which has progressively intruded into this area. The Russians failed in their attempt to secure the northern portion of Iran immediately after W. W. II, but they later succeeded in gaining considerable influence through more indirect means in the Arab world. By the mid-1960s they had stationed a considerable number of advisors in Syria, and after the Six Day War in the Middle East, in June 1967, approximately 7,000 advisors were stationed in Egypt.

Military intervention designed to maintain the *status quo* has occurred in all the five subordinate systems under discussion. In the Middle East, the American Sixth Fleet, whose major locus of operation is the Mediterranean Sea, has served to assure a continuing American presence in the area—even when it has not been used in a particular country. The American ships have been joined, since June 1967, by a Soviet fleet with similar purposes. A decade earlier, in 1958, American and British troops were used in Lebanon and Jordan, respectively, to prevent civil war and to abort the take-over of left-leaning Arab regimes. The British intervened on occasion throughout the Persian Gulf, from 1957 on, in order to maintain positions they were supporting. Similarly, the Russians supported Egyptian troops in Yemen from 1964 onwards, and when the Egyptians withdraw after the 1967 Arab-Israeli war, they intervened with Soviet pilots in order to prevent royalists from regaining power from the republicans in Yemen. Thus, the Russians used their advisors in the progressive regimes not only to extend their control, but also to prevent any loss of the gains they had made.

Military intervention by intrusive powers *in Southeast Asia* has been even more fluid and complex than in the Middle East. Vietnam, of course, is the most expensive case of military intervention in the post-World War II era. American involvement grew gradually, from support for the French in the pre-1954 period, to low-level backing of military and economic activities before 1961, to the stationing of slightly over 15,000 military advisors in the Kennedy administration, to massive participation, using American troops numbering over 500,000 in the Johnson administration (with accompanying contingents from Australia, New Zealand, South Korea, and Thailand). Soviet involvement in mainland Southeast Asia decreased dramatically under Khrushchev, but the inception of the Brezhnev-Kosygin regime and the American bombing of North Vietnam brought the Soviet Union into this area after February 1965, with progressively higher and more complicated levels of supply and support, and presumably larger numbers of personnel. For the North Vietnamese, their operations meant expansion into some degree of control of South Vietnam, but for the Russians it represented principally an attempt to maintain a position of prominence in the communist world vis-à-vis the Chinese and, if possible, to reassert their former superior position.

Unlike the Russian, American forces were active elsewhere in Southeast Asia, particularly in Thailand, the Philippines, and Laos. The U.S. used the air bases on Thai soil for the bombing of North Vietnam and assisted the Thai government in fighting the communist units concentrated in the northeastern section of the country. By the end of 1967, there were over 35,000 American troops stationed in Thailand. In the mid-1960's there were an additional 25,000 men stationed on four bases in the Philippines.

A small number of American forces had been active in Laos in the 1950's, in support of the right-wing Prince Boon Oum and General Phoumi Nosavan. President Kennedy altered the policy in favor of neutralist Prince Souvana Phouma and in 1962 signed the Geneva accord which supposedly neutralized the country. The United States later proceeded to increase its activity as the communists left the coalition government and as the war in neighboring Vietnam was accelerated, an acceleration accompanied by an exacerbation of overt conflict within Laos itself.

The Chinese have had noncombatant troops stationed in North Vietnam since the early 1960's, to assist in the movement and maintenance of equipment. Their activities in Laos, Thailand, and Burma appear to fall more clearly within the framework of subversion than military intervention.

Thus far, our discussion has primarily concentrated on the mainland core. *In the maritime core,* the British have until now been the most active in terms of military intervention, their activities being centered in Malaysia and at their base in Singapore. In the 1950's, the British assisted the Malaysians in defeating a communist insurgency. In the mid-1960's, the British were active in assisting the Malaysians when they were forced into a major confrontation with Indonesia over the future of the Federation (which President Sukarno opposed). When Sukarno lost power after the abortive October 1965 coup, the new leaders successfully sought a rapprochement with Malaysia, and British involvement gradually declined.

In Latin America, military intervention has been almost exclusively an

American privilege, except for a force of Russian military advisors in Cuba which numbered over 5,000 in the weeks preceding the Cuban missile crisis of 1962. In contrast to America's extensive and protracted military involvement in Southeast Asia, its recent actions in Latin America have generally been dramatic but shortlived. American military intervention has been especially difficult to justify because, from the Good Neighbor Policy through the Charter of the O.A.S., the U.S. has seemingly pledged not to intervene unilaterally in the internal affairs of a Latin American nation. Yet, in the 1960's, two of America's most significant political acts in Latin America were the near-intervention in the Cuban missile crisis, in October 1962, and the actual military intrusion into the Dominican Republic, in April 1965. In addition, the U.S. has undertaken the training of Latin American military officers in order to counteract the threat of communist subversion.[76] As in Bolivia in 1967, and in Guatemala in the mid-1960's, this assistance has occasionally led to the active involvement of American advisors in the field when the level of the insurrection seemed to merit such activities. In the Bolivian case, the insurrection was unsuccessful and resulted in the death of the near-legendary revolutionary hero, Che Guevara.

Active military intervention in the remaining two subordinate systems has been less frequent. American troops have been stationed regularly *in West Europe* since World War II. Since the Korean War there has been a heavy concentration of American forces in West Germany, increased or decreased in accordance with European developments, strategic doctrines, and American involvement outside of Europe. The Berlin blockade of 1948, the Korean War, and the Berlin crisis of 1961 stand out as moments of an increase of American force. American troops were also stationed at NATO headquarters in France, until President De Gaulle demanded their ouster in March 1966, and they were transferred to Belgium a year later. The closest the Russians have come to direct military intervention in West Europe is the Berlin blockade in 1948 and 1949, and the erecting of the Berlin Wall in August 1961.

In West Africa, the role of the French is comparable to that of the Americans in Latin America. They maintain a special military force near Paris for the purpose of intervention overseas, anywhere French interests are conceived to be involved. Their intervention in Niger in December 1963 was a show of force designed to discourage a military uprising against the incumbent government. In Togo, in December 1962, they intervened in a border conflict with Ghana. The most frequent use of French troops has occurred in the neighboring subordinate system of Central Africa, especially in the early 1960's. Since they controversially reversed a military coup in Gabon in February 1964, the French have been more restrained, and have in fact pulled most of their troops out of Africa. Nevertheless, they intervened

[76] Bailey, *Latin America in World Politics,* p. 108.

in the Central African Republic in November 1967, in order to bolster the government there, and they intervened in Chad, in August 1968, at the request of the government, to help subdue a rebellious group.[77]

SUBVERSION

As we indicated in our discussion in Chapter 1, subversion, by its very nature, is extraordinarily difficult to document. We can however provide some hints of operations which have or may be proceeding. Subversion is by definition most likely when an intrusive nation's purpose is to revert to a *status quo* which existed previously or to expand its own control. When the intrusive power is seeking to bolster the local government in power, subversion is rarely necessary. In our discussion of subversion, we will deal first with the four subordinate systems in which subversive activities are most frequent and politically significant, moving from those with the least to those with the most intense subversive activity. Finally we will deal with the unique case of West Europe.

West Africa

In West Africa there is considerable incentive for subversion, but the combination of French strength and local weakness has thus far limited any dramatic evidence of it, except perhaps in the most powerful and most contested countries. The French and British have been least in need of using the technique, the British because of declining involvement and the French because they were strong enough to act through established governments. In the early and mid-1960's, however, Kwame Nkrumah, the dictator of Ghana, progressively strengthened his ties with the Soviet Union, and also with China. By the time he was overthrown, in February 1966, the Western powers—particularly the United States—had several reasons for seeking his ouster. Indeed, he had consented to the use of his country as a base for subversion elsewhere in Africa. Whether or not the U.S. or any other country, however, was instrumental in the overthrow of Nkrumah, as of Indonesia's Sukarno, is almost impossible to document. Each had built up enough antagonism within his own political system to create a good deal of domestic incentive for a coup, without enlisting agents of intrusive powers. It should also be added that the Soviet Union and China both have an interest in returning Nkrumah to power in Ghana, but there is no evidence available as to whether or not they have pursued any acts of subversion in order to do so.[78]

[77] For further information on French military intervention in Africa, see "France's Military in Africa," *Africa Report*, IX (January, 1964), 10; and "Gabon: Putsch or Coup D'état?" *Africa Report*, IX (March, 1964), 14–15.

[78] The present regime has on several occasions accused the Soviet Union and more frequently, Communist China and Cuba, of attempting to overthrow its government and return Nkrumah to power.

As we have seen, the Chinese and Russians have both been active in Guinea and Mali. Indeed, the pattern of paramount powers with influence in these countries has sometimes resembled a revolving door. The combination of fluid domestic politics and the involvement of a variety of intrusive powers has resulted in the constant possibility of subversion from those who temporarily believed themselves to be out of influence.

The most volatile nation in West Africa, and relatively the most vulnerable to subversion, is Nigeria, a nation once considered Africa's strongest democracy. The civil war between the central government and the rebel region known as Biafra created a situation where the possibilities of subversion were increased, as were the number of active intrusive powers. The Soviet Union and Great Britain were among those contributing weapons and materiel to the central government cause, while the French and Portuguese aided the Biafrans. This somewhat chaotic situation has considerably heightened the likelihood of subversive plots and counterplots.

Latin America

In Latin America we find a region in which the motives for subversion have been strong, but the motives for self-control by the intrusive powers even stronger. The United States has attempted to overthrow an undesired regime —once successfully (the Arbenz government in Guatemala in 1954), and once unsuccessfully (the aborted Bay of Pigs operation against Cuba in 1961.) The Soviet Union, the challenger, has an interest in using subversion to expand its control; still, the expensiveness and unreliability of the Cuban experience has considerably cooled its zeal for the support of guerrilla movements, despite Cuban enthusiasm. Rather, the Russians seem to prefer to encourage the gradual development of nationalism, which in Latin America is likely to be distinctly anti-U.S. The Soviet Union seems to be walking a tightrope between increasing ties with the established governments, accommodation of traditional pro-Moscow communists, and occasional support of guerrilla movements.[79]

While these means, particularly support for guerilla movements, may involve subversive techniques, Russian policy in Latin America seems, at least for the moment, to have moved in a direction which embraces the more standard instruments of statecraft. The Chinese, who have even fewer means at their disposal than the Russians, are freer to espouse a less compromising, more revolutionary position. Since the cooling of their relations with the Cubans in January 1966, however, their influence in this region has been largely dormant.

The Middle East

In the Middle East, the importance of intrusive subversion has grown considerably since 1945. Soviet policy with respect to Iran and Turkey, in

[79] Dinerstein, *Soviet Policy in Latin America,* pp. 80–90.

the immediate post-World War II period, sought the overthrow of pro-American regimes. When a leader arose in Iran who might have pursued policies more congruent with Soviet interest (Mossadegh), the Americans promptly used the technique of subversion to have him overthrown. Within the Arab core, the Russians have used their favorable relations with the U.A.R. and Syria to encourage subversion by these states in Iraq in 1958, in Yemen in 1962, and in what is now South Yemen in 1967. The problem here, of course, has been that the more removed the Russians become from particular efforts, the less control they have over them. There is some evidence that the union of Egypt and Spria in 1958 stemmed in part from Nasser's concern over Soviet activity in Syria. In the current period, the Russians have been active in Egypt, Syria, Sudan, Yemen, and Iraq, but by more overt means than were previously considered necessary. The Russians also appear to have joined the Chinese in support of the Al-Fatah, the Palestine Liberation Organization and similar guerilla movements in the wake of the June 1967 War. The Chinese themselves have been active in Yemen. As for the Americans, it can be assumed that they would prefer to arrest the increase of Russian influence, but no hard evidence is available of any particular subversive activities which they may have been undertaking.

Southeast Asia

In Southeast Asia subversion has become a way of life. Here, it is difficult to distinguish evidence from allegation and subversion from actual military intervention. It appears that the Chinese and Americans are the most active, and that the Russians—in keeping with the traditionally low level of their participation in this subordinate system—have not been especially active outside of Vietnam. The Chinese have verbally supported opposition groups in South Vietnam, Burma, Thailand, and Laos. The degree to which they have actually provided materiel and personal support remains open to debate but it appears likely that, at the very least, agents who have received Chinese funds have at various times been present in South Vietnam, Laos and Thailand, and that since 1967 Burmese opposition groups have received aid and materiel. In Thailand, and especially in Laos, detection becomes especially complicated because of the presence of North Vietnamese nationals. Cambodia's Sihanouk has also accused the Chinese of activity against his regime. In addition, the Chinese appear to have encouraged the Indonesian communists in their unsuccessful quest for power in 1965, a disastrous error which resulted in their total loss of influence with the ruling forces in that country. Finally, the Chinese have at least verbally supported the incipient insurgent movements in the Philippines and Malaysia, as they had earlier movements in those countries.

The United States, the intrusive power most often aligned with the incumbent in Southeast Asia, has found subversion necessary less frequently. Whether or not American agents played any role in the Indonesian coup or the events leading up to it is a matter open to conjecture, but the coup occurred so quickly that it is hard to imagine a calculated American plan and it is doubtful that the Americans were themselves actively planning a coup. The two countries where American subversive involvement has been greatest are apparently Laos and South Vietnam. The U.S. is reported to have "...built up Ngo Dinh Diem as the pro-American head of South Vietnam after the French, through Emperor Bao Dai, had found him in a monastery cell in Belgium and brought him back to Saigon as Premier." In Laos, American support of the right-wing government in the 1950's was based, to a major extent, upon CIA activity. Its election was apparently engineered by CIA agents, who stuffed ballot boxes and planned local uprisings. Air America, an airline with major service to Laos, apparently operates with CIA funds.[80]

The profile of subversion in Southeast Asia which emerges from this brief analysis, then, is one of a broad level of subversive activities by China, a more limited but more in-depth program by the United States, and a considerably more limited program by the Soviet Union.

West Europe

Politics in West Europe are distinguished by a lack of subversive activities on the part of the intrusive powers, especially in the core and the Northern periphery. In the immediate post-World War II period, the communist parties of France and Italy were generally regarded as potential centers of Soviet subversion. However, with the communist defeats at the polls in Italy and France from 1946 to 1948, and with the subsequent thaw in the Cold War and its accompanying polycentrism, it can safely be said that this threat has largely been removed. Indeed, in the French disorders of the spring of 1968, the communists were faced with accusations by the young radicals that they were not revolutionary enough. Thus, the old-line communists in West Europe, as in Latin America, faced a generation gap similar to the one from which the old-line Humphrey liberals in the U.S. have suffered.

Whereas covert agents are likely to be active in subversion in the other four regions, overt espionage is a much more productive and frequent activity of these international sleuths in West Europe. It is here that governments suffer the routine embarrassment of revealing that one or another of their bureaucrats has been spying for the Soviet Union—a game played with similar results by the other side. Although the frequent exposés make pallid reading for the hardy seekers of nonfiction James Bond, espionage serves as a funnel of information for the two superpowers. West Europe functions as a central focus of an undesired, but apparently unceasing,

[80] The last three statements are based on "CIA: Maker of Policy or Tool," *New York Times,* April 25–29, 1966 (a five-part series).

exchange of secrets between the U.S. and the U.S.S.R. Occasionally, espionage plays a major role in domestic or international politics, as when the British spy scandals contributed to the defeat of the Tories in 1964, or when the Berlin crisis of 1961 was, in some degree, precipitated by Khrushchev's concern that West Berlin had become too great a center of espionage and subversion for the East. In general, however, espionage has become more normal for the superpowers in West Europe than either espionage or subversion in the other subordinate systems.

Only in the Southern periphery does subversion play a role in West European politics. Greece, from 1945 to 1949, was the stage of the first major internal war of the new era, involving communist insurgents and a Western-backed government; and, by the late 1960's, the right-wing coup of 1967 had again made Greece the central focus in West Europe for subversive activity. In addition, Franco's Spain, Salazar's Portugal, Turkey, and Cyprus could all be considered incipient or potential centers of concerted infiltration by opposing covert agents—a reflection of the greater fluidity of the South's internal politics despite the apparent political stability of Spain, Portugal, and Turkey.

CONCLUSIONS

We have seen that subversion is an important means of participation for intrusive powers which seek to expand their influence in particular subordinate systems. We have also seen that although there are active subversive forces at work in Latin America and West Africa, intrusive activities are confined to particular countries rather than being regionwide. Subversive activity is endemic to most of the Middle East, and organic to Southeast Asia. West Europe is a unique case where espionage is more important than subversion. In general, subversive activity follows the general patterns of intrusive activity we have witnessed throughout our discussion. The level of intrusive competition, the level of local conflict, and the degree of subversion seem to be directly related.

THE UNITED NATIONS

Intrusive powers may use the United Nations in a variety of ways to accomplish social, economic, or political goals within particular subordinate systems. There are a variety of U.N. agencies which serve social and economic needs of less-developed nations. The United Nations Economic and Social Council co-ordinates activities for regional economic commissions—ECE (Europe), ECAFE (Asia), ECLA (Latin America), and ECA (Africa) which do not grant aid but which gather information and provide other means of assistance to local members. In addition, such agencies as UNESCO and UNICEF and the U.N. Development Program fight illiteracy and disease, and provide measured amounts of technical assistance. The various communist nations in the U.N., associated with the U.S.S.R., have never been enthusiastic supporters of multilateral means of intrusive involvement, and have never contributed heavily. In part for this reason, but even more because of the very nature of the activities which they pursue, the political acts of the primary U.N. bodies have always been more important than the normal functions of its economic and social agencies.[81]

The Middle East

In the Middle East, the presence of the U.N. has been felt more closely than in any other subordinate system. From the creation of Israel onward, debates, votes, and acts of the United Nations have been critical instruments in the policies pursued by various intrusive powers. The British used the international organization to extricate themselves from their involvement in Palestine in 1948; the Russians voted for the establishment of the State of Israel because they sought to encourage British withdrawal. In 1956, a mutual Soviet-American desire to mute the Suez crisis led to the creation of a United Nation Expeditionary Force (UNEF), the first major peace-keeping force of the United Nations, which functioned on the Israeli-Egyptian border until May 1967. In the Six Day War of June 1967, the primary powers similarly used the U.N. as a means of arranging a cease fire they both believed to be in their interests. In the period following the War, the Soviet Union used the organization as a means of demonstrating its support for the Arab cause, in part in order to compensate for its unwillingness to enter the conflict. Both the U.S. and the U.S.S.R. sought to promote, through the U.N., a postwar settlement which each favored. In the Middle East, then, the major intrusive powers have viewed the United Nations as a means of projecting and pursuing their own policies. Their inability to control their own allies has often necessitated the use of the U.N., as a "neutral" body, to curtail local hostilities, inhibit the flexibility of intrusive powers, and thus restrict the possibility of confrontation between the primary powers. The U.N. has thus served both the United States and the Soviet Union, as a means of protecting them from their friends and removing them from their adversaries.

Latin America

In the Middle East, conditions have favored the intrusive use of the U.N. In Latin America and West Africa an opposite process is at work. Here American and French paramountcy, at least in the respective cores, has meant that neither wanted to involve the organization. To the United States, the OAS—which it controls—has always seemed a "more appro-

---

[81] For a recent account of the United Nations' role in the international system, see Evan Luard, *Conflict and Peace in the Modern International System* (Boston: Little, Brown and Company, 1968), Chap. 9.

priate" instrument for handling crises than the U.N., where its influence has gradually declined with the membership of a variety of Afro-Asian states; to the Soviet Union, the U.N. has afforded a cheap source of potential intrusion. Especially since the rise of Fidel Castro in Cuba, the U.N. has appeared to the Russians a means of embarrassing the U.S. and possibly even diminishing American influence—especially during the 1961 Bay of Pigs crisis. Nevertheless, the U.N. has not played a major role in any of the major Latin American crises or issues. In the aftermath of the Cuban missile crisis, the United States and the Soviet Union agreed to have U.N. observers stationed in Cuba to investigate whether or not the missiles had actually been removed, but they were never sent because Castro refused to accept them. Here the U.N. observers would have functioned as they do in the Middle East. Otherwise, the U.N. has largely been uninvolved in major Latin American issues.

West Africa

Similarly, the French have regarded involvement of the U.N. in West African disputes and conflicts as a counterproductive activity which might lead to their own loss of influence. It is instructive that even in the Nigerian civil war, the role of the U.N. has been minor—a further indication of the lack of its involvement and of the African disillusionment with it, caused in part by the U.N.'s involvement in the Congo. Indeed, the major intrusive role in the Nigerian civil war was played unsuccessfully by the Commonwealth, and the OAU seemed at times more effective.

The only importance of the U.N. in West Africa is related to the attempt to end the colonial status of Portuguese Guinea. This effort draws its importance, however, primarily from the more significant issues involved in attempting to oust the Portuguese from the far larger colonies of Angola and Mozambique in Southern Africa, to eject the South Africans from South West Africa, and to control the rebel regime in Rhodesia.

Southeast Asia

The intrusive use of the U.N. in Southeast Asia is midway between its considerable use in the Middle East and its comparative lack of involvement in West Africa and Latin America. The foremost obstacle to the active use of the U.N. by intrusive powers is that Communist China is not one of its members; thus the kind of dynamic mixture of competition and collusion that the U.S. and the Soviet Union pursue in the Middle East is impossible in Southeast Asia. Whether or not the Chinese would use the U.N. in a similar way is moot, but their importance as an intrusive power in Southeast Asia diminishes the role of the U.N. in this subordinate system. Moreover, the two Vietnams are not members of the organization. Both the U.S. and the U.S.S.R. have had to be sensitive to possible reactions in

Vietnam, should the conflict there have been discussed in the U.N. or should any action be taken by the U.N. The Soviet Union chose to ignore the U.N. completely, while the U.S. made several lukewarm and unsuccessful attempts to involve the U.N. indirectly in some type of negotiations to end the War. In the Laos issue (the foremost unsolved problem in the mainland core from 1959 to 1962), the organization's Secretary General sent a special representative (in 1959) to investigate the situation. Yet, the final agreements reached—tentative as they have turned out to be—were negotiated and signed in 1962 in Geneva, outside the framework of the U.N. These Geneva agreements were signed by Communist China as well as by the U.S. and the U.S.S.R.

In the maritime core, where the absence of China has been less significant and the involvement of the U.S.S.R. less penetrating, all members of the area are also members of the U.N.[82] The major involvement of the U.N. has been with Indonesia; first, to dispatch observers in 1948 and 1949, during the Dutch withdrawal; and second, to dispatch a force in 1962 and 1963 to West Irian, to supervise the transfer of authority from the Dutch to the Indonesians. Here the primacy of Western control has made the U.N. a convenient tool for use in delicate operations when no other equally neutral international organ appeared to be available. What the U.N.'s role might have been if a progressively left-leaning and pro-Chinese Indonesia had continued to confront Malaysia is difficult to estimate, but experience suggests that the U.N. would have become a less effective tool for the intrusive powers.

West Europe

The four intrusive systems we have discussed thus far have a vertical involvement with the U.N.: intrusive powers use the U.N. to act upon developments within the region. In West Europe, involvement is more horizontal: the U.N. is itself a theater for the interaction of various members of the subordinate and intrusive systems. This condition exists because of the importance of particular West European states within the U.N.— France and Great Britain in particular, but also several of the former and outgoing colonial powers as well. As an increasing number of newly independent states were admitted to the U.N. in the late 1950's and early 1960's, issues of past and present colonialism became more and more significant in United Nations' discussions. The prevalence of this issue, and the close involvement of the West Europeans, presented the U.S. with numerous delicate situations (e.g., West Irian, the former Belgium Congo, Angola, Mozambique, Algeria, Rhodesia) which offered America the alternative of supporting its allies at the expense of its position among the less developed

---

[82] Indonesia formally withdrew from the U.N. on January 21, 1965, but rejoined on September 28, 1966.

nations or of supporting the new countries at the cost of alienating its allies. American decisions have, in turn, had their effect upon the morale and elan within NATO. Thus, the U.N. became not merely a tool of American intrusion, but a part of its working relations with the members of the subordinate system.

When polycentrism increased in the early 1960's, the U.N. was an indicator of the changing environment in West Europe. As peacekeeping became more significant to the operation of the U.N., France and the Soviet Union began to share their disillusionment with many aspects of the U.N.'s activity— particularly after the Congo operations. The similar positions taken by these two countries were both cause and effect of the warming relations between them.

In the Southern periphery of West Europe, the U.N. has acted in ways more similar to other areas. From 1946 until 1954, the U.N. stationed observers on the Greek border. More importantly, however, a peace force was established (in 1964) in Cyprus, to attempt to control the seething chaos on that island from erupting into full-scale warfare between the Greek and Turkish communities. In this area, as in the maritime Southeast Asian core, Western powers with primary influence on both sides preferred to use the U.N. rather than any regional organization (e.g., NATO). In Cyprus, there was the additional factor that a peace keeping force was needed and was acceptable. The U.N. had already established mechanisms for a peace force, and thus its instrument appeared the most convenient.

CULTURAL AND EDUCATIONAL ACTIVITIES

When we speak of cultural and educational activities, we include the students, artists, and tourists who travel to the intrusive country as well as the teachers, students, tourists, entertainers, artists, volunteers, and various types of technical personnel who travel to the aided nation. We include the export of movies, the translation of books and magazines, and the publication of newspapers. Because of the breadth of the subject and the paucity of data, we will simply attempt to present a short résumé of some of the programs pursued by various intrusive powers, with particular emphasis on the destination of foreign students.

In 1966, the *UNESCO Statistical Yearbook* published a study of the location of foreign students in fifteen of the most popular countries.[83] Although the Soviet Union and China were not included in the study, it reveals much interesting information about the popularity of universities in some of the major intrusive powers around 1964. The United States is by far the most popular country in which to study, France possesses less than

---

[83] UNESCO Statistical Yearbook, 1966, (Paris: UNESCO, 1967), pp. 306–11. The remaining references to foreign students from non-Communist countries in this chapter are based on this source.

half as many foreign students, West Germany is third, and the U.A.R. and the United Kingdom vie for fourth place. The Soviet program, relatively small, has been complained against, both by Soviet citizens and by visiting students, and as a result, the number of enrollees has declined since the peak year of 1962.[84] The Soviet Union has appealed to students from less developed countries, particularly from Africa, but the other intrusive powers tend to have a broader base. Moreover, slightly fewer students from Asia, Africa, and Latin America have undertaken programs in the Soviet Union since 1955 than the number which were in the United Kingdom alone in 1964 (13,500 vs. 15,084).[85]

The United States is by far the most popular destination for *Latin American* students, and Spain is second.[86] France, Germany, and Italy are also frequent centers for Latin American youth studying abroad. Students from the British Caribbean, not surprisingly, favor the United States, Great Britain, and Canada.

In West Africa, students from the core study overwhelmingly in France, while students from the periphery study in the United States, Great Britain, and West Germany, in that order. The major exceptions include a sizable majority from Guinea in the United States, and contingents in communist countries from Mali, Guinea, and Ghana. There were over twice as many Ghanese in the major Western countries as in communist countries during Nkrumah's peak of power, the mid-1960's; almost twice as many Guineans in communist countries as in the West, at one point; and about half as many in communist countries as in Western countries from Togo and Mali, with a significant minority in communist nations from Niger.[87] The figures for Guinea, Ghana, and Mali are as high as they are because they include significant numbers of short-term technical trainees (up to half the figure for Ghana and about one-third of Guinea's). Moreover, unlike the UNESCO figures, these figures include secondary and vocational students.

As in West Africa, the destinations of *Middle Eastern* students follow patterns which, in terms of the intrusive system, are by now familiar. In the periphery the largest number of students journey to the U.S., then to Germany and France. Austria, Britain, and Switzerland are also popular.

---

84 Tansky, "Soviet Foreign Aid," pp. 963–64. "Since the peak year of 1962, when more than 3,400 students initiated academic programs, the number of new enrollees has declined each year with an estimated 1,300 students entering the Soviet Union in 1965."

85 This figure (for the Soviet Union) does not include students from European countries.

86 Portugal was not included in the UNESCO study; presumably it would have ranked high for Latin America because of the Portuguese background of Brazil.

87 Material on communist nations is for March 1962. U.S. Information Agency, Research Reference Service, *Communist Propaganda Around the World: Apparatus and Activities—1961,* ed. Murray G. Lawson, 1962 (Washington, D.C.: U.S.I.A.) p. 176.

In the core, the "progressive" Soviet-influenced countries have students much more frequently in communist nations than do the more "conservative" and neutral Arabs. In addition to an unusually large number reported from Iraq and Yemen in communist nations, there are significant minorities from the U.A.R. and Syria.[88] Germany, Austria, Great Britain, and France are also popular with students from these countries. The other more conservative Arab countries concentrate their studies, as their politics, in the West. When students leave the Middle East, they study primarily in the same Western countries as their Arab brethren.

In Southeast Asia, the United States—like everywhere else—has been popular, but otherwise there is a general following of colonial patterns. Especially in a country clearly allied with the U.S. (e.g., the Philippines, Thailand). Australia, Japan, West Germany, and Canada are also popular countries in which to study. Indonesia under Sukarno seems to have had the highest concentration of students (outside of North Vietnam) in communist countries-notably in the Soviet Union. Cambodia and Burma have also had contingents in communist countries.[89]

In *West Europe* there is considerable interchange among the core countries, but in addition the U.S., Switzerland and, to a lesser extent, Austria are popular, while Great Britain receives only a small minority of the core's foreign students. Most of the British foreign students study either in the U.S. or France, but significant minorities travel to Canada, Germany, and Australia. Students from the rest of the northern periphery go mainly to Germany, although large groups travel to the U.S., and also to France, Switzerland, Britain, and Austria. The only major differences in the southern periphery are a greater preference for Britain, and a greater diversity among the various countries of Europe as choices for study.

Thus, in the exchange of foreign students there is a unique coincidence of political patterns and educational choices. There seems to be a direct connection between intrusive political and economic programs, on the one hand, and cultural and educational programs, on the other. Colonial traditions are erased slowly, if at all. Moreover, when there are differences in educational preferences, these tend to revolve around regional choices, no matter what the divisions within the subordinate system itself. Thus, Latin Americans have an understandable preference for Spain; Middle Easterners of all varieties seem to prefer Germany, Austria, and Switzerland more than do

[88] As of December 1962, it was estimated that the following numbers were in communist-bloc countries: Iraq, 2,230; Yemen, 400; U.A.R.: 245; Syria: 290. Although the two charts should not necessarily be considered comparable, the UNESCO report provides a contrasting notion of students in particular Western countries. United States Information Agency, Research and Reference Service, *Communist Propaganda Activities in the Near East and South Asia: 1963,* (R-162-64), Oct. 20, 1964 (Washington, D.C.: U.S.I.A.) p. 100.

[89] Information on students in communist countries is for 1961, from United States Information Agency, *Communist Propaganda around the World,* p. 326.

people from other regions (except the West Europeans themselves). Ever-popular France is especially desirable to students from the West African core. Australia and Japan are more important in Southeast Asia than elsewhere. Above all, the United States is distinctive for its popularity—even in West Europe, where there seems to be a concentration on France and West Germany. Study in communist states seems to be almost directly related to current political conditions. At least this significant aspect of cultural and educational exchange seems to revolve around established patterns and conditions, American superiority, and occasional politically influenced communist inroads.

An examination of cultural and educational programs would not be complete without some consideration of teaching personnel abroad. Information was not available concerning the number of teachers in each country; hence, worldwide figures have had to be used. We can assume, for the sake of simplicity, that teachers travel roughly the same roads as students. Table 6-5 indicates the number of publicly financed experts and volunteers in education sent from OECD countries to less developed lands between 1965 and 1966. These figures show the former colonial powers emphasize publicly financed experts, while the newcomers (particularly the U.S. and Germany) stress volunteers. In formerly colonial areas, the colonial powers have obvious advantages.

As the communist programs are relatively new intrusive instruments, exporting educators tends to be a less important part of their programs than economic and technical assistance.[90] Still as the material in Table 6-5 suggests, Western programs also contain extensive technical aid. Moreover, it is extraordinarily difficult to compare communist programs to Western efforts, because they often resemble services made available by Western private enterprise. Leo Tansky reports that nearly 80% of the Soviet technicians who have been employed abroad (there were 9,500 in 1965) have been sent since 1960. About 45% have been employed in Asian countries and more than one-third in the Middle East, although the number in Africa is increasing. It is interesting to note that, as time goes on, more and more of the Soviet experts are engaged in educational and broader training activities (e.g. managerial, medical, agricultural activities), especially in Africa. The major Soviet programs include the construction of technical institutes and vocational training centers whose curricula tend to center around such subjects as engineering, agriculture, mining, and industrial production. These institutes are designed to produce highly skilled professional and technical personnel.[91]

The Chinese have also been active in the area of technical assistance. Milton Kovner explains that:

90 Tansky, "Soviet Foreign Aid," p. 906.
91 Tansky, "Soviet Foreign Aid," pp. 960–62.

Although Communist China accounted for less than 10 per cent of all Communist aid expenditures in less-developed countries, its share in the total number of Communist personnel in developing countries nearly doubled in 1965, exceeding the number of technicians from Eastern Europe, and numbering about half the 9,500 Soviet technicians in the field.[92]

The large number of manual laborers used in Chinese projects are chiefly responsible for the inflated figures. Kovner reports that Chinese technicians have been engaged primarily in agricultural projects, road building, and dam construction. Chinese student exchange programs accounted for only 3% of the more than 21,000 students trained in communist countries from the mid-1950's to the mid-1960's, and even this modest program was disrupted during the Cultural Revolution.[93]

No discussion of cultural and educational programs can be complete without some special mention of French efforts. Their activities are unique, not so much for their quantity as for the central importance of French *civilisation*. There are 177 French colleges and lycées abroad, some of which are linked directly to agencies of the French government or are sponsored by private French associations. In 1964, these schools enrolled nearly 310,000 students and had over 6,200 French-born teachers sent by the French government. In addition, France operates 43 institutes and 100 cultural centers in foreign countries, which, in 1964, were used by some 128,000 foreign students. The famous *Alliance Française* has recently been especially active in Latin America and in the English-speaking countries of Africa and Southeast Asia. Its headquarters are in Paris, and it 800 sections offer cultural activities to 120,000 members in all parts of the world.[94]

A final significant effort which should be mentioned before ending our analysis of cultural and educational programs is the American Peace Corps. Of course, the Peace Corps includes volunteers who are involved in such diverse activities as library work, surveying, biochemistry, speech therapy; nevertheless, the Peace Corps has become a symbol of American activities abroad and it is therefore interesting to analyze the geographical distribution of the volunteers.[95] From June 1961 to December 1967, the volunteers *in the five regions* were concentrated in Latin America (36% of the world-

[92] *The U.S.S.R. & Developing Countries* (Moscow, 1966) p. 37. Quoted in Milton Kovner, "Communist China's Foreign Aid to Less Developed Countries," in U.S. Congress, Joint Economic Committee, *An Economic Profile of Mainland China*, Part IV, 90th Cong. 1st Sess., February, 1967, (Washington, D.C.: Government Printing Office), pp. 614–15.

[93] *Ibid.*

[94] France, *Cultural & Technical Cooperation. Supplement to France: Aid and Cooperation*, 1965, (New York: Ambassade de France, Service de Press et d'Information, December 1965), pp. 25–27. For further information on exchanges of scientific and technical information, see also pp. 44–46.

[95] The information that follows is taken from Peace Corps, Office of Volunteer Support, *Quarterly Statistical Summary* (Washington, D.C.), December 31, 1967, pp. 1–2.

wide total); West Africa was second (16%); and Southeast Asia third (14%). The distribution of Peace Corps workers was widest in Latin America, ranging from 1,945 in Colombia to 58 in Guyana; the only two major countries in which volunteers were not stationed were Haiti and Argentina.[96] In West Africa, similarly, only Mali had not received vounteers; the programs ranged from 1,768 volunteers in Nigeria to a training program in Dahomey. In mainland Southeast Asia, only Thailand received volunteers, but heavy American involvement in Vietnam and Laos probably accounts for the Peace Corps being sent elsewhere. The Philippines, Thailand, and Malaysia all had heavy concentrations of Peace Corpsmen; indeed, the Philippines received the largest number in the world (2,120). Indonesia received a meager number (46) which will probably increase if her relations with the U.S. continue to improve. In the Middle East, Iran and Turkey received comparatively large numbers of volunteers (703 and 994 respectively) but none were sent to the core. The high degree of political and economic development in West Europe, as well as diminished American interest, is reflected in the fact that only Cyprus has been a host to volunteers (22). Thus, participation through the Peace Corps—as through the other cultural and educational activities we have surveyed—seems to follow traditional patterns, political dominance, and the broad framework we analyzed in our discussion of bilateral arrangements.

PROPAGANDA

Types of propaganda are also diverse and varied, and can easily be meshed with other types of methods of intrusive participation. For example, communist aid commitments (especially Chinese) are often widely advertised, even though the recipient may never actually use the funds allotted to him. Movies, magazines, books, and newspapers, are frequently vehicles—overt or covert—of propaganda activities, even while functioning as parts of cultural and educational programs. Some of the more spectacular recent propaganda efforts have included *Twenty Letters to a Friend*, the book by Stalin's daughter, Svetlana, published in the U.S.; the claim, in July 1966, that Chairman Mao Tse Tung, then 72 years old, had swum 8 miles in 65 minutes in the Yangtze River; and the Soviet celebration, in 1967, of the fiftieth anniversary of the October revolution.

One of the best means of measuring propagandistic activity is to record the weekly number of broadcast hours beamed at specific regions by the leading intrusive powers. The rise in the number of radio sets throughout the world, especially with the widespread use of transistors, has made this vehicle an especially significant one. As Table 6-6 shows, the Russians and Chinese have been particularly active in this area. The data are somewhat

---

[96] The periphery, outside of Jamaica and Guyana, is labeled "Eastern Caribbean" in *ibid.*

deceptive, however, in that they do not include broadcasts which are not announced as beamed at specific areas, so that many British Broadcast Corporation (BBC) General Overseas Service and Voice of America (VOA) World-Wide Service programs are omitted. Moreover, more important than shortwave broadcasts is the ability to place broadcasts on local stations, both radio and television, and the U.S. has been more active and more successful with this kind of activity than with shortwave broadcasts. Since television cannot be transmitted long distances onto home screens, the ability to place programs on local stations will become even more important in the future and the U.S. may be especially successful.[97]

Table 6-6 contains a comparison of the broadcasts of six of the major intrusive powers. The Table also provides at least an indication of the direction of present programming by broad areas, even though it was not possible to gain precise information about our five regions. The Table clearly reveals that broadcasts, especially to the developing world, have increased between 1956 and 1967. It also highlights the efforts of the communists, the fantastic advances of the Chinese, and the surprising decline of the United States in this field. The United States has actually expanded its worldwide services in English, though not its broadcasts beamed at specific areas.[98] Nevertheless, the Table shows that the communist nations are extraordinarily active, and it also shows that the Germans significantly expanded their programs between 1956 and 1967.

As to regional distribution, the proportion of programs to West Europe declined but there were increases in broadcasts to Latin America and Africa, reflecting the effect of Castro in the one and the increase in independence in the latter. There was a general increase in programs to the Far East and Middle East by the major intrusive powers except the United States. The Table shows that France, more than any of the other intrusive powers, concentrates on Africa, and information contained elsewhere suggests she also concentrates on Francophonic countries and prefers to supply radio and television programs for local use rather than broadcast on short wave.[99]

While this material is brief and general, it indicates the significance of propaganda in the intrusive system and shows that particular intrusive powers concentrate on specific areas. It also shows that there is a variety of instruments of propaganda chosen by the various intrusive powers.

THE INTRUSIVE SYSTEM AND THE PATTERN VARIABLES

Our study of the nine methods of participation in five subordinate systems may now permit us to make some tentative conclusions about the effects of

[97] _Britannica Book of the Year_ (Chicago: Encyclopedia Britannica, Inc.), 1967, p. 649.

[98] _Ibid._, 1968, p. 646.

[99] France, _Cultural and Technical Cooperation_, pp. 34–35.

intrusive actions upon the subordinate system, in terms of our four pattern variables. The following statements are not intended to be definitive, but they will indicate the direction in which further research and investigation might take us.

COHESION

We will first discuss the influence of intrusive powers upon social cohesion and then proceed to an analysis of their ability to affect the other three types of cohesion: economic, political, and organizational.

Social Cohesion

As we pointed out in Chapter 1, the creation of social cohesion by intrusive powers is extremely difficult and, consequently, rare.[100] The three factors which appear to be most important are timing, local conditions, and the degree of primacy of the intrusive power.

Thus, the Spanish and Portuguese were extremely effective in molding the social cohesion of *Latin America:* they possessed colonies, not simply influence; they were the first intrusive powers present; and they were also able to destroy the indigenous civilizations and to implant social forms of their own. Even now, when the U.S. is the primary intrusive power, its influence upon social cohesion is minimal compared to the Spanish and Portuguese. There is little doubt that the high percentage of Latin American students who study in the U.S. contributes to a solidification of American cultural influence within the subordinate system and has indirect repercussions upon Latin American states. Yet, these achievements cannot even be considered in the same light as the Iberian accomplishments.

In West Africa, the dominance of the French is related to their former colonial primacy. The French may not have been able to eradicate tribalism or the memory of ancient empire, but they were able to create a pattern of common concerns and traditions among the elite. This achievement appears even more considerable when we compare the French record in West Africa to the one in Indo-China.

When intrusive powers become involved with redirecting social cohesion failure is more frequent than success. *Indo-China* illustrates the failure of an intrusive power to provide a durable degree of social cohesion. *In the Arab and Malay areas,* moreover, the net effects of intrusion in the past half-millenium have been to deepen and aggravate divisions, and even to create new ones (e.g., the Catholic Philippines vs. Moslem Indonesia and Malaysia). The overseas Chinese, throughout *Southeast Asia,* should proba-

---

100 Throughout this discussion of social cohesion, we are dealing only with the success or failure of the policies of intrusive powers. We do not mean to attach any special value to social cohesion *per se.*

bly also be viewed as having an indirect corrosive effect upon social cohesion in this subordinate system.

Other Aspects of Cohesion

External powers may not be able to directly affect social cohesion, but through their intrusion they can help to sway regional conceptions which ultimately influence economic, political, and organizational cohesion. We can discuss these three elements of cohesion together, in terms of the patterns we uncovered through our analysis of the methods of participation. As a result of that earlier discussion, we would expect West Europe to be the subordinate system most susceptible to intrusive influence and Latin America second, because of the dominance of the U.S. The mixed pattern of bilateral relations leads us to expect that West Africa will be less malleable. The intrusive competition in the Middle East and Southeast Asia should make the creation of some sort of regionally cohesive unit extremely difficult.

In West Europe, America's encouragement of German democracy and Western orientation, of regional cooperation and integration, have contributed to cohesion. As subsequent developments have suggested, the Russians have inadvertently contributed through such actions as the Berlin blockade, the Czechoslovak coup, and Hungarian repression. These caused the West Europeans to recognize the commonality of their lot far more quickly, and in a more sustained fashion, than they might have done otherwise no matter how great the American encouragement. Moreover, the record of American support for regional cohesion has not been unmixed. America's suffrance of right-wing dictatorships in Spain, Portugal, and Greece has limited political cohesion. In the realm of economics, unless they cause the Europeans to unite against them, American private investments will continue to limit economic cohesion, but at the same time encourage its potentialities by creating European-wide industrial entities. Finally, even though the United States supported the European Defense Community (EDC), the American involvement in European defense throughout the postwar era (e.g. NATO, Nassau, MLF) has had the ultimate effect of inhibiting organizational cohesion. In sum, there can be little doubt that the U.S. has indeed abetted political, economic, and organizational cohesion in West Europe. Most likely, less would have been done without its presence; but its efforts have not resulted uniformly in increased cohesion.

In Latin America, the United States has made no thoroughgoing contribution to political or economic cohesion. The types of regimes it has supported have been varied and diverse, and its support has depended upon local conditions. The American policy has generally been one of supporting or suffering regimes which it believed would act in its own interests— political, economic and military. Such governments moved in a vaguely leftward and reformist direction immediately after Castro came to power (e.g., Bosch of the Dominican Republic, Betancourt of Venezuela, Frondizi of Argentina), but in the mid-1960's there was a turn, both in Latin American events and in American support, toward more military and conservative type regimes (e.g., Balaguer in the Dominican Republic, Branco in Brazil, Ongunia in Argentina). There was, however, no general pattern. The U.S. seemed capable of living with both Samosa, the old-style dictator of Nicaragua, and with the hope of the Democratic Left, Frei of Chile.

We have seen that the U.S. only recently joined the effort to encourage regional economic institutions. Its economic policies have resulted in trade being oriented toward the U.S. rather than within the Latin American core. The most positive results of its efforts, in terms of economic cohesion, may be the encouragement of industrialization as a result of aid and investment policies. Thus far, however, the ledger does not show a net encouragement of internal trade, although such encouragement is implied in the scheme for a Latin American common market and in the comparatively recent American support for the Central American common market.

No matter what its motivation, the strongest American effect upon Latin American cohesion has been in the organizational arena. The mere existence of the U.S. has given the Latin America nations reason enough for common interests and common concerns: to control the U.S. (e.g., the issue of non-intervention) and to seek whatever economic fruits might be possible (e.g., increased economic assistance).

No other state has contributed to Latin American cohesion in any major way. Certainly, Soviet support of Cuba has diminished political and economic cohesion to the extent that Cuba was removed from the Latin American core.

In West Africa, as our analysis of multilateral and bilateral arrangements and trade and economic investment showed, the political and organizational cohesion of the periphery has gradually declined as other powers continually chipped away at British hegemony and as conditions within the two most important peripheral countries—Ghana and Nigeria—swayed erratically on the sea of internal politics. Economically, the effect of intrusive activities in the periphery has been to stress domestic viability rather than regional interaction and complementarity. In the core, France has provided a measure of political and organizational, but little economic, cohesion. Here again, other powers—particularly the Soviet Union, China, and, to a lesser extent, the U.S.—have attempted to chip away at French dominance, but with mixed results. The pattern in this subordinate system has been a measure of cohesion provided by lingering colonial presences and traditions, with the newcomers—Western or communist—tending to break down old patterns and partially eroding what cohesion existed.

In Southeast Asia and the Middle East, none of the recent intrusive powers has enhanced cohesion, as our analysis of their methods of participation indicated. Britain encouraged the formation of the Arab League in the mid-1940's and urged the Egyptians to identify with the Arab cause, but the days of British suzerainty are gone and the Soviet-American competition which has replaced it has hardly abetted cohesion. Rather, it has tended to bifurcate political cohesion in the Arab core and has had little effect upon organizational cohesion—other than encouraging or discouraging a variety of alliances.[101] Neither of the superpowers has had a visible positive effect upon economic cohesion. At the very most, the intrusive powers have attempted to create their own units, within this subordinate system, which each hoped might form a nucleus for their future hegemony. In the process, whether or not they have aided national integration or political and economic development, they have certainly not advanced regional cohesion.

In Southeast Asia, a trace of organizational and political cohesion has been provided in the maritime core. By and large, however, the intrusive powers have only used the lack of cohesion throughout Southeast Asia to promote their own designs and interests, thereby exacerbating even further regional and national chaos. In short, intrusive powers in Southeast Asia have, in general, preferred to ride an ostrich of anarchy rather than fly a Pagasus of accord.

COMMUNICATIONS

As we have already noted, it is most difficult to obtain concrete information about communications. We can, however, base some general conclusions on our previous discussion of the nine methods of participation. The tentative character of these statements should become quickly apparent. We will first examine the special case of West Europe, and then move on to some examples of isolated effects of intrusion upon communications.

In West Europe, where communications are at their highest stage of development, the influence of intrusive powers reaches its highest level. The United States has provided political encouragement and platforms for an exchange among elite in NATO, OECD (and before it OEEC) and, to a lesser extent, in its own universities. As to transportation, TWA, Pan American Airlines, and Aeroflot (the Soviet airlines) fly to Europe. Several European airlines (e.g., Lufthansa, KLM, Alitalia) purchase part or all of their equipment from American companies, and a smaller number purchase from the Soviet Union (e.g. Swissair, KLM). As we noted in our discussion of private investment, in 1964 Americans owned 24% of Common Market automobile production, a major indication of intrusive influence upon trans-

---

[101] Even so, since 1967 the Soviet-sponsored U.A.R. and American-sponsored Jordan have found many common interests; the U.S. has had difficulty uniting Iran and Saudi-Arabia behind a common Persian Gulf policy; and the Russians have been unable to get the Syrians and Egyptians to agree on a common Israeli policy or a common Arab policy.

portation. In addition, the American-owned International Telephone and Telegraph Company (IT&T) owns the Avis Rent-A-Car subsidiaries in several West European countries. As to personal communications, IT&T owns a broad range of manufacturing plants for telephone and telegraphy equipment in West Europe.[102] As to mass media, the major contributions of the U.S. appear to have been television programs provided, research and development later sent to Europe (e.g., color TV) and, finally, satellite communications (which may, however, have greater implications for global than regional transmission). The Soviet Union's cooperation with France to develop color TV may be considered its major involvement in regional communications.

In the other four subordinate systems, the indigenous problems are entirely different. The small amount of trade within these regions (even in the cores) is indicative of the low level of communications. In these areas, internal communications are at so low a plane that the major thrust of the programs of intrusive powers is to improve national instruments before proceeding to regional development. Road building, or the development of airlines, radio broadcasting, or television transmission, is usually a national program—even when one intrusive power is primary in an entire subordinate system or sector (as the U.S. in Latin America or France in the West African core). As in West Europe, national programs may augur well for regional efforts, but this is still in the future. Nevertheless, there are some incipient intrusive effects upon regional communications, and we will mention a few examples as an indication of types of participation which may become more significant. We will discuss these in the following order: transportation, exchanges among the elite, mass media, and personal communications.

Transportation

Transportation is the most obvious vehicle of intrusion. The United States has assisted in a major project, the Pan-American Highway which potentially offers transportation by road throughout the Americas,[103] and its uniqueness is testimony to the paucity of communications within the core. In mainland Southeast Asia, the intrusive powers have played a major role in the Mekong development project and the Asian highway project which will, between them, improve internal water and road transportation, but these are isolated

---

102 Clyde H. Farnsworth, "ITT Carries Banner in U.S. Business Invasion of Europe," *The New York Times,* July 17, 1967, p. 41.

103 The American effort has concentrated on the Central American states rather than Mexico or South America. For further information, see Senate Committee on Public Works, *Report on Progress on Inter-American Highway, 1962,* 87th Congress, 2nd Sess., 1962 (Washington, D.C.: Government Printing Office) p. 3; also, Ellis Briggs, "The Inter American Highway," *Atlantic,* CCXXI (February, 1968), 126–29.

and rare endeavors. The effect of the intrusive powers upon regional air-line service can be seen, for example, in West Africa, where the few indigenous airlines which travel beyond their own borders are all assisted by intrusive powers. Air Guinea is assisted by the Czechs, the Russians, and the Americans; Air Mali, by the Czechs and the Russians; Ghana Airways, by the Russians, Swiss, British, and Italians; and Air Nigeria has agreements with BOAC and Pan American.[104] In addition, fourteen West European, Communist, and American airlines fly to West Africa. It is not surprising, for example, given our analysis of West African political relationships, that in 1965 Aeroflot and the Czechslovak airlines connected Senegal, Mali, Guinea, and Ghana.[105]

Exchanges Among the Elite

Universities, and externally sponsored international organizations and conferences, are important instruments for exchanges among the elite of each of the four regions. We explored these avenues when we discussed multilateral arrangements and cultural and educational programs. We saw that in West Africa and Latin America, for example, French, American, and Spanish universities, and French and American international institutions, foster communication among the elite.

Mass Media

The use of mass media by intrusive powers for the dissemination of propaganda has important implications for regional communications. Radio broadcasts, both taped and shortwave, are often prepared for more than a national audience. Moreover, television offers a unique chance for intrusive powers to attempt to create common attitudes and prejudices. This potentiality is being realized in the Middle East, where the common language and the relatively compact size of the core creates a special opportunity for an intrusive power to promote regional communications.

Personal Communications

The telephone and telegraph were themselves intially intrusive contributions to each of these four subordinate systems, as well as to West Europe. Today the local states are still often dependent upon external aid for such communication. IT&T still controls a wide range of domestic and regional outlets, even though it has sold many of its holdings since World War II and some have been expropriated (e.g., in Cuba). IT & T is especially strong in Latin America and, as we have seen, West Europe. In Latin America, it still controls the telephonic and telegraphic communications of several

---

[104] George Weeks, "Wings of Change: A Report on the Progress of Civil Aviation in Africa," *Africa Report,* X (February, 1965), 14–40.
[105] *Ibid.*

countries with the U.S. and Europe. It owns the communications instruments between several Latin American countries and, in addition, the Avis Rent-a-Car subsidiaries in a few Latin American countries. Most important, it manufactures most of the telephone and telegraph equipment used in Latin America.[106]

One of the most exciting instruments in this field at the present time is the communications satellite. In Latin America, for example, the U.S. is aiding a satellite program which will measurably assist regional communications, as part of the program for a core-wide Common Market by 1985.[107]

Despite these promises of future achievements, the demands of internal integration and development tend to take precedence over regional requirements in subordinate systems dominated by developing states. Political and physical restrictions mitigate in favor of the prior improvement of national communications. While communications can in turn increase regional cohesion, they must in general await improvements in domestic areas.

LEVEL OF POWER

We can relate our analysis of the effects of intrusion upon the level of power to the patterns we discussed earlier in our examination of the methods of participation. Because changes in military and motivational power are more dramatic, they tend to be more significant in subordinate systems where there is a high degree of competition among local and among intrusive powers. On the other hand, in regions where one intrusive power dominates, there is more potential effect upon material power. In general, the intrusive powers can far more easily raise a nation's military or motivational capacity than its material strength. We will discuss West Europe and Latin America first and the Middle East and Southeast Asia second, leaving the mixed case of West Africa to last.

West Europe

In West Europe, the United States has been dominant, and it has accomplished the most massive and effective example of externally furnished impetus to material power that has ever been witnessed.

Through the Marshall Plan, the U.S. played a central role in rehabilitating the several West European economies and societies after World War II, and thus visibly affected not only the regional distribution of power but the material power of the subordinate system as a whole. In this system, even the effects of military programs have been less successful and less dramatic, and, as we have seen, the American influence upon European material power continues. Not only do American companies operating in Europe

---

106 Stanley H. Brawn, "How One Man Can Move a Corporate Mountain," *Fortune,* LXXIV (July 1, 1966), 81–83.

107 Kathleen McLaughlin, "Latin Lands Prepare for Satellite Communications," *New York Times,* February 11, 1968, Part III, p. 1.

provide a means of increased communications, but as Servan-Schreiber stresses, in the short-run American investment is the principle vehicle for technological progress in Europe and has a generally beneficial effect upon the European standard of living.[108]

There can also be no question that American military intervention and military aid have substantially increased the military power of many members of this subordinate system. The resulting strength, however, has had the opposite of the usual effect: the European attainment, through American assistance and support of a deterrent capacity, has produced a decreased willingness to act in the general realm of international politics and has helped to tranquilize, rather than to exacerbate, European conditions. Even DeGaulle—who has represented the major exception to these generalizations —readily admitted that the American deterrent provided him with an umbrella in which he could safely play in the international rain.

Latin America

Whereas intrusive (American) aid to Europe has effectively raised the level of European power, created a military stalemate, and failed to increase Europe's desire for international involvement, the effects of such aid were quite different elsewhere. It is rather difficult to estimate the effect of American involvement upon material power in Latin America. Certainly, there has been no dramatic increase in the power of the indigenous states. In West Europe, the process was one of rehabilitation; in Latin America it has been one of construction. American programs were reviewed after Nixon's disastrous trip in 1958 and the coming of Castro, and, as we have seen, there has been an attempt in the 1960's to encourage projects (e.g., Alliance for Progress, Latin American integration), which might help to improve Latin American material power. As yet, these programs remain more promise than actuality.

American sales of arms to various Latin American states have increased the over-all quality of divergent armed forces, but have had little effect upon the balance of power in the system. Indeed, Geoffrey Kemp suggests that the Latin American air forces are equipped with far less sophisticated weapons (and in smaller numbers) than their counterparts in such subordinate systems as the Middle East and North Africa.[109]

The most dramatic intrusive effect upon Latin America in recent years

[108] Servan-Schreiber, p. 38. In the long run, he believes the effect of these corporations will be to increase Europe's dependence and backwardness.

[109] In "Rearmament in Latin America," *The World Today*, XXIII (September, 1967), Kemp writes: "First, the equipment of all Latin American air forces, apart from those of Cuba and Venezuela, is antiquated and far below the standards to be found even in some North African countries" (P. 377). "...Since 1955 the relative pace of rearmament in other areas has far exceeded modernization in Latin America, and today there are still more combat jets in Egypt, Iraq, and Israel than in the entire Latin American subcontinent *including* Cuba, who alone accounts for over 60 per cent of the total" (P. 378).

has resulted from the Russian arrangements with Cuba. Russian support for Cuba has enabled that regime to survive, since no anti-American government can exist in Latin America without external aid. The specific results of Soviet intrusion have been an increase in Cuba's military power, and a qualitative rise in her motivational power, far beyond her material base. As we have suggested earlier, this rise in motivational power is not completely controllable by the Russians.

Ironically, the most significant effect of the chain reaction of events set off by the Cuban experience has been to intensify and rigidify American involvement with Latin America. It has increased the relative priority of Latin America in the diminished American foreign aid program, but it has also increased American willingness to intervene militarily, directly and indirectly, to "prevent another Cuba."

In Latin America, then, intrusive actions have not generally contributed to a rise in material power, but they have not contributed to large increases in military or motivational power either (except in Cuba). Generally, arms sales to Latin America have had more consequences for domestic politics than for international relations.

The Middle East

The effects of intrusion in the Middle East are quite different than in either Latin America or West Europe. Oil profits resulting from the activities of intrusive powers have improved the material power of several states, especially Kuwait, Saudi Arabia, Iran, Iraq, and British protectorates in the Persian Gulf. Considerable Western aid, private and public, to the peripheral states has increased their material positions. There have been important material efforts by all external parties in the oil-poor Arab states, of which, as we have suggested, the Aswan Dam is only the most dramatic.

The most important intrusive event in this area since the Ottomans were ejected has been the rise in influence of the U.S.S.R. Economic aid, numerous trade agreements and, above all, generous military aid represent a substantial commitment on the part of the Soviet Union. The results of Russian material aid have themselves not been major, particularly when we consider, for example, that the Aswan Dam will only be able to absorb the effects of increased population. But the political effects of this commitment, on military and motivational power, have influenced the direction of Middle East international politics. They have complicated and exacerbated relations within the core as various Arab states have lined up with support from East or West. They have made it easier for President Nasser to remain the dominant force in Arab politics, but at the same time have provided the Syrians (and perhaps in the future the Iraqis) with an opportunity to oppose him. They have led to local adventurism and expansionism (e.g., the Egyptians in Yemen). Most important, they have aggravated Arab-Israeli relations and made some kind of *modus vivendi* extremely difficult, if not impossible. Russian arms granted to the Arabs have only been answered by Western (mainly French, and then American) aid to Israel, in order to create a balance which has never been achieved. Instead of creating a stalemate, the intrusive powers have constantly raised the price of conflict without decreasing its incentives. Their effect here in military and motivational terms must certainly be seen as the opposite of West Europe, and except for the influence of oil in material terms it is more similar to Latin America, especially in the Arab core.

Southeast Asia

In Southeast Asia the intrusive powers have, even more than in the Middle East, artificially raised the military and motivational power of combatants without reducing indigenous tensions. In *the mainland core,* neither South nor North Vietnam would have been able to continue the war through the mid-1960's without massive outside assistance—particularly, South Vietnam has needed American aid. Elsewhere in the mainland core, as we have seen, the U.S. has made considerable economic and military contributions to Thailand and Laos. It is always difficult to assess the material effects of aid (e.g., in South Vietnam they seem to have more than been offset by the costs of the war), but certainly all the mainland core countries would be far weaker militarily without it.[110]

In *the maritime core,* British and American aid to Malaysia and the Philippines has enabled these countries to remain competitive with Indonesia, even though Indonesia is potentially far stronger. The Indonesians, for their part, have turned to intrusive powers in accordance with the goals of their own foreign policy. The Russians, and then the Chinese, became a primary influence when Indonesian foreign policy grew more revanchist, but as internal conditions changed and the Indonesians were more willing to coexist with their neighbors, the Western powers again became more influential. They then took on the primary task of attempting to increase Indonesia's material power and guide its motivation in cooperative directions.

West Africa

In West Africa, the most important acts of an intrusive power occurred at the time of independence, when President DeGaulle decided to divide the core into a variety of small states instead of creating a sleeping giant. By doing so, he eased the task of the French in ensuing years but weakened the individual political entities. Besides dominant France, the Soviet Union pandered to Nkrumah's adventurism, and when the motivational bubble

---

[110] Cambodia, as Gordon indicates, is a special case because it is possible to suggest that intrusive conflicts—particularly in Vietnam—deter local states from putting pressure upon Prince Sihanouk's country. See Gordon, *The Dimensions of Conflict in Southeast Asia,* pp. 63–64.

broke there was little to show for either his (or their) material or military-oriented efforts.[111] The Russians may have failed in Ghana, but the Western showcase—Nigeria—was a similar failure as coup and counter-coup in 1966 led to civil war. In countries like the Ivory Coast, Liberia, and Senegal, the most significant effects of intrusive activity have been in the realm of material power. Here the intrusive powers were able to achieve some durable effects because internal stability provided an arena for material improvement.

Conclusions

Intrusive influence upon the level of power in West Africa has been mixed. Material improvement generally resulted when stability prevailed. Where there has been intrusive or local conflict, as in the Middle East and Southeast Asia, intrusive influences have chiefly affected military and motivational power. Where one intrusive power has dominated, material aid has been effective—although infrequently—as a comparison of West Europe and Latin America suggests.

THE STRUCTURE OF RELATIONS

In our discussion of power, we have already alluded to several elements in the structure of relations. It now remains for us to tie together the last segments of the analysis of this fourth pattern variable. We can divide our discussion between the regions where the primary effect of the intrusive powers is to exacerbate conflict (Southeast Asia and the Middle East), those in which the dominant influence is to proliferate the means of cooperation (West Europe and Latin America), and the region where there is a degree of balance between the two (West Africa).

West Europe and Latin America

In West Europe, the two superpowers have managed to temper the ever-present contingency of conflict over the two Germanies despite, or perhaps in part because of, the potential use of nuclear weapons should a conflict arise. By raising the level of the means of conflict, they muted the causes: a stalemate has resulted. The Soviet threat and American support helped create NATO in the 1950's; the apparent lessening of the Soviet threat and American diversion elsewhere allowed the loosening of the bloc and its transformation into an alliance in the 1960's. Through multilateral arrangements and broad-gauged economic assistance, the Americans have encouraged regional economic cooperation. The alliance-like relationship of both EEC and EFTA resulted indirectly from American efforts, but the U.S. has been unable thus far to effect an enlarging of the EEC by the inclusion of Great Britain. The net effect of intrusion has, therefore, been to encourage

---

[111] Goldman, *Soviet Foreign Aid,* p. 173.

cooperation—indeed collaboration—among many of the European nations, to muzzle conflict, and to promote a small degree of common European identification. Even in the Greek-Turkish dispute, which nearly erupted into open warfare in 1967, American mediation was able to prevent a military confrontation.[112]

In Latin America the hegemony of the United States has had a similar effect. International organizations and conferences encourage amelioration and cooperation, although on a less developed scale than in West Europe. Border disputes are stalemated through concentration on externally supported, internally oriented arms races. Regional alliance and stalemate severely limit international conflicts, but domestic tensions remain and are accented. Only where intrusive opposition is paramount (Cuba) does the type of international conflict typical of other systems begin to occur. Yet, sustained crisis through subversion is more typical of relations between the core and periphery than of intrusive participation. The depth of American supremacy and the basic caution which characterizes Soviet policy in this subordinate system result in Soviet dependence (outside Cuba) on trade, the U.N., and cultural and educational programs geared toward segments of the elite, rather than on military assistance, military intervention, or even primary reliance on subversion. In Latin America, then, the net effect of intrusive participation is to anesthetize the causes as well as the means of relations.

West Africa

In West Africa, as we have seen, the influence of France is comparable to that of the United States in Latin America. In the course of devising their new role in West Africa, the French have primarily used bilateral assistance, trade and economic investment, and cultural and educational programs, but they have also resorted to military intervention and propaganda. The result has been a considerable superiority despite challenges from other external powers.

Although they Balkanized the core, the French have managed to limit competition within it whether engendered between the Ivory Coast and Senegal or by the Guinean and Malian flirtation with diverse intrusive powers. Alliance has been the result, as well as a degree of equilibrium particularly between Guinea and her neighbors. In the periphery the symmetry imposed by France in the core has been lacking, and intrusive powers have served as a funnel through which Ghana and Nigeria have experienced internal transformations. Except for Nkrumah's designs (encouraged by the Soviet Union and China), which threatened sustained crisis with other

[112] That war came so close and could occur in the future is itself a major exception to American efforts in this area, and proves that even a powerful intrusive nation can at times be limited.

members of the system, intrusive powers have thus far concentrated upon the domestic level of power rather than the structure of international relations. In general, order and control have been contributed by the French, while the British efforts to create a viable polity in Nigeria failed. Ironically, Balkanization resulted in stability and federation, in chaos.

As the external states interacted with indigenous tribalism, the intrusive powers played a primary role in shaping the context of relationships in the first years of the West African subordinate system as we have now come to know it. Having defined the basis for relationships by their initial acts, the former colonial powers have attempted to control the causes and means of West African international relationships while new intruders on the scene tried to create novel issues by enhancing the instruments at the disposal of local friendly states (e.g., the Russians in Ghana) or to maintain the *status quo* while giving local states an alternative to French and British dominance (e.g., the United States).

The Middle East and Southeast Asia

In the Middle East and Southeast Asia (especially on the mainland), intrusive powers have directly aggravated indigenous relations. In both areas, local conflicts would exist without intrusive powers, but with them the level of violence and, therefore, destructive capability has been raised.

In the Middle East, the effect of the intrusive powers has by now become familiar to readers of this volume. The primary Western methods of participation have been trade and economic investment and military arrangements with some degree of military intervention; the Soviet Union has concentrated on bilateral assistance (both military and economic) and trade. The Russian presence has aggravated the smoldering sustained crisis within the Arab core, and their donations of arms have contributed to direct military conflict and sustained crisis between the Arabs and Israel. The Chinese have similarly aggravated the confrontation through support of Arab guerilla movements. In Turkey and Iran, on the other hand, gradual Soviet offers of assistance have resulted in a moderation of the stalemated conflict which had previously existed between these countries and the Russians. Except within a part of the periphery, then, the sale or donation of more and more dangerous weapons, and the political capital which goes with them, have tended not only to raise the level of the means of relations but have thereby caused the issues in contention to become less susceptible to resolution.

In the mainland Southeast Asia core, ancient conflicts have existed for centuries among the various peoples which now inhabit the area, and American, Chinese, and Soviet penetration has intensified local strife and aggravated local tensions. By creating and then supporting two Vietnams and by leaving Laos as a separate political entity, the intrusive powers have contributed their share to the already conflict-prone area. In raising the level of violence without multiplying the methods of amelioration, they have forced both ancient and recent quarrels to be fought with external (and more volatile) means. The high degrees of internal turmoil and external participation are indicated by the fact that subversion and military intervention have been more important here than in the other subordinate systems we have studied.

In the maritime core, the intrusive powers have served as moderating agents, except when Sukarno sought to use the Russian and, later, the Chinese club to pound Malaysia into docility. Malay core divisiveness, irritated by diverse colonial powers in the past, has been replaced by the present encouragement of containment of conflict and concrete means of cooperation offered by the Western powers associated with the various member states. Intrusive activity in this core has consequently tended to resemble that in West Europe, Latin America, and West Africa more than that in the mainland core or the Middle East—but the uncertain goals of the indigenous states, especially Indonesia, and the absence of a single dominant power has made (and, with British withdrawal, promises even more to make) control of conflict less stable here.

In West Europe, then, the intrusive powers have raised the means, but moderated the causes of conflict, while in Latin America and, less consistently in West Africa and the maritime Southeast Asian core, they have tempered both causes and means. On the Southeast Asian mainland and in the Middle East, on the other hand, the competition of intrusive powers has aggravated the basic issues dividing nations and provided more dangerous weapons with which to settle differences.

CONCLUSION

We thus come to the conclusion of this analysis of intrusive effects upon the five subordinate systems in terms of the four pattern variables. We can list our conclusions in broad terms as follows:

1. Intrusive powers are relatively weak in their ability to alter social *cohesion,* and only slightly stronger with respect to economic cohesion. Their main efforts are usually concentrated on political and organizational cohesion.
2. When internal *communications* have already been developed, intrusive powers tend to concentrate on aiding regional instruments of interaction. When the nation-states in a subordinate system distinctively lack internal communications, intrusive powers tend to concentrate on the domestic arena and support few regional projects.
3. Military aid, intervention, and subversion, which alter military and motivational power, have the most direct and dramatic effects upon regional distributions of *power.* Economic assistance, although potentially more significant in the long run, in general has less effect on immediate, short-run gains in power. Accord-

ingly, where intrusive powers are in competition, military aid and motivational influence tend to have more political relevance; in areas where one intrusive power is dominant or where the intrusive power collaborate, the prospect of raising material power is greater.

4. Finally, intrusive powers, as they affect *the structure of relations,* often are as important in limiting conflict and even, on occasion, encouraging cooperation as they are in intensifying strife. Where a dominant intrusive power operates—or, at least, intrusive powers are allied with each other—local conflict tends to be muted. Where intrusive powers compete, local conflict tends to be aggravated.

7

READINGS

INTRODUCTION

The dynamics of the intrusive system—including the methods of participation as well as the major issues encountered in each of the subordinate systems—are amply demonstrated in the five following articles. Together they provide a panorama of the processes and problems current in each of these systems, and individually they apply to each subordinate system one of the maxims of any investigation into great power intrusion: there are bound to be (or be perceived to be) fundamental contradictions between the interests of the indigenous states and those of the intrusive powers.

Marshall D. Shulman's widely quoted article, "'Europe' Versus 'Détente'?," provides an analysis of the role played in West Europe by the two intrusive powers of that area, the United States and the Soviet Union. It places in perspective the future of the American relationship to the Soviet Union in this crucial theatre of intrusive interaction. Shulman wrestles with the critical problem for the West European system: are universal instruments of cooperation between the United States and the Soviet Union incompatible with maintaining the solidarity and cooperativeness of the Western alliance?

In discussing the tensions between the policy choices of alliance and detente, Shulman considers what we have called political and organizational cohesion and the structure of relations. His discussion corroborates our stress, concerning methods of participation, on both multilateral and bilateral arrangements in the West European intrusive system, and he illustrates how military intervention is a crucial determinant of intrusive action in this region.

One of Shulman's most interesting points is his observation of the subtlety of the Russians' intrusive efforts within West Europe, a consequence of their having concentrated upon trade, cultural exchanges, and technological cooperation. Our analysis of the methods of participation showed that frequently these efforts may be more decisive in intrusive relations with a subordinate system than more visible methods like military intervention or mutlilateral arrangements are. Since this article was written, however, the Soviets have sought recourse to a dramatic act of military intervention in order to regain the status quo: Soviet occupation of Czechoslovakia in August 1968 created a political trauma throughout West Europe whose implications still cannot be completely known. There is little question that as a result of the Soviet action the position of the United States has been strengthened within the subordinate system; the capacity for successful Soviet manipulation of the more subtle modes of participation has been weakened.

Shulman's article suggests that the relationships among intrusive powers and the international relations of a subordinate system are closely connected. It is paradoxical that the destinies of the members of a region as powerful as West Europe should be as closely tied as they are to the acts of the intrusive powers. This close linkage in the West European case demonstrates why the intrusive system must be considered in any analysis of even the most powerful subordinate systems.

In comparing the two areas of American dominance, West Europe and Latin America, we have shown the differences in the American role in each subordinate system. In West Europe, the United States is a force primarily in security relationships. While its economic participation is essential and subtle, security predominates in its role because of the German problem, the oft-perceived Soviet threat, and the high level of power of the system's members. In Latin America (with the exception of Cuba), on the other hand, the United States is strategically so dominant that economic participation comes to the fore as security becomes less critical. Celso Furtado's article, "U.S. Hegemony and the Future of Latin America," discusses the implications of American predominance not only for the international relations of Latin America but for its economic development as well. Here is an attempt to assess current efforts toward economic integration in the context of American intrusive participation. Furtado skillfully demonstrates the interrelationship of what we have called the methods of multilateral and bilateral arrangements, economic investment, and subversion. He shows how various kinds of participation can interact—especially when a dominant power has a high degree of control within a subordinate system. Thus we see more clearly the close involvement of the United States in Latin American politics, economics, and society and its simultaneous alienation from what has been termed "the Latin American revolution."

The reader should consider carefully the importance of the economic means of intrusive participation, trade and economic investment, relative to such methods as subversion, military intervention, and propaganda. In particular, he should take into account the potentially enormous effects which intrusive powers can have upon the states of a subordinate system. As we pointed out earlier, intrusive powers may promote or inhibit cohesion, communications, cooperation, and conflict; in these situations the intrusive powers affect developments within the regional, subordinate system, and the local states are victims or beneficiaries of intrusive activities. In Latin America, the conditions of the intrusive system are typically complex. We must attempt to discern the degree of congruity of Latin American needs and American interests. Furtado points to the issues of economics and security that are basic to that determination and suggests a possible direction for United States policy to take in order to eliminate conflicts of interests between the United States and the Latin American nations. The reader may consider for himself whether Furtado's solutions are viable.

From Latin America, in which the United States is dominant, we move to a very different type of intrusive pattern in the Middle East. In his article, "The Consequences of Defeat," Bernard Lewis focuses on the Arab-Israeli Six-Day War in June 1967. As we saw previously, the competitions of both the intrusive and the subordinate systems here are acute and overlapping. Here military assistance and intervention are the most important aspects of the intrusive relationship to the subordinate system. Lewis shows us that in the Six-Day War the Arabs and Israelis cannot be considered alone, for, as he puts it, the Arabs, Israel, the Soviet Union, and the West were "the chief parties concerned."

In his analysis of the events of the War, Lewis points out what we might call "the intrusive condition": intrusive states can extricate themselves from an area, local states cannot. His analysis of the differences between the major intruders and the local competitors is patterned accordingly. He shows the effects of intrusive powers (past and present) on Arab and Israeli calculations and perceptions. We are given a unique view of the effect which both the absence and presence of intrusion can have on the cohesion, the power, and the relations of a subordinate system.

This article permits us to attempt to identify the ways in which the tensions of an intrusive system were demonstrated during the Six-Day War. In both the American-Israeli and the Soviet-Arab relationships, we must attempt to identify the manner in which actions by both the United States and the Soviet Union helped to precipitate first crisis, then war, and later led to an imposed cease fire. We must also seek to discern how the United Nations served as an instrument of participation by the intrusive powers in this subordinate system. Finally, we must attempt to assess the degree of independence of the members of this subordinate system from their intrusive allies and adversaries.

However Middle Eastern events develop in the future, the Six-Day War remains as a cardinal example of the dramatic interaction between the intrusive powers and the members of a subordinate system. It is a case where the destinies of all concerned were intertwined, where the actions both of the intruders and of the local states mutually affected one another. As such, the immediate consequences of the crisis—as described in the article by Bernard Lewis—provide a unique opportunity to test the operation of an intrusive system in turmoil, and they convey many of the typical patterns which operate in the Middle Eastern intrusive system itself.

While the article by Bernard Lewis concentrates on the one event of the Six-Day War to focus on Middle Eastern intrusive relations, the next article, "France's New Role in Africa," takes a much less dramatic act as a starting point for its analysis. As we have seen, in February 1964 the French intervened militarily in the central African state of Gabon to prevent an attempted military revolt against President M'ba. Yet this successful but blatant act led to a reappraisal of French policy towards Africa, which resulted in a greater reliance on less dramatic and more subtle methods of action: bilateral relations, trade and economic investment, cultural and educational activities, propaganda. In this discussion of Francophonic Africa, generally, the activities of the intrusive powers in West Africa are demonstrated.

Though it concentrates on French activities in the intrusive system, the article shows that in West Africa (as well as other subordinate systems of Africa) intrusive patterns are at present extremely volatile. Both the former colonial powers and the former colonies have been adjusting to the new relationships of independent states—of recipient and donor, subordinate system member and intrusive power—rather than those of colony and ruler. This analysis is consistent with the pattern suggested in Chapter VI, where we showed how emerging intrusive powers in Africa have frequently corroded the authority and influence of former colonial powers, especially those of the British.

The article suggests that, despite the fluidity of intrusive patterns in this area, of all the intrusive powers, France has remained dominant in West Africa. If more discreet methods of participation are necessary, either because of African sensitivities or internal economic constraints, France has thus far been prepared to adopt them. However, the French do not appear ready to relinquish their heavy activity in this area to any other intrusive power—and especially not to the United States. This discussion of the French role in Africa demonstrates the activities of a weaker intrusive power (weaker than the United States or the Soviet Union) in the relatively weak subordinate system of West Africa. It provides a useful contrast to the more dramatic and more powerful arenas that we have discussed.

Still more dramatic is the case of Southeast Asia. Compared to this turbulent region, West Africa is a placid island in a calm sea. William Chapin in "The Asian Balance of Power: An American View," considers a variety of alternatives in the future of Southeast Asia; his examination includes speculation on future relationships among the major intrusive powers in the area. In analyzing this article, the reader must consider what effects varying intrusive powers could have in the future Southeast Asian balance of power. He must also take into account what motivates the potential and present intrusive powers to seek influence, and perhaps even overt control, in Southeast Asia.

In addition to questions of motivations and goals, one must consider the diverse methods of participation by which the intrusive powers have influence in Southeast Asia. Mr. Chapin's discussion touches upon almost every element of the methods of participation, with special stress on multilateral and bilateral arrangements, trade and economic investments, subversion, and military intervention. He also stresses the importance of the means by which intrusive powers can and do affect economic and organizational cohesion and communications, as well as the more obvious level of power and structure of relations.

As each article in this chapter indicates, despite their considerable ability to influence events within a particular subordinate system, all of the external forces are, in the final analysis, removed from the system—whether physically near or far. It is their power combined with their lack of physical presence which shapes the context of what we have called the intrusive system as an element of the subordinate system.

Marshall D. Shulman

"EUROPE" VERSUS "DÉTENTE"?

I

It would be an exaggeration to describe the current discussion of our relations with the Soviet Union and with Western Europe as another Great Debate. Perhaps in the language of the times it might be called a Mini-Debate, distracted as it is and emotionally charged by events elsewhere which, however, may prove to be less fateful in the long run.

Implicit in almost every aspect of the discussion is one central issue: whether efforts to salvage or improve our relations with our West European allies work against our attempts to achieve some sort of a détente with the Soviet Union, and if so, which consideration ought to receive the higher priority in our policies.

The question is raised in many forms. In the debates as to whether the United States should proceed with the treaties regarding consular arrangements, the proliferation of nuclear weapons or the prohibition of certain military activities in space, the arguments tend to be less concerned with the specific merits of

Reprinted from Marshall D. Shulman, " 'Europe' versus 'Detente'?," *Foreign Affairs*, XLV (April, 1967, copyright by the Council on Foreign Relations, Inc., New York) 389–402, by special permission of the publisher.

the treaties themselves than with the symbolic significance of such arrangements as part of a rapprochement between the United States and the Soviet Union. The advocates assert that only old habits of thought about the cold war persist in keeping alive the "communist menace," that the new fluidity of European political life—East and West—has created a new situation ripe for a Soviet-American settlement, made more feasible by the mutuality of their concerns about China. It is often further implied that a lesser American involvement in European affairs and a contraction of our commitments elsewhere would be a desirable concomitant of such a rapprochement.

The main line of argument against this position has been that Soviet behavior does not yet evidence the good faith which would make such a settlement possible (witness the Soviet supply of war matériel to North Viet Nam and the National Liberation Front), and that the pursuit of an illusory rapprochement with the Soviet Union would hasten the final dismantling of the Atlantic Alliance, which ought to be the cornerstone of American policy in the present period.

In the background of the effort to reconcile these conflicting positions are shadowy uncertainties about recent political developments in Europe. Almost everyone agrees that something new has been happening in European political life, but it has not yet been possible to define what that "something" is, or how deeply it changes the nature of the political alignments in Europe. In the West, does the "European" drive still fundamentally conform to the Monnet vision, only temporarily interrupted by General de Gaulle? Or has the momentum in this direction now passed, and been replaced by a European idea which is essentially that of a loose relationship among nation-states desiring a role in international politics more independent of the United States? In Eastern Europe, has the fragmentation of Soviet control reached the point at which inter-bloc arrangements across Europe can supersede the further development of West European integration? The answers involve assessments of profound social transformations whose outlines may not become clear to us for some time; and they will have an obvious bearing on the kind of relationship to be sought across the Atlantic —whether an institutionalized integration or a gradual and pragmatic extension of certain economic functions during a period in which military and political integration may be less feasible. But whatever form or degree of Atlantic integration may be possible, the more immediate question remains whether we are compelled to choose between strengthening the alliance and achieving a détente with the Soviet Union.

One factor that has contributed to making these seem conflicting alternatives is that in practice the United States has adduced the Soviet military threat as the principal motivation for the Western Alliance. Other and more positive motivations are mentioned, but from the earliest days of NATO and particularly since 1950, American esti-mates of the military requirements have run substantially higher than those of our European allies, and our analysis of Soviet intentions and capabilities has furnished our main arguments in behalf of the alliance.

On both sides of the Atlantic there are wide differences in present estimates of the Soviet military threat, but it seems fair to say that the prevailing West European estimate has been diminishing relative to our official estimate, and that this has been a major factor in the weakening of the alliance. At the same time, the volatile nature of American responses to a potential détente with the Soviet Union has created uncertainty in Europe about the seriousness and steadiness of our own view of the Soviet problem. The net effect has been to counterpose the détente and the alliance as alternative policies. Can we clarify our understanding of the present character and extent of the dangers represented by Soviet policies, and work with our allies toward common language on the kind of a response now required for the West? Can we clarify our understanding of the kind of détente with the Soviet Union that may be possible in the present period, as distinguished from the longer-range settlements toward which we would like to work? The implication in the way these questions are posed is that a two-stage approach to the détente question may help to reduce some of the confusion regarding different time-scales and functions which lies at the root of this apparent contradiction.

II

The reasons why the Soviet military threat is now perceived by some in this country and many in Europe as substantially lower than before have to do more with impressions of Soviet intentions than with estimates of Soviet military strength. These estimates have been increasing of late, both absolutely and in some respects relative to our own, although our lead in strategic capabilities seems assured at least for several years to come. Among the factors generally cited are the following:

1. The fragmentation of the communist bloc is widely regarded as having eliminated or reduced the effectiveness of any serious challenge from the communist nations. "The communist bloc is no longer monolithic." The Chinese defiance of the Soviet leadership, the increased autonomy in foreign-policy matters asserted by some East European states and the lack of coördination of the foreign communist parties are cited as reasons for believing that the "containment" of communist expansionism is no longer necessary and that the possibilities for settlements with the Soviet Union are now greater.

2. The changes which have been taking place inside the Soviet Union are regarded by many as having transformed the Soviet system to the point that its foreign policies are expected to be essentially conservative and non-ideological,, rather than dynamic and disruptive.

3. In recent years, Soviet policies have tended, with some exceptions, to emphasize indirect and longer-term modes of advancing Soviet interests, rather than direct and militant challenges. This has lessened the incidence of dramatic confrontations which formerly stimulated cohesion and mobilization in the West. It is generally accepted that this evolution of Soviet policy is largely due to the success of the Western Alliance. The differences are in the interpretation of the ambiguities of "peaceful coexistence" in Soviet strategy.

4. In recent months the discussion of increased intercontinental missile production and anti-ballistic missile deployment in the Soviet Union has raised questions about whether we may be approaching the end of a stabilized plateau in the strategic arms race. Nevertheless it is widely assumed that the Soviet leadership has accepted, or must in logic accept, a common or parallel interest with the United States in restraining the arms race, at least at the strategic level.

Each of these factors has considerable force, but there is a tendency in public discussions to draw immoderate conclusions from them. Understandably, many in this country and in Europe react against the oversimplifications of the past by regarding the "communist menace" as having been a myth from the start, or as having become so negligible that little or no defense against it is now required. As a result, the discussion has become so polarized between assertions of "threat" and "no threat" that it has become difficult to get public attention to focus upon processes of change in international politics which are in fact complex and ambiguous. The net effect of these processes, I would argue, has not been to eliminate the conflict relationship with the Soviet Union but to change its character; and the starting point for any Western policy must be to find more appropriate terms for describing the nature of the political contest in which we are now engaged. What the Western Alliance faces in the present period is not, I suggest, the spectre of world communist revolution, nor of a Soviet effort to communize Western Europe, nor of Soviet forces preparing for the military conquest of Europe, but the problem of how to take the measure of a Soviet effort to use political, economic and military means to strengthen its influence on the European continent.

In evaluating the effects of the undeniable fragmentation of the communist bloc, it would be as mistaken to conclude that this process eliminates any serious challenge from the Soviet Union as it would be to say that the disarray in the Western Alliance disposes, for the Russians, of the challenge of American power. What this process of fragmentation does dispose of is the bogey of a unified, articulated threat, which was probably never as monolithic as we once saw it. It is useful to be reminded that local manifestations of communism have to be considered in their local contexts, and that differentiated responses are required in each case; but it does not follow that either local communist movements or Soviet or Chinese power are no longer matters of concern. It may even be that if Soviet policy can demonstrate the necessary resilience, the Soviet Union may turn to advantage the possibility of drawing upon increasingly nationalist sources of support for the separate elements of the communist movement.

It is clear that the recent developments in China have been a source of distraction, uncertainty and anxiety to the Soviet leadership. It is not yet possible to gauge the full effects of these developments upon Soviet policy, but predictions of a Soviet alliance with the West against China appear to be at the extreme edge of optimism, considering the residual suspicions in the Soviet-Western relationship. Clearly the Sino-Soviet dispute, together with the climate of reduced tension in Europe, has intensified nationalist trends in Eastern Europe, and has encouraged a greater degree of independence in the foreign policies of some East European countries. These countries have resisted the Soviet effort to isolate the United States in European politics, largely because

they fear this would reduce their own freedom of manœuvre. All this does certainly limit the Russians' freedom of action and requires them to exercise much more persuasion in intra-bloc relations than formerly. The opening up of Eastern Europe to Western influences and the development of trade and cultural ties across the European continent introduce ambiguity and movement in European politics which may have important long-run effects even in the Soviet Union itself. However, for the immediately foreseeable future the process has certain limits which are imposed by Soviet security conceptions and by the groups which exercise political control in these countries. Of course, the arrows point in both directions: Soviet diplomacy will seek to exploit the opportunities offered by the new fluidity in Europe to influence the political alignments in the West.

Regarding the assumption that domestic social transformations have begun to have a conservative effect on Soviet foreign policy—a large subject about which much has been written—perhaps it would be fair to say, by way of a summary contention, that this involves at least two uncertainties: one, the timespan required for qualitative changes to make themselves felt, and the other, the direction in which these changes are in fact moving. While the party and police bureaucracies are intact and in unchallenged political control, it does seem premature, at least, to argue as the Chinese and some Westerners do that the Soviet Union has already become something of a bourgeois state.

It is true that pockets of autonomy have developed here and there in Soviet society, and that the process of decision-making has grown more complex and bureaucratized in response to the requirements of advancing industrialization. But there is a distinction to be made between administrative decision-making and the exercise of political power, the devolution of which may take a very long time—if indeed the Soviet political structure is moving in that direction. It is also true that Soviet policy is and always has been fairly conservative in the sense that it has been cautious about risk-taking. The fundamental dynamism of Soviet policy, which arises partly out of national growth and partly out of ideology, may be diminished by domestic economic problems and by the reduction of external opportunities, but there is no evidence that it has yet been diminished by transformations within the Soviet system.

Soviet policies toward Western Europe increasingly reflect traditional methods of seeking national advantage, but this is not to say that the ideological factor in Soviet policy has become negligible. Here it is important to distinguish between the ideologically expressed goal of world revolution, which has gradually receded to a point at which it may have little operational significance, and other aspects of the ideology which have changed more slowly and which cannot be said to have lost their operational effect upon Soviet policy. The Marxist-Leninist framework of analysis of historical trends, although it has been evolving, remains an important factor in the Soviet view of Western systems as obsolescent and inherently a source of conflict. It is still an obstacle to genuinely coöperative relations with the West and particularly with the United States; it does not prevent limited coöperation in certain areas, but its assumption of fundamental incompatibility does set

limits on the degree of coöperation possible in the present period. This framework of perception is more strongly represented in certain age groups and in certain parts of the bureaucracy than in others, and it may therefore have a diminished effect in the future. In the meantime it forms one of the demarcations between present and future phases of East-West relations.

Turning now to an evaluation of "peaceful coexistence" in Soviet policy, the most striking paradox is how much Western policy has been the victim of its own success. The evolution of Soviet policy toward a more indirect and long-term mode of advancing its interests is a logical response to the facts of life which the Western Alliance helped to create: the West's strategic superiority, its high growth rates and its firmness in resisting direct militant pressures. Now, while the Western Alliance is trying to adapt to the removal of those overt pressures which formerly held the alliance together, the Soviet Union is groping for realistic ways of increasing its influence.

In practice, peaceful coexistence has meant an increasingly active diplomatic effort in the theater most likely to be decisive for the balance of power—Europe. The revival of Western Europe's economic power reduced the Soviet hope of revolutionary social transformations, but it opened up possibilities for political manœuvre amidst the tensions that accompanied the growing European desire for a role in international affairs more independent of the United States. Viet Nam introduced a qualitative leap forward for the Soviet Union in Western Europe, partly because of the unpopularity of the American position in Viet Nam, but even more because the war occupied so much of our attention and energy. Exploiting the advantages offered by the decline of American influence in Europe, the Soviets have intensified their efforts to weave a network of technological, trade, cultural and political relationships with the major countries of Western Europe, as well as with Canada and Japan.

How better to dramatize this campaign than to have the Soviet President visit the Pope! How better to symbolize the Soviet effort to reach across the political spectrum—the Russian revolutionary fist now unclenched into an outstretched hand! It has been an active year for Soviet diplomacy in Europe: de Gaulle to Moscow, Kosygin to Paris; Wilson to Moscow (twice), Kosygin to London; Gromyko and then Podgorny to Rome; Demichev and then Podgorny to Vienna—talking trade, cultural exchanges and technological coöperation.... Soviet-European coöperation to overcome the technological gap with the United States.... Europe for the Europeans—a low-keyed reiteration of the theme of the Bucharest communiqué of the Warsaw Pact powers last July, calling for a European conference to reach a settlement of European problems, liquidating NATO and the Warsaw Pact, merging the Common Market into an all-European arrangement, legitimizing the sovereign rights of the German Democratic Republic.

But here is the most difficult problem for Soviet diplomacy—what to do about Germany? The leverage offered by General de Gaulle is obviously useful in weakening the Western Alliance and reducing the American presence in Europe, but in their second thoughts the Soviets have wondered whether the "objective consequence" of this line of action might not be to leave the Federal Republic as the strongest power in Western Europe. No clear answer to this dilemma has appeared, but the tentative strategy has been to isolate the Federal Republic with the intensified themes of "revanchism" and "militarism," while implying that advantages might accrue from the recognition of the German Democratic Republic. The price held out to the Germans of détente with the Soviet Union is the continued division of Germany and detachment from the United States.

What is the purpose of this effort? The answer begins with the recognition that, in the absence of general war or the active threat of war, the decisive issue is the place of industrial Europe in the world power balance. The Soviet hope is that, as a result of the present fluidity in European political life and our diminished influence in Europe, it can increase its influence to the point where it can bring the individual European nation-states into some form of closer and perhaps subordinate relationship, thereby enhancing its power position relative to the United States. It should be stressed that this is mainly a political and economic effort over a period of time during which Soviet leaders hope they will have strengthened their economic base of power; it is not primarily a military threat, although Soviet military capabilities will of course lend support to Soviet diplomacy.

Whether this is a realistic expectation depends upon a number of imponderables. What is involved is an historic gamble. From the viewpoint of Western Europe, increased contacts in a climate of reduced tension offer an opportunity to soften the ideological barriers, to wean away the East European states, and to prepare the ground for a European settlement. From the Soviet point of view, the expectation is that these increased contacts will provide leverage to prod the West European states toward a loose coalition against the United States. What is in question is not whether there should be increased contacts between Eastern and Western Europe—for these are irresistible in the present tide of politics—but whether there can be enough coördination and political consciousness in the management of these contacts so that the effect will be a strengthening of European independence rather than fragmentation and subordination. Call it morbid optimism, perhaps, but such are the complexity and intractability of these matters that one is tempted to guess that whichever side gains the advantage, it is likely to be because the ineptitude of the adversary exceeded its own.

It was suggested at the start that a certain commonality of interest exists between the Soviet Union and the United States in reducing the hazard of general war. How far is the assumption warranted, and to the extent that it is, how far does it serve to limit the political rivalry just described?

There can be no doubt that if logic and rationality prevail, the two great powers must recognize the mutuality of their interest in preventing the outbreak of general nuclear war. Indeed, they have done so, within limits. The arms race has not as yet gone through the roof: tacit restraints have been accepted in practice, as each side has learned through experience the interacting effects of measures to improve its situation, and budgetary pressures have provided some constraints as well. There are some buts, however. It has proved impossible so far to translate this common interest into agreed limitations on armaments, for reasons which are all too familiar. The use of

military chips to support a diplomatic hand carries the constant risk that events may carry a crisis situation beyond rational control. The natural professional zeal of military interests on both sides to achieve a security based upon superiority provides a continuing dynamic to the arms race, as we see currently illustrated in the pressures for anti-ballistic missiles. The Viet Nam conflict, and the prospect of many other local conflict situations in Asia, Africa and Latin America, have weakened the emerging confidence that there was a low probability of general war. And the growth of Chinese military power has added a complicating factor which, for the present at least, makes the prospect for any arms-reduction agreements an academic question, as people are unfortunately fond of saying, by which they usually mean that it is without practical significance.

The important point to observe, however, is that even if we act on the assumption—as I believe we should—that with time the Soviet Union and the United States can and will find ways to stabilize and ease their military confrontation, this does not necessarily mean any easing of their political rivalry. There is not an inevitable continuum between arms control and a political truce. It has been an error, I believe, to argue in favor of particular arms-control measures as though they could remove tensions which arise from basic political conflicts of interest. Of course, the prevailing level of tension is not irrelevant to the arms race; however, symbolic measures designed to reduce tensions, but having nothing to do with the substance of our conflicting concerns, may prove to be worse than useless, for they lead to self-deception and miscalculation. Therefore, in striving to find practical ways of exploiting the common interest in preventing general war, it is essential to recognize that the mutuality of aims is limited, that rivalry on many fronts may continue, and that arms-control measures are not necessarily linked to a political rapprochement.

III

This brings us to the question of détente. What kind of a détente with the Soviet Union is possible in the present period? To begin with, the term itself is imprecise and often misleading. Although in its strict sense détente suggests only some reduction of tension, it is generally used to connote a political rapprochement. In retrospect, we see that even in the periods when "détente" was on everyone's lips, as in 1959 and again in 1963–64, the word had at best a qualified application, since the reduction of tension was accompanied by strenuous Soviet efforts to gain political and military advantages. It seems probable, for example, that the Soviet decision to increase production of intercontinental missiles was made during the post-Cuban "détente" of 1963–64.

In the present period, although a reduction of tension between the Soviet Union and the United States is obviously desirable, and would now be welcomed by our European allies, there are a number of factors which may set limits on the extent to which it is practicable, even if the Viet Nam issue were resolved or surmounted.

To begin with, the present fluidity in European politics tends to encourage an active rivalry for political advantage—in contrast to the provisional stabilization which sustained earlier periods of reduced tension. The previous Soviet emphasis on the status quo

(meaning American acceptance of the Soviet position in Eastern Europe) as a condition for peaceful coexistence has, except in the case of East Germany, given way to a more open game of political manœuvre across the entire continent. It is even more true in a period of movement than it was when lines seemed frozen that so long as the issue of a divided Germany remains, it sets effective limits on how much easing of tension can be expected.

Perhaps Viet Nam will prove to be a transitory factor, but the present diplomatic isolation of the United States on this issue encourages the Soviet Union to press for relative gains by further isolating the United States (détente toward Europe, but not toward the United States) rather than helping to relieve the estrangement by accepting bilateral forms of coöperation. Further limits are set by the Soviet view that American policy is increasingly militant and uncompromising—a view not relieved by recent speeches of the President. This is reinforced by the Soviet expectation that political turbulence throughout the underdeveloped world may lead to other conflict situations, and that a militant American response to these is likely. As for the present upheavals in China, whatever their outcome, it is evident that new lines of power and influence will be drawn in Asia, causing instability for some time to come. In this connection, the Chinese charges of Soviet collusion with "American imperialism" and of loss of revolutionary zeal in leading the international communist movement still evoke a defensive response in the Soviet Union, and for the present at least, inhibit Soviet contacts with the United States which could be used by the Chinese to lend credence to the charge.

However, let us assume optimistically that rising Soviet apprehensions about the conflict with China and concern about the mounting costs of the arms race may be gaining increasing weight in Soviet calculations, and may lead toward acceptance of some reduction of tension with the United States in the foreseeable future. How then should we respond? Above all, we should keep clearly in mind the distinction between the limited détente that may be possible in the present period and symbolic acts which seem to suggest a rapprochement but do not in fact moderate any fundamental causes of conflict. For these can only encourage our allies to trample each other on the road to Moscow.

The main function of a limited détente between the Soviet Union and the United States is to reduce the hazard of general nuclear war. It is unlikely that much more than this can be done at present. The possibility of common action arises not only out of a common appreciation of the destructiveness of general nuclear war and a mutual (although perhaps uneven) appreciation of the costs of the arms race, but also conceivably out of different estimates of the political effects of various arms-control measures. For example, joint action on a nonproliferation treaty may be possible because each side expects the political side-effects to advance its own interests more than those of its antagonist. Similarly, modest programs of trade and cultural relations may be possible and useful, not because of common interests, but because of different evaluations of the effects of such programs.

In time we may get to the point at which agreements to reduce arms may become feasible, but for the present perhaps the most effective measures open to us may be in the realm of tacit restraints and a restoration of channels of communication offering maximum privacy and confidence. The process of diffusion by which interested people in both countries are learning something about the interactions of politics, science and military technology has already demonstrated its long-term utility. Possibly the model of the Tashkent agreement can be encouraged in peripheral conflicts where the interests of the two powers are not arrayed against each other.

But it is unlikely that a settlement of European problems can be a feature of any détente in the immediate period ahead. The Soviet Union shows as little sign of being willing to relinquish its economic and military position in East Germany as the United States is willing to abandon the Federal Republic. This point is not always clearly understood. What the United States seeks is not to challenge the Soviet Union for the control of Germany, but to work toward a solution of the German problem under conditions which permit the continued development of democratic political institutions within Germany. This is a vital interest, for if discriminatory treatment breeds a revival of irrational nationalism in Germany, Europe's future stability will be again in jeopardy. A European settlement is impossible without a resolution of the German problem, and it is only in the framework of a European settlement that the problem of Germany can be resolved. Clearly, it will take time for this problem to become soluble; it cannot be encompassed by a limited détente now, but must await a more fundamental settlement in the future.

IV

The essential conception sketched above is that our present limited-adversary relationship with the Soviet Union is not inconsistent with the varied coöperative functions possible between the United States and Western Europe. The apparent contradiction between the two relationships becomes more manageable if the Soviet military threat is not made the major motivation for the Western Alliance. The Soviet problem is now neither the main reason for the Western Alliance nor a matter of unconcern to it. We must make an effort to discard the oversimplifications to which we have become accustomed in our public discourse and to find with our allies a common language for describing and understanding the more complex forms which the Soviet challenge takes in the present period. This approach implies that the political problems presented by Soviet policies should be given relatively more attention than the purely military threat, and, as a corollary, that the political vitality of the alliance may be more crucial than the level of its military readiness. There is much to build on in terms of shared values and common aspirations. More than this, we must together provide the nucleus for some kind of international system. We are bound together not by anti-communism but by common concern about the potential destructiveness of war, virulent nationalism and international anarchy. In this perspective, present Soviet policies may be seen as an obstacle to the degree of international coöperation required to deal with these problems, and we should make it a central objective of our association with Western Europe over the longer term to widen the area of coöperative relations with the Soviet Union.

To develop a conception of a second stage of détente is necessary for several reasons. First, the more clear we are as to what we can expect in the way of improved relations with the Soviet Union in the present period, the less we shall fluctuate between euphoria and disappointment, with confusing results for public opinion at home and our allies abroad. Second, by keeping steadily in mind the direction in which we would like to see the situation evolve, we shall avoid present actions which handicap the achievement of our long-term purposes.

What is now required of us is to prepare the ground for the next stage—to work at the outlines of a European settlement which can be realized in a series of phases over the next several decades. We know some of the conditions for that settlement: the reunification of Germany, the establishment of a framework of security guarantees, the broadening of economic interdependence across a continent not subject to the hegemony of any nation. In time, the Soviet Union will surely come to see its legitimate self-interest fulfilled in such a settlement; as it begins to accept this view, we shall find it possible to work together in reducing armaments and in building international stability and order.

Is two decades a reasonable guess for so profound a change in fundamental outlook? It is hard to say, even for ourselves. We are an impatient people, but we must learn to accept a longer-term perspective toward these problems.

LATIN AMERICA

Celso Furtado

U. S. HEGEMONY AND THE FUTURE OF

LATIN AMERICA

Within the group of nations termed the Third World—nations for whom the problems of development come before all others—Latin America occupies a special position, in view of the peculiarity of its relations with the United States. Almost all the underdeveloped African and Asian countries have achieved political independence within the last two decades and are at present led by a generation that emerged during the revolutionary struggle. The consciousness of victories achieved lends optimism to their behaviour and even leads them to overestimate their strength and capabilities in the effort to overcome underdevelopment. In Latin America, on the contrary, there is a general consciousness of living through a period of decline. On the one hand, the phase of 'easy' development, through increasing exports of primary products or through import substitution, has everywhere been exhausted. On the other, the region is becoming aware that the margin of self-determination, in its search for ways of coping with the tendency to-

Reprinted from Celso Furtado, "U.S. hegemony and the future of Latin America," *The World Today,* monthly journal of the Royal Institute of International Affairs, London, Vol. XXII (September, 1966) 375–85, by permission of the publisher.

wards economic stagnation, is being daily reduced as the imperative of U.S. 'security' calls for a growing alienation of sovereignty on the part of national governments. This difference in the historical situation explains, to some extent, the disparity between the psychological attitudes currently observable among the Latin American peoples and the other peoples of the Third World. To the optimism of the latter is opposed the feeling of revolt that prevails among Latin Americans, particularly in the younger generation. Latin American society is currently going through a revolutionary phase, as a consequence of the penetration of modern technology and the emergence of new collective aspirations within the framework of institutions ill-equipped to absorb this new technology or to interpret and satisfy these aspirations.

It is a notorious fact that the relevant political problems of Latin American countries are of direct interest to the authorities responsible for U.S. security, who are in a position to interfere decisively in the working out of a solution for these problems. It is only natural, therefore, that Latin Americans should become increasingly preoccupied with the following questions: (*a*) what exactly is understood by U.S. security? and (*b*) to what degree are the interests of this security compatible with the Latin American revolution?

U.S. SPHERE OF INFLUENCE

A new international order is now inevitably evolving as the methods of the cold war become obsolete, though what form it will take is not yet clear. It is perfectly obvious, however, that, without some basic understanding between the principal centres of power, the diplomatic processes envisaged in the United Nations Charter are of little value. The fundamental problem is, therefore, to discover the likely trends of this basic understanding. The Russians, having redefined their security problems in the light of their technological advance, are apparently no longer concerned with maintaining a strictly regimented sphere of influence. On the contrary, they now seem inclined to think that a return to a pluralist international system, necessarily implying the break-up of the Western bloc led by the United States, would increase their relative influence; this pluralism would probably lead to an aggravation of the 'contradictions' between the principal capitalist nations, and this could only operate to the Russian advantage. By progressively 'liberalizing' their sphere of influence, the Russians seem to be working towards the creation of a new international order in which the principle of self-determination will have a not altogether secondary role to play. Behind this lies the idea that, in the long run, capitalism, at least in the form propounded by the United States, is not viable for most of the countries of the Third World. The latter, in changing their social order, are much more likely to move away from American influence. In this way, a 'community of socialist nations' would tend to grow quite naturally and the Soviet Union would assume legitimate leadership as *primus inter pares* in such a community. The United States, on the other hand, conscious that a 'conclusive and world-wide victory over Communism' is no longer possible, seems to be inclined to define the supreme aim of her foreign policy as the defence of the integrity of the 'free world'.[1] This is a difficult aim to achieve, since it requires, on the one hand, strict delimitation of the perimeter of a sphere of influence extending over a number of continents and, on the other, the development and successful application within that sphere of influence of social techniques capable of preventing significant changes in the social structures of numerous countries at different stages of development.

The attempt by the United States to define her area of influence *vis-à-vis* the Soviet Union passed its conclusive test at the time of the so-called Cuban rocket crisis in October 1962. This confrontation established that the Soviet

[1] In cold-war jargon, the term 'free world' refers more or less vaguely to all the countries outside the Soviet and Chinese orbits of influence. By historical tradition, the Americans have a marked aversion for the concepts of 'empire' and 'imperialism' when used to explain their own policy. Recently an English political analyst attempted to demonstrate that this was an unfounded prejudice, since the Americans 'in the last 20 years, have been carrying out with unparalleled maturity and generosity, their imperial obligations.' (See Henry Fairlie, "A Cheer for American Imperialism," in the *New York Times Magazine,* July 11, 1965.) I prefer, however, to stick to the concept of a 'sphere of influence' which has been used by someone as well integrated in the North American political establishments as Walter Lippmann.

Union cannot give unlimited guarantees of defence to a country in the North American sphere of influence which attempts to break away from U.S. hegemony by means of effecting changes in its social structure. American victory in this decisive case consisted in conducting the crisis in such a way that the Soviet Union was faced with the alternatives of having to unleash a thermo-nuclear war or of recognizing the 'right' of the United States to limit the sovereignty of any country within her orbit, even after such a country had succeeded in changing its social structure. In the final analysis, therefore, this means that a country which changes its social structure and, in this way, moves out of the U.S. orbit of influence, can be 'tolerated' but will not be recognized by the dominant Power. The doctrine was established that defence of such a 'tolerated' country must always fall within the sphere of so-called 'limited' warfare, the possibility of a thermo-nuclear confrontation being excluded. To establish this doctrine, the United States paid the price of risking a nuclear holocaust; and it is by the price paid that the importance of the victory should be measured. All the indications are that the United States is pursuing a similar aim in the case of Vietnam: namely, to create a situation that, by the very nature of its dynamic, will force the principal contender—in this case China —to acknowledge the limits of its own strength.

PROBLEM OF SOCIAL INSTABILITY

Once the perimeter of the U.S. sphere of influence has been established and any outside military interference has been neutralized, the problem arises as to whether U.S. hegemony is able to maintain a high degree of social stability within its area of influence. In this respect, we must draw attention to two points: first, that the basic variable which determines the contemporary historic process is provided by technological development; secondly, that the speed with which modern technology must penetrate the underdeveloped world in order to overcome initial resistance and ensure continuity of development inevitably provokes a series of social reactions incompatible with the preservation of most of the preexisting structures.

In the United States, the nature of this problem is slowly coming to be understood. For a long time the problem was simply considered an aspect of the cold war: the social instability of the Third World was attributed to the 'Machiavellian' actions of the Soviet Union, and it was held that the only solution to the problem lay in 'containing' the 'aggressive' Power. Referring to the Eisenhower Administration, Professor Morgenthau writes: '...both the thought and actions of our government tend toward the assumption that the Soviet Union is not only the exploiter of world revolution —which is correct—but also its creator —which is a convenient absurdity.'[2] Later the doctrine emerged, formulated by MIT technicians led by W. W. Rostow, according to which the aims of U.S. foreign policy could more easily be fostered by properly organized 'for-

[2] Hans Morgenthau, *The Political and Military Strategy of the United States* (1954), reproduced in *Politics in the Twentieth Century* (Chicago: University of Chicago Press, 1962), Vol. II, p. 21.

[3] The ideas of this group are expressed in a study presented to a special Senate Committee in July, 1957, *The Objectives of United States Economic Assistance Programs.*

eign aid' programmes for underdeveloped countries.[3] It was accepted that the development process could be oriented from outside, the U.S. aim being to 'create independent, modern and developing States.'[4] The whole problem was to help underdeveloped countries to overcome their initial difficulties and attain a point of 'self-supporting development.' Implicit in this theory is the idea that, once the pains preceding 'take-off' have been assuaged, any serious risk of social instability would cease to exist.

This theory, which enjoyed a great vogue at one stage and produced its most brilliant efflorescence in the 'Alliance for Progress,' came in for serious criticism in the period that followed. It has been argued that one should not forget that development itself, even when oriented from outside, creates social instability since it 'undermines the cultural structure and religious order.'[5] This line of thought emphasizes the fact that the aim of U.S. policy, namely, to keep intact its sphere of influence, must never be lost sight of, and that any particular country's development should be considered as a means of attaining this end. 'As a rule,' writes Professor Wolfers, 'the most effective type of aid will be the aid that promises to give the greatest satisfaction to those élite groups who are eager to keep the country out of Communist or Soviet control.' In a recent book, political scientist John S. Pustay, a major in the U.S. Air Force, reminds us that 'the very programs designed to promote socioeconomic development (for example, the Alliance for Progress) will in themselves create tensions and dislocations as the old and indigenous way of life is replaced by a new and alien mode of living. Therefore, the military will be called upon to back the civil police in providing stability during this period of social turmoil.'[6] As the leading Power, the United States must concern herself with the creation of supranational structures to ensure this stability if she does not want to run the risk of growing defections inside her sphere of influence. Until such supranational structures are created, the United States herself will have to bear the responsibility for providing internal social stability in all countries falling within her orbit. In one of his last speeches in the United Nations, Adlai Stevenson made it clear that 'as long as the international community is not prepared to rescue the victims of clandestine aggression, national force will have to fill the gap.'

'SECURITY' VERSUS 'DEVELOPMENT'

For the United States, therefore, the basic problem in the second half of the twentieth century is the problem of her 'security,' that is to say, the question of the type of world-wide organization that will prevail as a consequence of the current technological revolution, and that must be compatible with the preservation of 'the American way of life' inside U.S. territory and the defence of American economic interests outside. From the Latin Amer-

---

[4] W. W. Rostow, *The Stages of Economic Growth* (1959), reproduced in W. F. Hahn and J. C. Ness, eds., *American Strategy for the Nuclear Age* (New York: Doubleday & Company, Inc., 1960).

[5] Arnold Wolfers, *Military or Economic Aid: Questions of Priority.* A report to the Presidential Committee for the Study of Military Aid, July 1959, reproduced in *ibid.,* p. 386.

[6] John S. Pustay, *Counter-insurgency Warfare* (New York: Free Press of Glencoe, Inc., 1965).

ican point of view, on the other hand, the great problem is that of 'development,' that is to say, the problem of gaining access to the fruits of this technological revolution.

It must be borne in mind that Latin America's political and social institutions were essentially transplanted from Europe and that, from the very beginning, the Latin American national economies existed as a frontier of the European or, at a more recent stage, of the European and North American economies. The characteristics of capitalist industrial development, which proceeded within the framework of powerful national States, provoked from the outset a heavy concentration of the fruits of technical progress; this inevitably created poles of technological advance, giving rise to geographical concentration of income and wealth. Such a process can be observed in the European continent itself, where, up to the second World War, the central, eastern, and southern European countries, despite their integration in the regional economy, had practically no access to the fruits of technological progress at the end of a century of industrial revolution. In Latin America, development induced by the industrial revolution in Europe and the United States was enough to transform part of the economic systems inherited from the colonial epoch, but not enough to create autonomous systems able to generate further growth. Hence, Latin America remained on the 'periphery' of advanced industrial economies at a time when markets for primary products were far from able to generate the dynamism required.

Attempt at industrialization of an 'import-substitution' type for a time provided an alternative and allowed further changes to be made in the economic structures of some countries. However, the type of industrial organization practicable in certain historical conditions cannot be independent of the type of technology to be adopted. The technology which Latin America has to assimilate in the second half of the twentieth century effects a considerable saving in manpower and is extremely exacting with regard to the size of the market. In the conditions at present prevailing in the region, the rule tends to be monopoly or oligopoly and progressive concentration of income; and this in turn, by conditioning the pattern of demand, directs investment towards certain industries, which are precisely those requiring a high capital coefficient and those most exacting with regard to the size of the market. In Latin America, experience has proved that this substitutive form of industrialization tends to lose its impulse once the phase of 'easy' substitutions has been exhausted, and leads eventually to stagnation.[7]

At present, Latin America is faced with the ineluctable necessity of introducing profound changes into its institutional framework in order to lay the foundations for development. These changes will have to be oriented in three directions: (a) in such a way that technological change is prevented from provoking concentration of income and distorting the allocation of

[7] Of the Latin American countries that have made substantial advances in the 'substitution' type of industrialization, Mexico is the only case which has not yet shown a clear tendency towards stagnation. It must, however, be taken into account that this is the only country in the group which has promoted far-reaching agrarian reform and eliminated the political influence of the feudally based oligarchy. On the other hand, Mexico is notable for the great development of her export of services (tourism), an activity that absorbs considerable manpower.

productive resources, thus reducing the efficiency of the economic system; (*b*) in the sense of widening the present and potential size of markets through schemes for regional economic integration; and (*c*) by influencing the actual orientation of technological development in terms of the specific requirements of the present phase of Latin America's modernization process. Obviously, therefore, development in Latin America cannot simply result from spontaneous market forces. Only the conscious and deliberate action of central decision-making organs can ensure that it is properly worked out. What is currently called the 'Latin American Revolution' is really the recognition of this problem and the attempt—intermittent and desultory as yet—to create a system of political institutions that can guide the social changes needed to make development viable. Since the present ruling classes fail to understand the nature of the problem and are determined to maintain the *status quo,* those in Latin America who are actually struggling for development are, whether consciously or not, playing a 'revolutionary' role.

Let us now see how the problems of U.S. 'security' tie in with those of Latin American development. Since the Latin American area is the innermost circle of the U.S. zone of influence, it is only natural that the latter country's policy of hegemony should be conducted there in exemplary fashion. From the Latin American point of view, the Cuban rocket crisis must be interpreted as bringing the Monroe Doctrine up to date. According to the new rules, two options are open to the countries of Latin America: political and economic integration under U.S. hegemony, each particular situation being defined within the sphere of influence of the super-

Power, or dislocation from this sphere of influence. In the latter event, however, the country in question can only hope to have its sovereignty 'tolerated' according to rules laid down for each individual case by the dominant Power. These rules can be rigid enough to render internal pressures uncontrollable, and they can make survival of the regime (as in the present case of Cuba) a heavy onus on any Powers outside the sphere of influence who become politically involved in the issue. The recent Dominican experience made it clear that the United States is not prepared to tolerate any further defections within the inner circle of her zone of influence. Until the external perimeter of the sphere of influence is more solidly established—and this could be a consequence of solving the Vietnam issue—it can be expected that a rigid line of intolerance will prevail in the Latin American area.

If we admit that the military aspects of the 'security' problem in the region have been solved by implicit Soviet acceptance of a new definition of the Monroe Doctrine, we can infer that the economic aspects will now come to the fore. It is likely, therefore, that the domestic problems of each individual Latin American country, particularly in the economic sphere, will become of increasing interest to the organs responsible for U.S. external security. As the most probable path (other than open 'subversion,' which would be dealt with on the military level) that a Latin American country can follow in order to move out of the U.S. sphere of influence is to effect changes in its economic policy, the latter will have to be strictly controlled from outside if stability is to be maintained. At the same time, since one of the prerequisites for averting major changes in economic policy is the preservation of existing power structures, strict vigilance will have to be maintained over the political processes and, in addition, a control mechanism for preventive action must be introduced into individual countries if the enormous cost of international police action is to be avoided.

As soon as U.S. 'security' is defined as implying the maintenance of the social *status quo* in Latin America, it becomes perfectly clear that the autonomy of the countries in the region (assuming that Latin American nations and States are something more than the temporary power structures) to supervise their own development is reduced to very little. This doctrine implies that fundamental decisions must be taken at a higher level, probably in the political centre of the sphere of influence or in some 'supranational' organ to which effective power may have been delegated by that political centre. We must therefore ask what type of 'development' the United States envisages for Latin America. This question has never been the subject of open discussion in government circles, since Congress has regarded 'economic aid' as a mere complement of 'military aid' which was defined strictly within the orbit of security policy. Recently the problem has been attracting some attention, but chiefly on the technical-administrative level. As Professor Edward Mason observes: 'Recently AID has given increased attention to this problem and has attempted to formulate for some of the principal aid-receiving countries a so-called Long-Range Assistance Strategy which spells out U.S. economic, political, and security interests in the countries in question, the conditions necessary to their attainment, and

the relevant instrument of foreign policy.'[8]

U.S. BUSINESS CORPORATIONS

Although no unanimous conclusion has been reached on all aspects of this complex problem, there is already an accepted doctrine in the United States in so far as at least one point is concerned: namely, that a decisive role in Latin American development is being undertaken by private American companies and that U.S. 'aid' policy should be conducted principally through them. The report of the Clay Committee was emphatic on this point, and in recent years both Congress and the Administration have shown considerable concern to create conditions for the effective operation of political guarantees and economic incentives to enable private U.S. firms to carry out this important function. 'Guarantee' agreements have been signed with Latin American governments permitting private U.S. companies operating in their territories to enjoy a privileged position in comparison with identical companies operating at home. At the same time, measures such as the Hickenlooper amendment create political 'super-guarantees' for U.S. companies by subjecting local governments to a permanent threat. In the words of Professor Mason: 'It would seem that the government has gone about as far as it can go to promote U.S. private foreign investment in Latin America without outright subsidization.'[9] In this context, private investment means, whether ex-

8 Edward S. Mason, *Foreign Aid and Foreign Policy* (New York: Harper & Row, Publishers, for Council on Foreign Relations, 1964), p. 48.

9 *Ibid.*, p. 90.

plicitly or implicitly, investment by the large corporations, since the small American business firm possesses neither the capacity nor the means to operate abroad.

The first problem that arises from the Latin American point of view is to establish what type of political organization is likely to be compatible with a regional economic system controlled chiefly by powerful American corporations. It is easy to infer that the most attractive sectors for these corporations are those producing goods or services in which technological development plays an important role. Without going into other aspects of the problem, we must remember that the large American corporation is a powerful private bureaucracy, exercising public or semi-public functions, whose integration into U.S. political society has up to now remained undefined. Professor Andrew Hacker reminds us that 'Unlike the religious and guild structures of earlier centuries, the large firm of today has no theoretical rationale linking power, purpose, and responsibility.'[10] Hence no way has yet been found of integrating these large corporations, whose functions are becoming increasingly public, into the structure of a pluralistic political society. At the same time, government is becoming increasingly powerless against these great corporations, since even in the United States 'government is weaker than the corporate institutions purportedly subordinate to it...'[11] Even Adolph Berle, the leading authority on this subject, who cannot

be suspected of animosity towards the large company, draws attention to the fact that the board of directors of a large corporation derives power from no one but itself, 'it is an automatic self-perpetuating oligarchy.'[12] The enormous power at present possessed by these large corporations has not the slightest claim to legitimacy. Professor Berle tells us that in the U.S. the doctrine is taking shape that 'where a corporation has the power to affect a great many lives (differing from the little enterprise which can be balanced out by the market) it should be subject to the same restraints under the Constitution that apply to an agency of the federal or state government.'[13] Called upon to operate in Latin America with a number of privileges, outside the control of U.S. anti-trust legislation, and with U.S. political and military protection, the great American corporation must of necessity become a super-Power in any Latin American country. Since a large proportion of the basic decisions on orientation of investment, location of economic activity, orientation of technology, and the degree of integration of the national economies rests in the hands of these large corporations, it is quite clear that the existing national States will come to play an increasingly secondary role.

Such a regional 'development project,' which tends to render obsolete the idea of nationality as the principal political force in Latin America, offers many attractions to important sectors of the local ruling classes, who see in it an ingenious formula for deflating

---

[10] Andrew Hacker, "Corporate America," Introduction to *The Corporation Take-Over* (New York, Harper & Row, Publishers, 1964), p. 2.

[11] *Ibid.*, p. 11.

[12] A. A. Berle, 'Economic Power and the Free Society,' included in *The Corporation Take-Over*, p. 91.

[13] *Ibid.*, p. 99.

the 'nationalism' which they hold responsible for most of the current social unrest. If most of the State's substantive functions in controlling the economic and social development process were taken away, then the current political 'ferment' characterizing many Latin American countries would in all probability tend to diminish and government could then function principally on the 'technical' level. We would have attained, by the opposite path, the Saint Simonian ideal of replacing the government of men by the administration of things.

Leaving aside the question of whether such a situation could be reconciled with the traditions of Latin American culture and merely considering some of the technical aspects of the problem, there is ample reason to believe that such a 'development project' is not viable in current Latin American conditions. The great U.S. corporation seems to be as inadequate an instrument for dealing with Latin American problems as is a powerful mechanized army faced with guerrilla warfare. The large corporation with its advanced technology and high capitalization, particularly when backed by numerous privileges, produces the same effect in an underdeveloped economy as large exotic trees introduced into an unfamiliar region: they drain all the water, dry up the land, and disturb the balance of flora and fauna. In effect, indiscriminate penetration into a fragile economic structure by large corporations, characterized by their high degree of administrative inflexibility and enormous financial power, tends to provoke a structural imbalance difficult to correct—for instance, a greater differentiation in living standards between groups of the population and a rapid increase of open or disguised unemployment. If control by the national governments is further reduced, allowing the large U.S. corporations to operate with even greater freedom than they now enjoy, the tendency to concentration of economic activity is likely to be accentuated, aggravating the existing differences in living standards between social groups and geographical areas, and the final result will be a real or potential increase of social tensions. Since economic decisions of a strategic nature would fall outside the scope of Latin American governments, these tensions would tend to be regarded, on the local political plane, solely from their negative viewpoint; State action would therefore have to be essentially repressive in character.

Economic development in the problematical conditions Latin America is called upon to face at the moment requires, however, the co-operation of large masses of the population and active participation by important sectors of this population. This is why the most difficult tasks are of a political rather than a technical nature. Hard political decisions must be taken and this can be done only if such action is supported by the existing national centres of political power. The principle of nationality is therefore vital for the present phase of Latin American development. Today, more than ever, this concept is extraordinarily functional and any measure taken to weaken the Latin American States as political centres, able to interpret national aspirations and to rally the people around common ideals, will limit the region's development possibilities. Thus, Latin America's economic integration can be justified only if it is conceived in terms of defining common policy between national States and not as a co-ordinating link between the great foreign enterprises operating in the region.

CONCLUSIONS

In conclusion, one can enumerate certain points:

(1) Under the conditions of nuclear equilibrium obtaining at present between the super-Powers, the exercise of supranational hegemony can be justified only in the light of the interest of the Power wishing to exercise such hegemony.

(2) Spheres of influence have no longer any significance for the super-Powers from the point of view of their military security.

(3) From the standpoint of the countries of the Third World, spheres of influence are nothing but systems of economic domination, which lessen their freedom of manœuvre as they seek to adapt their political and social structures to development requirements.

(4) U.S. hegemony in Latin America, by underpinning the anachronistic power structure, constitutes a serious obstacle to development for the majority of countries in the region.

(5) The U.S. Government's programme for development in Latin America, based as it is on the activities of the great American business corporations and on preventive control of 'subversion,' is not viable, except as a means of freezing the social *status quo*.

(6) The success of development policy in Latin America will depend first of all on the capacity of its promoters to mobilize the great mass of the population in the region. This can be done only from each national political centre and in conformity with national values and ideals.

(7) Economic integration will serve the development needs of the region only if it stems from a common policy formulated by really independent national governments and not from the co-ordination of the interests of the great foreign business enterprises operating in Latin America.

MIDDLE EAST

Bernard Lewis

THE CONSEQUENCES OF DEFEAT

I

Since the end of the third Arab-Israeli war the vocabulary of Middle Eastern

Reprinted from Bernard Lewis, "Consequences of Defeat," *Foreign Affairs,* XLVI (January, 1968, copyright by the Council on Foreign Relations, Inc., New York) 321–35, by special permission of the publisher.

politics has been enriched with a new formula—"the removal of the consequences of aggression." The phrase presents some obvious difficulties of definition concerning the origin of the aggression, the nature of its consequences and the manner of their removal. All these are subject to a wide diversity of interpretations. However, the meaning of the Arab states in putting forward this formula as a demand is quite clear; it is that Israel is the aggressor, that the occupation of Arab lands and the departure of their Arab inhabitants are the consequences of aggression, and that these consequences should be reversed.

It is possible that in certain circumstances the conquerors might be willing to give up their conquests; it is even conceivable that the refugees might return—though this would make them unique among the countless millions in Europe, Asia and Africa who have fled or been driven from their homes in our brutal century. But far more has happened than the occupation of lands and the movement of peoples, important as these may be. In the world of reality, events cannot be unmade, and their effects persist, even when their results vanish. Sometimes these events are of such dimensions as to involve radical reassessments: governments reassess policies at the periphery of their interests and people at the center of crisis reassess their governments. It seems likely that the war and crisis in the Middle East in the summer of 1967 formed such a turning point. The four chief parties concerned—the Arabs, Israel, the Soviet Union and the West—must have been pondering the significance of these events and the lessons to be learnt from them.

The Russians were involved in the crisis from the start—indeed, without descending to the conspiratorial conception of history or returning to the polemics of the cold war, we can say with reasonable assurance that they had no small part in creating it. One contribution, which they shared with other powers, was the dispatch of large quantities of modern, sophisticated weapons

to the area; another, more distinctively their own, was their unswerving support for the Arab states in any and every encounter, irrespective of circumstances. A good example of this is the recurrent problem of clashes on the Syrian-Israeli border. Most observers—and governments—were content to treat each incident on its merits and to blame one side or the other as seemed appropriate. But the Soviet Government invariably supported the Syrians, even when they were palpably in the wrong, and on several occasions even used its veto in the Security Council to save the Syrians from a mildly critical resolution. On November 3, 1966, the veto was applied against an inoffensive resolution sponsored, among others, by two African states—a remarkable indication of how far the Soviet Government was prepared to go in support of its Arab protégés.

This kind of action would in itself have led Arab governments to form a high—and, as it turned out, exaggerated—assessment of Soviet willingness to stand by them in a crisis. There is, in addition, some evidence of Soviet help at a more intimate level than the politics of the United Nations. Syrian gunnery on the border, it is said, showed a degree of professional efficiency out of accord with the previous and subsequent performances of the Syrian army; Syrian diplomacy, on both border issues and questions of oil transit payments, was conducted with a professional finesse that suggested greater reserves of skill and experience than are normally available to short-lived governments in Damascus.

In his television address on Friday, June 9, President Nasser explained how the crisis had begun. On May 15, he said, it had become clear from Israeli statements that they intended to attack

Syria. This was confirmed by information from Syrian sources and also by reports from the Egyptian intelligence services. Moreover, "our friends in the Soviet Union informed the parliamentary delegation which visited Moscow early last month that there was a premeditated intention to attack Syria. It was our duty not to stay with our arms crossed. It was a duty of Arab solidarity, and also a guarantee for our national security." It was for this reason, said the President, that he had sent his forces to the frontier. This had led successively to the withdrawal of [the United Nations Expeditionary Force] UNEF, the Egyptian occupation of Sharm el-Sheikh, and the declaration of a blockade of the Gulf of Aqaba, since "the passage of the enemy flag in front of our troops was intolerable, and inflicted the deepest wound on the feelings of the Arab nation."

President Nasser of course acted, as always, by his own choice, but we may believe him when he says that the original impetus came from Syrian and Russian warnings. Both Syrian and, what is more important, Russian spokesmen have throughout taken the same line. But were these warnings based on a genuine danger—or even on a genuine belief that such a danger existed? The evidence adduced, apart from vague references to information received, consisted of two points: an alleged concentration of large Israeli forces on the Syrian frontier, and menacing speeches by Mr. Eshkol. Neither piece of evidence amounts to much. The speeches were no more than routine warnings of reprisals in what had become a standardized pattern, intended to discourage Syrian and soothe Israeli hotheads—an exercise which should have been familiar to Arab leaders. The troop concentration,

as is clear from the reports of the U.N. truce observers, never took place. The Syrians may have misread the situation and panicked; the Russians will not have done so, and the conclusion is inescapable that the Soviet Government, for reasons of its own, either planned or connived at the launching of what became a new and dangerous crisis in Israel-Arab relations.

The suggestion has been made that the Soviet purpose was to provide a distraction in the Middle East and thus relieve the pressure on Viet Nam. This would assume, first, that they intended, from the start, to create a major international crisis, involving the powers and especially the United States, and, second, that they counted on the willingness of the United States to become involved. Both assumptions seem unlikely. A more probable explanation is that they aimed at something much more limited and local, a scare rather than a crisis, and that its purpose was to save the tottering Syrian régime from collapse. The Soviets had invested a good deal of time, effort and money in the left-wing Baathist government and had achieved a closer relationship with it than with any other government not under communist control. In May 1967, that government, and with it the Soviet position in Syria, was in grave danger. It was already more than a year old—a dangerous age in Damascus. Based on an uneasy alliance between members of Muslim religious minority groups, it was unpopular with the Sunnis,[1] and further weakened by the split between Alawis and Druzes. Worst of all, some of its supporters had gratuitously antagonized the powerful Islamic establishment. Like other "re-

[1] At one time the Baathist government was known as the *'Adas* (lentil) régime—an acronym of 'Alawis, Druzes and Isma'ilis.

volutionary" and "progressive" régimes in the Arab world, the Baathists had confined their radicalism to politics and economics and had usually refrained from attacking Islamic beliefs, traditions or institutions. They had therefore encountered nothing more than the grumbles of a population accustomed to acquiesce in the vagaries of authoritarian government. There are, however, limits to acquiescence, and at the beginning of May the publication in an army-sponsored magazine of an article denouncing religion and belief in God evoked a menacing wave of popular resentment against a régime which now seemed to be threatening the most cherished values of a Muslim people. The government beat a hasty retreat, attributing the article to the C.I.A., but the damage was already done. The Baathists and their Russian backers may well have decided that a little diversion, based on the unfailing theme of Palestine, might be useful. As the crisis developed, and seemed to be tending toward a diplomatic victory for the revolutionary Arab states, and therefore for Russia, wider and more tempting prospects appeared—the collapse of Western influence, the consolidation of Russian influence in the revolutionary Arab states, and its extension to the remaining Arab states in the Middle East and North Africa.

In backing them so far, the Russians were clearly assuming that the Arabs would win—if necessary in a war, but probably without one. The West would be hypnotized into accepting Arab demands; Israel, abandoned by her Western friends, perhaps even under their pressure, would be forced to give way. The dispatch of a Russian fleet to the eastern Mediterranean, of a strength obviously insufficient to confront the U.S. Sixth Fleet, can only have been intended to overawe Israel,

with American acquiescence. The world would learn that the friends of the Soviets prosper, while the friends of the West do not.

For a while the world seemed to be learning just that. The West faltered and fumbled; Israel, unsure of Western attitudes, hesitated; President Nasser, triumphant, threw caution to the winds. After nationalizing the Suez Canal in 1956, he had astutely sat back, declared himself satisfied and left the next move to his opponents. After closing the Straits of Tiran, he declared explicitly that this was a preliminary to the final confrontation with Israel, for which he was now ready. The other revolutionary Arab states were with him; even his Arab enemies felt obliged to make the necessary accommodations. That the Russians encouraged him to go so far is unlikely; they certainly did not prevent him.

The six-day war and its sequel showed that the Russians had failed badly in their military and political intelligence and assessments—not perhaps of the West, but of Israel and the Arabs. No doubt they were misled about the one by their own anti-Semitic stereotypes, about the other by the wishful thinking of their Arab informants. The correction of error is difficult in a dictatorship. By Monday evening, June 6, informed opinion—by Tuesday almost everyone in the free world—knew how the battle was going. It was not until Tuesday night (Wednesday morning in the Middle East) that the Soviet delegate to the U.N. agreed to an unconditional ceasefire. The extra time he had striven to gain for the Arabs served only to consolidate their defeat.

From Wednesday morning the signs multiplied that the Russians were engaged in a reappraisal—probably agonizing. They were surprised, disconcerted and very angry. Their public fury was directed against Israel; in addition, they were probably not unmoved by the swift collapse of Arab arms and by President Nasser's attempt, through the false charge of American and British participation, to drag them into war.

The Russians had reason to be angry. Soviet prestige—the reputation of Soviet arms and guidance, the value of Soviet friendship, the credibility of Soviet warnings—had received a damaging blow, with far-reaching repercussions. The Russians had suffered this blow because, through the extent of their commitment to the Arabs, they had in effect entrusted the safety of Soviet prestige to the keeping of Arab governments over which they had no real control. They had taken great chances, which turned out badly; they had done so for very dubious gains. The Arab leaders were very unwise to assume that the Soviets would accept, for their sake, risks which they had not accepted for Berlin or Viet Nam. This miscalculation was disastrous for the Arabs; it was also most unfortunate for the Soviet Union.

The root of the trouble was that the Arab governments, even that of Syria, were not satellites, and were therefore ultimately uncontrollable. The Soviet Government, in dealing with the Middle East, found itself in a position of responsibility without power—a reversal of its normal experience. It is not surprising that they were disturbed.

In this predicament, the Soviet leadership had, basically, a choice between two policies: either to consolidate its hold on the revolutionary Arab governments and transform them into satellites, or to attempt some measure of disengagement. This in turn is linked with the larger, global choice before them, between détente and coexistence,

on the one hand, and active hostility toward the United States on the other. Both choices are affected by changing and conflicting pressures within the collective leadership which succeeded Khrushchev.

One of these pressures is that of the so-called Stalinists—more precisely, the exponents of repression and chauvinism. These circles are strongly affected by old-fashioned anti-Semitism, which can become a powerful factor in determining attitudes both toward a Jewish state and toward its enemies. The point is sometimes made that Jewish or pro-Jewish sentiments can lead to unbalanced and unrealistic policies. This is of course true. It is equally true, though less obvious, that anti-Jewish sentiments can have the same effect. The hysterical violence and traditional anti-Semitic symbolism of Soviet attacks on Israel show that the offenses of the Israelis, in Soviet eyes, were greatly aggravated by the fact that they were Jews. These Soviet reactions also suggest that one of the motives of a pro-Arab policy may have been a desire to hurt the Jews, and that this emotional impulsion may have warped the judgment of policy-makers and led them to a degree of indulgence to Arab wishes which was ultimately harmful to Soviet and even Arab interests. This phenomenon is not unknown in other countries; in the Soviet Union it was not countered or corrected by any pressure, emotional or otherwise, in the opposite direction.

II

Anti-Jewish prejudice may have pushed the policy of supporting Arab nationalism to ill-judged extremes; it was not of course the sole or even the main motive for this policy, which rested on a fairly realistic assessment of the condition of the Arab world and the importance of the Middle Eastern bridgehead for Soviet activities in Asia and Africa.

This importance was enhanced, rather than reduced, by the Arab defeat, and for the moment there was much to tempt the Russians into a closer involvement. The régimes they had supported were in danger of overthrow, with further damaging effects to Soviet prestige. China seemed ready to usurp Russia's place as the patron of Arab nationalism, and was gaining the support of Arab communists. The blow to Western influence, on the other hand, was far heavier than to Russian influence, and affected even those countries that were under conservative régimes. For a while the Russians seem to have toyed with the idea of establishing communist régimes in the Arab lands—and then to have abandoned it as too dangerous.

It is not difficult to see why. To transform the Arab countries into satellites would be an expensive, difficult and hazardous operation, and would never be safe unless the régimes were sustained, as in Eastern Europe, by the threat or presence of Soviet force. Even in Eastern Europe, this policy has become precarious; it would be still more so in countries that have no land frontier with the Soviet Union. Moreover, such an intervention in the Arab lands would endanger the new, hard-won and greatly valued understanding with Turkey and Iran—both of them, despite their recent rethinking, still members of Western-oriented alliances. In addition, it soon became clear that the Chinese menace was not yet a serious factor, and that the collapse of Western influence was by no means as complete as had at first appeared. The Syrian episode had shown that Islam was still the strongest loyalty of the people, and that outraged Islamic feelings could still shake or destroy a government which really tried to enforce its "progressive" and "revolutionary" principles. An attempt to create "popular democracies" could arouse very powerful forces indeed.

Finally, and most important of all, the danger of a direct confrontation with the United States remained. It was this danger that had induced the Soviet Government, at the height of the crisis, to draw back from armed intervention to save the Arabs. An adventurous policy in the Middle East could easily lead to a new danger of confrontation—and to another withdrawal, with even more damaging effects on Soviet prestige. In avoiding an entanglement with the Arabs and a collision with the United States, the Soviet leadership would be faithful to tradition. During the centuries of expansion, by which the principality of Muscovy grew into the great Russian Empire, the greater Soviet Union and the still greater Soviet bloc, two principles were almost always respected: to advance by land into adjoining regions to which troops and settlers could easily be moved, and to avoid a clash with a superior or even an equal power.

The dilemma of the Soviet Government was acute. A closer involvement in the Middle East was too dangerous —yet disengagement seemed politically impossible. The collective leadership could not make the sudden changes of policy that were possible for Stalin or Khrushchev; the internal pressures were too strong, and the status of the Soviet Union as a superpower was heavily committed. The Russian demand to Egypt, at the time of President Podgorny's visit, for a purge of bourgeois elements in the Egyptian Government and army, could be interpreted either way—as a prelude to Bolshevization or to abandonment. As an emergency measure, an airlift of arms was organized, to save the Nasserist and Baathist régimes from collapse. But while Soviet prestige clearly required that these régimes survive the war and its immediate aftermath, it did not necessarily require their indefinite continuance, and there are some indications that the Soviets have begun to regard President Nasser as expendable. It is still too early to assess the future development of Soviet policy in the Middle East, nor indeed is it certain that this policy has yet been decided. Much will obviously depend on the attitudes of the Western powers and, above all, of the United States.

There are, however, some signs of its probable direction. The Soviets will certainly continue to give vociferous support to the Arab case against Israel, especially at the United Nations. They will try to salvage their battered prestige and hope that, as on previous occasions, they will find someone in the West to help them in this task. But in all probability they will take care not to get into a position again where their prestige can be endangered by governments and armies which they do not control. The most likely development is a policy based on relations with individual Arab states rather than on Arabism, and aimed at the kind of relationship that they have sought to establish with Turkey, Iran and Pakistan. The question is how far they will be allowed to extricate themselves if they desire to do so.

Like the Soviet Union, the Western powers have been able to draw certain inferences from what has happened. For a while it seemed that the West, and particularly the United States, had been outmanœuvred. The ring was closing around Israel; even pro-Western Arab rulers, whatever their real feelings, were lining up behind President Nasser. Communist Russia could support Arab nationalist demands to the full; the United States and Britain, captives of their own freedom and their own standards, could not, and were thus forced to appear as enemies of the Arabs. Their only choice was of what kind: as enemies to be respected and conciliated, or to be despised and ignored. For the United States, a far more terrible choice was being prepared—whether to abandon Israel to destruction, or to be trapped in a land war in Southwest as well as Southeast Asia.

Fortunately for the United States, no such choice was needed. Through no particular wisdom or merit of their own, the Western powers emerged from a dangerous situation with what turned out to be only minor injuries. Like the Russians, they had learned that their control over their friends was very limited. They were fortunate in that the state which was generally regarded as their protégé did not need to be rescued. The danger remained.

For a while, it seemed that despite their failure against Israel, the Russians had won a considerable political success against the United States and Britain, which found themselves being ignominiously evicted from most Arab countries. But even this was deceptive. The two most powerful Arab weapons against the West—the oil boycott and, for Britain, the sterling balances—both proved ineffective. The stoppage of oil exports did greater and swifter damage to the sellers than to the buyers. Arabian money transferred from London to Switzerland, at low or no interest rates, found its way back to London, to earn high interest for its new custodians. Even the closing of the Suez Canal did less harm than was feared, and for the United States even brought some marginal advantage—some additional exports and the slowing down of Russian supplies to North Viet Nam. The inconvenience to Britain was more serious, but much of this was of a transitional nature, until new arrangements could become fully effective. The heaviest sufferers were India, some other Asian and East African states, and above all the Egyptians themselves.

As the flames and the dust subsided, there were signs that the damage to Anglo-American diplomacy was less severe than had at first appeared. Some Arab leaders were beginning to wonder whether they were wise to identify themselves entirely with one camp in the global conflict, and whether indeed they had chosen the right one. Before very long, several Arab states began to make overtures to the West, and even President Nasser flew a kite, no doubt expecting, on the basis of past experience, that Western governments would respond with eager gratitude to the opportunity once again to feed his people and sustain his régime. This time, however, he had overestimated the American capacity to absorb calumny, abuse and injury, and the response from Washington was disappointing. In London he fared somewhat better, though the extent of British complaisance, and its value to Egypt, are still not clear.

That President Nasser should have found it necessary to seek London's good offices—for pressure in Jerusalem or intercession in Washington—is a measure of the failure of another kind of Western policy, that of General de Gaulle. Previous French policy toward Israel had been based on the assumptions that nothing could be achieved with the Arab states, and that one small ally in the Middle East was better than none at all. In a calculation unconnected with the Middle East, both as-

sumptions were now abandoned. By supporting the Russian and Arab line against Israel, the General incurred some immediate losses—in the political and commercial good will of Israel, and in the confidence of Europe, at a time when the credibility of his friendship was rather important to him. In compensation, he gained warm words from Moscow and the Arab capitals. Whether he will gain any more from them is dubious. They for their part have already learnt that his support made no real difference to them; they are unlikely to pay for more than they receive.

III

In the West as in Russia the question that arises is a basic and simple one—how much trouble is the Middle East worth? On both sides there seems to be a growing appreciation of the advantages of disengagement—as far as is feasible—from an area of high risks, great costs, dubious returns and, above all, of diminishing importance, as it is being bypassed by strategic, economic and technological developments and overshadowed by the urgent problems of East Asia. These must, increasingly, dominate political and strategic thinking in Washington and Moscow.

For the powers of the Communist and Western blocs the possibility exists, however remotely, of extricating themselves from the Middle Eastern quicksands. No such possibility is open to the countries of the Middle East, which must make the best they can of conditions in their area—including, for as long as may be necessary, the policies of the great and not-so-great powers. The lessons of the war will thus appear to these countries in a somewhat different form.

What Israel learnt is what victors

always learn from victory—that is, that they were right all along. On two points in particular the crisis and war confirmed Israeli beliefs: that their survival depended, ultimately, on their willingness and ability to fight for it, and that they could not trust the United Nations, where their enemies had a built-in position of advantage. The Soviet veto in the Security Council is always available to the Arabs, even on the most trivial matters; the combination of the Communist bloc and the quaintly named "nonaligned" states in the General Assembly is sufficient to prevent any solution acceptable to Israel, if not to enforce one acceptable to the Arabs. "If the Arabs table a resolution tomorrow that the earth is flat," said an Israeli minister, "they can count on at least 40 votes."

Reliance on their own military and political strength in the Middle East and mistrust of "United Nations auspices" are two basic Israeli conclusions from recent events. A third is that, of all the powers of the outside world, the only one that really matters to Israel is the United States. Even in the euphoria of victory, Israelis know that American good will is fundamental to them. Basically, there are three things that Israel wants from Washington: first, to deter the Russians, as in June 1967, from direct military intervention against them; second, to refrain from imposing, alone or with others, a solution which Israel judges contrary to her interests; third, to ensure that Israel's armaments do not fall dangerously below the level of the Arab states. In other words, they wish to be sure that the Americans will neither undermine their position nor allow Russia to do so. Given this assurance, they feel confident that they can cope with their Arab neighbors. The ultimately more serious problem of their Arab subjects, with its implica-

tions for the whole future of their state, society and ethos, remains unresolved, and there is little sign of agreement, inside Israel, on how to tackle it.

A victory, said the Duke of Wellington, is the greatest tragedy in the world, except a defeat. The Arabs suffered this greater tragedy, and the problems confronting them—problems of understanding and of action—have a terrible urgency quite different from the milder dilemmas of the Americans, the Russians, even of the Israelis.

The first and obvious question was—what went wrong? Why had they suffered a double defeat—a military defeat in the field, at the hands of a nation inferior in numbers, weapons, territory and resources, and a political defeat at the United Nations, despite every appearance of overwhelming political superiority? At the moment of crisis and war, it was the Arab states which found themselves isolated from world opinion, and even some of those governments which supported them were clearly acting against their own public opinion at home.[2] Even the full mobilization of the Soviet regular and auxiliary forces in the General Assembly failed to secure the necessary majority for the resolutions that the Arabs wanted. It was a political defeat hardly less striking than the military defeat which had preceded it.

War and defeat are the classical motors of social and political change. Sometimes they lead to major transformations, as in Germany and Russia after the First World War; sometimes to a mood of sullen resentment and withdrawal, as in the South after the American Civil War, and in Spain after 1898. Defeat is especially cogent

---

[2] The line-up raises difficult problems for those who believe that economics and ideology, not politics, are the determining factors in international as in other affairs.

when inflicted by the carriers of another civilization with a different and challenging religion or ideology. The defeat in Palestine in 1948 was the first such shock suffered directly by the Eastern Arabs. The earlier defeats at the hands of West and East European imperialism had been sustained by the Turks and Persians, who, as the dominant peoples of Islam, had shielded the Arabs from the realities of politics and war. The vague encounters of the Anglo-French period added little of value to their experience; on the contrary, by providing easy victories over embarrassed and halfhearted opponents they fostered a dangerous illusion of strength.

The shock of defeat in 1948, in place of the expected victory parade, was all the greater in that it was inflicted, not by the mighty imperial powers, but by the despised and familiar Jews. The *nakba* (disaster), as the Arabs called it, gave rise to an extensive literature, much of it concerned with the political and military blunders of Arab leaders, but some of it, as for example the well-known works by Mr. Musa Alami and Professor Constantine Zurayk, attempting to penetrate to the deeper social and cultural causes of the Arab failure.

Politically, the defeat was seen as a failure of the régimes—the parliamentary and constitutional monarchies and republics—which had conducted the war. The lesson learnt was the need for a more radical and more violent approach. The traditional and authoritarian régimes, as in Jordan and Saudi Arabia, managed to survive, but the régimes in Syria, Egypt and Iraq were swept away. They were succeeded by military governments, with programs of revolutionary change, later designated socialism, and of Arab nationalism. In international relations, their anti-West-

ern attitudes gradually became pro-Soviet, when the Soviet Union finally emerged as the most serious and dangerous antagonist of the West and of Western civilization.

The second defeat, in 1956, brought no comparable soul-searching or upheaval. This was because the military defeat was compensated by a great political victory, and because the significance of the struggle was blurred by myths. Three beliefs, in particular, shaped Arab thinking on these events: first, that Egypt was defeated by France and Britain, not just by Israel; second, that a cause of defeat was Arab disunity, which left Egypt alone to face the tripartite attack; third, that Egypt was saved from the consequences of defeat by the intervention of Russia, her new friend since the previous year.

The third of these is an obvious myth—a successful combined effort of delusion and self-delusion. The record of October and November 1956 makes it quite clear that the Soviet Government did not speak out until the American President and other spokesmen had explained, not once but several times, that the United States did not support Britain, France or Israel, and disapproved of their action. Then and only then did the Soviets take up the Egyptian cause and utter dire threats against the aggressors. And even after that, they were powerless to secure the Israeli withdrawal from Sinai, which was brought about by the American Government alone. Yet the myth of the Soviet rescue became an article of faith, and was reaffirmed by King Hussein in Moscow as late as October 3, 1967.

The military myths were more excusable, and were, in part at least, solidly based on fact. Egypt had indeed fought alone; Israel had not. The Egyptian interpretation of events was further encouraged by a flow of revelations and confessions.[3] The study of these revelations may well have contributed to President Nasser's—perhaps also to Moscow's—misjudgment of the relative military and political strengths of Israel and Egypt.

The myth of 1956—Egypt, alone, embattled and ultimately victorious against three enemies—stood for more than ten years. The events of 1967 should finally have dispelled it. This time the defeat was political as well as military. Three Arab states on Israel's borders, with help from others, were overwhelmed by Israel alone. There have been attempts to refurbish the old myths and create new ones; they have had only limited success.

There is still little willingness to face the facts—far less than in 1948–49, when discussion was still free and often realistic. The relatively minor defeat of that time was called *nakba,* disaster. The far greater defeat of 1967 is firmly labelled *naksa,* setback. This word is used even in press translations or summaries of foreign comments, and serves to render such terms as defeat and disaster, which are tabu. The universal adoption of this word is a striking example of the nationalization of language and its use to control thought and conceal reality.

Discussion so far has been mainly on the tactical level, and has concentrated on such things as military and political errors and unwise propaganda. In some Arab countries, as for example, in North Africa and South Arabia, rulers and leaders have been quick to draw inferences from the new balance of power within the Arab world, and to realign their policies accordingly. There are as yet few outward signs of any desire to examine the deeper causes of the Arab predicament: the basic weaknesses of Arab society in an age of disruption and transition; the inadequacy of Arab political structures and ideas;[4] the widening sociological and therefore technological gap.

What are the prospects of peace in the Middle East? In the outside world, the realists, like other people, are divided into two groups: the pro-Arab realists, who say that it is unrealistic to expect the Arabs to recognize Israel, and the pro-Israel realists, who say that it is unrealistic to expect Israel to relinquish her gains without substantial guarantees. Stated in this form, the two views are mutually exclusive—and both could well be right. There is, however, a faint hope that the Arabs may in the last resort prove less implacable than the pro-Arabs in their hostility to Israel. One Arab leader, President Bourguiba, was prepared, however reluctantly, to accept the fact of Israel's existence even before the war. Other leaders in the East may be coming to the conclusion that some form of recognition is the least disagreeable of the alternatives that face them. The problem remains whether, in a context of unstable régimes, contested succession and external incitement, they will have the courage and ability to act on such beliefs.

In the past, it has sometimes been argued that the Arab-Israeli conflict prevents great-power agreement, some-

---

[3] Notably by General Dayan's "Diary of the Sinai Campaign" (Hebrew, 1965; English translation, 1966) and by the publication in the spring of 1967, in *The Times,* of London, of Mr. Anthony Nutting's account of the Suez crisis, later brought out in book form, "No End of a Lesson: The Story of Suez."

[4] It is striking that, of the three Arab armies engaged, the Jordanian, with every disadvantage of numbers, terrain and armament, acquitted itself best. Simple, old-fashioned tribal and monarchical loyalties were more effective in maintaining morale than the revolutionary nationalism of Egypt and Syria.

times that the great-power conflict prevents the Arabs and Israelis from coming to terms. Certainly outside intervention has more than once increased tensions, provoked crises and prevented solutions. The effect of the United Nations on problems in the Middle East and elsewhere has often been like that of modern medicine on major diseases—enough to prevent the patient from dying of natural causes, but not enough to make him well. Chronic invalidism is not a happy state.

It may well be that the best hope for the Middle East lies in its diminishing importance, which may in time lead to the great powers losing interest in the area. This would not be the first time. The decline of European interest in the Middle East in the fifteenth and sixteenth centuries, and its effects, are well known. An earlier example may be found in the fourth century A.D.,

when the last of a long series of wars between Rome and Persia came to an end. While the struggle between the two great powers of the ancient world continued, both were active in Arabia —politically, militarily, commercially. During the long peace from 384 to 502 A.D., both lost interest. During the centuries of neglect, the trade routes were diverted, the caravan cities abandoned and much of Arabia reverted to nomadism.

It would not be easy for the great powers to lose interest and might well be painful for the Middle East, where the final fulfillment of the long-standing demand for the end of imperialism could have disconcerting political and economic effects. Without foreign stimulation, there would be grave danger of deterioration and regression; without foreign irritants, there might also be some hope of peace.

WEST AFRICA

FRANCE'S NEW ROLE IN AFRICA

Students of Gaullism are currently watching what appear to be very considerable changes in the General's policy towards Africa, in particular towards the succession States of France's colonial Empire. As with so much of

Reprinted from *The World Today*, monthly journal of the Royal Institute of International Affairs, London, XX (September, 1964) 382–86, by permission of the publisher.

the General's thinking and public statements, endless exegesis is possible, and only the rare dramatic events, such as the abortive *coup d'état* in Gabon last February, can give any clear guidance to the new role in Africa which de Gaulle is seeking to create for his country. Nevertheless, there are some pointers to the way in which France is seeking to draw back from the special position in Africa which began with

Jules Ferry and ran through the French Empire, the *Union française,* the *Communauté,* and the *Union Africaine et Malgache,* and to take up a new one in which Africa, even the French-speaking parts, will fit into the world-wide political, economic, and strategic attitudes which the General is developing.

THE CASE OF GABON

The new approach is a flexible one, with signs of enough opportunism to suggest that French policy in Africa, as elsewhere, is based much more on straightforward French interests than on the world mission which de Gaulle is keen to expound. Gabon is a good case in point. The military revolt against President M'ba was suppressed almost as a reflex action in order to defend the very considerable French economic interests in a wealthy country whose income per head is among the highest in Africa. It now seems that de Gaulle feels that he was mistaken— that the revolution could safely have been allowed to take place, and that M. Jean-Hilaire Aubame, replacing M. M'ba, could have provided greater stability, together with the specious respectability of a regime based on a popular uprising. There are well-founded reports in Paris that the next upheaval in Gabon will be given its head.

Gabon was a landmark, since it clearly showed that the question of whether or not to intervene in African upheavals is today answered in terms of purely French interests. The public apologia which followed the Gabon events was highly unacceptable to many African Heads of State, who are very concerned to show that their ties with France (or even their place in the

Organization of African Unity) are not, in fact, a 'Holy Alliance' designed to keep them in power, but are honourable working relations helping them to create and develop their nations. Many French observers, even among de Gaulle's friends, feel that he could just as well have taken the line that Equatorial Africa was an unstable area of the world in which France had special responsibilities, and that it was intolerable that, in a country like Gabon, an army of a few hundred men should be allowed to decide who should rule. This is an argument which can stand a lot of examination. Instead, the French Government announcement listed French interventions in other parts of Africa, most of which were indignantly denied by the countries in question.

In all this, the carefully elaborated *Quai d' Orsay* doctrine that French policy distinguished between risings with genuine popular support, in which intervention was inadmissible, and purely military or even criminal troubles, in which 'police'-type action was justified, went completely overboard. Since the advent of de Gaulle, the French Foreign Ministry has more and more the air of an academic organization explaining, after the event, the rationale of a policy it does not really understand and about which it was never consulted. In fact, during the Gabon events, the *Quai* seemed to have little idea of what was going on, and African policy was as usual in the hands of M. Foccart, Secretary-General for African Affairs at the Presidency.

It is worth noting that the argument of spheres of responsibility has currently much greater validity in Africa than in Europe or elsewhere, and is a line along which the continent's foreign relations could well develop over the next decade. Politically, the 'State' in Africa has come into existence before the 'Nation', whereas the converse was the case in Europe. The consequence is likely to be an explosive instability, in which many more rivalries than the simple and alien East–West one are likely to breed. Moreover, the re-emergence of a pre-colonial pattern of trade relations, and the recasting of economic ties of all kinds with the former colonial Powers, are likely to lead to a new form of outside participation which will be inevitable for almost all the African countries.

The failure of the French Government to put forward the perfectly sound legalistic basis for its intervention in Gabon was perhaps the most striking evidence of the change in French thinking on Africa. After independence, France made military agreements with her former colonies covering, among other things, the questions of military aid and cooperation. These are often less than clear in their range, but the one completely unequivocal one to have been published (many of the other countries are known to have secret agreements with France) is that of 17 August 1960, with Gabon, which provides that:

"Si la défense, tant intérieure qu'extérieure, du Gabon dépend de la seule République gabonaise, celle-ci peut, avec l'accord de la République française, faire appel aux forces armées françaises pour sa défense intérieure ou extérieure."

Instead, the French Information Minister, M. Peyrefitte (and not the Foreign Ministry), listed cases of French military action in recent months to help the Governments of other African countries. Two of the Heads of State involved, M. François Tombalbaye of Chad and M. Mokhtar ould Daddah of Mauritania, published strongly worded denials. In the first place, neither wished to be associated in the African mind with the clearcut Gabon incident, widely regarded in the continent as the use of external force to keep in power one of the most authoritarian rulers in Africa. And the Mauritanian President, still very preoccupied with asserting his Government's sovereignty over a country which Morocco claims as a part of her territory, is obviously concerned at the publication of any statement tending to show that his Government cannot measure up to the definition of statehood under international law, one of the elements of which is 'maintaining law and order in its territory'.

The Gabon coup was also of direct interest to those countries where jungle and desert, 'black' and 'white' Africa meet, notably Chad and the Niger Republic. These countries, especially Chad, are coping with a built-in Tuareg or Muslim opposition, whose basic, though rarely stated, view is that, while it was willing to be ruled by white Frenchmen (though even in the years of French rule the peace was often uneasily kept), government by negroes is unacceptable. As the white man withdraws from Africa, he is leaving behind him the artificial frontiers created little more than half a century ago and, within them, a resurgence of many of the basic ethnic and other African problems upon which they were imposed. The structures of the young States contained within these frontiers are certainly too fragile for them to deal unaided with the problems involved; French action is often welcome, but the rules of the game are that it should be much more discreet than was the case in Gabon.

AFRICA'S NEW PLACE IN FRENCH THINKING

Politically, economically, and strategically, the new place of Africa in French global policies is being worked out. First, the political aspect. Since General de Gaulle returned to power in 1958, the whole basis of French policy has been the renaissance of France as a world Power, with world responsibilities and world-wide ambitions. Africa is important to the General only in so far as it fits in with this plan, and all the evidences are that it is fitting less and less. It also appears to be less necessary to French designs. Until Algerian independence, France had a vital position to defend at the United Nations, for which African votes and African voices were needed. There is no such issue now. Still more important is the rapid emergence in the world of an African diplomatic personality, and the growing and natural tendency of the young French-speaking African States to strengthen their ties with their neighbours and to loosen those with France. A strong and active Organization of African Unity [OAU] will inevitably undermine the framework within which special links between France and her former colonies are possible. No country heavily dependent on any extra-African Power (whether France, Britain, the United States, the Soviet Union, or China) can hope to play a leading role in the OAU. This is the reason behind the transformation, decided in March at Dakar, of the *Union Africaine et Malgache* into the *Union Africaine et Malgache de Coopération Economique*. As the latter, fuller real membership of the OAU is possible. France appears to be swimming with this tide, or at least

reconciling and readapting herself to it.

The whole trend is complicated, however, by the fact that almost all the ex-French African States are led by the rulers who brought them to independence; they are closely associated in the public mind with France, and most of them were active in French political life before independence. Current Gaullist policy is caught in the dilemma of maintaining appropriate relations with the present leaders, and at the same time being prepared for successful relations with successors whose political stock-in-trade will certainly be much more radical.

Economically, the new French policy was defined in President de Gaulle's press conference of 31 January 1964, and in the Report on *La Politique de Coopération avec les Pays en Voie de Développement* published early this year.[1] The conclusion of the Report, accepted by the French Government, was that aid to under-developed countries will stay at roughly its present proportion of France's gross national product—which will certainly mean a considerable increase in the years to come as the national product increases. Aid to Africa, however, at about $700 m. a year, is unlikely to increase. The main effort will be directed elsewhere, notably towards South America, and much more stringent criteria for aid are likely, including a financial return for France.

In seeking to posit France's new economic policy in Africa, it is important not to be misled by '*Cartierisme*'—the view forcefully expounded by the journalist and polemicist Raymond Cartier that France is simply wasting on ungrateful and corrupt African countries money which would much better be

[1] *Ministère d'Etat Chargé de la Réforme Administrative,* January, 1964.

devoted to meeting the needs of her own restive peasantry. M. Cartier is a popular writer, who has his following in France, and it is perhaps worth recalling that he is not the French Government and does not represent its views. Nevertheless, France clearly intends to be much more careful about the aid she furnishes to Africa in the future. And if de Gaulle's world policy goes ahead, aid-relations with the former colonies are likely in the future to resemble relations with under-developed countries which are receiving help from France for the first time.

Another widely expected initiative is also to be noted. French aid is likely over the coming years to be concentrated on three countries, Senegal, the Ivory Coast, and Gabon. Senegal (French long before Savoy and Nice) could become a sort of African Lebanon; the Ivory Coast and Gabon are of course the most profitable to develop. The argument proffered in support of such a policy is that, at the present stage, development of all the countries involved is too great a task for France. She will therefore concentrate on the three, in the hope that their wealth will spread to neighbouring countries. In fact, it will be one large step on the road to withdrawal from tasks and responsibilities in which the General has lost interest.

Strategically, Africa is already becoming part of a global policy sketched out by de Gaulle in his speech of 23 November 1961, at Strasbourg:

Comme l'éloignement relatif des continents ne cesse pas de se restreindre, il n'est plus, où que ce soit, de danger, ni de conflit, qui n'intéressent une puissance mondiale et, par conséquent, la France. Au surplus, sous des formes nouvelles, adaptées à notre siècle, la France est, comme toujours, présente et active outre-mer. Il en résulte que sa sécurité, l'aide qu'elle doit à ses alliés, le concours qu'elle est engagée à fournir à ses associés, peuvent être mis en cause en une région quelconque du globe. Une force d'intervention terrestre, navale et aérienne, faite pour agir à tout moment, n'importe où, lui est donc, bel et bien necessaire. Nous commençons à la réaliser.[2]

In Africa this is being put into practice by a change from the old 'politique de présence' to a policy of strategic forces, ready to act where needed. Instead of the French garrisons in each country, all French troops are to be grouped in Mauritania, Chad, and the Ivory Coast; only instructors and technical-assistance personnel will be left elsewhere. This scheme fits in with France's world approach; it also meets the growing unacceptability of French forces stationed in African countries.

As has been said, two salient developments govern the new French policy in Africa: France's own search for a wider world position and the rapidity of fuller independence in the new Africa. It is most important, however, that French determination to keep a dominant position in her former colonies should not be underestimated, nor that of many of the Heads of State involved to keep close and friendly ties with France, as far as this is possible. France is changing her position *vis-à-vis* Africa, but is still much concerned that nobody shall replace her there, especially not the United States. Indeed the frictions between France and the United States in Africa are far more acute and important than the East-West conflicts which make the newspaper headlines. De Gaulle is realistic

2 *La documentation française,* December 9, 1961.

enough to see that the Russians and the Chinese, because of lack of technology and money, cannot hope to supplant France in Africa for many years, while the United States might well be able to do so.

William Chapin

THE ASIAN BALANCE OF POWER: AN AMERICAN VIEW

Asia seems fated to be the main centre of world tension for years to come. Its political conflicts are as difficult to resolve as they are dangerous to peace, and Asia, unlike most of the rest of the world, has only an uncertain relation to the central balance of power in which the United States and the Soviet Union play the dominant roles. This central balance can never fully cover Asia (Asia is too big and too important for that). But it is also unlikely that Asia will develop any really independent balance system, for the United States as well as the Soviet Union will probably remain heavily involved in Asian affairs for a long time to come. The important task now is to work towards a limited regional balance of

Reprinted from William Chapin, *The Asian Balance of Power: An American View* ("Adelphi Paper," No. 33 [London: Institute for Strategic Studies, 1967]), by permission of the author.

power in which Asian states assume greater responsibility for the peace of their continent and the freedom of the smaller states.

Today many of the Asian states are excessively dependent on an American military presence for their security. But if Communist aggression is defeated in South Vietnam, Asian states will probably take greater initiatives than they do today to achieve some economic and political cohesion, the lack of which has been one of Asia's chief weaknesses. And Asian states may also acquire greater confidence in their own ability to cope with security problems. As long as China is regarded as a serious threat, no arrangements that Asians can devise in the forseeable future can be more than a partial substitute for American strategic power in the Far East. Nevertheless, growing Asian confidence might permit a considerable reduction of American military power in the area without arousing alarm among the states that regard it as the linchpin of their security.

In reviewing the power-balance problem of Asia, I shall leave out the Middle East, but include Australia and New Zealand as part of the Indo-Pacific area. I shall assume that South Vietnam will remain an independent state and that the question of National-ist China and Taiwan will not be a critical issue in the coming decade, al-though it will doubtless be a serious and troublesome one. These assump-tions are probably not unreasonably optimistic.

Asia is a term the Europeans have used since classical times to designate the largely unknown lands stretching endlessly to the east of Europe's own limits, and Asians themselves at one time would have regarded the term as meaningless. The disparate cultures, vast distances and numerous racial groupings all seemed to demonstrate that Asia was at best only a loose geographic label, invented for Western convenience. The area has never known anything like the cultural unity of the Western world. Nevertheless, huge sub-regions of Asia have had many cen-turies of close cultural and political association. And Asians by now have come to regard themselves as having certain important things in common that distinguish them from other peo-ple. This has been stimulated in part by the example of the broad cultural base in the West, the common resent-ment against the Western domination of the past and a certain racist identifi-cation as a coloured people. But more important than any of these factors in making Asia a meaningful entity, in the past as today, is the enormous land mass and population of China. Almost all Asian countries border on China or

are reasonably close to it, and with China's emergence as a united and strong power the Middle Kingdom has again become the country around which the politics of Asia revolve.

THE CHINA PROBLEM

China is a dynamic and ambitious Communist state, but she is probably not bent on aggression in the sense that Nazi Germany and pre-war Japan were. Despite the talk of her coveting the rice bowls of South-East Asia, we have no good evidence that she wishes to occupy these lands either to control greater food resources or as an outlet for her surplus population. South-East Asia could not really alleviate her population pressure and could con-tribute only very marginally to her food needs. China apparently assumes, and has some good grounds for doing so, that she can continue for some time to meet most of the food needs of an expanding population if she applies more fertilizers and modernizes her agriculture. She is not at present pressing vigorously any of her border claims and seems disposed to raise them only when she judges that it would be expedient to do so. The short border war with India in 1962 seems to have been carried out as much to humiliate India, particularly in the eyes of the new nations, and to demonstrate China's strength as to gain control over disputed territory in a remote region. The repression in Tibet was a brutal example of repression, but again it cannot be considered aggression in the accepted sense of the term.

But if comparisons with Nazi Ger-many and Japan are misleading, China is still very much an expansionist state, much as the Soviet Union has been. Certainly the Asian states that live under China's huge shadow can be pardoned if they regard her as a threat to their security. For China seeks Asian hegemony not only as an end in itself, but as one means of establishing her claim to be the peer of the United States and the Soviet Union. And her ambitions go beyond that. China, with her still fanatic faith in the doctrines formed from her own revolutionary experience, believes she must bring down the decadent or heretical world around her by the militant spread of her credo. As this world collapses, she assumes, of course, that she will become the leader of a new revolutionary world order from which both capitalists and revisionists will be utterly banished.

The emphasis placed on this revolutionary or ideological objective has been so great as to suggest that it is her main foreign objective. Apparently it still ranks as one of her chief objectives, despite the discouraging record in the past two years of her efforts to foment rebellion in Africa, Latin America and South-East Asia. And a state that regards a high degree of instability and political chaos in the rest of the world as a condition advantageous to its interests is a menace to world peace. So also is a state that rushes to intervene in the quarrels of Asian powers, as China did with its ultimatum to India in 1965, that is prepared to run the risk of war to advance ideological objectives, that actively supports or initiates subversive movements in other countries, and that openly supports the aggressive policies of one Asian state against another, as China did by encouraging Indonesia's 'confrontation' with Malaysia. And China's threat may become more serious as she acquires a strong nuclear capability.

As long as China places such great emphasis on ideological objectives, regarding national interests as complementary to, if not identical with, them, the rest of the world and Asia in particular are going to find it hard to reach an acceptable accommodation with her. This is not to say that the Chinese Communists are inflexible bigots. Indeed, they have shown much tactical flexibility. They have ably exploited local situations, reached understandings with 'imperialist' as well as neutral states and have made a virtue of retreating before superior pressure. But the present turmoil in China, as Red Guards exalt the ideal of continuous revolution, suggests that zeal in the pursuit of ideological objectives, external as well as internal, is the highest good.

This is a depressing but not hopeless outlook. Mao Tse-tung and his immediate successor may for a time succeed in keeping revolutionary fervour at a high pitch, but at some point dogma and zeal are no longer enough. In a Communist state, as in any other, policies will ultimately be judged by their results. And if the Communists do not succeed in South Vietnam, as we assume will be the case, the present priorities and emphasis in foreign policy should change, at least after Mao's retirement. A Communist failure in South Vietnam could indeed become the Chinese equivalent of the Soviet experience of October 1962 in Cuba, even though the Vietnamese issue might not assume such dramatic form. We should not expect China to abandon the objective of world revolution any more than we would expect the Soviet Union to abandon her ultimate ideological objectives. But Soviet leaders do not appear disposed to run serious risks for the sake of remote ideological goals or to give them a high priority in the allocation of resources.

Much has changed since October 1962 as tacit understandings about the use of force have been reached. Similarly, if China reduces the energy and resources that until now she has been committing to her ideological objectives and pursues them only as long-range goals, and then more from considerations of doctrine than from any sense of conviction, the prospects of reaching a reasonable and durable settlement in Asia might improve.

We can assume that at this point China's basic national interests and objectives as these affect foreign relations would not differ very much from those of a strong and united Chinese state under a non-Communist regime. They would include adequate protection for the nation's frontiers; the expulsion of American and other external military forces from the mainland of Asia and, somewhat less urgently, from the island periphery as well; world recognition of China as the peer of the United States and the Soviet Union; and the predominant voice in Asian affairs.

China's ideological or revolutionary objectives may parallel or further some of the narrower national interests, but they work against others. Ideological considerations were a decisive factor in the break with the Soviet Union, whose economic and technical aid could be of great help to China's own struggling industries. Furthermore, the championship of 'people's war' has brought a powerful American army to China's southern flank, and the quarrel with the Soviet Union may be drawing a large Russian force to its northern borders as well. Despite China's official position, such forces must appear to many Chinese as a threat to China's borders and as a challenge to her ambitions to become the dominant Asian power. And the basically cautious atti-

tude China adopted when confronted with a large American force in Vietnam, despite the bluster, was a humiliating demonstration to the world of the country's considerable military limitations. Such considerations cannot have escaped the notice of many Chinese. Perhaps some of the revisionism denounced by the Red Guards is in fact criticism of a militant foreign policy that has failed to advance or, worse, has worked against, the national interests.

A Chinese state that gave priority to national objectives in her foreign policy would not be easy to live with, and the changed emphasis would not necessarily lead to reduce tensions. Nevertheless, rulers who subordinate ideological considerations presumably are psychologically more capable of adjusting aims to political and strategic realities. In any case, objectives of the kind just listed are not so disturbing that the rest of the world cannot look for some accommodation with China over a period of years. No nation today has designs on China's territory. If conditions in Indochina improve, there will be no need for the indefinite presence of American troops on the mainland of South-East Asia. Although it remains to be seen whether China will become the peer of the United States and the Soviet Union, she is already a great power in many respects. There must be acceptance of her right to play a key role in Asian affairs as long as she leaves her neighbours in peace.

THE AREA OF ACCOMMODATION

Containment of Chinese expansion has been the main theme of American policy towards China since 1950. An extensive system of alliances, including the South-East Asian Treaty, a powerful net of air, naval and logistic bases in the Western Pacific, the deployment of troops not only in Vietnam but elsewhere on the mainland, and the application of vigorous trade controls have all contributed to the containment of Chinese Communism in Asia. So, too, has the strong American opposition to Communist China's admission to the United Nations. The United States' Asian and other allies have generally supported containment as the most effective means of countering an ambitious and expansionist state, even though they criticize some of the means employed. Containment, however, has strict limitations as a long-term policy, and the United States and her allies should be looking for opportunities for reaching some accommodation as a complement to containment. At this point China is in no mood to be receptive to gestures from the United States, as her rejection of American proposals for limited contact has shown. But China is by no means closed to much broader contacts and trade with neighbouring states than exist today. Accommodation, of course, is not appeasement. It implies reciprocity of concessions and a process of adjustment on both sides of ambitions to political realities.

A number of steps might be taken over the years by the United States and her Asian and European allies as a means of reaching accommodation with China. Some could be profitably considered now, whereas others could be considered seriously only after Asian fears of Chinese intentions have greatly subsided. Such steps could include relaxation of some of the trade restrictions that limit China's access to Western markets and sources of supply; gradual moves by Asian states to put their relations with China on a normal basis; the formation of regional groupings led by the stronger Asian powers; increased European and international aid programmes; and a gradual withdrawal of American forces from South-East Asia as the security outlook in that area improves.

Trade restrictions of the kind supported by the United States and some of her allies probably have not had much success as a means of limiting China's economic development. China's development, indeed, has been obstructed less by external economic restrictions than by her own decisions, e.g. the break with the Soviet Union and such follies as the 'Great Leap Forward'. Expanded trade could be a useful if limited means of broadening contact with China. Greater exposure to the outside world, even if it is only commercial, is something China badly needs, and trade with her, within the restrictive limits established by the main Western trading nations, should be encouraged.

Japan's trade with China will probably continue to expand rapidly, despite such limitations as the Japanese Government's refusal to finance long-term commercial credit and some concern about possible dependence on China's raw materials. The trade between the two nations has grown from an insignificant $24 million in 1960 to more than $600 million in 1966. This is a faster rate of growth than that shown by Japan's trade with other partners, but trade with China still accounts for only a quite minor share of Japan's total trade. However, Japan is already China's largest trading partner. As long as this condition continues, it is unlikely that China will be able effectively to exploit Japanese trade for political purposes as she tried to do in 1958, when she stopped her trade with Japan. Indeed, it rather looks as though China were becoming heavily dependent upon her trade with Japan. Restricted as the commercial visits between Japan and China may be, they are increasing with the expansion of trade. About 4,000 Japanese businessmen and technicians visited China in 1965, although the number of Chinese visits to Japan was much smaller and declined somewhat from the previous year.

Putting relations with China on a better basis will prove to be a difficult and touchy thing for many Asian states. But eventually it may be done, even as the West European states have gradually improved their relations with the Soviet Union. This cannot come about very quickly, for mistrust on all sides is deep, and for some Asian countries the whole question of better relations with Communist China is closely tied to the recognition issue. But at some point in the next few years Communist China will probably take a seat in the United Nations despite the still strong opposition to her admission and her own contemptuous attitude towards the Organization. Whatever the drawbacks to China's admission may be, it will mark a step towards ending her semi-isolation and to some extent modify her outlook, just as participation in the affairs of the United Nations has modified every other member's.

REGIONAL SOURCES OF STRENGTH

In a recent article Alastair Buchan, the Director of the Institute for Strategic Studies, argued that a Japanese-Australian-Indian *entente* might form a countervailing force to China and thus provide the basis for an internal Asian power balance. He believed each of the three Asian powers could assume broad regional responsibilities while strengthening its military capability. He also thought that this essentially political approach would permit a limited withdrawal of American forces from

Asia once the Taiwan question was more or less resolved (Taiwan would be regarded as an American responsibility).[1] This is an interesting thesis. A proposal for any formal arrangement among these three powers probably would not find much support at this point, although their close co-operation ought to be encouraged. But the possibility that regional political arrangements under the aegis of Asian powers might develop into a countervailing force against China deserves examination. Any state that attempts to assert regional leadership will face intimidating problems, perhaps the worst of which is the unhappy state of Asian relations at even the regional level; but the approach might hold some promise. It is one that can be undertaken by Asians themselves, and no serious consequences should follow from an unsuccessful attempt.

JAPAN

Japan has been moving only slowly and hesitantly in assuming leadership in Asia, but she has the resources, the wealth and now apparently the inclination to take a leading role. Japan, whose recovery from the shambles of her defeat in 1945 has far exceeded anything that was expected twenty years ago, is today one of the world's richest nations, and her economic future looks better every year. But she owes much of her prosperity to the fact that only slight demands have so far been made on her resources for defence or for aid to the poor countries of Asia. Japan's alliance with the United States has sheltered her considerably from the many shocks of the outside world.

Disputes over foreign policy have had a divisive effect in Japanese politics, and Socialist criticism of the conserva-

1 *Encounter*, December, 1966.

tive governments and the close alliance with the United States have at times brought about internal crises. But unless there is a sharper shift in Japanese internal politics than most observers expect, it is probable that Japan will continue to regard her treaty with the United States as the keystone of her defence. However, she can and must assume a greater role in Asian and world politics if the alliance is to endure for many more years to come. It cannot be imagined that a people as vigorous and talented as the Japanese will be content for much longer to see other nations, even her mighty ally, take the initiative in the affairs of an area in which she should be assuming prime responsibility. Japan indeed could become the strongest power in Asia politically as well as economically. Fortunately, she is not out to challenge Communist China, but is looking for ways of reaching at least a limited accommodation with China through broadened trade relations. The Japanese also assume that they have insights into China's behaviour and thinking that Westerners cannot hope to have and for that reason they are the people best qualified to act as a bridge between China and the Western world. At the same time Japan is moving cautiously to improve her relations with the Soviet Union, and she sees no conflict in her efforts to strengthen her ties with both nations simultaneously. Indeed, she seems to assume that the Soviet Union and Communist China may soon be competing for her favour. Her trade relations with China raise some problems with Taipei, another important trading partner, but in time she should be able to reach some acceptable understanding regarding her trade with all the nations concerned.

Japan's recovery of leadership in Asia can only be built up patiently over a period of many years. As her political influence and strength increase, the suspicion of South Korea and the Philippines may grow correspondingly. The harsh Japanese occupation of the Philippines and the long period of colonization in Korea are not likely to be soon forgotten. Nor should it be overlooked that the American defence agreements with Australia, New Zealand and the Philippines were reached with Japan rather than China as a possible future enemy in mind. On the other hand, Japan's reputation in Thailand, South Vietnam, Indonesia and much of Malaysia does not present a serious political liability.

Japan is only beginning to give serious thought to the long-range implications of her initiatives in economic assistance in Asia. But the Ministerial Conference for Economic Development on economic problems in South-East Asia, held in Tokyo in April 1966 (followed by the agricultural meeting sponsored by Japan in December), could become the basis of a useful economic grouping that in time may assume some political substance. Any regional grouping in which Japan asserts leadership should have an economic rather than a political basis, and this is the approach that Japan is taking. As the Prime Minister, Eisaku Sato, said at the time of the April conference, Japan is 'resolved to engage in positive co-operation for the development of South-East Asian countries'. We have no clear notions yet about the organizational form that this Japanese regional aid will assume, but it could conceivably be something along the lines of the former Organization of European Economic Co-operation (OEEC) and include a large number of states. Japan, as chief donor, could become its leader without arousing serious suspicion of her political ambitions, but an organization of this kind would, if successful, acquire its own political importance. It would not lead the Philippines and South Korea to cut the painter with the United States, but it should encourage them to look more and more to Japan for help. And if Japan out of fear of Chinese power should decide to expand her own military forces, she may be able to allay Asian suspicions by establishing beforehand her readiness to contribute to the economic development of her Asian neighbours.

INDIA AND OTHER ASIAN POWERS

India is still suffering from the shock of her humiliating defeat in 1962 and the war with Pakistan in 1965. This is a state that is deeply disillusioned with the results of its efforts to assert moral and political leadership under Nehru and with the lack of sympathy it found during its quarrel with Pakistan. India's sense of dependence on foreign aid has been made all the more acute by the recent disastrous crop failures. As a consequence, she is turning in on herself and has shown little interest in asserting leadership or responsibility anywhere in Asia except in the areas along her north-east frontiers. But it is unlikely that she will indefinitely be content to play only a secondary role in Asian politics.

Although the expense of strengthening the armed forces has placed a heavy strain on her economy, India at least has the satisfaction of knowing she can rely basically on her own resources for the defence of her territory. Her defences against China are perhaps the most important element in the Asian power balance that is not dependent on American or other external support. Moreover, India through her defence system and her diplomatic efforts is also ensuring the protection of the smaller states. Nepal is today accepting Chinese aid, but its independence is strengthened by the close presence of a strong Indian army. Limited as it is, the regional defence responsibility that India has assumed extends to one of the most exposed areas in Asia.

As time goes on, India may be able to assert some leadership in South-East Asia, perhaps in concert with Japan and Australia. She will become a source of attraction to the small South-East Asian states if it becomes apparent that she has in fact the military strength to resist Chinese encroachments on her frontiers. But if she is to assume some regional responsibility, she cannot take the approach she did under Nehru, when she saw as her main task the defence of the newly won independence of the smaller states against Western interference. This is not much of a concern in South-East Asia today. India must show more readiness to support the South-East Asian states, at least diplomatically, against foreign Communist pressure (as she did in her support of Malaysia in 1965). And this could mean resistance to Hanoi as well as to China.

Close co-operation between India and Japan, if it comes about at all, will develop very slowly. The differences in background, outlook and resources are profound, and the two countries are separated by an enormous distance. Before the Chinese invasion, the Indians rather haughtily regarded the Japanese as an aligned nation with whom they had little in common. But today Indians and Japanese are finding some common ground, and periodic sub-ministerial consultations appear to be useful. India wants Japanese economic and technical help. Both nations are concerned about South-East Asia's future. But if India no longer regards Japan's alliance with the United States as a serious handicap to co-operation, she still distrusts the external powers and may encourage Japan to take a more independent line in Asian affairs. The Japanese at some point might find such prompting useful. The problem of nuclear weapons is also a matter of great interest to both countries.

AUSTRALIA

Despite her strong ties with the United Kingdom and the United States and her past traditions, Australia is becoming increasingly an Asian power. She occupies a huge land mass only a short distance from Indonesia. She holds the largest remaining colony in Asia—North-East New Guinea and Papua—and bears a very heavy responsibility for the colony's future. Australia's relations with most Asian states are good. She retains Commonwealth ties with several of them, has actively supported the Colombo Plan and has developed her own Asian aid programme. Her rapidly developing trade with Japan will probably assume great political importance in the years ahead.

Australia can play a key role in contributing to an Asian power balance. Although her population is small, her resources are impressive by Asian standards, and she can assume modest regional responsibilities. As many Australians will acknowledge, the country's great economic growth since the war should enable her to increase her defence and aid budgets. One rationale for the relatively low defence budgets of the past was that the savings would stimulate development and thus provide a broader base later for heavy military and aid expenditures.

Indonesia, Malaysia and Singapore are the areas of South-East Asia where Australia's regional interests most clearly lie. Thus far Australia has worked closely with the British in shoring up Malaysia's own defences. Presumably she will continue to take an active part in Malaysia's defence, as she did during the 'confrontation' period, even though the British might later reduce their forces in Asia. It would not be in the interest of Australia, the rest of non-Communist Asia or Europe to see the responsibility for Singapore's and Malaysia's security pressed upon the United States.

Although 'confrontation' is now officially ended, Malaysia doubtless has reasons to be concerned about a restless Indonesia that lies only a few miles across the straits. Indonesia's vast internal problems will make her a difficult neighbour under the best of forseeable conditions, but no country is in a better position to work closely and effectively with her than Australia. Good relations between Australia and Indonesia may help prevent another 'confrontation' and also act as a steadying force generally in Indonesian affairs.

Indonesia and Thailand are two other countries whose role as potential regional powers should be considered. Indonesia, which today is gradually recovering from her extended binge under Sukarno and the bloody settling of accounts that followed the attempted Communist coup in the autumn of 1965, is a desperately poor country for all her potential wealth. Furthermore, she is perhaps more a Javanese empire than a nation, and the divisive regionalism that has plagued her in the past will prove to be troublesome for a long time to come.

Indonesia's vast population, her widely scattered island territory, the poverty of Java and the whole pointlessness of her recent history weigh heavily on her. Her new leaders have rejected Sukarno's antics in both internal and foreign politics, but the Indonesians are an intensely proud people who are eager to make Indonesia a leading power in Asia; their ambition may outrun their capabilities indefinitely. Indonesia is far too big to be merely an equal in any local Asian grouping, and yet her own weaknesses and the Malaysian memories of 'confrontation' will make it very difficult for the country to assume leadership of a Malayan grouping. Indonesia may, indeed, prove to be a chronically unstable power. Certainly neither the West nor the Asian states should underrate her problems.

Thailand, a country with a long history as an independent state, has an imperial tradition of her own, and had the French not intervened in Indochina in the nineteenth century, she would probably have absorbed much of Laos and Cambodia. For a long time a backwater of Asian politics, Thailand is today widening her horizons. With her thirty million people, she is rapidly moving away from a subsistence to a diversified economy. A broad educational system, hydro-electric projects and an expanded road network are transforming the country's economy and society. Her oligarchic government is in the Thai tradition, and she enjoys a greater degree of unity than most Asian countries. She has also had more success than others in integrating a large Chinese minority. The current insurgency in the north-east provinces, though serious, is not alarming, and it can probably be brought under control. Thailand has been very sensitive to the pressure of the North Vietnamese troops in Laos, who at times have pushed to the Mekong itself, and to that of her huge Chinese neighbour. She has relied heavily on her special ties with the United States for her security and with American help has been strengthening her own military forces.

Thailand has already asserted some leadership in South-East Asian affairs. She took the lead in 1961 in forming the Association of South-East Asia (ASA),

an informal economic and political grouping of Thailand, Malaysia and the Philippines. With South Korea she is the most active supporter of the newly formed Asian and Pacific Council (see below). The Thais also played a useful role in bringing the confrontation between Malaysia and Indonesia to an end.

Thailand's relations with Cambodia and Laos, however, have not been good; indeed, in the case of Cambodia, they have been a highly disruptive element in Indochinese politics. Thailand is by no means entirely at fault, and she is working now to put her relations with her neighbours on a better footing. But she ought to be making still greater efforts to establish the closest relations with Laos, even though the latter is and should remain a neutralized state. Laos is a weak country occupying a strategic position in Asia and one of vital importance to Thailand. The Lao and the Thais have a similar cultural and ethnic background. But the Lao with some reason deeply distrust the Thais, whom they regard as exploiters. A number of gestures on Thailand's part, e.g. reducing the charges on Laos's overland transport, could do something to encourage the Lao to look more to their Mekong neighbour for support and to dispel some of the excessive distrust.

All regional or Asian-wide organizations have thus far relied chiefly on exchange programmes or aid as the basis for co-operation. Some of these organizational efforts, such as the Colombo Plan, the United Nations Economic Commission (ECAFE) and, more recently, the Asian Development Bank, rely heavily on Western financial support for their projects. The Association of South-East Asia, the Tokyo Conference proposal of April 1966 and the recently concluded Asian and Pacific Council (ASPAC) have thus far been limited to Asian participation and support. The Colombo Plan, which has co-ordinated Commonwealth aid programmes, has been one of the most successful regional and multilateral economic and technical aid programmes in Asia. ECAFE is establishing a habit of limited co-operation among Asian countries and makes available much important statistical data. It is the sponsor of the Asian highway programme and, more important, the huge Mekong development project. The Asian Development Bank, which was formed in 1966 with a subscribed capital of $1,000 million, may be the chief source of funds for major national or regional development projects.

The Association of South-East Asia was formed in 1961 largely through the efforts of Malaya and Thailand. It looked at first for a fairly broad regional association, but the Philippine Republic was the only other government to join it. It has some fairly ambitious common economic projects in mind, such as a jointly owned airline, but it also had a strong regional political orientation. It became moribund as an organization when the Philippines and Malaysia quarrelled over Sabah, an area of Borneo that formed a province of Malaysia. The collapse of confrontation, however, led to its revival, and it may yet move from its present shaky state to something more solid. There have been suggestions that ASA might later be expanded to include Indonesia. This is an approach that may prove to be practicable in the future, but at this point Indonesia would probably be far too much for an untried organization to handle.

ASPAC, an organization formed to further economic and social co-operation, was established largely at Korean initiative. With a membership consisting of Thailand, South Vietnam, Japan, South Korea, Nationalist China,

Australia and New Zealand, it is perhaps too far-ranging to acquire importance as a regional organization. But there is more support for it than was expected, and the Thais in particular are trying to give the organization some substance.

Regional co-operation in South-East Asia has been disappointing so far and we certainly should not even look for development on the model of the European Common Market. But useful if more modest institutions should evolve from the current interest in co-operation. There are several elements that should improve the outlook: President Johnson's offer of 7 April 1965 to provide $1,000 million for South-East Asian development, the growing interest in the development of the Mekong and the likelihood of increased Japanese assistance. A heavy American commitment to regional projects—and the Mekong may be only the most important—may stimulate some closer regional economic ties. The Japanese aid offer at the Tokyo Ministerial Conference of April 1966, as well as the $200 million subscription to the Asian Development Bank, should involve Japan more actively in South-East Asian affairs and prepare the way for her assumption of important regional responsibilities. She should be able to play an important role not only on the mainland of South-East Asia but in Indonesia as well. Here the interests of Japan and those of Australia should converge: it will be to both countries' advantage to help as well as to restrain Indonesia.

EXTERNAL AID

Non-Communist Asia, except for Japan and a few other countries, has been almost as dependent on American economic help as on an American military presence. This is an unhealthy condition, which Western Europe, Japan and even the USSR and the East European states can rectify, for they all have a heavy stake in Asian security. The European countries have enjoyed steadily rising national incomes, and defence expenditures for most of them have not shown a corresponding increase. Some nations are already making generous contributions, but the amount of European aid over the next decade ought to increase greatly. A generous and intelligent European aid programme could become a key element in an Asian power balance, particularly if the remaining European military presence is reduced. Not only would it contribute to the economic health of the shaky economies of many Asian states; by broadening the sources of aid, it might also reduce some of the polarization of Asian politics that has developed from the Chinese-American rivalry. This is something that the Communist Chinese themselves probably would not resist, for it would to some extent reduce the dependence of non-Communist Asia on the United States.

The Lower Mekong cuts across or borders four countries in the most sensitive area of South-East Asia: Laos, Thailand, Cambodia and South Vietnam. Its development, which is being co-ordinated under United Nations auspices, will be a costly programme, heavily dependent on foreign financing. Some of the projects have now been completed or are under construction, but the main ones are still in the study or planning stage. As the projects are completed, they will permit greatly expanded rice production, industrial development and flood control. The United States has offered large sums for the programme, but more than American and World Bank aid is needed. There is no area in Asia where heavy European aid can bring more

promising benefits, for an important international presence associated with the Mekong's development should in time damp down the international conflict that has plagued the area for so many years.

The neutralization of all former French Indochina (and even all South-East Asian mainland states) is an approach towards a broad Asian balance of power that is often suggested, particularly in Europe. But the record of neutralization has not been encouraging. North Vietnam's invasion of South Vietnam and Laos, with the support or at least the acquiescence of China, upset the efforts of the great powers to neutralize Indochina through the agreements reached at Geneva in 1954 and 1962. Nevertheless, the United States has left open the possibility of a neutral or non-aligned South Vietnam. President Johnson's offer at the Manila conference in October 1966 to withdraw American forces from South Vietnam as North Vietnamese support for the Viet Cong subsided leaves the way open to meet a basic condition of neutralization. The United States continues her efforts to make the present nominal neutralization of Laos a reality and is sympathetic to Cambodia's wish to remain neutral. But the United States cannot endorse only a face-saving settlement over Vietnam, whether it is based on neutralization or some other arrangement. And no one should overlook the dangers of concluding agreements that would be as easy to violate as were the Geneva Agreements of 1954 and 1962.

Burma has established what seems to be a satisfactory neutral status, and suggestions for neutralization elsewhere in mainland South-East Asia apply apparently to Thailand. With the example of 'neutral' Laos before it, much of whose territory is today occupied by North Vietnamese troops, Thailand is not likely to exchange her present security arrangements with the United States for the uncertainties of neutralization. It should be noted here that many units of the large North Vietnamese force in Laos are in the northern provinces, a region that has nothing to do with communications between North and South Vietnam. This strong presence in northern Laos therefore gives grounds for much concern about North Vietnam's intentions in Indochina generally. Thailand's disastrous failure to establish herself as a neutralized state just before the outbreak of the Pacific War is also still vivid in Thai memories. But if neutralization should prove to be workable in Indochina over an extended period, Thailand herself might later be prepared to consider neutralization seriously.

The position of the Soviet Union is a further important element affecting the Asian power balance. The Soviet Union's main interests are centred in Europe, but she is deeply concerned with Asian affairs by virtue of geography, her status as a major power and her ideological quarrel with China. Russia, after all, is by far the largest territorial power in Asia, and she has a long boundary with China that in the future may become a source of much political contention and even military concern. The proximity of her Pacific territories to Japan and Japan's increasing power make it likely that her relations with Japan will assume greater importance as time goes on. Moreover, the USSR almost touches the Indian sub-continent, and she has worked steadily over the years to increase her influence in India and Afghanistan, and more recently Pakistan. She also involved herself actively in the politics of Indochina and Indonesia, but gained little for her pains.

The Soviet Union views the Vietnamese war with deep misgivings. She wants to see the Americans suffer a setback, but a serious defeat for the United States would not necessarily further Soviet interests. The Soviet Union today enjoys a special position in Indochina by virtue of her position as a co-chairman of the Geneva Conferences of 1954 and 1962. Despite the treacherous politics of this area, which holds no vital interest for the USSR, she wants to keep that position. She perhaps recognizes that a serious defeat for the United States in Vietnam might mean the end of the Soviet as well as the American presence in Indochina as China staked out the area as her sphere of influence. Furthermore, a serious defeat for the United States could also have the most serious repercussions for the Soviet Union's ideological quarrel with China. All this suggests that the Soviet Union would be pleased to see Hanoi modify its position on negotiations with the United States and South Vietnam and thus bring a messy war to an end before it leads to deeper Soviet involvement.

The Soviet Union's approach to Asia has changed considerably since the confident days of 1955 when Khrushchev and Bulganin started their tour of India. She has learned by now that her interests are not served by provoking unrest in an area where she has no vital concern, but where conflict of any kind might develop into something serious enough to involve her with the United States. She has also learned that the nations of South-East Asia are not easy targets for Communist subversion. It is probably too much to expect that Soviet interest in or concern about South-East Asia over the next decade will reach the point at which the USSR will participate in any multilateral economic assistance programmes such as the Asian Development Bank or ambitious programmes under United Nations sponsorship. But the Soviet Union cannot evade her great power responsibilities in Asia without running the risk of losing her influence in much of the continent. She may, therefore, increase her own Asian aid programmes, particularly for India and Hanoi. And when she can do so, let us hope that she will again use her influence to bring about the kind of constructive settlement she worked for and got at Tashkent in January 1966.

THE AMERICAN PRESENCE

The presence of the vast American military force in the Far East is based formally on various agreements concluded with South Korea, Japan, the Philippines, Nationalist China, Australia and New Zealand, as well as on American obligations arising from the South-East Asia Treaty. These agreements are defensive only. Although, as we noted earlier, not all of them were concluded with a Communist threat in mind, the language has been broad enough to cover a changed situation. In a broader sense, however, the American military position in the Far East is the outgrowth of the Pacific War, the collapse of Japan, the decline of European power in Asia, the threat of Communist aggression and the emergence of new and weak Asian states. American forces today are deployed from South Korea and Japan to South Vietnam and Thailand. Between these points there are American bases in Okinawa, the Philippines and Guam. The Seventh Fleet's operations cover the Western Pacific and the Indian Ocean. But the United States has been a Pacific power for many years. Her forces in the Philippines formed part of that impressive pre-war military power, centred largely on British bases but with Dutch and French positions

as well, that controlled all Asia east of Suez to the islands and mainland of South-East Asia. Today Britain is the only other external power that retains a strong force in Asia. By supporting Malaysia against Indonesian aggressions, she recently played a key role in maintaining security in South-East Asia and could do so again. The British Government has stated its intentions to keep a strong military force in the Far East, but there is growing pressure in Britain to bring about not only a reduction but eventually a withdrawal of British forces in Asia.

The presence of American military power in Asia is both a source of tension and a source of stability or security. Tension is inherent in a power situation in which one of the main elements is expansionist, or is presumed to be, and the others resist it. It is the price that must be paid for security and it is something many nations have learned to live with. At this point many Asian nations, including some that might acknowledge it, see no substitute for the security provided by American military power. As long as China is regarded as a threat, it could not be withdrawn from the Western Pacific area without creating a highly unstable political situation. We noted earlier the lingering Asian suspicions of Japan. Here again American military forces may play an important role. The assurance to Asian states represented by the presence of these forces in the Far East will become more important if Japan strengthens her own military forces and assumes greater regional responsibilities. Indeed, a condition for Asian acceptance of a stronger Japanese role may be the presence of American military power in the Far East for an indefinite period.

Although the United States has alliances with a number of Asian states, she does not see herself as the leader of a grand military coalition. She has asked her allies to contribute military forces and other aid to Vietnam, but she has not proposed a counterpart to the North Atlantic Treaty Organizations as a military instrument for China's containment. She is encouraging many of the Asian states to strengthen their own military forces, for at some point they ought to rely on themselves to a greater degree than they do today for their defence. If the strength of Communist Asian states is formidable, it is not irresistible.

If political arrangements of the type discussed earlier should lead to stronger concentrations of political power along China's periphery and as Asian states improve their military forces, American military power might be reduced. There is nothing eternal about the presence of American troops on the mainland of South-East Asia. Moreover, there is nothing immutable about the strength of the American force on the island bases. We can assume it might eventually be reduced if the political outlook in Asia justified it. There is an analogy here with Western Europe. The reduction of American forces in Europe would not cause the concern today that it would have a few years ago. The fear of Soviet aggression has diminished, and in the prosperous Europe of today the possibility of any state's turning to Communism seems remote. But the withdrawal of American military forces would be quite a different matter, for it would raise the gravest doubts about the American commitment to Europe's defence. Similarly, we can foresee a reduction of American military forces in Asia if the general political outlook improves, but not a move, such as withdrawal of

American forces from the periphery of Asia, that would seriously call into question American defence commitments to Asia.

The war in Vietnam has centred the world's attention on the American might in South-East Asia, but this is only part of the American presence. As President Johnson emphasized in his speech of 12 July 1966, the United States is a Pacific power as well as an Atlantic power and has committed herself to helping Asia as she did to helping Europe. The responsibilities go far beyond military protection.

American economic aid to Asia since the end of the war totals billions of dollars, and aid will continue for an indefinite period. Bringing Asia out of its rut of poverty will be a task for generations to come, and the United States will be taking the lead in pressing the rest of the world to do its part.

COMMUNIST MILITARY STRENGTH

China's chief threat to Asia is the subversive one and this will lose most of its force if the Communist rebellion in South Vietnam fails. China's offensive military capability today is a limited one, although China has shown that she can bring heavy and effective pressure against some countries along her borders. Her Navy and Air Force are too weak to ensure the success of an invasion against her island neighbours or Taiwan. Her ground forces number about 2,250,000 officers and men. She has an Air Force of about 100,000 men and 2,300 aircraft, only a few of which are late models. The Navy has only a limited defence capability, except for a growing submarine force. China's military pressure along the borders of her non-Communist neighbours is limited pretty much to the Indian border and the Himalayan border states, and India can now or should soon be able to meet this pressure without recourse to outside help. China does not seem disposed to place military pressure on Burma, whose neutrality seems to satisfy her, or on Laos, much of which is today burdened by a North Vietnamese occupation. Thailand has no common border with her. China may continue indefinitely a campaign of subversion against Thailand without fear of retaliation, but she would face a serious logistic problem if she invaded Thailand through either Burma or Laos and would certainly find herself at war with the United States. Thailand's position would become dangerous only if the Communists succeeded in gaining control of all Vietnam. All this suggests that the exposed area of South-East Asia will not require an American presence on the mainland once the Vietnamese question is settled. The growing American capability of rapid air deployment of ground troops from peripheral bases and from bases much further back can also justify a later withdrawal. American protection would thus become basically a strategic one.

As China's nuclear capability expands and as she acquires long-range missiles in the next decade, her threat may become more serious. She may then hope to neutralize American military power by threatening American cities. But she has much to learn about the uses of nuclear power. For one thing she will learn that the bomb does not confer the power to act with impunity. She will also learn that the ultimate weapon is almost useless as a means of achieving a limited objective and that she probably cannot use it to achieve a major objective without the grave risk of a war that will bring about her own destruction. The American strategic protection will probably suffice for an indefinite time for any non-nuclear Asian country that feels threatened by China's nuclear weapons. But China's growing nuclear capability may yet bring Japan and India into the nuclear weapons race. In India there is an active debate over the pros and cons of developing weapons. Although Japan does not regard China as the threat to her security that India does, she, too, is showing concern. Both countries clearly have the capability to develop such weapons and a decision by either to take the step could be decisive in persuading the other to do the same.

No one can now do more than suggest possible approaches towards the forming of an Asian power balance. Such a balance will not be reached through some broad understanding between the Soviet Union and the United States, although it cannot be formed without that. And we cannot count on any general settlement between China and the external powers. China may never take this approach, even though we should assume that there will be some accommodation. If an Asian balance is established, it will probably come about only gradually as numerous local political arrangements are worked out and consolidated, as the non-Communist states acquire strength and confidence, as rules of conflict are made, and as more understandings are reached about the use of political and military power. In the meanwhile the most external powers can do is to work to improve the political climate and encourage Asians to play a greater part in their continent's affairs.

SUGGESTIONS FOR FURTHER READING

West Europe

Cerny, Karl H., and Henry W. Briefs, *NATO in Quest of Cohesion*. New York: Frederick A. Praeger, Inc., 1965.

Cleveland, Harold Van B., *The Atlantic Idea and Its European Rivals*. New York: McGraw-Hill Book Company, 1966.

Hassner, Pierre, *Change and Security in Europe. Part I: The Background*. "Adelphi Paper," No. 45. London: The Institute for Strategic Studies, 1968.

————, *Change and Security in Europe. Part II: In Search of a System*. "Adelphi Paper," No. 49. London: The Institutue for Strategic Studies, 1968.

Hoffmann, Stanley, *Gulliver's Troubles: Or the Setting of American Foreign Policy*. New York: McGraw-Hill Book Company, 1968.

Kaiser, Karl, "The US and the EEC in the Atlantic System," *Journal of Common Market Studies*, V (June 1967), 388–425.

Kissinger, Henry A., *The Troubled Partnership: A Reappraisal of the Atlantic Alliance*. New York: McGraw-Hill Book Company, 1965.

Shulman, Marshall D., "Recent Soviet Foreign Policy: Some Patterns in Retrospect," *Journal of International Affairs*, XXII, No. 1 (1968), 26–47.

Stanley, Timothy W., *NATO in Transition: The Future of the Atlantic Alliance*. New York: Frederick A. Praeger, Inc., 1965.

Steel, Ronald, *The End of Alliance: America and the Future of Europe*. New York: The Viking Press, Inc., 1964.

Windsor, Philip, "Nato and European Detente," *The World Today*, XXIII (September, 1967), 361–69.

Latin America

Dinnerstein, Herbert, "Soviet Policy in Latin America," *American Political Science Review*, LXI (March, 1967), 80–91.

Hill, Robert C., "U.S. Policy toward Latin America," *Orbis*, X (Summer, 1966), 390–407.

Johnson, John J., "The U.S. and the Latin American Left Wings," *Yale Review*, LVI (March, 1967), 321–35.

Lee, J. J., "Communist China's Latin American Policy," *Asian Survey*, IV (November, 1964), 1123–34.

Lieuwen, Edwin, *U.S. Policy in Latin America: A Short History*. New York: Frederick A. Praeger, Inc., 1965.

Maderiaga, Salvador de, *Latin America between the Eagle and the Bear*. New York: Frederick A. Praeger, Inc., 1962.

Matthews, Herbert L., ed., *The United States and Latin America*. Englewood Cliffs, N.J.: Prentice-Hall, Inc., 1959.

May, Ernest, "The Alliance for Progress in Historical Perspective," *Foreign Affairs*, XLI (July, 1963), 757–74.

Mecham, J. Lloyd, *A Survey of United States–Latin American Relations*. Boston: Houghton Mifflin Company, 1965.

Poppino, Rollie, *International Communism in Latin America*. London: Free Press of Glencoe, 1964.

Sears, Dudley, "Latin America and U.S. Foreign Policy," *Political Quarterly*, XXXIV (April/June, 1963), 200–10.

Schneider, Ronald M., "The U.S. in Latin America," *Current History*, XLVIII (January, 1965), 1–39.

The Middle East

Adie, W. C., "China's Middle East Strategy," *The World Today*, XXIII (August, 1967), 317–27.

Badeau, John S., *The American Approach to the Arab World*. New York: Harper and Row, Publishers, 1968.

Campbell, John C., *The Middle East in the Muted Cold War*. Denver, Colo.: University of Denver Press, 1964.

Hoagland, John H., Jr., and John B. Teeple, "Regional Stability and Weapons Transfer: The Middle Eastern Case," *Orbis*, IX (Fall, 1965), 714–28.

Khan Rais, "Israel and the Soviet Union," *Orbis*, IX (Winter, 1966), 999–1,012.

Lewis, Bernard, *The Middle East and the West*. New York: Harper and Row, Publishers, 1964.

Masaunat, George S., "Sino-Arab Relations," *Asian Survey*, VI (April, 1966), 216–26.

Rouleau, Eric, "French Policy in the Middle East," *The World Today*, XXIV (May, 1968), 209–17.

Schwadran, Benjamin, "Soviet Posture in the Middle East," *Current History*, LIII (December, 1967), 331–36.

West Africa

Brzezinski, Zbigniew, *Africa and the Communist World*. Stanford, Calif.: Stanford University Press, 1963.

Emerson, Rupert, *Africa and United States Policy*. Englewood Cliffs, N.J.: Prentice-Hall, Inc., 1967.

Gann, L. H., and Peter Duignan, *Burden of Empire: An Appraisal of Western Colonialism in Africa South of the Sahara*. New York: Frederick A. Praeger, Inc., 1967.

Goldschmidt, Walter, ed., *The United States and Africa*, rev. ed. New York: Frederick A. Praeger, Inc., 1963.

Hevi, John, *The Dragon's Embrace: The Chinese Communists and Africa*. New York: Frederick A. Praeger, Inc., 1967.

Little, I. M. D., *Aid to Africa: An Appraisal of U.K. Policy for Aid to Africa South of the Sahara*. London: Overseas Development Institute, 1964.

Morison, David L., *The USSR and Africa*. London: Oxford University Press, 1964.

Okigbo, P. N. C., *Africa and the Common Market*. Evanston, Ill.: Northwestern University Press, 1967.

Stokke, Baard R., *Soviet and East European Trade and Aid in Africa.* New York: Frederick A. Praeger, Inc., 1967.

Skurnik, Walter A. E., "New Motifs in West Africa," *Current History,* XLVIII (April, 1965), 207–12.

Yu, George T., "China's Failure in Africa," *Asian Survey,* VI (August, 1966), 461–68.

"France's African Children," *Round Table,* CCXXI (December, 1965), 29–37.

Southeast Asia

Bell, Coral, *The Asian Balance of Power: A Comparison With European Precedents.* "Adelphi Paper," No. 44. London: The Institute for Strategic Studies, 1968.

Buchan, Alastair, *China and the Peace of Asia.* New York: Frederick A. Praeger, Inc., 1965.

Butwell, Richard, "Southeast Asia: How Important—To Whom?," *Current History,* LII (January, 1967), 1–7.

Chapin, William, "The U.S. and S. E. Asia," *The World Today,* XXIII (August, 1967), 348–54.

Greene, Fred, *U.S. Policy and the Security of Asia.* New York: McGraw-Hill Book Company, 1968.

Hunter, Robert E., and Philip Windsor, "Vietnam and United States Policy in Asia," *International Affairs* (London), XLIV (April, 1968), 202–12.

Kennedy, D. E., *The Security of Southern Asia.* New York: Frederick A. Praeger, Inc., 1965.

Montgomery, John D., *The Politics of Foreign Aid: American Experience in Southeast Asia.* New York: Frederick A. Praeger, Inc., 1962.

Nicholas, H. G., "Vietnam and the Traditions of American Foreign Policy," *International Affairs* (London), XLIV (April, 1968), 189–201.

Reischauer, Edwin O., *Beyond Vietnam: The United States and Asia.* New York: Alfred A. Knopf, Inc., 1967.

Scalapino, R. A., ed., *The Communist Revolution in Asia: Tactics, Goals, and Achievements.* Englewood Cliffs, N.J.: Prentice-Hall, Inc., 1965.

Trager, Frank N., "Pax Asiatica?" *Orbis,* X (Fall, 1966), 673–89.

Zagoria, Donald S., *Vietnam Triangle: Moscow, Hanoi, Peking.* New York: Pegasus Publishers, 1967.

part four

THE
SUBORDINATE SYSTEM
AND
REGIONAL ORGANIZATION

8

TYPES OF REGIONAL ORGANIZATIONS

INTRODUCTION

At the outset of this book we distinguished between the comparative regional international politics approach, which studies the process of international politics within regions, and various other regional approaches, one of which attempts to study regions exclusively in terms of regional organizations. Professor Lynn H. Miller, in the following essay, attempts to apply the categories discussed in this volume to the study of international institutions and to show the relevance of regional organizations for regional international politics. In so doing he uses the concept of security orientation to arrive at a breakdown of regional organizations into three types: cooperative, alliance, and functional. His essay includes a brief discussion of the usefulness of systems analysis in explaining the internal dynamics of regional organizations.

Professor Miller, drawing on Table 8-1, discusses the relationship between the three types of regional organizations and the international politics of particular subordinate systems. He appraises the degree of identity between membership in a regional organization and presence in either a core, a periphery, an entire subordinate system, or even an intrusive system. He then uses the resulting correlations as a basis for analyzing the relationship between the structure of relations of a subordinate system and the strength of regional organizations. He also considers how focusing on these three types of regional organization assists in understanding inter-subordinate system relations.

This article permits the reader to assess how important regional organizations are to regional international relations. In particular, he should explore the interconnections between organizational cohesion and the degree of cooperation or conflict within a subordinate system. He should consider what effect participation in regional organizations has on the roles of specific states within their subordinate systems. He should also take into account how regional organization membership affects the independence of individual states relative to the remainder of the system, and for stronger states how it affects their ability to lead or organize alliances. He should contrast the international organizations that include states from more than one region with those whose members are in a single subordinate system. Finally, he should assess the role of regional organizations in what we called in Chapter I power-oriented and cohesive-oriented relations between subordinate systems. How do regional organizations facilitate or inhibit the activities of intrusive powers within a particular subordinate system, and how do they affect the relations of the members of subordinate systems in culturally and politically related systems? From Professor Miller's article the reader should gain an understanding of the role of regional organizations in international relations both within and among regions.

Lynn H. Miller

REGIONAL ORGANIZATIONS AND SUBORDINATE SYSTEMS

Since this volume is concerned with subordinate international systems, which the editors have distinguished carefully from regional organizations, the inclusion of an article which treats regional organizations may seem unnecessary and even contrary to their avowed purposes. What follows, first of all, is an attempt to indicate the potential relevance of regional organizations to the systemic study of the international relations of regions.[1] An effort is made to bring together here the two worlds of description and analysis based on formal-legal structures, on the one hand, and the more sociologically-oriented approach of the systems theorist, on the other. Second, this article is a partial attempt to consider the factors involved in intersubordinate system relations to the extent that they relate to the activities of regional international organizations. As Cantori and Spiegel have noted, "one of the most significant indices [of intersubordinate system relationships] is the degree of shared participation in international organizations, which may

operate either toward cohesion or toward power."[2] This is to say we may expect the participation of states in intergovernmental organizations to constitute one of the chief vehicles for the conduct of intersubordinate system relations, or for discovering the linkages which exist between subordinate systems.

A number of university level texts on international relations devote a section, usually brief, to a description of the more important regional organizations of the post-World War II period. While such descriptions often supply useful information to the student as to the contexts in which many important international decisions are made, no view of these structures alone permits an assessment of the vast complexities of the political and social process in which legal structures are set. To take an extreme case, a man stranded on a desert isle in 1950, with only a copy of the Charter of the North Atlantic Treaty organization in his pocket, would have no way of predicting, no matter how carefully he read that document, such things as the NATO debates on nuclear strategy that have been a continuing feature of the organization or the disaffection of General de Gaulle from the alliance structure. The analysis and praise of the League of Nations Covenant that was so com-

---

[1] Cantori and Spiegel have noted (Chap. 1, Footnote 3) their own deliberate avoidance of the technical vocabulary of systems theory as used by a number of contemporary political scientists. They also note, however, "the suggestiveness of what we have to say for systems theory in political science." The present essay, too, is meant to be primarily suggestive for systemic analysis of regional organizations, for reasons indicated above.

[2] See above, Chap. 1, p. 38.

mon during the 1920's and 1930's had little bearing upon the problems which beset and ultimately destroyed the League.

In contrast, the more complex, sociologically oriented approaches to the study of international political phenomena, of which the subordinate systems emphasis of the present volume is one example, have attracted the attention and interest of social scientists in recent decades because of their greater sophistication and methodological rigor. Their intelligent use may permit the gradual accumulation of a scientifically verifiable body of knowledge about social and political life out of which eventually might come greater understanding of these phenomena. Different approaches obviously have differing utilities, and must be selected with a view to the kinds of information needed in the problem area to be explored. The very complexity of a systemic approach, with its multiple variables and nearly limitless applicability to any congeries of social processes, may make it appear ill-suited to the interests of legal scholars and others concerned with international institutions. However, there are several reasons for dual attention to formal-legal structures and to trans-national systems and processes. When the subordinate international system is the object of attention, there are reasons also for focusing upon regional international organizations.

Before indicating what those reasons are, it would be useful to consider some of the confusions to be avoided over the term "regional organization."

I. THE CLASSIFICATION OF REGIONAL ORGANIZATIONS

Although international organization is by no means an exclusively contemporary invention, this phenomenon is probably more important today than ever before. Certainly, it is a more complex process today than at any time previously in the nation-state period, if for no other reason than that different kinds of international organizations have multiplied on a vastly greater scale in the last several decades. Since different organizations have very different purposes and memberships, certain basic distinctions must be made before any kind of comparison or generic treatment can be meaningful.

First, it is obvious that a fundamental distinction can be made between the universalistic international organization, the United Nations, and all of the "regional" international organizations.[3] In this connection, the regional organizational category is broad enough to include all limited-member associations, whether or not they are genuinely regional in the sense of comprising states that are geographically proximate. Thus, the Commonwealth, whose members are now scattered throughout the world, can be considered to be as much a regional organization as the Nordic Council, whose membership is limited to the countries within the geographically compact Scandinavian area. What all of these associations have in common is what distinguishes them from the United Nations—an absence of intention to become universalistic or nearly universalistic in scope. Although the reasons for the limited membership of these associations may vary widely, in general it is safe to assume that these reasons are historical

---

[3] It may not be too far-fetched to suggest an analogy between the concepts of dominant and subordinate international systems, on the one hand, and the United Nations and regional organizations, on the other. In both instances, study of the politics of the dominant system or universalistic organization alone tends to ignore, and sometimes distort, the politics of various subordinate systems (regional organizations).

in nature, the product of perceived political, cultural, economic, or military ties.[4]

Yet, even the distinction between the one universalistic organization and the limited-member associations is not as clear-cut as might be supposed, particularly in specific types of international activity. The United Nations system is itself a complex network, and some of its more important work in the area of economic development is carried out in the framework of regional Economic Commissions—for Europe, Latin America, Africa, and Asia and the Far East.[5] Participation in these Commissions is not limited to individuals representing countries within the area, although their purpose is to provide forums that are as efficient as possible for considering the economic problems—often very different from one region to another—of UN member states. The activities of certain UN Economic Commissions clearly may be relevant for certain types of investigation focussing upon subordinate systems, particularly those involving economic interrelationships. It may be found in some instances that they provide (a) an instrument for increasing

the stability or cohesion of the subordinate system (or systems), (b) an avenue for permitting the economic intrusion of the dominant system, or some members of the dominant system, into the area, or (c) a formalized link between the subordinate system and most of the rest of the world system as it is manifested in the United Nations Organization.[6]

The picture is further confused by the existence of numerous UN specialized agencies, whose memberships are not identical with, but approximate, that of the United Nations itself. These agencies all have specific "functional" concerns,[7] in the sense that each is designed to grapple with particular issues—from international postal problems, to health issues, to scientific and artistic projects—which are the common concerns of many states in an age of growing interdependence at many levels. While none of the specialized agencies is a regional organization in the sense that it has a deliberately limited membership, very often some of its activities, like those of ECOSOC's regional economic commissions, have a

---

[4] Thus, the Commonwealth is the product of the mutual experience of its members within the British imperial system; Benelux is almost purely the result of economic imperative for three small and highly developed European states confronted with the great economic competition of larger units in the mid-twentieth century; the Arab League reflects, at least to a limited extent, the common culture of its members; NATO is clearly the product of a commonly perceived security threat to the states of the North Atlantic area.

[5] As is typical in United Nations parlance, these Economic Commissions commonly are referred to by their alphabetic acronyms: ECE, ECLA, ECA, and ECAFE. All are technically under the jurisdiction of one of the principal organs of the United Nations, the Economic and Social Council, or ECOSOC.

[6] There may even be the possibility that the work of such regional commissions may aid in the creation of new regional systems where they have not previously existed. For example, a recent study on the ECE specifically describes it as fundamental to an emerging European system. See Jean Siotis, "ECE in the Emerging European System," *International Conciliation*, No. 561 (January, 1967).

[7] Here the term "functional" is used in the sense employed by David Mitrany and others, to describe international cooperative efforts, particularly on economic and social questions, intended to provide a basis for the ultimate solution of the most divisive political conflicts. For the classic elaboration of the functionalist thesis, see especially Mitrany's *The Progress of International Government* (New Haven: Yale University Press, 1933) and his *A Working Peace System* (London: Royal Institute of International Affairs, 1946).

distinctive impact upon a particular region or subordinate system. Examples might be the World Health Organization's campaign to eradicate the tsetse fly in tropical Africa, UNESCO's drive to save the ancient temples of Luxor from inundation by the Nile above Aswan in Egypt, or various of the technical assistance projects under the direction of the United Nations Development Programme.[8]

Other illustrations of ways in which activities originating in the United Nations system may bear upon the cohesion of subordinate systems no doubt could be found. Perhaps enough has been said, however, to indicate the reason for this brief excursion into some aspects of the UN organization, that is, various processes at work even within the universalistic international organization may relate directly and yet discretely to particular subordinate international systems. As such, they constitute part of the fabric of systemic, although not of regional organizational, analysis. Now we need to turn to the even greater challenge posed to rigorous analysis by the very diverse kinds of limited-member associations which go under the name of regional organizations.

Although many writers have objected to the ambiguous use of the term "regional organization," and some have attempted to make the concept more precise, most statesmen and many observers continue to use the term so loosely as to prevent general agreement upon its precise meaning.[9] As a result,

according to one writer on the subject, "ambiguity of definition has forced regional arrangements to bear a double burden they were never meant to assume. On the one hand, the very looseness of the term has made regional arrangements seem to be little more than a series of treaty structures creating bilaterally assumed obligations within a context limited as to area or as to function. There came, in popular parlance at least, to be a difference of degree, but not of kind, between the treaties and agreements similar to those traditionally signed among states and *organizations* created by a collectivity of states for security, economic, or other purposes."[10] Some have insisted, in the attempt to narrow somewhat the vast category of limited-member associations, that at a minimum a "regional" organization must be associated in some way with a particular geographic region of the world.[11] Others have applied the term to so dispersed an association as the Commonwealth, asserting that "regional" simply connotes a community of interest.[12]

J. Padelford, "Regional Organization and the United Nations," *International Organization*, VIII, 2 (May, 1954), 203–16; Amry Vandenbosch and Willard N. Hogan, *Toward World Order* (New York: McGraw-Hill Book Company, 1963); Ann Van Wynen and A. J. Thomas, Jr., *Non-Intervention: the Law and Its Import in the Americas* (Dallas: S. M. U. Press, 1956); J. Lloyd Mecham, *The United States and Inter-American Security, 1889–1960* (Austin: University of Texas Press, 1961); Peter Calvocoressi, *World Order and New States* (New York: Frederick A. Praeger, Inc., 1962); Edgar S. Furniss, Jr., "A Re-examination of Regional Arrangements," *Journal of International Affairs*, IX, 2 (May, 1955), 79–89.

[10] Furniss, "A Re-examination of Regional Arrangements," p. 81.

[11] Vandenbosch and Hogan, pp. 265–66.

[12] Thomas and Thomas, pp. 177–78.

[8] The UNDP is not a specialized agency of the United Nations, but is under the authority of the General Assembly and ECOSOC. Yet it is functionally oriented and its work is in many respects analogous to that of the specialized agencies.

[9] A sampling of the writers who have attempted definitions might include Norman

This last dispute is perhaps largely irrelevant to a concern with subordinate international systems which, by definition, are composed of states that are geographically proximate. Such concepts as core, periphery, and intrusive system are largely meaningless when applied to the Commonwealth. However, this does not mean that the Commonwealth or any other international association whose members are widely dispersed cannot be analyzed systemically; rather, to the extent that the analytic framework of the subordinate system applies to them at all, they probably must be considered as aggregators of such systems. For example, meetings of Commonwealth prime ministers no doubt constitute unusual opportunities for communication between the leaders of different subordinate systems.

Undoubtedly there are more useful ways to narrow the category of limited-member international organizations than simply by throwing out all those in which geographical proximity of the members is not a factor. A classificatory scheme is needed, based upon the isolation of a pattern variable crucial in all regional organizations. No single such variable—and hence, no single classificatory scheme—is preferable *a priori* to every other such variable. What follows is, therefore, but one possible approach which permits a classification of types of regional organizations.[13]

Three broad types of regional organization can be distinguished on the basis of the single variable of the *security orientation* of component states

as expressed through the organizational structure. We begin by assuming that, within the spectrum of international relations, regional organizations are most likely to come into being among states whose relations already have been marked by at least a modicum of cooperation. It is virtually a contradiction in terms to suggest that limited-member organizations are likely to be produced among states whose relations with each other typically are those of sustained crisis or direct military conflict. But if we are safe in assuming that regional organizations will only arise among states that interrelate on the cooperative side of the spectrum of relations, we still must acknowledge that there are obvious gradations in cooperation among the members of various regional groupings. The security orientation of the grouping gives some indication both of the degree and kind of cooperation perceived by the member states.

"Security orientation" is a broader and more inclusive term than "security capability"; the latter implies the existence of a distinctive military concern (for example, nation-states and traditional military alliances possess some sort of security capability), while the former does not *necessarily* do so. In the broadest sense, all contemporary international organizations are maintained, at least in part, because of a desire of participating states to enhance security through organization. Unless some measure of insecurity were perceived by national actors, there would be little reason for them to organize. Obviously, this insecurity is not always perceived simply in terms of a military threat from outside. It may also relate, for example, to economic instability or to political tension which is scarcely peace-threatening but, nonetheless, re-

---

[13] Note that Cantori and Spiegel, for example, demarcate the subdivisions of subordinate systems on the basic of four pattern variables: (1) nature and level of cohesion, (2) nature of communication, (3) level of power, and (4) structure of relations.

garded as unfortunate and unnecessary. The organizational response, then, to whatever the source of insecurity that is perceived by organizing state actors constitutes that organization's security orientation.

On this basis, several hypothetical orientations are possible. *First,* the organization's structure and practice may be designed to aid in settling disputes among its own members either through the diplomatic process or through more elaborate peacekeeping machinery. *Second,* the organization may be designed to present a common military and, perhaps, diplomatic front against an outside actor or actors. *Third,* both of the above issues may be regarded as irrelevant to the purposes of the organization (perhaps because other organizations with similar memberships respond to them). Hence, the rationale of this third type of organization is to be found in perceptions of what might be called "functional insecurity," that is, in the mutual desire to improve economic relations to deal with other technical problems resulting from proximity and growing interdependence. The functional organization's relationships with other groupings and processes concerned with security capabilities explains its lack of concern with military policy. All existing regional organizations can be classified on the basis of these three kinds of orientation: (1) Cooperative, (2) Alliance, and (3) Functional.

Cooperative. This group includes organizations that combine, to a greater or lesser extent, both the first and second security orientations described above. These are associations which have arisen as the expression of some sort of regional solidarity in the face of the politics of the outside world, and which also possess the machinery, at least in embryo, to control the use of force within their own region. In the most fully developed of these groups, the Organization of American States, the machinery involved permits both (a) the development of a common policy in the face of intervention from outside the organization, and (b) the settlement of disputes among member states. For the other two groupings which fall into this regional type (the Organization of African Unity and the Arab League), the provisions for settlement of inter-member disputes are less fully developed than are those for creating common policies. Characteristic of this type, however, is the fact that they are not alliances in the traditional sense, but are "ostensibly more permanent groups whose professed first aim is to keep the peace within a given area."[14] Their *raison d'etre* springs from territorial unity, which itself may contribute to an ethnic or ideological common ground. Yet, cooperation obviously has not advanced among the members to the point of their pluralistic integration,[15] or there would be no need for organizational machinery designed to facilitate the settlement of disputes in which force is used or threatened.

Alliance. A second group of associations sometimes labelled regional organizations is composed of states bound together by multilateral defense treaties. This category includes many of the

---

[14] Calvocoressi, p. 59.

[15] The term is employed here as defined by Karl W. Deutsch and his associates in *Political Community and the North Atlantic Area* (Princeton: Princeton University Press, 1957), pp. 5–6. A pluralistic security-community is one composed of two or more "sovereign" states, formally independent, whose interrelations are marked by "dependable expectations of 'peaceful change' among its population."

alliances of the postwar world, such as NATO, the Warsaw Pact, ANZUS, SEATO, and CENTO. The only treaty arrangements including a common defense pledge that do not fall within this category, in fact, are those which are bilateral and not multilateral. (These lack the so-called permanent institutions of the multilateral arrangements, such as secretariats, councils, and the like, and generally make no provisions at all for a coordination of military policy prior to outright military involvement with a third power.) As to the multilateral arrangements, it is evident that it is only the second kind of security orientation that is meant to be entailed here.[16] These are "outer-directed" associations which have come into being as the result of a felt threat from a common external enemy, and they do not possess the structures, unless, perhaps, incidentally, to regulate the use of force within the group.

Functional. The third group includes organs of economic and political consultation and action which make no attempt to provide military collaboration. Far more of the extant regional groupings in the world today—groupings which differ from each other in important respects—belong to this type than to the other two. Such organizations as the European Coal and Steel Community, the Common Market, the Nordic Council, have in common their "inner-directedness" as transnational ventures. They either (a) have come into being only after there is reasonable assurance that the participants will be able to resolve their own disputes without resorting to the use of force, or else they (b) are organs of economic or technical cooperation which presum-

ably would fail to function in the unlikely event of overt armed violence among the member states.[17] This type of organization is not concerned with presenting a united military policy to external actors. For these organizations, inter-member security and organizational security *vis-à-vis* external actors is irrelevant to the purposes of the organization. They may be closely associated with other regional associations which direct themselves toward security capability so that they may seem to possess it themselves, but in fact their concerns are not with the regulation of force.[18]

Some such classificatory scheme as this provides the basis for more precise

---

[16] *Supra,* p. 8.

[17] Organizations which might fall into the category of sub-type (a) above would include, in particular, the European Communities, wherein pluralistic integration already has proceeded some distance and the potentiality even exists that with increased integration the grouping will function, for all practical purposes, as a single actor in international affairs. In that event, such a development obviously would transcend the stage of organization, as that term is commonly used, and the analytic framework would have to be altered accordingly.

Sub-type (b) organizations of functional cooperation would include such groupings as the European Free Trade Association, the OECD, and other limited-member associations designed to promote mutual welfare and economic or technical assistance.

[18] For example, the Organization for Economic Cooperation and Development, like its predecessor, the Organization for European Economic Cooperation, "may appropriately be regarded as the framework for North Atlantic Community economic activities" in view of the fact that all NATO members are also members of the OECD. [Ruth D. Lawson, *International Regional Organizations, Constitutional Foundations* (New York: Frederick A. Praeger, Inc., 1962), p. 11.] Yet, the two organizations are constitutionally and functionally distinct, and OECD, as such, lacks the critical variable of the force-controlling potential.

analysis of the regional organizational phenomenon than is possible if the very different kinds of organizations are lumped together for study and generalization.[19] Once such distinctions are made, it is possible to examine particular regional organizations systemically, in terms of inputs, transformation processes, and outputs. Now, however, we need to consider some of the utilities of systemic analysis for the student of regional international organizations. While these are considerations which draw us away from the specific issue of subordinate international systems to some extent, they are meant to suggest an additional, rigorous approach to the study of regional organizations.[20]

[19] The only major international association, sometimes called a regional organization, which is difficult to classify on the basis of the above scheme, is the Commonwealth. It combines some of the characteristics of both the Functional and Cooperative organizations: it does not possess the force-regulating machinery of Cooperative organizations in any formal sense yet, unlike the Functional groups, Commonwealth members do concern themselves with the resolution of disputes among the members, and there is consultation on foreign policy to the extent that there is some unity on certain issues *vis-à-vis* external actors. Moreover, another of the characteristics of Cooperative organizations is lacking in the Commonwealth in the absence of territorial unity.

As the imperial experience which once bound Commonwealth members together continues to recede into the past, we probably may expect lesser, rather than greater, cohesion on political issues within the grouping. The day may soon come, if it has not already arrived, when the Commonwealth will cease to be a meaningful grouping with any discernible impact upon international affairs. Already, most of its states are members of various other regional associations, some of which appear to command their greater allegiance and attention than do the affairs and ties of the Commonwealth.

[20] See note #1, above.

II. SYSTEMS ANALYSIS AND REGIONAL ORGANIZATIONS

First, to state what should be perfectly evident, "systems" and "organizations" are by no means mutually exclusive terms. An organized unit is as much a system as is an integrated community, a biological organism, or world society. That is, all of these phenomena may be conceived of and studied as systems, even though their stability in systemic terms obviously will vary depending upon the amount and kind of cohesion that exists among component structures and functions. The real point is that the term "system" is instrumentally neutral as used in the social sciences: it neither assumes an inevitable growth in cohesion and stability on the part of the processes studied nor does it prescribe for such growth. Thus, within the international arena, it is possible to conceive, in systemic terms, of action taking place entirely within a bloc, at one extreme, and that involving direct military conflict, at the other.[21] In contrast, an organization is a more specific concept, entailing some form of legal structure binding several actors. When the organization in question is a regional international one, as noted earlier, it is most likely that it will be found to exist only at the most cooperative end of the spectrum of relations, that is, among states that interact either in terms of a bloc or an alliance framework.[22] It becomes difficult, if not impossible, to conceive of organizations other than as instruments *for*

[21] See above, Chap. 1, Table 1-2.
[22] *Ibid.* Obviously, on the other hand, a universal international organization such as the United Nations can and does encompass states, some of whose interrelationships are manifested from time to time in terms of the least cooperative categories of the spectrum of relations, those of sustained crisis and direct military confrontation.

something. As the conscious creations of individual men, organizations presumably are brought into being to produce certain results. Significantly, however, any very precise analysis of the organization's progress in achieving specified goals or even in self-maintenance must depend upon techniques other than mere exegesis of its formal-legal structure. It is systemic analysis which is preeminently suited for such a purpose, for while it is instrumentally neutral as an analytic technique, such analysis is specifically designed to permit examination of cohesive and disruptive aspects of social processes conceived as an interrelated unit. Any analyst of particular international organizations, then, would do well to follow the path of systemic analysis since, in general, such an approach is well suited to revealing the political and social development of such organizations.

A second point is to some extent the other side of the same coin. If systemic analysis is useful to the student of regional international organizations, so are many of these organizations potentially important in themselves as objects of systemic analysis. To focus upon regional organizations is to direct attention to certain international developments that are of undoubted importance in the contemporary period. While regional international organizations vary greatly in their viability and importance, the organizational phenomenon is one to be reckoned with in the international arena of today. It is increasingly evident that the traditional Hobbesian model of the international system—as a state of nature in which total anarchy prevails—is no longer fruitful as an explanatory concept for many of the actions that we witness today within the international arena. Much state conduct, not to mention many of the activities of various inter-

national agencies and institutions, is difficult to reconcile with the state of nature concept, in which all actors are "sovereign" nation-states and no political authority exists outside those nation-states. On the other hand, to view the international system in terms of the model of an integrated community is not very helpful. Transnational, integrated communities may indeed exist in the world today, but they quite clearly do not encompass all the world's people.[23]

More specifically, the concept of "organization" may permit practical analysis of a phenomenon which constitutes a sort of half-way house between the state of nature (that is, the absolute sovereignty of component states within the world arena) and the thoroughly integrated world community. It is no longer sufficient to attempt explanations of all international political behavior in terms which view all transnational associations as transitory aberrations from the state of nature, characterized by the war of all against all. Neither is it realistic to view all such transnational undertakings as inevitable first steps down the path to worldwide (or even regional) integration. To discuss regional organization solely from a traditionalist or state oriented point of view, as it relates to the conduct of multilateral diplomacy, to alliance policy, and so forth, is to assume as given what is open to question: that nation-states are to continue indefinitely as the only significant actors in international politics.[24] On the other hand, to ignore inter-member conflict within regional groupings, through analysis

[23] See Deutsch's formulations of "integration," *Political Community and the North Atlantic Area*, pp. 1–10.
[24] See Stanley Hoffmann's critique of Hans Morgenthau on this point, in his *Contemporary Theory in International Relations* (Englewood Cliffs, N.J.: Prentice-Hall, Inc., 1960), p. 36.

concerned only with organizations as integrated actors in the world community, is to assume the existence of a regional community where there may be none. Analysis which accounts for both viewpoints probably must answer ambiguously the question as to which units currently constitute the significant international actors. In some circumstances, state actors remain crucial; in others, it is the regional organizations that act as a unit; in still others, the universal international organization may play a dominant role.

A third general reason for the systemic analysis of regional organizations lies in the increased importance that constitutional analysis can achieve in such a context. Each organization is built upon a constitutional framework, a treaty structure which creates the organization and sets forth its basic goals and operative procedures. It is true that formal-legal analysis of the basic enabling documents of international organizations, when divorced from considerations of political practice, may in fact lead to distortions of political reality rather than accurate perceptions of it. But if the organization in question is examined as a system—which is to say, as an entity of interdependent parts which is developing and evolving or stagnating and disintegrating—it becomes useful to consider its formal constitutional structure as a model to compare to its systemic processes. If this is done, one may expect to learn two kinds of things, both crucial to meaningful political analysis. First, the direction of the organism's growth and evolution from its constitutional "birth" can be plotted with some accuracy (and if, in fact, it is not growing, but dormant, that too, should be ascertainable). Secondly, tools are provided for determining the

relative importance to the particular body politic of practice that conforms to the formalistic demands of the constitutional documents.

The latter is a point that can be of great importance in assessing the relative deference given in differing political groups to authoritative norms and rules. Such analysis may be able to account for at least three kinds of phenomena, all of which must be increasingly explored and understood by social scientists interested in the process of community building at transnational levels. First, such an approach can explore and, perhaps, define differences in personalistic versus legalistic considerations on the part of various groups in their creation and development of authority structures. For example, it may be that the nations of the West, with their traditions of domestic constitutionalism and development of positive international legal standards, would be rather inclined to emphasize formalistic criteria in their international organizational relationships. In contrast, perhaps, the personalism of the Middle Eastern political culture suggests that examination of the organic law of, say, the Arab League cannot permit very confident generalizations about Arab League practice in most areas. Yet this kind of cultural approach to the issue is not the only one involved.

In the second place, an awareness of the relative importance of practice that is "law-abiding" in different regional organizations can permit realistic treatment of the kinds of political relationships that do exist among the states within the organizations. If a particular relationship is clearly one of the overt domination and political control of quasi-sovereign entities by an imperial power, a constitutional organizational document which treats these units as equals is not likely to reveal much of importance about the structures and functions of the grouping. Systems analysis is needed for that. For instance, it has been customary in the West to dismiss the Warsaw Pact as a scrap of paper without genuine relevance to the political realities of the Soviet bloc. Only recently, with the clear loosening of the satellite status of the East European states, has it been suggested in the West that the Warsaw Pact may be evolving into a genuine political coalition somewhat more like NATO than it has been previously.[25] As this development continues, formal-legal analysis of the pact may become more meaningful because more closely related to operative political restraints within the area.

This example leads to the third relevant factor in this regard. The more complex the legal-political "mix" of relationships among member states, the more important formalistic provisions are likely to be as a basis for analyzing political practice. The study of U.S. constitutional law is an important approach to analysis of the American political process at least in part because the complexities of American federalism and separation of powers have forced more important political conflicts in this country into constitutional channels. Similarly, in the Organization of American States, international law has been relied upon strongly as a means of harmonizing the potentially very unharmonious relationships of the American states. The *de jure* equality

and *de facto* inequality of the members combine to make the political-legal status of the members complex in relation to each other, and to encourage reliance upon formalistic approaches to issues—a reliance that is also compatible with the political cultures of these nations.

Undoubtedly, other reasons could be adduced for combining an interest in regional international organizations with systems analysis. Perhaps the point has been made clearly enough, however, that attention now may be directed toward a few generalizations about regional organizations and the subordinate systems of this study.

III. REGIONAL ORGANIZATIONS AND SUBORDINATE SYSTEMS

In this connection it may be useful to reexamine the world's subordinate systems as these are defined by Cantori and Spiegel, in terms of membership by states listed in various regional international organizations.[26] What follows is only a brief overview, intended to indicate some of the kinds of issues which exhaustive treatment of particular organizations and subordinate systems may need to consider. There are, however, at least four kinds of gains which may be derived from such an overview of membership in regional organizations on the part of states which participate in subordinate systems. First, it may permit a more useful classification of regional organizations for purposes of their consideration in systemic analysis. Here, such factors as the relationship between organizational membership and membership in the subordinate system's core,

[25] See especially Thomas W. Wolfe, *Soviet Strategy at the Crossroads* (Cambridge: Harvard University Press, 1964). Chap. 17 treats the development of cooperation on military policy within the Warsaw Pact area.

[26] See Cantori and Spiegel, Table 1-1, "Subordinate Systems of the World and Their Subdivisions," Chap. 1.

Table 8-1   SUBORDINATE SYSTEMS AND REGIONAL ORGANIZATIONAL MEMBER-SHIP

Key:
Cooperative
Arab League: AL
Joint African and Malagasy Organization: OCAM[27]
Organization of American States: OAS
Organization of African Unity: OAU
Alliance
Central Treaty Organization: CENTO
North Atlantic Treaty Organization: NATO
Warsaw Pact: WP
Western European Union: WEU
Southeast Asia Treaty Organization: SEATO
Functional
A.[28]
East African Community: EAC
European Economic Community (Common Market):   EEC
European Coal and Steel Community: ECSC
European Atomic Energy Commission: Euratom
B.[29]
Association of Southeast Asian Nations: ASEAN
Belgium, Netherlands, Luxemburg Union: BENELUX
Conseil de l'Entente: CE
Council for Mutual Economic Assistance: COMECON
European Free Trade Association: EFTA
Guinea-Ghana-Mali Union: UAS (Union of African States)
Latin American Free Trade Association: LAFTA
Central American Common Market: CACM
Organization for Economic Cooperation and Development: OECD
Nordic Council: NC
* = *Peripheral states with core potential*
(Angola) = *Colony*
−Afghanistan− = States which could possibly be members of a second periphery

---

[27] OCAM ("Organisation commune africaine et malgache"), which was founded by thirteen French-speaking states in February, 1965, is intended to operate within the framework of the OAU and to reinforce cooperation among the African states and Madagascar. Its aim is to accelerate the development of these states in the political, economic, social, technical, and cultural spheres.

[28] This is the Functional sub-type wherein the organizations might be described as community-oriented, that is, as intended to eliminate the traditional barriers of state sovereignty in specified, functional areas. For this purpose, supranational authority is the ultimate goal.

[29] This is the Functional sub-type whose organizations are intended to improve functional conditions in such areas as trade and economic development, but without providing a supranational administrative authority in the process.

Table 8-1   (Cont'd)

REGION	CORE	PERIPHERY	INTRUSIVE SYSTEM
Western Europe	France EEC, ECSC, Euratom, NATO OECD, WEU W. Germany EEC, ECSC, Euratom, NATO, OECD, WEU Italy EEC, ECSC, Euratom, NATO, OECD, WEU Belgium EEC, ECSC, Euratom, NATO, OECD, WEU, BENELUX Netherlands EEC, ECSC, Euratom, NATO, OECD, WEU, BENELUX Luxemburg EEC, ECSC, Euratom, NATO OECD, WEU, BENELUX	*U. Kingdom EFTA, NATO, OECD, WEU *Ireland OECD *Switzerland EFTA, OECD *Austria EFTA, OECD Greece NATO, OECD Iceland NATO, OECD, NC –Turkey– NATO, OECD Cyprus *Spain OECD *Portugal EFTA, NATO, OECD *Denmark EFTA, NATO, OECD, NC *Sweden OECD, NC *Norway EFTA, NATO, OECD, NC Malta –Finland– NC, EFTA (Assoc. status)	U.S. NATO, OECD U.S.S.R. Canada[30] NATO, OECD
Eastern Europe	Poland COMECON, WP Czechoslovakia COMECON, WP Hungary COMECON, WP Rumania COMECON, WP Bulgaria COMECON, WP	*Albania[31] *Yugoslavia Finland EFTA E. Germany COMECON, WP	U.S. France W. Germany U.S.S.R. COMECON, WP P.R. China
North America	U.S. NATO, OAS, OECD	–Trinidad and Tobago– OAS	

[30] Canada is not included in the Cantori-Spiegel Table 1-1, but I have done so here, under the heading of "intrusive system" because of Canada's participation in two West European-oriented organizations.

[31] Albania originally was a member of both COMECON and the Warsaw Pact, but has not participated in either for several years.

Table 8-1 (Cont'd)

REGION	CORE	PERIPHERY	INTRUSIVE SYSTEM
	SEATO, (CENTO)[32] Canada NATO, OECD	–Jamaica– –Barbados– OAS –(West Indies Associated States)–	
Latin America	Argentina LAFTA, OAS	*Cuba[33] Trinidad and Tobago OAS	U.S. OAS
	Bolivia LAFTA, OAS	Jamaica Barbados OAS	U.S.S.R. U. Kingdom
	Brazil LAFTA, OAS	Guyana Haiti OAS	Netherlands France
	Chile LAFTA, OAS	(Surinam) (West Indies Associated States)	P. R. China
	Colombia LAFTA, OAS		
	Costa Rica OAS, CACM		
	Dominican Republic OAS		
	Ecuador LAFTA, OAS		
	El Salvador OAS, CACM		
	Guatemala OAS, CACM		
	Honduras OAS, CACM		
	(British Honduras)		
	Mexico LAFTA, OAS		
	Nicaragua OAS, CACM		
	Panama OAS		
	Paraguay LAFTA, OAS		
	Peru LAFTA, OAS		
	Uruguay LAFTA, OAS		
	Venezuela LAFTA, OAS		
East Asia	Peoples Republic of China	*Taiwan North Korea South Korea *Mongolia	U.S. Portugal U. Kingdom U.S.S.R.

32 The United States is not a treaty member of CENTO but is "associated" with it, and has participated fully in its activities.

33 Cuba remains officially a member of the OAS, but the Castro government has been prevented by vote of the members to participate in any of the organization's activities.

Table 8-1   (Cont'd)

REGION	CORE	PERIPHERY	INTRUSIVE SYSTEM
		Japan (Hong Kong) (Macao)	
Southwest Pacific	Australia SEATO New Zealand	(Islands of South Pacific) Western Samoa	U.S. SEATO France[34] U. Kingdom SEATO U.S.S.R. Japan
Southeast Asia	I. Maritime Indonesia ASEAN Malaysia ASEAN Philippines SEATO, ASEAN II. Mainland Laos North Vietnam South Vietnam Cambodia Thailand SEATO, ASEAN	Singapore ASEAN (Territory of New Guinea) (Territory of Portuguese Timor) Burma	P. R. China Japan Portugal Australia SEATO U.S. SEATO France[34] U. Kingdom SEATO U.S.S.R.
South Asia	India	*Ceylon *Nepal *Bhutan *Sikkim Afghanistan Maldive Islands Pakistan SEATO, CENTO –Burma–	U.S. SEATO U.S.S.R. U. Kingdom SEATO, CENTO P. R. China
Middle East	U.A.R. AL Yemen AL S. Arabia AL Kuwait AL Iraq AL Lebanon AL Sudan AL Jordan AL Syria AL	Israel Turkey CENTO Iran CENTO –Afghanistan–	U.S. (CENTO)[32] U.S.S.R. France U. Kingdom CENTO W. Germany P. R. China

[34] France is an original member of SEATO, but has refused to participate in   its activities for several years.

Table 8-1   (Cont'd)

REGION	CORE	PERIPHERY	INTRUSIVE SYSTEM
	S. Yemen AL		
North Africa	Morocco AL, OAU	Mauritania[35] OAU	France U.S.S.R.
	Tunisia AL, OAU	Libya AL, OAU	U.S. P. R. China
	Algeria AL, OAU	(Span. Sahara)	Spain Portugal
		U.A.R.[36] AL, OAU	
		Sudan[37] OAU	
West Africa	Ivory Coast OCAM, OAU, CE	Nigeria OAU	U.S. U.S.S.R.
	Dahomey OCAM, OAU, CE	Liberia OAU	France U. Kingdom
	Guinea UAS, OAU	Sierra Leone OAU	
	Senegal OCAM, OAU	Gambia OAU	
	Upper Volta OCAM, OAU, CE	Ghana UAS, OAU	
	Mali UAS, OAU	(Port. Guinea)	
	Niger OCAM, OAU, CE		
	Togo OCAM, OAU		
Southern Africa	South Africa	Malawi OAU	U.S. U.S.S.R.
	Rhodesia	Malagasy Rep. OCAM, OAU	France U. Kingdom
	(Angola)	Lesotho OAU	
	(Mozambique)		
	(South-West Africa)	Botswana OAU	
		Zambia OAU	
		Swaziland OAU	
		Mauritius	
Central Africa	Congo (Kinshasa) OCAM, OAU	Cent. Afric. Rep. OCAM, OAU	U.S. Belgium
	Rwanda OAU	Chad OCAM, OAU	P. R. China U.S.S.R.

[35] Mauritania was an original member of OCAM, but subsequently withdrew on grounds that its purposes would undermine those of the OAU.

[36] The UAR is not included by Cantori and Spiegel as a part of the North Africa subordinate system. I have included it here, however, because of its membership in the Arab League and the OAU.

[37] The Sudan is not included by Cantori and Spiegel in the North Africa subordinate system. I have included it as a peripheral state because of its membership in the OAU.

Table 8-1   (Cont'd)

REGION	CORE	PERIPHERY	INTRUSIVE SYSTEM
	Burundi	Cameroon	France
	OAU	OCAM, OAU	Spain
		Gabon	
		OCAM, OAU	
		Congo (Brazza.)	
		OCAM, OAU	
		Equatorial Guinea	
		OAU	
East	Uganda	Ethiopia	U.S.
Africa	EAC, OAU	OAU	U.S.S.R.
	Kenya	Somalia	France
	EAC, OAU	OAU	P. R. China
	Tanzania	(French Somali.)	U. Kingdom
	EAC, OAU		

periphery, or intrusive system sectors may reveal certain patterns useful for differentiating types of organizations. Secondly, such an overview may provide the basis for assessing the viability of regional organizations by examining their congruence or noncongruence with the parameters of subordinate systems. Thirdly, and conversely, it may permit an assessment of the viability of the subordinate system in relation to its congruence with particular regional organizations. Fourthly, and most importantly, it provides a graphic point of departure for a consideration of the role of regional organizations in inter-subordinate system relations.

Some twenty-two regional international organizations are included in the following table. This is not an exhaustive listing, but is meant to include important samplings of Cooperative, Alliance, and Functional types.

As previously indicated, this table permits a useful focus at several different levels. The first involves types of regional organizations and the kinds of distinctions among them that may be meaningful for analysis. In this connection, it is clear that only Functional organizations correlate effectively to the membership of subordinate systems. That is, every Functional organization listed (with the exception of Finland's membership in EFTA) possesses a membership exclusively contained within a particular subordinate international system, if core, periphery, and intrusive states all are included. Furthermore, only the "community-oriented" sub-type of Functional grouping[38] is composed of states all of which also constitute the entirety of the subordinate system's core (in West Europe, the members of the three European Communities). In contrast, both Cooperative and Alliance organizations tend to have memberships drawn from more than one subordinate system. Exceptions are the OAS among Cooperative groupings, and NATO and the Warsaw Pact among Alliance organizations, again if members of the intrusive system are included along with periphery and core members. The Arab League contains members included in two subordinate systems (the Middle East and North Africa); the OAU's members are drawn from the five sub-

[38] See above, notes 28 and 29.

ordinate systems of the African continent; CENTO states are included in both the Middle East and South Asia; and SEATO's membership is drawn from states ranging across three subordinate systems (Southwest Pacific, Southeast Asia, and South Asia).

In addition, important members of Alliance organizations generally are to be found within the intrusive system rather than either the core or periphery. This is true of the United States in CENTO, NATO and SEATO, of Britain and France in SEATO, of Britain in CENTO, and of the Soviet Union in the Warsaw Pact.

None of this constitutes a true "test" of the utility of classifying regional organizations as Cooperative, Alliance, or Functional. It at least suggests, however, that differences in the security orientations of the three types may relate directly to the position of member states in core, periphery or intrusive systems. With the addition of more regional organizations and associations than have been included here, it may be possible to distinguish other types, or varieties of types, for purposes of greater precision in the analysis of organizations.

Secondly, what of the viability of regional organizations as suggested by their relative congruence with divisions within and between subordinate systems? It is probably not accidental that the most highly integrated regional groupings in the world today are the European communities, all of whose members together constitute the core of a single subordinate system. In contrast, should we expect the least viable regional organizations to be those whose memberships do not correlate closely with particular subordinate systems? So sweeping a conclusion may not be warranted; yet, when the correlation factor is considered in the light

of differences in organizational type, some tentative conclusions may be possible.

Among Cooperative organizations, the OAS correlates most closely to a single subordinate system, the Arab League is included in two, and the OAU in five. Yet, Cooperative organizations, by definition, are created in part to deal with the peaceful resolution of inter-member conflicts. This may suggest that such groupings are capable, within limits, of containing members from more than one subordinate system. In other words, perhaps the existence of structures within these organizations for the resolution of disputes among the members reflects the fact that those members are not all situated within the core of a single system, but range into the periphery, the intrusive system, and even other systems. On the other hand, it is clear that the OAS has proceeded further in the direction of developing structures for the resolution of inter-member disputes than has either the Arab League or the OAU. Is this explainable in part because of the greater congruence of its membership with a single system than is the case for the other two organizations? It would be interesting to ascertain, for example, the extent to which conflicts within the Arab League tend to produce opposing alignments between the member states of the Maghreb and those of the area nearer the Red Sea.[39] Is there any likelihood of the OAU breaking up or evolving

[39] Tunisia was virtually read out of the Arab League when, several years ago, President Bourguiba called publicly for Arab accommodation with Israel. Both his action and the reaction it provoked within the League may be partially explainable in terms of Tunisia's comparative distance from Israel and relative uninvolvement through the years with the problems of the Israeli presence in the Middle East.

into several Cooperative and Functional organizations, whose membership would correspond more closely to those of the various African subordinate systems? Some such development may, in fact, be taking place in the creation of such infant groupings as the West African Regional Group, the Union of Central African States, and the Organization of Riparian States of the River Senegal.

In Alliance organizations, which theoretically are not concerned with treating issues of inter-member conflict, is a lack of congruence between subordinate system and organizational membership a more ominous sign of ultimate weakness than is the case where similar conditions exist in Cooperative organizations? The experience of the two Alliance groupings whose members are most widely scattered would seem to indicate this. Neither SEATO nor CENTO has shown marked effectiveness as an instrument of multilateral defense. In both, intrusive system members are the only important military powers involved; moreover, even the weaker, "regional" members of these groupings are not confined, in either treaty system, to a single subordinate system. This at least suggests that the interests of the states within the region may be rather different and that, therefore, organizational attempts to achieve a common military policy probably will not proceed very far. NATO is less divided in this respect, which may be another way of suggesting why NATO constituted a rather formidable defense establishment with an elaborate organizational system for a number of years. Yet here, too, the presence of an intrusive power as the most important member clearly has taken its toll (perhaps increasingly in recent years) on organization-wide harmony. As a result, there

is a growing tendency to question the long-range viability of NATO as an arrangement for formulating common defense policy, not to mention common foreign policy generally.

Thirdly, to reverse the viewpoint, what does this table suggest as to the viability of particular subordinate systems on the basis of their congruence with regional organizations? Clearly it would be misleading to suggest that the most stable systems are those with the most regional organizations. To do so would be to ignore the likelihood that imperial or quasi-imperial relationships may exist among certain states within a subordinate system, insuring a large measure of systemic stability even in the absence of formal, transnational structures. It also would ignore the possibility that historical factors and the foreign policy orientations of particular states inhibit their joining together in regional organizations, even though they may be members of relatively stable subordinate systems.[40]

With this in mind, it may be meaningful to explore the relationship between a subordinate system's stability and the number (or kind) of transnational organizations it has generated. A system all of whose core states are members of a Cooperative organization (such as West Africa and the OAU) may be somewhat less stable than one

---

[40] "Historical factors" have inhibited wide participation by the divided nations of Vietnam and Korea in international organizations, although this has been less true at the regional level of the two Germanies. The latter is, no doubt, largely due to the eagerness of states in both West and East Europe to integrate the Germanies as fully as possible into their own systems as an attempt to prevent future German imperialism.

"Foreign policy factors" certainly have inhibited India, and perhaps also the Peoples' Republic of China, from becoming involved in regional organizations.

whose core states are united in a community-oriented Functional grouping (such as West Europe and the European Communities). A subordinate system, some of whose core members belong to organizations that cross systemic boundaries while their relations with other core members are by no means cohesive, should no doubt prove to be rather unstable as a system (as, for example, Southeast Asia).

Moreover, the view of organizational membership presented here may suggest that certain states that have not previously been so considered ought to be regarded as members of particular subordinate systems. Thus, the membership of Sudan and the U. A. R. in the OAU may qualify both states as participants in the periphery of the North Africa subordinate system. Similarly, Canada's participation in both NATO and OECD may suggest a role within the intrusive system of Western Europe. Addition to the table of other regional groupings might suggest other potential participants.[41]

Finally, the table suggests the various roles regional organizations may play in *intersubordinate system relations*. The issue is obviously one ripe for fuller investigation, and only a few observations will be attempted here. It is clear that Cooperative and Alliance, but not Functional, organizations are most relevant to such relations. As we have noted, community-oriented Functional organizations, in particular, are confined to states within the core area of a single subordinate system. This is not to say that community-oriented Functional groupings may not have a considerable impact upon relations with other subordinate systems—by strengthening the grouping's political or economic potential *vis-à-vis* other such systems, for instance. But it is the Cooperative and Alliance organizations which include states from the core, periphery, and intrusive system of a single area, as well as those from more than one subordinate system in certain cases. These are the types of organization that can be expected to play important roles as agents of intersubordinate system relations.

Furthermore, the existence of these latter two types of regional organizations relates in interesting ways to the patterns of intersubordinate system relations described as power-oriented and cohesive-oriented.[42] The three Cooperative organizations—the OAS, the OAU, and the Arab League—all are instrumentalities for the conduct of intersubordinate system relations, since all three combine states from more than one system within the organization. Yet it is only the OAS which is the vehicle for the conduct of power-oriented relations in the Latin American system. Relations between the two systems encompassed within the Arab League and the five systems within the OAU are cohesive-oriented. In other words, none of the relations which occur between intrusive, external systems and either the Middle East or the African subordinate systems are channeled through a Cooperative organizational framework. While U.S. intrusion into the Latin American system historically has been characterized by sporadic tension and conflict, it remains, as manifested in the existence of the OAS, a more thoroughly regularized and accepted intrusion than is characteristic in other power-oriented relations throughout the world.

Clearly, however, some power-

41 For example, Finland is included in the periphery of West Europe by virtue of its participation, with Norway, Sweden, Denmark, and Iceland in the Nordic Council.

42 See the discussion above by Cantori and Spiegel, Chap. 1, pp. 37–39.

oriented relations may be marked by a good deal of harmony even in the absence of a Cooperative organization for the states involved. At present, Soviet intrusion into the Middle East appears to fit such a description. Yet it may be precisely because no institutional arrangements have yet been produced to "legitimize" this or some other intrusive relationship, that the Middle Eastern subordinate system remains the seat of such potentially explosive political rivalries. Thus, the quality of Soviet-Arab relations generally is perceived (at least by other actors) as more *ad hoc* and temporary than, say, U.S.-Latin American relations. One of the functions of Cooperative organizations, in other words, may be to signal potential intruders that existing power-oriented relationships generally are acceptable to all participant states.

But what of the fact that in several instances power-oriented intersubordinate system relations are marked by the existence of Alliance organizations (CENTO in the Middle East, SEATO in three different systems in Asia, NATO in West Europe, and the Warsaw Pact in East Europe)? Because of the fact that these organizations are of a different type, different kinds of problems for intersubordinate system relations are involved. Since Alliance organizations, by definition, do not possess the machinery for the resolution of intermember conflict, they are predicated upon the assumption that dependable expectations of peaceful change already exist among the members. Yet, because of the fact that they lack such machinery, Alliance organizations should not be expected to serve as particularly effective instruments for the conduct of intersubordinate system relations. As the postwar experience with NATO and other such groupings has shown, the existence of such Alliances may increase the level of relationships, yet when the conflicts of interest arise that are inevitable between states in different subordinate systems, Alliance machinery *per se* is not always capable of treating them effectively. In contrast to Cooperative organizations, Alliance groupings are more likely to increase the interrelationships that states of one subordinate system may have with those of another without promoting greater cohesiveness in the quality of those relations in the process.

The long-range effect of such a situation may be to undermine the effectiveness of the coalition as a single actor in the world arena even while intersubordinate system relations increase in scope and number. Among current groupings, this is perhaps most clearly true of SEATO, which is progressively less viable as a military alliance, even while it remains one of the principal vehicles of the power-oriented politics of the United States into the various subordinate systems of Asia. To a lesser extent, this phenomenon also appears to be true of all the other Alliance organizations of the postwar period. An increase in the "amount" of relations— whether cohesive- or power-oriented— among States in an Alliance organization may well create new problems with which a Cooperative organization is better equipped to deal. Moreover, an Alliance organization that is created as the instrumentality for the intrusion of the states of one subordinate system into another, such as SEATO or CENTO, may even prompt the strengthened resistance of rival state actors, thereby increasing rather than ameliorating tensions.

These are but a few of the most obvious questions and issues that can be raised, both about subordinate systems and regional organizations, when analysis proceeds along the lines suggested here. It is hoped that serious future attempts will be made to investigate the conditions involved in the development of social systems at transnational levels. While the mere existence of legal structures at regional levels by no means provides a certain catalyst in this development—as contemporary experience amply proves—neither may such structures safely be ignored in a period when many of them clearly are contributing to the transformation of the international political system.

SUGGESTIONS FOR FURTHER READING

General

Gregg, Robert W., "The UN Regional Economic Commissions and Integration in the Underdeveloped Regions," *International Organization,* XX (Spring, 1966), 208–32.

Miller, Linda B., "Regional Organization and the Regulation of Internal Conflict," *World Politics,* XIX (July, 1967).

Nye, J. S., "Patterns and Catalysts in Regional Integration," *International Organization,* XIX (Autumn, 1965), 870–84.

West Europe

Anderson, Stanley V., *The Nordic Council: A Study of Scandinavian Regionalism.* Seattle: University of Washington Press, 1967.

Aubrey, Henry G., *Atlantic Economic Cooperation: The Case of OECD.* New York: Frederick A. Praeger, Inc., 1966.

Beaufre, Andre, *NATO and Europe.* New York: Alfred A. Knopf, Inc., 1966.

Buchan, Alastair, *NATO in the 1960's: The Implications of Interdependence.* New York: Frederick A. Praeger, Inc., 1963.

Feld, Werner, "National Economic Interest Groups and Policy Formulation in the EEC," *Political Science Quarterly,* LXXXI (September, 1966), 392–411.

Fox, William T. R., and Annette B. Fox, *NATO and the Range of American Force.* New York: Columbia University Press, 1967.

Inglehart, Ronald, "An End to European Integration?" *The American Political Science Review,* LXI (March, 1967), 91–105.

Lindberg, Leon N., "Decision Making and Integration in the European Community," *International Organization,* XIX (Winter, 1965), 56–80.

Osgood, R. E., *NATO: The Entangling Alliance.* Chicago: University of Chicago Press, 1962.

Scheinman, Lawrence, "Euratom: Nuclear Integration in Europe," *International Conciliation,* No. 563 (May, 1967).

Latin America

Claude, Inis L., Jr., "The OAS, the UN, and the United States," *International Conciliation,* No. 547 (March, 1964), 1–67.

Connel-Smith, Gordon, *The Inter-American System.* New York: Oxford University Press, 1966.

———, "The OAS and the Dominican Crisis," *The World Today,* XXI (June, 1965), 229–39.

Fenwick, Charles G., *The Organization of American States: The Inter-American Regional System.* Washington: Pan American Union, 1963.

Haas, Ernst B., "The Uniting of Europe and the Uniting of Latin America," *Journal of Common Market Studies,* V (June, 1967), 315–43.

Montalva, Eduardo Frei, "The Alliance that Lost Its Way," *Foreign Affairs,* XLV (April, 1967), 437–39.

Nye, J. S., "Central American Regional Integration," *International Conciliation,* No. 562 (March, 1967).

Slater, Jerome, *The OAS and United States Foreign Policy.* Columbus: Ohio State University Press, 1967.

Wionczek, Miguel S., "Latin American Free Trade Association," *International Conciliation,* No. 551 (January, 1965), 1–80.

The Middle East

Boutros-Ghali, B. Y., "The Arab League: 1945–1955," *International Conciliation,* No. 498 (May, 1954).

Diab, Muhammed, "The Arab Common Market," *Journal of Common Market Studies,* IV (May, 1966), 238–50.

Khadduri, Majid, "The Arab League as a Regional Arrangement," *American Journal of International Law,* XL (October, 1946), 756–77.

MacDonald, Robert W., *The League of Arab States.* Princeton, N.J.: Princeton University Press, 1965.

Ramazani, Royhollah K., *The Middle East and the European Common Market.* Charlottesville: University of Virginia Press, 1964.

West Africa

Boutros-Ghali, B. Y., "The Addis Ababa Charter," *International Conciliation,* No. 546 (January, 1964), 5–62.

McKeon, Nora, "The African States and the OAU," *International Affairs,* XLII (July, 1966), 390–409.

Mazrui, Ali A., *Towards a Pax Africana: A Study of Ideology and Ambition.* Chicago: University of Chicago Press, 1967 .

Tevoedjre, Albert, *Pan Africanism in Action: An Account of the UAM.* Cambridge Mass.: Harvard University Center for International Affairs, "Occasional Paper," 1965.

Touval, Saadia, "The Organization of African Unity and African Borders," *International Organization,* XXI (Winter, 1966), 102–27.

Southeast Asia

Gordon, Bernard L., "Problems of Regional Cooperation in Southeast Asia," *World Politics,* XVI (January, 1964), 222–53.

Modelski, George, *SEATO: Six Studies.* Melbourne: F. W. Cheshire, 1962.

Schaaf, C. Hart, and Russel Fifield, *The Lower Mekong: Challenge to Cooperation in Asia.* Princeton, N.J.: Princeton University Press, 1963.

Sewell, W. R. Derrick, and F. White Gilbert, "The Lower Mekong," *International Conciliation,* No. 558 (May, 1966), 5–63.

9

CONCLUSION: TYPES OF SUBORDINATE SYSTEMS

We have explored the problems of comparing regional international systems; we have separated the globe into fifteen regions; we have applied four pattern variables to three subdivisions (the core, the periphery, and the intrusive system). We have analyzed, as thoroughly as was possible, each of these subdivisions within five subordinate systems. At this juncture—as our final endeavor—it seems plausible to use the information, techniques, and hypotheses acquired to develop a typology of subordinate systems.

In our examination of subordinate systems, we found vast differences among the five regions we studied and among the other ten to which we (or others) occasionally alluded. There are—among the states which compose regions—great differences of political and economic development, of national unity, of level of power, of culture of politics. Between regions as a whole, we discovered, there are similarly great differences in the homogeneity, complementarity, and compatibility of the members. Each subordinate system contains, as we saw, geographical, social, and political attributes peculiar to itself, but yet we simultaneously found that we could compare the processes and patterns within each to similar dynamics which were taking place in other regional international systems.

In this chapter, we will take our analysis to a slightly higher level of abstraction in an attempt to group together various subordinate systems. Our key instruments here, as before, are the four pattern variables; cohesion, communications, power, and relations. The combination of strong cohesion, communications, power, and cooperation, as we have seen, produce very divergent subordinate systems from those with weak cohesion, poor communications, little power, and great conflict. It is our contention that the manner and degree in which these four factors combine provide a profile of the subordinate system, and we can now proceed to suggest that those with similar profiles can be grouped together for the sake of more distinct analysis. We can also suggest that while a subordinate system as a whole may be rather disjointed, the core sector, taken separately, may indicate very different patterns. Thus, in addition to considering the fifteen subordinate systems, it is worthwhile to consider the various cores as well.

We can suggest four types of subordinate systems (or, in the case of the core, four sectors): integrative, consolidative, cohesive, and coherent. Each type of subordinate system or sector represents a lower level of rank with respect to the four pattern variables: Thus, *integrative systems* have relatively high degrees of cohesion, communications, power, and cooperation, and *coherent systems* are distinguished by comparatively low levels of each. In integrative systems, there is generally at work a process of economic, social, and political integration. This process is lacking in *consolidative systems,* but at least there is an absence of direct military conflict. In *cohesive systems* there is a high element of one of the pattern variables, usually cohesion, but conflict is possible. In coherent systems the minimal elements (a measure of distinctiveness with respect to at least one of the pattern variables) which produce system or sector identification are present, but little more. We proceed now to a more complete discussion of each of these four types of subordinate systems.

Table 9-1   TYPES OF SUBORDINATE SYSTEMS

INTEGRATIVE

Systems	*Cores*
North America	West Europe
The Soviet Union	East Asia (Communist China)
	South Asia (India)

CONSOLIDATIVE

Systems	*Cores*
West Europe	Southwest Pacific
Southwest Pacific	Southern Africa
East Europe	Latin America
	East Europe

COHESIVE

Systems	*Cores*
North Africa	Middle East
Latin America	North Africa
Southern Africa	Maritime Southeast Asia
	West Africa
	East Africa
	Central Africa

COHERENT

Systems	*Cores*
Middle East	Mainland Southeast Asia
South Asia	
East Asia	
West Africa	
East Africa	
Southeast Asia	
Central Africa	

INTEGRATIVE SYSTEMS

The reader may recall that, in Chapter 1, we took *integration* to mean the process of political unification or incorporation. Integration may include the unification of sectors of one nation-state, or the federation of more than one nation-state to form a new whole. In either case, the process of integrating assumes, but proceeds beyond, the absence of military conflict. An integrative system is one in which the component parts are integrated into a single nation-state, the process of integration is occurring among independent political entities, or the interaction among independent sovereignties with respect to political, economic, social, and organizational forces is extremely high. Consequently, an integrative system is not identical with integration, and can include extremely close relationships between particular states which have not formally amalgamated.

As a glance at Table 9-1 will indicate, we have ranked five systems and sectors in this grouping: North America,[1] the Soviet Union, the West European core, the East Asian core (Communist China), and the South Asian core (India). The cohesion, communications, and cooperation between *Canada and the United States* are extremely high. As a consequence, although there is no conscious political movement at work to produce one state, the level of cooperation and interaction between Canada and the United States is so great (compared to other regions) that we can consider these two states to constitute an integrative system. Indeed, it is possible to argue that in terms of social and economic cohesion and communications —abetted by a high level of political and economic development—a greater degree of interaction has been achieved between the U.S. and Canada than within India and Communist China.

The *South Asian (India) and East Asian (China) cores,* are significant for the degree of amalgamation these ancient systems have achieved.[2] It is, of course, possible that at some future point either core might disintegrate and begin to resemble the Arab or Malay cores. But for the present they must be classed as weaker, but remaining, integrative cores.

The one sector of these five which we have studied in detail is the West European core. Stanley Hoffmann has indicated the deficiencies of the integration movement in national terms.[3] Yet, as his analysis and others in this volume have suggested, compared to other cores a pronounced degree of cooperation, cohesion, and communications has been achieved. Even were

[1] For purposes of clarity, we will treat the Anglophonic Caribbean states as part of the Latin American periphery in this analysis.

[2] The integration of these systems is not complete, however. Taiwan (or Nationalist China) remains separated from the mainland; and Pakistan and India were divided at the time of independence.

[3] "Obstinate or obsolete? The Fate of the Nation State and the Case of Western Europe," pp. 73–99, this volume.

the West European integration movement to be arrested and the nation-state to remain an essential element of regional international politics, the degree of integration accomplished thus far allows us to classify this subordinate system as integrative. True, there are obvious differences, ethnically and linguistically; economic complementarity is, with all its progress, still deficient; and Franco-German competition still smolders, although sublimated, stifled, and muffled. Yet, on the positive side, this core has established institutional means of concrete and daily cooperation. It is successful enough, at least economically, that many states in the periphery seek to join. Military conflict is (at least for the present) no longer contemplated; the major bone of contention is the possible future direction of political activities. Thus, while the nation-state appears to be as obstinate as ever, the regional sector is highly developed, its interactions are sophisticated and ameliorative, and its organizations and communications are complicated and variegated. In short, the tendencies expressed in the last 20 years make this core integrative, even though the six states comprising it have not actually integrated and may never do so.

CONSOLIDATIVE SYSTEMS

We have called the second type of subordinate system "consolidative." *Consolidation* was defined, in Chapter 1, as a condition in which nations cease to prepare for war against one another but are not involved in a process of unification. In this type of system or sector there is no direct military conflict among the constituent states, or at least there is an amelioration of conflict; still, the processes of communications and cohesion necessary for movement toward integration are also either totally lacking or in a very rudimentary stage. These systems tend to rank high in more than one pattern variable (obviously including a low level of military conflict) or medium in several variables. As Table 9-1 shows, we have placed seven systems (including sectors) in this grouping: West Europe (the entire subordinate system); East Europe (the core and the system); the Southwest Pacific (the core and the system); the Southern African core; and the Latin American core.

We are dealing here with several diverse regional entities. *The Southwest Pacific and Southern African cores* manifest both a high degree of homogeneity and of common interests, but they have not yet reached the stage of regional amalgamation manifested in the integrative subordinate systems. *The East European core* has been undergoing a profound transformation. Since political cohesion is more crucial here than most, this region's consolidation may be slowly dissolving. The core and the system as a whole are not as consolidated as they were in the late 1940's or even the 1950's. The conflicts between Yugoslavia and Albania, Rumania and Hungary, and liberal Czechoslovakia and East Germany (in 1968) are indicative of the erosion of consolidation. Indeed, were it not for Soviet willingness to use force (including the nominal participation of its East European allies) in the form of the Czechoslovak occupation of August 1968 to maintain political cohesion, this region would be on the verge of developing into two competing *ententes* (Yugoslavia, Rumania, and Czechoslovakia vs. the more orthodox communist states). Thus, the presence and interest of the Soviet Union provides a measure of insurance against too precipitous a decline of consolidative tendencies, at some cost in local flexibility and in the freedom of the East European states.

As we have seen, *West Europe* as a whole is complex and diverse. When the northern periphery grouping and the core are taken together, the system is highly consolidative. Indeed, the primary candidates for membership in the core and for close attachment with it come from this section of the periphery.[4] When the system is taken as a whole, however, and the southern periphery added, the level of consolidation achieved is greatly reduced. Turkey and Greece have, on several occasions, been close to military conflict over Cyprus. Portugal and Spain (joined in 1967 by Greece) are considered by many other West European statesmen as political outcasts because they are dictatorships. Nevertheless, we have tried to show that these states' ties with the core and with various sections of the northern periphery are very strong, though not as strong as between the other core and the northern periphery.

The Latin American core can, without serious question, be considered a consolidative system. There is strong social and organizational cohesion, but little political and economic cohesion. Communications are few, but growing. The distribution of power is diverse but the level of power is gradually rising—especially among the stronger states. There is potential military conflict, but domestic turmoil is currently more significant than international disputes and so there is no warfare. Finally, there is talk of economic integration, but the obstacles to its accomplishment remain at present formidable.

COHESIVE SYSTEMS

In *cohesive systems* there is a high level in one pattern variable or a medium level in at least two. Some form of direct military conflict is possible, and in general these systems have not achieved the level of cohesion, communications, level of power, and cooperation distinctive of consolidative and integrative systems. We have considered several systems and sectors as being cohesive: the cores of the Middle East, maritime Southeast Asia, West

[4] Although Greece and Turkey have already achieved "associated" membership with the Common Market, this relationship does not necessarily lead to full membership. For example, several African countries—especially the Francophonic states—have become loosely associated with the EEC, but they are certainly not candidates for full membership.

Africa, East Africa, and Central Africa, and the regions of North Africa, Latin America, and Southern Africa.

All these systems have some distinguishing characteristics. The Middle East, maritime Southeast Asia, and North Africa (core and system) are socially cohesive. The West, East, and Central African cores each have similar colonial histories—which provide a measure of social cohesion and communication among the elite. The Latin American core is tied to Cuba by social cohesion, and to the remainder of the periphery by organizational cohesion and the effects of similar intrusive hegemonies. In Southern Africa, the black nations of the periphery have economic ties to the core which distinguish them from other African states in their approach to the Southern African core.

We have seen that *the Middle East* contains a very uneven and perhaps contradictory core. The level of social cohesion is very high, of organizational cohesion, moderate; but of economic and political cohesion, low. Communications—via the mass media and among the elite—are only moderate, but power is small and the level of conflict within the core itself very great. This core does not have the cooperative elements present in the Latin American core, even though those cooperative elements are in large part provided by a hegemonic external power. Indeed, the conflict between Cuba and the core may be compared to the progressive-conservative Arab conflict, so that with reference to the structure of relations, Latin America as a whole is more similar to the Arab core than the two cores are to each other.

We pointed out, in Chapter 2, that there were many similarities between the West African and the maritime Southeast Asian cores which, like the Middle East, have not achieved the level of communication, cohesion, power, and cooperation typical of consolidative and integrative systems. In the *West African core,* the consolidating effect of the recent French empire is offset by the memory of competing empires and the reality of conflicting tribes. In the *maritime Southeast Asia core,* the consolidating effect of ancient empire is offset by the recency of diverse colonialisms and the reality of competing nation-states.

COHERENT SYSTEMS

The fourth type of subordinate system may be labeled simply as "coherent." *Coherence* represents the minimum quality of a subordinate system which is diffuse and difficult to delineate. Coherent subordinate systems are distinguished by little cohesion and communications, a low level of power, and usually a high degree of conflict—including frequent resort to military force. The regions which we have considered coherent include Southeast Asia (and the mainland core as well), East Africa, South Asia, East Asia, the Middle East, Central Africa, and West Africa. *In the mainland Southeast Asian core,* as we have pointed out, there is little cohesion of any type;

the level of communications, power, and cooperation is low while that of conflict is high, with respect to both the domestic and regional settings. The system as a whole is even more diffuse. In *West Africa,* the elements of cohesion provided by the French imprint within the core largely dissolve when we consider the system as a whole. In *the Middle East,* the relative cohesion of the Arab core becomes basically blurred when we consider the periphery as well. Taken as one, this system is distinctive for its lack of homogeneity and interaction, although were the conflict between the core and the periphery to be ameliorated it could become a consolidative region, since differences are no greater than in East Europe.

INTRUSIVE POWERS

It is interesting to compare the four types of subordinate systems with the activities of intrusive powers. We find that as we move from integrative to coherent regions, the conflict among the intrusive powers becomes greater. Thus, integrative regions are distinctive for the near absence of competition among external nations. Within North America and the Soviet Union there is no intrusive conflict, for these systems contain the two primary powers. China has shut out intrusion, while India has achieved relatively compatible coexistence. Only in the West European core is there instrusive competition, but a competition muted and oriented by the American superiority. Similarly, in the consolidative systems there is no case of extensive intrusive competition. Indeed, the unilateral abstention of one of the superpowers is more important in these cases than any other pattern.

It is only in the cohesive systems that pronounced competition among intrusive powers begins—and, to be sure, there have been recent examples of intrusive contest and competition in each area. For example, in the Middle Eastern core the Russians and Americans have lined up on opposite sides as Great Britain and France scrambled for mediating roles. In the maritime Southeast Asian core, until 1965, the communist states were aligned in varying degrees with Indonesia; the West with Malaysia and the Philippines. In the West African core the Russians, Chinese, Americans and, most of all, the French have supported individual states as events and fortunes allowed. Only in Latin America did the kind of confrontation more distinctive of coherent regions once occur (the 1962 Cuban missile crisis). It is interesting to note that in the wake of this event there have been no serious and dramatic confrontations in this subordinate system, nor do any appear likely.

In the majority of coherent regions, however, competition between intrusive powers has been exacerbated and often volatile. Although there are plenty of examples of the day-to-day type of great-power competition which occurs in cohesive systems, there are also an ample number of military conflicts and crises (e.g., Vietnam, Arab states vs. Israel, Korea, Taiwan vs.

Communist China). Of the four types of systems, the level of conflict between intrusive powers has been highest in the coherent regions.

Of course, the generally low level of power in the cohesive and coherent regions contributes to the ease with which external powers intrude. Yet, local competition and the lack of regional cohesion—if not also consolidation —facilitates intrusion, as the examples of the more powerful East and South Asian regions suggest. Thus, the nature of the core, of the periphery, and of the dynamic relations between them is closely related to the role played by intrusive powers in a particular subordinate system.

REGIONAL INTERNATIONAL POLITICS :
A SUMMARY

The core, the periphery, the intrusive system, and the four types of subordinate systems that we have defined, should serve as a means of integrating the several parts of this analysis. They help us to see the critically significant roles that regional subordinate systems play in the functioning of the current international system. And they provide a framework that permits us to compare systematically the international political dynamics of the actual regional subordinate systems of today's world. Although we chose to concentrate on five of these actual systems, we have tried to demonstrate that our schema of regional international systems is sufficiently detailed to classify and explain every area of the globe.

Our purpose has been to provide a perspective from which to consider the operations of international politics and a method for understanding the international scene more fully. No one needs to agree precisely with the memberships that we have assigned to particular regions to acknowledge that, overall, our method makes possible systematic comparisons of dynamic political realities. Nor should any proposed subordinate systems be viewed as static entities: their memberships change—especially on their peripheries —as political circumstances change with time.

We believe that our method synthesizes various approaches to the study of both international and comparative politics, and, where it seemed appropriate, we have borrowed also from studies of international organizations; where international integration seemed important, we have applied the insights of studies in that field in our assessment of particular subordinate systems. But most important, we have tried to understand specific events and their causes in particular, actual, subordinate systems. How could we explain the international politics of a locality? How important were political, economic, or social elements? What role did the factors of communications and the level of power of the states play in explaining the dynamics of those politics? What accounted for the cooperation and conflict in a specific area?

And how did these factors join with geography to help define an area? These are the large questions that have been constantly before us.

The task of understanding regional international politics is just beginning. While we know that we have not answered all the interesting questions that are emerging in this field, we hope that our building-block like approach has enabled the reader of the articles collected here to appreciate the dynamic processes of regional politics in a time when the international system is changing from a bipolar to a more globalized form.

APPENDIX: TABLES
TO CHAPTERS 2, 4, AND 6

Table 2-1a CORE SECTOR COHESION

WEST EUROPE

| COUNTRIES | Social | | | MAJOR EXPORTS | Economic | | Political | Organizational |
	ETHNICITY	LANGUAGE	RELIGION		TRADE WITHIN THE COREb (% TOTAL TRADE)	TRADE BETWEENb THE CORE & PERIPHERY	REGIME TYPEc	REGIONAL ORGANIZATIONSd
Belgium	Flemish, Walloon	Flemish (54.5) French (44.5) German (1.0)	Catholic (99) Prot. Jewish	manufactured products (57) medicines & transport equipment (15)	63/57*	14.5/14.5*	R.S.	EEC, Benelux, NATO, Council of Europe, ECSC, EURATOM, OECD, WEU.
France	French, Bretons, Alsatians, Basques	French	RC-(93) Prot.}(7) Jewish}	semifinished (20) consumer goods (15)	42.5/41	16/9	R.S.	EEC, Council of Eur, SEATO, NATO, ECSC, Euratom, OECD, WEU
Italy	Italian, German Sardinian	Italian	RC (99) Prot., Jew	industrial products foodstuffs	41/32.5	20.5/15	R.S.	EEC, Council of Eur, NATO ECSC, OECD, WEU, EURATOM
Luxembourg	French, German	Letzeburghish Fr. & Ger.	RC (98) Prot. (1)	iron & steel (75)	63/57*	14.5/14.5*	R.S.	EEC, Benelux, Council of Europe, NATO, WEU, ECSC, EURATOM, OECD
Netherlands	Dutch (predom.) Frisians	Dutch (some Frisian)	RC (51) Prot. (49)	machinery foodstuffs manufactured goods	55.5/54	21.5/15	R.S.	EEC, Benelux, Council of Eur, NATO, WEU, ECSC, EURATOM, OECD.
West Germany	German	German	Prot. (55) RC (44)	finished goods (85)	36.5/37	31.5/21	R.S.	EEC, Council of Eur, NATO, EURATOM, OECD, WEU.

*Belgium & Luxembourg combined.
aFor Sources see pp. 407-8.
bPercentage of total trade (1966).

cR.S. = Reconciliation System; M.S. = Mobilization;
M.O. = Military Oligarchy; N.S. = Neo-mercantilist Society. See p. 12.
dFor key on organizations see p. 407.

Table 2-1 (Cont'd)

LATIN AMERICA

	Social			Economic		Political	Organizational
COUNTRIES	ETHNICITY	LANGUAGE	RELIGION	EXPORTS	TRADE WITHIN THE CORE[e]	REGIME TYPE	REGIONAL ORGANIZATIONS
Argentina	white (86) Indian (2) mestizo & mulatto (12)	Spanish	RC (99)	cereal-linseed (33) meat (33) wool (8)	16/22.5	M.O.	LAFTA, OAS, AP, DB
Bolivia	Indian (46) mestizo (44) white (10)	Spanish (official) Quechua/Aymara	RC (95)	tin (67) silver (5) antimony	5/12.5	M.O.	OAS, AP, DB LAFTA
Brazil	Indian (3) white (60) negro (15) mestizo (22)	Portuguese elite (Eng. or Fr.) German	RC (93) animism, Buddhism	coffee (44) cotton (6) cocoa, iron, (6) wood	11/16	M.O.	LAFTA, OAS, AP, DB
Chile	mestizo (68) white (30) Indian (2)	Spanish German	RC (95) Shamanism (5)	copper (70) iron (11) nitrates (4)	7/22.5	R.S.	LAFTA, OAS, AP DB
Colombia	mestizo (68) white (26) mulatto(14)	Spanish Indian dial.	RC (96)	coffee (59) petrol (13)	7.5/10.5	R.S.	LAFTA, OAS, AP DB
Costa Rica	mestizo (98) white (2)	Spanish Eng. (mid. classes)	RC (98)	coffee (38) bananas (24)	22.5/19.5	R.S.	ODECA, CACM, OAS, AP, DB,
Ecuador	Indian (48) mestizo (44) white (8)	Spanish (93) Quechua (7)	RC (94)	bananas (47) cocoa (12) coffee (22)	7.5/10.5	R.S.	LAFTA, OAS, AP DB
El Salvador	mestizo (52) Indian (40) white (8)	Spanish Nahvatl (some Indians)	RC (predom.)	coffee (46) cotton (12)	24/32	R.S.	CACM, OAS, AP, DB, ODECA
Guatemala	Indian (54)	Spanish	RC (predom.)	coffee (49)	22.5/23	R.S.	CACM, OAS, AP,

[e]Since trade between the core and periphery is minimal as a percentage of core states' trade, figures were not included here.

Table 2-1 (Cont'd)

	Ethnic	Language	Religion	Exports		Status	Organizations
	white (9) mixed (35)	Indian dialects		cotton (18) bananas (5)			DB, ODECA
Honduras	mestizo (70) white (10) Indian (20)	Spanish (off.) English (widely spoken)	RC (97)	bananas (60) coffee (14) wood (7) cotton (3)	14/23.5	R.S.	CACM, OAS, DB, ODECA
Mexico	Indian (28) mestizo (70) white & negro (2)	Spanish (88) Indian dial (3.6) Spanish & Ind. (7)	RC (96) Prot. (3)	cotton (89) corn (7) coffee (7) sugar (6)	7.5/3	R.S.	LAFTA, OAS, AP, DB
Nicaragua	mestizo (75) white (10) Indian (10) negro (5)	Spanish (96) Indian dialect	RC (predom.)	cotton (41) coffee (16) sesame (7) meat (6)	12/25	N.S.	CACM, OAS, AP, DB, ODECA
Panama	mestizo/mulatto (65) negro (13) white (11) Indian (10)	Spanish (91.8) English (7.8)	RC (93) Prot. (6)	petrol. (29) bananas (50) shrimps (10)	4/25	R.S.	OAS, AP, DB
Paraguay	mestizo (97) Indian (3)	Spanish Guarani (Ind)	RC (state religion)	meat (28) wood (22)	38/22.5	M.O.	LAFTA, OAS, AP, DB
Peru	Indian (50) mestizo (33) white (12)	Spanish (off.) Quechua (31)	RC (95)	fish (24) copper (24) cotton (11)	8/13	M.O.	LAFTA, OAS, AP, DB
Uruguay	mestizo (10) white (88)	Spanish	RC ("majority")	meat (24) wool (45)	14.5/35	R.S.	LAFTA, OAS, AP, DB
Venezuela	mestizo (69) white (17) negro (7) Indian (7)	Spanish	RC ("majority")	petrol. (92)	8.5/3	R.S.	LAFTA, OAS, AP, DB
Dominican Repub.	mixed (65) negro (20) white (15)	Spanish	RC	sugar (56) coffee (15) cocoa (8) tobacco (5)	n.a./n.a.	R.S.	OAS, AP, DB

Table 2-1 (Cont'd)

MIDDLE EAST

	Social				Economic		Political	Organizational
					TRADE WITHIN THE CORE	TRADE BETWEEN THE CORE & PERIPHERY		
COUNTRIES	ETHNICITY	LANGUAGE	RELIGION	MAJOR EXPORTS			REGIME TYPE	REGIONAL ORGANIZATIONS
UAR	Arab	Arabic (98)	Muslim (91) Christian (8)	cotton (55) rice (8)	7.5/5.5	n.a.	M.S.	AL, CM, FI, OAU
Yemen	Arab	Arabic	Muslim	sheep	42.5/77	n.a./n.a.	M.S.	AL, AEU, FI
Saudi Arabia	Arab	Arabic	Muslim	oil (76) petrol. prods. (13)	2.5/3.5	1/n.a.	M.A.	AL, AEU, FI
Kuwait	Arab	Arabic, English	Sunni (Muslim) (54)	oil (97)	3/5.5	.5/2.5	M.A.	AL, AEU, CM, FI
Iraq	Arab (80) Kurdish (20)	Arabic (80) Kurd, Turk, Persian (20)	Sunni (Muslim) (90) Christian	oil (93)	6.5/4.5	2/1	M.S.	AL, AEU, CM, FI
Lebanon	Arab	Arabic, French & English (2nd lang.)	Muslim (50) Christian (50)	vegetables (9) fruit (15) textile (6)	57/13	1.5/4.5	R.S.	AL, FI
Sudan	Arab Nilo-hamitic	Arabic various tribal	Muslim Christian Animism	cotton (49) peanuts (13)	11/4.5	—/—	R.S.	AL
Jordan	Arab	Arabic	Sunni (Muslim) (80)	phosphates (30) tomatoes (18)	44/21	/1	M.A.	AL, AEU, CM, FI
Syria	Arab (predom.) Kurdish	Arabic (91) Kurdish	Sunni (Muslim) (60) Alamites	cotton (43) barley (8)	30.5/11.5	3.5/2	M.S.	AL, AEU, CM
South Yemen	Arab	Arabic English	Muslim	fish	9/28	/13.5	M.S.	AL

Table 2-1 (Cont'd)

WEST AFRICA

	Social				Economic		Political	Organizational
					TRADE WITHIN THE CORE	TRADE BETWEEN THE CORE & PERIPHERY	REGIME TYPE	REGIONAL ORGANIZATIONS
COUNTRIES	ETHNICITY	LANGUAGE	RELIGION	MAJOR EXPORTS				
Ivory Coast	Ashanti (15) Mande (12)	French (off.), Agni, Kru, Malinke, Mande	Animist (65) Muslim (23) Christian (12)	coffee (39) timber (24) cocoa (17)	4.5/2.5	—/—	N.S.	OAU, EEC (assoc.) CE, FZ, OCAM
Dahomey	Fon (29) Adja (9) Bariba (7)	French (off.), Kwa	Animist (predom.)	palm prods (69) cotton (5)	1/4.5	4.5/2	M.O.	OAU, EEC (assoc.), CE, OCAM, FZ
Guinea	Fulani (14) Mande (7) Susu (3)	French (off.), English, Mande, Fulani	Muslim(predom.)	bananas (10) alumina (60)	n.a.	n.a.	M.S.	OAU, FZ
Senegal	Wolof (20) Serer (8) Fulani (9)	Outof (33) French (10) Polar	Muslim (75) Animist, Christian	peanuts (42) peanut oil (36) phosphates (6)	inf./—	—/—	M.S.	OAU, EEC (assoc.), FZ, OCAM
Upper Volta	Mossi (42) Bobo (3) Fulani (3)	French, More, Bambara	Animist (87) Muslim (11)	livestock (58) peanuts (5)	7/18	41/	M.O.	OAU, EEC (assoc.), CE, FZ, OCAM
Mali	Bambara (22) Fulani (10) Senefou (6)	French, Fulani, Bambara, Songnai	Muslim (90) Christian Animist	cotton (24) fish (23) peanuts (11)	64/10.5	24/1	M.S.	OAU, EFC (assoc.), FZ (reentering)
Niger	Hausa (42) Djeima Songhai (20)	French, Arabic, Hausa	Muslim (65) Animist (30)	peanuts (62) livestock (14)	2/8	18/1.5	M.S.	EEC (assoc.), CE, FZ, OAU, OCAM
Togo	Ewe (20) Kubrai (12) Watyi (11)	French, Ewe, Twi	Animist (66) Catholic (20) Muslim 8	cocoa (19) palm kernels (6) phosphates (42) coffee (22)	—/—	1/3.5	M.O.	OAU, EEC (assoc.), FZ, OCAM

Table 2-1   (Cont'd)

SOUTHEAST ASIA

| | | | | | Economic | | Political | Organizational |
| | Social | | | | TRADE WITHIN THE CORE | TRADE BETWEEN THE CORE & PERIPHERY | REGIME TYPE | REGIONAL ORGANIZATIONS |
COUNTRIES	ETHNICITY	LANGUAGE	RELIGION	MAJOR EXPORTS				
Maritime Core:								
Indonesia	Indonesian (88) Chinese (2)	Bahasa Indonesian, English	Muslim (90) Christian (4) Hindu (3)	rubber (31) oil prods. (37)	3.4/inf.	—/—	M.O.	Colombo ASEAN,
Malaysia	Malay (44) Chinese (36) Ind. & Pakist. (11) (mostly Tamils)	Malay English	Muslim (50) Hindu Buddhist, Confu-sionism, Taoist	rubber (38) tin (23) timber (12)	inf.	23/11	M.A.	Commonwealth Colombo, ASEAN, ASPAC
Philippines	Filipinos (99)	Tagalog (37) English (37)	Christian (90) Muslim (5)	sugar (14) coconuts (34) timber (25)	.5/4.3	—/—	R.S.	SEATO, ASEAN, ASPAC
Mainland Core:								
Laos	lowland Lao (66) Vietnamese Chinese	Lao (66) French English	Buddhist (state)	tin (61) resins (11) timber (8)	30/33	—/—	M.A.	Colombo, Mekong
N. Vietnam	Vietnamese (85)	Vietnamese	Buddhist Catholic (9)	cement	n.a.	n.a.	M.S.	
S. Vietnam	Vietnamese (5) Chinese (5)	Vietnamese French & English	Taoism Buddhist, Christian Catholic	rubber (71)	n.a.	n.a.	M.O.	Colombo, Mekong
Cambodia	Khmer (85) Vietnamese (5) Chinese (6)	Khmer (83) French	Buddhist (off.)	rice (63) rubber (22) corn (8)	inf./4.4	—/—	M.A.	Colombo, Mekong
Thailand	Thai (80) Chinese (10)	Thai English/Chinese	Buddhist Spirit Worship	rice (28) rubber (13) tin (9)	11.1/1.3inf./1.3	—/—	M.A.	ASEAN, ASPAC SEATO, Colombo, Mekong

Table 2-2 CORE SECTOR POWER

WEST EUROPE[a]

COUNTRY	POPULATION (THOUSANDS) 1965	GNP ($ THOUSANDS) 1965	ENERGY CONSUMPTION (MILLION METRIC TONS COAL EQUIVALENCY) 1965	TOTAL MILITARY 1967–68	% GNP ON DEFENSE 1967–68	RANKING
		Material		*Military*		*Motivational*
Belgium	9,449	16,740,000	44.32	102,000	2.9	Middle
France	49,450	93,460,000	142.08	520,000	4.4	Secondary
Italy	52,931	56,740,000	84.75	416,000	3.3	Middle
Luxembourg	333	628,000	Incl. w/ Belgium	800	1.3	Micro-state
Netherlands	12,377	18,960,000	39.98	130,000	3.8	Middle
West Germany	59,297	112,200,000	246.59	460,000	3.6	Secondary

LATIN AMERICA

COUNTRY	POPULATION (THOUSANDS)	GNP ($ THOUSANDS)	ENERGY CONSUMPTION (MILLION METRIC TONS COAL EQUIVALENCY)	TOTAL MILITARY	% GNP ON DEFENSE	RANKING
		Material		*Techno-Military*		*Motivational*
Argentina	22,352	16,050,000	29.98	120,000	2.1	Minor
Bolivia	3,698	599,000	0.68	15,000	2.0	Micro-state
Brazil	81,301	21,970,000	28.52	194,000	3.2	Middle
Chile	8,567	4,257,000	9.33	60,000	2.5	Minor
Colombia	17,787	5,103,000	9.62	63,000	1.3	Regional
Costa Rica	1,433	593,000	0.44	1,200 (1962)	0.489 (1962)	Micro-state
Ecuador	4,960	1,128,000	1.08	20,000	2.0	Micro-state
El Salvador	2,929	795,000	0.49	5,000	1.2	Micro-state
Guatemala	4,438	1,410,000	0.81	9,000	0.9	Micro-state
Honduras	2,284	504,000	0.35	4,700	1.2	Micro-state
Mexico	40,913	19,415,000	41.71	68,500	0.8	Minor
Nicaragua	1,655	588,000	0.39	7,100	1.6	Micro-state
Panama	1,246	617,000	1.39	3,400 (1962)	0.269 (1959)	Micro-state
Paraguay	1,927	443,000	0.26	20,200	2.1	Micro-state
Peru	11,650	4,281,000	6.84	55,100	3.1	Regional
Uruguay	2,715	1,555,000	2.49	15,400	1.5	Micro-state
Venezuela	8,722	7,691,000	25.94	30,500	2.2	Regional
Dominican Republic	4,619	960,000	0.70	19,300	3.9	Micro-state

[a] *For sources, see pp. 407–8.*

Table 2-2 (Cont'd)

MIDDLE EAST

	Material			Techno-Military	Motivational	
COUNTRY	POPULATION (THOUSANDS)	GNP ($ THOUSANDS)	ENERGY CONSUMPTION (MILLION METRIC TONS COAL EQUIVALENCY)	TOTAL MILITARY	% GNP ON DEFENSE	RANKING
U.A.R.	30,083	4,700,000	9.2	166,000	11.1	Minor
Yemen	5,000	489,000	0.04	23,000	n.a.	Micro-state
Saudi Arabia	6,000	1,521,000	2.1	36,000	12.1	Regional
Kuwait	467	1,518,000	4.9	n.a.	n.a.	Regional
Iraq	8,261	1,909,000	4.6	82,000	10.5	Regional
Lebanon	2,152	1,120,000	1.6	10,800	4.2	Regional
Sudan	14,148 (1967)	1,387,000	0.9	18,400	4.4	Regional
Jordan	2,016	462,000	0.5	31,800	12.2	Regional[b]
Syria	5,467	1,125,000	1.9	60,500	11.9	Regional
South Yemen	1,250	n.a.	0.5	n.a.	n.a.	Micro-state

WEST AFRICA

	Material			Techno-Military	Motivational	
COUNTRY	POPULATION (THOUSANDS)	GNP ($ THOUSANDS)	ENERGY CONSUMPTION (MILLION METRIC TONS COAL EQUIVALENCY)	TOTAL MILITARY	% GNP ON DEFENSE	RANKING
Ivory Coast	3,835	963,000	.58	4,000	2.5	Regional
Dahomey	2,365	165,000	.07	1,000	0.6	Micro-state
Guinea	3,500	257,000	.34	4,800	3.1	Regional
Senegal	3,490	680,000	.51	2,500	3.7	Regional
Upper Volta	4,858	257,000	.05	1,000	0.6	Micro-state
Mali	4,576	297,000	.09	3,100	2.1	Regional
Niger	3,328	250,000	.04	1,200	1.2	Micro-state
Togo	1,638	156,000	.07	250	0.9	Micro-state

SOUTHEAST ASIA

	Material			Techno-Military	Motivational	
COUNTRY	POPULATION (THOUSANDS)	GNP ($ THOUSANDS)	ENERGY CONSUMPTION (MILLION METRIC TONS COAL EQUIVALENCY)	TOTAL MILITARY	% GNP ON DEFENSE	RANKING
Maritime Core:						
Indonesia	105,500	10,450,000	11.59	357,000	n.a.	Minor
Malaysia	9,400	2,866,000	3.36	32,600	4.3	Minor
Philippines	32,300	5,198,000	6.75	30,500	1.8	Minor
Mainland Core:						
Laos	2,600	173,000	0.09	67,000	6.9	Micro-state
North Vietnam	18,900 (1964)	n.a.	n.a.	421,000	n.a.	Minor
South Vietnam	16,100	1,810,000 (1964)	1.18	325,000	10.5	Regional
Cambodia	6,100	830,000	.28	36,900	5.9	Micro-state
Thailand	31,400	3,854,000	3.37	126,330	2.3	Minor

[b]Were Jordan to lose the West Bank permanently, it would be reduced to a micro-state.

Table 4-1a PERIPHERAL SECTOR COHESION

WEST EUROPE

	Social			Economic			Political	Organizational
	ETHNICITY	LANGUAGE	RELIGION	MAJOR EXPORTS	TRADE WITHIN THE PERIPHERY[b]	TRADE BETWEEN THE PERIPHERY AND CORE[b]	REGIME TYPE[c]	REGIONAL ORGANIZATION[d]
Austria	Austrian (99) Slovenian Croatian Magyar	German (99) Slovene (.5) Hungarian (.5) Croatian	Cath. (94) Prot. (6)	Machinery (20) Iron & steel (13) Textiles (8) Lumber (7) Chemicals (5)	17/21.5	45/59	R.S.	EFTA, C of E, OECD
Denmark	Danish	Danish	Prot. (99)	Meat (25) Machinery (17) Dairy Products (9)	41/42.5	24.5/35	R.S.	Nordic Council, EFTA, C of E, NATO
Great Britain	English, Scotch, Welsh, Irish	English (99)	Prot. (82) Cath. (16) Jews, Muslim	Machinery (43) Chemicals (9) Textiles (5) Iron steel (4)	17.5/19.5	20/18.5	R.S.	EFTA, C of E, NATO, Commonwealth SEATO, OECD, WEU
Iceland	Icelandic	Icelandic	Lutheran (96)	Fish & Fish Products (92)	45/42.5	20.5/22.5	R.S.	Nordic Council, C of E, NATO, OECE C of E, OECD
Ireland	Irish Anglo-Irish	English (73) Gaelic (27)	Cath. (96) Prot. (4)	Livestock (21) Meat (17) Textiles (8)	71.5/58	11/14	R.S.	C of E, NATO, OECD

aFor sources, see pp. 407–8.
bPercentage of total trade exports/imports (1966)
cFor explanations of regime types see p. 12.
dFor key on organizations see p. 407.

Table 4-1 (Cont'd)

Norway	Norwegian (99) Finnish Lapp	Norwegian (99) Finn Lapp	Prot. (99)	Manufactured goods (23) Aluminum (11) Fish (9) Paper (3)	56.5/43.5	24.5/28	R.S.	C of E, NATO, EFTA, OECD, Nordic Council
Sweden	Swede (99) Finnish, Lapp	Swedish (99) Finn, Lapp	Prot. (99)	Machinery (36) Wood pulp (11) Paper (9)	45/43	30.5/36	R.S.	Nordic Council, EFTA, C of E, OECD
Switzerland	German, French, Italian	German (74) French (20) Italian (4)	Prot. (53) Cath. (46)	Machinery (30) Watches (14) Chemicals (20) Textiles (8)	23.5/17	38/60.5	R.S.	EFTA, C of E, OECD
Cyprus	Greek (79) Turk (18) Armenian Maronite (4)	Greek (80) Turk (20) English	Orthodox (80) Muslim (19)	Potatoes (12) Copper concentrates (31) Oranges (8) Iron Pyrites (7)	47.5/44	29/28.5	R.S.	C of E, Commonwealth
Greece	Greeks (93) Turk (4) Macedonian	Greek (98)	Orthodox (97) Muslim	Tobacco (27) Dried fruit (11) Fresh fruit (6) Cotton (7)	14.5/21	35.5/41	M.O.	C of E, NATO, OECD
Malta	Jewish Maltese	Maltese	Catholic	Petrol. products (11) Textiles (26) Clothing (11) Vegetables (6)	45.5/45	16/27	R.S.	C of E, Commonwealth
Portugal	Portuguese	Portuguese	Catholic	Fish (7) Textiles (20) Cork (9) Wine (7)	33.5/28.5	20/34.5	N.S.	EFTA, C of E, OECD, NATO
Spain	Castilian Galician Andalusian Basque Catalan	Spanish Castilian Basque	R.C. (99) Prot., Jew	Citrus fruit (12) Ships & boats (7) Chemicals (6) Elect. machines (5)	21/19	33.5/37.5	N.S.	OECD

Table 4-1 (Cont'd)

LATIN AMERICA

COUNTRY	ETHNICITY	LANGUAGE	RELIGION	MAJOR EXPORTS	TRADE WITHIN THE PERIPHERY	TRADE BETWEEN THE PERIPHERY AND CORE	REGIME TYPE	REGIONAL ORGANIZATION
Barbados	African & Mixed (88) European & Asiatic Indian (12)	English	Anglican (70) Meth. & Morav. (30)	Sugar (70) Molasses (9) Rum (6)	3/5.5	—/10.5	R.S.	OAS, Commonwealth
Cuba	White (73) Negro (12) Mestizo (15)	Spanish	R.C.	Sugar (88)	0/0	inf./1	M.S.	OAS (Suspended)
Guyana	East Indian (50) African (33)	English (off.)	Christian, Hindu, Muslim	Sugar (30) Bauxite (23) Rice (13) Alumina (17)	11.5/11.5	.5/—	R.S.	Commonwealth
Jamaica	African (90)	English	Prot., R.C.	Bauxite (23) Sugar (22) Alumina (24) Bananas (8)	1/1	.5/7	R.S.	Commonwealth
Trinidad & Tobago	Negro (60) Asiatic Indian (35)	English (off.) Creole	R.C. (30) Prot. (27) Hindu (20) Muslim (6)	Petrol. (79) Sugar Chemicals	4/1.5	2/38	R.S.	OAS, AP, DB, Commonwealth
Haiti	Negro (95) Mulatto (5)	French (off.) Creole (80)	R.C. (state) Prot., Voodoo	Coffee (55) Sugar (7)	n.a.	n.a.	N.S.	OAS, AP, DB

Table 4-1 (Cont'd)

MIDDLE EAST

COUNTRY	ETHNICITY	LANGUAGE	RELIGION	MAJOR EXPORTS	TRADE WITHIN THE PERIPHERY	TRADE BETWEEN THE PERIPHERY AND CORE	REGIME TYPE	REGIONAL ORGANIZATION
Israel	Jewish (89) Arabic (10)	Hebrew (90) Arabic (10)	Jewish (89) Muslim (8) Christian (2)	Citrus fruits (18) Diamonds (38) Textiles (9)	3/1	0/0	R.S.	None
Turkey	Turkish(predom.) Kurdish Greek Arabic	Turkish (91)	Muslim	Cotton (26) Tobacco (22) Hazel nuts (11) Raisins (5)	2/1	5/5	R.S.	CENTO, C of E, EEC, NATO, OECD
Iran	Iranian, Kurdish, Azerbaijan	Farsi Azari	Muslim	Petroleum (88)	.33/.5	6/2	M.A.	Colombo, CENTO
WEST AFRICA								
Nigeria	Yoruba (23) Ibo (12) Hausa (12)	English (off.) Hausa, Yoruba, Ibo.	Muslim, Christian, Animist	Peanuts (18) Palm kernels (12) Crudeoil (32) Cocoa (10)	.5/inf.	.5/inf.	M.O.	OAU, Commonwealth
Liberia	Vai, Kru, Golas Kpelle	English (20) Vai, Bassa Lorma	Prot. (most) R.C. Animists	Rubber (20) Iron ore (69)	n.a.	n.a.	R.S.	OAU
Sierra Leone	Mende Temme } (60)	English (off.) Hausu Mende Temme	Animists (mostly) Christian, Muslim	Palm kernels (8) Coffee (6) Diamonds (53) Iron ore (17)	n.a.	n.a.	M.O.	OAU, Commonwealth

404

Table 4-1 (Cont'd)

WEST AFRICA

COUNTRY	ETHNICITY	LANGUAGE	RELIGION	MAJOR EXPORTS	TRADE WITHIN THE PERIPHERY	TRADE BETWEEN THE PERIPHERY AND CORE	REGIME TYPE	REGIONAL ORGANIZATION
Gambia	Manding (38) Fula (13) Wolof (12)	English (off.) Wolof, Fula, Mandinga	Muslim (50) Animist Christian	Peanuts (49) Peanut prod. (45)	n.a.	n.a.	R.S.	OAU, Commonwealth
Ghana	Twi, Fanti, Ashanti	English, Twi, Ewe, Ga	Animist Christian (41) Muslim (12)	Cocoa (59) Timber (12) Manganese (7) Diamond (6)	1/1	1/2.5	M.O.	OAU, Commonwealth

SOUTHEAST ASIA

Mainland Periphery

COUNTRY	ETHNICITY	LANGUAGE	RELIGION	MAJOR EXPORTS	TRADE WITHIN THE PERIPHERY	TRADE BETWEEN THE PERIPHERY AND CORE	REGIME TYPE	REGIONAL ORGANIZATION
Burma	Burmese (75) Karen (12) Kayan	Burmese (80)	Buddhist (75) Animists, Muslim, Hindu, Christian	Rice (61) Teak (13)	—/—	inf./.8	M.O.	Colombo

Maritime Periphery

COUNTRY	ETHNICITY	LANGUAGE	RELIGION	MAJOR EXPORTS	TRADE WITHIN THE PERIPHERY	TRADE BETWEEN THE PERIPHERY AND CORE	REGIME TYPE	REGIONAL ORGANIZATION
Singapore	Chinese (80) Malay (12) Indian (7)	4 official langs.: Malay, English, Mandarin Chinese, Tamil	Buddhism, Muslim	Rubber (23) Petroleum (12)	—/—	32/23	R.S.	Colombo, ASEAN, Commonwealth

405

Table 4-2[a] PERIPHERAL SECTOR POWER

WEST EUROPE

	POPULA-TION (000's) (1965)	GNP ($000's) (1965)	ENERGY CONSUMED (MILL, METRIC, TONS, EQUIV.) (1965)	TOTAL MILITARY (1967–68)	% GNP DEFENSE (1967–68)	RANKING
	Material			*Military*	*Motivational*	
Great Britain	54,595	99,180,000	282.1	429,000	6.4	Secondary
Ireland	2,876	2,805,000	6.56	14,600	1.4	Regional
Switzerland	5,945	13,930,000	15.86	31,000	2.5	Middle
Austria	7,555	9,190,000	19.08	21,000	1.6	Minor
Greece	8,551	5,550,000	6.7	158,000	3.4	Regional
Iceland	192	475,000	.76	—	—	Micro-state
Cyprus	594	417,000	.5	n.a.	n.a.	Micro-state
Spain	31,604	21,750,000	32.47	275,000	2.2	Middle
Portugal	9,199	3,740,000	4.8	148,500	5.7	Middle
Denmark	4,758	9,990,000	19.9	45,500	2.6	Minor
Sweden	7,734	19,320,000	34.9	82,200	4.5	Middle
Norway	3,273	7,000,000	13.4	35,000	3.6	Minor
Malta	319	319,000	.23	—	—	Micro-state

LATIN AMERICA

Barbados	244	97,000 (1964)	.10	250[66]	n.a.	Micro-state
Cuba	7,631	2,800,000	7.25	121,000	7.2	Minor
Guyana	646	193,000	n.a.	1,000	2.1	Micro-state
Jamaica	1,788	873,000	1.59	1,500	0.6	Micro-state
Trinidad and Tobago	975	639,000	3.39	1,000	0.4	Micro-state
Haiti	4,660	327,000	0.15	5,500	2.1	Micro-state

MIDDLE EAST

Israel	2,580	3,397,000	3.96	71,000	12.2	Minor
Turkey	31,391	8,123,000	10.35	482,000	4.3	Minor
Iran	25,781	5,933,000	8.83	180,000	3.6	Minor

WEST AFRICA

Nigeria	57,500	4,852,000	18.46	54,000*	n.a.	Minor
Liberia	1,070	213,000	.28	3,200	1.8	Micro-state
Sierra Leone	2,290	344,000	.16	1,850 (1965)	1.2 (1965)	Micro-state
Gambia	330	28,000	.01	n.a.	n.a.	Micro-state
Ghana	7,740	1,743,000	.81	16,000	2.5	Minor

SOUTHEAST ASIA

Maritime Periphery: Singapore	1,913[66]	1,062,000	1.08	n.a.	n.a.	Regional
Mainland Periphery: Burma	25,200[67]	1,760,000	1.15	139,200	6.4	Regional

aFor sources, see pp. 407–8.
*Excludes Biafra

ORGANIZATION KEY

AEU—Council of Arab Economic Unity
AL—Arab League
AP—Inter American Common Alliance for Progress
ASEAN—Association of Southeast Asian Nations
ASPAC—Asian & Pacific Council
BENELUX—Belgium-Netherlands-Luxembourg
CACM—Central American Common Market
CE—Conseil de l'Entente
CENTO—Central Treaty Organization
CM—Arab Common Market
COLOMBO PLAN—Colombo Plan for Cooperative Economic Development in South & Southeast Asia
COMMONWEALTH
COUNCIL OF EUROPE (C of E)
DB—Inter-American Development Bank
ECSC—European Coal & Steel Community
EEC—European Economic Community
EFTA—European Free Trade Association
EURATOM—European Atomic Energy Community
FI—Arab Financial Institute
FZ—Franc Zone
LAFTA—Latin American Free Trade Association
MEKONG—Mekong Development Committee
NATO—North Atlantic Treaty Organization
NORDIC COUNCIL
OAS—Organization of American States
OAU—Organization of African Unity
OCAM—Organisation Commune Africaine et Malgache
ODECA—Organization of Central American States
OECD—Organization for Economic Cooperation and Development
SEATO—Southeast Asia Treaty Organization
WEU—Western European Union

SOURCES FOR STATISTICS ON CORE AND PERIPHERAL SECTORS (TABLES 2-1, 2-2, 4-1, 4-2)

Agency for International Development. *Proposed Economic Assistance Programs, 1967.* Washington, D.C.: Agency for International Development, 1966. (Major Exports, Population)

———, Statistics & Reports Division—Office of Program Coordinator. *Estimates of GNP.* Washington, D.C.: Agency for International Development, February 6, 1967. (GNP)

Coward, H. Robert. *Military Technology in Developing Countries.* (Cambridge, Mass.: Massachusetts Institute of Technology, 1964. (GNP, Total Military, Percentage GNP on Defense)

de Blij, Harm. *A Geography of Sub-Saharan Africa.* Chicago: Rand McNally & Co., 1964. (Major Exports)

Europa Yearbook—1967, Vols. I & II. London: Europa Publications, Ltd., 1967. (Religion, Regional Organizations, Population, Ethnicity, Language, GNP, Energy Consumption, Major Exports, Total Military)

Howard, Michael and Robert Hunter. *Israel and the Arab World: the Crisis of 1967.* London: Institute for Strategic Studies, 1967. Adelphi Papers, No. 41. (Total military)

Hunter, Guy. *South-East Asia—Race, Culture, and Nation.* London: Oxford University Press, 1966. (Ethnicity)

Information Please Almanac, 1967. New York: Simon and Schuster, Inc., 1966. (Ethnicity)

Institute for Strategic Studies. *Military Balance: 1965–66.* London: Institute for Strategic Studies, 1965. (Total Military, Percentage of GNP on Defense)

————. *Military Balance: 1966–67.* London: Institute for Strategic Studies, 1966. (Total Military, Percentage of GNP on Defense)

————. *The Military Balance: 1967–1968.* London: Institute for Strategic Studies, 1967. (Total Military)

International Monetary Fund and International Bank for Reconstruction and Development. *Direction of Trade—Annual.* Washington, D.C., 1966 (Trade)

Kitchen, Helen (ed.). *A Handbook of African Affairs.* New York: Frederick A. Praeger, Inc., 1964. (Language, Regional Organizations, Total Military)

Lambert, Jacques. *Latin America: Social Structures and Political Institutions.* Trans. Helen Katel. Los Angeles: University of California Press, 1967. (Ethnicity)

Oxford Economic Atlas of the World. London: Oxford University Press, 1965. (Major Exports)

Roberts, C. Paul and Takako Kohda (ed.). *Statistical Abstract of Latin America—1966.* Los Angeles: University of California, 1967. (Population)

Statesman's Yearbook, 1967–68. New York: St. Martin's Press, Inc., 1967. (Language, Religion, Total Military, Regional Organizations, Percentage GNP on Defense)

United Nations. *Statistical Yearbook, 1966,* 18th issue. New York: Statistical Office of the United Nations, 1967. (Population, Energy Consumption, GNP)

West African Directory, 1966–67. London: Thomas Stinner and Company, 1966. (Ethnicity, Religion, Major Exports.)

Wood, David. *Armed Forces in Central and South America.* London: Institute for Strategic Studies, 1967. Adelphi Papers, No. 34. (GNP, Total Military, Percentage GNP on Defense)

————. *The Middle East and the Arab World: The Military Context.* London: Institute for Strategic Studies, 1965. Adelphi Papers, No. 20. (Total Military)

Worldmark Encyclopedia of Nations: Africa. New York: Harper & Row, Publishers, 1967. (Ethnicity, Language, Religion, Major Exports, GNP)

Worldmark Encyclopedia of Nations: Asia and Australia. New York: Harper & Row, Publishers, 1967. (Ethnicity, Language, Religion, Major Exports, Regional Organizations, GNP, Total Military)

Worldmark Encyclopedia of Nations: Europe. New York: Harper & Row, Publishers, 1966. (Ethnicity, Language)

Worldmark Encyclopedia of Nations: the Americas. New York: Harper & Row, Publishers, 1965. (Ethnicity, Language, Religion, Major Exports, Regional Organizations)

Worldmark Encyclopedia of Nations: United Nations. New York: Harper & Row, Publishers, 1965. (Regional Organizations)

Zaborski, Bagdan. "European Languages." *Goode's World Atlas,* 12th edition. Chicago: Rand-McNally & Co., pp. 108–9. (Ethnicity)

Table 6-1 AMERICAN, SOVIET AND COMMUNIST CHINESE AID
(In millions of U.S. dollars)

WEST EUROPE	UNITED STATES			USSR	CHINA
	Total Economic	Total Military	Total Economic & Military 1945–65[1]	Economic Aid Committed 1946–67[2]	Economic Aid Committed 1946–66[3]
Austria	1,152.3	Classified	1,152.3		
Belgium-Luxembourg	510.3	1,247.1	1,757.4		
Denmark	262.4	621.3	883.7		
France	3,077.6	4,180.8	7,258.4		
West Germany	2,789.7	951.6	3,741.3		
Ireland	91.2	—	91.2		
Italy	3,069.2	2,311.1	5,380.3		
Netherlands	817.1	1,240.3	2,057.4		
Norway	288.6	852.6	1,141.2		
Portugal	154.2	333.7	487.9		
Spain	1,132.9	583.8	1,716.7		
Sweden	82.0	—	82.0		
U.K.	6,310.4	1,034.6	7,345.0		
Greece	1,733.1	1,779.9	3,513.0		
Iceland	64.0	—	64.0		
Turkey	1,998.9	2,635.3	4,634.2		
Cyprus	19.0	—	19.0		
Malta	—	—	—		
Switzerland	—	—	—		

Sources:

[1] *For U.S. Aid:*

Agency for International Development, Office of Program Coordination, Statistics and Reports Division, "U.S. Overseas Loans & Grants & Assistance for International Organizations, July 1, 1945–June 30, 1965," Special Report for the House Foreign Affairs Committee, 1966.

The figures are less repayments and interest. For figures before repayments and interest see same source.

[2] *For Soviet Aid:*

Marshall I. Goldman, *Soviet Foreign Aid* (New York: Frederick A. Praeger, Inc., 1967), p. 206.

U.S. Congress, New Directions in the Soviet Economy, Report by Leo Tansky, "Soviet Foreign Aid to the Less Developed Countries," J.E.C., Part IV (Washington, D.C.: U.S. Govt. Printing Office, 1966), p. 974.

U.S. Congress, "Soviet Economic Performance 1966–67," J.E.C. (Washington, D.C.: U.S. Govt. Printing Office, 1968), p. 127.

[3] *For Communist Chinese Aid:*

Alexander Eckstein, *Communist China's Economic Growth and Foreign Trade* (New York: McGraw-Hill Book Company, 1966), p. 307.

Marshall I. Goldman, *Soviet Foreign Aid* (New York: Frederick A. Praeger, Inc., 1967), p. 206.

U.S. Congress, An Economic Profile of Mainland China, Report by Milton Kovner, "Communist China's Foreign Aid to Less Developed Countries," J.E.C., Vol II (Washington, D.C.: U.S. Govt. Printing Office, 1967), p. 612.

Table 6-1 (Cont'd)

LATIN AMERICA	UNITED STATES			USSR	CHINA
	Total Economic	Total Military	Total Economic & Military	Economic Aid Committed	Economic Aid Committed
Argentina	322.9	63.1	386.0	115	
Bolivia	403.9	13.0	416.9		
Brazil	1,589.9	269.5	1,859.4	100	
Guyana	17.0	—	17.0		
Barbados	—	—	—		
Chile	796.2	110.5	906.7	57	
Colombia	484.3	78.4	562.7		
Costa Rica	120.7	2.0	122.7		
Cuba	33.2	10.6	43.8	592	60
Dominican Republic	188.5	14.2	202.7		
Ecuador	178.7	42.2	220.9		
El Salvador	88.2	4.3	92.5		
Guatemala	188.6	10.0	198.6		
Haiti	92.0	4.3	96.3		
Honduras	63.1	4.4	67.5		
Jamaica	36.4	.6	37.0		
Mexico	553.2	6.2	559.4		
Nicaragua	93.6	7.6	101.2		
Panama	145.0	1.6	146.6		
Paraguay	74.7	6.0	80.7		
Peru	319.1	107.4	426.5		
Trinidad & Tobago	41.8	—	41.8		
Uruguay	66.7	35.4	102.1		
Venezuela	239.9	62.4	302.3		

MIDDLE EAST	UNITED STATES			USSR	CHINA
Iran	704.7	712.2	1,416.9	330	
Iraq	50.7	46.4	97.1	184	
Israel	780.1	20.3	800.4		
Jordan	471.4	37.0	508.4		
Lebanon	75.7	8.7	84.4		
Saudi Arabia	25.1	39.9	65.0		
Syria	81.9	Less than 50,000.	81.9	237	16–20
U.A.R.	1,010.3	—	1,010.3	1,011	85
Yemen	39.1	Less than 50,000	39.1	92	44–49
Turkey	1,998.9	2,635.3	4,634.2	210	
Sudan	89.4	.4	89.8	22	
Kuwait	—	—	—		
So. Yemen (n.a.)	—	—	—		

WEST AFRICA	UNITED STATES			USSR	CHINA
Dahomey	8.6	.1	8.7		
Gambia	.1	—	.1		
Ghana	163.6	Less than 50,000	163.6	89	42
Guinea	69.3	.8	70.1	85	32
Ivory Coast	25.8	.1	25.9		

410

Table 6-1 (Cont'd)

WEST AFRICA

	Total Economic	Total Military	Total Economic & Military	Economic Aid Committed	Economic Aid Committed
Liberia	200.5	5.4	205.9		
Mali	13.6	2.2	15.8	61	19.6
Niger	8.7	.1	8.8		
Nigeria	157.0	1.0	158.0		
Senegal	16.5	2.6	19.1	7	
Sierra Leone	27.1	—	27.1	28	
Togo	9.8	—	9.8		
Upper Volta	5.4	.1	5.5		

SOUTHEAST ASIA	UNITED STATES			USSR	CHINA
Burma	101.5	—	101.5	14	84–88
Cambodia	256.0	87.1	343.1	25	55–60
Indonesia	618.9	68.9	687.8	372	123
Laos	418.5	Classified	418.5	4	4
Malaysia	31.7	0.1	31.8		
Philippines	1,221.5	467.7	1,689.2		
Thailand	403.1	Classified	403.1		
S. Vietnam	2,375.1	″	2,375.1		
No. Vietnam	—	—	—		457*
Singapore	—	—	—		

*Total until 1964.

Table 6-2 ARMS SUPPLIERS

DONORS/RECIPIENTS	OWN	USA	UNITED KINGDOM	FRANCE	W. GERMANY	SWEDEN NORWAY	ITALY	USSR NETHER-LANDS	CANADA
West Europe									
France	(W) (P) (S) (M)	W, P, S, (M)	P, S	W, P, S		S(N)	W, P, S		S
W. Germany	W, (S) (M)	W, P, S, (M)	S			W	W		S
Italy	W, P, (S)	W, P, S, (M)	P, S	W, P	W, S				
Belgium	W, S	W, P, S, (M)	S	W, P					
Netherlands	W, S	W, P, S, (M)	W, P, S						
Luxembourg									
PERIPHERY									
North									
United Kingdom	(W) (P) (S) (M)								
Ireland		P, M	S						
Switzerland	W	P, S, (M)	W, P, M	W, P		W	W	W (USSR)	
Austria	W		W, P, S	W, P		P			
Denmark	(S) (P) (S)	M	W, S, M	S		P	W, S		
Sweden	S	P, S, (M)	S	M					
Norway							W	S	
Iceland									
South									
Greece	W, S	W, (P) (S)	S		S	S(N)			
Cyprus					S				
Spain	W, S	W, P, S, M	S	S	S				
Portugal		W, P, S		P, S			P, S	W (USSR)	P
Malta									
Middle East	USSR	USA	UNITED KINGDOM	FRANCE		WEST GERMANY	ITALY	CANADA	BELGIUM NETHERLANDS
UAR	Post 1955: W, P, (S) M, A		Pre 1955: W, S	W			W		
Yemen	W, P	S					W		
Saudi Arabia		W, P, S, M	W, P, M, S	W					

	Post 1958: USSR	USA	UNITED KINGDOM	FRANCE	COMMUNIST CHINA / JAPAN	WEST GERMANY	ITALY / SPAIN	CANADA / SWEDEN	BELGIUM / NETHERLANDS
Kuwait			W, P, S, M						
Iraq	W, P, S, M	W, P	W, P, S						
Lebanon		W, P, S	P, W	W, P, S					
Sudan	W, P, S, M		P						
Jordan		W, P	W, P	P					
Syria	n.a.			S					
South Yemen									
Israel		W, P, S, M	W, S	Ⓦ, Ⓟ, S, M		W			
Turkey	S	W, P, S, M	S			S	S	S, P	S(N)
Iran	W	W, P, S, M	P, S, M				S		
West Africa									
Ivory Coast				W, P, S					
Dahomey				W, P					
Guinea	W, P			W, P, S					
Senegal		W, P		W, P					
Upper Volta				P					
Mali	W, P			W, P					
Niger				W, P					
Togo				P					
Nigeria	P		W, S			P			S(N)
Liberia		S							
Sierra Leone									
Gambia									
Ghana	P, S		W, P, S				W, P	P	P
Latin America									
Argentina		W, Ⓟ, Ⓢ	P, S	W, P			S	S	S(N)
Bolivia		W, Ⓟ, Ⓢ	W	W					S(N)
Brazil		W, Ⓟ, Ⓢ, Ⓜ	P, S, M	P	S (Jap.)		W	(S)	S(N)
Chile		W, Ⓟ, Ⓢ	P, S, M	S		S	S(S)		P
Colombia		W, Ⓟ, Ⓢ	S	P					S
Costa Rica	[No Armed Forces]								
Dominican Republic		W, Ⓟ, Ⓢ	P, S	W, P			W	S	P

413

Table 6-2 (Cont'd)

DONORS / RECIPIENTS	USSR	USA	UNITED KINGDOM	FRANCE	COMMUNIST CHINA JAPAN	W. GERMANY	ITALY SPAIN	CANADA SWEDEN	BELGIUM NETHER- LANDS
Ecuador		W, P, S	P, S			S		P	
El Salvador		P, S	S					S(S)	
Guatemala		P					S(S)		
Honduras		P	P	P					
Mexico		W, P, S							
Nicaragua		W, P							
Panama		W, S			S(J)				S(N)
Paraguay		W, P, S	P, S	P, S			S		
Peru		W, P, S	S	P, S			S(S)	S	
Uruguay		W, P, S	P, S				S		P
Venezuela		W, P, S	P	W, P, S		P			W
Cuba	W, P, M, A, S	P, S	S						
Trinidad & Tobago		S	A						
Jamaica									
Barbados									
Guyana									
Haiti		W, P, S							
S. E. Asia									
Indonesia	W, P, S M	P, S	W, S(Austr.)	W, M	S(J)	S	W, S	P	S(N)
Malaysia		W, P, S M	W, P, S	P			S		
Philippines		W, P, S A		P	W, S(J)		S		
Laos	W				W, S				
North Vietnam	W, P, S M, A								

414

South Vietnam	W, P, S	Ⓦ Ⓟ Ⓢ Ⓐ	P	W, P	W, S(J)	W, S
Cambodia		P, S	P, S	P	S	P
Thailand		W, P, S, M	Ⓦ Ⓟ Ⓢ			
Singapore	S	P, S	P, S			
Burma						

ARMS FURNISHERS

Key W—Arms for ground forces—(small weapons—artillery—armor).

P—Airplanes at all categories and helicopters.

S—Ships

M—Missiles—(Surface-to-surface—Surface-to-air).

A—Advisory body operating in the country.

D—Direct intervention.

O—Major Supplying Power

SOURCES

Blackman, R.V.B. ed., *Jane's Fighting Ships, 1966–1967*, London: S. Low, Marston and Co., Ltd., 1967 or McGraw-Hill Book Co., New York, N.Y., 1967.

The Military Balance, 1967–1968, London: Institute for Strategic Studies, 1968.

The Control of Local Conflict, Vol. II, US Arms Control & Disarmament Agency, WEC—98, Washington, D.C., June 30, 1967.

Arms to Developing Countries, 1945–1965, London: Institute for Strategic Studies.

Europe-France-Outremer, Vol. XLIV, No. 447, April 1967.

Interavia, Vol. XXIII, Nos. 2 and 3, February and March, 1968.

Frank, Lewis A., *The Arms Trade in International Relations*, New York, N.Y.: Frederick A Praeger, 1969.

The authors with to thank Mr. Georges Vitry for his assistance in the preparation of this table.

Table 6-3 THE TEN MOST IMPORTANT RECIPIENTS OF NET OFFICIAL ASSISTANCE FROM SELECTED DONOR COUNTRIES
(Annual Average 1960–1965—in Millions U.S. Dollars)

FRANCE (1)		GERMANY	
Recipients	Amount	Recipients	Amount
Algeria	158.7	India	71.7
D.O.M. and T.O.M. in America	118.4	Israel	65.5
		Pakistan	25.9
D.O.M. and T.O.M. in Africa	69.5	Turkey	24.2
		Brazil	16.4
Morocco	49.9	Liberia	14.7
Senegal	36.9(2).	Greece	10.3
Madagascar	31.2(2)	Chile	7.0
T.O.M. in Oceania	25.6	Indonesia	6.7
Ivory Coast	24.9(2)	U.A.R.	6.3
Tunisia	20.3		
Cameroon	13.4(2)		
Total	548.8		248.7
Overall Total	769.9		360.4
Per Cent	71.3		69.0

JAPAN		UNITED KINGDOM		UNITED STATES	
Recipients	Amount	Recipients	Amount	Recipients	Amount
India	28.2	India	70.5	India	649.1
Indonesia	20.3	Kenya	44.9	Pakistan	313.7
Burma	19.2	Tanzania	24.5	Korea	212.1
Philip.	18.5	Pakistan	19.2	Vietnam	204.4
Pakistan	10.3	Uganda	18.9	Brazil	158.6
Korea	8.6	Malawi	16.8	Turkey	151.6
Vietnam	7.7	S. Arab. Fed.	14.2	U.A.R.	141.8
Brazil	5.8	Malta	13.8	Yugoslavia	98.8
Thailand	2.4	Br. W. Indies	11.9	Chile	86.5
Cambodia	0.7	Malaysia	10.3	China (Taiwan)	81.3
Total	121.7		245.0		2097.9
Overall Total	119.4		392.3		3242.8
Per Cent	101.9(3)		62.0		65.0

Note: *Those countries have been underlined which figure in the list of more than one donor.*
(1) *As detailed information for previous years is not available, the annual average 1964–1965 has been used.*
(2) *These figures do not take account of $69.70 million extended to African and Malagasy states and for which no separate breakdown is available.*
(3) *Japan received repayments from some countries not mentioned in this list.*
Source:
   O.E.C.D., *The Flow of Financial Resources to Less-Developed Countries 1961–65* (Paris, 1967), p. 154.

Table 6-4 INTRUSIVE TRADE WITH THE FIVE SUBORDINATE SYSTEMS
(In Percentages of Trade) 1966

	WESTERN EUROPE U.S.S.R.		United States	
	EXPORT	IMPORT	EXPORT	IMPORT
France	.5	1.5	6	10
Belgium-Luxembourg	2	2	8.5	8
Netherlands	.5	.5	4.5	11.5
West Germany	.5	1.5	7	12.5
Italy	1	2	9	12.5
United Kingdom	3.5	4.5	12.5	12
Ireland	—	.5	7	9.5
Switzerland	1	.5	11	9
Austria	15	10	4.5	4.5
Spain	.5	inf.	13	17
Portugal	—	—	11.5	8
Denmark	1	1.5	8.5	7
Sweden	1	2	7	9.5
Norway	1	1.5	9	7.5
Malta	—	.5	11	4.5
Greece	7	3	10.5	11
Iceland	7	7	16.5	14.5
Turkey	4	3.5	16.5	24
Cyprus	6	3	1	4.5

Table 6-4 (Cont'd)

LATIN AMERICA

	United States		United Kingdom		France		West Germany		U.S.S.R.		China	
	EXP.	IMP.	EXP.	IMP.	EXP.	IMP.	EXP.	IMP.	EXP.	IMP.	EXP.	IMP.
Mexico	53	64	1	3	1.5	5	2	7.5	inf.	inf.	—	—
Guatemala	31	41.5	1	5	1.5	2	14.5	8.5	—	—	—	—
Honduras	56.5	50	inf.	3	1	1	15.5	5	—	—	—	—
El Salvador	26.5	32.5	inf.	3.5	inf.	1.5	24.5	8	—	—	—	1.2
Costa Rica	46	39	.5	5	1	2.5	11.5	10	—	—	—	—
Nicaragua	22.5	46	2.5	3.5	.5	.5	15	7	—	—	—	—
Panama	68	41.5	2	3	—	1	2.5	3	—	—	—	—
Colombia	43.5	48	4	5.5	.5	1.5	13.5	11	—	—	—	—
Venezuela	37	51	7	5.5	1	3	1.5	10	—	—	—	—
Ecuador (1)	42.5	47	.5	5	2.5	3	22	11.5	—	—	—	—
Peru	42.5	39.5	3	4.5	2	2	11	13	—	—	—	—
Bolivia	39.5	41.5	45.5	4.5	inf.	1	5.5	12.5	—	—	—	—
Paraguay	23	21	8.5	6	2	2	3.5	19	—	—	—	—
Argentina	8	23	9.5	6	3	3.5	5.5	9.5	5.5	1.5	5.5	inf.
Uruguay	12.5	12	14	5.5	4.5	2	8	11	3.5	.5	—	—
Brazil	33.5	39	4.5	3	3.5	2.5	7.5	9	2	2.5	—	—
Dominican Republic	88	47	.5	4.5	1	1.5	1	6.5	—	—	—	—
Haiti (1)	47	61	2	4.5	12.5	4.5	3.5	4	—	—	—	—
Cuba (2)	—	—	2	6	1.5	2	inf.	2.5	47.5	49.5	14.5	14.5
Trinidad and Tobago	37.5	14	14.5	17	inf.	.5	.5	1	—	—	—	—
Jamaica	38.5	36.5	26.5	22	inf.	2	1.5	3.5	—	—	—	—
Barbados	9	18.5	45	31.5	—	—	—	2.5	—	—	—	—
Guyana	22	23	22	33	.5	1	.5	3	—	—	—	—
Chile	25	39.8	15	5.6	4.3	2.7	9.5	12.3	—	—	inf.	inf.

WEST AFRICA

	United States		United Kingdom		France		West Germany		U.S.S.R.		China	
	EXP.	IMP.	EXP.	IMP.	EXP.	IMP.	EXP.	IMP.	EXP.	IMP.	EXP.	IMP.
Ivory Coast	17	8	3	2	40.5	58	6.5	6.5	inf.	inf.	—	—
Dahomey	9.5	5	1	3.5	53.5	53	.5	3.5	inf.	—	—	—

Table of trade percentages by country and trading partner. Each trading partner has two value columns.

	United States		United Kingdom		France		West Germany		U.S.S.R.		China	
Guinea	23	22	4	5	4	21.5	7	11		12*	10*	2
Senegal	inf.	4	1	1	77.5	51.5	2.5	5				
Upper Volta (5)			.5	.5	15.5	32.5						
Mali	.5	2	2	2	3	21		1.5		13		28.5
Niger		4	1	3.5	55.5	52		3				5.5
Togo	2	3	2	8	40	31	6	12.5				2.5
Nigeria	9	15.5	37	30.5	7.5	6	10.5	11.5	inf.	inf.		1.4
Liberia (6)	39	40	10	10			32	20				
Sierra Leone	6	6.5	62.5	28.5	.5	7.5	6.5	6				1.5
Gambia			50	46.5								
Ghana	14.5	17	25	29	1	4.5	7.5	7.5	9.5	6	1.9	2.1

MIDDLE EAST

	United States		United Kingdom		France		West Germany		U.S.S.R.		China	
Syria	2.0	8	1	6	4.5	6	4.5	9	11	7.5	11.5	5.5
Lebanon (3)	6.5	17	5	9.5	5.	9.5	5.5	10.5	1.5	1.5		
Jordan		15.5		12		2.5	3.5	4.5		2	1.1	3
Iraq	2.5	10	15	13.5	15	2	5.5	12	2.6	5	.5	4.5
U.A.R.	2.5	20	3	5	2	5	4	8	23.5	9	5.5	4
Sudan	3	8	6.5	21	5	2	8.5	7	4.5	5	5.5	6
Kuwait	2	21	17.5	16	10	2.5	2	8		2		3.5
Saudi Arabia	6.5	29.5	6.5	11.5	3.5	4.5	8.5	8.5				
Yemen (4)			.5	inf.	2	4	.5	2.5				
South Yemen (Aden)	.5	1.5	22	11.5	1	1	inf.	3	inf.	1		.5
Iran	6.5	18.5	14.5	12.5	4.5	4	3.5	22	1	3		1
Turkey	16.5	24	9.5	11	5	6	15.5	15.5	4	3.5		inf.
Israel	15.5	26.5	12.5	18.5	4	4.5	9.5	8	inf.	inf.		

SOUTHEAST ASIA

	United States		United Kingdom		Japan		France		U.S.S.R.		China	
Indonesia (7)	26.4	11.3	1.9	1.9	23.2	22.4	3.5	2.9	8*			
Malaysia (8)	14	4.5	6.5	14	21.5	9.5	4	2				
Philippines	39.5	34	1	4.5	33	27.5	inf.	1				
Singapore (8)	1.5	4	3.5	9.5	4	11.5					7*	

Table 6-4 (Cont'd)

	United States		United Kingdom		Japan		France		U.S.S.R.		China	
	EXP.	IMP.	EXP.	IMP.	EXP.	IMP.	EXP	IMP.	EXP.	IMP.	EXP.	IMP.
Laos	—	14.5	—	10	—	13	—	5.5	—	—	—	—
North Vietnam (7)												
South Vietnam	4	39.5	16	1.5	14.5	13	39	3	—	—	—	—
Cambodia	2	2.5	2	4.5	7.5	13.5	16	25.5	1	3	—	—
Thailand	7	41	3.5	6	20.5	25.5	1	1	—	inf.	8.5	16.5
Burma	1	11	6.5	12	6.5	24	1	1	.5	2.5	8.5	7

Source for Table 6–4

International Monetary Fund and the International Bank for Reconstruction and Development. *Direction of Trade: A Supplement to International Financial Statistics*, Annual 1962–66.

(*)Starred items are from *Britannica Book of the Year, 1968.*

Notes:

1. Based on derivative data; only approximate.
2. Data for 1965 only.
3. Figures for U.S.S.R. and China are for 1965, others are for 1966.
4. No data for Soviet and Chinese trade with Yemen; total Sino-Soviet-Eastern Europe trade probably 30% of exports, 15% of imports approximately. Data for Yemen, Lebanon (exports), Kuwait and Saudi Arabia is derivative and, therefore, percentages are only approximate.
5. Based on derivative data, only approximate; does not include data for U.S.S.R. trade which is unknown. Where available, from Encyclopedia Britannica.
6. Liberian data is from Britannica Book of the year, 1968, p. 475.
7. No data.
8. Data only approximate; no data available for Soviet and Chinese trade.

Although it was not possible to include them here, it is important to add that the East European states together frequently compose a substantial trade percentage especially in those countries where the Soviet Union trades heavily. As a counteracting factor, it is worth noting that some of the smaller states (e.g., Austria, Belgium, Switzerland) also add to the trade percentage of Western-oriented states.

Table 6-5 INTRUSIVE PERSONNEL IN DEVELOPING COUNTRIES

	EXPERTS IN EDUCATION[a]		OPERATIONAL PERSONNEL[b]		ADVISORS[c]		VOLUNTEERS[d]	
	1965	1966	1965	1966	1965	1966	1965	1966
France	29,235	30,190	10,016	13,207	3,939	1,118	339	400
Germany	762	806	429	473	476	835	893	1,566
Japan	39	17	—	—	526	600	40	151
U.K.	3,628	4,355	10,554	11,346	426	408	911	1,323
U.S.A.	2,594	2,328	—	—	6,726	7,537	11,843	17,912

Source: OECD, Development Assistance Efforts and Policies: 1967 Review, Report by Willard L. Thorp, September, 1967, pp. 202–9.

[a] *Experts in education include teachers of primary and secondary, university and higher technical education; teacher training; technical and vocational training; other and educational administrators and educational advisors.*

[b] *Operational personnel include persons in economic planning, surveys, etc; public administration; power, transport and communication; industry, mining and handicraft; trade, banking, insurance, tourism; agriculture; health services and labor relations.*

[c] *Advisors are in the same fields of activity as operational personnel are found.*

[d] *Volunteers include teachers in primary and secondary education, university and higher technical education, technical and vocational training; volunteers are also in the fields of economic planning, surveys, etc; public administration; power, transport, and communication, industry, mining and handicraft; trade, banking, insurance, tourism; agriculture; health services; social services and labor relations.*

Table 6-6 WEEKLY NUMBER OF BROADCAST HOURS TO DISTINCT TARGET AREAS BY LEADING INTERNATIONAL BROADCASTERS

	USSR		CHINA		VOA		BBC		WEST GERMANY		FRANCE
	1956	1967	1956	1967	1956	1967	1956	1967	1956	1967	1968
Non-Communist Europe	217	216	21	64	23[a]	[a]	112	84		70	91
Communist Europe	70	121		365	538	178.5	90.5	124		132	
Far East	133	389	115.5	455.5	251.5	196	28	61	21	49	42
Middle East[b]	45.5	205	3.5	28	161	49	39.5	105.5	21	61	24.15
Africa[c]		147	3.5	77		67	12	97	21	171.5	290.5
Latin America	21	101.5		56	2	71.5	30	44	21	66	70

Note: Several of the above broadcasts were services that are not announced for any specific target area (e.g., BBC's General Overseas Service or VOA's World-Wide Service). The totals given here thus will not agree with totals published in other sources.

[a] These areas are reached primarily by pre-packaged programs aired over local networks.
[b] From the Arab Maghreb to West Pakistan.
[c] South of the Arab Maghreb.

Sources: All figures excluding France from Britannica Book of the Year 1968: Events of 1967 (Chicago: Encyclopedia Britannica, Inc., 1968), p. 647. For France: Paris vous parle, November 15, 1968, p. 15 (O.R.T.F. broadcasts).

INDEX